The Growth of
INCARCERATION
in the United States

Exploring Causes and Consequences

Committee on Causes and Consequences of High Rates of Incarceration

Jeremy Travis, Bruce Western, and Steve Redburn, *Editors*

Committee on Law and Justice

Division of Behavioral and Social Sciences and Education

NATIONAL RESEARCH COUNCIL
OF THE NATIONAL ACADEMIES

THE NATIONAL ACADEMIES PRESS
Washington, D.C.
www.nap.edu

THE NATIONAL ACADEMIES PRESS   500 Fifth Street, NW   Washington, DC 20001

NOTICE: The project that is the subject of this report was approved by the Governing Board of the National Research Council, whose members are drawn from the councils of the National Academy of Sciences, the National Academy of Engineering, and the Institute of Medicine. The members of the committee responsible for the report were chosen for their special competences and with regard for appropriate balance.

This study was supported by Award No. 11-99472-000-USP from the MacArthur Foundation and Award No. 201I-DJ-BX-2029 from the U.S. Department of Justice. Any opinions, findings, conclusions, or recommendations expressed in this publication are those of the author(s) and do not necessarily reflect the views of the organizations or agencies that provided support for the project.

Additional copies of this report are available from the National Academies Press, 500 Fifth Street, NW, Keck 360, Washington, DC 20001; (800) 624-6242 or (202) 334-3313; http://www.nap.edu.

Suggested citation: National Research Council. (2014). *The Growth of Incarceration in the United States: Exploring Causes and Consequences.* Committee on Causes and Consequences of High Rates of Incarceration, J. Travis, B. Western, and S. Redburn, Editors. Committee on Law and Justice, Division of Behavioral and Social Sciences and Education. Washington, DC: The National Academies Press.

First Printing, April 2014
Second Printing, July 2014

THE NATIONAL ACADEMIES
Advisers to the Nation on Science, Engineering, and Medicine

The **National Academy of Sciences** is a private, nonprofit, self-perpetuating society of distinguished scholars engaged in scientific and engineering research, dedicated to the furtherance of science and technology and to their use for the general welfare. Upon the authority of the charter granted to it by the Congress in 1863, the Academy has a mandate that requires it to advise the federal government on scientific and technical matters. Dr. Ralph J. Cicerone is president of the National Academy of Sciences.

The **National Academy of Engineering** was established in 1964, under the charter of the National Academy of Sciences, as a parallel organization of outstanding engineers. It is autonomous in its administration and in the selection of its members, sharing with the National Academy of Sciences the responsibility for advising the federal government. The National Academy of Engineering also sponsors engineering programs aimed at meeting national needs, encourages education and research, and recognizes the superior achievements of engineers. Dr. C. D. Mote, Jr., is president of the National Academy of Engineering.

The **Institute of Medicine** was established in 1970 by the National Academy of Sciences to secure the services of eminent members of appropriate professions in the examination of policy matters pertaining to the health of the public. The Institute acts under the responsibility given to the National Academy of Sciences by its congressional charter to be an adviser to the federal government and, upon its own initiative, to identify issues of medical care, research, and education. Dr. Harvey V. Fineberg is president of the Institute of Medicine.

The **National Research Council** was organized by the National Academy of Sciences in 1916 to associate the broad community of science and technology with the Academy's purposes of furthering knowledge and advising the federal government. Functioning in accordance with general policies determined by the Academy, the Council has become the principal operating agency of both the National Academy of Sciences and the National Academy of Engineering in providing services to the government, the public, and the scientific and engineering communities. The Council is administered jointly by both Academies and the Institute of Medicine. Dr. Ralph J. Cicerone and Dr. C. D. Mote, Jr., are chair and vice chair, respectively, of the National Research Council.

www.national-academies.org

Preface

The growth of incarceration rates in the United States for more than four decades has spawned commentary and a growing body of scientific knowledge about its causes and the consequences for those imprisoned, their families and communities, and U.S. society. Recognizing the importance of summarizing what is known (and not known) about the many questions this phenomenon has raised, the National Institute of Justice (NIJ) of the U.S. Department of Justice and the John D. and Catherine T. MacArthur Foundation requested a study by the National Research Council (NRC). We are grateful for support throughout the study from the current and former NIJ directors, John Laub and Greg Ridgeway, and from our program officers at the MacArthur Foundation, Laurie Garduque and Craig Wacker. This report is the product of that 2-year effort, conducted by an ad hoc committee created by the National Research Council to assess the evidence and draw out its implications for public policy. I and the other members of the study committee hope it will inform an extensive and thoughtful public debate about and reconsideration of the policies that led to the current situation.

Special thanks are owed to the late James Q. Wilson who chaired the Committee on Law and Justice (CLAJ) at the time the study was conceived more than 5 years ago. Recognizing the importance of this issue, he organized a subcommittee of Phil Cook, Duke University; Glenn Loury, Brown University; Tracey Meares, Yale Law School; and myself to develop a study idea for CLAJ's approval. At a meeting held at John Jay College of Criminal Justice in January 2009, led by former CLAJ director Carol Petrie, a group of scholars helped develop parameters for a study of high rates of incarceration. NIJ and the MacArthur Foundation subsequently recognized that such a study would come at an important moment in the nation's history and could make a significant contribution to public understanding and to improving the justice system.

On the committee's behalf, I thank the many individuals and organizations who assisted us in our work and without whom this study could not have been completed. Several scholars conducted original analyses and working papers for the committee. Alfred Blumstein, Carnegie Mellon University, and Alan Beck, Bureau of Justice Statistics, U.S. Department of Justice, updated their classic analysis of changes in incarceration levels. Other contributors included Doris MacKenzie, Penn State University; Richard Rosenfeld, University of Missouri, St. Louis; Susan Turner, University of California, Irvine; Sara Wakefield, University of California, Irvine; and Christopher Wildeman, Yale University, who provided detailed analyses on various topics of interest to the committee ranging from crime rates to prison programs to research needed to address knowledge gaps identified in the report. Bettina Muenster, John Jay College of Criminal Justice, was a valuable consultant to the committee, most especially in her reviews of several important parts of the literature. Peter Reuter, University of Maryland, College Park, and Jonathan Caulkins, Carnegie Mellon University, provided insights from their work on drug crime. Eric Cadora and Charles Swartz of the Justice Mapping Center, Rutgers University School of Criminal Justice, provided community maps of incarceration. Steven Raphael, University of California, Berkeley, and Michael Stoll, University of California, Los Angeles, generously shared advanced text of their now-published book on why so many people are in prison. In addition, a number of colleagues reviewed the research literature and prepared data for specific chapters: Scott Allen, University of California, Riverside; Anthony Bator, Harvard University; Dora Dumont, Miriam Hospital, Providence, RI; Wade Jacobsen, Princeton University; Becky Pettit, University of Washington; Jessica Simes, Harvard University; Catherine Sirois, Harvard University; and Bryan Sykes, University of Washington.

Sixteen individuals participated in a December 2012 public workshop on health and incarceration, organized by committee member Josiah Rich, which informed that element of the committee's work. Other participants were committee members Craig Haney, Bruce Western, and Scott Allen, University of California, Riverside; Redonna Chandler, National Institute on Drug Abuse; Jennifer Clarke, Brown University Medical Center; Jamie Fellner, Human Rights Watch; Robert B. Greifinger, John Jay College of Criminal Justice, CUNY; Newton Kendig, Federal Bureau of Prisons; Marc Mauer, The Sentencing Project; Fred Osher, Council of State Governments; Steven Rosenberg, Community Oriented Correctional Health Services; Faye S. Taxman, George Mason University; Emily Wang, Yale University;

Christopher Wildeman, Yale University; and Brie Williams, University of California, San Francisco. The Robert Wood Johnson Foundation provided support for the preparation and publication of a summary of that workshop (available through the National Academies Press, http://www.nap.edu/catalog.php?record_id=18372).

All of us recognize that the study would not be what it is—in the depth of analysis, quality of writing, or force of its conclusions—without the efforts of the committee's vice chair, Bruce Western. I thank him not only for his innumerable substantive contributions to the report, but also for his thoughtful leadership at critical times during the committee's deliberations.

One member of the study committee, Jeffrey Beard, resigned in late 2013. He concluded that his obligations as secretary of the California Department of Corrections and Rehabilitation, a position he assumed after having been appointed to the committee, precluded him from participating in the final stages of the committee's deliberations. We are indebted to him for his contributions to the committee's early work.

Committee member Ricardo H. Hinojosa has written a supplementary statement, which is Appendix A. In it he expresses concerns about the report's discussion and certain conclusions related to the causes of high rates of incarceration and their effect on crime prevention, based on his judicial experience. However, he does support the panel's recommendations and the importance of their consideration by the public and policy makers.

This study and report have benefited from the valuable assistance of many NRC staff within CLAJ. Steve Redburn, scholar and study director, oversaw meeting agendas and schedules for the production of this report. In the assembly of the report, he was assisted by Malay Majmundar, senior program officer, and Julie Schuck, senior program associate, to work collaboratively with the committee members to integrate their ideas, analyses, writings, and conclusions into a sound report. Barbara Boyd, administrative coordinator, made sure the committee's study and meetings ran smoothly, gathered data and created several figures in this report, as well as provided bibliographic assistance. The former CLAJ director, Jane Ross, offered wise guidance at the start of the committee's deliberations. The current CLAJ director, Arlene Lee, provided leadership and intellectual rigor in the final phases of production of this report to ensure that its complex messages were well-grounded. Conversations with Robert Hauser, executive director, and Mary Ellen O'Connell, deputy executive director, of the Division of Behavioral and Social Sciences and Education helped the committee strengthen the presentation of its conclusions and the articulation of normative principles for the use of incarceration.

We also thank the many other NRC staff members who assisted the committee in its work. Anthony Mann provided administrative support as needed. Kirsten Sampson Snyder shepherded the report through the NRC review process; Eugenia Grohman helped edit the draft report; Yvonne Wise processed the report through final production; and Patty Morison offered guidance on communication of the study results. The staff of the NRC library and research center, Daniel Bearss, Colleen Willis, Ellen Kimmel, and Rebecca Morgan, provided valuable assistance on the report bibliography. We also appreciate the efforts of Rona Briere and Alisa Decatur in their editing of the final text.

This report has been reviewed in draft form by individuals chosen for their diverse perspectives and technical expertise, in accordance with procedures approved by the NRC's Report Review Committee. The purpose of this independent review is to provide candid and critical comments that will assist the institution in making its published report as sound as possible and to ensure that the report meets institutional standards for objectivity, evidence, and responsiveness to the charge. The review comments and draft manuscript remain confidential to protect the integrity of the deliberative process.

I thank the following individuals for their review of this report: Anthony A. Braga, Program in Criminal Justice Policy and Management at Harvard Kennedy School, Harvard University, and School of Criminal Justice, Rutgers University; Shawn Bushway, Program on the Economics of Crime and Justice Policy, School of Criminal Justice, University at Albany, State University of New York; Michael Flamm, Department of History, Ohio Wesleyan University, Delaware, Ohio; Michael Gottfredson, University of Oregon; Peter Greenwood, Advancing EBP, Agoura, California; Martin F. Horn, John Jay College, City University of New York, and New York State Sentencing Commission; Randall L. Kennedy, School of Law, Harvard University; Kenneth C. Land, Department of Sociology, Duke University; Marc Mauer, The Sentencing Project, Washington, DC; Theda Skocpol, Scholars Strategy Network and Department of Government and Sociology, Harvard University; Cassia Spohn, School of Criminology and Criminal Justice, Arizona State University; Christopher Uggen, Department of Sociology, University of Minnesota; Lester N. Wright, School of Population Health, University of Adelaide, and School of Medicine, Flinders University, Adelaide, South Australia; Mark H. Moore, John F. Kennedy School of Government, Harvard University; and Sara Rosenbaum, Department of Health Policy, School of Public Health and Health Services, George Washington University.

Although the reviewers listed above provided many constructive comments and suggestions, they were not asked to endorse the conclusions and recommendations nor did they see the final draft of the report before its release. The review of this report was overseen by Mark Moore, Harvard University, and Sara Rosenbaum, George Washington University. Appointed by the NRC, they were responsible for making certain that an independent examination of this report was carried out in accordance with institutional procedures and that all review comments were carefully considered. Responsibility for the final content of this report, however, rests entirely with the authoring committee and the institution.

More than 5 years ago, CLAJ recognized that the time had come to marshal the best science and gain insight into how incarceration had reached exceptional levels and with what consequences. To that end, we on the study committee committed ourselves to reaching the consensus presented in this report through open-hearted deliberation and collaborative spirit. Our work will be judged a contribution to the extent that it informs a robust public discourse on these matters with scientific evidence and thoughtful reflection on the purposes and proper limits of incarceration.

Jeremy Travis, *Chair*
Committee on Causes and Consequences of
High Rates of Incarceration in the United States

Contents

Summary

After decades of stability from the 1920s to the early 1970s, the rate of incarceration in the United States more than quadrupled in the past four decades. The Committee on the Causes and Consequences of High Rates of Incarceration in the United States was established under the auspices of the National Research Council, supported by the National Institute of Justice and the John D. and Catherine T. MacArthur Foundation, to review evidence on the causes and consequences of these high incarceration rates and the implications of this evidence for public policy.

Our work encompassed research on, and analyses of, the proximate causes of the dramatic rise in the prison population and the societal dynamics that supported those proximate causes. Our analysis reviewed evidence of the effects of high rates of incarceration on public safety as well as those in prison, their families, and the communities from which these men and women originate and to which they return. We also examined the effects on U.S. society.

After assessing the evidence, the committee found that the normative principles that both limit and justify the use of incarceration as a response to crime were a necessary element of the analytical process. Public policy on the appropriate use of prison is not determined solely by weighing evidence of costs and benefits. Rather, a combination of empirical findings and explicit normative commitments is required. Issues regarding criminal punishment necessarily involve ideas about justice, fairness, and just deserts. Accordingly, this report includes a review of established principles of jurisprudence and governance that have historically guided society's use of incarceration.

1

Finally, we considered the practical implications of our conclusions for public policy and for research.

FINDINGS AND CONCLUSIONS

From 1973 to 2009, the state and federal prison populations that are the main focus of this study rose steadily, from about 200,000 to 1.5 million, declining slightly in the following 4 years. In addition to the men and women serving prison time for felonies, another 700,000 are held daily in local jails. In recent years, the federal prison system has continued to expand, while the state incarceration rate has declined. Between 2006 and 2011, more than half the states reduced their prison populations, and in 10 states the number of people incarcerated fell by 10 percent or more.

The U.S. penal population of 2.2 million adults is the largest in the world. In 2012, close to 25 percent of the world's prisoners were held in American prisons, although the United States accounts for about 5 percent of the world's population. The U.S. rate of incarceration, with nearly 1 of every 100 adults in prison or jail, is 5 to 10 times higher than rates in Western Europe and other democracies.

CONCLUSION: The growth in incarceration rates in the United States over the past 40 years is historically unprecedented and internationally unique.

Those who are incarcerated in U.S. prisons come largely from the most disadvantaged segments of the population. They comprise mainly minority men under age 40, poorly educated, and often carrying additional deficits of drug and alcohol addiction, mental and physical illness, and a lack of work preparation or experience. Their criminal responsibility is real, but it is embedded in a context of social and economic disadvantage. More than half the prison population is black or Hispanic. In 2010, blacks were incarcerated at six times and Hispanics at three times the rate for non-Hispanic whites. The emergence of high incarceration rates has broad significance for U.S. society. The meaning and consequences of this new reality cannot be separated from issues of social inequality and the quality of citizenship of the nation's racial and ethnic minorities.

Causes

By the time incarceration rates began to grow in the early 1970s, U.S. society had passed through a tumultuous period of social and political change. Decades of rising crime accompanied a period of intense political conflict and a profound transformation of U.S. race relations. The problem of crime gained a prominent place in national policy debates. Crime and race were sometimes conflated in political conversation.

In the 1960s and 1970s, a changed political climate provided the context for a series of policy choices. Across all branches and levels of government, criminal processing and sentencing expanded the use of incarceration in a number of ways: prison time was increasingly required for lesser offenses; time served was significantly increased for violent crimes and for repeat offenders; and drug crimes, particularly street dealing in urban areas, became more severely policed and punished. These changes in punishment policy were the main and proximate drivers of the growth in incarceration. In the 1970s, the numbers of arrests and court caseloads increased, and prosecutors and judges became harsher in their charging and sentencing. In the 1980s, convicted defendants became more likely to serve prison time. More than half of the growth in state imprisonment during this period was driven by the increased likelihood of incarceration given an arrest. Arrest rates for drug offenses climbed in the 1970s, and mandatory prison time for these offenses became more common in the 1980s.

During the 1980s, the U.S. Congress and most state legislatures enacted laws mandating lengthy prison sentences—often of 5, 10, and 20 years or longer—for drug offenses, violent offenses, and "career criminals." In the 1990s, Congress and more than one-half of the states enacted "three strikes and you're out" laws that mandated minimum sentences of 25 years or longer for affected offenders. A majority of states enacted "truth-in-sentencing" laws requiring affected offenders to serve at least 85 percent of their nominal prison sentences. The Congress enacted such a law in 1984.

These changes in sentencing reflected a consensus that viewed incarceration as a key instrument for crime control. Yet over the four decades when incarceration rates steadily rose, U.S. crime rates showed no clear trend: the rate of violent crime rose, then fell, rose again, then declined sharply. The best single proximate explanation of the rise in incarceration is not rising crime rates, but the policy choices made by legislators to greatly increase the use of imprisonment as a response to crime. Mandatory prison sentences, intensified enforcement of drug laws, and long sentences contributed not only to overall high rates of incarceration, but also especially to extraordinary rates of incarceration in black and Latino communities. Intensified enforcement of drug laws subjected blacks, more than whites, to new mandatory minimum sentences—despite lower levels of drug use and no higher demonstrated levels of trafficking among the black than the white population. Blacks had long been more likely than whites to be arrested for violence. But three strikes, truth-in-sentencing, and related laws have likely increased sentences and time served for blacks more than whites. As a consequence, the absolute disparities in incarceration increased, and imprisonment became common for young minority men, particularly those with little schooling.

> CONCLUSION: The unprecedented rise in incarceration rates can be attributed to an increasingly punitive political climate surrounding criminal justice policy formed in a period of rising crime and rapid social change. This provided the context for a series of policy choices —across all branches and levels of government—that significantly increased sentence lengths, required prison time for minor offenses, and intensified punishment for drug crimes.

Consequences

Relationships among incarceration, crime, sentencing policy, social inequality, and numerous other variables influencing the growth of incarceration are complex, change across time and place, and interact with each other. As a result, estimating the social consequences of high rates of incarceration, including the effects on crime, is extremely challenging. Because of the challenge of separating cause and effect from an array of social forces, studies examining the impact of incarceration on crime have produced divergent findings. Most studies conclude that rising incarceration rates reduced crime, but the evidence does not clearly show by how much. A number of studies also find that the crime-reducing effects of incarceration become smaller as the incarceration rate grows, although this may reflect the aging of prison populations.

> CONCLUSION: The increase in incarceration may have caused a decrease in crime, but the magnitude of the reduction is highly uncertain and the results of most studies suggest it was unlikely to have been large.

Much research on the crime effects of incarceration attempts to measure reductions in crime that might result from deterrence and incapacitation. Long sentences characterize the period of high incarceration rates, but research on deterrence suggests that would-be offenders are deterred more by the risk of being caught than by the severity of the penalty they would face if arrested and convicted. High rates of incarceration may have reduced crime rates through incapacitation (locking up people who might otherwise commit crimes), although there is no strong consensus on the magnitude of this effect. And because offending declines markedly with age, the incapacitation effect of very long sentences is likely to be small.

CONCLUSION: The incremental deterrent effect of increases in lengthy prison sentences is modest at best. Because recidivism rates decline markedly with age, lengthy prison sentences, unless they specifically target very high-rate or extremely dangerous offenders, are an inefficient approach to preventing crime by incapacitation.

The distribution of incarceration across the population is highly uneven. As noted above, regardless of race or ethnicity, prison and jail inmates are drawn mainly from the least educated segments of society. Among white male high school dropouts born in the late 1970s, about one-third are estimated to have served time in prison by their mid-30s. Yet incarceration rates have reached even higher levels among young black men with little schooling: among black male high school dropouts, about two-thirds have a prison record by that same age—more than twice the rate for their white counterparts. The pervasiveness of imprisonment among men with very little schooling is historically unprecedented, emerging only in the past two decades.

Much of the significance of the social and economic consequences of incarceration is rooted in the high absolute level of incarceration for minority groups and in the large racial disparities in incarceration rates. In the era of high incarceration rates, prison admission and return have become commonplace in minority neighborhoods characterized by high levels of crime, poverty, family instability, poor health, and residential segregation. Racial disparities in incarceration have tended to differentiate the life chances and civic participation of blacks, in particular, from those of most other Americans.

CONCLUSION: People who live in poor and minority communities have always had substantially higher rates of incarceration than other groups. As a consequence, the effects of harsh penal policies in the past 40 years have fallen most heavily on blacks and Hispanics, especially the poorest.

Coming from some of the most disadvantaged segments of society, many of the incarcerated entered prison in unsound physical and mental health. The poor health status of the inmate population serves as a basic marker of its social disadvantage and underlines the contemporary importance of prisons as public health institutions. Incarceration is associated with overlapping afflictions of substance use, mental illness, and risk for infectious diseases (HIV, viral hepatitis, sexually transmitted diseases, and others). This situation creates an enormous challenge for the provision of health care for inmates, although it also provides opportunities for screening, diagnosis, treatment, and linkage to treatment after release.

Prison conditions can be especially hard on some people, particularly those with mental illness, causing severe psychological stress. Although levels of lethal violence in prisons have declined, conditions have deteriorated in some other ways. Increased rates of incarceration have been accompanied by overcrowding and decreased opportunity for rehabilitative programs, as well as a growing burden on medical and mental health services.

Many state prisons and the Federal Bureau of Prisons operate at or above 100 percent of their designed capacity. With overcrowding, cells designed for a single inmate often house two and sometimes three people. The concern that overcrowding would create more violent environments did not materialize during the period of rising incarceration rates: rather, as the rates rose, the numbers of riots and homicides within prisons declined. Nonetheless, research has found overcrowding, particularly when it persists at high levels, to be associated with a range of poor consequences for health and behavior and an increased risk of suicide. In many cases, prison provides far less medical care and rehabilitative programming than is needed.

Incarceration is strongly correlated with negative social and economic outcomes for former prisoners and their families. Men with a criminal record often experience reduced earnings and employment after prison. Fathers' incarceration and family hardship, including housing insecurity and behavioral problems in children, are strongly related. The partners and children of prisoners are particularly likely to experience adverse outcomes if the men were positively involved with their families prior to incarceration. From 1980 to 2000, the number of children with incarcerated fathers increased from about 350,000 to 2.1 million—about 3 percent of all U.S. children. From 1991 to 2007, the number of children with a father or mother in prison increased 77 percent and 131 percent, respectively.

The rise in incarceration rates marked a massive expansion of the role of the justice system in the nation's poorest communities. Many of those entering prison come from and will return to these communities. When they return, their lives often continue to be characterized by violence, joblessness, substance abuse, family breakdown, and neighborhood disadvantage. The best evidence to date leaves uncertain the extent to which these conditions of life are themselves exacerbated by incarceration. It is difficult to draw strong causal inferences from the research, but there is little question that incarceration has become another strand in the complex combination of negative conditions that characterize high-poverty communities in U.S. cities.

Given the evidence, crime reduction and socioeconomic disadvantage are both plausible outcomes of increased incarceration, but estimates of the size of these effects range widely. The vast expansion of the criminal justice system has created a large population whose access to public benefits, occupations, vocational licenses, and the franchise is limited by a criminal conviction. High rates of incarceration are associated with lower levels of civic and political engagement among former prisoners and their families and friends than among others in their communities. Disfranchisement of former prisoners and the way prisoners are enumerated in the U.S. census combine to weaken the power of low-income and minority communities. For these people, the quality of citizenship—the quality of their membership in American society and their relationship to public institutions—has been impaired. These developments have created a highly distinct political and legal universe for a large segment of the U.S. population.

CONCLUSION: The change in penal policy over the past four decades may have had a wide range of unwanted social costs, and the magnitude of crime reduction benefits is highly uncertain.

The consequences of the decades-long build-up of the U.S. prison population have been felt most acutely in minority communities in urban areas already experiencing significant social, economic, and public health disadvantages. For policy and public life, the magnitude of the consequences of incarceration may be less important than the overwhelming evidence of this correlation. In communities of concentrated disadvantage—characterized by high rates of poverty, violent crime, mental illness and drug addiction—the United States embarked on a massive and unique intensification of criminal punishment. Although many questions remain unanswered, the greatest significance of the era of high incarceration rates may lie in that simple descriptive fact.

Policies regulating criminal punishment cannot be determined only by the scientific evidence. The decision to deprive another human being of his or her liberty is, at root, anchored in beliefs about the relationship between the individual and society and the role of criminal sanctions in preserving the social compact. Thus, sound policies on crime and incarceration will reflect a combination of science and fundamental principles.

GUIDING PRINCIPLES

A broad discussion of principles has been notably absent from the nation's recent policy debates on the use of imprisonment. Beginning in the early 1970s, in a time of rising violence and rapid social change, policy makers turned to incarceration to denounce the moral insult of crime and to deter and incapacitate criminals. As offender accountability and crime control were emphasized, principles that previously had limited the severity of punishment were eclipsed, and punishments became more severe. Yet a balanced understanding of the role of imprisonment in society recognizes that the deprivation of personal liberty is one of the harshest penalties society can impose. Even under the best conditions, incarceration can do great harm—not only to those who are imprisoned, but also more broadly to families, communities, and society as a whole. Moreover, the forcible deprivation of liberty through incarceration is vulnerable to misuse, threatening the basic principles that underpin the legitimacy of prisons.

The jurisprudence of punishment and theories of social policy have sought to limit public harm by appealing to long-standing principles of fairness and shared social membership. We believe that as policy makers and the public consider the implications of the findings presented in this report, they also should consider the following four principles whose application would constrain the use of incarceration:

- *Proportionality:* Criminal offenses should be sentenced in proportion to their seriousness.
- *Parsimony:* The period of confinement should be sufficient but not greater than necessary to achieve the goals of sentencing policy.
- *Citizenship:* The conditions and consequences of imprisonment should not be so severe or lasting as to violate one's fundamental status as a member of society.
- *Social justice:* Prisons should be instruments of justice, and as such their collective effect should be to promote and not undermine society's aspirations for a fair distribution of rights, resources, and opportunities.

These principles ought to be seen as complementing rather than conflicting with the recent emphasis on offender accountability and crime control. Together, they help define a balanced role for the use of incarceration in U.S. society.

CONCLUSION: In the domain of justice, empirical evidence by itself cannot point the way to policy, yet an explicit and transparent expression of normative principles[1] has been notably missing as U.S. incarceration rates dramatically rose over the past four decades. Normative principles have deep roots in jurisprudence and theories of governance and are needed to supplement empirical evidence to guide future policy and research.

---

[1]Political theorists and legal analysts have often observed that public policy necessarily embodies ethical judgments about means or ends. These judgments are informed by normative principles: basic ideals or values—often embedded in history, institutions, and public understanding—that offer a yardstick by which good governance is measured (see, e.g., Gillroy and Wade 1992).

POLICY IMPLICATIONS AND RECOMMENDATION

We have looked at an anomalous period in U.S. history, examining why it arose and with what consequences. Given the available evidence regarding the causes and consequences of high incarceration rates, and guided by fundamental normative principles regarding the appropriate use of imprisonment as punishment, we believe that the policies leading to high incarceration rates are not serving the country well. We are concerned that the United States has gone past the point where the numbers of people in prison can be justified by social benefits. Indeed, we believe that the high rates of incarceration themselves constitute a source of injustice and, possibly, social harm. A criminal justice system that made less use of incarceration might better achieve its aims than a harsher, more punitive system

RECOMMENDATION: Given the small crime prevention effects of long prison sentences and the possibly high financial, social, and human costs of incarceration, federal and state policy makers should revise current criminal justice policies to significantly reduce the rate of incarceration in the United States. In particular, they should reexamine policies regarding mandatory prison sentences and long sentences. Policy makers should also take steps to improve the experience of incarcerated men and women and reduce unnecessary harm to their families and their communities.

We recommend such a systematic review of penal and related policies with the goals of achieving a significant reduction in the number of people in prison in the United States and providing better conditions for those in prison. To promote these goals, jurisdictions would need to review a range of programs, including community-based alternatives to incarceration, probation and parole, prisoner reentry support, and diversion from prosecution, as well as crime prevention initiatives.

Given the evidence that incarceration has been overused when less harmful alternatives could plausibly achieve better individual and social outcomes, we specifically urge consideration of changes in sentencing and other policies. We also propose that policy makers and citizens rethink the role played by prisons in addressing public safety and seek out crime reduction strategies that are more effective and less harmful. In many cases, alternatives to incarceration would be more practical and efficient ways to achieve the same objectives. Although a comprehensive review of the research on noncustodial sanctions and treatments was not part of our charge, that research could provide policy makers with guidance on when and how to substitute these alternatives for incarceration.

To minimize harm from incarceration, we urge reconsideration of the conditions of confinement and programs in prisons. Given that nearly all prisoners are eventually released, attention should be paid to how prisons can better serve society by addressing the need of prisoners to adjust to life following release and supporting their successful reintegration with their families and communities. Reviews of the conditions and programs in prisons would benefit from being open to public scrutiny. One approach would be to subject prisons to systematic ratings related to their public purposes. Such ratings could incorporate universal standards that recognize the humanity and citizenship of prisoners and the obligation to prepare them for life after prison.

We offer more specific suggestions for reconsideration of incarceration policies in three domains—sentencing policy, prison policy, and social policy.

- **Sentencing policy.** The evidence does not provide explicit guidance for a comprehensive reexamination of current sentencing policies. Details of strategies for reducing incarceration levels will depend on a complex interplay between the public and policy makers. Yet the evidence points to some sentencing practices that impose large social, financial, and human costs; yield uncertain benefits; and are inconsistent with the long-standing principles of the jurisprudence of punishment. Specifically, the evidence suggests that long sentences, mandatory minimum sentences, and policies on enforcement of drug laws should be reexamined.
- **Prison policy.** Given how damaging the experience of incarceration can be for some of those incarcerated and in some cases for their families and communities, we propose that steps be taken to improve the conditions and programs in prisons in ways that will reduce the harmful effects of incarceration and foster the successful reintegration of former prisoners when they are released.
- **Social policy.** Reducing the severity of sentences will not, by itself, relieve the underlying problems of economic insecurity, low education, and poor health that are associated with incarceration in the nation's poorest communities. Solutions to these problems are outside the criminal justice system, and they will include policies that address school dropout, drug addiction, mental illness, and neighborhood poverty—all of which are intimately connected to incarceration. If large numbers of intensely disadvantaged prime-age men and women remain in, or return to, poor communities without supports, the effects could be broadly harmful. Sustainably reducing incarceration may depend, in part, on whether services and programs are sufficient to meet the needs of those who would

otherwise be locked up. Thus, policy makers and communities will need to assess and address the availability, accessibility, and quality of social services, including drug treatment, health care, employment, and housing for those who otherwise would be imprisoned.

RESEARCH RECOMMENDATION

Recognizing that the knowledge base for many policies related to incarceration is limited, we urge the research community to work closely with the national and state governments and nongovernmental institutions to develop an ambitious and multifaceted portfolio of study to fill knowledge gaps in this field. For policy and public understanding, more studies are needed of the effects of various sanction policies, including those involving incarceration, on crime. The availability and effectiveness of alternatives to help achieve a just and safe society without a heavy reliance on incarceration need to be thoroughly studied.

The design and evaluation of promising alternatives to incarceration are of critical importance to this proposed research portfolio. Such a research program would expand the options of state officials for responding to the problem of crime. Scholars should also be engaged in policy discussions about the costs and benefits of various changes in sentencing policy that would reduce rates of incarceration. Researchers should expand the number of systematic evaluations of prison-based programs, aid in the development of evidence-based policies that promote humane prison conditions, and help design and evaluate reentry programs that support successful reintegration. Finally, when these interventions have proven effective, the research community should offer its expertise to assist in bringing them to scale.

RECOMMENDATION: Given the prominent role played by prisons in U.S. society, the far-reaching impact of incarceration, and the need to develop policies that reduce reliance on imprisonment as a response to crime, public and private research institutions and statistical agencies should support a robust research and statistics program commensurate with the importance of these issues.

Research aimed at developing a better understanding of (1) the experience of being incarcerated and its effects, (2) alternative sentencing policies, and (3) the impact of incarceration on communities is outlined in the report's final chapter and expanded on in Appendix C.

1

Introduction

After decades of stability from the 1920s to the early 1970s, the rate of incarceration in the United States has increased to a rate more than four times higher than in 1972. In 1972, the U.S. incarceration rate—the number in prisons and local jails per 100,000 population—stood at 161. After peaking in 2009, the number of people in state and federal prisons fell slightly through 2012. Still, in 2012, the incarceration rate was 707 per 100,000, a total of 2.23 million people in custody (Glaze and Herberman, 2013). With nearly 1 of every 100 adults in prison or jail, the U.S. rate of incarceration is 5 to 10 times higher than the rates in Western European and other liberal democracies.[1]

The large racial disparity in incarceration is striking. Of those behind bars in 2011, about 60 percent were minorities (858,000 blacks and 464,000 Hispanics) (Carson and Sabol, 2012; Maguire, n.d., Table 6.17.2011). The largest impact of the prison buildup has been on poor, minority men. African American men born since the late 1960s are more likely to have served time in prison than to have completed college with a 4-year degree (Pettit and Western, 2004; Pettit, 2012). And African American men under age 35 who failed to finish high school are now more likely to be behind bars than employed in the labor market. The rise in incarceration

---

[1]The 1972 incarceration rate is calculated from counts of the prison and jail population reported in Hindelang et al. (1977, Tables 6.1 and 6.43). The 2012 prison and jail incarceration rates and the incarcerated population are reported in Glaze and Herberman (2013, Table 2). International incarceration rates for European countries are from Aebi and Delgrande (2013), and data on Australia, Canada, New Zealand, and the United States are from Walmsley (2012), as well as updates from the International Centre for Prison Studies (2013).

transformed not only the criminal justice system, but also U.S. race relations and the institutional landscape of urban poverty.

The U.S. justice system has charted a unique path to crime control that
traverses poor and minority communities across the country. A number of
research literatures explore the sources of rising incarceration rates in policy
and social change; the relationship between crime and incarceration; and
the effects of incarceration on the employment, health, and family life of
the formerly incarcerated and more broadly on U.S. civic life. Yet there has
been no comprehensive effort to date to assess the causes, scope, and consequences of contemporary incarceration rates. Four questions stand out:

1.   What changes in U.S. society and public policy drove the rise in
     incarceration?
2.   What consequences have these changes had for crime rates?
3.   What effects does incarceration have on those in confinement; on
     their families and children; on the neighborhoods and communi-
     ties from which they come and to which they return; and on the
     economy, politics, structure, and culture of U.S. society?
4.   What are the implications for public policy of the evidence on
     causes and effects of high levels of incarceration?

An ad hoc committee of the National Research Council was asked to
review the scientific evidence on these questions. By weighing the evidence
on both the causes and consequences of high rates of incarceration, the
committee's work may help the public and policy makers decide whether
the current rates are too high and, if so, to explore policy alternatives. And
if the evidence is wanting or inconsistent, then this study can indicate directions for future research.

THE COMMITTEE'S CHARGE

The committee's statement of task (see Box 1-1) describes in greater
detail the scope of its efforts.

Incarceration is a unique state function. The forcible deprivation of
liberty and detention in a facility designed for the purpose is a restriction
on the individual freedom to which liberal societies aspire. Incarceration
represents a collective decision that some among us are too dangerous, or
their crimes too serious, to circulate freely in the community. To preserve
order and safety, to affirm norms of lawful conduct, and to help remedy
criminal behavior, we built lockups, detention centers, asylums, jails, and
prisons. These institutions reflect how a society through its political process
has negotiated a compromise between order and freedom. Incarceration
is in many ways a foundational institution, being the last resort of a state's

authority in the performance of its many other functions. As many have remarked, the use and character of incarceration thus reveals something fundamental about a society's level of civilization and the quality of citizenship (de Beaumont and de Tocqueville, 1970; Churchill, 1910; Dostoevsky, 1861).

Imprisonment lies at one end of a continuum of legally ordered restraints on liberty, some imposed not as punishment but as part of the criminal justice process prior to a possible charge or conviction or following release from confinement. At the other end of the continuum are forms of community supervision, such as probation and parole, as well as in-home detention. Compared with punishment outside a facility, confinement in a local jail or detention facility for short periods is likely to be seen and experienced as a more severe form of punishment. Prison incarceration then follows. Of course, imprisonment itself varies in severity, depending on the specifics of confinement and treatment.

Contemporary incarceration takes many forms. The juvenile justice system has developed a special set of rules and protocols for the detention of children. Criminally convicted adults are held in state or federal prisons, generally serving more than a year for a felony. Local jails typically detain those serving short sentences or awaiting trial. Immigrants awaiting deportation may be held in federal detention facilities. The mentally ill may be housed under civil commitment to state hospitals. The conditions of incarceration, like those who are confined, thus show considerable variation.

The primary focus of this report is on adults incarcerated in prisons and jails. Prisoners form an important subset of this group because of their large numbers among the total incarcerated population and the long terms of their confinement. Throughout the report, therefore, we often focus specifically on prison incarceration. The size of the prison population depends not only on the number of crimes, arrests, convictions, and prison commitments but also on the use of alternatives to incarceration and on responses to violations of the terms of parole or probation. Although other forms of incarceration outside of the adult criminal justice system are undeniably important, they have been less important to the steep rise in incarceration over the past four decades that forms our main charge.

This study differs from many conducted by committees of the National Research Council with respect to its scope and the number of questions posed about a complex social phenomenon. The causes of the increase in incarceration rates are disputed, and its consequences are not fully understood. Nevertheless, a rigorous review of the evidence is now timely. A burgeoning research literature helps explain why the U.S. incarceration rate grew so dramatically and examines the consequences for those incarcerated, their families, communities, and U.S. society. For several decades, enthusiasm for incarceration dominated crime policy and the related public

BOX 1-1
Causes and Consequences of High Rates of Incarceration
Statement of Task

An ad hoc panel will conduct a study and prepare a report that will focus on the scientific evidence that exists on the use of incarceration in the United States and will propose a research agenda on the use of incarceration and alternatives to incarceration for the future. The study will explore the causes of the dramatic increases in incarceration rates since the 1970s, the costs and benefits of the nation's current sentencing and incarceration policies, and whether there is evidence that alternative policies would more effectively promote public safety and community well-being.

Recognizing that research evidence will vary in its strength and consistency, the panel will undertake the following tasks:

1. Describe and assess the existing research on the causes, drivers, and social context of incarceration in the United States over the past 30-40 years. To what extent does existing research suggest that incarceration rates were influenced by historical and contemporary changes in:
   a. operations of criminal justice system and other public sector systems that may affect rates of arrest or conviction, and nature and severity of sanctions: such as patterns of policing, prosecution, sentencing, prison operations, and parole practices;
   b. legal and judicial policies, such as changes in law, institutional policies and practices, and judicial rulings affecting conditions for arrest, sanctions for various crimes, drug enforcement policies, and policies regarding parole and parole revocation; and
   c. social and economic structure and political conditions, such as criminal behavior, cultural shifts, changes in political attitudes and behavior, changes in public opinion, demographic changes, and changes in the structure of economic opportunity.

conversation. Commentators on both the left and the right are now reacting critically to the incarceration boom, partly out of concern for growing correctional budgets, partly because of questions about the effectiveness of incarceration in reducing crime, and partly out of misgivings about the values that have come to dominate penal policy (e.g., Gramlich, 2013; Kabler, 2013; Alexander, 2010). Reform, it appears, is under way. At the state level and in the federal government, many elected officials are supporting initiatives aimed at reducing prison populations and are turning to the research evidence for guidance. In this context, the committee hopes to inform a critical conversation about the significance of high incarceration rates for U.S. society and the future of the nation's penal and social policies.

2. Describe and assess the existing research on the consequences of current U.S. incarceration policies. To what extent does the research suggest that incarceration rates have effects on:
   a. crime rates, such as to what extent this is due to deterrence and incapacitation, to rehabilitation, or to criminogenic effects of incarceration;
   b. individual behavior and outcomes, during imprisonment and afterward, such as changes in mental and physical health, prospects for future employment, civic participation, and desistance/reoffending;
   c. families, such as effects on intimate partners and children, patterns of marriage and dating, and intergenerational effects;
   d. communities, such as geographic concentrations, neighborhood effects, effects on specific racial and ethnic communities, high rates of reentry and return in some communities, labor markets, and patterns of crime and policing; and
   e. society, such as (in addition to effects on the crime rate) the financial and economic costs of incarceration, effects on U.S. civic life and governance, and other near-term and longer-term social costs and benefits.
3. Explore the public policy implications of the analysis of causes and consequences, including evidence for the effectiveness and costs of alternative policies affecting incarceration rates. What does the research tell us about:
   a. efficacy of policies that may affect incarceration or serve as alternatives to incarceration, including their effects on public safety and their other social benefits and costs;
   b. the cost-effectiveness of specific programmatic approaches to reducing the rate of incarceration;
   c. how best to measure and assess the potential costs and benefits of alternative policies and programs; and
   d. ways to improve oversight and administration of policies, institutions, and programs affecting the rate of incarceration.

To address the study charge, the National Research Council assembled a committee of 20 scholars and practitioners to review and assess the research evidence. The committee members include not only criminologists and sociologists who have conducted original research on these issues but also representatives of other academic disciplines, including economics, political science, psychology, law, medicine, and history, who brought to bear different methods and perspectives. The members include those whose professional experience gives them practical insights into the workings of the judicial and corrections systems and the policy debates in the legislative and executive branches of government. To aid in this study, the committee also enlisted several other scholars with specialized expertise to review

particular subsets of questions, such as the health and public health implications of incarceration; the policy shifts and system dynamics leading to
higher incarceration rates; and the availability in prisons of rehabilitative
education, training, treatment, and work experience.

We hope the result of the committee's work will be seen as a fair summary of what is known today about the sources of the rise of incarceration
in the United States; how it has affected people, communities, and society;
and the implications of that knowledge for public policies determining
future rates of incarceration.

A central question for public policy is whether increasing the incarceration rates affect public safety and, conversely, whether crime rates
contributed to the growth of imprisonment in America. The historical relationship between crime and incarceration is complex. On the one hand, the
decades-long rise in incarceration rates began following a substantial rise
in crime rates in the United States. Yet the growth of the prison population
continued through and after a major decline in crime rates in the 1990s.
In reviewing the evidence, the committee paid attention to the effects of
changes in state and federal policy and practice over the period of the rise
in incarceration rates, including the relationship of policy changes to crime
rates. We noted that in many instances, these policy choices reflected and
resulted from broader political and social currents, including, for a variety
of reasons, a marked tendency to resort to imprisonment, and harsh punishments generally, as society's preferred response to crime, even when crime
rates were falling.

Understanding the impact of high rates of incarceration on crime is
challenging. Incarceration can reduce crime by incapacitating those who
would otherwise be committing crimes in free society. Incarceration may
also deter or rehabilitate those who are punished from committing future
crimes. Fear of such punishment may deter others from committing crimes.
On the other hand, the prison experience and its aftermath may in some
cases contribute to future criminal activity. The net effect of incarceration
on crime will vary depending, for example, on who is sent to prison, the
type of crime, the length of sentences, and how people are treated while
in prison and after release. Despite a large and growing body of studies
exploring the complex relationship between crime and incarceration rates
over recent decades, then, a precise quantification of the impact of high
rates of incarceration on U.S. crime rates remains a significant scientific
challenge.

In this report, we are not simply concerned with explaining changes
in the rates of incarceration. Nor are we limited to analyzing the effects
of imprisonment on individuals who serve prison sentences during the
era of high incarceration. We also consider the aggregate, cumulative
effects of the nation's incarceration policies. America's high rates of

incarceration have changed the meaning and consequences of a prison sentence for those who go to prison and for the families and communities to which they return. Over time, high incarceration rates may increase or decrease public safety, alter the functioning of labor markets and the economy, strengthen or weaken the fabric of communities, and skew the distribution of income and opportunity. Higher rates of incarceration also affect U.S. civic life, influence the nation's pursuit of racial justice, and tip the balance in close elections. At the most basic level, more incarceration uses resources that could be spent for other purposes. Finally, we also assess the evidence on how high incarceration rates and their consequences affect the quality of American democracy.

MEANINGS AND USES OF INCARCERATION

Incarceration—legally imposed deprivation of personal liberty, typically in a facility specially designed for the purpose—is one of the most severe forms of punishment a society can impose. Prison terms usually are reserved for those found guilty of more serious crimes, defined as felonies by state and federal legislatures.

The scale of incarceration can be measured in a variety of ways. The incarceration rate is usually presented as a ratio of those in prison (or prison and jail) at a given time to a society's (or state's) population. The incarceration rates can be calculated for specific demographic groups in the population—by race or age, for example—and for small geographic areas, such as neighborhoods or blocks. The incarceration rate describes the footprint of the penal system in society. The magnitude of incarceration also might be measured by scaling prison admissions by crimes or arrests rather than by population. Such measures reflect the impact of prosecution and sentencing policies on the overall punitiveness of the criminal justice system. Both kinds of statistics are reported in Chapter 2.[2]

We are concerned in this report not only with the numbers behind bars but also with the nature and meaning of that experience and how it has changed over the period of the rise in incarceration rates. How one views the increasingly frequent resort to prison in the United States also depends in part on how one understands the purposes served by imprisonment for society and for the sentenced individual.[3]

---

[2]The committee considered and rejected the notion that the incarceration rate might also be presented as a ratio of those in prison to crimes reported. There is no analytical connection between one year's crimes and a prison population sentenced for crimes committed years ago.

[3]A convenient summary history of thinking about incarceration and its uses can be found in Simon and Sparks (2013, Chapters 1-7).

Crime and punishment are social and legal constructs. Their nature and meanings change over time and differ from one society (and one person) to another. In American jurisprudence, a prison sentence serves three possible purposes. First, the purpose of a prison sentence may be understood primarily as retribution, or "just deserts," meaning that the severity of a given crime requires deprivation of the liberty of the person found guilty of that crime. Second, a prison sentence may be justified as a way of preventing crime, either through deterrence of the individual sentenced (specific deterrence), deterrence of others in society at large who may be inclined to offend (general deterrence), or avoidance of crimes that might otherwise have been committed by that individual absent incarceration (incapacitation). Finally, a prison sentence may be deemed justified as a means of preventing future crimes through the rehabilitation of the individual incarcerated. Of course, these rationales are not mutually exclusive.

Throughout U.S. history, the emphasis on one or another rationale for incarceration has shifted significantly, and it continues to change. As a consequence, the conditions of confinement and the experience of returning to society also have changed. To understand the effects of the rise in incarceration, one must examine how prison environments have changed as the numbers of prisoners have increased and how this changed environment may lead to different outcomes for the individuals incarcerated.

Whereas the jurisprudence of incarceration emphasizes the purposes of retribution, deterrence, incapacitation, and rehabilitation, criminal punishment also provides a vivid moral symbol, publicly condemning criminal conduct. Thus the French sociologist Emile Durkheim (1984) argued that penal law affirms basic values and helps build social solidarity. By this account, punishment activates society's moral sentiments and reinforces the collective sense of right and wrong. Critics have objected that, rather than reflecting "society as a whole," institutions of punishment under real conditions of social and economic inequality burden the disadvantaged (Spitzer, 1991; Lukes and Scull, 1983; Garland, 2013). From this perspective, prisons and jails reflect and perhaps exacerbate social inequalities rather than promote social solidarity. Legal principle has grappled with the penal system's innate potential for injustice. Rules of constraint were developed to restrict the unbridled and arbitrary application of punishment. Expressed in the language of Western jurisprudence, justice requires that society's decision to deprive a citizen of liberty through imprisonment be constrained by two countervailing principles: proportionality (punishment should be tailored to the severity of the crime) and parsimony (punishment should not be more severe than required to achieve a legitimate public purpose) (see the discussion of guiding principles below).

Some scholars have argued that, in light of this nation's long history of troubled race relations, it is especially important to consider whether prison and other punishments unfairly burden African Americans and other minority groups. If so, the justice system only reinforces historical inequalities, thereby undermining the social compact that should undergird the nation's laws. Other scholars have stressed the utilitarian value of prison for achieving socially desired ends. From this societal viewpoint, the use of incarceration is assessed according to whether its social benefits exceed its social costs. By this instrumental view, imprisonment can be used, for example, to contain and discourage crime—directly by confining those prone to commit further crimes or by deterring them or, by example, others from committing future crimes. Assessments of the effectiveness of policies favoring incarceration would therefore depend on an empirical understanding of its purported benefit of crime prevention or other social benefits, weighed against the direct costs of the prisons themselves and the indirect social costs incurred by removing incarcerated individuals from society.

Prisons also can support the rehabilitation of those incarcerated so that after release, they are more likely to live in a law-abiding way and reintegrate successfully into the rhythms of work, family, and civic engagement. In this narrower view of the instrumental value of incarceration policies, the effectiveness of prisons is measured by such outcomes as lower rates of recidivism and higher rates of employment, supportive family connections, improved health outcomes, and the standing of the formerly incarcerated as citizens in the community. The relevant scholarly literature focuses on issues of the availability and effectiveness of programs; the impact of the prison environment on the self-concept, behavior, and human capital of those incarcerated; and the experience of leaving prison and returning home.

Yet another stream of scholarly inquiry examines the role of the criminal justice system, and in particular the role of prisons, in controlling entire categories or communities of people. In this view, the laws of society and the instruments of punishment have been used throughout history to sustain those in power by suppressing active opposition to entrenched interests and deterring challenges to the status quo. This scholarly literature has examined the role of the justice system—including the definition of crimes by legislatures, enforcement of laws by the police, and uses of incarceration—in dealing with new immigrant groups, the labor and civil rights movements, the behavior of the mentally ill, and the use of alcohol and illegal drugs, to cite some examples. In recent years, scholars in this tradition have focused on the impact of the justice system on racial minorities in the United States and specifically on the impact of recent high rates of incarceration on the aspiration for racial equality. Researchers who study the power relations of society reflected in the criminal justice system often observe that the poor, minorities, and the marginal are seen as dangerous or undeserving. In these cases, the majority will support harsh punishments entailing long sentences and the use of imprisonment for lesser offenses. The effect of incarceration and other punishments used in this way may be to reproduce and deepen existing social and economic inequalities.

Because incarceration imposes pain and loss on both those sentenced and, frequently, their families and others, these costs also must be weighed against its social benefits in determining when or whether the deprivation of liberty is justified. This equation must consider as well the harms caused by those sent to prison. These harms include those experienced by individual victims and the broader negative social effects emanating from the criminal act. By punishing breaches of the social compact, vindicating the victims of crime often is viewed as an important purpose of the criminal sanction. Such an analysis of costs and benefits must be both normative and empirical. While there are no scientific solutions to normative problems, evidence on the effects of incarceration can inform that analysis. Moreover, given the pain imposed by imprisonment and other harsh punishments, it may be reasonable to minimize their use when alternatives can achieve the same social benefits at lower cost to society. High incarceration rates may signal that in many instances, prison is being used when alternatives would achieve equal or better outcomes for society.

Because incarceration encompasses a range of experiences that vary widely across individuals and from one era or place to another, its effects are difficult to assess. This variation arises not only from differences in the legal terms of sentences, such as length and conditions for release, but also from differences in the conditions of confinement and after release. Harsh or abusive prison environments can cause damage to those subjected to them, just as environments that offer treatment and opportunities to learn and work can provide them with hope, skills, and other assets. So while we talk about incarceration as a single phenomenon, it in fact describes a wide range of experiences that may have very different effects.

STUDY APPROACH

For each set of questions posed in its statement of task, the committee reviewed and weighed the published research and, where the evidence permitted, summarized what is known about the phenomenon of high rates of incarceration, its causes, its effects, and the implications of that knowledge for public policy. In many respects, the body of published research on these topics is now substantial and continues to grow quickly. On some questions, the weight of evidence from empirical studies is compelling. For others, it is suggestive but not definitive. In still other cases, it is thin or conflicting. An important part of our work involved identifying the limits of current knowledge and therefore of its usefulness as a guide to the public and policy makers.

In light of the challenges to empirical research in this area, our approach was first to identify the strongest, most methodologically rigorous individual studies and then, where possible, to review multiple studies using differing methods to establish the extent to which there is compelling evidence, and some degree of agreement, on the causes or effects of high rates of incarceration in the United States. Although there is something to be learned from the experience of other affluent societies that have followed a different path, our main point of reference was earlier in this country's history, when incarceration rates were a fraction of what they are today.

Guiding Principles

A discussion of values has been notably missing from the nation's recent policy debates on the use of prison. Although policies on criminal punishment necessarily embody ideas about justice, fairness, and desert, the recent policy discourse often has been characterized by overheated rhetoric or cost-benefit calculations that mask strong but hidden normative assumptions. Basic principles for penal reform should be transparent and open to debate.

In the period of rising incarceration rates and public concerns about safety, elected officials and other policy makers have argued that those committing crimes should be held accountable and punished severely. These values of offender accountability and crime control have become paramount, and older principles that balance the tendency to harsh punishment have receded from the policy debate. In undertaking this study, the committee reviewed the scholarly literature on the role of prison in society and the principles governing correctional policy generally. Based on this review, the committee articulated a set of guiding normative principles that, if observed, would restore balance to the discussion of criminal justice values. The following four normative principles helped the committee interpret the scientific evidence and guided the committee in carrying out its charge to recommend new policy alternatives:

1. *Proportionality:* Criminal offenses should be sentenced in proportion to their seriousness.
2. *Parsimony:* The period of confinement should be sufficient but not greater than necessary to achieve the goals of sentencing policy.
3. *Citizenship:* The conditions and consequences of imprisonment should not be so severe or lasting as to violate one's fundamental status as a member of society.
4. *Social justice:* Prisons should be instruments of justice, and as such their collective effect should be to promote and not undermine society's aspirations for a fair distribution of rights, resources, and opportunities.

Rather than describing the positive goals of imprisonment, each of these principles describes a different kind of constraint. These principles also set firm limits on one of the main impulses behind the dramatic rise in incarceration—the desire for retribution. We recognize that the urge to express public disapproval of criminal behavior is a legitimate purpose of punishment, but the disapproval of crime must be expressed within the bounds set by other normative convictions. The state's authority to deliberately deprive people of their liberty through incarceration may be abused, and its misuse may undermine its legitimacy. We elaborate on the scholarly basis for each of the above principles in Chapter 12.

Understanding Causes

Researchers seeking to understand the causes of the rise in incarceration (discussed in detail in Chapters 3 and 4) have been able to identify and estimate the effects of several proximate causes, including specific state and federal policy choices. These include not only legislated policies but also changes in police practice, the behavior of prosecutors and judges, and the administration of parole, as well as other changes in how laws are implemented. These direct influences on the numbers incarcerated, however, have a social and historical context, including public concerns about crime and disorder, political incentives to respond to or exploit those concerns, and a complex history and evolution of racial and ethnic group relationships and politics.

Understanding the deeper sources of the rise in incarceration rates calls for other kinds of evidence and analysis than those applied in exploring proximate causes, along with a more subjective set of judgments about how to interpret that evidence. For example, it is not always possible to assess the motivation and incentives of leaders or voters that contributed to putting more people behind bars. The analytical problem is complicated by the largely autonomous decisions and actions taken by multiple actors in the states and the federal government. Nevertheless, the committee devoted considerable effort to exploring such questions of causality in the belief that a better understanding of how the United States reached this point is essential to understanding where the country should go from here.

Our analysis of both causes and consequences (discussed below) must remain provisional because the growth of incarceration is so recent, its effects are still unfolding, and the level and uses of incarceration at a given moment in time are the result of a complex set of past and ongoing social and political changes. Beginning in the 1960s, a complex combination of organized protests, urban riots, violent crime and drug use, the collapse of urban schools, and many other factors contributed to declining economic opportunities in many neighborhoods and too often to greater fear of crime. After 1970, a wave of heavy industry closings and mass layoffs resulting from technological changes, international competition, and shifting markets contributed to the elimination of many relatively high-paying jobs for less educated workers with specialized skills. Places hardest hit by the wave of industrial losses also experienced large and sustained increases in crime (National Research Council, 2008, p. 5). In the 1980s, a wave of crack cocaine use and related street crime hit many of the nation's already distressed inner cities.

In the wake of these and other structural shifts, employment fell among young people with little schooling and work experience. The income gap between unskilled and skilled workers widened. Large-scale migrations from rural to urban areas and an influx of lower-skilled undocumented workers from Mexico and Central America coincided with this widening inequality. In past decades, then, as growing percentages of all ethnic and racial groups have graduated from high school and went on to higher education, those who dropped out were left further behind with fewer options for earning a living.

In response to the protests and turmoil of the 1960s, major national commission reports examined the causes of racial division and the historical roots of violence in the United States (President's Commission on Law Enforcement and the Administration of Justice, 1967; National Advisory Commission on Civil Disorders, 1968; U.S. National Commission on the Causes and Prevention of Violence, 1969; National Advisory Commission on Criminal Justice Standards and Goals, 1973). These and other experts recommended renewed efforts to address poverty and racial inequality at its roots. Following initial support for "Great Society" programs designed to tackle poverty, both an increase in violent crime starting in the 1960s and periodic civil disorder contributed to public fears of crime and support for tougher sanctions.

These fears and their political uses contributed in turn to a series of changes in criminal laws and prescribed punishments; changes in law enforcement and criminal justice procedures; and other changes affecting the frequency and severity of punishments, including incarceration. Pessimism emerged, among professionals as well as the larger public, about the potential of prisons to rehabilitate their occupants. Those affected most directly by changes in the criminal justice system lived in the neighborhoods most severely affected by the loss of economic opportunity and other kinds of distress, including high rates of violent crime and drug dealing. And in the past two decades of the period of the rise in incarceration rates, new attention to illegal immigration and to sex offenses led to new laws and penalties, contributing to growing numbers detained, convicted, and sentenced to prison for these offenses.

A full description of this complex and evolving social context for the expanded use of prison as a response to crime in the United States is beyond the scope of this study. Nonetheless, it is important to examine this history to better understand the rising use of imprisonment over nearly four decades. The committee does not view the growth of incarceration as an inevitable product of these larger social changes. The United States has experienced other periods of sweeping social change and disorder in which incarceration rates did not rise. During the recent period, moreover, the United States stood apart from other modern industrial democracies in the direction it took. To understand how U.S. incarceration rates reached their current level, the committee examined and weighed evidence of various kinds, drawing on the methods of historians, economists, and political scientists, as well as other social scientists.

Assessing Consequences

The committee's efforts to isolate the effects of the high rates of incarceration (discussed in Chapters 5 through 11) likewise faced a series of analytical challenges. For purposes of this study, we were interested in the aggregate effects of higher incarceration rates on individuals, their families and children, the communities from which they come, and U.S. society. Our ability to measure these effects depends in part on inferences drawn from numerous studies examining how the lives of those incarcerated differ from the lives of those otherwise like them who have not experienced incarceration. If, for instance, those who go to prison fare worse than others, is this then due to incarceration or some other factor, such as illiteracy or drug addiction, which is correlated with incarceration? Because the personal characteristics or behaviors that put people at greater risk of incarceration may cause them to do poorly in other ways, researchers may find it difficult to isolate the effects of incarceration.

To the extent that the effects of incarceration on individuals and their families can be measured, one may infer that a rise in incarceration rates will cause those effects to be more widespread. However, measurement of aggregate effects over time poses a second set of research challenges. One of these is the need to separate effects leading to or arising from the growth of incarceration in the United States from other, more or less contemporaneous social changes, such as changes in crime rates or labor market conditions. For example, if homicide rates fell in the United States after 1980, is it methodologically feasible to determine whether any part of that decline can be attributed to increased incarceration, taking into account all the simultaneous changes in other aspects of the society and the environment that have been shown to influence homicide? This was a central question for the committee to address, but the methodological challenges make it a difficult one to answer.

As rates of many major crime types rose and fell for more than five decades, incarceration rates started to rise nationally in 1973 and continued to rise for 40 years, stabilizing only recently (Tonry, 2012; see Figure 1-1). Some may compare the decline in crime rates after 1980 and again in the 1990s with the increase in incarceration rates and infer that incarceration greatly reduces crime. However, studies of crime trends that consider many possible influences, including changes in incarceration rates, have had limited success separating different causes. Evidence concerning the complex relationship between crime and incarceration rates is reviewed in Chapter 5.

In a society or community where incarceration rates rise significantly, the experience of incarceration and/or its meaning for individuals and families may change, altering its effects. Given the demographic and geographic concentration of the rise in incarceration in the United States, the greatest impact has been felt by those living in the poorest communities. If the

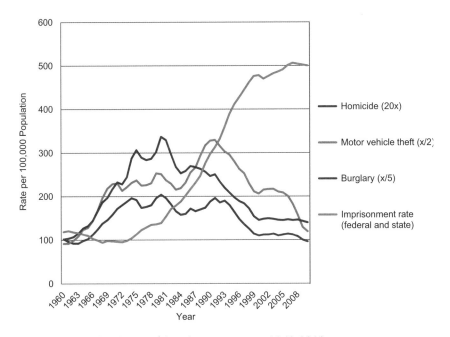

FIGURE 1-1 U.S. crime and imprisonment rates, 1960-2010.
NOTE: The different crime rates have been rescaled, as noted in the figure, to facilitate comparison of time trends.
SOURCE: Tonry (2012).

incarceration experience has become more common in some communities than others, does this new reality alter the cumulative or marginal effects of incarceration on the rates of certain types of crime, or the deterrent effects of the criminal justice system, or the employment rates of those released back into those communities? As the rate of incarceration rises, its average and marginal effects may change as well, because those being locked up may include individuals who have different responses to incarceration relative to those imprisoned when the rate was lower. Therefore, an inquiry into the consequences of high rates of incarceration might focus on whether the incarceration of larger numbers has provided diminishing returns to U.S. society—smaller benefits at higher costs—at the margin. Finally, family dynamics, marriage, and labor markets may also function differently in communities with high rates of incarceration.

Another research challenge is posed by the diverse conditions of incarceration. The experience of incarceration varies from prison to prison, from state to state, and between the state and federal systems. It is also likely that the prison experience has changed over time, in particular over the period when incarceration rates rose and prison administrators were struggling to stay abreast of the rapid expansion of their systems. Furthermore, because incarceration is not a single, uniform experience but is highly varied, even to some degree unique to each prisoner, generalizing about its effects is difficult. Depending, among other things, on the conditions and duration of confinement and release, imprisonment can be humane and even helpful. Incarceration can provide time for reflection and personal growth, access to better health care and treatment of drug dependency or illness, respite from toxic environments or situations, and opportunities to learn and acquire skills. Alternatively, prison can be harmful and degrading, exposing the confined to criminal influence, violence, and humiliation; isolating them from nurturing human contact and personal responsibility; and leaving them poorly equipped for life outside. Generalization about prison's effects requires more sophisticated measures of the nature of that experience than are often readily available to researchers, especially given ethical and practical barriers to conducting controlled studies inside prisons. Moreover, the prior characteristics of those incarcerated and their behavior help determine the nature of the prison experience both objectively and subjectively. Understanding the effects of incarceration thus requires specifying in some detail the nature of that experience, as well as distinguishing its effects from the effects of these preexisting characteristics and concurrent behaviors.

Not only is the base of knowledge about the prison experience constrained by a paucity of studies, but also even the extant literature may be of limited value. Because prison conditions and sentencing practices are continually evolving, sometimes in response to the level of incarceration and related budget pressures, some findings of earlier studies may not be applicable to later periods. As typical prison conditions and the number and types of people exposed to them change over time, even strong empirical findings must be viewed as provisional. For example, if there has been a shift since the 1970s from a more rehabilitative to a more punitive prison management regime, the effects of incarceration may have changed as a result.

A further limit on analysis of prison conditions is imposed by barriers to researchers' access to prisons. In earlier times, scholars were given broad access to prisons, prisoners, and corrections officers. By contrast, the contemporary prison has not been the subject of sustained empirical inquiry, perhaps reflecting less interest on the part of researchers and wariness on the part of prison administrators. The lack of research access, combined with cutbacks in other forms of outside review—journalistic investigations of life on the inside and judicial review of legal challenges to prison conditions—means that the nation's prison systems are less open than before to public scrutiny. Finally, prisons have not been subjected to the same degree of regular reporting and public scrutiny based on transparent, published standards of performance as some other major public institutions, such as schools and hospitals.

Because the scientific study of a social phenomenon contributes to new understanding or interpretations, it has the potential to change the phenomenon itself. Indeed, a major purpose of the committee's work is to provide the public and policy makers with new insights that could lead to new policies. In this period of evolving public opinion and policy and rapid expansion of the role of incarceration in U.S. society, there may be more reason than usual to regard all findings on the rise in the incarceration rate, including those of this study, as provisional and a new starting point for further research.

Weighing the Evidence

Summarizing research across a variety of disciplines—from history, to economics, to medicine, to law—and across a range of questions—from the historical sources of policy change to incarceration's effects on individuals—defies any single standard of evidence or method of synthesis. Historians and economists, for example, work with different empirical materials, and each discipline treats social context differently. Assessing employers' responses to formerly incarcerated job seekers, an area in which randomized trials are possible, enables strong causal inferences for which statistical certainty can be estimated. Analysis of the development of punitive crime policy, an area in which history is run just once in all its complexity, is no less rigorous and empirical, but the findings will be of a different nature. In executing a charge that ranged so widely, the committee encountered methodological challenges in three areas: data, consequences, and historical interpretation.

Although the incarcerated population is reasonably well accounted for during our period of study, the data landscape often is seriously incomplete. There are no complete data series on the ethnicity and education of prison inmates, for example, so we frequently rely on estimates throughout this report. Longitudinal data following people in and out of prison and other contexts, such as schooling, work, and family, would have greatly improved our understanding of the effects of incarceration. Beyond these challenges, summarizing data from 51 prison jurisdictions (and thousands of localities) often involves glossing over the great institutional and statutory variation across the country. In this report, then, we attempt to paint a general national picture while recognizing that U.S. criminal justice is a matter largely for state and local governments. When we rely on case studies, we take care to extrapolate their lessons in light of the particular institutional context in which those lessons were generated. In general, many of the data gaps can be filled by using estimates or by pooling different data sources, but doing so necessarily adds uncertainty to the conclusions that are drawn. The major published data series on incarceration used in this report are described and assessed in Appendix B.

Besides providing an accurate portrait of the penal system, a key part of the committee's charge concerned the consequences of incarceration. In a variety of different empirical domains—in the study of employment, health, families, and communities—incarceration is closely correlated with multiple measures of social and economic disadvantage. In rare cases, controlled experiments are possible. Just as rarely, so-called natural experiments—such as those arising from changes in law in some places but not others, or from variations in judicial interpretation or sentencing practice—produce variation in incarceration that is independent of the background conditions that are usually closely related to serving time in prison. More narrowly, the committee, like empirical researchers, was challenged to fully disentangle the effects of incarceration from those of conviction or other operational aspects of criminal justice, such as the conditions of confinement.

Finally, the committee confronted the problem of historical interpretation. For a large and regionally variable phenomenon such as the emergence of high incarceration rates, unfolding for more than four decades across 50 states and at the federal level, the historical record often does not point unambiguously to a single chain of events propelling its occurrence. As the historical narrative reaches back in time, from sentencing policy in the 1980s to the politics and social change of the 1960s and even earlier, the number of plausible rival explanations is multiplied. Both where causal inference about incarceration is threatened by correlated measures of socioeconomic disadvantage and where the historical record is open to alternative interpretations, we have, whenever possible, tried to look at multiple sources of empirical evidence, generated by different research designs subject to different flaws and strengths. Pulling a variety of findings together, we have attempted to characterize the weight of the evidence, often describing the scientific consensus as a plausible range of conclusions instead of a unique inference.

Empirical studies have wrestled with the methodological challenges outlined above with varying success, so a major task of this committee was to separate stronger from weaker evidence. We have tried to describe carefully the limits of current knowledge so that readers of this report can form their own judgments about the strength of the evidence and therefore its usefulness as a basis for public policy and their own actions. We have taken care to indicate where uncertainty exists in research results, clarifying what is not known as much as what is.

Applying the Evidence to Policy

Based on a weighing of the evidence and its limits, the committee's final task was to assess its implications for public policy. As already noted, these implications depend on both normative and scientific analysis. People hold differing views regarding the outcomes of policy, including the balancing of risks to public safety against both the potential social benefits and reduced costs of alternatives to the policies that have led to the current high rate of incarceration.

Members of this committee share the view that the inherent severity of incarceration as a punishment—including the harm it often does to prisoners, their families, and communities—argues for limiting its use to cases where alternatives are less effective in achieving the same social ends. The evidence reviewed in this report reveals that the costs of today's unprecedented rate of incarceration, particularly the long prison sentences imposed under recent sentencing laws, outweigh the observable benefits. We are conscious as well that a key feature of today's high rate of incarceration is that large proportions of poor, less educated African American and Hispanic men are likely to be in jail or prison at some time in their lives. Indeed, for many poorly educated African American and Hispanic men, coercion is the most salient of their encounters with public authority. These findings led us to look for better policy choices.

The committee's role is not to decide what level or use of incarceration is appropriate for the nation or a given state. Regardless of one's values or preferences, however, choices can be informed by our assessment of the effects of and trade-offs among different policies. To the extent that trade-offs can be quantified, alternative policy regimes can be compared in terms of the levels of incarceration and public safety and other effects they may produce. To the extent that evidence is conflicting or suggests a range of possible effects, alternative sets of assumptions will show a range of likely results of alternative policies.

ORGANIZATION OF THE REPORT

The remainder of this report is organized around the major sets of questions posed in the committee's charge. Chapter 2 provides an overview of the rise in the incarceration rate since the early 1970s, its components, and accompanying changes in society. Chapters 3 and 4 explore evidence regarding the complex set of factors contributing directly and indirectly to the high rate of incarceration in the United States. Chapters 5 through 11 examine evidence regarding the impacts of the rise in incarceration on crime (Chapter 5); the nature of the experience of prison for those incarcerated (Chapter 6); the effects of incarceration on prisoners' health and mental health (Chapter 7) and employment and earnings after release (Chapter 8); the effects on children and families (Chapter 9) and on the communities from which prisoners come and to which they return (Chapter 10); and wider consequences for U.S. society (Chapter 11). Chapter 12 reviews the principles and values that determine the proper role of prisons in society and traces their intellectual lineage including the modern application of these foundational concepts. Chapter 13 summarizes the implications of the evidence on causes and consequences for public policy, applies the guidance provided by the principles that constrain the use of incarceration, and presents the committee's findings and recommendations for policy makers and the public. This final chapter also presents our recommendations for research to address gaps in knowledge on many questions pertinent to the policy choices facing leaders and the public. A more detailed research agenda is provided in Appendix C.

2

Rising Incarceration Rates

In 1973, after 50 years of stability, the rate of incarceration in the United States began a sustained period of growth. In 1972, 161 U.S. residents were incarcerated in prisons and jails per 100,000 population; by 2007, that rate had more than quintupled to a peak of 767 per 100,000. From its high point in 2009 and 2010, the population of state and federal prisoners declined slightly in 2011 and 2012. Still, the incarceration rate, including those in jail, was 707 per 100,000 in 2012, more than four times the rate in 1972. In absolute numbers, the prison and jail population had grown to 2.23 million people, yielding a rate of incarceration that was by far the highest in the world.[1]

This chapter begins the committee's exploration of this expansion of incarceration in the United States. It starts by tracing trends in American

---

[1]Small differences in incarceration rates from different sources result mainly from whether jurisdiction counts (prisoners under the jurisdiction of the state, a small number of whom may be housed in county facilities) or custody counts (the actual number housed in state facilities) are used. Only jurisdiction counts are available in a continuous series from 1925 to 2012. A total incarceration rate that includes the jail population should be based on custody counts; otherwise some double counting will occur whereby prisoners housed in county jails are also counted as being under state jurisdiction. Rates in Figure 2-1 are based on jurisdiction counts, while rates in Figure 2-2 are based on custody counts. As noted in Appendix B, the rates of state and federal imprisonment, 1925-2012 (Figure 2-1), were taken from Maguire (n.d., Table 6.28.2011) and from Glaze and Herberman (2013, Table 2). Data for jail incarceration, 1980-2012, were taken from Maguire (n.d., Table 6.1.2011) and from Glaze and Herberman (2013, Table 2). Data on jail incarceration, 1972-1979, were taken from Hindelang et al. (1977, p. 632) and Parisi et al. (1979). Missing years were interpolated. International incarceration rates (Figure 2-2) were taken from International Centre for Prison Studies (2013).

imprisonment rates through the twentieth century and by comparing rates of incarceration in the United States with those in other countries. The chapter then explores the fundamental question of the relationship of the growth in incarceration to crime. To this end, it summarizes two lines of research: the first relates trends in imprisonment to trends in rate of arrests per crime and the chances of prison admission, while the second focuses on the high rate of incarceration among African Americans, calculating how much of the racial disparity in incarceration can be explained by racial disparities in arrests and offending. The following section elaborates on the analysis of racial disparity in incarceration by reporting incarceration rates for whites and minorities, at different ages and different levels of education. That analysis reveals that incarceration rates among prime-age, minority men with very low levels of schooling are extraordinarily high.

The empirical portrait presented in this chapter points strongly to the role of changes in criminal justice policy in the emergence of historically and comparatively unprecedented levels of penal confinement. As a result of the lengthening of sentences and greatly expanded drug law enforcement and imprisonment for drug offenses, criminal defendants became more likely to be sentenced to prison and remained there significantly longer than in the past. The policy shifts that propelled the growth in incarceration had disproportionately large effects on African Americans and Latinos. Indeed, serving time in prison has become a normal life event among recent birth cohorts of African American men who have not completed high school.

U.S. INCARCERATION IN HISTORICAL AND COMPARATIVE PERSPECTIVE

The Bureau of Justice Statistics (BJS) has reported the incarceration rate for state and federal prisons from 1925 to 2012 (see Figure 2-1). Through the middle of the twentieth century, from 1925 to 1972, the combined state and federal imprisonment rate, excluding jails, fluctuated around 110 per 100,000 population, rising to a high of 137 in 1939. As noted earlier, after this period of relative stability, the imprisonment rate grew rapidly and continuously from 1972, increasing annually by 6 to 8 percent through 2000. The rate of growth slowed in the first decade of the 2000s, reaching a peak of 506 per 100,000 in 2007 and 2008. This high plateau was sustained through the end of the decade. In 2012, the imprisonment rate of 471 per 100,000 was still 4.3 times the historical average of 110 per 100,000. If the numbers in jail are added, the incarceration rate totaled 767 per 100,000 in 2007 and 707 per 100,000 in 2012 (Glaze and Herberman, 2013). When stated in absolute numbers rather than rates, the growth in the size of the penal population has been extraordinary: in 2012, the total of 2.23 million people held in U.S. prisons and jails was nearly seven times the number in

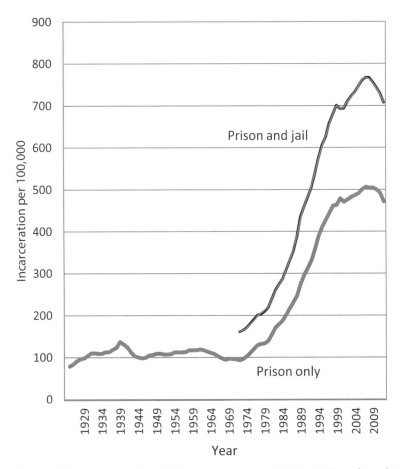

FIGURE 2-1 U.S. state and federal imprisonment rate (1925-2012) and total in-carceration including prison and jail inmates (1972-2012) per 100,000 residents. SOURCES: The 1925-2011 imprisonment series is from the *Sourcebook of Criminal Justice Statistics* (Maguire, n.d., Table 6.28.2012). The jail population series was constructed from various Sourcebook tables on the total adult correctional population, including Table 6.1.2011, which encompasses the period 1980-2011. (See also Appendix B.) Prison and jail population figures, 2012, are from Glaze and Herberman (2013). U.S. population estimate for 2012 is from the U.S. Census Bureau (n.d.-b).

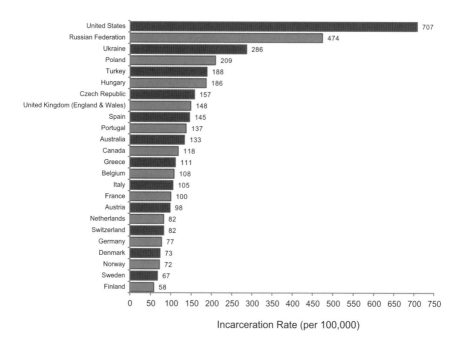

FIGURE 2-2 Incarceration rates per 100,000 population of European and selected common law countries.
NOTES: Rate estimates vary slightly from those of other sources for the United States. Year of reporting for the United States is 2012; years for other nations range from 2011 to 2013.
SOURCE: International Centre for Prison Studies (2013).

1972.[2] The three levels of government together had expanded the nation's penal population by more than 1.9 million people since 1972.

The historically high U.S. incarceration rate also is unsurpassed internationally. European statistics on incarceration are compiled by the Council of Europe, and international incarceration rates are recorded as well by the International Centre for Prison Studies (IPS) at the University of Essex in the United Kingdom. The 2011 IPS data show approximately 10.1 million people (including juveniles) incarcerated worldwide. In 2009, the United States (2.29 million) accounted for about 23 percent of the world total. In 2012, the U.S. incarceration rate per 100,000 population was again the

---

[2]Here "incarceration" is used to refer to the numbers in prison or in jail at a given time. Consistent with the committee's charge and main focus on those sentenced to prison, generally for periods of a year or more, the term "incarceration" is used in much of the report to refer only to those in prison. However, where jails are discussed or the context does not make the usage clear, the terms "prison" and "jail" are used.

highest reported (707), significantly exceeding the next largest per capita rates of Rwanda (492) and Russia (474) (International Centre for Prison Studies, 2013). Figure 2-2 compares the U.S. adult incarceration rate with the rates of European countries, Australia, and Canada. The Western European democracies have incarceration rates that, taken together, average around 100 per 100,000, one-seventh the rate of the United States. The former state socialist countries have very high incarceration rates by European standards, two to five times higher than the rates of Western Europe. But even the imprisonment rate for the Russian Federation is only about two-thirds that of the United States.

In short, the current U.S. rate of incarceration is unprecedented by both historical and comparative standards.

Trends in Prison and Jail Populations

Discussion and analysis of the U.S. penal system generally focus on three main institutions for adult penal confinement: state prisons, federal prisons, and local jails. State prisons are run by state departments of correction, holding sentenced inmates serving time for felony offenses, usually longer than a year. Federal prisons are run by the U.S. Bureau of Prisons and hold prisoners who have been convicted of federal crimes and pretrial detainees. Local jails usually are county or municipal facilities that incarcerate defendants prior to trial, and also hold those serving short sentences, typically under a year.

This sketch captures only the broad outlines of a penal system with enormous heterogeneity. For example, several small states (Alaska, Connecticut, Delaware, Hawaii, Rhode Island, Vermont) hold all inmates (including those awaiting trial and those serving both short and long sentences) under the jurisdiction of a single state correctional agency. In Massachusetts, county houses of correction incarcerate those serving up to 3 years. Many prisons have separate units for pretrial populations. But this simple description does not encompass the nation's entire custodial population. Minors, under 18 years old, typically are held in separate facilities under the authority of juvenile justice agencies. Additional adults are held in police lockups, immigration detention facilities, and military prisons and under civil commitment to state mental hospitals.

Despite the great institutional complexity, prisons and jails account for the vast majority of penal confinement. It is here that the transformation of American criminal justice has been most striking, and it is here that the U.S. incarceration rate increased to historically and internationally unprecedented levels.

Trends in the State Prison Population

State prisons accounted for around 57 percent of the total adult incarcerated population in 2012, confining mainly those serving time for felony convictions and parolees reincarcerated for violating their parole terms. Later in the chapter, we examine trends in state prison dynamics in greater detail, by offense categories, and decompose the effect of increased admission rates and increased time served on the rise in the rate of state imprisonment. The state prison population can be broadly divided into three offense categories: violent offenses (including murder, rape, and robbery), property offenses (primarily auto vehicle theft, burglary, and larceny/theft), and drug offenses (manufacturing, possession, and sale). In 2009, about 716,000 of 1.36 million state prison inmates had been convicted of violent crimes.

The most marked change in the composition of the state prison population involves the large increase in the number of those convicted for drug offenses. At the beginning of the prison expansion, drug offenses accounted for a very small percentage of the state prison population. In 1996, 23 percent of state prisoners were convicted of drug offenses (Mumola and Beck, 1997, p. 9). By the end of 2010, 17.4 percent of state prisoners had been convicted of drug crimes (Carson and Sabol, 2012, Table 9).

Trends in the Federal Prison Population

Federal prisons incarcerate people sentenced for federal crimes, so the mix of offenses among their populations differs greatly from that of state prisons. The main categories of federal crimes involve robbery, fraud, drugs, weapons, and immigration. These five categories represented 88 percent of all sentenced federal inmates in 2010.[3]

Federal crimes are quite different from those discussed above for state prisons. Robbery entails primarily bank robbery involving federally insured institutions; fraud includes violations of statutes pertaining to lending/credit institutions, interstate wire/communications, forgery, embezzlement, and counterfeiting; drug offenses typically involve manufacturing, importation, export, distribution, or dispensing of controlled substances; weapons offenses concern the manufacturing, importation, possession, receipt, and licensing of firearms and cases involving a crime of violence or drug trafficking when committed with a deadly weapon; and immigration offenses include primarily unlawful entry and reentry, with a smaller fraction involving misuse of visas and transporting or harboring of illegal entrants (Bureau of Justice Statistics, 2012a).

---

[3]At least one-half of the remainder comprised those sentenced for possession/trafficking in obscene materials (3.7 percent) or for racketeering/extortion (2.7 percent) (Bureau of Justice Statistics, n.d.-b).

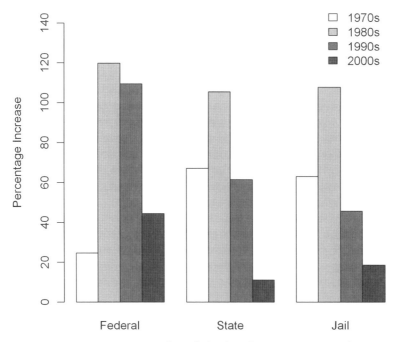

FIGURE 2-3 Percentage growth in federal and state prison populations and the local jail population by decade, 1972 to 2010.
NOTE: Growth is measured as the percentage change from 1972 to 1980, from 1981 to 1990, from 1991 to 2000, and from 2001 to 2010.
SOURCE: See Appendix B.

Figure 2-3 shows the percentage growth in federal and state prison populations and the local jail population over the period of the incarceration boom. In the first decade, 1972 to 1980, the state prison and jail populations each grew by about 60 percent. In the 1980s, the incarcerated population more than doubled in size across all three levels. By 1990, the incarcerated population had increased to more than four times its 1972 level. By 2000, state prison and jail populations were about six times higher than in 1972, and their growth through the 2000s slowed significantly. Beginning from a much smaller base, the federal prison population grew at a much faster rate than the state prison and local jail populations in the 1980s and 1990s. Even in the 2000s, when penal populations in state and local institutions had almost ceased to grow, the population of the federal system increased in size by more than 40 percent from 2001 to 2010.

Trends in the Jail Population

In 2012, one-third of the adult incarcerated population was housed in local jails. Jail is often the gateway to imprisonment. Jails serve local communities and hold those who have been arrested, have refused or been unable to pay bail, and are awaiting trial. They also hold those accused of misdemeanor offenses—often arrested for drug-related offenses or public disorder—and those sentenced to less than a year. John Irwin's (1970) study of jail describes its occupants as poor, undereducated, unemployed, socially detached, and disreputable. Because of their very low socioeconomic status, jail inhabitants, in Irwin's language, are "the rabble," and others have similarly described them as "social trash," "dregs," and "riff raff" (Irwin, 1970, pp. 2-3; see also Cornelius, 2012).

The jail population is about one-half the size of the combined state and federal prison population and since the early 1970s has grown about as rapidly as the state prison population. It is concentrated in a relatively small number of large urban counties. The short sentences and pretrial detention of the jail population create a high turnover and vast numbers of admissions. BJS estimates that in 2012, the jail population totaled around 745,000, with about 60 percent of that population turning over each week (Minton, 2013, Table 7; Glaze and Herberman, 2013). In 2010, the nation's jails admitted around 13 million inmates (Minton, 2011). With such high turnover, the growth of the jail population has greatly expanded the footprint of penal confinement.

The Increasing Scope of Correctional Supervision

The significant increase in the number of people behind bars since 1972 occurred in parallel with the expansion of community corrections. Figure 2-4 shows the scale of the entire adult correctional system. Correctional supervision encompasses prisons and jails and also the community supervision of those on probation and parole. Probation usually supervises people in the community who can, following revocation for breach of conditions, be resentenced to prison or jail. Like the incarcerated population, the probation population increased greatly in absolute terms, from 923,000 in 1976 to 4.06 million in 2010, declining slightly to 3.94 million in 2012. Parole agencies typically supervise people who have served part of their sentence in prison and have been released back to the community, subject to such conditions as reporting to a parole officer, staying drug-free, and maintaining employment. Therefore, parole supervision can be expected to increase as its source, the numbers in prison, grows. From 1975 (the earliest year for which data are available) to 2010, the population under parole

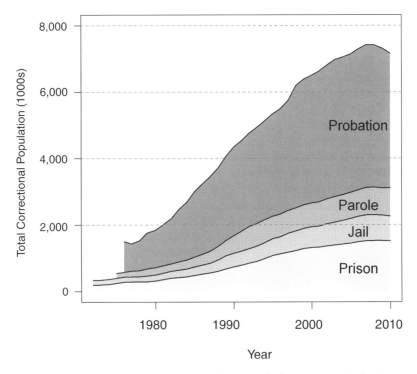

FIGURE 2-4 Total adult correctional population, including state and federal prison, local jail, and probation and parole populations, 1972 to 2010.
SOURCE: See Appendix B.

supervision grew by a factor of six, from 143,000 to 841,000. In 2012, it stood at 851,000.

The large probation and parole populations also expand a significant point of entry into incarceration. If probationers or parolees violate the conditions of their supervision, they risk revocation and subsequent incarceration. In recent decades, an increasing proportion of all state prison admissions have been due to parole violations (Petersilia, 2003, pp. 148ff). As a proportion of all state prison admissions, returning parolees made up about 20 percent in 1980, rising to 30 percent by 1991 and remaining between 30 and 40 percent until 2010. This represents a significant shift in the way the criminal justice system handled criminal offenses, increasing reliance on imprisonment rather than other forms of punishment, supervision, or reintegration. Parole may be revoked for committing a new crime or for violating the conditions of supervision without any new criminal conduct ("technical violators"), or someone on parole may be charged with a new crime and receive a new sentence.

The rising numbers of parole violations contributed to the increase in incarceration rates. The number of parole violators admitted to state prison following new convictions and sentences has remained relatively constant since the early 1990s. The number of technical violators more than doubled from 1990 to 2000. In 2010, the approximately 130,000 people reincarcerated after parole had been revoked for technical violations accounted for about 20 percent of state admissions (Carson and Sabol, 2012, Table 12; Glaze and Bonczar, 2011, Table 7). These returns accounted for 23 percent of all exits from parole that year (Glaze and Bonczar, 2011, Table 7).

The overall correctional population—including probationers and parolees—has grown substantially since 1972. By 2010, slightly more than 7 million U.S. residents, 1 of every 33 adults, were incarcerated in prison or jail or were being supervised on parole or probation. At the end of 2012, the total was 6.94 million, or 1 of every 35 adults. The rise in incarceration rates should thus be understood as just part of a broad expansion of the criminal justice system into the lives of the U.S. population.

Variation in Incarceration Rates Among States

Trends in incarceration rates vary greatly among states. While the national imprisonment rate increased nearly 5-fold from 1972 to 2010, state incarceration rates in Maine and Massachusetts slightly more than doubled. At the other end of the spectrum, the rates in Louisiana and Mississippi increased more than 6-fold.

To see the change in trends, it is useful to divide the period since 1972 into two parts: from 1972 to 2000 and from 2000 to 2010 (see Figure 2-5). As discussed above, the period from 1972 to 2000 was a time of rapid growth for state prison populations; the change in incarceration rates in this period is indicated for each state in blue. The largest increases in this period generally occurred in southern and western states. From 1972 to 2000, incarceration rates grew most in Louisiana, Mississippi, Oklahoma, and Texas. In Louisiana, the rate grew by 700 per 100,000 population—more than 10-fold—rising to 801 per 100,000 by 2000, then climbing further to 867 by 2010. Growth in state incarceration rates was much slower in the northeast and midwest. In Maine and Minnesota, the rates grew by only around 100 per 100,000. These two states had the lowest incarceration rates by 2010—148 for Maine and 185 for Minnesota. In the period since 2000, incarceration rates have grown more slowly across the country. As shown by the red circles in Figure 2-5, a few states have registered very large declines, including Delaware, Georgia, and Texas in the south and New Jersey and New York in the northeast.

The growth in the incarcerated population represents a broad transformation of penal institutions extending across the federal, state, and local

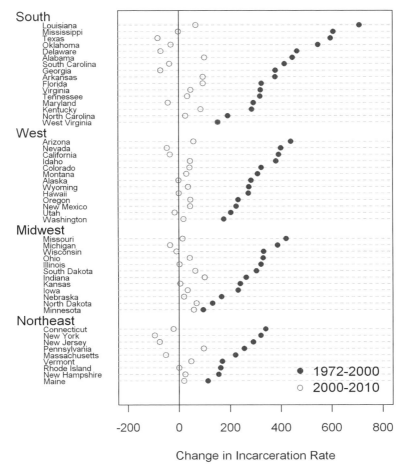

FIGURE 2-5 Change in state imprisonment rates per 100,000 population, 50 states, 1972-2000 and 2000-2010.
SOURCE: See Appendix B.

levels and all regions of the country. Incarceration rates grew most from 1972 to 2000 and in the south and the west. Some evidence indicates a new dynamic emerging over the last decade, as growth in state incarceration rates has slowed significantly across the nation.

CRIME AND THE DYNAMICS OF THE GROWTH
OF THE PENAL POPULATION

The link between crime and the growth of the penal population is neither immediate nor direct. Incarceration trends do not simply track trends in crime, although trends in crime have clearly been an important part of the context in which incarceration rates have grown.

Research on the population dynamics of incarceration illuminates the link between incarceration and crime and provides a description of how the system has grown. Analysis of population dynamics offers a simple model in which the growth of incarceration has two main causes: the level of crime in society and the policy response to crime (Raphael and Stoll, 2013). Criminal offending determines the number of people who might be arrested and then serve time in prison, while criminal justice policy determines the likelihood and duration of incarceration for those arrested. As detailed in the following chapter, spreading across the United States and the federal government, the approach to sentencing quickly shifted over the four decades of the incarceration rise. The diffusion of new sentencing policies focused at first on the development of sentencing guidelines and determinate sentencing policies, and more recently included initiatives designed to increase the certainty and severity of prison sentences. In the first phase, primarily from the mid-1970s to the mid-1980s, a wave of reforms aimed to make sentencing procedures fairer and outcomes more predictable and consistent. In the second phase, from the mid-1980s through 1996, changes in sentencing policy were aimed primarily at making sentences for drug and violent crimes harsher and their imposition more certain. The principal mechanisms to these ends were mandatory minimum sentences, "three strikes" laws, laws labeled "truth-in-sentencing," and laws mandating life without possibility of parole for certain offenses. Since the mid-1990s, no states have created new comprehensive sentencing systems, none has enacted new truth-in-sentencing laws, and only one has enacted a three strikes law. New mandatory minimum sentence laws have been narrowly targeted at such crimes as carjacking, human smuggling, and child pornography.

In the sections that follow, the way these policy changes affected incarceration levels for more than three decades after 1980 is decomposed by stages of the criminal justice process in an effort to quantify, to the extent possible, how the changes in sentencing policy cumulatively contributed to higher levels of incarceration at both the state and federal levels. The analysis, which draws extensively on work by Alfred Blumstein and Allen Beck conducted at the committee's request, also provides a rough estimate of the extent to which the incarceration increase over the period is attributable to changes in sentencing policy rather than other factors, including changes in crime rates. The following sections decompose the growth in the penal population from 1980 to 2010 into components related to crime, the rate of arrests per crime, the chances of prison admission per arrest, and the length of time served. Trends in incarceration can be decomposed for specific crime categories and for state and federal prisons separately. (The jail population, about a third of all those incarcerated, has not been analyzed in this way because detailed data on jail admissions are lacking.) Slightly different decompositions have been reported by others (Blumstein and Beck, 1999; Beck and Blumstein, 2012; Raphael and Stoll, 2013; Neal and Armin, 2013). The analyses differ in their details but yield similar results for the three decades since 1980.

In the context of the U.S. prison boom, the main limitation of the decomposition analysis concerns the treatment of drug crimes. Drug crimes (incidents of possession, sale, and manufacture) are not recorded in crime statistics. In any case, the level of drug arrests depends significantly on the level of enforcement efforts. For drug offenses, then, one can see how penal policy has changed, but analysis cannot specify the contribution of drug crime to the drug-related incarceration rate, only to drug arrests. Below we summarize Beck and Blumstein's (2012) analysis of trends in the state prison population. Their analysis examines trends in crime, arrests admissions, and time served for drug offenses, burglary, aggravated assault, robbery, rape, and murder.

Trends in Crime

Changes in crime rates affect the numbers of people subject to arrest, conviction, and sentencing and are thus a key source of changes in incarceration rates. A large research literature and several National Research Council reports have investigated crime trends and their measurement (e.g., Lynch and Addington, 2006; National Research Council, 2008). Research has been based largely on the Uniform Crime Reports (UCR) and the National Crime Victimization Survey (NCVS). The UCR, based on police reports and compiled by the Federal Bureau of Investigation (FBI), provide long time series and an accurate count of homicide rates, while the NCVS provides a count of crime victims, measurement of the circumstances of victimization, and a detailed demographic portrait of crime victims. The analysis below is based on the UCR crime rates that can be associated with a parallel series of arrest statistics.[4]

---

[4]Care must be taken in interpreting historical trends in crime rates; for example, homicide rates are affected by improvements over time in emergency medical treatment that have reduced deaths from violence; and changing treatment of domestic violence affects counting of simple versus aggravated assault. Various so-called "white collar" offenses contribute in small numbers to the prison population. Exact, consistent counts of such crimes, and therefore of their impact on incarceration levels, are hampered by difficulties of definition and measurement (Barnett, 2000; Hagan, 2010; Simpson, 2011).

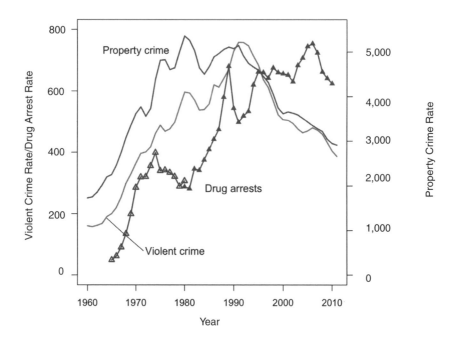

FIGURE 2-6 Violent and property crime rates per 100,000 population, 1960 to 2011, and the drug arrest rate per 100,000, 1980 to 2010.
SOURCES: Uniform Crime Reports. Drug crime rate, 1965-1980; Federal Bureau of Investigation (1993); Maguire (n.d., Table 3.1062.2011, property and violent crime rates); Uniform Crime Reports (drug arrest rates).

Trends in crime measured by the UCR are reported in Figure 2-6. The figure shows trends for three series: for the overall violent crime rate (including assault, murder, rape, and robbery) for 1960 to 2011, the overall property crime rate (including burglary, larceny/theft, and motor vehicle theft) for 1960 to 2011, and the drug arrest rate for 1965 to 2010.

The country experienced a large increase in crime from the early 1960s until the 1980s. From the early 1990s, crime rates began to fall broadly for the following two decades. Property and violent crime show roughly similar trends, although the property crime rate peaked in 1979, while violence continued to rise through the mid-1980s after falling in the first half of the decade. Following the broad trends in crime, the homicide rate—widely thought to be the most accurately measured—began to increase from the 1960s, peaking in 1981. Similar to the property crime rate, the homicide rate fluctuated through the 1980s until peaking again in 1991, just below the 1981 level.

Trends in drug arrests followed a different pattern. The drug arrest rate grew very sharply in the 1980s, more than doubling from 1980 to 1989. After a 2-year decline, the drug arrest rate again increased over the next decade, and by 2010 was more than double its level in 1980.

In summary, the growth in incarceration rates beginning in 1973 was preceded for about a decade by a very large increase in crime rates. Incarceration rates showed their strongest period of growth in the 1980s, as violent crime fell through the first half of the decade and then increased in the second. Incarceration rates continued to climb through the 1990s as the violent crime rate began to fall. Finally, in the 2000s, crime rates have remained stable at a low level, while the incarceration rate peaked in 2007, and the incarcerated population peaked in 2010. Thus the very high rates of incarceration that emerged over the past decades cannot simply be ascribed to a higher level of crime today compared with the early 1970s, when the prison boom began.

Linking Crime to the Trend in Imprisonment

One can think of the size of the prison population as depending on the level of crime, the probability of arrest given a crime, the probability of a prison admission given an arrest, and the time served in prison. If crime increases but all else is unchanged, then the prison population will increase because a larger number of individuals with a fixed probability of apprehension will yield more arrests. Similarly, if the probability of arrest given a crime goes up, then the prison population also will increase, all else being equal. Increases in the chances of prison admission and time served in prison also increase the prison population when all else is unchanged. Each step in the process of incarceration influences the overall trend, which in turn can be decomposed into the contribution of crime, arrest, prison admission, and time served. Here we summarize the analysis of Blumstein and Beck (1999, 2005) and Beck and Blumstein (2012) for state prison populations, looking separately at trends for drug offenses, burglary, aggravated assault, robbery, and murder for the period 1980 to 2010.

The analysis aims to account for the changes in incarceration rates across the different crime categories. The states' combined incarceration rates increased across all crime categories (see Figure 2-7). Most striking, however, is the dramatic increase in the incarceration rate for drug-related crimes. In 1980, imprisonment for drug offenses was rare, with a combined state incarceration rate of 15 per 100,000 population. By 2010, the drug incarceration rate had increased nearly 10-fold to 143 per 100,000. Indeed, the rate of incarceration for the single category of drug-related offenses, excluding local jails and federal prisons, by itself exceeds by 50 percent

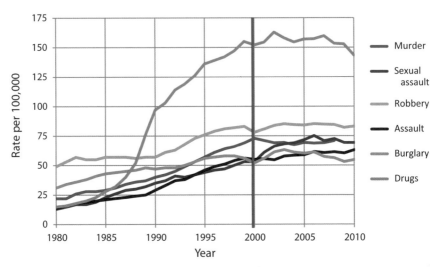

FIGURE 2-7 Combined state incarceration rate by crime type, 1980 to 2010.
SOURCE: Beck and Blumstein (2012).

the average incarceration rate for all crimes of Western European countries
and is twice the average incarceration rate for all crimes, including pretrial
detainees, of a significant number of European countries.

Trends in Arrests per Crime

The first point at which the criminal justice system can affect the incarceration rate is through the likelihood of arrest of someone who has committed a crime. The ratio of arrests to crimes is sometimes interpreted as a
measure of policing effectiveness or efficiency. Despite significant changes
in police technology and management from 1980 to 2010, the ratio of arrests to crimes for the major crime types handled by states and localities
has shown little change (see Figure 2-8). For example, the arrest rate for
burglaries remained at about 14 arrests per 100 adult offenses. Arrest rates
for rape declined rather steadily after 1984 (dropping from a peak of 44
arrests per 100 adult offenses to 24 per 100 by 2010). Robbery arrest rates
were steady until 2000 and then increased slightly from 26 to 31 arrests per
100 reported offenses by 2010. In contrast, the arrest rate for aggravated
assault grew until 2000 and then remained flat (around 52 arrests per 100
offenses). Murder is the exception, showing a decline in the arrest rate
per crime after 2000: arrests for murder were close to 100 per 100 adult
offenses until 1998 and then declined to 80 per 100 after 2000. Overall,

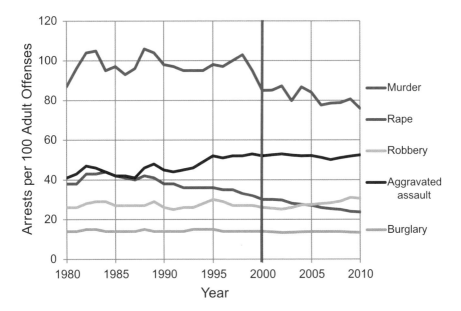

FIGURE 2-8 Arrests per 100 adult offenses by crime type, 1980 to 2010.
SOURCE: Blumstein and Beck (2012).

by the measure of the ratio of arrests to crimes, no increase in policing effectiveness occurred from 1980 to 2010 that might explain higher rates of incarceration.[5]

A significant shortcoming of the accounting framework applied here is that the analysis cannot describe the probability that drug crimes—chiefly for possession, sale, and manufacture—are converted into arrests. Although data are available on self-reported drug use, there are no national trend data describing the level of felony possession, sale, and manufacture offenses. This absence of data also reflects a conceptual limitation in that drug crimes typically are not discrete events like most other crimes but part of a continuous pattern of drug use and dealing. The underlying level of crime that provides the basis for arrest is not only difficult to measure but also difficult to define.

Despite these conceptual difficulties, it is clear that drug law enforcement efforts escalated substantially over the period of the prison boom. From 1980 to 1989, the arrest rate for possession and use offenses increased by 89 percent. After a 2-year period of decline, the drug arrest rate

---

[5]At the federal level, the increase in incarceration has been closely correlated with the increase in numbers of convictions.

climbed again to peak in 2006, 162 percent above the 1980 level. The arrest rate fell slightly from this peak, but in 2009 was still more than double the rate in 1980. In 2009, 1.3 million arrests were reported to the UCR for drug use and possession, and another 310,000 arrests were made for the manufacture and sale of drugs (Snyder, 2011).

To foreshadow our later discussion of racial disparity, drug arrest rates, at least since the early 1970s, have always been higher for African Americans than for whites. In the early 1970s, when drug arrest rates were low, blacks were about twice as likely as whites to be arrested for drug crimes. The great growth in drug arrests through the 1980s had a large and disproportionate effect on African Americans. By 1989, arrest rates for blacks had climbed to 1,460 per 100,000, compared with 365 for whites (Western, 2006). Throughout the 1990s, drug arrest rates remained at historically high levels. It might be hypothesized that blacks may be arrested at higher rates for drug crimes because they use drugs at higher rates, but the best available evidence refutes that hypothesis. A long historical trend, dating back to the 1970s, is available from the Monitoring the Future survey of high school seniors. Self-reported drug use among blacks is consistently lower than among whites, a pattern replicated among adults in the National Survey on Drug Abuse. Fewer data are available on drug selling, but self-reports in the National Longitudinal Survey of Youth, 1979 and 1997, show a higher level of sales among poor white than poor black youth. In short, the great escalation in drug enforcement that dates from the late 1970s is associated with an increase in the relative arrest rate among African Americans that is unrelated to relative rates of drug use and the limited available evidence on drug dealing.

Prison Admissions per Arrest

A second point of criminal justice intervention is the sentencing of those who have been arrested, charged, and convicted. Because national trend data are not readily available for charging and conviction, analysis of imprisonment population dynamics has examined the probability of prison admission given an arrest (Blumstein and Beck, 1999, 2005; Beck and Blumstein, 2012; Raphael and Stoll, 2013). For the major crime types handled at the state level, the probability that arrest would lead to prison rose over the three decades from 1980 to 2010. The number of prison commitments per 100 adult arrests showed a significant and nearly steady increase (see Figure 2-9). For example, the rate of commitment to state prison for murder rose from 41 to 92 per 100 arrests, an increase of more than 120 percent. The percentage changes for three other categories of

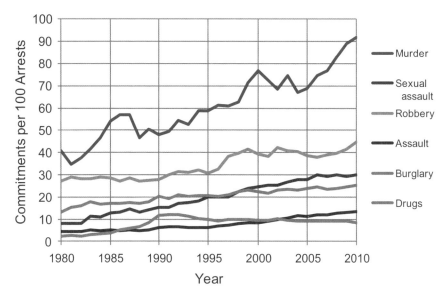

FIGURE 2-9 State prison admissions per 100 adult arrests, 1980-2010.
NOTE: Commitments include only new court commitments (which include new offenders and parole violators with new sentences only).
SOURCE: Beck and Blumstein (2012).

offenses—sexual assault,[6] aggravated assault, and drug crimes—were well over 200 percent; however, those changes were less dramatic because the rates for these offenses started from such low levels. Between 1980 and 2010, prison commitments for drug offenses rose 350 percent (from 2 to 9 per 100 arrests); commitments for sexual assault rose 275 percent (from 8 to 30 per 100 arrests); and commitments for aggravated assault rose 250 percent (from 4 to 14 per 100 arrests). State prison commitment rates for burglary and robbery also increased, but these increases were below 100 percent. These figures indicate that an increased probability that arrest would lead to prison commitment contributed greatly to the rise in incarceration rates between 1980 and 2010.

---

[6]Estimates for rape and other sexual assaults were combined because of difficulties in distinguishing rape from other sexual assaults in administrative data collected in BJS's National Corrections Program.

Time Served

The final component of assessing the contribution of changes in criminal justice policy to the rise in incarceration rates is the duration of incarceration for those given prison sentences. Time served must be estimated because it is not completely observed: the duration of incarceration is not known for those who have not been released. One could calculate time served from a cohort of releases, but this method would overrepresent those serving short sentences and underrepresent those serving long sentences. At the limit, those serving life without parole will never be released, and time served will be known only at their death. Calculating time served from release cohorts will thus underestimate the average. Blumstein and Beck (1999; Beck and Blumstein, 2012) base estimates of time served on the ratio of the stock population—the number of people in prison on the day of the annual population count—to new court commitments in that year. If commitment rates were reasonably constant over time, that estimate of time served would be reasonably accurate. But admission rates, of course, have not been stationary and were increasing, especially during the 1980s and 1990s, which introduces error in the time-served estimates. To reduce that error, the admission process is smoothed by being approximated in each year as the 3-year average of the number of new court commitments in that year and the 2 adjoining years.[7]

Given that sentence lengths for serious crimes have increased greatly since 1980, the full impact of lengthy sentences on the level of incarceration has yet to be felt. The contribution of long sentences to rising incarceration rates can be fully observed only over a very long period. Without a sufficient observation period for lengthy sentences, average sentence lengths will also be underestimated. Very long sentences have increased in number since the proliferation of enhancements for those convicted of second and third felonies, the institution of truth-in-sentencing requirements, and other shifts in sentencing policy discussed in greater detail in Chapter 3. BJS's analysis of recent trends in the state prison population reveals the growing population serving life and other long sentences. As of the end of 2000, BJS estimated that about 54,000 state prison inmates were serving life sentences, with a median age of under 30. Using a different methodology, a 2013

---

[7]Estimates for 1980 and 2010 are omitted because one of their adjoining years is not available for the three-point smoothing. This estimation model (the ratio of stock population to new court commitments) is based on all new court commitments, including those parole violators arriving with a new sentence, but not counting technical parole violators. This approach contrasts with other measures based on using the number of exits in each year rather than new court commitments. (See Patterson and Preston, 2008.) Counting exit flow would count parolees only on the most recent increment of their total time served and would not take account of the earlier time served, prior to readmission on a parole violation. Thus, it would underestimate the total time served on the original sentence.

survey report by the Sentencing Project estimates that more than 150,000 people were serving life sentences in state prison in 2012 (Nellis, 2013).[8] Because of nonstationarity in admission rates and the growing prevalence of very long sentences, the estimates of time served presented below should be viewed as a lower bound on the increase in time served. The downward bias is likely to be largest for violent crimes, for which the growth in very long sentences has been greatest.

The most dramatic change in average time served was for murder, which climbed from 5.0 years in 1981 to 16.9 years in 2000, an increase of 238 percent. The second largest growth was in time served for sexual assault, which increased 94 percent, from 3.4 years in 1981 to 6.6 years in 2009; the rate of increase for this crime type was the largest observed during the 2000-2010 decade, adding about 2.5 months each year. The slowest rate of increase in time served was for drug offenses, increasing from 1.6 years in 1981 to 1.9 years in 2000 and then remaining nearly steady through 2009. The stability of time served by those committing drug offenses contrasts with the significant growth in rates of arrest and commitment for drug offenses discussed earlier. Time served may have changed little because short prison sentences were imposed on those committing drug offenses who may previously have served probation or time in jail. Trends in time served for the other three crime types—aggravated assault, burglary, and robbery—showed somewhat similar growth patterns. Averaging 4.0, 2.8, and 2.0 years, respectively, over the entire 1980-2010 period, all had some growth from 1980 to 2000 (83, 41, and 79 percent, respectively), and all remained nearly stable after 2000 (see Figure 2-10).

The decomposition of the growth in incarceration rates is summarized in Table 2-1. From 1980 to 2010, the state imprisonment rate for six main crime types grew by 222 percent. Setting aside drug-related incarceration, for which offending rates are difficult to define and measure, changes in crime trends or in police effectiveness as measured by arrests per crime contributed virtually nothing to the increase in incarceration rates over the 30-year period. Rather, the growth can be attributed about equally to the two policy factors of prison commitments per arrest and increases in time served. These results are based on consideration of changes in all six crime types. Because the response to drug-related crimes is so distinctive and significant, Beck and Blumstein (2012) examined the other five crime

---

[8]This number should be viewed as an approximation. The estimate was obtained by surveying state and federal prison authorities. It is unclear whether the count of prisoners serving life sentences includes those in custody or under jurisdiction. Custody and jurisdiction definitions typically yield slightly different counts of prison populations. In 2012, the same survey estimated that another 5,420 people were serving life sentences in federal prisons.

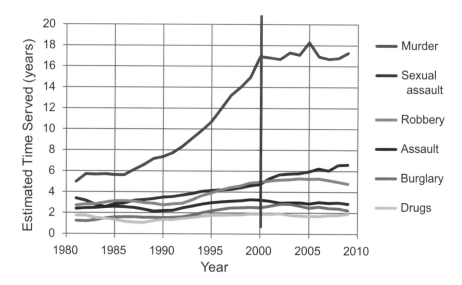

FIGURE 2-10 Estimated time served in state prison, 1980 to 2010.
NOTE: See text for a discussion of calculations of time served.
SOURCE: Beck and Blumstein (2012).

types omitting drug offenses and found similar results, albeit with a slightly greater contribution from time served.

When each decade is examined separately, different factors are found to contribute to the growth in incarceration rates. The first decade, 1980-1990, saw the largest increase in the state incarceration rate (107 percent). The largest share of this growth is attributable to changes in commitments per arrest, which accounted for 79 percent of the growth in the six-offense analysis and 50 percent when drug offenses were excluded. The time-served effect was fairly small (14 percent) when drug crimes were included but more than doubled (38 percent) when they were omitted. The significant growth in enforcement for drug-related offenses in the 1980s thus is associated with a large increase in prison admissions, but those convicted of drug offenses were serving relatively short sentences.

During the second decade, the 1990s, when the state incarceration rate grew by 55 percent (from a much-enlarged base compared with 1980), considerable attention was paid to increasing sentences, and especially time served, through various legislative actions, such as truth-in-sentencing. This is shown by the fact that in the 1990s, time served replaced imprisonments per arrest as the leading factor in growth in incarceration rates, accounting for 74 percent of the growth for all six crimes and 62 percent when drug crimes are excluded. The final decade, 2000-2010, was a period of

TABLE 2-1 Decomposing the Growth in State Imprisonment Rates, 1980-2010

	Entire Period 1980-2010 (%)	Three Decades		
		1980-1990	1990-2000	2000-2010
Change to Be Explained (%)	222	107	55	1
All Six Offenses				
Crime trends	—	—	—	—
Arrests per crime	—	7	—	—
Imprisonments per arrest	49	79	27	100
Time served	51	14	73	—
Five Offenses, Excluding Drug Crimes				
Crime trends	—	3	—	—
Arrests per crime	—	10	<1	—
Imprisonments per arrest	44	50	38	96
Time served	56	38	62	4

SOURCE: Beck and Blumstein (2012).

negligible growth (0.65 percent) in the overall incarceration rate in state prisons, and whatever growth occurred is attributable almost entirely to increases in imprisonments per arrest.

Trends in the Federal System

Growth in the incarceration rate has been larger and more sustained in the federal system than in the states. Between 1980 and 2000, the federal prison population increased by nearly 500 percent, from 24,363 to 145,416, surpassing the growth in state prison systems. By 2000, the federal system was the third largest prison system in the nation, behind those of Texas and California. Moreover, while the rapid growth of the states' prison populations tapered off after 2000, the federal system continued to see a steady increase, becoming the largest system by midyear 2002. By 2010, the federal system, with a population of 209,771 inmates, had grown to be larger than the next largest system, the Texas Department of Criminal Justice, by more than 36,000 inmates (Guerino et al., 2011). The federal system thus accounts for roughly 10 percent of the total prison population, but its share has been growing during the prison boom.

Nearly all incarceration in federal prisons is due to federal convictions for robbery; fraud; and drug, weapon, and immigration offenses.[9] During 1980-2000, as with the states, the most dramatic change was in drug-related offending, for which the incarceration rate increased more than 10-fold, from 3 per 100,000 in 1980 to 35 in 2000. The other two crime types that saw comparably large growth are weapon and immigration offenses, which also increased more than 1,000 percent; that growth is less apparent because incarceration rates for these offenses started at such low levels in 1980. The incarceration rate for fraud grew considerably (about 227 percent) over this period, but still much less than the rates for the other three crime types. The incarceration rate for robbery rose steadily from 2.9 per 100,000 adults and then peaked at 4.6 per 100,000 in 2000.

Since 2000, the patterns of growth in incarceration rates have changed.[10] With an already high rate of incarceration for drug offenses (35 per 100,000 adults), the increase for these offenses was more modest, up 16 percent (to 41 per 100,000 adults). At the same time, the dominant source of growth was weapon offenses, up 135 percent (from 5.2 to 12.2 per 100,000 adults) and immigration offenses, up 40 percent (from 6.5 to 9.1 per 100,000 adults). Fraud showed little change (up 5.5 percent), while robbery declined (from 4.6 to 3.2 per 100,000).

RACIAL DISPARITY IN IMPRISONMENT

The discussion thus far has examined the growth in incarceration rates, linking it to trends in crime, arrests, prison admissions, and time served. The data point clearly to the increased rate of prison admission (particularly marked for drug crimes) and the increase in time served (especially for violent offenses) as sources of increased incarceration rates.

A parallel set of questions about the relative contributions of crime and the criminal justice system has been raised in the analysis of racial disparities in incarceration. As noted earlier, the rise in incarceration rates has had a disproportionately large effect on African Americans and Latinos. Having higher rates of poverty and urbanization and a younger age distribution, minority populations—at least for some categories of offenses—also show higher rates of offending and victimization. As incarceration rates were increasing, how much of the evolving racial and ethnic disparity in those

---

[9]Note that BJS's federal justice statistics program includes all sentenced federal prisoners, regardless of sentence length; moreover, all counts are based on fiscal years, ending September 30 of each reference year.

[10]The Urban Institute recently completed a report examining growth in incarceration rates from 1998 to 2010, using a similar approach but applying it to estimates of growth in numbers of inmates by crime type rather than growth in incarceration rates by crime type (see Mallik-Kane et al., 2012).

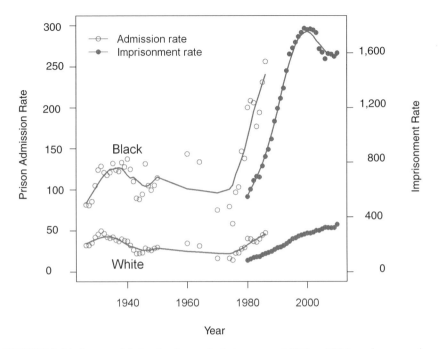

FIGURE 2-11 State and federal prison admission rates, 1926 to 1986, and state and federal imprisonment rates, 1980 to 2010, for blacks and whites.

NOTES: A smooth line indicates the trend. Hispanics are included among both racial groups.

SOURCES: Admissions rates are from Langan (1991b). Black and white imprisonment rates are from Beck and Blumstein (2012).

rates can be explained by racial and ethnic differences in offending? This question, of course, is not just of descriptive interest; it is central to understanding the social significance of the emergence of high incarceration rates. The sources of racial and ethnic disparities in incarceration are discussed in Chapter 3.

Trends in black and white imprisonment are shown in Figure 2-11.[11] BJS compiled state and federal prison admission rates for blacks and whites separately in a historical series extending from 1926 to 1986 (Langan, 1991b). The data are available annually from 1926 to 1946 and then intermittently for the post-World War II period until 1986. They show an

---

[11]Trends in imprisonment for Hispanics are discussed in a later section of this chapter. Note that Hispanics are not counted separately and are therefore included in the numbers for blacks and whites presented here.

increase in African American imprisonment from 1926 to 1940, while imprisonment rates were declining for whites. Prison admission rates climbed steeply in the mid-1970s but much more in absolute terms for African Americans than for whites.

The disparity in incarceration can be measured in both absolute and relative terms. The absolute disparity is measured by the difference between black and white incarceration rates, while the relative disparity is measured by the black-white ratio in incarceration rates. Table 2-2 shows the trend in absolute and relative disparity for imprisonment and admission rates for selected years from 1970 to 2010. Through the 1970s and 1980s, racial disparities increased in both absolute and relative terms. The increase in absolute disparities is especially striking, growing more than 3-fold from 1970 to 1986 for prison admission rates and more than doubling from 1980 to 1990 for imprisonment rates. The large increase in absolute disparities reflects the extraordinarily high rates of incarceration among African Americans that emerged with the overall growth of the incarceration rate. From 1990 onward, the white incarceration rate increased more rapidly than the incarceration rate for blacks, and the relative disparity declined. Still, the absolute disparity increased significantly in the 1990s as black incarceration rates continued to grow, and serving time in state or federal prison became commonplace for young African American men in poor communities.

Because of the large disparity—which was already high in 1972—the steep increase in incarceration rates produced extremely high rates of incarceration for blacks but not whites. In 2010, the imprisonment rate for blacks was 4.6 times that for whites—the lowest disparity in imprisonment

TABLE 2-2 Absolute and Relative Racial Disparities in Rates of Prison Admission and Imprisonment, 1970 to 2010

	Disparity	
	Absolute	Relative
Prison Admission Rates		
1970	58.7	4.6
1986	208.9	5.4
1970	58.7	4.6
Imprisonment Rates		
1980	465	6.5
1990	1,018	6.8
2000	1,487	6.3
2010	1,252	4.6

SOURCES: Admission rates are from Langan (1991b). Black and white imprisonment rates are from Beck and Blumstein (2012).

over the entire period for which race-specific incarceration rates are available. Although the disparity had declined from its peak in the early 1990s, it was still very large—of a magnitude that exceeds racial differences for many other common social indicators. For example, black-white ratios for indicators as varied as wealth, employment, poverty, and infant mortality are significantly smaller than the 4.6 to 1 ratio in imprisonment (Beck and Blumstein, 2012; Western, 2006).

Violent Crimes

The relative involvement of blacks in violent crimes has declined significantly since the late 1980s (see Figure 2-12). From 1972 to 1980, the relative share of blacks in arrests for rape and aggravated assault fell by around one-fourth; more modest declines in their share of arrests were recorded for murder and robbery from the 1970s to the 2000s. In the 1970s, blacks

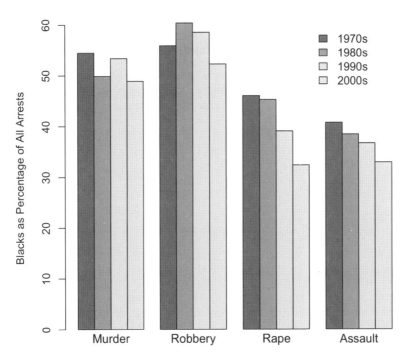

FIGURE 2-12 Average percentage of blacks among total arrests for murder and non-negligent manslaughter, robbery, forcible rape, and aggravated assault, by decade, 1972 to 2011.
SOURCE: Uniform Crime Reports race-specific arrest rates, 1972 to 2011.

accounted for about 54 percent of all homicide arrests; by the 2000s, that share had fallen below half. For robbery, blacks accounted for 55 percent of arrests in the 1970s, falling to 52 percent by the 2000s. For rape, blacks accounted for about 46 percent of all arrests in the 1970s, declining by 14 percentage points to 32 percent by the 2000s. The declining share of blacks in violent arrests also is marked for aggravated assaults, which constitute a large majority of violent serious crimes: 41 percent in the 1970s and just 33 percent in the 2000s.

These figures show that arrests of blacks for violent crimes constitute smaller percentages of absolute national numbers that are less than half what they were 20 or 30 years ago (Tonry and Melewski, 2008). Violent crime has been falling in the United States since 1991. In absolute terms, involvement of blacks in violent crime has followed the general pattern; in relative terms, it has fallen substantially more than the overall averages. Yet even though participation of blacks in serious violent crimes has declined significantly, disparities in imprisonment between blacks and whites have not fallen by much; as noted earlier, the incarceration rate for non-Hispanic black males remains seven times that of non-Hispanic whites.

Drug Crimes

The situation for drug offenses is similar to that for violent crime in some respects, but there is a critical difference. Although, according to both arrest and victimization data, blacks have higher rates of involvement than whites in violent crimes, the prevalence of drug use is only slightly higher among blacks than whites for some illicit drugs and slightly lower for others; the difference is not substantial. There is also little evidence, when all drug types are considered, that blacks sell drugs more often than whites (Tonry, 2011a, Chapter 3).

In recent years, drug-related arrest rates for blacks have been three to four times higher than those for whites (see Figure 2-13). In the late 1980s, the rates were six times higher for blacks than for whites (Blumstein and Wallman, 2006). The recent relative decrease in racial disparity in drug arrests did not result from reduced police emphasis on black sellers but from increases in total drug arrests and greater emphasis on crimes related to marijuana. Marijuana arrestees are preponderantly white and are much less likely than heroin and cocaine arrestees to wind up in prison (Room et al., 2013). Absolute numbers of blacks arrested for trafficking in cocaine and heroin have not fallen significantly; they simply make up a smaller percentage of overall arrest numbers that are rising.

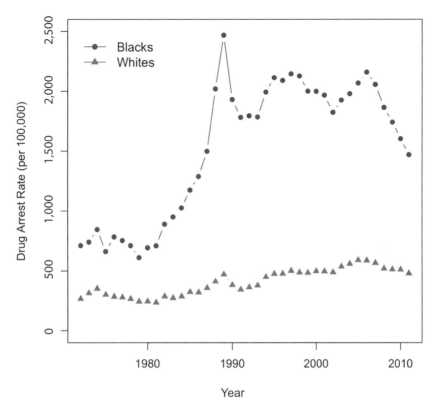

FIGURE 2-13 Drug arrest rates for blacks and whites per 100,000 population, 1972 to 2011.
SOURCES: Uniform Crime Reports race-specific arrest rates, 1980 to 2011 (accessed from BJS). 1972 to 1979 is taken from Federal Bureau of Investigation (1990).

Incarceration of Hispanics

In the discussion of black and white incarceration rates thus far, Hispanics have been included in those two racial groups. Distinguishing incarceration rates for Hispanics helps underline ethnicity as another source of disparity. Separating Hispanics from non-Hispanics also modifies understanding of the racial disparity in incarceration rates between non-Hispanic blacks and whites. In 1974, only 12 percent of the white state prison population and a negligible proportion of blacks reported being of Hispanic origin. By 2004, 24 percent of the white prison population and around 3 percent of blacks reported being Hispanic.

As the white prison population has come to include more Hispanics, the raw black-white disparity in incarceration has tended to shrink because of the relatively high incarceration rate among Hispanics. An alternative approach that separates race and ethnicity entails studying incarceration among Hispanics and non-Hispanic blacks and whites. Most published data on incarceration trends distinguish racial groups but not ethnicities. The data reviewed earlier on prison admission and imprisonment rates by race were taken from the National Prisoner Statistics (NPS) Series, an annual survey of state and federal departments of correction conducted by BJS. The NPS survey was first administered in 1926 and has gathered counts of the prison populations by race and sex. Data on Hispanics have been collected since 1974 in the BJS Survey of Inmates of State Correctional Facilities and since 1972 in the Survey of Inmates in Local Jails. Data also are available from the decennial census, which collects information on the entire U.S. population, including information on national origins and, for immigrants, country of birth. By combining NPS counts with survey data, BJS has constructed state and federal imprisonment rates for Hispanics since 2000, and rates can be constructed back to 1990 using the BJS methods (Guerino et al., 2011; Beck and Blumstein, 2012). With additional assumptions about the Hispanic fraction of the federal prison population (which is never more than about 10 percent of the total prison population), estimates of the prison and jail incarceration rates for Hispanics, non-Hispanic whites, and non-Hispanic blacks can be constructed for the entire period of the growth in incarceration from 1972 to 2010 (see Appendix B).

Figure 2-14 reports incarceration rates separately for Hispanics, non-Hispanic whites, and non-Hispanic blacks aged 18 to 64. These age-specific incarceration rates account usefully for differences in the age distribution among the three race-ethnicity groups, adjusting for the relative youth of the black and Hispanic populations. The series before 1990 are represented by dashed lines indicating estimates based on 1991 surveys of federal prisoners.

Hispanic incarceration rates fall between the rates for non-Hispanic blacks and whites. Over the period of the growth in incarceration rates, the rate has been two to three times higher for Hispanics than for non-Hispanic whites. From 1972 to 1990, the Hispanic rate grew strongly along with incarceration in the rest of the population. Through the 1990s, the Hispanic rate remained roughly flat at around 1,800 per 100,000 of the population aged 18 to 64. Since 2000, the incarceration rate for Hispanics has fallen from 1,820 to just under 1,500.

The Hispanic population itself is heterogeneous, including U.S. citizens and noncitizens and a large number of different national origins. Ruben Rumbaut has explored variation in incarceration within the Hispanic population, relying mainly on census data and survey data on the immigrant

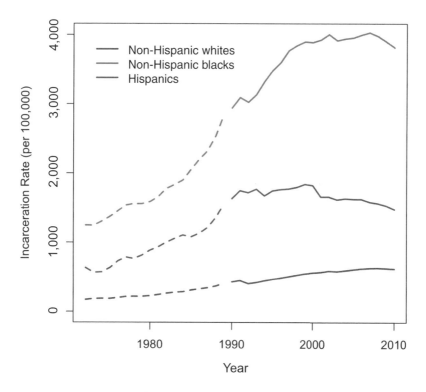

FIGURE 2-14 Prison and jail incarceration rates per 100,000 population for non-Hispanic whites, non-Hispanic blacks, and Hispanics, aged 18 to 64, 1972 to 2010. SOURCE: See Appendix B in this report.

population (Rumbaut and Ewing, 2007; Rumbaut, 2009). Rumbaut finds that incarceration rates (and arrest rates) for the immigrant population are relatively low given their poverty rates and education. The highest incarceration rates are found among long-standing national groups—Puerto Ricans and Cubans. For national groups with large shares of recent immigrants—Guatemalans and Salvadorans for example—incarceration rates are very low. The largest national group, Mexicans, includes significant native-born and foreign-born populations. The incarceration rate indicated in the 2000 census is more than five times higher for native-born U.S. citizens of Mexican descent than for U.S. immigrants born in Mexico. In fact, U.S.-born Mexicans have higher incarceration rates than any other U.S.-born Hispanic group (Rumbaut, 2009). Overall, the incarceration rate for those of Mexican origin is lower than that for either Puerto Ricans or Cubans.

This discussion of incarceration of Hispanics has been limited to those in prisons or local jails, and does not encompass immigrant detention outside of those institutions. There is evidence that the latter form of detention has increased significantly in the past decade in specialized immigrant detention facilities (Dingeman and Rumbaut, 2010; Meissner et al., 2013; National Research Council, 2011, Chapter 4), but this type of incarceration lies beyond the committee's charge.

CONCENTRATION OF INCARCERATION BY AGE, SEX, RACE/ETHNICITY, AND EDUCATION

Although racial and ethnic disparities in incarceration are very large, differences by age, sex, and education are even larger. The combined effects of racial and education disparities have produced extraordinarily high incarceration rates among young minority men with little schooling. The age and gender composition of the incarcerated population has changed since the early 1970s, but the broader demographic significance of the penal system lies in the very high rate of incarceration among prime-age men. The prison population also has aged as time served in prison has increased, but 60 percent of all prisoners still were under age 40 in 2011 (Sykes, 2013).

Incarceration rates have increased more rapidly for females than for males since the early 1970s. In 1972, the prison and jail incarceration rate for men was estimated to be 24 times higher than that for women. By 2010, men's incarceration rate was about 11 times higher. Women's incarceration rate had thus risen twice as rapidly as men's in the period of growing incarceration rates. Yet despite the rapid growth in women's incarceration, only 7 percent of all sentenced state and federal prisoners were female by 2011 (Carson and Sabol, 2012, Table 5). In comparison, 13 percent of local jail populations were women by that year (Maguire, n.d., Table 7.17.2011). The racial disparity in incarceration for women is similar to that seen for men. As with the trends for men, the very high rate of incarceration for African American women fell relative to the rate for white women, although the 3 to 1 black-white disparity in women's imprisonment in 2009 was still substantial (Mauer, 2013).

Figure 2-15 shows estimates of prison and jail incarceration rates for male non-Hispanic whites, non-Hispanic blacks, and Hispanics aged 20 to 39 in 1972 and in 2010. For these series, we used survey data to calculate incarceration by different levels of schooling; we also used information on self-reported ethnicity in surveys dating from the early 1970s to separate Hispanics from non-Hispanic blacks and whites (see Appendix B). For each racial and ethnic group, the incarceration rate is shown for those with at least some college education, for those with no college education (including high school graduates and high school dropouts), and for those who had not

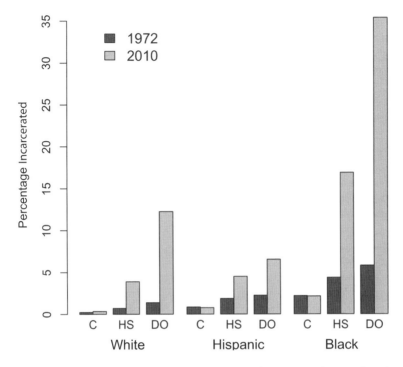

FIGURE 2-15 Prison and jail incarceration rates for men aged 20-39 by education and race/ethnicity, 1972 and 2010.
NOTES: C = at least some college; HS = all noncollege men; DO = less than 12 years of completed schooling.
SOURCE: See Appendix B in this report.

completed high school or received a general equivalency diploma (GED). From 1972 to 2010, the U.S. population's educational attainment, including levels of college attendance, increased. In particular, high school dropout rates declined substantially over this period, so the high school dropouts of 2010 are likely to be a narrower and certainly more educationally disadvantaged population than those who dropped out in 1972. Still, the proportions of college attendees and those with no college education in the population remained more stable than the proportion of high school dropouts over this period.

Extremely high incarceration rates had emerged among prime-age non-college men by 2010 (see Figure 2-15). Around 4 percent of noncollege white men and a similar proportion of noncollege Hispanic men in this age group were incarcerated in 2010. The education gradient is especially significant for African Americans. Among prime-age black men, around 15 percent of those with no college and fully a third of high school dropouts were incarcerated on an average day in 2010. Thus at the height of the prison boom in 2010, the incarceration rate for all African Americans is estimated to be 1,300 per 100,000. For black men under age 40 who had dropped out of high school, the incarceration rate is estimated to be more than 25 times higher, at 35,000 per 100,000.

Educational inequalities in incarceration rates have increased since 1972 (see Figure 2-15). Incarceration rates have barely increased among those who have attended college; nearly all the growth in incarceration is concentrated among those with no college education. Some may argue that the rise in incarceration rates is related to increased selectivity, as the non-college group shrank as a fraction of the population. The noncollege group may have been less able to work and more prone to crime in 2010 compared with 1972. Still, any such selection effect may have been somewhat offset by rising educational attainment in the noncollege population. Higher rates of high school graduation increased the schooling of those without college, perhaps negating the criminal propensity of the low-educated population. Although it is difficult to say precisely how much of the rising educational inequality in incarceration is due to shifts in selectivity, the statistics clearly show that prison time has become common for men with little schooling.

Educational disparities also shed light on the relatively high level of incarceration among Hispanics. Hispanics are incarcerated at a lower rate than non-Hispanic whites at every level of education. Because Hispanics—and new immigrants in particular—tend to have very low levels of education, there are relatively more Hispanics than whites in the high incarceration group of those with less than a high school education.

The statistics discussed above are for incarceration rates at a single point in time. BJS developed estimates of the lifetime probabilities of imprisonment for men and women in different racial and ethnic groups (Bonczar and Beck, 1997; Bonczar, 2003). Those estimates assume a stable underlying rate of prison admission for all the birth cohorts in prison at a given time. Pettit and Western (2004; Western, 2006; Western and Wildeman, 2009; Pettit, 2012) developed this work further, estimating cumulative risks of imprisonment for men and women in different birth cohorts and at different levels of education. These estimates show how the experience of imprisonment has become more prevalent for successive cohorts as the incarceration rate has risen.

It is instructive to compare the risks of imprisonment by age 30-35 for men in two birth cohorts: the first born in 1945-1949, just before the great increase in incarceration rates, and the second born in the late 1970s, growing up through the period of high incarceration rates (see Figure 2-16). Because most of those who go to prison do so for the first time before

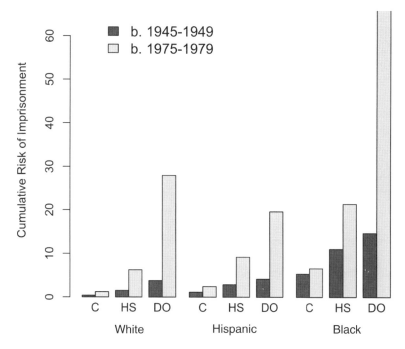

FIGURE 2-16 Cumulative risks of imprisonment by 1979 for men born in 1945-1949 and by 2009 for men born in 1975-1979, by race and education.
NOTES: C = at least some college; HS = completed high school or general equivalency diploma (GED); DO = no high school diploma or GED.
SOURCE: Data from Pettit et al. (2009, Table 37).

age 30 to 35, these cumulative proportions can be interpreted roughly as lifetime risks of going to prison. Education, for these cumulative risks, is recorded in three categories: for those who attended at least some college, for high school graduates or GED earners, and for those who did not complete high school.

Similar to the increases in incarceration rates, cumulative risks of imprisonment have increased substantially for all men with no college education and to extraordinary absolute levels for men who did not complete high school. The prison system was not a prominent presence in the lives of white men born just after World War II. Among high school dropouts, only 4 percent had been to prison by their mid-30s. The lifetime risk of imprisonment was about the same for Hispanic high school dropouts at that time. For African American men who dropped out of high school and reached their mid-30s at the end of the 1970s, the lifetime risk of imprisonment was about 3 times higher, at 15 percent.

The younger cohort growing up through the prison boom and reaching their mid-30s in 2009 faced a significantly elevated risk of imprisonment. Similar to the rise in incarceration rates, most of the growth in lifetime risk of imprisonment was concentrated among men who had not been to college. Imprisonment risk reached extraordinary levels among high school dropouts. Among recent cohorts of African American men, 68 percent of those who dropped out of school served time in state or federal prison. For these men with very little schooling, serving time in state or federal prison had become a normal life event. Although imprisonment was less pervasive among low-educated whites and Hispanic men, the figures are still striking. Among recent cohorts of male dropouts, 28 percent of whites and 20 percent of Hispanics had a prison record by the peak of the prison boom.

In sum, trends in these disaggregated rates of incarceration show that not only did incarceration climb to historically high levels, but also its growth was concentrated among prime-age men with little schooling, particularly low-educated black and Hispanic men. For this segment of the population, acutely disadvantaged to begin with, serving time in prison had become commonplace.

CONCLUSION

This chapter has painted a broad statistical portrait of the trends in incarceration since 1972, the beginning of the U.S. prison boom. After a lengthy period of stability in incarceration rates, the penal system began a sustained period of growth beginning in 1973 and continuing for the next 40 years. U.S. incarceration rates are historically high, and currently are the highest in the world. Clues to the causes and consequences of these high rates lie in their community and demographic distribution. The characteristics of the penal population—age, schooling, race/ethnicity—indicate a disadvantaged population that not only is involved in crime but also has few economic opportunities and faces significant obstacles to social mobility. Through its secondary contact with families and poor communities, the penal system has effects that extend far beyond those who are incarcerated (as discussed in Chapters 9 and 10).

The review of the evidence in this chapter points to four key findings:

1. Current incarceration rates are historically and comparatively unprecedented. The United States has the highest incarceration rates in the world, reaching extraordinary absolute levels in the most recent two decades.
2. The growth in imprisonment—most rapid in the 1980s, then slower in the 1990s and 2000s—is attributable largely to increases in prison admission rates and time served. Increased admission rates

are closely associated with increased incarceration for drug crimes and explain much of the growth of incarceration in the 1980s, while increased time served is closely associated with incarceration for violent crimes and explains much of the growth since the 1980s. These trends are, in turn, attributable largely to changes in sentencing policy over the period, as detailed in Chapter 3. Rising rates of incarceration for major offenses are not associated with trends in crime.

3. The growth in incarceration rates in the 1970s and 1980s was associated with high and increasing black-white disparities that subsequently declined in the 1990s and 2000s. Yet despite the decline in racial disparity, the black-white ratio of incarceration rates remained very high (greater than 4 to 1) by 2010.

4. Racial and ethnic disparities have combined with sex, age, and education stratification to produce extremely high rates of incarceration among recent cohorts of young African American men with no college education. Among recent cohorts of black men, about one in five who have never been to college and well over half of all high school dropouts have served time in state or federal prison at some point in their lives.

The following chapters explore in greater detail the causes and consequences of high rates of incarceration, but these chapters should be read against the backdrop of the following facts thus far established. First, the recent period of high incarceration rates is historically unprecedented and unmatched abroad. Second, incarceration is now pervasive among young men who are both acutely disadvantaged socially and economically and involved in crime. Third, today's penal system, by virtue of its size and demographic concentration, has a broad social significance, reshaping the institutional landscape of poverty in America. We next begin to explore the causes of the growth in incarceration rates by studying the most proximate changes in criminal processing and sentencing that precipitated and drove 40 years of prison growth.

3

Policies and Practices Contributing to High Rates of Incarceration

High rates of incarceration in the United States and the great numbers of people held in U.S. prisons and jails result substantially from decisions by policy makers to increase the use and severity of prison sentences. At various times, other factors have contributed as well. These include rising crime rates in the 1970s and 1980s; decisions by police officials to emphasize street-level arrests of drug dealers in the "war on drugs"; and changes in prevailing attitudes toward crime and criminals that led prosecutors, judges, and parole and other correctional officials to deal more harshly with individuals convicted of crimes. The increase in U.S. incarceration rates over the past 40 years is preponderantly the result of increases both in the likelihood of imprisonment and in lengths of prison sentences—with the latter having been the primary cause since 1990. These increases, in turn, are a product of the proliferation in nearly every state and in the federal system of laws and guidelines providing for lengthy prison sentences for drug and violent crimes and repeat offenses, and the enactment in more than half the states and in the federal system of three strikes and truth-in-sentencing laws.

The increase in the use of imprisonment as a response to crime reflects a clear policy choice. In the 1980s and 1990s, state and federal legislators passed and governors and presidents signed laws intended to ensure that more of those convicted would be imprisoned and that prison terms for many offenses would be longer than in earlier periods. No other inference can be drawn from the enactment of hundreds of laws mandating lengthier prison terms. In the federal Violent Crime Control and Law Enforcement

Act of 1994, for example, a state applying for a federal grant for prison construction was required to show that it:

> (A) has increased the percentage of convicted violent offenders sentenced to prison; (B) has increased the average prison time which will be served in prison by convicted violent offenders sentenced to prison; (C) has increased the percentage of sentence which will be served in prison by violent offenders sentenced to prison.

Yet while individual laws clearly reflected a policy choice to increase the use and length of incarceration, it is unlikely that anyone intended, foresaw, or wanted the absolute levels of incarceration that now set the United States far apart from the rest of the world.

In this chapter, we describe and then assess the development of U.S. sentencing and punishment policies and practices since the early 1970s. The first section reviews the profound shifts in the U.S. approach to sentencing over the four decades of the incarceration rise, including the development of sentencing guidelines and determinate sentencing policies and more recent initiatives designed to increase the certainty and severity of prison sentences. The second section details principles of justice that have undergirded punishment policies in the United States and other democratic countries since the Enlightenment and demonstrates that many policies enacted over the past 40 years are inconsistent with those principles. The third section examines the disjunction in recent decades between policy-making processes and the available social science evidence on the effects of punishment policies. The fourth section surveys and analyzes disproportionate and damaging effects of recent U.S. punishment policies on members of minority groups. In the committee's view, the nation's policy choices that increased the incarceration rate to unprecedented levels violated traditional jurisprudential principles, disregarded research evidence that highlighted the ineffectiveness and iatrogenic effects of some of those policies, and exacerbated racial disparities in the nation's criminal justice system.

CHANGES IN U.S. SENTENCING LAWS

American sentencing policies, practices, and patterns have changed dramatically during the past 40 years. In 1972, the incarceration rate had been falling since 1961 (see Figure 2-1 in Chapter 2). The federal system and every U.S. state had an "indeterminate sentencing" system premised on ideas about the need to individualize sentences in each case and on rehabilitation as the primary aim of punishment. Indeterminate sentencing had been ubiquitous in the United States since the 1930s. Statutes defined crimes and set out broad ranges of authorized sentences. Judges had discretion to decide whether to impose prison, jail, probation, or monetary sentences. Sentence appeals were for all practical purposes unavailable. Because sentencing was to be individualized and judges had wide discretion, there were no standards for appellate judges to use in assessing a challenged sentence (Zeisel and Diamond, 1977). For the prison-bound, judges set maximum (and sometimes minimum) sentences, and parole boards decided whom to release and when. Prison systems had extensive procedures for time off for good behavior (Rothman, 1971; Reitz, 2012).

Few people questioned the desirability of indeterminate sentencing. The American Law Institute (1962) in the *Model Penal Code*, the National Commission on Reform of Federal Criminal Laws (1971) in its *Proposed New Federal Criminal Code*, and the National Council on Crime and Delinquency (1972) in the *Model Sentencing Act* all endorsed the approach.

Within a few years, however, the case—and support—for indeterminate sentencing collapsed. University of Chicago law professor Albert Alschuler described the sea change: "That I and many other academics adhered in large part to a reformative viewpoint only a decade or so ago seems almost incredible to most of us today" (Alschuler, 1978, p. 552).

Criticisms of indeterminate sentencing grew. Judge Marvin Frankel's (1973) *Criminal Sentences—Law without Order* referred to American sentencing as "lawless" because of the absence of standards for sentencing decisions and of opportunities for appeals. Researchers argued that the system did not and could not keep its rehabilitative promises (Martinson, 1974). Unwarranted disparities were said to be common and risks of racial bias and arbitrariness to be high (e.g., American Friends Service Committee, 1971). Critics accused the system of lacking procedural fairness, transparency, and predictability (Davis, 1969; Dershowitz, 1976). Others asserted that parole release procedures were unfair and decisions inconsistent (Morris, 1974; von Hirsch and Hanrahan, 1979).

Not all objections focused primarily on consistency and procedural fairness. Conservatives objected that indeterminate sentencing allowed undue "leniency" in individual cases (van den Haag, 1975) and paid insufficient attention to punishment's deterrent and incapacitative effects (Fleming, 1974; Wilson, 1975). Policy histories of California's Uniform Determinate Sentencing Law of 1976 describe an alliance of liberals and conservatives favoring determinate sentencing and abolition of parole (Messinger and Johnson, 1978; Parnas and Salerno, 1978). A first set of sentencing guidelines developed by the Pennsylvania Sentencing Commission was rejected by the legislature after conservatives characterized them as being insufficiently severe (Martin, 1984).

Those criticisms sparked major changes in American sentencing and punishments, and ultimately in the scale of imprisonment. In retrospect, three distinct phases are discernible. During the first, principally from

1975 to the mid-1980s, the reform movement aimed primarily to make sentencing procedures fairer and sentencing outcomes more predictable and consistent. The problems to be solved were "racial and other unwarranted disparities," and the mechanisms for solving it were various kinds of comprehensive sentencing and parole guidelines and statutory sentencing standards (National Research Council, 1983).

The second phase, from the mid-1980s through 1996, aimed primarily to make sentences for drug and violent crimes harsher and their imposition more certain.[1] The principal mechanisms to those ends were mandatory minimum sentence, three strikes, truth-in-sentencing, and life without possibility of parole laws.[2] Mandatory minimum sentence laws required minimum prison terms for people convicted of particular crimes. Three strikes laws typically required minimum 25-year sentences for people convicted of a third felony. State truth-in-sentencing laws typically required that people sentenced to imprisonment for affected crimes serve at least 85 percent of their nominal sentences.

The third phase, since the mid-1990s, has been a period of drift. The impetus to undertake comprehensive overhauls or make punishments substantially harsher has dissipated. No states have created new comprehensive sentencing systems, none has enacted new truth-in-sentencing laws, and only one has enacted a three strikes law. Mandatory minimum sentence laws have been enacted that target carjacking, human smuggling, and child pornography, but they are much more narrowly crafted than were their predecessors.[3] According to annual reports issued by the National Conference of State Legislatures, several hundred state laws have been enacted since 2000 that in various ways make sentencing less rigid and less severe. Most of these laws are relatively minor and target less serious offenses. In

---

[1]A wide variety of other harsh criminal justice policies were adopted during this period, including registration, notification, and residence laws for sex offenders and a variety of "dangerous offender" and "sexual psychopath" laws. Similar initiatives affecting the juvenile justice system lowered the top age of juvenile court jurisdiction, made discretionary transfers to adult courts easier, and excluded some violent offenses from juvenile court jurisdiction regardless of the defendant's age.

[2] Laws authorizing sentences without the possibility of parole were enacted for a number of reasons, including as part of a strategy by opponents of capital punishment to create a credible alternative to the death penalty.

[3]Summaries such as this must be hedged because no organization maintains a comprehensive database on changes in sentencing laws. The National Conference of State Legislatures for many years compiled annual summaries (of uncertain comprehensiveness) and maintains a searchable database beginning with developments in 2010 (http://www.ncsl.org/issues-research/justice/state-sentencing-and-corrections-legislation.aspx [February 28, 2014]). The Sentencing Project (e.g., Porter, 2013), the Vera Institute of Justice (e.g., Austin, 2010), and the Public Safety Performance Project of the Pew Charitable Trusts issue occasional selective summaries. None of these, however, is comprehensive or cumulative.

few cases have major punitive laws of the second period been repealed or substantially altered. High-profile changes to totemic tough-on-crime laws such as New York's 1973 Rockefeller Drug Laws and the 1986 federal 100-to-1 law for sentencing crack and powder cocaine offenses were partial. In the first of these examples, severe mandatory penalties for many offenses continued to be required (New York State Division of Criminal Justice Services, 2012); in the second, a lower but still high—18-to-1—drug quantity differential for offenses involving pharmacologically indistinguishable crack and powder cocaine was established (Reuter, 2013).[4] More typically, changes in state sentencing laws created exceptions to the coverage of mandatory minimum sentence laws or slightly narrowed their scope,[5] expanded prison officials' authority to grant time off for good behavior, made earlier release possible for narrow categories of prisoners, or reduced the probability of parole and probation revocations for technical offenses (Austin et al., 2013).

Phase I: Changes Aimed at Increased Consistency and Fairness

Sentencing reform initiatives proliferated in the aftermath of the rejection of indeterminate sentencing. The earliest and most incremental sought to reduce disparities through the development and use of parole guidelines and "voluntary" sentencing guidelines. These initiatives were followed by statutory determinate sentencing systems and presumptive sentencing guidelines.

Parole Guidelines

Parole guidelines were the first major policy initiative of the sentencing reform movement, although one foot remained firmly in the individualization logic of indeterminate sentencing. In the 1970s, the U.S. Parole Board and boards in Minnesota, Oregon, and Washington created guideline systems for use in setting release dates. They sought to increase procedural fairness through the publication of release standards, reductions in

---

[4]Although the introduction of crack cocaine was associated with an increase in drug-related violence, subsequent reductions in violence have been consistent with the aging of the crack cocaine user and trafficker populations (U.S. Sentencing Commission, 2007, p. 83).

[5]Many recent changes in state mandatory minimum sentences laws authorize the imposition of some other sentence on selected offenders (Austin, 2010; Porter, 2013). Federal law long has provided such a "safety valve" for mandatory minimum sentence laws for drug crimes committed by first-time offenders who did not use violence or possess a gun and told the government all about their crime. In federal fiscal year 2012, nearly 40 percent of defendants sentenced under mandatory minimum sentence laws benefited from this provision (U.S. Sentencing Commission, 2013b, Table 44).

disparities in time served by those convicted of comparable crimes, and the linking of release decisions in part to empirical evidence on prisoners' probabilities of subsequent offending (Gottfredson et al., 1978). The parole guidelines movement quickly lost steam, however, despite evidence of the guidelines' effectiveness, when well implemented, in improving consistency in the setting of release dates and in time served for similar offenses (Arthur D. Little, Inc., and Goldfarb and Singer, Esqs., 1981; National Research Council, 1983, pp. 194-196). The four pioneering systems were abandoned in the 1980s, replaced in each case by presumptive sentencing guideline systems that also sought to achieve greater procedural fairness and consistency.

One advantage of parole guidelines is that they can make case-by-case decision making within a well-run administrative agency faster, less costly, and more easily reviewable than decisions made by judges. A second advantage is that, as commonly happened during the indeterminate sentencing era, parole boards can address prison overcrowding problems by adjusting release dates (e.g., Messinger et al., 1985). A major disadvantage, however, is that parole boards have authority only over those sentenced to imprisonment. Parole guidelines can reduce unwarranted sentence-length disparities among prisoners, but not between them and others sentenced to local jails or community punishments.

Voluntary Sentencing Guidelines

During the 1970s, local courts and, occasionally, state judiciaries in most states created systems of voluntary sentencing guidelines (Kress, 1980; National Research Council, 1983). Today, they would usually be referred to as "advisory" guidelines. Judges were not bound to follow them and needed to give no reasons if they did not; a defendant could not appeal the judge's decision. Most early voluntary guideline systems were abandoned or fell into desuetude. Evaluations through the late 1980s, most notably of judicially crafted systems in Maryland and Florida, showed that they had few or no effects on sentencing decisions or disparities (Rich et al., 1982; Carrow et al., 1985; Tonry, 1996, Chapter 3).

Voluntary guidelines have attracted renewed interest because of two recent U.S. Supreme Court decisions (*U.S. v. Booker*, 543 U.S. 220 [2005], and *Blakely v. Washington*, 542 U.S. 296 [2004]), which created new procedural requirements for presumptive sentencing guideline systems. A small number of states now operate voluntary guideline systems, but credible research evidence on their effects on sentencing disparities is not available. However, prison population growth in two especially well-known systems using voluntary guidelines—in Delaware and Virginia—has long been below national averages.

Determinate Sentencing Laws

The most influential reform proposals during this phase called for the abolition of parole release and the creation of enforceable standards to guide judges' decisions in individual cases and provide a basis for appellate review (e.g., Morris, 1974; Dershowitz, 1976; von Hirsch, 1976). Policy makers responded. Maine in 1975 abolished parole release and thereby became the first modern "determinate" sentencing state in the sense that the length of time to be served under a prison sentence could be known, or "determined," when it was imposed. California came second, enacting the Uniform Determinate Sentencing Act of 1976; the act abolished parole release and set forth recommended normal, aggravated, and mitigated sentences for most offenses. Other states—including Arizona, Illinois, Indiana, and North Carolina—quickly followed California's lead in enacting such laws. Evaluations concluded, however, that the laws had little if any effect on sentencing disparities (Cohen and Tonry, 1983; Tonry, 1996). No additional states have created comprehensive statutory determinate sentencing systems since the mid-1980s.

Presumptive Sentencing Guidelines

In 1978, Minnesota enacted legislation to create a specialized administrative agency—a sentencing commission—with authority to promulgate presumptive sentencing guidelines. Judges were required to provide reasons for sentences not indicated in the guidelines; the adequacy of those reasons could be appealed to higher courts. Minnesota's guidelines took effect in 1980. Oregon, Pennsylvania, and Washington created similar systems in the 1980s. Evaluations showed that well-designed and -implemented presumptive guidelines made sentencing more predictable, reduced racial and other unwarranted disparities, facilitated systems planning, and controlled correctional spending (Tonry, 1996, Chapter 3). Kansas, North Carolina, and Ohio created similar systems.

The Minnesota, North Carolina, and Washington commissions operated under "population constraint" policies; the aim was to ensure that the number of inmates sentenced to prison would not exceed the capacity of state prisons to hold them. The population constraint policies worked. During the periods when they were in effect, those states experienced prison population growth well below national averages.

The primary policy goal of the early presumptive guideline systems was to reduce disparities and unfairness (Lieb and Boerner, 2001; Frase, 2005; Kramer and Ullmer, 2008). The approach was proceduralist and technocratic, focusing primarily on the development of procedures for improving consistency and predictability and of population projection models for use in financial and facilities planning. The primary aim of North Carolina's guidelines was to control the size of the prison population (Wright, 2002). This aim was realized: after the guidelines took effect in 1994, North Carolina's incarceration rate through 2011 fluctuated between 340 and 370 per 100,000 population, while most other states' rates rose substantially. Population constraint policies made obvious sense to the early sentencing commissions and the legislatures that established them.

Things quickly changed. From the mid-1980s through 1996, policy making in this area ceased to be significantly influenced by concerns about evidence, fairness, and consistency. In Minnesota, the legislature in 1989 instructed the commission to abandon its population constraint policy. In Oregon, the committee that had drafted and monitored the guidelines was disbanded, and the guidelines were trumped by a broad-based mandatory minimum sentence law enacted in 1994. The Pennsylvania Commission on Sentencing survived, but state supreme court decisions effectively converted the nominally presumptive guidelines into voluntary ones (Reitz, 1997; Kramer and Ulmer, 2008).

More generally, presumptive sentencing guidelines fell from favor. The three most recent presumptive guideline systems—those of Kansas, North Carolina, and Ohio (abandoned in 2006)—were established in the mid-1990s. A few voluntary systems have been developed since then. Sentencing commissions in Florida, Louisiana, Tennessee, and Wisconsin were abolished, and Washington's lost its staff and budget in 2011 (Frase, 2013).

A number of studies have concluded that sentencing guidelines, especially with population constraints, help control the size of the prison population. Marvell (1995) compared prison population growth from 1976 to 1993 in nine states that had voluntary or presumptive guidelines with the national average and concluded that guidelines based on population constraints produced lower rates of population increase. Nicholson-Crotty (2004), using prison data for 1975-1998 in a 50-state analysis, concluded that guidelines based on capacity constraints tend to moderate growth in incarceration and that guidelines not based on such constraints exacerbate it. Stemen and colleagues (2006) analyzed state sentencing patterns in the period 1975-2002 and concluded that states that adopted presumptive guidelines and abolished parole release had lower incarceration and prison population growth rates than other states.

The promulgation of federal sentencing guidelines, which took effect in 1987, signaled the end of the phase of modern U.S. sentencing reform that targeted disparities and the beginning of a phase focused on increased certainty and severity. The Sentencing Reform Act of 1984 directed the U.S. Commission on Sentencing to develop guidelines for reducing disparities, to provide for nonincarcerative punishments for most nonviolent and nonserious first offenses, and to be guided by a prison population constraint policy.

The commission ignored the directives concerning first offenses and prison capacity and instead promulgated "mandatory" guidelines that greatly increased both the percentage of individuals receiving prison sentences and the length of sentences for many offenses (Stith and Cabranes, 1998). The federal guidelines were effectively converted from presumptive to voluntary by the U.S. Supreme Court in *U.S. v. Booker*, 543 U.S. 220 (2005).

Presumptive sentencing guidelines developed by a sentencing commission are the most promising means available to jurisdictions that want to reduce or avoid unwarranted sentencing disparities, improve budgetary and policy planning, or both. The well-documented successes of the Minnesota, Oregon, and Washington guidelines in the 1980s and of the North Carolina guidelines since their promulgation in 1994 show that both sets of goals are attainable.

Phase II: Changes Aimed at Increased Certainty and Severity

Sentencing laws enacted from the mid-1980s through the mid-1990s differed substantially from most of those enacted in the preceding period. Whereas the earlier initiatives were aimed principally at making sentences more predictable and consistent and making processes fairer and more transparent, initiatives in the second phase of change in modern sentencing law typically targeted making sentences harsher and more certain and preventing crime through deterrence and incapacitation. The focus shifted from fairness to certainty, severity, crime prevention, and symbolic denunciation of criminals. The shift toward severity took place despite three generations of efforts, often with federal demonstration project funding, to develop alternatives to incarceration (sometimes synonymously called "intermediate sanctions" or "community penalties") (Morris and Tonry, 1990).

The policy initiatives of the second phase, symbolized by the proliferation of mandatory minimum sentence laws, undermined pursuit of the aims of the first phase. Two centuries of experience has shown that mandatory punishments foster circumvention by prosecutors, juries, and judges and thereby produce inconsistencies among cases (Romilly, 1820; Reekie, 1930; Hay, 1975; Tonry, 2009b). Problems of circumvention and inconsistent application have long been documented and understood.

To illustrate this point with modern experience, we draw on the findings of the American Bar Foundation's Survey of the Administration of Criminal Justice in the United States, which was conducted in the 1950s. According to Frank Remington, director of the project, "Legislative prescription of a high mandatory sentence for certain offenders is likely to result in a reduction in charges at the prosecution stage, or if this is not done, by a refusal of the judge to convict at the adjudication stage. The issue . . .

thus is not solely whether certain offenders should be dealt with severely, but also how the criminal justice system will accommodate to the legislative charge" (Remington, 1969, p. xvii). Newman (1966, p. 179) describes how Michigan judges dealt with a lengthy mandatory minimum sentence for drug sales: "Mandatory minimums are almost universally disliked by trial judges. . . . The clearest illustration of routine reductions is provided by reduction of sale of narcotics to possession or addiction. . . . Judges . . . actively participated in the charge reduction process to the extent of refusing to accept guilty pleas to sale and liberally assigning counsel to work out reduced charges." Newman (1966, p. 182) tells of efforts to avoid 15-year mandatory maximum sentences: "In Michigan conviction of armed robbery or breaking and entering in the nighttime (fifteen-year maximum compared to five years for daytime breaking) is rare. The pattern of downgrading is such that it becomes virtually routine, and the bargaining session becomes a ritual. The real issue in such negotiations is not whether the charge will be reduced but how far, that is, to what lesser offense" (Newman, 1966, p. 182). Dawson (1969, p. 201) describes "very strong" judicial resistance to a 20-year mandatory minimum sentence for the sale of narcotics: "Charge reductions to possession or use are routine. Indeed, in some cases, judges have refused to accept guilty pleas to sale of narcotics, but have continued the case and appointed counsel with instructions to negotiate a charge reduction."

Many individuals committing offenses targeted by mandatory punishments do, of course, receive them, but others on whose behalf officials circumvent the laws do not. Mandatory punishments transfer dispositive discretion in the handling of cases from judges, who are expected to be nonpartisan and dispassionate, to prosecutors, who are comparatively more vulnerable to influence by political considerations and public emotion.[6] The following subsections review sentencing policy initiatives in the second phase of change in modern sentencing law.

Truth-in-Sentencing Laws

The term "truth-in-sentencing," a 1980s neologism, alludes to federal "truth-in-lending" laws of the 1970s that required consumer lenders and merchants to disclose interest rates and other key financing terms. The implication is that there is something untruthful about parole release and other mechanisms that allow discretionary decisions about release dates

---

[6]The evidence suggests that changes in sentencing laws have only short-term effects on the probability of plea-bargaining versus going to trial. Once the system adjusts to new standards, usually within 1 year or 2, traditional patterns reemerge (Feeley, 1983; Tonry, 1996, Chapter 5).

to be made. Under the indeterminate sentencing systems that pervaded the United States before 1975, however, there was nothing unwarranted or untruthful about parole release. The system was meant to allow tailoring of prison terms to the rehabilitative prospects and other circumstances of individuals. Maximum sentences—for example, in the American Law Institute's (1962) *Model Penal Code*—were not meant to indicate how long individuals should remain in prison but by what final date they must be released.

Policy advocates in the second phase of sentencing reform, however, defined the differences between the sentences announced by judges and the time served by prisoners as a problem that needed fixing. For example, U.S. Attorney General William Barr, writing a preface to a U.S. Department of Justice (1992) report titled *The Case for More Incarceration*, for example, argued that "prison works," urged that the number of people in prison be increased, and proposed a major national program of prison construction. Barr emphasized that most prisoners were released before their maximum sentences expired, pointed out that some committed offenses after release that would not have occurred had they been locked up, and implicitly urged that discretionary parole release be abandoned as a way to achieve more incarceration.[7]

Proposals like Barr's were later enacted in the Violent Crime Control and Law Enforcement Act of 1994. The act authorized $8 billion for distribution to states to pay for the construction of additional prisons, although much less was ultimately appropriated.[8] To qualify for a substantial portion of these funds, states had to demonstrate that violent offenders would be required to serve at least 85 percent of the sentence imposed. Twenty-eight states and the District of Columbia satisfied this and the other federal criteria (Sabol et al., 2002, Table 1.3).

Evaluators at the Urban Institute sought to determine how truth-in-sentencing laws affected sentencing patterns and prison populations. They were unable "to draw general conclusions about the effects of truth-in-sentencing on sentencing practices throughout the nation" (Sabol et al., 2002, p. vi), but found that the laws had large projected effects in some of the seven states they examined closely. When implemented as part of a comprehensive change to the sentencing system, "truth-in-sentencing laws were associated with large changes in prison populations." In one state, "the increase in the percentage of sentences required to be served before

---

[7]Parole abolition was also a goal of policy advocates in the first sentencing reform phase but for different reasons—because parole release disparities were unfair to prisoners and frustrated achievement of the goals of consistency and proportionality in sentencing (von Hirsch and Hanrahan, 1979). Sixteen states abolished parole for those reasons from the 1970s through the 1990s.

[8]The average annual state grant was $7,885,875, which U.S. Department of Justice officials estimated would pay for construction of space for 50 prisoners (Sabol et al., 2002, p. 28).

release led to larger increases in length of stay and consequently a larger effect of length of stay on the expected number of prisoners" (Sabol et al., 2002, p. vii).

In the seven case study states, the percentages of terms to be served under truth-in-sentencing were much higher than the actual percentages of sentences served by prisoners released in 1993 and the estimated percentages for those entering prison in 1991, as Table 3-1 shows. In most cases, the percentages at least doubled. The Urban Institute evaluators observed that the effects on the prison population would have been much greater had violent crime rates not fallen substantially after 1991: "Were the sentencing practices of 1996 to persist during a time when the number of violent offenses increases, the impacts on prison populations and corrections management could be dramatic" (Sabol et al., 2002, p. 31).

The RAND Corporation carried out another federally funded assessment of the effects of the federal truth-in-sentencing initiative (Turner et al., 2001). The assessment covered data only through 1997. Even so, the authors concluded, "We do know that nationwide, the imposed maximum sentence length, the average length of prison term, and the percent of term served for violent offenses have increased for TIS [truth-in-sentencing] states between 1993 and 1997. For non-TIS states, sentence lengths have been dropping, and months served have dropped slightly" (Turner et al., 2001, p. 134).

A 50-state analysis by the Vera Institute of Justice looked at the prison population effects of a wide range of sentencing policy changes (Stemen

TABLE 3-1 Actual and Estimated Percentages of Sentences Served Prior to Enactment of Truth-in-Sentencing and Percentages Expected to Be Served Under Truth-in-Sentencing, Seven Case Study States

State	Percentage of Sentence Served by Those Released from Prison During 1993	Estimated Percentage for Those Entering Prison During 1991	Expected Percentage Under Truth-in-Sentencing
Georgia	42	51	100
Washington	76	76	85
Illinois	44	43	85
Ohio	26	83*	97
New Jersey	39	37	85
Pennsylvania	46	108*	100*
Utah	36	32	Indeterminate

NOTES: Percentages marked by an asterisk refer to minimum sentences; all others refer to maximum sentences.
SOURCES: Ditton and Wilson (1999); Sabol et al. (2002, Table 3.3).

et al., 2006). Truth-in-sentencing laws were included among a variety of changes that increased time-served requirements for violent crimes. The authors found that "states with separate time served requirements for violent offenders had higher incarceration rates than other states" (Stemen et al., 2006, p. iii).

Concluding one of the most comprehensive 50-state analyses of the effects of the changes in sentencing law of the past four decades, Spelman (2009, p. 59) offers the following observation:

> Truth-in-sentencing laws have little immediate effect but a substantial long-run effect. This analysis makes sense: Truth-in-sentencing laws increase time served and reduce the number of offenders released in future years; the full effect would only be observed after prisoners sentenced under the old regime are replaced by those sentenced under the new law.

The authors of the Urban Institute study (Sabol et al., 2002) defined any state that had eliminated the possibility of parole release for some or all prisoners as a "truth-in-sentencing state." Marvell and Moody (1996) examined the prison population effects of parole abolition and, using 1971-1993 state prison data, found that only 1 of 10 abolition states experienced a higher rate of increase in the prison population than the 50-state average.[9] The lowest rates of growth were in Minnesota and Washington. The states included in that study, however, abolished parole release as part of the first phase of modern sentencing reform when no state had enacted a modern truth-in-sentencing law. The early parole abolition initiatives were aimed at greater transparency and in some cases at reductions in unwarranted sentencing disparities. Findings that the early abolitions of parole release operated to restrain growth in prison populations thus are not inconsistent with the findings of the Urban Institute (Sabol et al., 2002), the Vera Institute of Justice (Stemen et al., 2006), RAND (Turner et al., 2001), and Spelman (2009) that truth-in-sentencing laws operated to increase growth. Unlike the truth-in-sentencing initiatives, the earlier parole abolitions typically were not intended to increase the durations of prison sentences.

The Urban Institute, Vera, and RAND studies underestimate the effects of truth-in-sentencing laws on prison population growth because they cover periods ending, respectively, in 1996-1998 (for Ohio), 2002, and 1997. Mandatory minimum sentence, truth-in-sentencing, and three strikes laws requiring decades-long sentences inevitably have a "sleeper" effect. For many years, newly admitted prisoners accumulate; their numbers are not offset by others being released. The ultimate effects of the enactment

---

[9]Reitz (2006) concluded that parole abolition states generally had lower rates of prison population increase than parole retention states.

of truth-in-sentencing legislation in the mid-1990s thus are not yet apparent. This is true of many laws mandating decades-long sentences that were enacted during the second phase of sentencing reform. Under the three strikes laws of California and other states mandating 25-year minimum sentences, for example, most of which were enacted during 1993-1996, not a single prisoner's 25-year term expired by 2014. Under an 85 percent rule, a prisoner serving a 25-year sentence is not eligible for release before 21 years and 3 months. Only after several more years pass will newly admitted prisoners begin to be offset by the release of others admitted decades earlier.

Mandatory Minimum Sentence and Three Strikes Laws

Mandatory minimum sentence and three strikes laws have little or no effect on crime rates, shift sentencing power from judges to prosecutors, often result in the imposition of sentences that practitioners believe to be unjustly severe, and for those reasons foster widespread circumvention.

Between 1975 and 1996, mandatory minimums were the most frequently enacted change in sentencing law in the United States. By 1983, 49 of the 50 states had adopted such laws for offenses other than murder or drunk driving (Shane-DuBow et al., 1985, Table 30). By 1994, every state had adopted mandatory minimum sentences; most had several (Austin et al., 1994). Mandatory minimum sentences apply primarily to drug offenses, murder, aggravated rape, felonies involving firearms, and felonies committed by people who have previous felony convictions.

Knowledge about mandatory minimum sentences has changed remarkably little in the past 30 years. Their ostensible primary rationale is deterrence. The overwhelming weight of the evidence, however, shows that they have few if any deterrent effects. Analyses finding deterrent effects typically observe, as we do in Chapter 5, that existing knowledge is too fragmentary or that estimated effects are so small or contingent on particular circumstances as to have no practical relevance for policy making.

Modern findings on case processing under mandatory minimum sentence laws are consistent with the findings of the American Bar Foundation Survey and the historical studies cited above. The evidence is overwhelming that practitioners frequently evade or circumvent mandatory sentences, that there are stark disparities between cases in which the laws are circumvented and cases in which they are not, and that the laws often result in the imposition of sentences in individual cases that everyone directly involved believes to be unjust. The evidence concerning case processing comes primarily from six major studies (Beha, 1977; Joint Committee on New York Drug Law Evaluation, 1978; Rossman et al., 1979; Loftin et al., 1983; McCoy and McManimon, 2004; Merritt et al., 2006). All found that prosecutors and judges (and sometimes police) in many cases changed their practices to avoid the imposition of newly enacted mandatory minimum sentences, that prescribed harsher punishments were imposed in the remaining cases, and that overall the laws had few effects on conviction rates.[10]

To illustrate, New York State's Rockefeller Drug Laws required lengthy mandatory minimum sentences for a wide range of drug offenses. With great publicity, the legislature authorized and funded 31 new courts to handle drug cases and expressly forbade some forms of plea bargaining. Practitioners made vigorous efforts to evade the mandatory sentences and often succeeded; the remaining cases were dealt with as the law dictated (National Research Council, 1983, pp. 188-189). Drug felony arrests, indictment rates, and conviction rates all declined after the law took effect. For those convicted, the likelihood of being imprisoned and the average length of prison term increased. But the likelihood that a person arrested for a drug felony would be sent to prison remained the same after the law took effect—11 percent—as before (Joint Committee on New York Drug Law Evaluation, 1978).

Massachusetts' Bartley-Fox Amendment required imposition of a 1-year mandatory minimum prison sentence, without suspension, furlough, or parole, for anyone convicted of unlawful carrying of an unlicensed firearm. Two major evaluations of the law's effects were conducted (Beha, 1977; Rossman et al., 1979), as well as an ambitious secondary analysis of the data produced by those two studies (Carlson, 1982). The primary findings were that police altered their behavior, becoming more selective about whom to frisk, making fewer drug offense arrests, and seizing many more weapons without making an arrest; charge dismissals and acquittals increased significantly; and the percentage of defendants who entirely avoided a conviction rose from 53.5 to 80 percent.

The Michigan Felony Firearms Statute created a new offense of possessing a firearm while engaging in a felony, and specified a 2-year mandatory prison sentence that could not be suspended or shortened by release on parole and had to be served consecutively with a sentence imposed for the underlying felony. The Wayne County prosecutor established and enforced a ban on plea bargaining and launched a major "One with a Gun Gets You Two" publicity campaign. Findings on the statute's effects paralleled those of the above studies. Sizable increases in dismissals occurred; the probability of conviction declined; and the probability of imprisonment did not increase, but lengths of sentences increased for those sent to prison. Cases often were resolved by means of an adaptive response, the "waiver trial,"

---

[10]See also Crawford et al. (1998), Crawford (2000), Ulmer et al. (2007), and U.S. Sentencing Commission (1991) for a discussion of habitual offender laws in Florida and mandatory minimum sentences in Pennsylvania and in the federal courts, and of how prosecutors often do not file charges that trigger these sentences.

in which the judge would convict the defendant of a misdemeanor rather than the charged felony or, with the prosecutor's acquiescence, acquit the defendant on the firearms charge. Another avoidance technique was to decrease by 2 years the sentence that otherwise would have been imposed and then add back the mandatory 2-year increment (Heumann and Loftin, 1979; Loftin et al., 1983).

Oregon's Measure 11, adopted by referendum in 1994, required the imposition of mandatory minimum prison sentences ranging from 70 to 300 months for anyone convicted of 16 designated crimes (and eventually 5 more). RAND Corporation evaluators hypothesized that judges and lawyers would alter previous ways of doing business, especially in filing charges and negotiating plea bargains, to achieve results they deemed sensible and just. The evaluators expected that relatively fewer people would be convicted of Measure 11 offenses and more of non-Measure 11 offenses and that those convicted of Measure 11 offenses would receive harsher sentences. Their research confirmed these hypotheses. Sizable changes were observed in charging decisions (fewer Measure 11 crimes, more lesser crimes) and plea bargaining (fewer pleas to initially charged offenses, more pleas to lesser included offenses) (Merritt et al., 2006).

New Jersey's truth-in-sentencing law required those affected to serve 85 percent of their announced sentence. This was not a mandatory minimum sentence law, but similar hypotheses apply: that charging and bargaining patterns would change to shelter some defendants and that sentences would be harsher for those not sheltered. Both hypotheses were confirmed (McCoy and McManimon, 2004).

Truth-in-sentencing and mandatory minimum sentence (including three strikes) laws are difficult to reconcile with any mainstream, or even coherent, theory of punishment, as the discussion in the next section shows. Many of the laws require sentences that are highly disproportionate to sentences received by prisoners convicted of other offenses and, as we show in Chapter 5, cannot be justified on the basis of their crime prevention effects.

We now step back from this period of policy turbulence and shifting objectives to assess the changes detailed in this section against three yardsticks—the principles of justice that underlie ideas about punishment in Western thought, the role of scientific evidence in the adoption of sentencing policies, and the unprecedented racial disparities that have resulted from the past four decades of policy changes.

PRINCIPLES OF JUSTICE

Reasonable people, including members of this committee, hold differing views on the purposes and goals of sentencing and punishment. We believe it is important to discuss principles of justice in relation to criminal punishment not to promote any particular view or set of views, but to make four points.

The first is that normative principles of justice are relevant to deciding whether a sentencing policy or a decision in an individual case is justifiable and appropriate. Criminal punishment is the paradigm instance of conflict between the interests of the state and those of the individual; criminal convictions can result in losses of property, liberty, and life. Few people want such decisions to be made casually, arbitrarily, or capriciously. That this is so can be seen by recognizing how any individual, law-abiding or not, would want criminal charges against himself or herself handled— evenhandedly, fairly, and justly. Principles of justice are inherently germane to thinking about punishments meted out for crime. The second and third points concern core ideas that recur in coherent sets of views about just punishments—that punishments should ordinarily be proportionate to the severity of crimes and that they should not be more severe, or cost more to administer, than makes sense in relation to the goals they are intended to achieve. These ideas are often (as in the guiding principles articulated in Chapter 1) referred to as the principles of "proportionality" and "parsimony."[11] The fourth point is that proportionality and parsimony have long been widely recognized as important considerations in punishment in all Western countries, including the United States.

Considerations of proportionality and parsimony have fallen into neglect in the United States. Many laws enacted in the 1980s and 1990s required less serious crimes to be punished more severely than more serious ones. Examples include mandatory minimum sentence laws requiring longer terms for people convicted of small sales of drugs than terms typically imposed for many violent offenses, and the sentencing of people to 25-year minimum terms for property misdemeanors under California's three strikes law. Such laws violate the fundamental principle that punishments should be proportionate to the seriousness of crimes. Other laws mandating prison sentences vastly longer than can be justified by their crime prevention effects violate the principle of parsimony.

Proportionality has been a requirement of every mainstream normative theory of punishment since the Enlightenment. Retributivists, who believe that those who commit offenses deserve to be punished for moral reasons, also believe that punishments must be proportional to the seriousness of crimes. If, for example, shoplifting were punished more severely than robbery or rape, the law on its face would send the perverse moral message that

---

[11]In earlier times, as in the Model Sentencing Act of the Advisory Council of Judges of the National Council on Crime and Delinquency (1972), parsimony often was referred to as "the least restrictive alternative" principle: if several possible punishments would achieve their goals equally well, the least restrictive or costly one should be used.

shoplifting is the most serious of the three offenses. Punishing a street-level seller of a few grams of an illicit substance more harshly then someone who commits a violent offense likewise implies that an act of violence is less serious or important than a small sale of drugs.

As an idea and as a term of art, proportionality is commonly associated with retributivist views.[12] Proportionality, however, is not just a retributive value. Some form of proportionality is a major component of all mainstream theories of punishment. Consequentialists, who believe that punishments can be justified by their crime prevention or other good effects, also endorse a conception of proportionality (Frase, 2009).[13] They typically believe that punishment can be justified if the suffering imposed on a convicted individual prevents greater suffering by others. Thus for consequentialists, punishments should be proportional to the good effects they will produce. Punishments more severe than is necessary to achieve those effects waste public resources and impose suffering for no good purpose.

Some people, probably most, subscribe to mixed theories in which punishments can be justified by their crime prevention effects, but only if they do not exceed what would be warranted by the seriousness of the crime. That is, retributive ideas about deserved punishment set upper limits on what can justly be done to a particular individual, but anticipated crime prevention effects may be appropriate considerations in deciding what to do within those limits (e.g., Morris, 1974; Tonry, 1994).[14]

Restorative justice theories typically take the same position, although based on different reasoning. John Braithwaite, the most influential restorative justice theorist, offers a negative retributivist account. Proportionality per se, he argues, is not important. The important objectives are to treat offenders and victims with respect and concern and to try to repair broken or damaged relations among the victim, the offender, and the community. If restorative processes culminate in unanimous agreement among participants on substantially different consequences for offenders in comparable

---

[12]Modern retributivist theorizing dates from the nineteenth-century writings of Kant (1965) and Hegel (1991). Modern theories differ in details but agree on the core propositions that offenders deserve to be punished for moral reasons and that punishments should be proportionate to the degree of wrongdoing. Ashworth and colleagues (2009, Chapter 4) and Tonry (2011b, Part II) survey contemporary theories and theorists.

[13]Modern consequentialist theorizing dates from the eighteenth- and nineteenth-century writings of Beccaria (2007) and Bentham (1970, 2008). Modern theories differ in details but agree on the core propositions that punishments must be justified by their beneficial effects and should not be more severe than is required to achieve those effects. Ashworth and colleagues (2009) and Tonry (2011b) survey contemporary theories and theorists.

[14]Philosophers refer to this as "negative" retributivism (proportionality concerns set maximum but not minimum limits on punishment), in contrast to "positive" retributivism, in which proportionality concerns define the appropriate deserved punishment and thus set both maximums and minimums (Duff, 2001).

cases, then so be it. At the same time, Braithwaite argues, there is a human rights limit—the upper bound of proportionate sentences the justice system might impose (Braithewaite and Pettit, 1990; Braithwaite, 2001).

The ideas just summarized are consistently represented in the philosophical literature as fundamental principles of punishment, but they also reflect widely held beliefs among the general public. There are good reasons to believe that most Americans share the notions that punishments should generally be proportionate to the seriousness of crimes in the retributive sense and not be wasteful or excessive in the consequentialist sense (Roberts and Stalans, 1997). A sizable body of public opinion research, for example, shows that lay people believe punishments should be proportionate to the seriousness of crimes (e.g., Robinson, 2008, 2013), and there is widespread agreement within the United States and other countries about the relative seriousness of different crimes (e.g., Roberts et al., 2003; Darley and Pittman, 2003; Aharoni and Friedland, 2012).

The principles of justice outlined here provide a useful lens through which to evaluate sentencing changes over the past 40 years. Many sentences mandated and imposed under current laws are neither proportionate nor justifiable in terms of their preventive effects. Many street-level drug traffickers, for example, are mandated to receive minimum prison terms of 5, 10, 20, or more years—more severe than punishments received by many people convicted of robbery, rape, or aggravated assault. These laws violate retributive ideas about proportionality given that the general public typically views robberies, rapes, and aggravated assaults as more serious than most drug sales and deserving of greater punishment (Robinson, 2008). Nor can such laws be justified in consequentialist terms. Most drug policy analysts agree that, as discussed further below, imprisoning individual drug dealers seldom reduces the availability of drugs or the number of traffickers (Caulkins and Reuter, 2010; Kleiman et al., 2011).

Some three strikes laws—for example, California's—mandate lengthier sentences for some property and drug offenses than are required for violent offenses. These laws violate retributive ideas about proportionality; few people believe property and drug crimes, even when repeated, are more serious than violence. These laws also fail consequentialist tests. If the goal is deterrence, then it makes little sense to threaten harsher penalties for theft or a small-scale drug sale than for rape; to do so implies that rape is a less serious offense. If the goal is incapacitation, then it makes little sense to protect the community by confining those convicted of drug or property offenses longer than those convicted of violent ones. If the goal is rehabilitation, then it makes little sense to use longer prison terms and incur greater expense to treat those convicted of property offenses compared with those convicted of violent offenses. If the goal is reinforcing norms, clarifying values, or reassuring the public, then it makes little sense to undermine norms and obfuscate values by suggesting that theft is more serious than rape, or to imagine that such perverse messages will reassure the public.

We have summarized these principles to provide a normative framework for thinking about the policies that led to high rates of incarceration in the United States. In the committee's view, many of the nation's policy decisions that have contributed to high rates of incarceration are inconsistent with the principles of parsimony and proportionality. In Chapter 12, we argue for a reaffirmation of these fundamental and widely supported principles in setting punishment policies in the future.

EVIDENCE AND POLICY

Social science evidence has had strikingly little influence on deliberations about sentencing policy over the past quarter century. Many factors combined to increase sentence lengths in U.S. prisons. They include enactment of mandatory minimum sentence, truth-in-sentencing, three strikes, and life without possibility of parole laws; discretionary decisions by prosecutors to charge and bargain more aggressively and by judges to impose longer sentences; and decisions by parole boards to hold many prisoners longer, deny discretionary release altogether more often, and revoke parole more often. Some of these decisions were premised on beliefs or assumptions about deterrence, incapacitation, or both. From a crime control perspective, those beliefs and assumptions were largely mistaken (see Chapter 5).

We acknowledge that the relationship between scientific knowledge and policy making is complex, as a specialized literature on "research utilization" has long made clear (e.g., Cohen and Lindblom, 1979). A 1978 National Research Council report, *Knowledge and Policy: The Uncertain Connection,* notes that numerous social science studies of policy interventions had by then accumulated and that numerous efforts had been made to increase their relevance to and use for policy making. But the report observes that "we lack systematic evidence as to whether these steps are having the results their sponsors hope for . . ." (National Research Council, 1978b, p. 5). The committee responsible for a subsequent National Research Council report, *Using Science as Evidence in Public Policy,* concluded that the connection between social science knowledge and policy remained "uncertain" and that "despite their considerable value in other respects, studies of knowledge utilization have not advanced understanding of the use of evidence in the policy process much beyond the decades-old National Research Council (1978b) report" (National Research Council, 2012b, p. 51).

Scholars of policy making have long been skeptical of rational models of the relationship between research and policy, of the idea that policy decisions do or even should flow more or less directly from scientific evidence concerning the likely effects of alternative policy choices. The 2012 National Research Council report observes that "some mixture of politics, values, and science will be present in any but the most trivial of policy choices. It follows that use of science as evidence can never be a purely 'scientific' matter . . . a dependable and defensible reason will not necessarily be used just because it is available. Re-election concerns, interest group pressure, and political or moral values may be given more weight and may draw on reasons outside the sphere of what science has to say about likely consequences" (National Research Council, 2012b, pp. 15, 17).

We do not disagree with the preceding observations, but note nonetheless that consideration of social science evidence has had little influence on legislative policy-making processes concerning sentencing and punishment in recent decades. The consequences of this disconnect have contributed substantially to contemporary patterns of imprisonment.[15] Evidence on the deterrent effects of mandatory minimum sentence laws is just one such example. Two centuries of experience with laws mandating minimum sentences for particular crimes have shown that those laws have few if any effects as deterrents to crime and, as discussed above, foster patterns of circumvention and manipulation by prosecutors, judges, and juries (Hay, 1975). Three National Research Council studies have examined the literature on deterrence and concluded that insufficient evidence exists to justify predicating policy choices on the general assumption that harsher punishments yield measurable deterrent effects (National Research Council, 1978a, 1993, 2012a). Nearly every leading survey of the deterrence literature in the past three decades has reached the same conclusion (e.g., Cook, 1980; Nagin, 1998, 2013b; Doob and Webster, 2003). Despite those nearly unanimous findings, during the 1970s, 1980s, and 1990s the U.S. Congress and every state enacted laws calling for mandatory minimum sentences (Shane-Dubow et al., 1985; Austin et al., 1994; Stemen et al., 2006).

---

[15]We do not mean to imply that scholars at particular times unanimously subscribed to certain views of what the evidence showed. Wilson (1975) and others (e.g., Bennett et al., 1996) argue that scientific evidence broadly supported many of the sentencing policy changes of the 1980s and early 1990s. However, they represented a minority viewpoint. A claim by Bennett and colleagues (1996), for example, that proposed policies were justified by the existence of youthful "superpredators" was widely repudiated—including recently by a National Research Council panel (National Research Council, 2013). The weight of the evidence supporting the conclusions we offer in this section was clear during the 1980s and 1990s, as is shown by the findings of a series of National Research Council studies (e.g., on deterrence and incapacitation [National Research Council, 1978a]; on criminal careers [National Research Council, 1986]; and on sentencing reform initiatives, including mandatory penalties [National Research Council, 1983]) and elsewhere (e.g., Cohen's [1983] influential survey of the state of knowledge about incapacitation).

In Chapter 5, we also discuss at considerable length the evidence on the important question of the relationship between high rates of incarceration and crime. That assessment leads to the conclusion that although the growth in incarceration rates may have caused a decrease in crime, the magnitude of the reduction is highly uncertain and the results from most studies suggest that it was unlikely to have been large. The social science evidence available in the 1980s and 1990s would have predicted such a result.

RACIAL DISPARITIES

Many features of U.S. criminal justice systems—including unwarranted disparities in imprisonment, invidious bias and stereotyping, police drug arrest practices, and racial profiling[16]—disproportionately affect blacks and Hispanics (Tonry, 2011a). Table 3-2 shows the most recent available national data on racial disparities in imprisonment, capital punishment, life sentences, and sentences of life without possibility of parole for adults and minors. The disparities are enormous. Racial disparities in imprisonment and the absolute numbers of black people, especially men, now or formerly behind bars are major impediments to the creation of an America in which race does not matter (Alexander, 2010).

Higher rates of black and Hispanic than white imprisonment were demonstrated in Chapter 2. They are partly caused and substantially exacerbated by the mandatory minimum sentence, three strikes, truth-in-sentencing, life without possibility of parole, and similar laws enacted in the 1980s and 1990s. All of these laws mandate especially severe—in recent decades unprecedentedly severe—punishments for offenses for which black and Hispanic people often are disproportionately arrested and convicted.[17]

---

[16]We do not discuss racial profiling by the police in this chapter because the extent to which it significantly contributes to high levels of incarceration is unclear. Police profiling results in many more arrests of black people than would otherwise occur. Research on profiling generally concludes that police stop blacks disproportionately often on sidewalks and streets, but find contraband at lower rates for blacks than for whites (e.g., Engel and Calnon, 2004; Center for Constitutional Rights, 2009; Engel and Swartz, 2013).

[17]In discussing data on race and ethnicity in this chapter, we sometimes refer to "blacks" and "whites." At other times, we present data on "Hispanics," "non-Hispanic whites," and "non-Hispanic blacks." The terms used depend on the data sources on which we draw. Prison and jail data published by the Bureau of Justice Statistics (BJS) through 1991 classify people as black and white, with no separate Hispanic category. Since then, national data on jail and prison populations have used a black, white, and Hispanic classification system. National arrest data compiled in the Federal Bureau of Investigation's Uniform Crime Reports and BJS data on criminal courts and sentencing use only black and white categories, which include Hispanics.

TABLE 3-2 Black, White, and Hispanic Inmates in Prison, on Death Row, and Serving Life Sentences, Recent Years

	Year	Total	White	Black	Hispanic	Other
Imprisonment, Jail[a]	Mid-2011	735,601	329,400 (45%)	276,400 (38%)	113,900 (15%)	15,900 (2%)
Imprisonment, State and Federal[b]	2011	1,537,415	516,200 (34%)	581,600 (38%)	349,900 (22%)	
Death row[c]	2010	3,158	1,750 (55%)	1,316 (41%)		
Executed	2010	46	33	13		
Received	2010	104	45	42		
Life Sentence	2008		47,032	66,918	20,309	
Life Without Possibility of Parole	2008		13,751	23,181	3,052	
Life Without Possibility of Parole, Minor	2008		497	984	206	

[a]Jail total includes Alaska Natives, American Indians, Asians, Native Hawaiians, and other Pacific Islanders. White and black subtotals exclude persons of Hispanic or Latino origin.

[b]Imprisonment total includes Alaska Natives, American Indians, Asians, Native Hawaiians, other Pacific Islanders, and persons identifying two or more races; white and black subtotals exclude persons of Hispanic or Latino origin.

[c]Death row total includes Alaska Natives, American Indians, Asians, Native Hawaiians, other Pacific Islanders, and Hispanic inmates for whom no other race was identified. White and black inmates include persons of Hispanic or Latino origin.

SOURCES: Nellis and King (2009, life without possibility of parole); Carson and Sabol (2012, prisoners); Snell (2011, death row).

We focus here primarily on disparities affecting blacks, only occasionally adverting to Hispanics, for several reasons.[18] The most important is that disparities affecting blacks have long been much more acute than those for any other group. Second, the unique history of slavery, Jim Crow laws, and legally sanctioned discrimination that ended only 50 years ago gives particular salience to patterns of disparate treatment affecting blacks. Third, for the first two reasons, the literature on disparities affecting blacks is vastly larger.

Understanding extraordinary racial disparities in imprisonment is a critical challenge facing the nation. As described in Chapter 4, the political and social context in which current policies unfolded has a pronounced racial dimension. In this section, we discuss three different kinds of racial disparity.

The first concerns differences in the probability that blacks and whites are in prison on an average day. In 2011, for example, the combined federal and state incarceration rate for non-Hispanic black men (3,023 per 100,000) was more than six times higher than that for non-Hispanic white men (478). The Hispanic rate (1,238) was slightly more than two-and-one-half times the white rate (Carson and Sabol, 2012, Table 8).

The second kind of disparity concerns racial differences in rates of imprisonment relative to group differences in offending. People are sent to prison because they are convicted of crimes, so it is natural to ask whether disparities in imprisonment rates correspond to disparities in criminality. In the 1980s and early 1990s, racial differences in arrests appeared to correspond closely to racial differences in imprisonment for serious violent crimes but not for property or drug crimes (Blumstein, 1982, 1993). In the 2000s, racial differences in arrests do not correspond closely to racial differences in imprisonment for violent, property, or drug crimes (Tonry and Melewski, 2008; Baumer, 2010).

The third kind of disparity concerns racial differences in sentencing and case processing after controlling for legally relevant differences among offenses. A sizable literature has long shown and continues to show that blacks are more likely than whites to be confined awaiting trial (which increases the probability that an incarcerative sentence will be imposed), to receive incarcerative rather than community sentences, and to receive longer

---

[18]Demographic differences explain in part why imprisonment rates are higher for Hispanics than for non-Hispanic whites (Tonry, 2012). The Hispanic population is much younger, and, consistent with research on age-crime curves, proportionately more Hispanics are in their high-crime ages. In 2008, nearly 44 percent of U.S. Hispanics were under 25, compared with 30 percent of non-Hispanic whites (U.S. Department of Commerce, 2010, Table 10). In 2010, among people arrested for violent crimes, 42.8 percent were under 25 (Maguire, n.d., Table 4.7.2010).

sentences. Racial differences found at each stage are typically modest, but their cumulative effect is significant (Tonry, 2011a; Spohn, 2013).

Disparities in Imprisonment Rates Relative to Population

Racial disparities in imprisonment are of long standing but worsened substantially in the 1980s and early 1990s. For a century before the 1960s, black people had been more likely to be held in prison than whites. As shown in Chapter 2, racial disparities in imprisonment began to rise in the 1960s and reached all-time highs in the 1980s and early 1990s. In recent years, differences in incarceration rates have slightly lessened. In absolute numbers, however, federal and state prisons in 2011 held more non-Hispanic black (581,000) than non-Hispanic white (516,000) inmates. In 2012, 13 percent of U.S. residents were non-Hispanic blacks, and 63 percent were non-Hispanic whites.

Disparities in Imprisonment Rates Relative to Offending

The critical question about imprisonment disparities is whether they result from group differences in criminality or from group differences in how cases are handled. If racial disparities in imprisonment perfectly mirrored racial patterns of criminality, then an argument could be made that the disparities in imprisonment were appropriate.[19] However, if racial disparities in imprisonment resulted entirely from differences in case processing, then they would violate principles of fairness and equal treatment.

Disparities in imprisonment result from a combination of differences in offending patterns and case processing. Disentangling in detail the respective roles of each is difficult. Some insights can be gained from comparing data from victimization surveys on the characteristics of assailants whom victims can identify, but those data are limited and cover only a small category of offenses. The closest scholars have come is to compare racial patterns of arrests for particular offenses with racial patterns in imprisonment for those offenses. As Table 3-3 shows, racial disparities in imprisonment have worsened substantially since the early 1990s relative to racial patterns of involvement in serious crimes.

A classic and influential analysis of racial disparities in imprisonment in 1979 (Blumstein, 1982) concluded that racial patterns of arrests "explained" a large proportion of the disparities, especially for serious violent

---

[19]As Chapter 2 shows, however, group differences in imprisonment are strongly associated with racial and economic differences in education and employment. Important policy issues concerning the sources of those differences and their remediability would remain to be addressed.

TABLE 3-3 Racial Disparities in Imprisonment Not "Explained" by Arrests, 1979-2008

Offense	1979 (%)	1991 (%)	2004(%)	2008 (%)
Murder and Non-negligent Homicide	2.8	−35	11.6	40
Forcible Rape	26.3		23.2	18.2
Robbery	15.6	11	37.2	44.7
Aggravated Assault	5.2		58.8	54.7
Larceny			44.3	
Larceny/Auto Theft	45.6			39.0
Burglary	33.1	25	45.5	44.3
Auto Theft			16.7	
Drug Offenses	48.9	50	57.4	66.2
All Offenses	20.5	24	38.9	45.0

NOTE: "All offenses" includes, in addition to the categories shown, "other violence," "other property," "public order," and "other/unspecified" offenses.
SOURCES: For 1979: Blumstein (1982); for 1991: Blumstein (1993, Table 2); Baumer (2010); for 2004: Tonry (2011a, Table 2.4); for 2008: Baumer (2010).

crimes, and for all offenses left only 20.5 percent "unexplained." For three serious violent crimes, small fractions of disparities in imprisonment were unexplained: murder and non-negligent homicide (2.8 percent), aggravated assault (5.2 percent), and robbery (15.6 percent). For larceny and auto theft (combined) and drug offenses, nearly half the racial disparity in imprisonment was unexplained.

Blumstein reasoned that if the percentages of black and white people held in prison for a particular offense, say, homicide, closely paralleled black and white percentages among those arrested, it would be reasonable to infer that racial patterns of involvement in crime were the primary reason for disparities in imprisonment. Blumstein's analysis cannot prove that racial bias and stereotyping had no or little influence on sentencing patterns. He argued, though, that it was reasonable to infer that their influence was relatively small. His conclusions were confirmed by Langan (1985), who used victim data instead of arrests and prison admission data rather than population data. Blumstein's (1982) conclusions also were confirmed by his subsequent analysis of 1991 data, which found that arrest patterns explained all but 24 percent of overall disparities in imprisonment (Blumstein, 1993).

Arrest data may be potentially misleading indicators of crime to the extent that they are distorted by bias in victims' decisions to report alleged crimes and in police decisions to record them. Yet there are good reasons to believe that the racial patterns shown by arrest data are reasonably accurate indicators of crimes committed, at least for serious violent crimes. Victims' descriptions of the racial characteristics of assailants and police data on victim-offender relationships in homicides have for 30 years indicated, at least for serious crimes, that racial offending patterns shown in arrest data do not deviate far from reality (Langan, 1985; Tonry, 2011a, Figure 2.7).

Other, more rigorous methods might be imagined for assessing relationships between racial patterns in crime rates and imprisonment over time at the aggregate national level, but such studies have not been carried out and published. Blumstein's analysis was widely cited over several decades as providing convincing evidence that bias and stereotyping are not the primary cause of racial disparities in imprisonment. However, replications using data for more recent years have found that arrests explain much lower percentages of imprisonment disparities relative to Blumstein's early studies. These findings are consistent with data reported in Chapter 2 on the increasing disjunction between racial patterns in crime and in imprisonment. Analyses for 2004 (Tonry and Melewski, 2008) and 2008 (Baumer, 2010) using the same method as that used by Blumstein show that, relative to arrest patterns, racial disparities in imprisonment became much worse in the twenty-first century compared with those found by Blumstein for 1979 and 1991. For 2004, 39 percent of overall disparities in imprisonment could not be explained by reference to arrests, and for 2008, 45 percent. Baumer (2010) concluded that for 2008, 40 percent of disparities in imprisonment for murder, 45 percent for robbery, 55 percent for aggravated assault, and 66 percent for drug offenses could not be explained by arrest patterns.

Different racial patterns of involvement in violent crime thus are part of the reason for disparities in imprisonment, but they can explain neither why disparities increased in the 1970s and 1980s nor why they remain so high in the twenty-first century. First, no significant shifts in racial patterns in arrests for violent crimes occurred in the 1970s and 1980s that could explain why black incarceration rates rose after the 1960s. Second, as discussed in Chapter 2, the relative over involvement of blacks in violent crimes has declined significantly since the 1980s.

The reason for increased racial disparities in imprisonment relative to arrests is straightforward: severe sentencing laws enacted in the 1980s and 1990s greatly increased the lengths of prison sentences mandated for violent crimes and drug offenses for which blacks are disproportionately often arrested. These two offense categories, however, raise different behavioral issues. For reasons of social disadvantage, neighborhood residence, and limited life chances that disproportionately affect them, blacks relative to whites have been more involved in violent crime and are more frequently arrested for such crimes (e.g., Sampson, 1987; Sampson and Wilson, 1995; Land et al., 1990; see Sampson and Lauritsen [1997] for a review). Thus one reason why black Americans are disproportionately affected by tougher sentencing policies for violent crime is that they are more often arrested for such crimes—even though the black-white difference in these arrest rates has been declining since the 1980s.

For drug crimes, the situation is different. As suggested in Chapter 2, the disproportionate numbers of arrests of black people for drug crimes bear little relationship to levels of black Americans' drug use or involvement in drug trafficking (e.g., Western, 2006, pp. 41, 45-48; a detailed case study of racial disparity in drug arrests is provided by Beckett and colleagues [2006]). Black people are, however, arrested for drug offenses at much higher rates than whites because of police decisions to emphasize arrests of street-level dealers (Beckett et al., 2005, 2006; Mitchell and Caudy, 2013). Legislative decisions also have specified the longest sentences for crack cocaine offenses, for which blacks are arrested much more often than whites. As the late Senator Daniel Patrick Moynihan (1993, p. 362) observed: "It is essential that we understand that by choosing prohibition [of drugs] we are choosing to have an intense crime problem concentrated among minorities."

Disparities in Sentencing and Case Processing

The committee's review of the literature justifies the conclusion that racial bias and discrimination are not the primary causes of disparities in sentencing decisions or rates of imprisonment. There are differences, but they are relatively small. No doubt they result partly from the various forms of attribution and stereotyping discussed below. Minority defendants are, however, treated differently at several stages of the criminal justice process, and those differences influence resulting disparities. We agree with the National Research Council's panel on sentencing research that "even a small amount of racial discrimination is a matter that needs to be taken very seriously, both on general normative grounds and because small effects in the aggregate can imply unacceptable deprivations for large numbers of people. Thus even though the effect of race in sentencing may be small compared to that of other factors, such differences are important" (National Research Council, 1983, p. 92).

The empirical literature on sentencing documents relatively small racial differences in the justice system experiences of black and white individuals with comparable criminal records and convicted of the same crime. Blacks and Hispanics are more likely than whites to be detained before trial; as noted earlier, being detained increases the probability that a prison sentence will be imposed (e.g., Demuth and Steffensmeier, 2004; Spohn, 2009). Although the evidence is not entirely consistent, the clear weight of research findings is that race and ethnicity affect charging and plea bargaining decisions in both capital and noncapital cases (Crutchfield et al., 1995; Miller and Wright, 2008; Spohn, 2013).

Black and Hispanic defendants, all else being equal, are somewhat more likely than whites to be sentenced to incarceration, and among those sentenced to incarceration in federal courts to receive somewhat longer sentences (Crutchfield et al., 2010; Spohn, 2013). Blacks are less likely than whites to be diverted to nonincarcerative punishments. In states that have sentencing guidelines, blacks are more likely than whites to receive sentences at the top rather than at the bottom of the guideline ranges (Tonry, 1996). Individual studies present divergent findings, often showing small disparities by race and ethnicity for men but not for women (or to different extents), for Hispanics but not for blacks, and for young but not for older offenders (or in each case vice versa) (e.g., Walker et al., 2006; Harrington and Spohn, 2007, pp. 40-45). Overall, when statistical controls are used to take account of offense characteristics, prior criminal records, and personal characteristics, black defendants are on average sentenced somewhat but not substantially more severely than whites. As noted above, however, small differences in this area matter. Spohn (2013, p. 168) concludes her recent exhaustive survey of disparity research thus: "Whether because of conscious bias, unconscious stereotypes linking race with crime, or colorblind application of racially tinged policies, judges' and prosecutors' decisions regarding bail, prosecution, and sentencing are not racially neutral."

While there is not convincing evidence of widespread racial bias in sentencing, there is, in contrast with several decades ago, credible evidence that black defendants are treated differently. Before 1980, many studies appeared to show systematic bias in sentencing of black defendants, but subsequent analyses concluded that failure to control for legally relevant sentencing factors, such as prior criminal record, seriously undermined the persuasiveness of those findings (e.g., National Research Council, 1983; Hagan and Bumiller, 1983). Reviews of subsequent research, however, concluded that blacks were treated less favorably than whites at a number of stages—for example, in pretrial detention decisions, prosecutorial charging decisions, and decisions to impose community rather than incarcerative punishments—and that the cumulative effect of small differences at each stage was substantial (e.g., Zatz, 1987; Chiricos and Crawford, 1995; Mitchell, 2005). Research on death penalty decisions similarly shows that the race of the victim plays a role in both charging and sentencing decisions (Sorensen and Wallace, 1999; Lee, 2007); this is especially evident in cases of interracial violence (Gross and Mauro, 1989; Baldus et al., 1990).

The finding that discernible racial differences exist in sentencing and case processing is disheartening. Race should not matter when criminal sentences are imposed. Viewed differently, however, the finding is not surprising. Americans of every racial and ethnic group are influenced by stereotypes about black people's involvement in crime. This is not to say that most Americans are bigoted or racist. Few white Americans still believe in the racial inferiority of black people, and most believe racial discrimination is wrong. Among earlier generations of white Americans, the belief that blacks are racially inferior to whites was commonplace. Those beliefs largely disappeared after the 1960s, sometimes to be replaced by other unflattering stereotypes (Unnever, 2013). Since the 1970s, large majorities of whites have favored integrated schools, accepted having blacks as neighbors, and believed that blacks and whites are of equal intelligence (Thernstrom and Thernstrom, 1997, pp. 498-501). One typical and detailed survey of research on racial attitudes concluded that Americans' endorsement of racial equality norms is nearly universal:

> Almost all whites genuinely disavow the sentiments that have come to be most closely associated with the ideology of white supremacy—the immutable inferiority of blacks, the desirability of segregation, and the just nature of discrimination in favor of whites. In this sense, nearly every white person today has a genuine commitment to basic racial equality in the public sphere (Mendelberg, 2001, pp. 18-19).

Comprehensive recent surveys of a range of literatures on racial attitudes have reached similar conclusions (e.g., Krysan, 2012).[20]

Whites, and members of other groups, nonetheless are influenced by racial stereotypes (Kirschenman and Neckerman, 1991). Sociologists use the term "statistical discrimination" to describe the attribution of characteristics of groups to individuals (Wilson, 1987) as when, for example, employers' preconception that inner-city minority men are less likely than others to be reliable workers leads them to reject reliable applicants (Pager, 2007). These issues are discussed further in Chapter 8.

Several literatures document the existence and force of racial stereotyping about crime and criminals. The media commonly portray a world of black offenders and white victims. When asked to describe typical violent criminals and drug dealers, white Americans often describe black individuals (e.g., Entman, 1992; Reeves and Campbell, 1994; Beckett and Sasson, 2004). Research on the influence of skin tone and stereotypically African American facial features shows that negative stereotypes operate to the detriment of blacks in the criminal justice system. They cause black individuals to be punished more severely than whites, and among blacks they cause dark-skinned people and people with distinctively African American facial

---

[20]This does not mean that racial anxieties and attitudes toward criminal justice have ceased to matter. Racial resentments and anxieties are major predictors of whites' support for harsh sentencing and punishment policies and their opposition to increased public expenditure on social welfare programs (Bobo and Johnson, 2004; Bobo and Thompson, 2006; Peffley and Hurwitz, 2010; Unnever, 2013).

features to be punished more severely than light-skinned people and people with more European features.

This form of stereotyping, known as "colorism," places darker-skinned American blacks at a comparative disadvantage in most spheres of life (Hochschild and Weaver, 2007).[21] Dark skin evokes fears of criminality (Dasgupta et al., 1999) and is an easily remembered characteristic of a purportedly criminal face (Dixon and Maddox, 2005). For example, an analysis of more than 67,000 male felons incarcerated in Georgia showed that controlling for type of offense, socioeconomic characteristics, and demographic factors, dark-skinned blacks received longer sentences than light-skinned blacks: light-skinned black defendants received sentences indistinguishable from those of whites, while longer sentences were received by medium-skinned (a year longer on average) and dark-skinned (a year and a half longer on average) black defendants (Hochschild and Weaver, 2007, p. 649).

Studies of Afrocentric feature bias take the analysis one step further (Blair et al., 2004). The evidence confirms the hypothesis that stereotypically African American facial features (e.g., dark skin, wide nose, full lips) influence decision makers' judgments (Blair et al., 2002, 2005; Eberhardt et al., 2004). Pizzi and colleagues (2005, p. 351) measured facial features of black and white defendants and concluded that practitioners treated differently not only black but also white defendants with such features:

> Racial stereotyping in sentencing decisions still persists. But it is not a function of the racial category of the individual; instead, there seems to be an equally pernicious and less controllable process at work. Racial stereotyping in sentencing still occurs based on the facial appearance of the offender. Be they white or African American, those offenders who possess stronger Afrocentric features receive harsher sentences for the same crimes.

Even death penalty decisions are influenced by facial features. Looking at cases in Philadelphia in which death had been a possible sentence, Eberhardt and colleagues (2006, p. 383) "examined the extent to which perceived stereotypicality of black defendants influenced jurors' death-sentencing decisions in cases with both white and black victims." With stereotypicality as the only independent variable, 24.4 percent of black defendants rated below the median in having stereotypical black features

---

[21]Colorism is defined as the "tendency to perceive or behave toward members of a racial category based on the lightness or darkness of their skin tone" (Maddox and Gray, 2002, p. 250). Empirical research on the subject is comparatively new, but the phenomenon is old. Seventy years ago, Myrdal (1944, p. 697) observed in *An American Dilemma: The Negro Problem and Modern Democracy*, "Without a doubt a Negro with light skin and other European features has in the North an advantage with white people."

were sentenced to death, compared with 57.5 percent of those rated above the median.

The Implicit Association Test (IAT),[22] which has been taken by millions of people, was developed by psychologists to assess people's attitudes toward members of different groups. The IAT results have consistently shown that implicit bias against blacks is "extremely widespread" (Jolls and Sunstein, 2006, p. 971) and demonstrate the existence of unconscious bias by whites against blacks (Rachlinski et al., 2009).[23] It would be remarkable if criminal justice practitioners were not affected by this bias.[24]

CONCLUSION

A number of lessons emerge from this look back at the past four decades of changes in sentencing policy. Successive waves of change swept the nation, some affecting all or most states. During the 1970s, experiments with voluntary sentencing guidelines were undertaken in many states, and all but one state enacted mandatory minimum sentence laws typically requiring minimum 1- or 2-year sentences or increases of 1 or 2 years in the sentences that would otherwise have been imposed. During the 1980s, the federal government and nearly every state enacted mandatory minimum sentence laws for drug and violent crimes, typically requiring minimum sentences of 5, 10, and 20 years or longer. During the 1990s, the federal government and more than half the states enacted truth-in-sentencing and three strikes laws. Almost all of the states now have life without possibility of parole laws. Voluntary guidelines and statutory determinate sentencing laws proved ineffective at achieving their aims of increasing consistency and diminishing racial and other unwarranted sentencing disparities. There is

---

[22]The IAT asks individuals to categorize a series of words or pictures into groups. Two of the groups—"black" and "white"—are racial, and two are characterizations of words as "good" or "pleasant" (e.g., joy, laugh, happy) or "bad" or "unpleasant" (e.g., terrible, agony, nasty). To test for implicit bias, one version of the IAT asks respondents to press one key on the computer for either "black" or "unpleasant" words or pictures and a different key for "white" or "pleasant" words or pictures. In another version, respondents are asked to press one key for "black" or "pleasant" and another key for "white" or "unpleasant." Implicit bias is defined as faster responses when "black" and "unpleasant" are paired relative to "black" and "pleasant."

[23]People taking the IAT at the Project Implicit website are regularly warned that they may find the results of their own test disturbing: "Warning: This test has been taken more than one million times, and the results usually reveal some degree of bias" (http://www.understanding-prejudice.org/iat/ [February 28, 2014]).

[24]Almost all demographic groups show a significant implicit preference for whites over blacks. The major exception is blacks: equal proportions show implicit preferences for blacks and for whites, but unlike whites they do not show a preference for their own group. The consensus view of the existence of implicit racial bias is based on the results of millions of tests of every imaginable group in the population.

little convincing evidence that mandatory minimum sentencing, truth-in-sentencing, or life without possibility of parole laws had significant crime reduction effects. But there is substantial evidence that they shifted sentencing power from judges to prosecutors; provoked widespread circumvention; exacerbated racial disparities in imprisonment; and made sentences much longer, prison populations much larger, and incarceration rates much higher.

The policy initiatives that swept the nation were by and large ineffective at creating just, consistent, and transparent sentencing systems. The more targeted approaches—parole and presumptive sentencing guidelines, especially when incorporating prison capacity constraints—were effective. Both parole and presumptive sentencing guidelines, when well designed and implemented, can demonstrably improve consistency, reduce disparity, and make these critical decisions more transparent. Presumptive sentencing guidelines incorporating prison capacity constraints offer a proven method for setting sentencing priorities, minimizing disparities, controlling prison population growth, and managing correctional budgets.

The evidence discussed in this chapter points to four main findings.

First, law reform initiatives aimed at achieving greater fairness, consistency, and transparency in sentencing have achieved their goals more successfully than initiatives aimed at achieving greater severity, certainty, and crime prevention.

Second, social science evidence on the effectiveness of sanctions and the operation of the justice system informed the development of parole and sentencing guidelines but had little influence on the development of initiatives aimed at achieving greater severity, certainty, and crime prevention. The evidence base on sentencing is broader and deeper now than in the 1980s and 1990s, but the primary findings have not changed significantly since they were disseminated in a series of National Research Council reports between 1978 and 1986.

Third, initiatives aimed at achieving greater severity, certainty, and crime prevention were largely incompatible with fundamental and widely shared ideas about just punishment that have characterized the United States and other Western countries since the Enlightenment. Many of the punishments imposed under the new laws have violated the principle of proportionality—that punishment should be proportionate to the individual's culpability and the gravity of the offense. Many also have violated the principle of parsimony—that punishments should be no more severe than is required to achieve their legitimate purposes.

Fourth, racial and ethnic disparities in imprisonment reached extreme and unprecedented levels in the 1980s and 1990s and have since remained at deeply troubling levels. They are partly caused and significantly exacerbated by recent sentencing laws aimed at achieving greater severity, certainty, and crime prevention and by law enforcement strategies associated with the war on drugs. They also result partly from small but systematic racial differences in case processing, from arrest through parole release, that have a substantial cumulative effect. And they are influenced by conscious and unconscious bias and stereotyping that remain pervasive in America despite the near disappearance of widespread beliefs about racial superiority and inferiority.

4

The Underlying Causes of Rising Incarceration: Crime, Politics, and Social Change

The growth of the penal system and high rates of incarceration did not occur by accident. As discussed in Chapter 3, they resulted from a series of policy decisions that were intended to increase the severity of sanctions. Less well understood are the underlying causes of this turn toward tougher sanctions.

This chapter examines the social, political, economic, and institutional forces that help explain why politicians, policy makers, and other public figures responded to changes in U.S. society in the decades after World War II by pursuing harsher practices, policies, and laws—and why they succeeded. Running through those explanations is a uniquely American combination of crime, race, and politics that shaped the adoption of more punitive criminal justice policies. The salient forces include social and political unrest following World War II, especially in the 1960s; a major electoral realignment as the Democratic Party divided over civil rights and other issues and as the Republican Party became competitive in the south for the first time since Reconstruction; a decades-long escalation in national crime rates beginning in 1961; and major transformations in urban economies that included the disappearance of many well-paid jobs for low-skilled workers. They also include distinctive features of American political institutions, including the election and partisan political appointment of judges and prosecutors, a winner-take-all two-party electoral system, and the use of ballot initiatives and referenda in some states to develop criminal justice policy. These conditions made the United States more vulnerable than other developed democracies to the politicization of criminal justice in a punitive direction.

The shift in criminal justice practices, policies, and laws in the postwar era that resulted in high incarceration rates was distinctive. It was a departure in some important ways from the historical experience of the United States prior to World War II. It was also distinct from the experience of many other Western countries during the latter part of the twentieth century.

Before World War II, the making, implementation, and enforcement of criminal justice policy in the United States were almost exclusively within the purview of the states or local authorities, not the federal government. From the 1940s onward, public officials and policy makers at all levels of government—from federal to state to local—increasingly sought changes in judicial, policing, and prosecutorial behavior and in criminal justice policy and legislation. These changes ultimately resulted in major increases in the government's capacity to pursue and punish lawbreakers and, beginning in the 1970s, in an escalation of sanctions for a wide range of crimes. Furthermore, criminal justice became a persistent rather than an intermittent issue in U.S. politics. To a degree unparalleled in U.S. history, politicians and public officials beginning in the 1960s regularly deployed criminal justice legislation and policies for expressive political purposes as they made "street crime"—both real and imagined—a major national, state, and local issue.

Although rising crime rates are a key part of this story, it is only by examining those trends within their social, political, institutional, and historical context that one can understand the underlying causes of the steep increase in incarceration rates. Most other Western countries experienced rising crime rates beginning in the 1960s. However, because of underlying differences in the social, political, economic, and institutional context, other Western countries did not respond to increased crime by adopting markedly harsher policies and laws.[1]

This chapter examines the conditions for the emergence of a criminal justice system characterized by harsh policies, practices, and laws and unprecedented high rates of incarceration: the beginnings in the 1940s of efforts made at the federal level to change criminal justice policies and practices nationally; a growing federal role in crime policy, the political impact of rising crime rates after 1961, the subsequent political and electoral realignment triggered by the civil rights movement, the wars on drugs declared by President Nixon and his successors, rising public anxiety about crime and the influence of racial factors on those attitudes, U.S. political

---

[1]As discussed in Chapter 2, the U.S. incarceration rate is approximately 5 to 12 times the rates in other Western countries and Japan. That said, some Western countries have embraced harsher policies in recent years, but nowhere near the extent of the United States (Tonry, 2007a).

institutions and culture, and growing economic distress in U.S. cities in the 1970s and 1980s.

THE POLITICS OF CRIME AND CRIMINAL JUSTICE FROM THE 1940S TO THE EARLY 1960S

Concerns about crime and criminal justice have surfaced periodically as major issues in U.S. politics at the national, state, and local levels, dating back to the nation's founding. While the committee members varied in their views on the weight to be given to the political origins of crime policy before the 1960s, it is clear that the poor and racial and ethnic minorities often were associated with the problem of crime in policy debates and popular culture throughout the nation's history.

The problem of crime has been central to discussions of a number of leading issues, including the meaning and significance of the American Revolution, the rise and fall of slavery and the convict-leasing system, Reconstruction, the modernization of the south, economic development, and race relations. In the late nineteenth and early twentieth centuries, national campaigns were waged against specific categories of crimes and types of lawbreakers, including family violence, prostitution, alcohol, gangsters, ransom kidnappings, marijuana use, sexual psychopaths, juvenile delinquents, and organized crime. These highly publicized campaigns often marked certain groups as inherently "criminal," including, depending on the moment, the Irish, Mexicans, African Americans, and single women (Gross, 2006; Hicks, 2010, Chapter 7; Muhammad, 2010; Chávez-Garcia, 2012; Blackmon, 2009; Stewart-Winter, forthcoming; Gottschalk, 2006, Chapter 3; Musto, 1999).

The country's criminal justice apparatus developed fitfully in the course of these intense and often morally and racially charged campaigns. These efforts typically produced at most a relatively small rise in the incarcerated population—not the very large and sustained shift toward harsher penal policies and consequences of the sort witnessed since the 1970s. Nevertheless, they left increasingly fortified law enforcement institutions in their wake (McLennan, 2008; Blue, 2012; Janssen, 2009; Murch, 2010, Chapter 3; Gottschalk, 2006). This proved important in the second half of the twentieth century as a growing number of politicians, policy makers, and other public figures chose to respond to the social and political turmoil that gripped the country from the 1940s to the 1970s and to the rise in crime rates in the 1960s by greatly expanding the nation's penal capacity.

How issues of crime and disorder were framed and debated in the context of this turmoil helps explain why the United States embarked on an unprecedented prison expansion that has lasted for four decades. The country had experienced crime waves prior to the 1960s, but they did not result in a sustained and increasing reliance on incarceration in criminal justice policy. Furthermore, these earlier crime waves did not spur sustained and wide-scale political attacks on judges, other public figures, and experts who sought to stem crime by addressing its structural causes and who emphasized the rehabilitation of lawbreakers rather than increased incapacitation and retribution.

There is a long history in the United States of debates over criminal justice policy, often in relation to the issues of race and civil rights. To many African Americans and Mexican Americans, dramatic, often violent confrontations in the years immediately after World War II illustrated serious problems of bias on the part of police forces. These confrontations included the lynching of black veterans returning home to the south after World War II; the numerous clashes between long-time white residents and new black and other migrants in U.S. cities, notably the infamous "Zoot Suit Riots" in Los Angeles in 1942[2] and the 1943 race riot in Detroit; and rising urban-suburban tensions with the rapid expansion of suburbia after the war (Sugrue, 1996; Murakawa, forthcoming; Mazon, 1984; Kruse and Sugrue, 2006; Theoharis and Woodard, 2003). These developments led many to demand that more attention be paid to episodes of police brutality as well as to police inaction in the face of organized and wide-scale white violence.

During this period, whites in the south and increasingly in the north also demanded that greater attention be paid to problems of crime and disorder. Many of them believed that these problems could be solved only with tougher laws; tougher sanctions; and tougher police, prosecutors, and judges. They sought greater protection from what they perceived to be disorderly protests by blacks and their allies seeking to desegregate U.S. society. Arguing that integration breeds crime, they sought an expanded criminal justice apparatus as a way to stem what they perceived as the increased lawlessness of blacks and their supporters who were challenging the Jim Crow regime (Sugrue, 1996; McGirr, 2002; Biondi, 2006; Countryman, 2007; Thompson, 2001; Jones, 2010; Murakawa, forthcoming; Weaver, 2007).

In response to this unrest and other political pressures at home and abroad, President Harry S. Truman and his supporters invoked the need for more "law and order" as they sought a greatly expanded role for the federal government in the general administration of criminal justice and law enforcement at the local and state levels and in the specific prosecution

---

[2]In the Zoot Suit Riots, Mexican American youths became the targets of violence by rioting white sailors following the release of inflammatory reports by government agencies suggesting that Mexicans had a greater propensity to crime because of their cultural inferiority and certain psychological characteristics (Grebler et al., 1970).

and punishment of civil rights crimes.[3] They introduced a flurry of bills in the 1940s and 1950s aimed at offering federal assistance to improve local and state police forces by making them more professional and providing them better equipment and training. They also proposed numerous measures to expand the federal role in areas that historically had been almost exclusively within the purview of states and municipalities, such as regulation of police brutality, antilynching measures, and anticonspiracy statutes (Murakawa, forthcoming).

Most of these bills were not enacted. However, all this legislative activity in the 1940s and 1950s deeply influenced how future discussions of law and order, crime, and the federal role in law enforcement would unfold. In advocating these measures, Truman and his allies helped establish a federal role in state and local law enforcement. They also hoped that greater procedural protections would ensure that members of minority groups would be treated fairly in the criminal justice system. By rendering the criminal justice system more legitimate in the eyes of minority groups, such protections, in their view, would eliminate a main source of protests and political discontent and also an important cause for criminal behavior on the part of groups that did not view the system as fair and legitimate (Murakawa, 2008).

The American Bar Foundation's expansive research agenda in the 1950s and 1960s on the problem of discretion and arbitrary power also was a contributing factor to the political push for more uniformity, neutrality, and proceduralism in law enforcement and sentencing. Two other key factors were the American Legal Institute's project to devise a Model Penal Code (to guide sentencing policy) and the Warren Court's series of decisions expanding the procedural rights of suspects, defendants, and prisoners (Stuntz, 2011, pp. 266-267; Murakawa, forthcoming).

This was the context in which Barry Goldwater, the Republican presidential nominee, ran a stridently law-and-order campaign in 1964 that sought white electoral support through explicit and implicit race-based appeals and denunciations of the civil rights movement.[4] From then on, the law-and-order issue became a persistent tripwire stretching across national and local politics. Politicians and policy makers increasingly chose to trigger that wire as they sought support for more punitive policies and for expansion of the institutions and resources needed to make good on promises to "get tough." In the past, crime and punishment concerns would burst on

---

[3]In signing the executive order creating the Presidential Committee on Civil Rights in December 1946, Truman lamented how in some places "the local enforcement of law and order has broken down, and individuals—sometimes ex-servicemen, even women—have been killed, maimed, or intimidated" (President's Committee on Civil Rights, 1947, p. vii).

[4]See Appendix A for a supplementary statement by Ricardo Hinojosa on this sentence and other similar committee findings in this chapter.

the scene and then usually recede without leaving behind a massive increase in the state's penal capacity. After 1964, however, the issue of law and order did not ebb, for several reasons discussed below.

THE JOHNSON ADMINISTRATION AND THE WAR ON CRIME

The social, political, and economic pressures that northern and southern whites felt from the Second Great Migration and from the civil rights movement persisted and intensified in the 1960s and 1970s. Leading public figures and their supporters—including mayors of large northern cities, such as Frank Rizzo of Philadelphia and Richard J. Daley of Chicago, and conservative southern Democrats, such Sen. Sam Erwin and Sen. Strom Thurmond—began calling for even more law enforcement power in response to rising crime rates and the demands of blacks for greater rights in the cities to which they had migrated. In response to these pressures, the Johnson Administration reformulated the law-and-order problem and expanded federal support for crime policy. Because Johnson-era initiatives expanded the role of the federal government in state and local crime policy but did not directly promote harsher penal policy, there are a variety of views on the significance of these measures for later policy. For some of the committee members, Johnson's initiatives laid some of the most important foundations for the "war on crime."

When President Johnson launched the war on crime,[5] he linked it to his war on poverty and to the need to address the "root causes" of crime. This approach suggested investing more in education, health, welfare, and other social and economic programs, not just law enforcement. Numerous presidential and other national commissions assembled in the late 1960s and early 1970s also highlighted the social and ecological dimensions of crime prevention.[6] But the root causes approach lost out for several reasons.

While conservatives fashioned a coherent point of view on the crime and punishment issue during these years, liberals had trouble finding a clear voice on the issue (Flamm, 2005, p. 124). As mentioned earlier, some liberals had been arguing since the 1940s for greater investments in law enforcement. They also had been arguing for more neutral procedures to

[5]See http://www.presidency.ucsb.edu/ws/?pid=27478 [February 2014] for President's Johnson's "Special Message to the Congress on Crime and Law Enforcement" in 1966.
[6]The President's Commission on Law Enforcement and Administration was convened in March 1965 and issued its report in 1967; the National Advisory Commission on Civil Disorders—known more frequently as the "Kerner Commission" or the "Riot Commission"—was formed in the summer of 1967 and issued its report in 1968; the National Commission on the Causes and Prevention of Violence was formed in 1968 and issued its report in 1969 (Haney, 2010; Flamm, 2005); and the National Advisory Commission on Criminal Justice Standards and Goals was created in 1971 and issued six reports in 1973.

resolve the law-and-order problem, which they characterized primarily as an issue of police brutality, organized white violence against those who challenged the color line, and discriminatory enforcement of laws. Others had been arguing for this greater investment in law enforcement, but for more punitive reasons. In short, strengthening investments in cities and social programs to mitigate the stresses and strains of the Great Migration had long been a secondary priority for many liberals, along with enhancing law enforcement and professionalizing the police.

In 1965, with strong support from the Johnson Administration, Congress enacted the Law Enforcement Assistance Act. This legislation established the Office of Law Enforcement Assistance to award grants and administer other programs aimed at improving and expanding law enforcement, court administration, and prison operations at the state and local levels. The dollar amounts involved were small, but the political significance was considerable. This measure engaged the federal government in criminal justice and law enforcement, both rhetorically and substantively, to an unprecedented degree (Flamm, 2005; Thompson, 2010).

The 1965 act garnered strong support spanning the political spectrum. Liberal Democrats, who had been ardently pushing since the 1940s for more proceduralism, neutrality, and uniformity in policing practices and sentencing policies, generally supported the act. Some of them rallied for greater police professionalism in the hope that this would yield racial fairness and thus reduce political unrest and crime among minority groups. Some of them also viewed an increase in expenditures on the police as complementing the recent series of Supreme Court decisions that had expanded procedural rights for suspects and defendants. In contrast, conservatives in both parties sought to use the expansion of federal involvement in law enforcement as a means of empowering police to deal forcefully with urban unrest. Many of them also hoped to counteract the Warren Court decisions that in their view had procedurally handcuffed the police and prosecutors (Kamisar, 2005; Allen, 1975). Thus, with mixed motivations, both liberals and conservatives helped clear the political ground for this and subsequent measures that expanded the criminal justice system and ultimately gave local, state, and federal authorities increased capacity for arrest, prosecution, and incarceration.

In 1965, Johnson also established the President's Commission on Law Enforcement and Administration of Justice. Three years later, Congress enacted the controversial Omnibus Crime Control and Safe Streets Act of 1968 in response to the commission's findings. Liberals were generally supportive of initial drafts of this legislation, which provided federal grants to police for equipment, training, and pilot programs and also greater federal investments in rehabilitation, crime prevention, and alternatives to incarceration. But as the bill moved through the legislative process, southern

Democrats and their Republican allies were able to substantially modify the final bill (Flamm, 2005, Chapter 7). They added funding formulas that gave state governments—not cities or the federal government—great leeway to distribute the large amounts of federal money that would be funneled over the years through the new Law Enforcement Assistance Administration. Furthermore, they successfully inserted provisions on wiretapping, confessions, and use of eyewitnesses that curtailed the procedural protections that had been extended by Supreme Court decisions (Flamm, 2005).

Still, some liberals viewed passage of the Safe Streets Act as another important step toward modernizing, professionalizing, and federalizing the criminal justice system. A number of them also saw it as an important mechanism for containing the growing social and political unrest in their own cities and states (Murakawa, forthcoming; Hinton, 2012). However, many other liberals were strongly opposed to the measure. They objected to what they saw as an emphasis on law enforcement solutions as the cost of addressing the "root causes" of crime. They also were strongly opposed to several provisions in the bill that they viewed as an inappropriate erosion of core civil liberties.

The assassination of Robert F. Kennedy in June 1968, near the end of the primary season, helped tip the balance in favor of the Safe Streets Act (Flamm, 2005, pp. 138-140; Simon, 2007, pp. 49-53). Two weeks after the assassination, Johnson signed the Safe Streets Act, though with considerable reluctance. He calculated that a veto might result in even harsher legislation and could irreparably harm Vice President Hubert Humphrey's campaign for the presidency (Flamm, 2005, p. 140).

LAW AND ORDER AND THE RISING CRIME RATE

The national crime rates had started to turn upward in 1961, and they continued rising through 1981. The lack of political consensus at the time on the causes of the increase in violent crime and what to do about it served to increase public concern. Fear of crime continued to provide political opportunities for candidates and office-holders even after crime rates began to fall. The responses of politicians, policy makers, and other public figures to rising crime rates were political choices not determined by the direction in which the crime rate was moving. Certain features of the social, political, and institutional context at the time help explain why in the U.S. case, those choices ultimately entailed embracing harsher policies rather than emphasizing other remedies (such as greater public investment in addressing the root causes of crime and in developing alternatives to incarceration), as well as stoking public fears of crime even after crime rates had ceased to increase.

Republican Party leaders were in an especially good position during these years to tap into public fears and anxieties about crime and to turn crime into a wedge issue between the two parties. As the Democratic Party split over civil rights issues, the south became politically competitive for the first time since the end of Reconstruction a century earlier. This development ushered in a major political realignment. Furthermore, key features of the political structure of the United States, which are discussed in greater detail below, made it especially vulnerable to politicians seeking to exploit public fears concerning crime and other law-and-order issues.

Rates for most serious crimes counted in the Uniform Crime Reports (UCR), compiled by the Federal Bureau of Investigation (FBI), increased significantly after 1961. Between 1964 and 1974, the U.S. homicide rate nearly doubled to 9.8 per 100,000,[7] and rates of other serious crimes also jumped. The homicide rate continued to oscillate around a relatively high rate of 8 to 10 per 100,000 until the early 1990s, before beginning a steady and significant drop that has since continued. Other Western countries have experienced strikingly similar patterns in their crime rates, although from smaller bases (Tonry, 2001).

The rise in homicide rates was concentrated geographically and demographically. As far back as the 1930s, the homicide rate for blacks in northern cities was many times the rate for whites (Lane, 1989). The gap in black-white homicide rates widened further over the course of the Second Great Migration as millions of blacks moved to urban areas outside the south, and it continued to grow thereafter (Jacoby, 1980).[8] The homicide rates in poor neighborhoods of concentrated disadvantage often were many times higher than those in affluent urban neighborhoods. Before crime rates began their steep drop in the early 1990s, the homicide rate among young black men aged 18 to 24 was nearly 200 per 100,000, or about 10 times the rate for young white men and about 20 times the rate for the U.S. population as a whole (Western, 2006, p. 170). Unfortunately, historical data on homicides among Latinos have been largely missing or unreported in existing official sources such as the UCR. Still, homicide rates for Latinos in 2005 were 7.5 per 100,000, as compared with 2.7 for white non-Latinos (Vega et al., 2009). The disparities are more pronounced for young men aged 15 to 24, with 31 deaths per 100,000 for Latinos compared with 10.6 for white non-Latinos.

Like the Great Migration, earlier waves of immigration from Ireland and southern and central Europe that flowed into U.S. cities in the

---

[7]The national homicide rate stood at 5.1 in 1960 and fluctuated around that level until 1964, when it was at 4.9.

[8]Pre-1980 homicide data are from the Historical Violence Database, available: http://cjrc. osu.edu/researchprojects/hvd/ [February 2014]; post-1980 homicide data are from the annual volumes of the UCR.

nineteenth and early twentieth centuries prompted "widespread fears and predictions of social deterioration," including public alarm that crime would rise as the number of immigrants rose in U.S. cities (MacDonald and Sampson, 2012, p. 7). Yet in the early twentieth century, a "hopeful vision of white criminality" eventually took hold in the wake of waves of immigration from Europe (Muhammad, 2010, p. 98). This vision grew out of the view that white criminality in urban areas was rooted primarily in the strains of industrial capitalism and urban life. Thus, policy makers, legislators, and social activists in the Progressive era sought to ameliorate those strains by pressing for greater public and private investments in education, social services, social programs, and public infrastructure in urban areas with high concentrations of European immigrants. The empirical findings of leading sociologists of the early twentieth century (Sutherland, 1947; Sellin, 1938) bolstered claims in the public sphere that "it was not immigration per se that accounted for social ills" but the poor living conditions in those overcrowded, unhealthy urban areas that tended to be magnets for immigrants entering the United States (MacDonald and Sampson, 2012, p. 7).

In contrast, the country responded to the rise in urban crime rates that followed the influx of many African Americans into U.S. cities and of many Mexicans into southwestern states by adopting increasingly punitive policies. For example, the rise in Mexican immigration to communities in the southwest was associated with increases in arrests without cause, denial of legal counsel, and harsh tactics ranging from interrogation sessions to beatings (Grebler et al., 1970). Research also suggests that the federal anti-marijuana law of 1937 was directed primarily against Mexican Americans (Hoffman, 1977).

POLITICAL AND ELECTORAL REALIGNMENT

Democrats were divided on how to respond to the increase in the crime rate. This split, together with deep differences over civil rights, the Vietnam War, and a series of controversial U.S. Supreme Court decisions that extended the rights of defendants, created a ripe opportunity for the political ascent of the Republican Party in states and localities where the Democratic Party had long been dominant, notably in the south and the southwest and in the growing suburbs around northern cities. Many leading Republican candidates and office-holders began developing political strategies that used the crime issue to appeal to white racial anxieties in the wake of the burgeoning black power movement and the gains of the civil rights movement.[9]

Some liberals interpreted the rise in the crime rate that occurred in the 1960s-1970s as a less serious threat to public safety than it was being

---

[9]See Appendix A for a supplementary statement by Ricardo Hinojosa on this sentence and other similar committee findings in this chapter.

depicted by conservative politicians and in the media. They viewed height-ened public fears over crime as a by-product of political posturing and an artifact of inaccurate and misleading statistics. For example, Nicholas Katzenbach, who served as U.S. attorney general in the early years of the Johnson Administration, maintained that the crime figures were inconclu-sive and that false information about crime often intimidated or misled the general public (Flamm, 2005, p. 125).

It does appear that the UCR data exaggerated the extent and duration of the crime increase for certain offense categories (Flamm, 2005, pp. 125-126; Ruth and Reitz, 2003).[10] Prior to 1973, when the U.S. Department of Justice began its yearly household survey of crime victims (the National Crime Victimization Survey), the UCR were the major source of national-level crime statistics. These data, which were recorded and collated by local police departments and then reported to the FBI, were often systematically skewed in recording and reporting, due in part part to incentives to record more crime in order to receive more government funding to combat crime (Ruth and Reitz, 2003; Thompson, 2010).[11]

Those liberals who did take the crime jump seriously often failed to challenge conservatives when they conflated riots, street crime, and political activism, especially on the part of African Americans and their supporters, and when they attributed the crime increase to the launch of the Great Soci-ety and to the mixing of the races due to the demise of segregation. Indeed, some key liberals contended that the "crime problem" was predominantly a race and civil rights problem, suggesting that entrenched segregation had created black cultural dysfunction and social disorder that, among other things, contributed to higher crime rates in urban areas (Murakawa, forthcoming).

The rise in national crime rates beginning in the 1960s coincided with an exceptional period in which punishments for many crimes were eas-ing. During this time, moreover, the U.S. Supreme Court issued a series of landmark decisions that restricted the authority of the police, established protections for suspects and those in custody, and overturned criminal

---

[10]Trends in UCR robbery rates correspond closely with the National Crime Victimization Survey (NCVS) over the past 50 years, but trends in aggravated assault do not. The UCR ag-gravated assault series trended upward from the early 1970s through the early 1990s, while the NCVS aggravated assault series (which is defined similarly) was trending downward. The difference likely is due to an increase in the recording of assaults as "aggravated" by the police during that period. Since the early 1990s, the UCR and NCVS aggravated assault series have trended similarly (Rosenfeld, 2007).

[11]After 1965, for example, "thanks to a new federal commitment to fighting crime, local enforcement could net substantial infusions of money and equipment by demonstrating that crime was on the rise in their area. Significantly, when crime rates began to inch up in Detroit in the later 1960s, even the city's mayor admitted that 'new methods of counting crime' had played an important role in 'distorting the size of the increase'" (Thompson, 2010, p. 727).

convictions that violated newly articulated constitutional principles. Conservative critics of the Warren Court charged that these "soft on crime" rulings, together with misguided liberal social welfare policies, had contributed to the increase in the crime rate.

Taken together, these developments helped foster a receptive environment for political appeals for harsher criminal justice policies and laws. So, too, did the escalation of clashes between protesters and law enforcement authorities during the 1960s and 1970s. In many cases—most notably the police crackdown on protesters at the 1968 Democratic National Convention in Chicago, the shooting deaths of antiwar student protesters at Kent State and Jackson State in 1970, and the bloody assault on New York's Attica prison in 1971 that left dozens dead—a degree of public sympathy was fostered for protesters and prisoners, at least initially.[12] That sympathy dissipated, however, as civil rights opponents continued to link concerns about crime with anxieties about racial disorder; the transformation of the racial status quo; and wider political turmoil, including the wave of urban riots in the 1960s and large-scale demonstrations against the Vietnam War (see, e.g., Beckett, 1997; Flamm, 2005; Weaver, 2007; Thompson, 2010).

Internal Democratic Party divisions over civil rights and the law-and-order question created new opportunities for the Republican Party in the south and elsewhere. In the north, many urban white voters initially maintained a delicate balance on civil rights. Although personally concerned over and often opposed to residential integration at the local level, they supported national pro-civil rights candidates. This balance was undermined as crime and disorder were depicted as racial and civil rights issues; together they "became the fulcrum points at which the local and national intersected" (Flamm, 2005, p. 10; see also Thompson, 2010).

In response to this altered political context, Republican Party strategists developed what has been termed the "southern strategy."[13] Centered in racially coded appeals to woo southern and working-class white voters, this strategy gradually transformed the landscape of American politics (see, e.g., Phillips, 1969; Tonry, 2011a). As historians make clear, the term "southern strategy" is somewhat misleading. At least some Republicans and even some Democrats had been associating crime with both "black-

---

[12]For example, the 1971 Attica uprising in New York State spurred a wellspring of public and scholarly interest in how to make prisons more humane and how to decrease the prison population. It also prompted numerous calls for a national moratorium on prison construction (Gottschalk, 2006, p. 181).

[13]Although Richard Nixon's presidential campaign in 1968 involved a law-and-order message combined with a tacit racial appeal to white voters (Edsall and Edsall, 1992), George Wallace's third-party run also contributed significantly to a climate in which issues of race, protest, and disorder were joined to build a conservative constituency in the south and across the country (Carter, 1995).

ness" and civil disorder more broadly, in locations outside the south. They had done so, with some success, long before Nixon political operative Kevin Phillips popularized the idea of a southern strategy in the late 1960s (Shermer, 2013; McGirr, 2002; Schoenwald, 2002; Thompson, 2001; Kruse and Sugrue, 2006).

The southern strategy was different in that it rested on politicizing the crime issue in a racially coded manner. Nixon and his political strategists recognized that as the civil rights movement took root, so did more overt and seemingly universally accepted norms of racial equality.[14] In this new political context, overtly racial appeals like those wielded by Goldwater's supporters in the 1964 campaign would be counterproductive to the forging of a new winning majority. Effectively politicizing crime and other wedge issues—such as welfare—would require the use of a form of racial coding that did not appear on its face to be at odds with the new norms of racial equality. As top Nixon aide H.R. Haldeman explained, Nixon "emphasized that you have to face the fact that the *whole* problem is really the blacks. The key is to devise a system that recognizes this while appearing not to [emphasis in original]" (Haldeman, 1994, p. 53).

The widespread loss of popular faith in liberalism's ability to ensure public safety, declining confidence in elite- and expert-guided government policies, and deeply felt anxieties and insecurities related to rapid social change and the economic stagflation of the 1970s fostered a political environment conducive to the southern strategy and populist law-and-order appeals (Flamm, 2005; Edsall and Edsall, 1992). Tough law-and-order agendas appealed to whites' anxieties about the rising crime rate, which were entangled with other anxieties about their "loss of stature and privileges as economic opportunities narrowed and traditionally marginalized groups gained new rights" (Kohler-Hausmann, 2010, p. 73; see also Rieder's [1985] classic account of whites' anxieties about crime in the 1960s and 1970s).

Furthermore, the increase in the crime rate coincided with the heyday of Lyndon Johnson's Great Society programs. Although there were many factors contributing to the rise in crime, this coincidence created an opportunity for claims that greater investment in social and other programs did not reduce crime. Some commentators argued that social programs actually contributed to rising crime rates by fostering a host of personal pathologies they claimed were the "real" roots of crime (O'Connor, 2008). A number of politicians contended that a weak work ethic, poor parenting practices, and a culture of dependency had all been created or exacerbated

---

[14]See Appendix A for a supplementary statement by Ricardo Hinojosa on the passage, which begins on the previous page beginning with "In the north . . ." and ends here, and other similar committee findings in this chapter.

by expanded public assistance and other social programs, and that these personal and cultural shortcomings were the major sources of the rise in disorder and violence.

OTHER POLITICAL FACTORS

Emerging research is helping to illuminate why the southern strategy was so effective in politicizing and further racializing the law-and-order issue, and why the war on drugs and other shifts toward harsher penal policies did not face more effective countervailing pressures and coherent counterarguments in opposition. The southern strategy was soon followed by the rise of a number of new social movements and interest groups whose messages and actions in some ways reinforced the punitive direction in which the nation was beginning to move. They included the victims' rights movement, the women's movement, the prisoners' rights movement, and organized opposition to the death penalty. Advocating for victims and against criminal defendants became a simple equation that helped knit together politically disparate groups.[15] Unlike prisoners' movements in other Western countries at the time, the movement in the United States was closely associated with broader issues involving race, class, and various struggles around injustice. As a consequence, criminal activity became associated in the public mind with controversial issues relating to race and rebellion, which fostered zero-sum politics that reduced public sympathy for people charged with crimes and thus was conducive to the promotion of harsher penal policies (Gottschalk, 2006, Chapter 7). Finally, legal battles over the death penalty "legitimized public opinion as a central, perhaps *the* central, consideration in the making of penal policy," which further enshrined the zero-sum view of victims and defendants in capital and noncapital cases (Gottschalk, 2006, p. 12 and Chapters 8-9).

Although African Americans experienced the largest absolute increases in incarceration rates, there is evidence that the black community was divided in its support for tough crime control policy. On the one hand, as discussed in further detail below, blacks have been generally less supportive than whites of punitive criminal justice policies, and survey data from as early as 1977 and 1982 show that blacks are less likely than whites to support severe sentences for violent crimes (Blumstein and Cohen, 1980; Miller et al., 1986; Secret and Johnson, 1989; Bobo and Johnson, 2004; Western and Muller, 2013). And while the attitudes of both black and white Americans have become less punitive over the past few decades, whites are

---

[15]For further discussion of how the political mobilizations against rape and domestic violence contributed to a more punitive political atmosphere, see Gottschalk (2006, Chapters 4-6), Bumiller (2008), and Richie (2012).

consistently more likely than blacks to report that court sentences are not harsh enough (Blumstein and Cohen, 1980; Miller et al., 1986; National Center for State Courts, 2006; Secret and Johnson, 1989; Western and Muller, 2013).

On the other hand, new research also finds that some black leaders supported tougher laws, most notably in the early years of the war on drugs, while others were fierce opponents. The growing concentration of violence, drug addiction, and open-air drug markets in poor urban neighborhoods; disillusionment with government efforts to stem these developments; and widening class divisions among blacks help explain why some African American community leaders endorsed a causal story of the urban crisis that focused on individual flaws, not structural problems, and that singled out addicts and drug pushers as part of the "undeserving poor" who posed the primary threat to working- and middle-class African Americans (Fortner, 2013; Barker, 2009, p. 151; Gottschalk, forthcoming; Cohen, 1999; Dawson, 2011).[16]

Other black leaders endorsed what Forman (2012) describes as an "all-of-the-above" approach, calling for tougher sanctions and aggressive law enforcement but also for greater attention and resources to address underlying social and economic conditions. According to Forman, this helps explain why African American political, religious, and other leaders in Washington, DC, the only black-majority jurisdiction that controlled its sentencing policies (after home rule was granted in 1973), supported tougher crime policy. Opposition to these policies remained muted, even after their disproportionate toll on blacks, especially young black men, became apparent. Forman (2012) attributes this stance to the stigmatizing and marginalizing effects that contact with criminal justice had on former prisoners and their families, inhibiting them from taking public positions or engaging in political debates about these policies. Black leaders, politicians, and advocacy groups clearly were not the main instigators of the shift to harsh crime policy, but at least in some instances, their actions helped foster this turn, in many cases unwittingly.

THE WAR ON DRUGS

As discussed in Chapters 2 and 3, the war on drugs has disproportionately affected African Americans and Latinos and has been an important contributor to higher U.S. rates of incarceration. Researchers have related racial considerations to the war on drugs in much the same way that social

---

[16]Similar attitudes often are seen among segments of the Latino community that favor stronger drug and anticrime laws. This is evident in how Latinos split their vote on Proposition 19—the State of California's proposition to legalize marijuana—in 2010 (Hidalgo, 2010).

and status conflicts between native Protestants and newly arrived Irish Catholics provided context for the temperance and prohibition movements in the late nineteenth and early twentieth centuries (see, e.g., Gusfield, 1963). In the war on drugs, politicians characterized addicts and pushers as "responsible not only for their own condition" but also for many of the problems plaguing inner-city neighborhoods where blacks predominated, including crime, eroding urban infrastructure, and widespread social and economic distress (Kohler-Hausmann, 2010, p. 74).

President Nixon declared the war on drugs in 1971 after initially having embraced greater investment in treatment, rehabilitation, and public health to combat substance abuse (Musto and Korsmeyer, 2002, Chapter 2). Two years later, Republican Governor Nelson Rockefeller of New York, who had authorized the assault on Attica and was trying to reposition himself politically in the face of the southern strategy and a possible run for the White House, led the state in enacting some of the nation's toughest drug laws. These new laws mandated steep minimum sentences for the sale and use of controlled substances, notably heroin and cocaine.[17] New York's new drug laws also influenced other states that sought to enact tough lengthy sentences for drug offenses.

These opening salvos in the war on drugs drew significant support from some leading black politicians and community leaders, as well as from some residents in poor urban areas (Kennedy, 1997, pp. 370-371; Barker, 2009; Fortner, 2013; Forman, 2012; Meares, 1997). For example, some black activists in Harlem supported the Rockefeller drug laws, as did the city's leading black newspaper (Barker, 2009; Fortner, 2013). In New York City and elsewhere, black leaders called for tougher laws for drug and other offenses and demanded increased policing to address residents' demands that something be done about rising crime rates and the scourge of drug abuse, especially the proliferation of open-air drug markets and the use of illegal drugs such as heroin and then crack cocaine (Barker, 2009; Fortner, 2013; Forman, 2012).

The Reagan Administration dramatically escalated the war on drugs even though drug use had been falling for most illicit substances since

---

[17]For much of the 1970s, New York's new drug laws had only a modest impact on the state's incarceration rate, thanks to "selective pragmatic enforcement" by local criminal justice authorities (Weiman and Weiss, 2009, p. 95). That situation changed in the 1980s and 1990s as incoming mayor Ed Koch of New York City sought to "retake the streets" and made a highly publicized shift toward "quality-of-life" policing in 1979, and Governor Hugh Cary promised significant additional support for prison construction, state prosecutors, local law enforcement, and a new joint state-local initiative to target drug trafficking. As a result, the proportion of all inmates serving time in New York State prisons for felony drug convictions soared as the Rockefeller laws belatedly became a major driver of the state's prison population (Weiman and Weiss, 2009).

1979.[18] After President Reagan launched his own version of the war on drugs in 1982 and renewed the call to arms 4 years later, public opinion surveys in 1986 indicated that fewer than 2 percent of the American public considered illegal drugs to be the most important problem facing the country (Beckett, 1997, p. 25). Surveys conducted 2 years later, however, showed that a majority of the public now identified drug abuse as a leading problem (Roberts et al., 2003). The shift in public opinion was partly a consequence of the enactment of tough new federal drug laws in 1986 and 1988, spurred by reports that crack cocaine had been introduced into urban drug markets.

These new drug laws resulted in historically unprecedented rates of imprisonment for drug use and possession (Reuter, 1992; Thompson, 2010). People convicted of drug offenses grew to make up about one-fifth of all state prison inmates and nearly two-thirds of all federal inmates by 1997 (Mumola and Karberg, 2006, p. 4). Since then, the portion of state prisoners serving time for drug offenses has stabilized at about the same rate, while the portion of federal inmates serving time for drug offenses has declined somewhat, to about one-half (Carson and Sabol, 2012, p. 1).

In the 1980s, some Democratic politicians notably joined the war on drugs effort that had been initiated by the Republican administration in the 1970s. The two parties embarked on periodic "bidding wars" to ratchet up penalties for drugs and other offenses. Wresting control of the crime issue became a central tenet of up-and-coming leaders of the Democratic Party represented by the center-right Democratic Leadership Council, most notably "New Democrat" Bill Clinton (Stuntz, 2011, pp. 239-240; Murakawa, forthcoming, Chapter 5; Schlosser, 1998; Campbell, 2007).[19]

Statistical analyses indicate that Republican Party control, especially at the state level, generally has been associated with larger expansions of the prison population (Western, 2006; Jacobs and Helms, 2001; Smith, 2004; Jacobs and Carmichael, 2001).[20] However, it is also the case that some leading Democrats—including Governor Mario Cuomo of New York in the 1980s and early 1990s (Schlosser, 1998), Governor Ann Richards of Texas in the early 1990s (Campbell, 2007), and President Clinton in the 1990s— presided over large increases in prison populations or the adoption of harsh sentences. As criminal justice policy in the United States continued to rely more heavily on incarceration, official party positions on crime control differed less and less. For example, Murakawa (forthcoming) observes that the

---

[18]Reported drug use reached its peak in the late 1970s and continued to fall until the early 1990s, when it turned upward but remained considerably below the late 1970s peak (Johnston et al., 2012, p. 167).

[19]See Appendix A for a supplementary statement by Ricardo Hinojosa on this paragraph and other similar committee findings in this chapter.

[20]However, Greenberg and West (2001, p. 634) found that "the party of the state's governor was essentially irrelevant" in explaining prison growth from 1971 to 1991.

Democratic Party platforms of the 1980s and 1990s invoked law-and-order rhetoric that differed little from what Richard Nixon had expressed two decades earlier, and extolled the long list of harsh penal policies the party had been instrumental in enacting.[21]

CRIME, PUNISHMENT, RACE, AND PUBLIC OPINION

As shown above, the role of public opinion in penal policy is complex, and public concern about crime and support for punitive crime control policy does not necessarily rise and fall in tandem with fluctuations in the crime rate (Beckett, 1997). Important intervening variables include the kind of crime-related initiatives that are promoted by politicians, the nature and amount of media coverage of crime, and the interplay of racial and ethnic conflict and concerns.

Consequently, crime-related public opinion can be volatile. Public opinion surveys and electoral outcomes demonstrate clear public support for certain hard-line policies, such as "three strikes" laws and increased use of incarceration (Cullen et al., 2000). But support for such punitive policies often is soft and therefore highly malleable, partly because public knowledge about actual criminal justice practices and policies is so limited (Cullen et al., 2000; Roberts and Stalans, 1998). For example, the public consistently overestimates the level of violent crime and the recidivism rate (Gest, 2001). Perhaps because people in the United States and elsewhere possess limited knowledge of how the criminal justice system actually works, they generally believe the system is far more lenient toward lawbreakers than it actually is (Roberts, 1997; Roberts and Stalans, 2000; Roberts et al., 2003).

Public opinion surveys that use simplistic approaches tend to reinforce the assumption that the U.S. public is unflinchingly punitive (Cullen et al., 2000). They also mask significant differences in the perspectives of certain demographic groups—especially African Americans and whites—on issues of crime and punishment. For example, African Americans are more likely than whites to perceive racial bias in the criminal justice system (Bobo and Thompson, 2006, 2010; Peffley and Hurwitz, 2010). And as noted above, African Americans also are traditionally less likely to support harsh punishments for violent crime. Moreover, some evidence suggests that public officials and policy makers misperceive or oversimplify public opinion on crime, focusing on Americans' punitive beliefs but deemphasizing or

---

[21]Although the Republican Party's southern strategy promoted harsher crime policy and the Republican administrations of Presidents Nixon and Reagan encouraged tougher drug enforcement and sentencing, the committee members varied in their views of the role played by Democratic Party policy makers in this process.

ignoring their support for rehabilitative goals (Gottfredson and Taylor, 1987; Cullen et al., 2000).

The influence of race on public opinion about crime and punishment is particularly complex, as discussed in Chapter 3. Research on racial attitudes suggests a decline in overt racism—or what Unnever (2013) calls "Jim Crow racism"—founded in beliefs about the innate inferiority of blacks and in adamant support for racial segregation. Survey research also shows that people generally believe racial discrimination is wrong and that they almost universally endorse norms of racial equality (see, e.g., Tonry, 2009a; Thernstrom and Thernstrom, 1997; Mendelberg, 2001; Bobo, 2001). Nonetheless, there are large and in some cases widening gaps in white, black, and Hispanic public opinion on racial issues. Nearly 50 percent of white Americans surveyed in 2008 said they believed blacks had achieved racial equality, compared with only 11 percent of blacks. Nearly three-quarters of blacks surveyed agreed that racism is still a major problem, compared with more than half of Latinos and about one-third of whites (Dawson, 2011, pp. 12-13, 148). Racial bias often is revealed implicitly as well. As discussed in Chapter 3, results from the Implicit Association Test (IAT), designed to measure people's implicit attitudes, demonstrate consistent bias against African Americans (Greenwald and Krieger, 2006).

Although overt racial hostility is less pervasive than it was years ago, latent and often unconscious stereotypes and prejudices still influence political and policy choices in subtle but powerful ways. Such subtle but powerful prejudice may play an important role in public policy preferences on crime and punishment. For example, results of both experimental and survey research suggest that racial resentment is a strong predictor of whites' support for capital punishment (Unnever et al., 2008; Bobo and Johnson, 2004) and that whites' support for the death penalty is undiminished even when they are reminded of racial disproportionality and bias in its application (Peffley and Hurwitz, 2010; Bobo and Johnson, 2004). Research also shows that racial prejudice is associated with increased support for punitive penal policies (Johnson, 2008).

Deeply held racial fears, anxieties, and animosities likely explain the resonance of coded racial appeals concerning crime-related issues, such as the infamous "Willie Horton ad" aired during the 1988 presidential election (see, e.g., Mendelberg, 2001). But racial indifference and insensitivity—as distinguished from outright racial hostility—may help explain the long-term public support for criminal justice policies that have had an adverse and disproportionate impact on blacks (and Latinos). For example, policing practices with large racially disparate impacts, such as the war on drugs and New York City's "stop-and-frisk" policies, are much more likely to be supported by whites than by blacks. In 2011, 85 percent of the approximately 685,000 stop-and-frisks conducted by the New York City police involved people who were black or Latino. In recent polling, whites approved of stop-and-frisk policies at more than twice the rate of blacks (57 percent versus 25 percent) (Quinnipiac University, 2012).[22]

In short, a sizable body of research supports the thesis that public opinion about crime and punishment is highly racialized. Whites tend to associate crime and violence with being black and are more likely than blacks to support harsh penal policies. Whites who harbor racial resentments are especially likely to endorse tougher penal policies and to reject claims that the criminal justice system discriminates against blacks. Blacks are much more likely than whites to say the criminal justice system is racially biased and much less likely to endorse capital punishment and other tougher sanctions (Unnever, 2013).

POLITICAL INSTITUTIONS AND CULTURE

Trends in crime rates and public opinion had much larger effects on criminal justice policy in the United States, compared with other Western countries, because they interacted with and were filtered through specific institutional, cultural, and political contexts that facilitated the growth in incarceration. As discussed in detail in Chapter 3, during the decades-long rise in imprisonment, determination of sentencing and other penal policies increasingly became the domain of the legislative branches of government. Legislators gained power over sentences from the executive branch by, among other things, eliminating parole, limiting commutation powers, and reducing early release programs. They also gained power over the judicial branch by, among other things, eliminating indeterminate sentencing, setting mandatory minimum sentences, and enacting truth-in-sentencing legislation. These shifts allowed the more populist impulses in the United States to have direct impacts on sentencing and other criminal justice policies. The most vivid example of this—what some have called the "democratization of punishment"—is the direct enactment of more punitive measures through ballot initiatives, most notably the three strikes ballot initiative in California (Barker, 2009; Zimring et al., 2001; HoSang, 2010).

Compared with the criminal justice systems of many other developed countries, the U.S. system is more susceptible to the influence of "short-term

---

[22]As noted above, studies show that blacks who are stopped and frisked are less likely than whites to be in possession of guns or other contraband and are no more likely to be arrested. Because so many more blacks than whites are stopped in the first place, however, many more blacks are taken into police custody as a result of being stopped (Center for Constitutional Rights, 2009). The racial gap in support of stop-and-frisk did not keep a federal judge from ruling in *Floyd v. New York* (2013) that the policy violated the constitutional rights of minorities and from recommending a series of reforms (including a monitor) to oversee changes. This controversial ruling had been stayed and was under appellate review at the time this report was being written.

emotionalism" and partisan and interest group politics (Gottschalk, 2006; Tonry, 2011a; Garland, 2010). As Murakawa (forthcoming, Chapter 5) shows, the U.S. House and U.S. Senate have been far more likely to enact stiffer mandatory minimum sentence legislation in the weeks prior to an election. Because of the nation's system of frequent legislative elections, dispersed governmental powers, and election of judges and prosecutors, policy makers tend to be susceptible to public alarms about crime and drugs and vulnerable to pressures from the public and political opponents to quickly enact tough legislation. Such actions serve an expressive purpose over the short run but may have negative long-term consequences (Tonry, 2007b, p. 40).[23] Incentives for supporting certain kinds of crime-related initiatives also tend to be misaligned across different levels of government. For example, it is relatively easy for local government officials to advocate increased sentence lengths and higher incarceration rates that state government officials are typically responsible for funding (including the building and running of state penitentiaries). Yet, despite taking hard-line positions on crime control, local governments often hire too few police officers (since cities and counties are responsible for paying nearly all local police budgets) (Stuntz, 2011, p. 289; Lacey, 2010, p. 111).

Lappi-Seppälä (2008) finds that democracies that are "consensual" (i.e., having a larger number of major political parties, proportional representation, and coalition governments) have lower rates of incarceration and have experienced smaller increases in incarceration since 1980 than winner-take-all, two-party democracies, such as the United States. Lacey (2008) and others (Cavadino and Dignan, 2006; de Giorgi, 2006) find that countries (such as Germany) with consensual electoral systems and coordinated market economies tend to be less punitive and more conducive to inclusionary and welfarist policies than the United States and Britain, whose electoral systems are less consensual and whose market economies are relatively less regulated.

In the United States, most prosecutors are elected, as are most judges (except those who are nominated through a political process). Therefore, they are typically mindful of the political environment in which they function. Judges in competitive electoral environments in the United States tend to mete out harsher sentences (Gordon and Huber, 2007; Huber and Gordon, 2004). In contrast, prosecutors and judges in many European countries are career civil servants who have evolved a distinctive

---

[23]It is also important to note, however, that in England and Wales, the *concentration* of political power rather than its dispersal has made it possible to adopt and implement a wide range of punitive policies. And although Switzerland shares many of the dispersed and populist features of the U.S. system, its penal policies generally have been stable over the past several decades (Tonry, 2007b).

BOX 4-1
Regional Variation in U.S. Incarceration: Historical Context

In the late nineteenth and early twentieth centuries, the nation's northeastern cities tended to have large police forces, small and stable prison populations, and low rates of criminal violence. The south, in contrast, tended to have small police forces, larger but highly variable prison populations, and high crime rates.* The west mimicked the south for most of the nineteenth century but came to resemble the northeast by century's end; as its police forces grew, crime rates shrank, and mob justice faded (Stuntz, 2011).

Although the nature and operation of penal systems today vary among the states, there is no scholarly consensus on the extent to which regional identity, history, or culture may have led either the criminal justice system of a given state or that of the nation as a whole in a much more punitive direction over the past four decades. Some scholars make strong arguments that regional history and culture matter a great deal. For example, they suggest that the nation's overall tough-on-crime policy should be seen as the eventual embrace of the south's more punitive form of justice, originally created and maintained in a region not only marked by slavery but also with a criminal justice system that treated African Americans with notable brutality following the Civil War (Perkinson, 2010; Lichtenstein, 1996; Oshinsky, 1997; Blackmon, 2009; Butterfield, 1995). Other scholars, however, point to the long history of punitive justice policies that were directed as well at communities of color in the north and west; they see the nation's embrace of unprecedented high rates of incarceration as an extension of policies and practices that were less narrowly regional in nature (Gross, 2006; Muhammad, 2010; Hicks, 2010; Chávez-Garcia, 2012, Chapter 1; Lynch, 2010). Recent research also suggests that any difference between the racial ethos of the south and the north became much less marked as African Americans moved in record numbers between 1880 and 1950 from the south to the north, where they were greeted by white northerners (particularly by European immigrants, who themselves were struggling for full rights of citizenship) with suspicion, hostility, and even violence (Muller, 2012).

---

*According to Gottschalk (2006, p. 48), "the association in the South of crime and race made it impossible to embrace rehabilitation, the *raison d'être* for the penitentiary. . . . The roots of the penitentiary were shallow in the South" and were uprooted by the Civil War. After the Civil War, the convict leasing system was widely adopted in the south as an alternative means of punishment and played an important role in the region's economic life.

---

occupational culture with a less punitive orientation, partly as a result of differences in legal training and career paths between the United States and European countries (Savelsberg, 1994).

Cultural differences—in particular, the degree of social and political trust and cohesion—also help explain some of the variation in incarceration rates, both cross-nationally and within the United States. (Box 4-1 provides some historical context for understanding regional variation in incarceration.) In cross-national comparisons, Lappi-Seppälä (2008) finds a negative relationship (which has grown stronger over time) between punitiveness and social and political trust, and a positive cross-sectional relationship between high levels of social and political trust and more generous welfare policies. Within the United States, incarceration rates generally have been lower in states with higher levels of social capital, voter participation, and other forms of complex civic engagement (Barker, 2009).

In examining the underlying causes of high rates of incarceration, it is important to keep in mind that the factors that sparked the increase may not be the same as those that currently sustain it. Economic interests, for example, initially did not play a central role in the upward turn in incarceration rates. Over time, however, the buildup created new economic interests and new political configurations. By the mid-1990s, the new economic interests—including private prison companies, prison guards' unions, and the suppliers of everything from bonds for new prison construction to Taser stun guns—were playing an important role in maintaining and sustaining the incarceration increase. The influence of economic interests that profit from high rates of incarceration grew at all levels of government, due in part to a "revolving door" that emerged between the corrections industry and the public sector. Another factor was the establishment of powerful, effective, and well-funded lobbying groups to represent the interests of the growing corrections sector. The private prison industry and other companies that benefit from large prison populations have expended substantial effort and resources in lobbying for more punitive laws and for fewer restrictions on the use of prison labor and private prisons (Elk and Sloan, 2011; Thompson, 2010, 2012; Gilmore, 2007; Hallinan, 2001; Herival and Wright, 2007; Gopnik, 2012; Abramsky, 2007). Many legislators and other public officials, especially in economically struggling rural areas, became strong advocates of prison and jail construction in the 1990s, seeing it as an important engine for economic development. The evidence suggests, however, that prisons generally have an insignificant, or sometimes negative, impact on the economic development of the rural communities where they are located (Whitfield, 2008).[24]

---

[24]Residents of rural counties, which have been the primary sites for new prison construction since the 1980s, are no less likely to be unemployed than people living in counties without prisons, nor do they have higher per capita incomes. New jobs created by prisons tend to be filled by people living outside the county where the prison is built. Prisons also fail to generate significant linkages to the local economy because local businesses often are unable to provide the goods and services needed to operate penal facilities. Furthermore, new prison construction often necessitates costly public investments in infrastructure and services, such as roads, sewers, and courts, where the prisons are sited (Gilmore, 2007; King et al., 2003).

URBAN ECONOMIC DISTRESS

While the political developments discussed above were marked by specific events—for example, elections, campaigns, and policy developments—long-term structural changes in urban economies also formed part of the context for the growth in incarceration rates. In American cities, problems of violence, poverty, unemployment, and single parenthood came together in minority neighborhoods as a focus of debates on crime and social policy. The connections among crime, poverty, and criminal punishment have been a long-standing interest of social theorists. They have argued that the poor are punished most because their involvement in crime and life circumstances are seen as threatening to social order. (Rusche [1978] provides a classic statement of the connection between incarceration and unemployment; Garland [1991] reviews the literature on the political economy of punishment.) In this view, the scale and intensity of criminal punishment fluctuate with overall economic cycles.

The social and economic decline of American cities in the 1970s and 1980s is well documented. William Julius Wilson (1987) provides a classic account in *The Truly Disadvantaged*. In Wilson's view, the decline of manufacturing industry employment combined with the out-migration of many working- and middle-class families to the suburbs. These economic and demographic changes left behind pockets of severe and spatially concentrated poverty (see also Jargowsky, 1997). It was in these poor communities that contact with the criminal justice system and incarceration rates climbed to extraordinary levels, particularly among young minority men with little schooling. Rates of joblessness, births to single or unmarried parents, and violent crime all increased in poor inner-city neighborhoods. These social and economic trends unfolded in the broader context of deteriorating economic opportunities for men with low levels of education, especially those who had dropped out of high school (Goldin and Katz, 2008), and the decline of organized labor and the contraction of well-paying manufacturing and other jobs in urban areas for low-skilled workers.

Rising incarceration rates overall appear to be produced primarily by the increased imprisonment of uneducated young men, especially those lacking a college education (see Chapter 2). In the wake of the civil rights movement, improved educational and economic opportunities appeared to foreshadow a new era of prosperity for blacks in the 1960s. However, the decline of urban manufacturing undermined economic opportunities for those with no more than a high school education. Fundamental changes also were unfolding in urban labor markets as labor force participation declined among young, less educated black men (Smith and Welch, 1989; Offner and Holzer, 2002; Fairlie and Sundstrom, 1999). In a careful review of labor market data from the 1970s and 1980s, Bound and Freeman

(1992) found growing racial gaps in earnings and employment that extended from the mid-1970s to the end of the 1980s.

The connections among urban unemployment, crime, and incarceration have been found in ethnographic and quantitative studies. With fewer well-paying economic opportunities available, some young men in poor inner-city neighborhoods turned to drug dealing and other criminal activities as sources of income. Ethnographers have documented the proliferation of drug dealing and violence in high-unemployment urban neighborhoods in the 1980s and 1990s (Bourgois, 2002; Anderson, 1990; Levitt and Venkatesh, 2000; Black, 2009). Qualitative researchers also argue that in poor urban areas, drunkenness, domestic disturbances, and the purchase and consumption of illegal drugs are more likely to take place in public places, whereas in suburban and more affluent urban areas, these activities tend to transpire in private homes and other private spaces. Consequently, poor urban residents are more exposed to police scrutiny and are more likely to be arrested than people residing in the suburbs or in wealthier urban neighborhoods (Duneier, 1999, pp. 304-307; Anderson, 1990, pp. 193-198). Field observation is consistent with the finding of quantitative studies that, controlling for crime, incarceration rates increased with joblessness among African American men with no college education (Western, 2006; Western et al., 2006).

In short, poor inner-city neighborhoods were increasingly plagued by higher rates of unemployment among young men, crime, and other social problems. These same neighborhoods were the focal points of debates over crime and social policy, and the places where incarceration became pervasive.

CONCLUSION

The policies and practices that gave rise to unprecedented high rates of incarceration were the result of a variety of converging historical, social, economic, and political forces. Although debates over crime policy have a long history in the United States, these various forces converged in the 1960s, which served as an important historical turning point for prison policy. Crime rates also increased sharply beginning in the 1960s, with the national homicide rate nearly doubling between 1964 and 1974. The relationship between rising crime trends and increased incarceration rates unfolded within, and was very much affected by, the larger context in which debates about race, crime, and law and order were unfolding.

The powerful institutional, cultural, political, economic, and racial forces discussed in this chapter helped propel the United States down a more punitive path. Yet the unprecedented rise in incarceration rates in the United States over this period was not an inevitable outcome of these forces.

Rather, it was the result of the particular ways in which the political system chose to respond to the major postwar changes in U.S. society, particularly since the 1960s. Unlike many other Western countries, the United States responded to escalating crime rates by enacting highly punitive policies and laws and turning away from rehabilitation and reintegration. The broader context provides a set of important explanations for both the punitive path that many politicians, policy makers, and other public figures decided to pursue and, perhaps more important, why so many Americans were willing to follow.

5

The Crime Prevention Effects of Incarceration[1]

As discussed in previous chapters, the growth in U.S. incarceration rates over the past 40 years was propelled by changes in sentencing and penal policies that were intended, in part, to improve public safety and reduce crime. A key task for this committee was to review the evidence and determine whether and by how much the high rates of incarceration documented in Chapter 2 have reduced crime rates. In assessing the research on the impact of prison on crime, we paid particular attention to policy changes that fueled the growth of the U.S. prison population—longer prison sentences, mandatory minimum sentences, and the expanded use of prison in the nation's drug law enforcement strategies.

We are mindful of the public interest in questions regarding the relationship between incarceration and crime. Indeed, as discussed in Chapters 3 and 4, the assertion that putting more people in prison would reduce crime was crucial to the political dynamic that fueled the growth in incarceration rates in the United States. In recent years, policy initiatives to reduce state prison populations often have met objections that public safety would be reduced. There is of course a plausibility to the belief that putting many more convicted felons behind bars would reduce crime. Yet even a cursory examination of the data on crime and imprisonment rates makes clear the complexity of measuring the crime prevention effect of incarceration. Violent crime rates have been declining steadily over the past two decades, which suggests a crime prevention effect of rising incarceration rates. For

---

[1]This chapter draws substantially on Durlauf and Nagin (2011a, 2011b) and Nagin (2013a, 2013b).

the first two decades of rising incarceration rates, however, there was no clear trend in the violent crime rate—it rose, then fell, and then rose again.

There are many explanations for the lack of correspondence between rates of incarceration and rates of violent crime and crime rates more generally. However, one explanation deserves special emphasis: the rate of incarceration, properly understood, is not a policy variable per se; rather, it is the outcome of policies affecting who is sent to prison and for how long (Durlauf and Nagin, 2011a, 2011b). The effect of these policies on crime rates is not uniform—some policies may have very large effects if, for example, they are directed at high-rate offenders, while others may be ineffective. Thus, the committee's charge was to dig below the surface and review the research evidence on the impact of the specific drivers of the rise in U.S. incarceration rates on crime in the hope that this evidence would inform the larger policy discourse. In this regard, one of our most important conclusions is that the incremental deterrent effect of increases in lengthy prison sentences is modest at best. Also, because recidivism rates decline markedly with age and prisoners necessarily age as they serve their prison sentence, lengthy prison sentences are an inefficient approach to preventing crime by incapacitation unless the longer sentences are specifically targeted at very high-rate or extremely dangerous offenders.

A large body of research has studied the effects of incarceration and other criminal penalties on crime. Much of this research is guided by the hypothesis that incarceration reduces crime through incapacitation and deterrence. Incapacitation refers to the crimes averted by the physical isolation of convicted offenders during the period of their incarceration. Theories of deterrence distinguish between general and specific behavioral responses. General deterrence refers to the crime prevention effects of the *threat* of punishment, while specific deterrence concerns the aftermath of the failure of general deterrence—that is, the effect on reoffending that might result from the *experience* of actually being punished. Most of this research studies the relationship between criminal sanctions and crimes other than drug offenses.[2] A related literature focuses specifically on enforcement of drug laws and the relationship between those criminal sanctions and the outcomes of drug use and drug prices.

This chapter presents the results of the committee's examination of the crime prevention effects of imprisonment through deterrence or incapacitation. The first section provides an overview of deterrence and reviews

---

[2]Drug sales, use, and possession are, of course, widely criminalized. While there are some long-standing national data collections on drug use and a few national surveys have asked about drug sales, there are no national time series on overall levels of drug crime. Thus, analyses of the relationship of imprisonment rates to crime rates provide no insight into impacts on drug crimes.

evidence on the deterrent effect of incarceration. The second section describes the theory of incapacitation and summarizes empirical research on incapacitation's effects. We then review panel studies examining the association between rates of incarceration and crime rates across states and over time. These studies do not distinguish between deterrence and incapacitation and might be viewed as estimating a total effect of incarceration on crime. The fourth section summarizes research on specific deterrence and recidivism. This is followed by a review of research on the effects of incarceration for drug crimes on drug prices and drug use. We then offer observations regarding gaps in knowledge about the crime prevention effects of incarceration.

DETERRENCE: THEORY AND EMPIRICAL FINDINGS

In the classical theory of deterrence, crime is averted when the expected costs of punishment exceed the benefits of offending. Much of the empirical research on the deterrent power of criminal penalties has studied sentence enhancements and other shifts in penal policy.

Theory

Most modern theories of deterrence can be traced to the Enlightenment-era legal philosophers Cesare Beccaria (2007) and Jeremy Bentham (1988). Their work was motivated by a mutual abhorrence of the administration of punishment without constructive purpose. For them that constructive purpose was crime prevention. As Beccaria observed, "It is better to prevent crimes than punish them" (1986, p. 93). Beccaria and Bentham argued that the deterrence process has three key ingredients—the severity, certainty, and celerity of punishment. These concepts, particularly the severity and certainty of punishment, form the foundation of nearly all contemporary theories of deterrence. The idea is that if state-imposed sanctions are sufficiently severe, criminal activity will be discouraged, at least for some. Severity alone, however, cannot deter; there must also be some probability that the sanction will be incurred if the crime is committed. Indeed, Beccaria believed that the probability of punishment, not its severity, is the more potent component of the deterrence process: "One of the greatest curbs on crime is not the cruelty of punishments, but their infallibility. . . . The certainty of punishment even if moderate will always make a stronger impression . . ." (1986, p. 58).

In contemporary society, the certainty of punishment depends on the probability of arrest given a criminal offense and the probability of punishment given an arrest. For a formal sanction to be imposed, the crime must be brought to official attention, typically by victim report, and the offender must then be apprehended, usually by the police.[3] The offender must next be charged, successfully prosecuted, and finally sentenced by the courts. Successful passage through all of these stages is far from certain. The first step in the process—reporting of the crime—is critical, yet national surveys of victims have consistently demonstrated that only half of all crimes are brought to the attention of the police. Once the crime has been reported, the police are the most important factors affecting certainty—absent detection and apprehension, there is no possibility of conviction or punishment. Yet arrests ensue for only a small fraction of all reported crimes. Blumstein and Beck (1999) find that robberies reported to police outnumber robbery arrests by about four to one and that the offense-to-arrest ratio is about five to one for burglaries. These ratios have remained stable since 1980. The next step in the process is criminal prosecution, following which the court must decide whether to impose a prison sentence. In light of the obstacles to successful apprehension and prosecution, the probability of conviction is quite low, even for felony offenses (although it has increased since 1980). Moreover, because the majority of felony convictions already result in imprisonment, policies designed to increase the certainty of incarceration for those convicted—through mandatory prison sentences, for example—will have only a limited effect on the overall certainty of punishment.

The third component of the theory of deterrence advanced by Bentham and Beccaria, and the least studied, is the swiftness, or "celerity," of punishment. The theoretical basis for its impact on deterrence is ambiguous, as is the empirical evidence on its effectiveness. Even Beccaria appears to have based his case for celerity more on normative considerations of just punishment than on its role in the effectiveness of deterrence. He observed: "the more promptly and the more closely punishment follows upon the commission of a crime, the more just and useful will it be. I say more just, because the criminal is thereby spared the useless and cruel torments of uncertainty, which increase with the vigor of imagination and with the sense of personal weakness . . ." (Beccaria, 1986, p. 36).

Deterrence theory is underpinned by a rationalistic view of crime. In this view, an individual considering commission of a crime weighs the benefits of offending against the costs of punishment. Much offending, however, departs from the strict decision calculus of the rationalistic model. Robinson and Darley (2004) review the limits of deterrence through harsh punishment. They report that offenders must have some knowledge of criminal penalties to be deterred from committing a crime, but in practice often do not. Furthermore, suddenly induced rages, feelings of threat and paranoia, a desire for revenge and retaliation, and self-perceptions of

---

[3]Crime may also be sanctioned entirely outside of the criminal justice system through retaliation by the victim or by others on the victim's behalf.

brilliance in the grandiose phase of manic-depressive illness all can limit a potential offender's ability to exercise self-control. Also playing a role are personality traits and the pervasive influence of drugs and alcohol: in one study, 32 percent of state prison inmates reported being high on drugs at the time of their crime, and 17 percent committed their crime to get money to buy drugs (Mumola and Karberg, 2006). The influence of crime-involved peers who downplay the long-term consequences of punishment is relevant as well.

Taken together, these factors mean that, even if they knew the penalties that could be imposed under the law, a significant fraction of offenders still might not be able to make the calculation to avoid crime. Because many crimes may not be rationally motivated with a view to the expected costs of punishment, and because offenders may respond differently to the severity, certainty, and swiftness of punishment, the magnitude of deterrent effects is fundamentally an empirical question. Furthermore, deterrent effects may depend on the type of sanction and its severity. Sanctions may be effective in some circumstances for some people but ineffective in other circumstances or for others.

Empirical Findings

Empirical studies of deterrence have focused primarily on sentence enhancements that introduce additional prison time for aggravating circumstances related to the crime or the defendant's criminal history. The earliest attempts after the 1970s to measure the effects of severity examined the deterrent effects of sentence enhancements for gun crimes. A series of studies (Loftin and McDowell, 1981, 1984; Loftin et al., 1983) considered whether sentence enhancements for use of a gun when engaged in another type of crime (such as robbery) deter gun use in the commission of a crime. While this research yielded mixed findings, it generally failed to uncover clear evidence of a deterrent effect (but see McDowall et al. [1992] for evidence of reductions in homicides).[4]

There is, however, an important caveat to keep in mind when extrapolating from these studies to understand the link between severity and deterrence: studies that failed to find a deterrent effect for sentence enhancements for use of a gun in committing a crime also found that the sentences ultimately imposed in these cases were in fact not increased.

---

[4]Pooling city-specific results to obtain a combined estimate of the impact of mandatory sentence enhancements for gun crimes, McDowall and colleagues (1992, p. 379) suggest that "the mandatory sentencing laws substantially reduced the number of homicides; however, any effects on assault and robbery are not conclusive because they cannot be separated from imprecision and random error in the data."

Thus, criminals may not have been deterred from using a gun because the real incentives were not changed. This observation is a reminder of Tonry's (2009b) commentary on the inconsistent administration of mandatory minimum sentencing.

Kessler and Levitt (1999) examine the deterrent impact of California's Proposition 8, passed in 1982. Proposition 8 anticipated the three strikes laws passed by many states, including California, in the 1990s, which substantially increased sentences for repeat commission of specified felonies. Kessler and Levitt estimate a 4 percent decline in crime attributable to deterrence in the first year after the proposition's enactment. Within 5 to 7 years, the effect grew to a 20 percent reduction, although the authors acknowledge that this longer-term estimate includes incapacitation effects.

The findings of Kessler and Levitt (1999) are challenged by Webster and colleagues (2006). They point out that Kessler and Levitt's findings are based on data from alternate years. Using data from all years, Webster and colleagues find that crime rates in the relevant categories started to fall before Proposition 8 was enacted and that the slope of this trend remained constant during the proposition's implementation.[5] (See Levitt [2006][6] for a response and Raphael [2006] for analysis that supports Webster and colleagues [2006].)

One exception to the paucity of studies on the crime prevention effects of sentence enhancements concerns analyses of the deterrent effect of California's "Three Strikes and You're Out" law, which mandated a minimum sentence of 25 years upon conviction for a third strikeable offense.[7] Zimring and colleagues (2001) conclude that the law reduced the felony crime rate by at most 2 percent and that this reduction was limited to those individuals with two strikeable offenses. Other authors (Stolzenberg and D'Alessio, 1997; Greenwood and Hawken, 2002), who, like Zimring and colleagues (2001), examine before-and-after trends, conclude that the law's crime prevention effects were negligible. The most persuasive study of California's three strikes law is that of Helland and Tabarrok (2007). As discussed below, this study finds an effect but concludes that it is small.

---

[5]In other words, the drop in crime after the passage of Proposition 8 "may simply be the result of a preexisting decline over time," consistent with the possibility that "by the time that legislative change is enacted, levels of crime have often already begun to drop for reasons not tied to variations in threatened punishment" (Webster et al., 2006, p. 441).

[6]According to Levitt (2006, p. 451), the arguments made by Kessler and Levitt (1999) "were based on the fact that after Proposition 8, eligible crimes fell more in California than noneligible crimes, and most importantly, the relative movements of eligible and noneligible crimes in California systematically differed from those in the rest of the United States after Proposition 8, but not before."

[7]Strikeable offenses include murder, robbery, drug sales to minors, and a variety of sexual offenses, felony assaults, other crimes against persons, property crimes, and weapons offenses (Clark et al., 1997).

One challenge for research on sentence enhancements is that because entire jurisdictions are affected by a sentencing reform, the "treated" defendants are necessarily compared with those in other times or places who are likely to differ in unmeasured ways. Six recent studies present particularly convincing evidence on the deterrent effect of incarceration by constructing credible comparisons of treatment and control groups, and they also nicely illustrate heterogeneity in the deterrence response to the threat of imprisonment. Weisburd and colleagues (2008) and Hawken and Kleiman (2009) studied the use of imprisonment to enforce payment of fines and conditions of probation, respectively, and found substantial deterrent effects. Helland and Tabarrok (2007) analyzed the deterrent effect of California's third-strike provision and found only a modest deterrent effect. Ludwig and Raphael (2003) examined the deterrent effect of prison sentence enhancements for gun crimes and found no effect. Finally, Lee and McCrary (2009) and Hjalmarsson (2009) examined the heightened threat of imprisonment that attends coming under the jurisdiction of the adult courts at the age of majority and found no deterrent effect. These studies are described further below.

Weisburd and colleagues (2008) present findings of a randomized field trial of different approaches to encouraging payment of court-ordered fines. Their most salient finding involves the "miracle of the cells"—that the imminent threat of incarceration provides a powerful incentive to pay delinquent fines, even when the incarceration is only for a short period. This finding supports the notion, discussed earlier, that the certainty rather the severity of punishment is the more powerful deterrent. It is true that in this study, there was a high certainty of imprisonment for failing to pay the fine among the treatment group. Nonetheless, the term used by Weisburd and colleagues—the "miracle of the cells" and not the "miracle of certainty"—emphasizes that certainty is a deterrent only if the punishment is perceived as costly enough.

This point is further illustrated by Project HOPE (Hawaii's Opportunity Probation with Enforcement). In this randomized experiment, the treatment group of probationers underwent regular drug testing (including random testing). The punishment for a positive test or other violation of conditions of probation was certain but brief (1-2 days) confinement. The intervention group had far fewer positive tests and missed appointments and significantly lower rates of arrest and imprisonment (Kleinman, 2009; Hawken and Kleiman, 2009; Hawken, 2010).[8]

---

[8]The success of Project HOPE has brought it considerable attention in the media and in policy circles. Its strong evaluation design—a randomized experiment—puts its findings on a sound scientific footing and is among the reasons why its results are highlighted in this report. Still, there are several reasons for caution in assessing the significance of the results.

Helland and Tabarrok (2007) examine the deterrent effect of California's "Three Strikes and You're Out" law among those convicted of strikeable offenses. They compare the future offending of those convicted of two previous strikeable offenses and those convicted of one strikeable offense who also had been tried for a second strikeable offense but were convicted of a nonstrikeable offense. The two groups had a number of common characteristics, such as age, race, and time spent in prison. The authors find an approximately 20 percent lower arrest rate among those convicted of two strikeable offenses and attribute this to the much more severe sentence that would have been imposed for a third strikeable offense.

Ludwig and Raphael (2003) examine the deterrent effect of sentence enhancements for gun crimes that formed the basis for a much-publicized federal intervention called Project Exile in Richmond, Virginia. Perpetrators of gun crimes, especially those with a felony record, were the targets of federal prosecution, which provided for far more severe sanctions for weapon use than those imposed by Virginia state law. The authors conducted a careful and thorough analysis involving comparison of adult and juvenile homicide arrest rates in Richmond and comparison of the gun homicide rates of Richmond and other cities with comparable preintervention homicide rates. They conclude that the threat of enhanced sentences had no apparent deterrent effect.

The shift in jurisdiction from juvenile to adult court that occurs when individuals reach the age of majority is accompanied by increased certainty and severity of punishment for most crimes. Lee and McCrary (2009) conducted a meticulous analysis of individual-level crime histories in Florida to see whether felony offending declined sharply at age 18—the age of majority in that state. They report an immediate decline in crime, as predicted, but it was very small and not statistically significant.[9]

As of this writing, the results have yet to be replicated outside of rural Hawaii. This is also a complex intervention, and the mechanisms by which compliance with conditions of probation is achieved are not certain. Specifically, a competing interpretation to deterrence for the observed effects is that probationers were responding to an authoritative figure. Nevertheless, the interpretation that certain but nondraconian punishment can be an effective deterrent is consistent with decades of research on deterrence (Nagin, 1998, 2013b). That such an effect appears to have been found in a population in which deterrence has previously been ineffective in averting crime makes the finding potentially very important. Thus, as discussed later in this chapter, research on the deterrent effectiveness of short sentences with high celerity and certainty should be a priority, particularly among crime-prone populations.

[9]The finding that the young fail to respond to changes in penalties associated with the age of majority is not uniform across studies. An earlier analysis by Levitt (1998) finds a large drop in the offending of young adults when they reach the age of jurisdiction for adult courts. For several reasons, Durlauf and Nagin (2011a, 2011b) judge the null effect finding of Lee and McCrary to be more persuasive in terms of understanding deterrence. First, Levitt (1998) focuses on differences in age measured at annual frequencies, whereas Lee and McCrary mea-

In another analysis of the effect, if any, of moving from the jurisdiction of juvenile to adult courts, Hjalmarsson (2009) uses the 1997 National Longitudinal Survey of Youth to examine whether young males' perception of incarceration risk changed at the age of criminal majority. Youth were asked, "Suppose you were arrested for stealing a car, what is the percentage chance that you would serve time in jail?" The author found that subjective probabilities of being sent to jail increased discontinuously on average by 5.2 percentage points when youth reached the age of majority in their state of residence. While youth perceived an increase in incarceration risk, Hjalmarsson found no convincing evidence of an effect on their self-reported criminal behavior.

In combination, the above six studies demonstrate that debates about the deterrent effect of legal sanctions can be framed in terms argued by Beccaria and Bentham more than two centuries ago: Does the specific sanction deter or not, and if it does, are the crime reduction benefits sufficient to justify the costs of imposing the sanction? The Helland and Tabarrok (2007) study is an exemplar of this type of analysis. It concludes that California's third-strike provision does indeed have a deterrent effect, a point conceded even by Zimring and colleagues (2001). However, Helland and Tabarrok (2007) also conclude, based on a cost-benefit analysis, that the crime-saving benefits are so small relative to the increased costs of incarceration that the lengthy prison sentences mandated by the third-strike provision cannot be justified on the basis of their effectiveness in preventing crime.

The above six studies suggest several important sources of the heterogeneity of the deterrent effect of imprisonment. One source relates to the length of the sentence. Figure 5-1 shows two different forms of the response function that relates crime rate and sentence length. A downward slope is seen for both, reflecting the deterrence effect of increased severity. Both curves have the same crime rate, C_1, at the status quo sentence length, S_1. Because the two curves are drawn to predict the same crime rate for a zero sanction level, the absolute deterrent effect of the status quo sanction level is the same for both. But because the two curves have different shapes, they also imply different responses to an incremental increase in sentence length to S_2. The linear curve (A) is meant to depict a response function in which there is a sizable deterrent effect accompanying the increase to S_2, whereas the nonlinear curve (B) is

---

sure age in days or weeks. At annual frequencies, the estimated effect is more likely to reflect both deterrence and incapacitation; hence Levitt's results may be driven by incapacitation effects rather than deterrence per se. Second, the analysis by Lee and McCrary is based on individual-level data and therefore avoids the problems that can arise because of aggregation (Durlauf et al., 2008, 2010). The individual-level data studied by Lee and McCrary also are unusually informative on their own terms because they contain information on the exact age of arrestees, which allows for the calculation of very short-run effects of the discontinuity in sentence severity (e.g., effects within 30 days of turning 18).

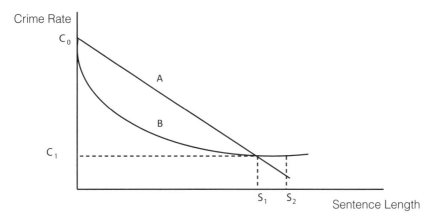

FIGURE 5-1 Marginal versus absolute deterrent effects.
SOURCE: Nagin (2013a).

meant to depict a small crime reduction response due to diminishing deterrent returns to increasing sentence length. In curve B in Figure 5-1, the largest reductions in crime will be obtained with small increases in short sentences.

The evidence on the deterrent effect of sentence length suggests that the relationship between crime rate and sentence length more closely resembles curve B in Figure 5-1 than curve A. Ludwig and Raphael (2003) find no deterrent effect of enhanced sentences for gun crimes; Lee and McCrary (2009) and Hjalmarsson (2009) find no evidence that the more severe penalties that attend moving from the juvenile to the adult justice system deter offending; and Helland and Tabarrok (2007) find only a small deterrent effect of the third strike of California's three strikes law. As a consequence, the deterrent return to increasing already long sentences is modest at best.

The fine payment (Weisburd et al., 2008) and Project HOPE (Kleiman, 2009; Hawken and Kleiman, 2009; Hawken, 2010) experiments also suggest that that curve B, not curve A, more closely resembles the dose-response relationship between crime and sentence length. Although these programs were designed to achieve behavioral changes other than simple crime prevention (payment of criminal fines and cessation of drug use, respectively), in both cases the subjects of the program demonstrated increased compliance with court orders, an important justice system goal. In the case of Project HOPE, subjects also showed substantially reduced levels of criminal offending. The results of these studies suggest that, unlike increments to long sentences, short sentences do have a material deterrent effect on a crime-prone population.

The conclusion that increasing already long sentences has no material deterrent effect also has implications for mandatory minimum sentencing. Mandatory minimum sentence statutes have two distinct properties. One is that they typically increase already long sentences, which we have concluded is not an effective deterrent. Second, by mandating incarceration, they also increase the certainty of imprisonment *given conviction*. Because, as discussed earlier, the certainty of conviction even following commission of a felony is typically small, the effect of mandatory minimum sentencing on certainty of punishment is greatly diminished. Furthermore, as discussed at length by Nagin (2013a, 2013b), all of the evidence on the deterrent effect of certainty of punishment pertains to the deterrent effect of the certainty of apprehension, not to the certainty of postarrest outcomes (including certainty of imprisonment given conviction). Thus, there is no evidence one way or the other on the deterrent effect of the second distinguishing characteristic of mandatory minimum sentencing (Nagin, 2013a, 2013b).

INCAPACITATION

Crime prevention by incapacitation has an appealing directness—the incarceration of criminally active individuals will prevent crime through their physical separation from the rest of society. In contrast with crime prevention based on deterrence or rehabilitation, no assumptions about human behavior appear to be required to avert the social cost of crime.

Despite the apparent directness and simplicity of incapacitation, estimates of the size of its effects vary substantially. Most estimates are reported in terms of an elasticity—the percentage change in the crime rate in response to a 1 percent increase in the imprisonment rate. Spelman (1994) distinguishes between two types of incapacitation studies—simulation and econometric studies. Simulation studies are based on the model of Avi-Itzhak and Schinnar (1973), described below. The earliest simulation-based estimates are reported by Cohen (1978). Her elasticity estimates range from −0.05 to −0.70, meaning each 1 percent increase in imprisonment rates would result in a crime reduction of 0.05 to 0.7 percent. Later estimates by DiIulio and Piehl (1991), Piehl and DiIulio (1995), and Spelman (1994) fall within a narrower but still large range of about −0.10 to −0.30—a 0.1 to 0.3 percent crime reduction for a 1 percent increase in imprisonment.

Econometric studies also examine the overall relationship between the crime rate and the imprisonment rate. These studies are discussed in greater detail in the next section. The range of elasticity estimates from these studies is similarly large—from no reduction in crime (Marvell and Moody, 1994; Useem and Piehl, 2008; Besci, 1999) to a reduction of about −0.4 or more (Levitt, 1996). These divergent findings are one of the key reasons the committee concludes that we cannot arrive at a precise estimate, or even a modest range of estimates, of the magnitude of the effect of incarceration on crime rates.

Many factors contribute to the large differences in estimates of the crimes averted by incapacitation. These factors include whether the data used to estimate crimes averted pertain to people in prison, people in jail, or nonincarcerated individuals with criminal histories; the geographic region from which the data are derived; the types of crimes included in the accounting of crimes averted; and a host of technical issues related to the measurement and modeling of key dimensions of the criminal career (National Research Council, 1986; Cohen, 1986; Visher, 1986; Piquero and Blumstein, 2007). Here we focus on two issues that are particularly important to estimating and interpreting incapacitation effects: the estimate of the rate of offending of active offenders and the constancy of that rate over the course of the criminal career.

Research on incapacitation effects derives from what has come to be called the "criminal career" model first laid out in a seminal paper by Avi-Itzhak and Schinnar (1973). These authors assume that active offenders commit crimes at a mean annual rate (denoted by λ) over their criminal career (averaging τ years in length).[10] The extent of punishment is described by the probability of arrest, conviction, and incarceration for a given crime and the length of time spent in prison.

At the level of the population, this framework yields an accounting model that calculates the hypothetical level of crime in society in the absence of incarceration and the fraction of that level prevented by incarceration as a function of the probability of incarceration and the average length of the sentence served. The theory, as already noted, is appealingly simple. The model has no behavioral component. It views the prevention of crime not as a behavioral response to punishment, as in deterrence, but as the result of the simple physical isolation of offenders. We return to the implications of these behavioral assumptions below, but first consider two other key assumptions of the Azi-Itzhak and Shinnar framework that has been so influential in research on incapacitation. The first concerns the assumption that λ is constant across offenders, and the second is that it remains unchanged over the duration of the criminal career.

Constancy of λ Across the Population

The most influential source of data for calculating λ—or the average rate at which active offenders commit crimes—has been the RAND Second

---

[10]It is further assumed that, while the offenders were active, they committed crimes according to a Poisson process and that career length was exponentially distributed.

Inmate Survey, for which a sample of 2,190 incarcerated respondents in California, Michigan, and Texas was interviewed in the 1970s. The survey recorded respondents' criminal involvement in the 3 years before their current incarceration (Petersilia et al., 1978). The most important finding of this survey was that λ is far from being constant across inmates; to the contrary, it is highly skewed. Table 5-1 is taken from Visher's (1986) reanalysis of the RAND data. For robbery, the mean to median ratio is 8.3, 12.6, and 5.2 for California, Michigan, and Texas, respectively. For burglary, these respective ratios are 15.9, 17.2, and 11.0. The difference between the median and the 90th percentile is even more dramatic. With the exception of robbery in Texas, that ratio always exceeds 20 to 1. The skewness of the offending rate distribution has crucial implications for the calculation of incapacitation effects: as a matter of accounting, the estimated size of incapacitation effects will be highly sensitive to whether the mean, median, or some other statistic is used to summarize the offending rate distribution.

Skewness in the offending rate distribution also has important implications for projecting the marginal incapacitation effect of changes in the size of the prison population. This is due to the important concept of "stochastic selectivity" (Canela-Cacho et al., 1997). Stochastic selectivity formalizes the observation that unless high-rate offenders are extremely skillful in avoiding apprehension, they will be represented in prison disproportionately relative to their representation in the population of nonincarcerated

TABLE 5-1 Differences in Distributions of λ for Inmates Who Reported Committing Robbery or Burglary, by State

Statistic	California	Michigan	Texas
Robbery			
25th pct.	2.1	1.4	0.9
50th pct.	5.1	3.6	2.5
75th pct.	19.8	13.1	6.2
90th pct.	107.1	86.1	15.2
Mean	42.4	45.4	13.1
Burglary			
25th pct.	2.3	1.9	1.2
50th pct.	6.2	4.8	3.1
75th pct.	49.1	24.0	9.9
90th pct.	199.9	258.0	76.1
Mean	98.8	82.7	34.1

NOTE: Data were computed as part of the reanalysis.
SOURCE: Visher (1986).

offenders. This is the case because they put themselves at risk of apprehension so much more frequently than lower-rate offenders.

Thus, surveys of offending among the incarcerated will overstate the crime prevention benefits of further increases in the imprisonment rate. The basis for this conclusion is straightforward: because most of the high-rate offenders will already have been apprehended and incarcerated, there will be relatively few of them at large to be incapacitated by further expansion of the prison population. The implication is that the crime control benefits of incapacitation will decrease with the scale of imprisonment. Canela-Cacho and colleagues (1997) use the RAND Second Inmate Survey to estimate the actual magnitude of the model's prediction. Their findings are dramatic—they conclude that offending rates of the incarcerated are on average 10 to 50 times larger than those of the nonincarcerated. Figure 5-2 compares projections of the distribution of robbery offense rates for offenders who are and are not incarcerated. The distributions are starkly different—few high-rate robbers are at large because most have already been apprehended and represent a large share of the prison population.

Direct evidence of stochastic selectivity is reported by Vollaard (2012), who studied the introduction of repeat-offender sentence enhancements in the Netherlands. These enhancements increased sentences from 2 months to 2 years for offenders with 10 or more prior convictions—mainly older men with histories of substance abuse who were involved in shoplifting and other property crimes. The sentence enhancements initially had a large crime-reducing effect, but the effect declined as they were administered to less serious offenders with fewer prior convictions. Recent work by Johnson and Raphael (2012) on the crime prevention effect of imprisonment also suggests that the size of the effect diminishes with the scale of imprisonment. They estimate substantial declines in the number of crimes averted per prisoner over the period 1991 to 2004 compared with 1978 to 1990. This finding also is consistent with the results of an earlier analysis by Useem and Piehl (2008), who conclude that crime reduction benefits decline with the scale of imprisonment, and with Owens' (2009) finding of modest incapacitation effects based on her analysis of 2003 data from Maryland.

Constancy of λ Over the Criminal Career

The criminal career model assumes that the offending rate is constant over the course of the criminal career. However, large percentages of crimes are committed by young people, with rates peaking in the midteenage years for property offenses and the late teenage years for violent offenses, followed by rapid declines (e.g., Farrington, 1986; Sweeten et al., 2013); in an application of group-based trajectory modeling (Nagin, 2005), Laub and Sampson (2003) show that the offending trajectories of all identified groups

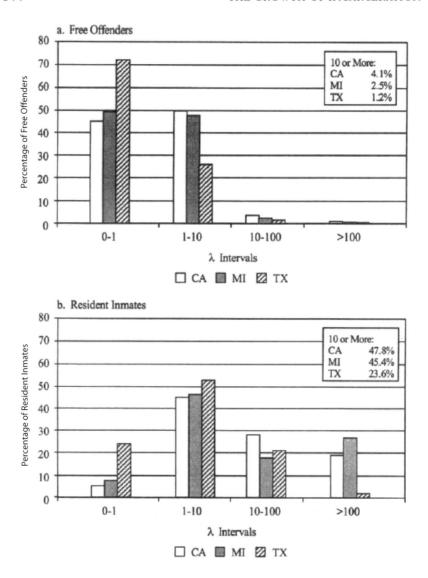

FIGURE 5-2 Distribution of offense rates (λ) among free offenders and resident inmates.
SOURCE: Canela-Cacho et al. (1997).

decline sharply with age. The implication is that estimates of offending rates of prison inmates based on self-reports or arrest data for the period immediately prior to their incarceration will tend to substantially overstate what their future offending rate will be, especially in their middle age and beyond. This conclusion is reinforced by the criminal desistance research of Blumstein and Nakamura (2009), Bushway and colleagues (2011), and Kurlychek and colleagues (2006). Blumstein and Nakamura (2009), for example, find that offending rates among the formerly arrested are statistically indistinguishable from those of the general population after 7 to 10 years of remaining crime free.[11]

Other Considerations

Beyond the constancy of the offending rate across offenders and over the criminal career, several other assumptions relate to the effectiveness of imprisonment as a public safety strategy. Three assumptions are particularly relevant here.

The first has to do with the phenomenon of replacement, as discussed in Box 5-1. From the inception of research on incapacitation, it has been recognized that incarceration of drug dealers is ineffective in preventing drug distribution through incapacitation because dealers are easily replaced. Miles and Ludwig (2007) argue that analogous market mechanisms may result in replacement for other types of crime.

Second, the criminal career model assumes that the experience of incarceration has no impact, positive or negative, on the intensity and duration of postrelease offending. As discussed later in this chapter, evidence of this effect is generally poor, but there is reason to suspect that the experiences of imprisonment may exacerbate postrelease offending.

Third, the criminal career model assumes away co-offending, a phenomenon that is particularly common among juveniles and young adults. In so doing, the model implicitly assumes that incapacitation of one of the co-offenders will avert the offense in its entirety—a dubious assumption. Indeed, Marvell and Moody (1994) conclude that failure to account for co-offending may inflate incapacitation estimates by more than a third.[12]

---

[11]Most active career offenders also desist from crime at relatively early ages—typically in their 30s (Farrington, 2003). The "age-crime curve" and the short residual lengths of criminal careers are among the principal reasons why it can be difficult to implement ideas about "selective incapacitation" of high-rate offenders—it is easy to identify high-rate serious offenders retrospectively but not prospectively.

[12]We also note that in their reanalysis of the RAND data, Marvell and Moody make further adjustments for many of the other factors already discussed. The adjustments result in a 77 percent reduction in their estimate of the incapacitation effect compared with the RAND estimate.

BOX 5-1
Replacement Effects and Drug Arrests

For several categories of offenders, an incapacitation strategy of crime pre-vention can misfire because most or all of those sent to prison are rapidly replaced in the criminal networks in which they participate. Street-level drug trafficking is the paradigm case. Drug dealing is part of a complex illegal market with low barriers to entry. Net earnings are low, and probabilities of eventual arrest and imprisonment are high (Levitt and Venkatesh, 2000; Caulkins and Reuter, 2010; Reuter, 2013). Drug policy research has nonetheless shown consistently that arrested dealers are quickly replaced by new recruits (Dills et al., 2008; MacCoun and Martin, 2009). At the corner of Ninth and Concordia in Milwaukee in the mid-1990s, for example, 94 drug arrests were made within a 3-month period. "These arrests, [the police officer] pointed out, were easy to prosecute to conviction. But . . . the drug market continued to thrive at the intersection" (Smith and Dickey, 1999, p. 8).

Despite the risks of drug dealing and the low average profits, many young disadvantaged people with little social capital and limited life chances choose to sell drugs on street corners because it appears to present opportunities not otherwise available. However, such people tend to overestimate the benefits of that activity and underestimate the risks (Reuter et al., 1990; Kleiman, 1997). This perception is compounded by peer influences, social pressures, and deviant role models provided by successful dealers who live affluent lives and manage to avoid arrest. Similar analyses apply to many members of deviant youth groups and gangs: as members and even leaders are arrested and removed from circulation, others take their place. Arrests and imprisonments of easily replaceable offenders create illicit "opportunities" for others.

ESTIMATING THE TOTAL EFFECT OF INCARCERATION ON CRIME

Instead of studying policy changes in specific jurisdictions or asking offenders about their levels of criminal involvement, another commonly used design analyzes the relationship between imprisonment rates and crime rates across states and over time. The usual specification regresses the logarithm of the crime rate on the logarithm of the incarceration rate, yielding an elasticity of the crime rate with respect to incarceration. This elasticity measures the expected percentage change in the crime rate for a 1 percent increase in the incarceration rate. Because the estimated elasticity does not distinguish between the effects of incapacitation and the effects of deterrence, researchers in this domain interpret it as estimating a "total effect" of incarceration on crime.

A key challenge for studies in this research tradition is the prob-lem of endogeneity—crime rates may affect incarceration rates even as incarceration rates affect crime rates because an increase in crime may increase the numbers of arrests and prison admissions. Under these conditions, a coefficient from a regression of crime rates on imprisonment rates will reflect both the reductions in crime due to incapacitation and deterrence and the increase in incarceration due to increased crime. Estimates of the negative incarceration effect that do not adjust for this endogeneity will thus be biased toward zero, underestimating the degree to which imprisonment reduces crime.

Adjustment for endogeneity of this kind usually involves instrumental variables. In this problem context, an instrumental variable is a variable that (1) is not affected by the crime rate but (2) does affect the incarceration rate, and (3) has no effect on the crime rate separate from its effect on the incarceration rate. Although instrumental variables generally are difficult to find, researchers have argued that some policy changes meet these three conditions. Such policy changes may thus be useful instruments for identifying the causal effect of incarceration on crime, purged of the influence of crime on incarceration. We discuss these studies below.

A review by Donohue (2007) identifies eight studies of the relationship of crime rates to incarceration rates. Six of the eight studies use data from all or nearly all of the 50 states for varying time periods from the 1970s to 2000, and the remaining two use the RAND inmate surveys and county-level data from Texas. All find statistically significant negative associations between crime rates and incarceration rates, implying a crime prevention effect of imprisonment. However, the magnitudes of the estimates of this effect vary widely, from nil for a study allowing for the possibility that prevention effects decline as the scale of incarceration increases (Liedka et al., 2006) to –0.4 percent for each 1 percent increase in the incarceration rate (Spelman, 2000). Apel and Nagin (2011), Durlauf and Nagin (2011a, 2011b), and Donohue (2007) discuss the main limitations of these studies.

Western (2006) performed a Bayesian sensitivity analysis that adjusted regressions not accounting for endogeneity according to different beliefs about the effect of crime on incarceration. In an analysis of 48 states for the period 1971 to 2001, the assumption that crime had no effect on incarceration yielded an elasticity of the index crime rate to state incarceration rates of –0.07. Assuming strong endogeneity—that a 1 percent increase in crime produced a 0.15 percent increase in incarceration—yielded an elasticity of –0.18 that was more than twice as large, although this estimate was statistically insignificant. In short, the estimated elasticity of crime with respect to incarceration is acutely sensitive to beliefs about the dependence of incarceration on crime. The highest estimates of crime-incarceration elasticity imply that crime has a large effect on incarceration rates.

Explicit adjustment for endogeneity with instrumental variables is provided by Levitt (1996), Spelman (2000), and Johnson and Raphael (2012).

Levitt (1996) uses court-ordered prison releases and indicators for over-crowding litigation to form a set of instrumental variables. (Spelman [2000] uses the same instruments applied to a slightly longer time series.) Levitt argues that such court orders meet the test for providing a valid estimate of the effect of the incarceration rate on the crime rate. The orders are not affected by and have no direct effect on the crime rate, affecting it only insofar as they affect the imprisonment rate. Levitt's instrumental variables-based point elasticity estimates vary by specification and crime type, but some are as large as –0.4.

Even if one accepts Levitt's arguments about the validity of the prison overcrowding instrument, the estimated effects have only limited policy value. The instrument, by its construction, likely is measuring the effect on crime of the early release of selected prisoners, probably those nearing the end of their sentenced terms. It may also reflect the effect of diverting indi-viduals convicted of less serious crimes to either local jails or community supervision. In either case, the estimates are not informative about the crime prevention effects, whether by deterrence or incapacitation, of sentence enhancements related to the manner in which a crime is committed (e.g., weapon use), to the characteristics of the perpetrator (e.g., prior record), or to policies affecting the likelihood of incarceration. More generally, the uncertainty about what is actually being measured inherently limits the value of the estimated effects for both policy and social science purposes.

A more recent instrumental variables-based study by Johnson and Raphael (2012) specifies a particular functional dependence of prison ad-missions on crime and uses this information to identify the incarceration effect. Identification is based on the assumption that prison populations do not change instantaneously in response to changes in the size of the criminal population. As in the non-instrumental variables-based analysis of Liedka and colleagues (2006), Johnson and Raphael conclude that the crime prevention effect of imprisonment has diminished with the scale of imprisonment, which was rising steadily over the period of their analysis (1978 to 2004). Their conclusion also is consistent with previously dis-cussed findings of Canala-Cacho and colleagues (1997), Vollaard (2012), and Owens (2009).

In light of the incapacitation studies, evidence reported by Johnson and Raphael (2012) that the crime-incarceration elasticity is smaller at higher incarceration rates suggests that relatively low-rate offenders are detained by additional incarceration when the incarceration rate is high. However, even the incapacitation interpretation is cast in doubt by the aging of the U.S. prison population. Between 1991 and 2010, the percentage of prison-ers in state and federal prisons over age 45 nearly tripled, from 10.6 percent to 27.4 percent (Beck and Mumola, 1999; Guerino et al., 2011). Thus, the apparent decline in the incapacitative effectiveness of incarceration with scale may simply be reflecting the aging of the prison population (regardless of whether this is attributable to longer sentences), which coincided with rising imprisonment rates. Further complicating the decreasing returns interpretation is the changing composition of the prison population with respect to the types of offenses for which prisoners have been convicted. For more than four decades, the percentage of prisoners incarcerated for non-Part I Federal Bureau of Investigation (FBI) index crimes[13] has increased substantially (Blumstein and Beck, 1999, 2005). Thus, the reduction in crime prevention effectiveness may be due to the types of prisoners incarcerated rather than the high rate of incarceration itself.

All of these studies, whether instrumental variables-based or not, also suffer from an important conceptual flaw that limits their usefulness in understanding deterrence and devising crime control policy. Prison population is not a policy variable per se; rather, it is an outcome of sanction policies dictating who goes to prison and for how long—the certainty and severity of punishment. In all incentive-based theories of criminal behavior in the tradition of Bentham and Beccaria, the deterrence response to sanction threats is posed in terms of the certainty and severity of punishment, not the incarceration rate. Therefore, to predict how changes in certainty and severity might affect the crime rate requires knowledge of the relationship of the crime rate to certainty and severity as separate entities. This knowledge is not provided by the literature that analyzes the relationship of the crime rate to the incarceration rate.

These studies also were conducted at an overly global level. Nagin (1998) discusses two dimensions of sanction policies that affect incarceration rates. The first—"type"—encompasses three categories of policies: those that determine the certainty of punishment, such as by requiring mandatory imprisonment; those that affect sentence length, such as determinate sentencing laws; and those that regulate parole powers. The second dimension—"scope"—distinguishes policies with a broad scope, such as increased penalties for a wide range of crimes, from policies focused on particular crimes (e.g., drug offenses) or criminals (e.g., repeat offenders).

The 5-fold growth in incarceration rates over the past four decades is attributable to a combination of policies belonging to all cells of this matrix. As described in Chapter 3, parole powers have been greatly curtailed and sentence lengths increased, both in general and for particular crimes (e.g., drug dealing), and judicial discretion to impose nonincarcerative sanctions has been reduced (Tonry, 1996; Blumstein and Beck, 1999, 2005; Raphael and Stoll, 2009). Consequently, any impact of the increase in prison population

---

[13]Part I index crimes are homicide, rape, robbery, aggravated assault, burglary, larceny/theft, motor vehicle theft, and arson.

on the crime rate reflects the effect of an amalgam of potentially interacting factors.

There are good reasons for predicting differences in the crime reduction effects of different types of sanctions (e.g., mandatory minimum sentences for repeat offenders versus prison diversion programs for first-time offenders). Obvious sources of heterogeneity in offender response include such factors as prior contact with the criminal justice system, demographic characteristics, and the mechanism by which sanction threats are communicated to their intended audience.

THE CRIMINAL INVOLVEMENT OF THE FORMERLY INCARCERATED

Research on incapacitation and deterrence focuses largely on the contemporaneous effect of incarceration—the crime prevented now by today's incarceration.[14] However, today's incarceration may also affect the level of crime in the future. In studying the lagged effects of incarceration on crime, researchers generally have focused on the criminal involvement of people who have been incarcerated. Two competing hypotheses appear plausible. On the one hand, people who have served time in prison may be less likely to be involved in crime because the experience of incarceration has deterred them or because they have been involved in rehabilitative programs. On the other hand, the formerly incarcerated may be more involved in crime after prison because incarceration has damaged them psychologically in ways that make them more rather than less crime prone, has brought them into contact with criminally involved peers, has exposed them to violent or other risky contexts, or has placed them at risk of crime because of imprisonment's negative social effects on earnings and family life (discussed in Chapters 8 and 9, respectively). A recent review of the literature on imprisonment and reoffending by Nagin and colleagues (2009) concludes that there is little evidence of a specific deterrent or rehabilitative effect of incarceration, and that all evidence on the effect of imprisonment on reoffending points to either no effect or a criminogenic effect.[15]

---

[14]The committee is not aware of any research estimating the lagged effects of incapacitation on crime.

[15]It is important to distinguish the effect of imprisonment on recidivism from the effect of aging on recidivism. Studies of the effect of aging on recidivism examine how rates of recidivism change with age, whereas studies of the effect of imprisonment on recidivism examine how imprisonment affects recidivism compared with a noncustodial sanction such as probation. Thus, the conclusion that rates of recidivism tend to decline with age does not contradict the conclusion that imprisonment, compared with a noncustodial sanction, may be associated with higher rates of recidivism.

Whatever the effects of incarceration on those who have served time, research on recidivism offers a clear picture of crime among the formerly incarcerated. The Bureau of Justice Statistics has published two multistate studies estimating recidivism among state prisoners. Both take an annual cohort of prison releases and use state and federal criminal record databases to estimate rates of rearrest, reconviction, and resentencing to prison. Beck and Shipley (1989) examine criminal records for a 1983 cohort of released prisoners in 11 states, while Langan and Levin (2002) analyze a 1994 cohort in the 11 original states plus 4 others. Although the incarceration rate had roughly doubled between 1983 and 1994, the results of the two studies are strikingly similar: the 3-year rearrest rate for state prisoners was around two-thirds in both cohorts (67.5 percent in 1994 and 62.5 percent in 1983).

Research on recidivism recently has been augmented by studies of "redemption"—the chances of criminal involvement among offenders who have remained crime free (Blumstein and Nakamura, 2009; Kurlychek et al., 2006, 2007; Soothill and Francis, 2009). Although none of these studies examines desistance among the formerly incarcerated, their findings are suggestive and point to the need for research on long-term patterns of desistance among those who have served prison time. Using a variety of cohorts in the United States and the United Kingdom, this research finds that the offending rate of the formerly arrested or those with prior criminal convictions converges toward the (age-specific) offending rate of the general population, conditional on having been crime free for the previous 7 to 10 years. The redemption studies also show that the rate of convergence of the formerly incarcerated tends to be slower if ex-offenders are younger or if they have a long criminal history.

Rehabilitative programming has been the main method for reducing crime among the incarcerated. Such programming dates back to Progressive-era reforms in criminal justice that also produced a separate juvenile justice system for children involved in crime, indeterminate sentencing laws with discretionary parole release, and agencies for parole and probation supervision. For much of the twentieth century, rehabilitation occupied a central place in the official philosophy—if not the practice—of U.S. corrections. This philosophy was significantly challenged in the 1970s when a variety of reviews found that many rehabilitative programs yielded few reductions in crime (Martinson, 1974; National Research Council, 1978a). By the late 1990s, consensus had begun to swing back in favor of rehabilitative programs. Gaes and colleagues (1999) report, with little controversy, that well-designed programs can achieve significant reductions in recidivism, and that community-based programs and programs for juveniles tend to be more successful than programs applied in custody and with adult clients. Gaes and colleagues also point to the special value of cognitive-behavioral therapies that help offenders manage conflict and aggressive and impulsive behaviors.

Since the review of Gaes and colleagues, there have been several important evaluations of transitional employment and community supervision programs (Hawken and Kleiman, 2009; Redcross et al., 2012). Results for transitional employment among parole populations have been mixed. Over a 3-year follow-up period, prison and jail incarceration was significantly reduced by a 6-week period of transitional employment, but arrests and convictions were unaffected. Parole and probation reforms involving both sanctions that are swift and certain but mild and sanctions that are graduated have been shown to reduce violations and revocations. Because evaluation of such programs is ongoing, information about other postprogram effects is not yet available.

Researchers and policy makers often have claimed that prison is a "school for criminals," immersing those with little criminal history with others who are heavily involved in serious crime. Indeed, this view motivated a variety of policies intended to minimize social interaction among the incarcerated in the early nineteenth-century penitentiary. Much of the research reported in Chapters 6 through 9 on the individual-level effects of incarceration suggests plausible pathways by which prison time may adversely affect criminal desistance. Research suggests the importance of steady employment and stable family relationships for desisting from crime (Sampson and Laub, 1993; Laub and Sampson, 2003). To the extent that incarceration diminishes job stability and disrupts family relationships, it may also be associated with continuing involvement in crime. As previously indicated, Nagin and colleagues (2009) found that a substantial number of studies report evidence of a criminogenic effect of imprisonment, although they also conclude that most of these studies were based on weak research designs.

EFFECTS OF INCARCERATION FOR DRUG OFFENSES ON DRUG PRICES AND DRUG USE

As discussed in Chapter 2, a large portion of the growth in state and federal imprisonment is due to the increased number of arrests for drug offenses and the increased number of prison commitments per drug arrest. Law enforcement efforts targeting drug offenses expanded greatly after the 1970s, with the arrest rate for drugs increasing from about 200 per 100,000 adults in 1980 to more than 400 per 100,000 in 2009 (Snyder, 2011). Sentencing for drug offenses also became more punitive, as mandatory prison time for these offenses was widely adopted by the states through the 1980s and incorporated in the Federal Sentencing Guidelines in 1986. Expanded enforcement and the growing use of custodial sentences for drug offenses also produced a large increase in the incarceration rate for these offenses. From 1980 to 2010, the state incarceration rate for drug offenses grew from 15 per 100,000 to more than 140 per 100,000, a faster rate of increase than for any other offense category. State prison admissions for drug offenses grew most rapidly in the 1980s, increasing from about 10,000 in 1980 to about 116,000 by 1990 and peaking at 157,000 in 2006 (Beck and Blumstein, 2012, Figures 12 and 13).

As discussed in Chapter 4, successive iterations of the war on drugs, announced by the Nixon, Reagan, and Bush administrations, focused drug control policy on both the supply side and the demand side of the illegal drug market. The intensified law enforcement efforts not only were aimed chiefly at reducing the supply of drugs, but also were intended to reduce the demand for drugs. On the supply side, the specific expectation of policy makers has been that, by taking dealers off the streets and raising the risks associated with selling drugs, these enforcement strategies and more severe punishments would reduce the supply of illegal drugs and raise prices, thereby reducing drug consumption. On the demand side, penalties for possession became harsher as well, and criminal justice agencies became actively involved in reducing demand through the arrest and prosecution of drug users. As a result of this twin focus on supply and demand, incarceration rates for drug possession increased in roughly similar proportion to incarceration rates for drug trafficking (Caulkins and Chandler, 2006).

Much of the research on drug control policy—and specifically, on the effectiveness of law enforcement and criminal justice strategies in carrying out those policies—is summarized in two reports of the National Research Council (2001, 2011). On the supply side of the drug market, the 2001 report finds that "there appears to be nearly unanimous support for the idea that the current policy enforcing prohibition of drug use substantially raises the prices of illegal drugs relative to what they would be otherwise" (p. 153). However, the combined effect of both supply- and demand-side enforcement on price is uncertain (Kleiman, 1997; Kleiman et al., 2011; Reuter, 2013) because effective demand-suppression policies will tend to decrease rather than increase price. Thus, the well-documented reduction in the price of most drugs since the early 1980s (Reuter, 2013) may, in principle, be partly a reflection of success in demand suppression.[16] Nevertheless,

---

[16]National data on drug price trends come from the System to Retrieve Information from Drug Evidence (STRIDE), which combines information on acquisitions of illegal drugs by the Drug Enforcement Administration (DEA) and the Metropolitan Police of the District of Columbia (MPDC). The underlying reporting base from DEA field offices is very sparse, and earlier National Research Council reports warn of the acute limitations of the STRIDE data. The data show large declines in the prices of cocaine and heroin since the early 1980s, and prices have largely been fluctuating around a historically low level over the past two decades. A typical estimate records a decline in the price of a pure gram of powder cocaine from $400

the ultimate objective of both supply- and demand-side enforcement efforts is to reduce the consumption of illicit drugs, and there is little evidence that enforcement efforts have been successful in this regard. The National Research Council (2001, p. 193) concludes: "In summary, existing research seems to indicate that there is little apparent relationship between severity of sanctions prescribed for drug use and prevalence or frequency of use, and that perceived legal risk explains very little in the variance of individual drug use." Although data often are incomplete and of poor quality, the best empirical evidence suggests that the successive iterations of the war on drugs—through a substantial public policy effort—are unlikely to have markedly or clearly reduced drug crime over the past three decades.

KNOWLEDGE GAPS

We offer the following observations regarding gaps in knowledge of the crime prevention effects of incarceration and research to address those gaps.

Deterrence and Sentence Length

The deterrent effect of lengthy sentences is modest at best. We have pointed to evidence from the Project HOPE experiment (Kleiman, 2009; Hawken and Kleiman, 2009; Hawken, 2010) and a fine enforcement experiment (Weisburd et al., 2008) suggesting that the deterrent effect of sentence length may be subject to decreasing returns. Research on the relationship between sentence length and the magnitude of the deterrent effect is therefore a high priority. Related research is needed to establish whether other components of the certainty of punishment beyond the certainty of apprehension, such as the probability of imprisonment given conviction, are effective deterrents.

Sentencing Data by State

A National Research Council report on the deterrent effect of the death penalty (National Research Council, 2012a) describes large gaps in state-level data on the types of noncapital sanctions legally available for the punishment of murder and on their actual utilization. Comparable gaps exist for other serious crimes that are not subject to capital punishment. As a consequence, it is not possible to compare postconviction sentencing practices across the 50 states. Development of a comprehensive database

---

in 1981 to under $100 in 2007 (Fries et al., 2008). Similar price declines are found for heroin and crack cocaine.

that would allow for such cross-state comparisons over time is therefore a high priority.

CONCLUSION

Many studies have attempted to estimate the combined incapacitation and deterrence effects of incarceration on crime using panel data at the state level from the 1970s to the 1990s and 2000s. Most studies estimate the crime-reducing effect of incarceration to be small and some report that the size of the effect diminishes with the scale of incarceration. Where adjustments are made for the direct dependence of incarceration rates on crime rates, the crime-reducing effects of incarceration are found to be larger. Thus, the degree of dependence of the incarceration rate on the crime rate is crucial to the interpretation of these studies. Several studies influential for the committee's conclusions in Chapters 3 and 4 find that the direct dependence of the incarceration rate on the crime rate is modest, lending credence to a small crime-reduction effect on incarceration. However, research in this area is not unanimous and the historical and legal analysis is hard to quantify. If the trend in the incarceration rate depended strongly on the trend in crime, then a larger effect of incarceration on crime would be more credible. On balance, panel data studies support the conclusion that the growth in incarceration rates reduced crime, but the magnitude of the crime reduction remains highly uncertain and the evidence suggests it was unlikely to have been large.

Whatever the estimated average effect of the incarceration rate on the crime rate, the available studies on imprisonment and crime have limited utility for policy. The incarceration rate is the outcome of policies affecting who goes to prison and for how long and of policies affecting parole revocation. Not all policies can be expected to be equally effective in preventing crime. Thus, it is inaccurate to speak of the crime prevention effect of incarceration in the singular. Policies that effectively target the incarceration of highly dangerous and frequent offenders can have large crime prevention benefits, whereas other policies will have a small prevention effect or, even worse, increase crime in the long run if they have the effect of increasing postrelease criminality.

Evidence is limited on the crime prevention effects of most of the policies that contributed to the post-1973 increase in incarceration rates. Nevertheless, the evidence base demonstrates that lengthy prison sentences are ineffective as a crime control measure. Specifically, the incremental deterrent effect of increases in lengthy prison sentences is modest at best. Also, because recidivism rates decline markedly with age and prisoners necessarily age as they serve their prison sentence, lengthy prison sentences are an inefficient approach to preventing crime by incapacitation unless they are specifically targeted at very high-rate or extremely dangerous offenders. For these reasons, statutes mandating lengthy prison sentences cannot be justified on the basis of their effectiveness in preventing crime.

Finally, although the body of credible evidence on the effect of the experience of imprisonment on recidivism is small, that evidence consistently points either to no effect or to an increase rather than a decrease in recidivism. Thus, there is no credible evidence of a specific deterrent effect of the experience of incarceration.

Our review of the evidence in this chapter reaffirms the theories of deterrence first articulated by the Enlightenment philosophers Beccaria and Bentham. In their view, the overarching purpose of punishment is to deter crime. For state-imposed sanctions to deter crime, they theorized, requires three ingredients—severity, certainty, and celerity of punishment. But they also posited that severity alone would not deter crime. Our review of the evidence has confirmed both the enduring power of their theories and the modern relevance of their cautionary observation about overreliance on the severity of punishment as a crime prevention policy.

6

The Experience of Imprisonment

This chapter summarizes what is known about the nature of prison life and its consequences for prisoners. The dramatic rise in incarceration rates in the United States beginning in the mid-1970s has meant that many more people have been sent to prison and, on average, have remained there for longer periods of time. Therefore, the number of persons experiencing the consequences of incarceration—whether helpful or harmful—has correspondingly increased. Although this chapter considers the direct and immediate consequences of incarceration for prisoners while they are incarcerated, many of the most negative of these consequences can undermine postprison adjustment and linger long after formerly incarcerated persons have been released back into society.

In examining this topic, we reviewed research and scholarship from criminology, law, penology, program evaluation, psychiatry, psychology, and sociology. These different disciplines often employ different methodologies and address different questions (and at times come to different conclusions). In our synthesis of these diverse lines of research, we sought to find areas of consensus regarding the consequences of imprisonment for individuals confined under conditions that prevailed during this period of increasing rates of incarceration and reentry.

Prisons in the United States are for the most part remote, closed environments that are difficult to access and challenging to study empirically. They vary widely in how they are structured and how they operate, making broad generalizations about the consequences of imprisonment difficult to formulate. It is possible, however, to describe some of the most significant trends that occurred during the period of increasing rates of incarceration that affected the nature of prison life. After reviewing these trends and acknowledging the lack of national and standardized data and quality-of-life indicators, we discuss aspects of imprisonment that have been scientifically studied. From the available research, we summarize what is known about the experience of prison generally, how it varies for female prisoners and confined youth, its general psychological consequences, and the particular consequences of extreme conditions of overcrowding and isolation, as well as the extent of participation in prison programming. We also consider, on the one hand, what is known about the potentially criminogenic effects of incarceration and, on the other hand, what is known about prison rehabilitation and reentry in reducing postprison recidivism.

VARIATIONS IN PRISON ENVIRONMENTS

Classic sociological and psychological studies have underscored the degree to which prisons are complex and powerful environments that can have a strong influence on the persons confined within them (Sykes, 1958; Clemmer, 1958; Toch, 1975, 1977). However, it is important to note at the outset of this discussion of the consequences of imprisonment that not all "prisons" are created equal. Not only are correctional institutions categorized and run very differently on the basis of their security or custody levels, but even among prisons at the same level of custody, conditions of confinement can vary widely along critical dimensions—physical layout, staffing levels, resources, correctional philosophy, and administrative leadership—that render one facility fundamentally different from another. One of the important lessons of the past several decades of research in social psychology is the extent to which specific aspects of a context or situation can significantly determine its effect on the actors within it (e.g., Haney, 2005; Ross and Nisbett, 1991). This same insight applies to prisons. Referring to very different kinds of correctional facilities as though the conditions within them are the same when they are not may blur critically important distinctions and result in invalid generalizations about the consequences of imprisonment (or the lack thereof). It also may lead scholars to conclude that different research results or outcomes are somehow inconsistent when in fact they can be explained by differences in the specific conditions to which they pertain.

This chapter focuses primarily on the consequences of incarceration for individuals confined in maximum and medium security prisons, those which place a heavier emphasis on security and control compared with the lower-custody-level facilities where far fewer prisoners are confined (Stephan and Karberg, 2003). Prisoners in the higher security-level prisons typically are housed in cells (rather than dormitories), and the facilities themselves generally are surrounded by high walls or fences, with armed guards, detection devices, or lethal fences being used to carefully monitor and control the "security perimeters." Closer attention is paid to the surveillance of inmate activity and the regulation of movement inside housing units and elsewhere in the prison. Obviously, these, too, are gross categorizations, with countless variations characterizing actual conditions of confinement among apparently similar prisons. The assertions made in the pages that follow about broad changes in prison practices and policies, normative prison conditions, and consequences of imprisonment all are offered with the continuing caveat that as prisons vary significantly, so, too, do their normative conditions and their consequences for those who live and work within them.

TRENDS AFFECTING THE NATURE OF PRISON LIFE

Although individual prisons can vary widely in their nature and effects, a combination of six separate but related trends that occurred over the past several decades in the United States has had a significant impact on conditions of confinement in many of the nation's correctional institutions: (1) increased levels of prison overcrowding, (2) substantial proportions of the incarcerated with mental illness, (3) a more racially and ethnically diverse prisoner population, (4) reductions in overall levels of lethal violence within prisons, (5) early litigation-driven improvements in prison conditions followed by an increasingly "hands-off" judicial approach to prison reform, and (6) the rise of a "penal harm" movement.

The first and in many ways most important of these trends was due to the significant and steady increase in the sheer numbers of persons incarcerated throughout the country. As noted in Chapter 2, significant increases in the size of the prisoner population began in the mid-to-late 1970s in a number of states and continued more or less unabated until quite recently. The resulting increases in the numbers of prisoners were so substantial and occurred so rapidly that even the most aggressive programs of prison construction could not keep pace. Widespread overcrowding resulted and has remained a persistent problem. Congress became concerned about prison overcrowding as early as the late 1970s (Subcommittee on Penitentiaries and Corrections, 1978). Overcrowding was described as having reached "crisis-level" proportions by the start of the 1980s and often thereafter (e.g., Finn, 1984; Gottfredson, 1984; Zalman, 1987), and it was addressed in a landmark Supreme Court case as recently as 2011.[1] At the end of 2010, 27 state systems and the Federal Bureau of Prisons were operating at 100 percent design capacity or greater (Guerino et al., 2011).

In addition to the rapid expansion of the prisoner population and the severe overcrowding that resulted, recent surveys of inmates have shown

---

[1]*Brown v. Plata*, 131 S. Ct. 1910 (2011).

high prevalence of serious mental illness among both prisoners and jail inmates (James and Glaze, 2006). Although the reasons for this high prevalence are not entirely clear, some scholars have pointed to the effect of the deinstitutionalization movement of the 1960s (e.g., Hope and Young, 1984; Hudson, 1984; Scull, 1977), which effectively reduced the amount of public resources devoted to the hospitalization and treatment of the mentally ill. Some have suggested that untreated mental illness may worsen in the community, ultimately come to the attention of the criminal justice system, and eventually result in incarceration (Belcher, 1988; Whitmer, 1980). However, Raphael and Stoll (2013) have estimated that deinstitutionalization accounted for no more than approximately "7 percent of prison growth between 1980 and 2000" (p. 156). Even this low estimate of the contribution of deinstitutionalization to the overall rise in incarceration indicates that in the year 2000, "between 40,000 and 72,000 incarcerated individuals would more likely have been mental hospital inpatients in years past" (p. 156). Other scholars and mental health practitioners have suggested that the combination of adverse prison conditions and the lack of adequate and effective treatment resources may result in some prisoners with preexisting mental health conditions suffering an exacerbation of symptoms and even some otherwise healthy prisoners developing mental illness during their incarceration (e.g., Haney, 2006; Kupers, 1999). In any event, the high prevalence of seriously mentally ill prisoners has become a fact of life in U.S. prisons. Further discussion of mental illness among the incarcerated is presented in Chapter 7.

Another trend resulted from the high incarceration rates of African Americans and Hispanics, which changed the makeup of the prisoner population and altered the nature of prison life. As discussed in Chapters 2 and 3, during the past 40 years of increasing imprisonment, incarceration rates for African Americans and Hispanics have remained much higher than those for whites, sustaining and at times increasing already significant racial and ethnic disparities. Racially and ethnically diverse prisoner populations live in closer and more intimate proximity with one another than perhaps anywhere else in society. In some prison systems, they also live together under conditions of severe deprivation and stress that help foment conflict among them. Despite this close proximity, racial and ethnic distinctions and forms of segregation occur on a widespread basis in prison—sometimes by official policy and practice and sometimes on the basis of informal social groupings formed by the prisoners themselves. Race- and ethnicity-based prison gangs emerged in part as a result of these dynamics (Hunt et al., 1993; McDonald, 2003; Skarbek, 2012; van der Kolk, 1987; Valdez, 2005). Estimates of gang membership vary greatly from approximately 9 percent to as much as 24 percent of the prison population during the past two decades (Hill, 2004, 2009; Knox, 2005; Wells et al., 2002). However, these different estimates mask the wide variation in the proportion of gang members within different prison systems and locations and the level of organization of the gangs themselves (Skarbek, 2011).

A number of scholars predicted that many of the above changes would result in prisons becoming more disorderly and unsafe (e.g., Blomberg and Lucken, 2000; Hagan, 1995). However, some key indicators of order and safety in prisons—including riots, homicides, and suicides—showed significant improvement instead. For example, in a study of reported riots, Useem and Piehl (2006, p. 95) find that "both the absolute number of riots and the ratio of inmates to riots declined." The number of riots declined from a peak in 1973 (about 90 riots per 1,000,000 inmates) to become a rare event by 2003, even though the prison population significantly increased over this period. The rate of inmate homicides likewise decreased, declining 92 percent from more than 60 per 100,000 inmates in 1973 (Sylvester et al., 1977) to fewer than 5 per 100,000 in 2000 (Stephan and Karberg, 2003). Useem and Piehl (2006) also report a similar drop in the rate of staff murdered by inmates—a rare but significant event that fell to zero in 2000 and 2001. In addition, as discussed further in Chapter 7, suicide rates in prison declined from 34 per 100,000 in 1980 to 16 per 100,000 in 1990, and largely stabilized after that (Mumola, 2005). Although these measures of lethal violence do not encompass the full measure of the quality of prison life (or even the overall amount of violence that occurs in prison settings), these significant declines during a period of rising incarceration rates are noteworthy, and the mechanisms by which they were accomplished merit future study.

In the early years of increased rates of incarceration in the United States, many of the most important improvements in the quality of prison life were brought about through prison litigation and court-ordered change. Thus, as part of the larger civil rights movement, a period of active prisoners' rights litigation began in the late 1960s and continued through the 1970s. It culminated in a number of federal district court decisions addressing constitutional violations, including some that graphically described what one court called "the pernicious conditions and the pain and degradation which ordinary inmates suffer[ed]" within the walls of certain institutions,[2] and that also brought widespread reforms to a number of individual prisons and prison systems. As prison law experts acknowledged, this early prison litigation did much to correct the worst extremes, such as uncivilized conditions, physical brutality, and grossly inadequate medical and mental health services within prison systems (e.g., Cohen, 2004).

By the beginning of the 1980s, as state prison populations continued to grow and correctional systems confronted serious overcrowding problems,

---

[2] *Ruiz v. Estelle*, 503 F. Supp. 1265 (S.D. Tex. 1980), p. 1390.

the Supreme Court signaled its intent to grant greater deference to prison officials. In a landmark case, *Rhodes v. Chapman* (1981),[3] for example, the Court refused to prohibit the then controversial practice of "double-celling" (housing two prisoners in cells that had been built to house only one). Even so, at least 49 reported court cases decided between 1979 and 1990 addressed jail and prison overcrowding, a majority of which resulted in court-ordered population "caps" or ceilings to remedy unconstitutional conditions (Cole and Call, 1992). By the mid-1990s, there were only three states in the country—Minnesota, New Jersey, and North Dakota—in which an individual prison or the entire prison system had not been placed under a court order to remedy unacceptable levels of overcrowding or other unconstitutional conditions (American Civil Liberties Union, 1995).

In 1995, Congress passed the Prison Litigation Reform Act (PLRA), which greatly limited prisoners' access to the courts to challenge their conditions of confinement. Among other things, the law prohibited prisoners from recovering damages for "mental or emotional injury suffered while in custody without a prior showing of physical injury" [at 42 U.S.C. Section 1997e(3)], and it also required prisoners to "exhaust" all "administrative remedies" (no matter how complicated, prolonged, or futile) before being permitted to file claims in court. Legal commentators concluded that the PLRA had helped achieve the intended effect of significantly reducing the number of frivolous lawsuits; however, it also instituted significant barriers to more creditable claims that could have drawn needed attention to harmful prison conditions and violations of prisoners' rights (Cohen, 2004; Schlanger and Shay, 2008). By the late 1990s, the average inmate could find much less recourse in the courts than the early years of prison litigation had appeared to promise (Cohen, 2004). Schlanger and Shay (2008, p. 140) note that the "obstacles to meritorious lawsuits" were "undermining the rule of law in our prisons and jails, granting the government near-impunity to violate the rights of prisoners without fear of consequences."

The final trend that affected the nature of prison life in the United States over the past several decades was both an independent factor in its own right and the consequence of several of those previously mentioned. It is somewhat more difficult to document quantitatively but has been vividly described in a number of historical accounts of this era of American corrections (e.g., Cullen, 1995; Garland, 2001; Gottschalk, 2006). The mid-1970s marked the demise of the pursuit of what had come to be called the "rehabilitative ideal" (Lin, 2002; Vitiello, 1991). Rehabilitation—the goal of placing people in prison not only as punishment but also with the intent that they eventually would leave better prepared to live a law-abiding life—had served as an overarching rationale for incarceration for nearly a

---

[3]*Rhodes v. Chapman*, 452 U.S. 337 (1981).

century (e.g., Allen, 1959). In this period, as discussed in Chapters 3 and 4, the dominant rationale shifted from rehabilitation to punishment.

As the manifest purpose of imprisonment shifted, aspects of prison life changed in some ways that adversely affected individual prisoners. Once legislatures and prison systems deemphasized the rehabilitative rationale, and as they struggled to deal with unprecedented overcrowding, they were under much less pressure to provide prison rehabilitative services, treatment, and programming (e.g., California Department of Corrections and Rehabilitation Expert Panel on Adult Offender Reentry and Recidivism Reduction Programs, 2007; Office of Inspector General, 2004; Government Accountability Office, 2012). We examine the available data on the decline in opportunities to participate in such services later in this chapter and also in Chapter 7.

As discussed in Chapters 3 and 4, during the period of incarceration growth, politicians and policy makers from across the political spectrum embraced an increasingly "get tough" approach to criminal justice. Eventually, advocates of these more punitive policies began to focus explicitly on daily life inside the nation's prisons, urging the implementation of a "no frills" approach to everyday correctional policies and practices. Daily life inside many prison systems became harsher, in part because of an explicit commitment to punishing prisoners more severely. What some scholars characterized as a "penal harm" movement that arose in many parts of the country included attempts to find "creative strategies to make offenders suffer" (Cullen, 1995, p. 340).

As Johnson and colleagues (1997) point out, political rhetoric advocated "restoring fear to prisons," among other things through a new "ethos of vindictiveness and retribution" that was clearly "counter to that of previous decades, which had emphasized humane treatment of prisoners and the rehabilitative ideal" (pp. 24-25). In some jurisdictions, "get tough" policies addressed relatively minor (but not necessarily insignificant) aspects of prisoners' daily life, such as, in one southern state, "removing air conditioning and televisions in cells, discontinuing intramural sports, requiring inmates to wear uniforms, abolishing furloughs for inmates convicted of violent crimes, and banning long hair and beards" (Johnson et al., 1997, p. 28). In 1995 and several times thereafter, Congress considered an explicit No Frills Prison Act that was designed to target federal prison construction funds to states that "eliminate[d] numerous prison amenities—including good time, musical instruments, personally owned computers, in-cell coffee pots, and so on" (Johnson et al., 1997, p. 28).[4] Although the No Frills Prison Act

---

[4]See H.R. 663 (104th), whose stated purpose was "to end luxurious conditions in prisons." Congress also considered No Frills Prisons Acts in 1999 [H.R. 370 (106th)] and again in 2003 [H.R. 2296 (108th)]. A bill by the same name, limiting food expenditures and restrict-

never became law, it did reflect prevailing attitudes among many citizens and lawmakers at the time. As described in more detail below, a number of restrictions on "prison amenities" were imposed through changes in correctional policy rather than legislation.

PRISON DATA

Before discussing the consequences of imprisonment for individuals, it is useful to describe contemporary conditions of confinement—the physical, social, and psychological realities that prisoners are likely to experience in the course of their incarceration. However, attempts to characterize the overall conditions of confinement are constrained by the lack of comprehensive, systematic, and reliable data on U.S. prison conditions. The best evidence available often is limited to specific places or persons. As noted at the outset of this chapter, any generalizations about typical prison conditions must be qualified by the fact that prisons differ significantly in how they are structured, operated, and experienced. Official national statistics that address certain aspects of imprisonment are useful for many scholarly purposes, but they have two important limitations: a lack of standardization and sometimes questionable reliability, on the one hand, and the fact that they typically focus on few meaningful indicators of the actual quality of prison life. We discuss each of these limitations in turn.

Lack of National and Standardized Data

Concerns about the accuracy or reliability of official compilations of general criminal justice data—including data collected in and about the nation's correctional institutions—are long-standing. More than 45 years ago, the President's Commission on Law Enforcement and the Administration of Justice (1967) concluded that regional and national criminal justice data often were inaccurate, incomplete, or unavailable and recommended a number of reforms. Similar concerns were voiced by the National Advisory Committee on Criminal Justice Standards and Goals and the General Accounting Office in reports published in the early 1970s (Comptroller General of the United States, 1973; National Advisory Commission on Criminal Justice Standards and Goals, 1973). Although a number of reforms and new standards were implemented, a report sponsored by the Bureau of Justice Statistics (BJS) that was published almost two decades after the 1967 Commission report acknowledged that "significant data quality problems still remain" (Bureau of Justice Statistics, 1985, p. 28).

---

ing living conditions, recreational activities, and property, was enacted in at least one state. See Alaska S.B. 1 (1997).

Notwithstanding the many improvements made in the intervening years and reasonably reliable data on a number of important criminal justice indicators collected by BJS and other government agencies, on which researchers justifiably rely, the collection and reporting of data from official sources measuring actual living conditions and overall quality of life inside the nation's correctional institutions remain problematic. No mandatory reporting requirement exists for most key indicators or measures, and many prison systems do not systematically assess or report them. In addition, there is little or no standardization of this process (so that different systems often use different definitions of the indicators); little or no quality control over the data; and no outside, independent oversight. As recently as 2005, for example, Allen Beck, chief statistician at BJS, testified that, because of this imprecision and unreliability, "the level of assaults [in prison] is simply not known" (Gibbons and Katzenbach, 2006, p. 418).

A National Research Council panel critically examined the nature and quality of data collection performed by BJS—the agency responsible for providing perhaps the nation's most reliable and relied upon criminal justice data. The panel concluded that "the lack of routine evaluation and quality assessments of BJS data is problematic because of the wide variety of sources from which BJS data series are drawn" (National Research Council, 2009, p. 253). Using BJS's prison-related data as an example, the panel noted that "much of the correctional data are collected from agencies and institutions that rely on varied local systems of record-keeping" that, among other things, include "varying definitions" of even basic facts such as race and level of schooling. The panel recommended that BJS "work with correctional agencies" to "promote consistent data collection and expand coverage beyond the 41 states covered in the most recent [National Corrections Reporting Program]" (p. 253).

Few Quality-of-Life Indicators

Few official or comprehensive data collection efforts have attempted to capture the quality-of-life aspects of prison confinement. The above National Research Council panel acknowledged the additional challenge of providing reliable descriptive data addressing contextual factors.[5] It rec-

---

[5]The National Research Council panel commented on the special challenges that are faced in trying to capture statistically the dimensions of "social context"—whether the context in which crime occurs or the context in which punishment is meted out. For example, the panel noted that one of the major limitations in the statistical data collected by BJS and other agencies on the various factors that influence criminality derives from the fact that "contextual factors associated with crime are inherently difficult to describe—and even characterize consistently" (National Research Council, 2009, p. 55). The panel elaborated further on the fact that the "geography of crime . . . including social and physical conditions and community

ommended that BJS "develop a panel survey of people under correctional supervision" that would allow researchers and policy makers to better "understand the social contexts of correctional supervision" both in prison and following release (National Research Council, 2009, Recommendation 3.6, p. 140), but that recommendation has not been implemented.

Ambitious attempts to estimate and compare the overall "punitiveness" of individual state criminal justice systems (e.g., Gordon, 1989; Kutateladze, 2009) have been constrained by not only the quality but also the scope of the data on which they were based. For example, Gordon's (1989) initial effort to construct a punitiveness or "toughness" index includes no data that pertained directly to conditions of confinement. Kutateladze's (2009) more recent and more elaborate analysis includes six categories of measurable indicators of conditions of confinement—overcrowding, operating costs per prisoner, food service costs per prisoner, prisoner suicide and homicide rates, sexual violence between inmates and between staff and inmates, and rate of lawsuits filed by prisoners against correctional agencies or staff members. But these indicators, too, were derived from data of questionable reliability; in addition, the analysis omits many important aspects of prison life.

No comprehensive national data are routinely collected on even the most basic dimensions of the nature and quality of the prison experience, such as housing configurations and cell sizes; the numbers of prisoners who are housed in segregated confinement and their lengths of stay and degree of isolation; the amount of out-of-cell time and the nature and amount of property that prisoners are permitted; the availability of and prisoners' levels of participation in educational, vocational, and other forms of programming, counseling, and treatment; the nature and extent of prison labor and rates of pay that prisoners are afforded; and the nature and amount of social and legal visitation prisoners are permitted. Moreover, the subtler aspects of the nature of prison life tend to be overlooked entirely in official, comprehensive assessments,[6] including those that Liebling (2011) finds are most important to prisoners: treatment by staff and elements of safety, trust, and power throughout the institution.

---

resources in an area" is difficult to specify and therefore tends not to be included in BJS and other government data collection efforts (p. 67).

[6]Lacking is what might be called a "national prison quality-of-life assessment" roughly comparable to the national performance measurement system that the Association of State Correctional Administrators has begun to implement to ensure greater levels of correctional accountability. See Wright (2005).

CONDITIONS OF CONFINEMENT

As noted above, no truly comprehensive, systematic, and meaningful assessment of prison conditions in the United States exists.[7] The lack of high-quality national data on prison life is due in part to the closed nature of prison environments and the challenges faced in studying the nature and consequences of life within them. Nonetheless, a substantial body of scholarly literature provides important insights into prevailing conditions of confinement and the experience of incarceration. Our review of that literature proceeds in the context of internationally recognized principles of prisoner treatment (see Box 6-1) and the long-established standards and guidelines adopted by the American Correctional Association and the American Bar Association.[8]

We agree with the observation that "some of the most valuable knowledge we have about corrections is the product of in-depth and sometimes qualitative research conducted by academics and policymakers inside our correctional institutions" (Gibbons and Katzenbach, 2006, p. 528). For example, Lynch's (2010) historical and qualitative study of the Arizona prison system chronicles a series of changes in correctional policies and practices that took place in that state over the previous several decades, many of which had direct consequences for the nature and quality of life inside Arizona prisons. These changes included significant increases in the length of prison sentences meted out by the courts, the introduction of mandatory minimum sentences, and the implementation of truth-in-sentencing provisions to ensure that prisoners would serve longer portions of their sentences before being released (see the discussion in Chapter 3). The prison population was reclassified so that a greater percentage of prisoners were housed under maximum security conditions. The nation's first true "supermax" prison was opened, where prisoners were kept in specially designed, windowless solitary confinement cells, isolated from any semblance of normal social contact nearly around the clock and on a long-term basis (a practice discussed later in this chapter). Investments in security measures expanded in Arizona during this era, including the use of trained attack dogs to extract recalcitrant prisoners from their cells, while rehabilitative program opportunities declined (Lynch, 2010).

Lynch also shows the ways in which Arizona prison officials modified many aspects of day-to-day prison operations in ways that collectively worsened more mundane but nonetheless important features of prison life.

---

[7]Some scholars have questioned the feasibility of such a national system. For example, see Kutateladze (2009).

[8]For further articulation of these principles, see http://www.aca.org/pastpresentfuture/principles.asp and http://www.americanbar.org/publications/criminal_justice_section_archive/crimjust_standards_treatmentprisoners.html#23-1.1 [July 2013].

BOX 6-1
Basic Principles for the Treatment of Prisoners

Adopted and proclaimed by General Assembly resolution 45/111 of 14 December 1990:

1. All prisoners shall be treated with the respect due to their inherent dignity and value as human beings.
2. There shall be no discrimination on the grounds of race, colour, sex, language, religion, political or other opinion, national or social origin, property, birth or other status.
3. It is, however, desirable to respect the religious beliefs and cultural precepts of the group to which prisoners belong, whenever local conditions so require.
4. The responsibility of prisons for the custody of prisoners and for the protection of society against crime shall be discharged in keeping with a State's other social objectives and its fundamental responsibilities for promoting the well-being and development of all members of society.
5. Except for those limitations that are demonstrably necessitated by the fact of incarceration, all prisoners shall retain the human rights and fundamental freedoms set out in the Universal Declaration of Human Rights, and, where the State concerned is a party, the International Covenant on Economic, Social and Cultural Rights, and the International Covenant on Civil and Political Rights and the Optional Protocol thereto, as well as such other rights as are set out in other United Nations covenants.
6. All prisoners shall have the right to take part in cultural activities and education aimed at the full development of the human personality.
7. Efforts addressed to the abolition of solitary confinement as a punishment, or to the restriction of its use, should be undertaken and encouraged.
8. Conditions shall be created enabling prisoners to undertake meaningful remunerated employment which will facilitate their reintegration into the country's labour market and permit them to contribute to their own financial support and to that of their families.
9. Prisoners shall have access to the health services available in the country without discrimination on the grounds of their legal situation.
10. With the participation and help of the community and social institutions, and with due regard to the interests of victims, favourable conditions shall be created for the reintegration of the ex-prisoner into society under the best possible conditions.
11. The above Principles shall be applied impartially.

SOURCE: United Nations (1990).

The changes included housing two prisoners in cells that had been designed to hold only one, reducing prisoners' access to higher education, removing certain kinds of exercise equipment from the prison yard, reducing the time prisoners could spend watching television, placing greater limits on the amount and kind of personal property prisoners could have in their cells, requiring prisoners to pay fees for medical services and for the electricity needed to run their electrical appliances, charging room and board to those engaged in compensated inmate labor, greatly reducing the number of "compassionate leaves" that had allowed prisoners to be escorted outside prison to attend to urgent family matters (such as funerals), placing additional restrictions on prison visits in general and on contact visits in particular, requiring prisoners' visitors to consent to being strip searched as a precondition for prison visitation, instituting the tape recording of all prisoner phone calls and adding the expense of the recording process to the fees paid by prisoners and their families for the calls, and returning to the use of "chain gangs" in which groups of shackled prisoners were publicly engaged in hard labor under the supervision of armed guards on horseback. (See Lynch [2010, pp. 116-173], for a more complete description of these changes and the political dynamics that helped bring them about.)

Arizona may be near the far end of the spectrum of prison systems that implemented an especially severe regime of "penal harm" over the period of increasing rates of incarceration in the United States, but other observers have documented severe conditions in other states as well and reached sobering conclusions about the outcomes of incarceration. For example, in an ethnographic study of a modern and otherwise apparently well-run prison in California, Irwin (2005, p. 168) finds:

> For long-termers, the new situation of doing time, enduring years of suspension, being deprived on material conditions, living in crowded conditions without privacy, with reduced options, arbitrary control, disrespect, and economic exploitation is excruciatingly frustrating and aggravating. Anger, frustration, and a burning sense of injustice, coupled with the crippling processing inherent in imprisonment, significantly reduce the likelihood [that prisoners can] pursue a viable, relatively conventional, non-criminal life after release.

Irwin (2005, p. 149) concludes that such conditions did "considerable harm to prisoners in obvious and subtle ways and [made] it more difficult for them to achieve viability, satisfaction, and respect when they are released from prison."

One of the most recent and comprehensive summaries of the current state of the nation's prisons was provided by the bipartisan Commission on Safety and Abuse in America's Prisons (Gibbons and Katzenbach, 2006). In 2005, the Commission held a series of information-gathering hearings in several locations around the country in which it heard live testimony and received evidence from correctional, law enforcement, and other government officials; representatives of interested community agencies and citizens' groups; and a wide array of academic and legal experts. Witness testimony provided the most informed "snapshot" of prison conditions across the country available at that time and since. In its final report, the Commission acknowledges that "America's correctional facilities are less turbulent and deadly violent than they were decades ago," noting that "many correctional administrators have done an admirable job" in bringing these improvements about (Gibbons and Katzenbach, 2006, p. 390). However, the Commission also observes that, despite the decreases nationally in riots and homicides,

> there is still too much violence in America's prisons and jails, too many facilities that are crowded to the breaking point, too little medical and mental health care, unnecessary uses of solitary confinement and other forms of segregation, a desperate need for the kinds of productive activities that discourage violence and make rehabilitation possible, and a culture in many prisons and jails that pits staff against prisoners and management against staff. (p. 390)

Thus, the authors argue that "steady decreases nationally in riots and homicides do not tell us about the much larger universe of less-than-deadly violence" or the "other serious problems that put lives at risk and cause immeasurable suffering" (p. 390).

Imprisonment of Women

Although most of the research conducted on the effects of imprisonment on individuals focuses on male prisoners (e.g., Fletcher et al., 1993), approximately 1 of every 14 prisoners in the United States is female (Carson and Golinelli, 2013). In fact, the incarceration rates of white and Hispanic women in particular are growing more rapidly than those of other demographic groups (Guerino et al., 2011). Compared with men, women are sentenced more often to prison for nonviolent crimes: about 55 percent of women sentenced to prison have committed property or drug crimes as compared with about 35 percent of male prisoners (Guerino et al., 2011). Women also are more likely than men to enter prison with mental health problems or to develop them while incarcerated: about three-quarters of women in state prisons in 2004 had symptoms of a current mental health problem, as opposed to 55 percent of men (James and Glaze, 2006).

There are many similarities between men's and women's prisons and some notable differences, as depicted in a number of ethnographic studies and first-hand accounts by women prisoners (e.g., Morash and

Schram, 2002; Ritchie, 2004; Solinger et al., 2010). For example, Ward and Kassenbaum's (2009) ethnographic study of a women's prison finds that, although women were subjected to virtually the same pains and deprivations of imprisonment as men (albeit with less pressing threats of victimization by other inmates), they felt the loss of familial roles and affectional relationships much more acutely and adapted to the prison environment in ways that reflected this.

Owen's (1998) ethnographic study of the very large women's prison in California (the Central California Women's Facility [CCWF]) reveals an inmate culture that developed "in ways markedly different from the degradation, violence, and predatory structure of male prison life"; that is, "in some ways, the culture of the female prison seeks to accommodate these struggles rather than to exploit them" (Owen, 1998, p. 2). Yet despite the gendered nature of these accommodations, "the social organization of women in a contemporary prison is created in response to demands of the institution and to conditions not of their own making." Thus, just as in male prisons, the typical female prisoner's "subsequent immersion in this culture" has a temporal dimension that "shapes one's level of attachment to prison culture as one becomes prisonized . . . or socialized into the normative prison structure" (Owen, 1998, p. 2). Also as in male prisons, Owen reports that overcrowding permeated the conditions of daily life at CCWF.

Although there are a number of parallels between life in men's and women's prisons, women prisoners face a number of additional hardships that complicate their experience of incarceration. For one, women's prisons historically have been underresourced and underserved in correctional systems, so that women prisoners have had less access to programming and treatment than their male counterparts (e.g., Smykla and Williams, 1996). Women prisoners also are more likely to be the targets of sexual abuse by staff (e.g., Buchanan, 2007). Specifically, women victims of sexual coercion and assault in prison are much more likely than their male counterparts to report that the perpetrators were staff members (e.g., Struckman-Johnson and Struckman-Johnson, 2006). Beck (2012) finds that of all reported staff sexual misconduct in prison, three-quarters involved staff victimizing women prisoners.

A majority of women prisoners are mothers, who must grapple with the burden of being separated from their children during incarceration (e.g., Phillips and Harm, 1997). In 2004, 62 percent of female state and federal inmates (compared with 51 percent of male inmates) were parents. Of those female inmates, 55 percent reported living with their minor children in the month before arrest, 42 percent in single-parent households; for male inmates who were parents, the corresponding figures were 36 and 17 percent (Glaze and Maruschak, 2008).

Imprisonment of Youth

In the 1980s and 1990s, new laws and changing practices criminalized many juvenile offenses and led more youth to be placed in custody outside the home,[9] including many who were tried as adults and even incarcerated in adult prisons. Confining youth away from their homes and communities interferes with the social conditions that contribute to adolescents' healthy psychological development: the presence of an involved parent or parent figure, association with prosocial peers, and activities that require autonomous decision making and critical thinking. In addition, many youth face collateral consequences of involvement in the justice system, such as the public release of juvenile and criminal records that follow them throughout their lives and limit future education and employment opportunities (National Research Council, 2013).

Youth transferred to the adult criminal justice system fare worse than those that remain in the juvenile justice system (Austin et al., 2000; Task Force on Community Preventive Services, 2007). The number of juveniles held in adult jails rose dramatically from 1,736 in 1983 to 8,090 in 1998, a 366 percent increase. In the late 1990s, 13 percent of confined juveniles were in adult jails or prisons (Austin et al., 2000); the proportion of confined juveniles who end up in adult jails or prisons is about the same today. According to Deitch and colleagues (2009), "once a [youth] has been transferred to adult court, many states no longer take his or her age into consideration when deciding where the child is to be housed before trial and after sentencing. . . . Although federal law requires separation of children and adults in correctional facilities, a loophole in the law does not require its application when those children are certified as adults. On any given day, a significant number of youth are housed in adult facilities, both in local jails and in state prisons" (p. 53). In 2008, 7,703 youth were counted in jails (Minton, 2013), and 3,650 prisoners in state-run adult prisons were found to be under 18 (Sabol et al., 2009). The number of juvenile inmates has declined in recent years, with 1,790 in prisons (Carson and Sabol, 2012)

---

[9]Juveniles are considered to be confined (as opposed to incarcerated) when they are adjudicated delinquent and ordered to be placed in residence outside the home—for example, in a group home or juvenile correctional facility. In an overall trend that is very similar to the one we have described for adults, the confinement rate of juveniles increased through the 1980s and 1990s. By 1997, the juvenile confinement rate had reached a peak of 356 juveniles in placement per 100,000 population. The confinement rate of juveniles rose steadily from 167 in 1979, to 185 in the mid-1980s, to 221 in 1989, reaching a peak in 1997 before starting to decline (Allen-Hagen, 1991; Child Trends, n.d.; Kline, 1989; Office of Juvenile Justice and Delinquency Prevention, 1983; Sickmund et al., 2011). It is worth noting that the placement rate did not change substantially between 1985 and 2008; the increased confinement rate is due largely to the growth of delinquency referrals handled by juvenile courts during that period rather than greater use of placement (National Research Council, 2013).

and 5,900 in jails (Minton, 2013) in 2011. With the growth in prison and jail populations, juveniles still represent less than 1 percent of the overall incarcerated population.

When youth are confined in jails, detention centers, or prisons designed for adults, they have limited access to educational and rehabilitative services appropriate to their age and development. Living in more threatening adult correctional environments places them at greater risk of mental and physical harm (Deitch et al., 2009; National Research Council, 2013). Research also has shown that placing youth in the adult corrections system instead of retaining them in the juvenile system increases their risk of reoffending (Bishop and Frazier, 2000; Mulvey and Schubert, 2011; Redding, 2008).

These disadvantages are borne disproportionately by youth of color, who are overrepresented at every stage of the juvenile justice process and particularly in the numbers transferred to adult court. Youth of color also remain in the system longer than white youth. Minority overrepresentation within the juvenile justice system raises at least two types of concerns. First, it calls into question the overall fairness and legitimacy of the juvenile justice system. Second, it has serious implications for the life-course trajectories of many minority youth who may be stigmatized and adversely affected in other ways by criminal records attained at comparatively young ages (National Research Council, 2013).

Congress first focused on these kinds of racial disparities in 1988 when it amended the Juvenile Justice and Delinquency Prevention Act of 1974 (P.L. 93-415, 42 U.S.C. 5601 et seq.)[10] to require states that received federal formula funds to ascertain the proportion of minority youth detained in secure detention facilities, secure correctional facilities, and lockups compared with the general population. If the number of minority youth was disproportionate, then states were required to develop and implement plans for reducing the disproportionate representation. Despite a research and policy focus on this matter for more than two decades, however, remarkably little progress has been made toward reducing the disparities themselves. On the other hand, at least in the past decade, some jurisdictions have begun to take significant steps to overhaul their juvenile justice systems to reduce the use of punitive practices and heighten awareness of racial disparities (for more discussion, see National Research Council [2013]). The steady decline in the juvenile confinement rate, from 356 per

---

[10]In 2002, Congress modified the disproportionate minority confinement requirement and mandated that states implement juvenile delinquency prevention and system improvement efforts across the juvenile justice system. Thus, the requirement was broadened from disproportionate minority confinement to disproportionate minority contact, and states were required to implement strategies aimed at reducing disproportionality.

100,000[11] in 1997 to 225 in 2010, is one indication that these reforms may be having the desired impact (Child Trends, n.d.; Sickmund et al., 2011).

General Psychological Observations

Imprisonment produces negative, disabling behavioral and physical changes in some prisoners, and certain prison conditions can greatly exacerbate those changes. Although imprisonment certainly is not uniformly devastating or inevitably damaging to individual prisoners, "particular vulnerabilities and inabilities to cope and adapt can come to the fore in the prison setting, [and] the behavior patterns and attitudes that emerge can take many forms, from deepening social and emotional withdrawal to extremes of aggression and violence" (Porporino, 1990, p. 36). As discussed further below, numerous empirical studies have confirmed this observation. Even one review of the literature (Bonta and Gendreau, 1990) reaching the overall conclusion that life in prison was not necessarily as damaging to prisoners as many had previously assumed nonetheless cites a number of studies documenting a range of negative, harmful results, including these empirical facts: "physiological and psychological stress responses . . . were very likely [to occur] under crowded prison conditions"; "a variety of health problems, injuries, and selected symptoms of psychological distress were higher for certain classes of inmates than probationers, parolees, and, where data existed, for the general population"; studies show that long-term incarceration can result in "increases in hostility and social introversion . . . and decreases in self-evaluation and evaluations of work" for some prisoners; and imprisonment itself can produce "increases in dependency upon staff for direction and social introversion," "deteriorating community relationships over time," and "unique difficulties" with "family separation issues and vocational skill training needs" (Bonta and Gendreau, 1990, pp. 353-359).

Coping with the Stresses of Incarceration

Many aspects of prison life—including material deprivations; restricted movement and liberty; a lack of meaningful activity; a nearly total absence of personal privacy; and high levels of interpersonal uncertainty, danger, and fear—expose prisoners to powerful psychological stressors that can

---

[11]Rates are calculated per 100,000 juveniles ages 10 through the upper age limit of each state's juvenile court jurisdiction (Child Trends, n.d.; Sickmund et al., 2011).

adversely impact their emotional well-being.[12] Toch and Adams (2002, p. 230) conclude that the "dictum that prisons are stressful cannot be overestimated" and identify patterns of "acting out" and other forms of apparently "maladaptive" behavior in which prisoners sometimes engage as they attempt to cope with the high levels of stress they experience in confinement.

Prison stress can affect prisoners in different ways and at different stages of their prison careers. Some prisoners experience the initial period of incarceration as the most difficult, and that stress may precipitate acute psychiatric symptoms that surface for the first time. Preexisting psychological disorders thus may be exacerbated by initial experiences with incarceration (e.g., Gibbs, 1982). Other prisoners appear to survive the initial phases of incarceration relatively intact only to find themselves worn down by the ongoing physical and psychological challenges and stress of confinement. They may suffer a range of psychological problems much later in the course of their incarceration (Taylor, 1961; Jose-Kampfner, 1990; Rubenstein, 1982).

For some prisoners, extreme prison stress takes a more significant psychological toll. Posttraumatic stress disorder (PTSD) is a diagnosis applied to a set of interrelated, trauma-based symptoms, including depression, emotional numbing, anxiety, isolation, and hypervigilance.[13] In a review of the international literature, Goff and colleagues (2007) find that the prevalence of PTSD in prisoner populations varies across studies from 4 to 21 percent, suggesting a rate that is 2 to 10 times higher than the prevalence found in community samples (Kessler et al., 1995; Stein et al., 1997). Studies conducted in the United States have observed the highest prevalence: PTSD is reported in 21 percent of male prisoners (Gibson et al., 1999; Powell et al., 1997) and in as many as 48 percent of female prisoners (Zlotnick, 1997), and in 24 to 65 percent of male juvenile inmates (Heckman et al., 2007; see also Gibson et al., 1999).

Herman (1992) proposes an expanded diagnostic category that appears to describe more accurately the kind of traumatic reactions produced by certain experiences within prisons. What she terms "complex PTSD" is brought about by "prolonged, repeated trauma or the profound

---

[12]Early studies of the impact of exposure to extreme forms of environmental stress in general concluded that it "may result in permanent psychological disability" and that "subjection to prolonged, extreme stress results in the development of 'neurotic' symptoms" in persons exposed to it (Hocking, 1970, p. 23).

[13]Four criteria must be met for the diagnosis of PTSD to be applied. A person must (1) be exposed to a severe stressor resulting in intense fear or helplessness; (2) undergo psychic reexperiencing or reenacting of the trauma; (3) engage in avoidance behavior or experience psychic numbing; and (4) experience increased arousal, typically in the presence of stimuli related to or reminiscent of the original trauma (American Psychiatric Association, 2000). For additional discussion of the disorder, see Wilson and Raphael (1993).

deformations of personality that occur in captivity" (p. 118). As reported in Haney (2006, p. 185), "unlike classic PTSD—which arises from relatively circumscribed traumatic events—complex PTSD derives from chronic exposure that is more closely analogous to the experience of imprisonment. Complex PTSD can result in protracted depression, apathy, and the development of a deep sense of hopelessness as the long-term psychological costs of adapting to an oppressive situation."

Of course, the unique and potent stresses of imprisonment are likely to interact with and amplify whatever preexisting vulnerabilities prisoners bring to prison. Prisoners vary in their backgrounds and vulnerabilities and in how they experience or cope with the same kinds of environments and events. As a result, the same prison experiences have different consequences for different prisoners (e.g., Hemmens and Marquart, 1999; Gullone et al., 2000). Many prisoners come from socially and economically marginalized groups and have had adverse experience in childhood and adolescence that may have made them more rather than less vulnerable to psychological stressors and less able to cope effectively with the chronic strains of prison life than those with less problematic backgrounds (e.g., Gibson et al., 1999; Greene et al., 2000; McClellan et al., 1997; Mullings et al., 2004; Zlotnick, 1997).

As noted earlier, significant percentages of prisoners suffer from a range of serious, diagnosable psychological disorders, including clinical depression and psychosis as well as PTSD. The exact onset and causal origins of these disorders cannot always be determined—some are undoubtedly preexisting conditions, some are exacerbated by the harshness and stress of incarceration, and others may originate in the turmoil and trauma generated by prison experiences. The incidence of psychological disorders among prisoners is discussed further in Chapter 7.

Prisonization: Adaptation to the Nature of Prison Life

Clemmer (1958, p. 299) defined "prisonization" as "the taking on in greater or less degree of the folkways, mores, customs, and general culture of the penitentiary" (see also Gillespie, 2003; Ohlin, 1956; Pollock, 1997). Incorporating these mores is a matter less of choice than of necessity. As one prisoner put it: "Those who adhere to the main tenets of prison culture— never 'rat' on another prisoners, always keep your distance from staff, 'do your own time'—have the best chance of avoiding violence" (quoted by Morris [1995, p. 211]). In addition to the internalizing of cultural aspects of the prison, prisonization occurs as prisoners undergo a number of psychological changes or transformations to adapt to the demands of prison life. It is a form of coping in response to the abnormal practices and conditions that incarceration entails. The nature and degree of prisonization will vary among prisoners, depending, in part, on their personal identity, strengths and weaknesses, and individual experiences both prior to prison and during the course of their prison stay (e.g., MacKenzie and Goodstein, 1995; Paterline and Petersen, 1999; Walters, 2003).

Two notable characteristics of the prison environment contribute to the process of prisonization: the necessary structure and routines that can erode personal autonomy and the threat of victimization. Maintaining order and safety within prisons often requires that routines and safeguards be established. As a result, daily decisions—such as when they get up; when, what, or where they eat; and when phone calls are allowed—are made for prisoners. Over long periods, such routines can become increasingly natural (Zamble, 1992), and some prisoners can become dependent on the direction they afford. As Irwin (2005, p. 154) put it, because "prison life is completely routinized and restricted," over time "prisoners steadily lose their capacity to exert power and control their destiny. . . ." He elaborates: "Months or years of getting up at a certain time to certain signals, going about the day in a routine fashion, responding to certain commands, being among people who speak a certain way, and doing things repetitively inures prisoners to a deeply embedded set of unconscious habits and automatic responses" (p. 166). Those who succumb to prisonization may have trouble adjusting to life back in the community, which is more unstructured and unpredictable. In extreme cases, some lose the capacity to initiate activities and plans and to make decisions (Haney, 2006).

In addition, prisoners often are aware of the threat of victimization, especially in overcrowded institutions. As part of the process of prisonization, prisoners develop strategies for coping with or adjusting to this threat (McCorkle, 1992). Some prisoners become hypervigilant. Some cope with the threat of victimization by establishing a reputation for toughness, reacting quickly and instinctively even to seemingly insignificant insults, minor affronts, or slightest signs of disrespect, sometimes with decisive (even deadly) force (Haney, 2011; Phillips, 2001). Other prisoners adopt aggressive survival strategies that include proactively victimizing others (King, 1992; Rideau and Sinclair, 1998). For example, sexual assault in prison has been described as a tragic and extreme adaptation to prison's harsh context, with severe, traumatic consequences for others (Coggeshall, 1991). As King (1992, pp. 68-69) put it: "Men who have been deprived of most avenues of self-expression and who have lost status by the act of imprisonment may resort to the use of sexual and physical power to reassert their uncertain male credentials."

The process of adapting to the prison environment has several psychological dimensions. Prisonization leads some prisoners to develop an outward emotional and behavioral demeanor—a kind of "prison mask"—that conceals internal feelings and reactions. Often unable to trust anyone, they disconnect and withdraw from social engagement (Jose-Kampfer, 1990; Sapsford, 1978). Some prisoners can become psychologically scarred in ways that intensify their sense of anger and deepen their commitment to the role of an outsider, and perhaps a criminal lifestyle (Irwin, 2005).

The prisonization process has additional psychological components. In discussing the "degradation ceremonies" that are a common feature of prison life, Irwin (2005, pp. 163-164) emphasizes that "treating prisoners with contempt and hostility and persistently and systematically casting them as unworthy harms them in complicated and somewhat unexpected ways," including leaving them psychologically scarred; deepening their commitment to an outsider, criminal lifestyle; and intensifying a sense of anger that collectively "leaves them ill-equipped for assuming conventional life on the outside."

Finally, as Lerman (2009b, pp. 154-155) notes, the experience of prison may also socialize prisoners "toward the entrenchment or adoption of antisocial norms, which reinforce attitudes that undermine compliance. Similarly, it may build an 'us against them mentality' that leads individuals to feel isolated from correctional workers, law-abiding citizens, or society as a whole." This aspect of prisonization may rigidify once a prisoner is released.

Prisoners who have deeply internalized the broad set of habits, values, and perspectives brought about by prisonization are likely to have difficulty transitioning to the community. Indeed, the ability to adapt successfully to certain prison contexts may be inversely related to subsequent adjustment in one's community (Goodstein, 1979). Not surprisingly, according to Haney (2006, p. 179), "a tough veneer that precludes seeking help for personal problems, the generalized mistrust that comes from the fear of exploitation, and the tendency to strike out in response to minimal provocations are highly functional in many prison contexts and problematic virtually everywhere else."

Extreme Conditions of Imprisonment

We have repeatedly emphasized that even maximum and medium security prisons vary widely in how they are physically structured, in the procedures by which they operate, and in the corresponding psychological environment inside. We have focused our analysis primarily on what can be regarded as the common features of prison life, lived under ordinary circumstances. Living in prison necessarily includes exposure to deprivation, danger, and dehumanization, all experienced as part of what might be termed the "incidents of incarceration." The experience is not (and is not intended to be) pleasant and, as we have shown, can be harmful or damaging when endured over a long period of time. However, the aphorism that "persons are sent to prison *as* punishment not *for* punishment" (MacDonald and Stöver, 2005, p. 1) is a reminder that certain extremes of incarceration can exacerbate its adverse consequences. In this section, we consider two prison conditions that are at the extreme ends of the social spectrum of experiences within prison—overcrowding and isolation.

Overcrowding

As noted earlier, the rapid increase in the overall number of incarcerated persons in the United States resulted in widespread prison overcrowding. The speed and size of the influx outpaced the ability of many states to construct enough additional bedspace to meet the increased demand (Haney, 2006). Despite recent declines in the populations of some state prison systems, many state systems, as well as the Federal Bureau of Prisons, remain "overcrowded," defined as operating at or very near their design capacity and many cases well above it.[14]

Specifically, as of the end of 2010, only 20 state prison systems were operating at less than 100 percent of design capacity, while 27 state systems and the Federal Bureau of Prisons were operating at 100 percent of design capacity or greater (see Guerino et al., 2011, Appendix Table 23).[15] At the extremes, statewide prison systems in Alabama and California were operating at nearly 200 percent of design capacity in 2010. California has experienced significant prison population reductions since then, largely in response to the federal court directive issued in *Brown v. Plata* (2011).[16] The Federal Bureau of Prisons was operating at 136 percent of its design capacity in 2010 (Guerino et al., 2011).

In the mid-1970s, the average prisoner in a maximum security prison in the United States was housed in a single cell that was roughly 60 square feet in dimension (slightly larger than a king size bed or small bathroom). That relatively small area typically held a bunk, a toilet and sink (usually fused into a single unit), a cabinet or locker in which prisoners stored their personal property (which had to be kept inside the cell), and sometimes a small table or desk. After the 1970s, double-celling (or, in extreme cases, triple-celling, dormitory housing, or even the use of makeshift dormitories

---

[14]There are several ways to specify a prison's or prison system's "capacity." The "design capacity" of a prison is the number of prisoners that planners or architects designed it to hold. "Operational capacity" generally refers to the number of inmates that can be accommodated based on a facility's staff, existing programs, and services. The term "rated capacity" is sometimes used to refer to the number of prisoners that a rating official in a jurisdiction has indicated the prison or system can or should hold. See Carson and Sabol (2012, p. 18).

[15]Guerino and colleagues (2011) could not obtain data for three states—Connecticut, Nevada, and Oregon.

[16]*Brown v. Plata*, 131 S. Ct. 1910 (2011).

located in converted gymnasiums or dayrooms) became the norm in prisons throughout the country as correctional systems struggled to keep pace with unprecedented growth in the prison population. The use of double-celling can place a significant strain on prison services if not accompanied by commensurate increases in staffing, programming resources and space, and infrastructure to accommodate the larger population of prisoners in confined spaces. During the period of rapidly increasing rates of incarceration, legislators, correctional officials, and prison architects came to assume that double-celling would continue, and as noted earlier, the Supreme Court in essence authorized its use.[17] The new prisons that were built during this period provided somewhat larger cells, responding to the revised American Correctional Association (2003) standards calling for a minimum of 80 square feet of space for double-bunked cells, which typically housed two prisoners.

Despite the initial widespread concern over double-celling among correctional professionals, prison litigators, and human rights groups, this practice became common in prison systems across the United States. Although many prisoners have a decidedly different view, correctional officials report that it causes a minimum of disruption to basic prison operations (Vaugh, 1993). Several correctional practices have perhaps ameliorated the dire consequences that were predicted to follow widespread double-celling. One such practice is use of the larger cells mentioned above. These are smaller than the previously recommended 60 square feet of space per prisoner, and not all prisons adhere to this new standard. However, those that do—typically prisons built more recently—provide double-celled prisoners with more space than they had in the small cells common in older facilities. In addition, even in some older facilities that do not meet the newer standard, the adverse consequences of double-celling can be mitigated by extending the amount of time prisoners are permitted to be out of their cells and increasing the number of opportunities they have for meaningful programming and other productive activities.

A large literature on overcrowding in prison has documented a range of adverse consequences for health, behavior, and morale, particularly when overcrowding persists for long periods (e.g., Gaes, 1985; Ostfeld, 1987; Paulus et al., 1988; Thornberry and Call, 1983). Early research observed elevated blood pressures (D'Atri, 1975) and greater numbers of illness complaints (McCain et al., 1976). More recently, British researchers found that overcrowding and perceived aggression and violence were related to increased arousal and stress and decreased psychological well-being (Lawrence and Andrews, 2004). In another study, Gillespie (2005) observed that prior street drug use and degree of overcrowding could explain the

---

[17]*Rhodes v. Chapman*, 452 U.S. 337 (1981).

likelihood of in-prison drug use. In addition, several studies have made a connection between overcrowding and the increased risk of suicide (Huey and McNulty, 2005; Leese et al., 2006; Wooldredge, 1999). According to Huey and McNulty (2005, p. 507), "the reduced risk of suicide found in much prior research to be evident in minimum security facilities is in fact voided by the deleterious effects of high overcrowding." Overcrowding within prisons may lead to increased risk of suicide because it decreases the level of "purposeful activity" in which prisoners are able to engage (Leese et al., 2006; see, also, Wooldredge, 1999).

Establishing empirical relationships between overcrowding and inmate disciplinary infractions and violence has proven challenging (e.g., Bleich, 1989). Some studies have found a causal relationship, while others have not (for a review, see Steiner and Wooldredge, 2009). The apparent inconsistency in outcomes may be due in part to other factors of prison life that complicate research in this area, including the level of analysis at which crowding is measured and its effects are assessed (e.g., whether crowding is measured in an individual housing unit, institution, or system); the extent to which prison practices actually change (and/or are perceived by prisoners to have changed) in response to overcrowding, altering such things as classification and security procedures; and the frequency with which disciplinary infractions and victimization are reported. Prison operations adjust and institutional actors adapt in multiple ways in attempts to deal with overcrowding-related pressures. Inmate violence levels themselves are known to be affected by a complex set of forces and factors (Steiner, 2009), and even undercrowded conditions, prisoner behavior can be managed through exceptional means, such as an especially high concentration of staff (Tartino and Levy, 2007). These and other complexities likely help explain the lack of definitive research results on this issue.

According to Haney (2006, p. 202), "overcrowding may affect prisoners' mental and physical health by increasing the level of uncertainty with which they regularly must cope. . . . Crowded conditions heighten the level of cognitive strain prisoners experience by introducing social complexity, turnover, and interpersonal instability into an environment in which interpersonal mistakes or errors in social judgment can be detrimental or dangerous" (Cox et al., 1984; DiCataldo et al., 1995). Overcrowding is likely to raise collective frustration levels inside prisons by generally decreasing the amount of resources available to prisoners. In addition, overcrowding has systemic consequences for prison systems. Prisons and prison systems may become so crowded that staff members struggle to provide prisoners with basic, necessary services such as proper screening and treatment for medical and mental illnesses (see Chapter 7). In fact, the Supreme Court recently concluded that overcrowding in the large California prison system was the primary cause of the state's inability to provide its prisoners with constitutionally adequate medical and mental health care.[18]

Prison administrators can take steps to ameliorate the potentially harmful impact of overcrowding, and many of them have done so. To deal with drug use, for example, prison officials have effectively employed increased surveillance and interdiction of the flow of drugs into prisons, increased the number and effectiveness of internal searches, implemented more random drug testing of prisoners, provided significant disincentives for drug possession or use, made treatment more accessible to prisoners with substance abuse problems, and closely monitored the continued application of these measures and their outcomes. Such control efforts have proven effective as part of a comprehensive drug interdiction program in reducing overall levels of drug use even in overcrowded prisons (e.g., Feucht and Keyser, 1999; Prendergast et al., 2004).

Heightened staffing levels may allow prisons to approximate the kind of programming and increased out-of-cell time that less crowded prisons would afford (at least to the point where the sheer lack of space impedes or prevents doing so) and may serve to counteract some of the adverse consequences of overcrowding. Similarly, the introduction of improved mental health monitoring and suicide prevention programs may lessen the harmful psychological consequences of overcrowding.

As noted earlier, there is evidence that at least since the 1990s, prisons generally have become safer and more secure along certain measurable dimensions. Specifically, the number of riots and escapes and per capita rates of staff and inmate homicides and suicides all have decreased sharply from the early 1970s. Thus, however much the severe overcrowding and lack of programming may have adversely affected the quality of life for prisoners, certain basic and important forms of order and safety were maintained and even improved in some prison systems (Useem and Piehl, 2006, 2008).

There are a number of plausible explanations for this unexpected finding. For one, during the period in which rates of imprisonment rapidly increased, a greater proportion of prisoners were incarcerated for nonviolent, less serious crimes. In addition, the architecture and technology of institutional control became much more sophisticated and elaborate over this period, so that correctional systems may have become more effective at responding to and thwarting disruptive or problematic behavior. A number of commentators also have acknowledged the important ways in which decisive judicial intervention and continuing oversight contributed significantly to maintaining prison order and stability, as well as ameliorating the most inhumane practices and conditions during the period of the prison buildup (Feeley and Rubin, 1998; Schlanger, 2003). Finally, other

---

[18] *Brown v. Plata*, 131 S. Ct. 1910 (2011).

commentators have concluded that political and correctional leadership made an important contribution to the safer and more secure prisons (Carroll, 1998; DiIulio, 1987; Useem and Piehl, 2008).

As Useem and Piehl (2006) have noted, research is still needed to better understand the full range of factors that help explain the maintenance of prison order and "to develop a more differentiated view of how some systems succeed and others fail" (p. 108). Also deserving of further study is the extent to which prisoner characteristics, modern forms of architectural and institutional control, decisive judicial intervention, and the use of more sophisticated prison management practices have successfully offset the negative consequences of overcrowding discussed above. Whether and to what degree some or all of these ameliorating factors may have entailed significant trade-offs in other aspects of the quality of prison life should be investigated as well (e.g., Liebling, 2011).

Long-Term Isolation

Historically, to maintain order and safety within facilities, prison administrators have placed individuals exhibiting assaultive, violent, or disruptive behaviors in housing units separate from the general prison population. Segregation or isolated confinement goes by a variety of names in prisons in the United States—solitary confinement, security housing, administrative segregation, close management, high security, closed cell restriction, and others. Isolated units may also be used for protective custody, for those inmates that need to be protected from others but do not necessarily pose a threat to the population. Such units have in common the fact that the prisoners they house have limited social contact in comparison with the general prison population. Among prison systems, there are different types of isolation units, ranging from less to more restrictive in terms of social contact and security. For example, the Bureau of Prisons has three types of segregated housing: special housing units, special management units, and administrative maximum. Referral to and placement in these units are governed by policies for determining the level of security and supervision the Bureau of Prisons believes is required (Government Accountability Office, 2013).

In less restrictive units, inmates may have limited congregate activity with others, be provided access to programming (e.g., educational and vocational training), and even be permitted to have work assignments. In more restrictive units, isolated inmates rarely if ever engage in congregate or group activity of any kind, have limited if any access to meaningful programming, are not permitted contact visits, and have most or all of their social contact limited to routine interactions with correctional staff. The social contact permitted with chaplains, counselors, psychologists, and medical personnel may occur under conditions in which prisoners are confined in cages, separated by bars or security screens, in mechanical restraints, or sometimes all three. The same is typically true of whatever limited contact they may be permitted to have with other inmates. Even under the best of circumstances, such restrictions mean that social contact or social interaction can hardly be considered "normal." This applies to instances in which prisoners in isolation units are double-celled with others. Although they have more social contact of a certain sort, in some ways double-celled prisoners in "isolated" confinement experience the worst of both worlds—they are deprived of even the minimal freedoms and programming opportunities afforded to mainline prisoners while at the same time being housed virtually around the clock with another person, inside a small space barely adequate for one.

Estimates of the number and rates of prisoners in isolated housing are limited by variations in the definitions and terms used to denote solitary-type confinement across different prison systems, as well as the fact that few systems regularly and reliably provide access to data on these issues. With those limitations in mind, it appears that about 5 percent of the U.S. prison population resides in isolated housing units at any given time. Although it is impossible to calculate precisely and reliably whether and how much overall change has occurred in the rate at which prison systems have resorted to isolated confinement during the period of increased rates of incarceration, the fact that there are many more persons in prison means that significantly more of them have been subjected to isolated confinement. Prison censuses conducted by BJS have yielded estimates of increased numbers of prisoners in "restricted housing," growing from 57,591 in 1995 to 80,870 in 2000 and then 81,622 in 2005 (Stephan, 2008). In these data, restricted housing includes disciplinary segregation, administrative segregation, and protective custody, and these figures represent a 1-day count. In each case, some facilities simply failed to respond to this census item, which may make these figures low-end estimates (e.g., in 2005 the Bureau of Prisons simply did not answer the relevant questions, whereas in 2000 it reported 5,000 in restricted housing). A recent review by the Government Accountability Office (2013) found that 7 percent of the federal prison population was held in segregated housing units in 2013 (5.7 percent in special housing units, 1.1 percent in special management units, and 0.3 percent in administrative maximum). This represents an increase of approximately 17 percent over the numbers held in 2008 and, based on the current Bureau of Prisons prisoner population, indicates that approximately 15,000 federal inmates are confined in restricted housing.

There is general agreement that over the past several decades, prison systems in the United States began to rely more heavily on the practice of confining prisoners on a long-term basis inside the most restrictive kind of isolation units—so-called "supermax prisons." Thus, as Useem and Piehl (2006, p. 101) note: "Supermax prisons, once a novelty, have become common. In 1984, the U.S. Penitentiary in Marion, Illinois, was the only supermax prison in the country. By 1999, 34 states and the federal system had supermax prisons, holding just over 20,000 inmates or 1.8 percent of the total prison population. . . ."

The average lengths of stay within isolation units are also difficult to calculate precisely and, because of sporadic reporting by state and federal prisons administrations, impossible to estimate overall. Indeed, only a handful of states have collected data on time spent in isolation. In one public report, Colorado's fiscal year 2011 review found that prisoners spent a mean of 19.5 months in isolation (14.1 months for those with mental health needs) (Colorado Department of Corrections, 2012). Jurisdictions vary widely in the degree to which they impose determinate and indeterminate terms of isolated confinement, whether there are mechanisms or "steps" by which prisoners can accelerate their release from such restrictive housing, and whether "step-down" or transitional programming is provided for prisoners who are moving from isolated confinement to mainline prison housing or being released from prison. There have been a number of reported cases of isolated confinement for periods of 25 or more years.[19]

The rest of this section focuses on what is known about long-term confinement in these most restrictive "supermax"-type isolated housing units. By policy, these special units are reserved for inmates believed by correctional officials to pose serious problems for prison operations. The supermax prison represents an especially modern version of an old practice—prison isolation—but now paired with increasingly sophisticated correctional technology.[20] Many supermax prisoners are subjected to these conditions for years (and, in extreme cases, for decades), an official practice that had not been widely used in the United States for the better part of a century. (See, for example, In re Medley, 134 U.S. 160 [1890]). Indeed, many penologists and correctional legal scholars have condemned the practice as "draconian, redolent with custodial overkill, and stultifying" (Toch, 2001, p. 383) and concluded that this kind of confinement "raise[d] the level of punishment close to that of psychological torture" (Morris, 2000, p. 98).

---

[19] *Ruiz et al. v. Brown et al.*, CA, Case No. 4-09-cv-05796-CW; *Silverstein v. Federal Bureau of Prisons*, Civil Action No. 07-CV-02471-PMB-KMT; *Wilkerson et al. v. Stalder et al.*, Civil Action Number 00-304-RET-DLD.

[20] "Supermax prison" most commonly refers to modern solitary confinement or segregation units that are often free-standing facilities dedicated entirely (or nearly so) to long-term isolation and that employ particularly technologically sophisticated forms of correctional surveillance and control.

The possibility that supermaxes may have contributed to a reduction in misbehavior in prisons has been characterized as "speculative" by some analysts (Useem and Piehl, 2006), and the existing empirical evidence suggests that these facilities have done little or nothing to reduce system-wide prison disorder or disciplinary infractions (Briggs et al., 2003). At least one prison system that greatly reduced the number of segregated prisoners by transferring them to mainline prisons reported experiencing an overall *reduction* in misconduct and violence systemwide (Kupers et al., 2009). Moreover, some empirical evidence indicates that time spent under supermax prison conditions contributes to elevated rates of recidivism (Lovell et al., 2007; Mears and Bales, 2009). Further research is needed on the relationship between levels of use of long-term isolation of prisoners and both overall behavior within prisons and recidivism rates.

There are sound theoretical bases for explaining the adverse effects of prison isolation, including the well-documented importance of social contact and support for healthy psychological and even physical functioning (e.g., Cacioppo and Cacioppo, 2012; Festinger, 1954; Hawkley and Cacioppo, 2003; Schachter, 1959; Turner, 1983; Thornicroft, 1991). The psychological risks of sensory and social deprivation are well known and have been documented in studies conducted in a range of settings, including research on the harmful effects of acute sensory deprivation, the psychological distress and other problems that are caused by the absence of social contact, and the psychiatric risks of seclusion for mental patients. (See Cacioppo and Cacioppo [2012] and Haney and Lynch [1997], for reviews of a broad range of these and other related studies on the adverse effects of social isolaton.) As Cooke and Goldstein (1989, p. 288) note:

> A socially isolated individual who has few, and/or superficial contacts with family, peers, and community cannot benefit from social comparison. Thus, these individuals have no mechanism to evaluate their own beliefs and actions in terms of reasonableness or acceptability within the broader community. They are apt to confuse reality with their idiosyncratic beliefs and fantasies and likely to act upon such fantasies, including violent ones.

An extensive empirical literature indicates that long-term isolation or solitary confinement in prison settings can inflict emotional damage (see Haney, 2003; Haney and Lynch, 1997; Scharf-Smith, 2006; Shalev, 2009, for summaries). The overwhelming majority of studies document the painful and potentially damaging nature of long-term prison isolation.[21] Occa-

---

[21] According to Haney (2003, p. 130), "Despite some methodological limitations that apply to some of the individual studies, the findings are robust. Evidence of these negative psychological effects comes from personal accounts, descriptive studies, and systematic research on solitary and supermax-type confinement, conducted over a period of four decades, by

sional studies have found little or no harm—Zinger and colleagues (2001) document no ill effects from as much as 60 days in isolation, while O'Keefe and colleagues (2013) report that a year in administrative segregation actually benefited prisoners (including those who were mentally ill). However, numerous methodological concerns have been expressed that limit any straightforward interpretation of these counterintuitive results (e.g., Grassian and Kupers, 2011; Lovell and Toch, 2011; Rhodes and Lovell, 2011; Shalev and Lloyd, 2011; Scharf-Smith, 2011).

One noteworthy example of research in this area is Toch's (1975) large-scale psychological study of prisoners "in crisis" in New York state correctional facilities, which includes important observations about the consequences of isolation. In-depth interviews with a large sample of prisoners led Toch to conclude that "isolation panic"—whose symptoms included rage, panic, loss of control and breakdowns, psychological regression, and a buildup of physiological and psychic tension that led to incidents of self-mutilation—was "most sharply prevalent in segregation." Moreover, Toch reports that the prisoners he interviewed made an important distinction "between imprisonment, which is tolerable, and isolation, which is not" (Toch, 1975, p. 54).

Other direct studies of prison isolation document a broad range of harmful psychological effects (e.g., Brodsky and Scogin, 1988; Cormier and Williams, 1966; Gendreau et al., 1972; Grassian, 1983; Grassian and Friedman, 1986; Korn, 1988a, 1988b; Scott and Gendreau, 1969; Walters et al., 1963). These effects include heightened levels of "negative attitudes and affect, insomnia, anxiety, panic, withdrawal, hypersensitivity, ruminations, cognitive dysfunction, hallucinations, loss of control, irritability, aggression and rage, paranoia, hopelessness, depression, a sense of impending

---

researchers from several different continents who had diverse backgrounds and a wide range of professional expertise. . . . Specifically, in case studies and personal accounts provided by mental health and correctional staff who worked in supermax units, a range of similar adverse symptoms have been observed to occur in prisoners, including appetite and sleep disturbances, anxiety, panic, rage, loss of control, paranoia, hallucinations, and self-mutilations. Moreover, direct studies of prison isolation have documented an extremely broad range of harmful psychological reactions. These effects include increases in the following potentially damaging symptoms and problematic behaviors: negative attitudes and affect, insomnia, anxiety, withdrawal, hypersensitivity, ruminations, cognitive dysfunction hallucinations, loss of control, irritability, aggression, and rage, paranoia, hopelessness, lethargy, depression, a sense of impending emotional breakdown, self-mutilation, and suicidal ideation and behavior. In addition, among the correlational studies of the relationship between housing type and various incident reports, again, self-mutilation and suicide are more prevalent in isolated housing, as are deteriorating mental and physical health (beyond self-injury), other-directed violence, such as stabbings, attacks on staff, and property destruction, and collective violence" [internal citations omitted].

emotional breakdown, self-mutilation, and suicidal ideation and behavior" (Haney, 2003, pp. 130-131).

Beyond these discrete negative consequences of isolation, a number of significant transformations appear to occur in many prisoners who have been placed in long-term segregation (see Box 6-2) that, although more difficult to measure, may be equally if not more problematic over the long term (Haney, 2003). These transformations come about because many prisoners find that they must change their patterns of thinking, acting, and feeling to survive the rigors of penal isolation. Such changes are perhaps best understood as forms of "social pathology"—brought about by the absence of normal social contact—that can become more or less permanent and limit the ability of those affected to integrate with others when released from segregation.

Some of the social pathologies that are adopted in reaction to and as a way of psychologically surviving the extreme rigors and stresses of long-term segregation can be especially dysfunctional and potentially disabling if they persist in the highly social world to which prisoners are expected to adjust once they are released. These psychological consequences speak to the importance of regularly screening, monitoring, and treating; sometimes removing prisoners who show signs of psychological deterioration; limiting or prohibiting the long-term isolation of prisoners with special vulnerabilities (such as serious mental illness);[22] and providing decompression, step-down, and/or transitional programs and policies to help those held in isolation acclimate to living within the prison population and/or the community upon release.

Idleness and Programming

In recounting a day of his maximum security prison routine to the late Norval Morris (1995, p. 203), one prisoner observed:

> For me, and many like me in prison, violence is not the major problem; the major problem is monotony. It is the dull sameness of prison life, its idleness and boredom, that grinds me down. Nothing matters; everything is inconsequential other than when you will be free and how to make time pass until then. But boredom, time-slowing boredom, interrupted by occasional bursts of fear and anger, is the governing reality of life in prison.

---

[22]For example, the American Psychiatric Association (2012) issued a Position Statement on Segregation of Prisoners with Mental illness stating that "prolonged segregation of adult inmates with serious mental illness, with rare exceptions, should be avoided due to the potential for harm to such inmates." The Position Statement also explains that "the definition of 'prolonged segregation' will, in part, depend on the conditions of confinement. In general, prolonged segregation means duration of greater than 3-4 weeks."

BOX 6-2
Consequences of Long-term Segregation: Social Pathologies

Haney (2003, pp. 138-140) describes "several of the social pathologies that [he and others found] can and do develop in prisoners who struggle to adapt to the rigors of [isolation in] supermax confinement. . . .

"First, the unprecedented totality of control in supermax units forces prisoners to become entirely dependent on the institution to organize their existence . . . because almost every aspect of the prisoners' day-to-day existence is so carefully and completely circumscribed in these units, some of them lose the ability to set limits for themselves or to control their own behavior through internal mechanisms. . . .

"Second, prisoners may also suffer a seemingly opposite reaction [in that] they may begin to lose the ability to initiate behavior of any kind—to organize their own lives around activity and purpose—because they have been stripped of any opportunity to do so for such prolonged periods of time. Chronic apathy, lethargy, depression, and despair often result. . . .

"Third, [in] the absence of regular, normal interpersonal contact and any semblance of a meaningful social context . . . prisoners are literally at risk of losing their grasp on who they are, of how and whether they are connected to a larger social world. Some prisoners act out literally as a way of getting a reaction from their environment, proving to themselves that they are still alive and capable of eliciting a genuine response—however hostile—from other human beings.

"Fourth, the experience of total social isolation can lead, paradoxically, to social withdrawal for some. . . . That is, they . . . move from, at first, being starved for social contact to, eventually, being disoriented and even frightened by it. As they become increasingly unfamiliar and uncomfortable with social interaction, they are further alienated from others and made anxious in their presence. . . .

"Fifth, and finally, the deprivations, restrictions, the totality of control, and the prolonged absence of any real opportunity for happiness or joy fills many prisoners with intolerable levels of frustration that, for some, turns to anger and then even to uncontrollable and sudden outbursts of rage. Others . . . occupy this idle time by committing themselves to fighting against the system and the people that surround, provoke, deny, thwart, and oppress them.

Measuring the extent to which idleness persists across U.S. prisons is difficult, in part because of the uneven and unreliable reporting practices discussed earlier. Most inmates usually are engaged in some kind of activity during an average day in prison. The issue of whether and how much that activity is designed to produce positive rehabilitative change is more difficult to assess. Nonetheless, prison officials have long recognized that programs aimed at preventing idleness and encouraging inmates to develop skills and social behaviors are beneficial for institutional security as well as public safety (Government Accountability Office, 2012). Our best estimates suggest that during the period of increasing rates of incarceration in the United States, the availability of prison programs (such as education, vocational training, and work assignments) and the extent of prisoners' participation in these programs have improved in some respects but decreased in many others.

Many people enter prison with educational deficits and could benefit from education while incarcerated. Literacy rates among prisoners generally are low, and substantially lower than in the general population (National Institute for Literacy, 2002; Greenberg et al., 2007). Over the past 40 years, the percentage of prisoners having completed high school at the time of their incarceration fluctuated between about one-quarter and more than one-third for state prison inmates, with higher rates for those housed in federal facilities. On a positive note, basic correctional education programs have been enhanced in response to "mandatory education laws" at both the state and federal levels, requiring prisoners who score below a certain threshold on a standardized test to participate while in prison. Since the Federal Bureau of Prisons implemented the first mandatory literacy program in the early 1980s, 44 percent of states have instituted such requirements (Coley and Barton, 2006). On the other hand, as part of the "get tough" movement discussed earlier, in 1994 Congress restricted inmates from receiving Pell grants, which had been enacted and funded by Congress in the 1970s as a way for disadvantaged groups to obtain postsecondary education. Moreover, reductions in federal funding under the Workforce Investment Act cut funding for correctional education to a maximum of 10 percent (from a minimum of 10 percent).

Data from BJS's Survey of State and Federal Correctional Facilities indicate that the percentage of state prisons offering basic and secondary education programs grew between the 1970s and 1990 and has remained fairly high (more than 80 percent). The percentage of facilities offering basic and secondary education is consistently higher for federal than for state prisons (more than 90 percent). However, the proportion of facilities offering college courses dropped after 1990, reflecting the elimination of Pell grants for inmates (Jacobson, 2005; Tewksbury et al., 2000). Most prison systems now offer at least some academic or educational programs for inmates targeting different literacy and academic levels. The most common types of programs are adult basic education, general education development (GED) certificate programs, special education, and (less often) college.

The *existence* of prison educational programs does not directly translate into *participation* by prisoners. Analyses of data from the Survey of Inmates in State and Federal Prisons reveal a decline in inmate participation in academic programs from 45 percent in 1986 to about 27 percent in 2004 (see also Phelps, 2011; Useem and Piehl, 2008), with the majority of inmates participating in those focused on secondary education. These reductions may reflect reduced funding in the 1990s as more of correctional budgets went to prison operations, as well as reduced support for rehabilitation programming among policy makers and the public (Messemer, 2011; Crayton and Neusteter, 2008). In addition, not all prisoners are eligible to participate in educational or other kinds of programming. Prisoners who have committed disciplinary infractions, been placed in isolation, or been convicted of certain kinds of crimes may be restricted or prohibited from enrolling. Priority may be given to prisoners with upcoming release dates or those with relatively greater educational needs. The availability of offerings within prisons is seldom sufficient to meet demand, meaning that individual prisoners often are wait-listed until a course opening occurs (Klein et al., 2004).

In addition to more academically oriented education, many prisons offer instruction in vocational or work-related skills. As prison systems moved from contract labor to in-house production of goods, vocational education was seen as a way to keep prisoners busy and keep idleness at a minimum (Schlossman and Spillane, 1994). However, funding for prison vocational programs decreased during the period of increasing rates of incarceration. In 1998, federal Perkins Act funding was reduced from a required minimum of 1 percent to a maximum of 1 percent of funds spent on correctional education. Nonetheless, most prisons now do manage to offer some kind of vocational training to improve the occupational skills of at least some prisoners. Training is provided in specific trade areas such as carpentry, electronics, welding, office skills, food service, horticulture, and landscaping. The best prison vocational training classes teach inmates skills that are currently in demand and are technologically sophisticated enough to transfer to viable job opportunities outside prison. More recently, certification in specific trades has become important as a way to ensure that skills learned in prison help prisoners transition into the outside labor market.

The percentage of state prisons offering vocational training programs has increased slightly over the past 20 years, from about 51 percent to just over 57 percent. The percentage of federal prisons offering vocational training also has been increasing, from 62 percent in 1990 to 98 percent in 2005. As with educational programming, however, the percentage of prisoners actually participating is low, generally ranging from 27 percent to 31 percent in state prisons from 1974 to 2004 and decreasing between 1997 and 2004. The percentage participating in federal prisons has been relatively flat—approximately 30 percent in 1990 and 32 percent in 2004.

In addition to educational and vocational training, prisons offer opportunities for work experience. Work can serve as a rehabilitative tool as inmates develop and improve work habits and skills. Participation in work assignments among state prison inmates dropped from 74 percent in 1974 to 66 percent in 2005. Participation in federal prisons has remained much higher than in most state prisons—around 90 percent over the past 20 years. Most assignments are "facility support" jobs. Other options include prison industry and work release programs.

Consistently large percentages of prisoners work only in facility support jobs. These low-paid work assignments are especially useful to the prison—they include general janitorial services, food preparation, laundry, and grounds or road maintenance—but not likely to enhance the future employment options of the prisoners. In fact, the most common work assignments for both state and federal inmates are in food preparation, followed by general janitorial work. Not all prisoners are paid for their work, and wages paid for prison labor generally are very low—only cents per hour. Over the past 40 years as incarceration rates have increased, the median number of hours of work per week for state inmates has dropped from 40 to 20.

Prison industry programs produce goods and services for the prison as well as outside vendors. Such work can include a wide range of activity, such as manufacture of license plates, textiles, or furniture or refurbishing of computers for use outside of schools. In 1979, Congress created the Prison Industry Enhancement Certification program as "a cost-effective way of reducing prison idleness, increasing inmate job skills, and improving the success of offenders' transition into the community" (Lawrence et al., 2002, p. 17). Slightly more than one-third of state prisons offer prison industry programs; in contrast, more than three-quarters of federal prisons have offered prison industry programs over the past 20 years.

Some prisoners participate in work release programs that allow them to leave the facility during the day for jobs in the community and return to the facility at night, but these opportunities have declined sharply over the period of the incarceration rise. States' work release offerings have fallen dramatically, from almost 62 percent of state prisons in 1974 to 22 percent in 2005. As of 2005, only 2 percent of federal prisons offered work release programs.

In summary, the 2004-2005 figures cited above indicate that only about one-quarter of state prisoners were involved in educational programming, fewer than a third were involved in vocational training, and about two-thirds had work assignments of any kind (most of these in facility support jobs).

Given the increasing rate of incarceration and declining rates of participation in these programs, larger numbers of prisoners are going without programming or work assignments. In addition, the quality of the programs and work is likely to be undermined by the disjunction between the number of prisoners who need them and the resources devoted to meeting those needs. For example, Irwin (2005, p. 75) studied vocational training programs in a medium security California prison—in which fewer than 20 percent of the prisoners participated—and characterizes the quality of these programs in this way:

> Several conditions greatly weaken the efficacy of these vocational training programs, most important, the lack of funds and resources. Instructors report that they have great difficulty obtaining needed equipment and materials. . . Instructors are fired, or they quit and are not replaced. . . Further, the training programs are regularly interrupted by lockdowns [and inclement weather] during which prisoners cannot be released to the hill for vocational training.

Further discussion of educational and work programs within prisons is provided below and in Chapter 8.

POTENTIAL POSTPRISON CRIMINOGENIC EFFECTS

Petersilia (2003, p. 53) describes the challenges faced by prisoners being released during the period of high rates of incarceration:

> The average inmate coming home will have served a longer prison sentence than in the past, be more disconnected from family and friends, have a higher prevalence of substance abuse and mental illness, and be less educated and less employable than those in prior prison release cohorts. Each of these factors is known to predict recidivism, yet few of these needs are addressed while the inmate is in prison or on parole.

A number of recent empirical studies, literature reviews, and meta-analyses report the potentially "criminogenic" effects of imprisonment on individuals—that is, the experience of having been incarcerated appears to increase the probability of engaging in future crime (e.g., Bernburg et al., 2006; Jonson, 2010; Nagin et al., 2009; Nieuwbeerta et al., 2009; Petrosino et al., 2010; Smith et al., 2004; Spohn and Holleran, 2002). For example, Vieraitis and colleagues (2007, p. 614) analyzed panel data from 46 states for the period 1974 to 1991 and found that "increases in the number of prisoners released from prison seem to be significantly associated with increases in crime," a finding they attribute to the "criminogenic effects of prison" and the fact that "imprisonment causes harm to prisoners." A related meta-analysis found that imprisonment had a modest criminogenic effect, and that the effect increased with longer amounts of time served (Smith et al., 2004).

The psychological mechanisms involved are not difficult to understand. The changes brought about by prisonization—including dependence on institutional decision makers and contingencies, hypervigilance, and incorporation of the most exploitive norms of prison culture—may be adaptive in the unique environment of prison but become maladaptive or dysfunctional if they persist in the very different world outside prison. Cullen and colleagues (2011, p. 53S) summarize some aspects of the "social experience" of imprisonment that help explain its criminogenic effect:

> For a lengthy period of time, [prisoners] associate with other offenders, endure the pains of imprisonment, risk physical victimization, are cut off from family and prosocial contact on the outside, and face stigmatization as "cons," a label that not only serves as a social obstacle or impediment with others but also can "foster anger and a sense of defiance" among prisoners themselves.

Thus, the negative individual-level changes that often result from imprisonment can adversely affect the interpersonal interactions in which prisoners engage once they are released, closing off opportunities to obtain badly needed social, economic, and other kinds of support. Sampson and Laub (1993, p. 256) conclude that the indirect criminogenic effects of long periods of incarceration on the men they studied stemmed from how the experience ensured that they were "simply cut off from the most promising avenues of desistance from crime."

Moreover, some studies indicate that prisoners confined in higher security prisons appear to be more likely to recidivate once they are released. To some extent, this can be attributed to the characteristics of persons sentenced to these kinds of facilities. However, researchers have concluded that negative labeling effects and environmental influences play a separate, independent role. As Bench and Allen (2003, p. 371) note, in general, a prisoner "classified as maximum security instantly obtains an image of one who is hard to handle, disrespectful of authority, prone to fight with other inmates, and at high risk for escape." To control for this negative initial "labeling effect," the authors conducted a double-blind experiment in which neither prison staff nor inmates knew the inmates' original classification scores. They found that when a group of prisoners originally classified as maximum security were randomly assigned to be housed in a medium security facility, the risk of disciplinary problems did not increase. This was true even though, at the outset, the maximum security prisoners "[stood] out on a number of dimensions such as length of sentence, severity of offense, prior incarcerations, and propensity to for violence" (p. 378). The authors conclude that, in addition to positive labeling effects (so that prisoners labeled and treated as "medium security" were more likely to behave as such), "it seems naïve to assume that the classification at any level is not affected by factors such as environmental influences, behavioral expectations, and contextual situations" (p. 378). Prisoners who are placed in environments structured to house better-behaved prisoners may also help elicit such behavior.

Lerman (2009a, 2009b) discusses other ways in which exposure to certain aspects of prison life can have criminogenic effects on prisoners. Her study revealed that, "among those [prisoners] with a relatively limited criminal past—with little experience in the criminal justice system and few past offenses—placement in a higher-security prison appears to have a criminogenic effect on both cognitions and personality" (Lerman, 2009b, p. 164). She also found that the severity of the prison environment appeared to influence prisoners' self-reported "social network," so that higher security prisons place prisoners in environments where they are surrounded by "significantly more friends who have been arrested, friends who have been jailed, and friends involved in gangs" (p. 19). In addition, she found that the likelihood that prisoners who were unaffiliated with a gang before entering prison would eventually join a gang increased with the security level of the prison to which they were assigned. Even those whom prison officials identified as gang members at the time they were admitted to the prison system were influenced by the security level of the prison to which they were assigned and were more likely to self-identify as gang members in higher security than in lower security prisons.

Other researchers have found similar results and concluded that time spent in higher security prisons and living under harsher prison conditions is associated with a greater likelihood of reoffending after release (e.g., Chen and Shapiro, 2007; Gaes and Camp, 2009). As a group of Italian researchers conclude, "overall, prison harshness, measured by overcrowding and numbers of deaths in prison, exacerbates recidivism" (Drago et al., 2011, p. 127).

WHAT WORKS IN PRISON REHABILITATON AND REENTRY

In any given year, approximately three-quarters of a million prisoners leave prison and return to free society (Petersilia, 2003). Research on reentry includes evaluations of prisoner reentry programs, as well as more basic research on how individuals navigate the reentry process. The most significant barriers to successful reentry include the difficulties faced in obtaining satisfactory employment and housing, arranging successful family reunification, and obtaining health care and transportation (e.g., Travis,

2005). (Further discussion of consequences after release from prison with respect to health care, employment, and families is provided in Chapters 7, 8, and 9, respectively.)

Many corrections agencies have created special offices with staff assigned to deal specifically with prisoner reentry. National organizations, including the Council of State Governments and the National Governors Association, have established working groups to address reentry, such as the Reentry Policy Council. The federal Serious and Violent Offender Reentry Initiative in 2003 awarded more than $100 million to 69 jurisdictions for the establishment of reentry programs. In the 2004 State of the Union address, President Bush included a promise of federal support for reentry efforts. More than $13 million was granted to 20 states in 2006 through the Prisoner Reentry Initiative Award program. And more than $270 million in federal funding has been dedicated to reentry over the past 4 years through the Second Chance Act of 2007.

Some research suggests that certain kinds of proactive programs of prison rehabilitation can be effective in neutralizing or even reversing the otherwise criminogenic effects of incarceration. The advent of so-called "evidence-based corrections" has encouraged correctional administrators, policy makers, and officials to place increased reliance on program evaluation and quantitative outcome measures to determine "what works" in prison rehabilitation and postprison reentry programs—both being evaluated primarily on the basis of how well they reduce recidivism (Cullen and Gendreau, 2000; MacKenzie, 2000; Sherman, 1998; Sherman et al., 1997).

One especially promising model of prison rehabilitation, known as risk-need-responsivity or RNR (Andrews and Bonta, 2006), has been successful in reducing recidivism when (1) prisoners at medium to high risk of recidivating are targeted, (2) they are assessed to determine their "criminogenic needs" (individual issues known to be associated with future criminal behavior), and (3) they are placed in rehabilitative programs designed to address those needs in a manner consistent with their learning styles to ensure their responsivity.

In addition, cognitive-behavioral therapy, which focuses on the way "an individual perceives, reflects upon, and, in general, thinks about their [sic] life circumstances" (Dobson and Khatri, 2000, p. 908)—has been shown to improve postrelease outcomes in some studies. The therapy is premised on the notion that "criminal thinking" is an important factor in deviant behavior (e.g., Beck, 1999). Cognitive-behavioral therapy has been used with a range of juvenile and adult prisoners inside institutions or in the community, and has been administered alone or as part of a multifaceted program (Lipsey et al., 2007). Meta-analyses of numerous and diverse studies of program effectiveness indicate that under the appropriate circumstances, when conducted by appropriately trained professionals, this kind of therapy can significantly reduce recidivism (e.g., Lipsey et al., 2007; Losel and Schmucker, 2005). Perhaps not surprisingly, better results were obtained for programs that were rated as better quality, had participants spend longer amounts of time in treatment, and were combined with other services.

Medical treatment, particularly for drug addictions, combined with a "continuum of care" that includes follow-up or aftercare services in the community for prisoners once they have been released, has been found to be effective in controlling substance abuse and reducing recidivism. Further discussion of this issue is included in Chapter 7. Education and work programming have long been viewed as essential components of rehabilitation. They also serve other purposes, such as eliminating idleness and thereby reducing management problems. Moreover, when work assignments directly support the needs of the institution, they decrease the costs of incarceration. Support for such programs comes in part from research demonstrating a strong relationship between criminal activity and low levels of schooling and unemployment. However, the quantity and quality of research examining the effectiveness of such programs in reducing recidivism and increasing employment are extremely limited.

Despite the widely recognized importance of prisoner education, comprehensive, reliable data are not available on the nature and quality of programs offered, the levels of actual participation, and the overall effectiveness of various approaches (MacKenzie, 2008). Studies often examine numbers of prisoners participating in such programs but overlook the actual amount of time spent in the classroom, specific program components, and the level of academic achievement attained. Other than documenting the impressive success of certain postsecondary prison education programs, research has as yet not resolved the critical issues of what works for whom, when, why, and under what circumstances, as well as the way in which special challenges faced by inmate-students in prison, such as lockdowns, transfers between facilities, and restricted movement, affect their learning and undermine their educational progress.

The available research indicates that, when carried out properly, certain forms of cognitive-behavioral therapy, drug treatment, academic programs, and vocational training appear to reduce recidivism. As yet, fewer studies have demonstrated positive outcomes for prison work programs (such as correctional industries) and "life skills" programs. (See, generally, Cecil et al., 2000; Fabelo, 2002; Gerber and Fritsch, 1995; MacKenzie, 2006, 2012; Steurer et al., 2001; Western, 2008; Wilson et al., 2000.)

KNOWLEDGE GAPS

As discussed earlier, attempts to characterize the overall conditions of confinement and analyze their impact on prisoners in general have been somewhat constrained by the relative lack of overarching, systematic, and reliable data. The best evidence available often is limited to specific places or persons, and any generalizations about typical prison conditions must be qualified by the significant differences in how prisons are structured, operated, and experienced. Because individual prisons are different and distinct institutions, useful knowledge about any one of them must often be case-specific and tied to actual conditions. Some of the limitations in knowledge and generalizability stem from the fact that, despite the substantial national investment in the use of incarceration, there has been no parallel investment in systematically studying its nature and consequences. Official national statistics addressing certain aspects of imprisonment have been useful for the present review, but they are limited by their lack of standardization and of focus on meaningful indicators of the actual quality of prison life. We offer the following observations regarding the gaps in knowledge about the issues examined here.

Data Improvement and Standardization

During the period of rising use of incarceration, the treatment of prisoners and the opportunities available to them have varied notably across prisons. The ability to rigorously measure the extent of that variation is currently lacking. Available national-level data rely on records intermittently submitted with varying degrees of reliability by a variety of local sources. The collection of records does not cover all correctional agencies, and each source uses slightly different definitions, so even basic "facts" are not comparable. A concerted effort to promote standard and reliable data collection with expanded coverage is needed.

A national database is needed for the routine, reliable, and standardized collection of information on basic dimensions of the nature and quality of the prison experience. This database should include but not necessarily be limited to data on housing configurations and cell sizes; the numbers of prisoners confined in segregated housing, their lengths of stay, and their degree of isolation; the amount of out-of-cell time and the nature and amount of property that prisoners are permitted; the availability of and prisoners' levels of participation in educational, vocational, and other forms of programming, counseling, and treatment; the nature and extent of prison labor and rates of pay that prisoners are afforded; the nature and amount of social and legal visitation prisoners are permitted; the nature and frequency of disciplinary infractions, violence, and assaults, as well as mental health and medical contacts, more frequent and nuanced than existing data on homicides, suicides, and prison riots; and a range of more subjective (but nonetheless reliably and precisely assessed) aspects of prison life, such as the nature and quality of prisoner and staff interactions, prisoners' overall level of participation in prison decision making, and the nature and quality of grievance resolution mechanisms to which they have access.

Mechanisms for Observed Consequences

Numerous studies have documented the adverse impact of imprisonment on prisoners. Yet some individuals are known to have benefited from imprisonment, and some problematic and potentially damaging prison conditions have been ameliorated or eliminated in some jurisdictions. The extent to which prisoner characteristics, modern forms of architectural and institutional control, decisive judicial intervention, certain kinds of rehabilitative and other programming, and the use of more sophisticated prison management practices have successfully offset the negative impacts of imprisonment, such as those due to overcrowding, deserves further study. Research should also address whether, to what degree, and in what ways improved institutional control and reductions in certain indicators of institutional dysfunction have entailed significant trade-offs in other aspects of the quality of prison life. Similarly, the ways in which changes in specific conditions of confinement affect postprison adjustment also warrant further study. As noted, for example, some empirical evidence indicates that time spent in isolated, supermax-type housing contributes to elevated rates of recidivism. The degree to which higher levels of institutional control and security contribute to increased recidivism in the long term also merits additional research.

Diversion Programs

One way of limiting the adverse consequences of imprisonment for individuals is to ensure that fewer people are incarcerated. It appears especially important to consider the option of relying on alternative sanctions or programs in cases of nonviolent crime and for lawbreakers who suffer from substance abuse problems or serious mental illness. Thus, there is a continuing need for research on evidence-based diversion programs that address both societal needs for safety and protection and the social, psychological, and medical needs of those convicted, but do so in ways that are less psychologically damaging and more cost-effective than incarceration.

CONCLUSION

Increased rates of incarceration may have altered the prison experience in ways that are, on balance, appreciably harmful to some prisoners and undermine their chances of living a normal life when released. Prisons are powerful social settings that can incur a variety of psychological, physical, and behavioral consequences for the persons confined within them. In general, those consequences include the ways in which prisoners can be adversely affected by the severe stressors that characterize prison life (e.g., danger, deprivation, and degradation), albeit to different degrees, and the many accommodations prisoners make to adjust to and survive the psychological pressures they confront and the behavioral mandates with which they must comply while incarcerated. On the other hand, prisons also can have positive impacts on some prisoners, especially when they provide effective programming that prepares them for life after release.

Conditions of confinement vary widely from prison to prison along a number of dimensions discussed in this chapter. Those variations affect the nature and degree of the changes prisoners undergo in the course of their incarceration. Some poorly run and especially harsh prisons can cause great harm and put prisoners at significant risk. Individual prisoners also vary in the degree to which they are affected by their conditions of confinement. Persons who enter prison with special vulnerabilities—for example, having suffered extensive preprison trauma or preexisting mental illness—are likely to be especially susceptible to prison stressors and potential harm.

The commitment of at least some prison systems to the goal of rehabilitation fluctuated over the period during which rates of incarceration rose in the United States—ranging from outright rejection in many jurisdictions at the outset of that period to greater acceptance and commitment in at least some places in more recent years. As a result, the potential of prisons to provide prisoners with meaningful opportunities for educational, vocational, and other forms of programming has been only partially realized (and in some places, and for some prisoners, not at all).

The individual consequences summarized in this chapter underscore the importance of moving beyond the admittedly significant interrelated issues of who is incarcerated, for how long, and under what conditions; what is done with them while they are there; and whether and how their postprison reintegration is supported. It is also important to consider the possibility that less restrictive and potentially less psychologically damaging alternatives are more appropriate for a number of those who are currently incarcerated. These alternatives also may be more cost-effective and contribute as much or even more than imprisonment to the overall goal of ensuring public safety.

In many ways, the use of long-term segregation needs to be reviewed. It can create or exacerbate serious psychological change in some inmates and make it difficult for them to return to the general population of a prison or to the community outside prison. Although certain highly disruptive inmates may at times need to be segregated from others, use of this practice is best minimized, and accompanied by specific criteria for placement and regular meaningful reviews for those that are thus confined. Long-term segregation is not an appropriate setting for seriously mentally ill inmates. In all cases, it is important to ensure that those prisoners who are confined in segregation are monitored closely and effectively for any sign of psychological deterioration.

Regardless of how many people are sent to prison and for how long, the nation's prisons should be safe and humane. The physical and psychological needs of prisoners should be properly addressed in a manner that is mindful of the reality that virtually all of them eventually return to free society. The way prisoners are treated while they are imprisoned and the opportunities they are provided both in prison and upon release will have a direct impact on their eventual success or failure and important consequences for the larger society.

7

Consequences for Health and Mental Health

The incarcerated population overrepresents socially marginalized and disadvantaged individuals with a high burden of disease. Health and mental health are prominent issues in debates about incarceration, both because in many cases health issues contributed to incarcerated individuals' involvement with the criminal justice system and because the vast majority of prisoners eventually return to the community (Travis, 2000), bringing their health conditions with them (Rich et al., 2011). In addition to the causes of incarceration described elsewhere, the inadequate community treatment of drug addiction and, to a lesser extent, mental illness can be viewed as underlying contributors to behaviors leading to incarceration (and reincarceration) in many cases (Rich et al., 2011).

The public health literature has documented the existence of a set of "social determinants of health," meaning a wide range of factors beyond individual behaviors and conditions that affect health (Bambra et al., 2010; Braveman et al., 2011; Centers for Disease Control and Prevention, 2013; Commission on Social Determinants of Health, 2008; Marmot, 2005). An example is unemployment: people without jobs frequently lack the health insurance that allows them to seek medical care and the income that allows them to eat healthfully, buy medicines, and otherwise address their health needs. Housing is another example of a social determinant of health: people without access to stable, adequate housing are at higher risk of a host of physical and mental stressors, from asthma to anxiety. As discussed elsewhere in this report, prisoners, as well as jail inmates, are more likely than the general U.S. population to be unemployed, poor, black or Hispanic, homeless, and uninsured, and these social variables are all strongly associated with poor health.

Increasing incarceration rates have drawn greater attention among health care professionals to the relationships between incarceration and health.[1] They have been presented with a dilemma in that the high rates of incarceration have offered an opportunity to identify and treat vulnerable people who might otherwise not have access to (or seek) health care; but at the same time, partly for the reasons discussed in Chapter 6, prisons are not the ideal setting for medical treatment (National Research Council and Institute of Medicine, 2013).

In this chapter, we present the current state of knowledge on the health and health care of inmates and the postrelease health of prisoners and their communities. Although gaps in knowledge in this area remain, the evidence base compiled over the past 10 years makes clear that current challenges in incarceration and community health are strongly connected for some of the most vulnerable communities, and ideally should be addressed in concert. Increased rates of incarceration, affecting these communities in particular, have only magnified these challenges. We begin with a review of key aspects of the health profile of inmates. This is followed by a description of the health care provided in correctional facilities. Next, we look at the impact of incarceration on both physical and mental health, and then at health following release. We conclude the chapter with a review of knowledge gaps in these areas and concluding remarks.

The main focus of inquiry for this committee was incarceration in state and federal prisons. For this chapter's discussion of health and incarceration, however, we believe it is important to include inmates from both jails and prisons. Although there are important differences between the two types of institutions, the similarities are striking from a health perspective. Both jails and prisons house a high-risk population with a heavy burden of disease; both present health perils as well as health opportunities; and in nearly all cases, the individuals held in these institutions are then released back into the community. For jails, the turnover often is quite rapid and the numbers are much greater; although the average daily jail census in 2011 was under 750,000, there were nearly 12 million admissions to jails from July 2011 to June 2012 and as many releases (Minton, 2013). By contrast, there were under 700,000 releases from state and federal prisons in 2011 (Carson and Sabol, 2012).

---

[1]These relationships were explored during a workshop conducted jointly by the Institute of Medicine and the National Research Council in December 2012. A summary of the views and analysis presented at this workshop informed this committee's work, and this chapter in particular (National Research Council and Institute of Medicine, 2013).

HEALTH PROFILE OF INMATES

The high burden of disease among jail and prison inmates (Binswanger et al., 2009; Fazel and Baillargeon, 2011; Wilper et al., 2009) poses challenges for the provision of care but also opportunities for screening, diagnosis, treatment, and linkage to treatment after release. Much of the disease in incarcerated populations can be attributed to overlapping synergistic epidemics (syndemics) of substance use, infectious diseases, and mental illness in the context of poverty, violence, homelessness, and limited access to health care. In this section, we address in turn the following aspects of the health profile of the incarcerated population: mental health, substance abuse, infectious diseases, chronic conditions, aging prisoners, and the health of female inmates.

Mental Health

A recent survey by the Bureau of Justice Statistics (James and Glaze, 2006) found that more than half of all inmates had some kind of mental health problem (see Table 7-1). For the survey, identification of a mental health problem was based on either a clinical diagnosis or treatment by a mental health professional within the past 12 months or having presented with symptoms of a mental disorder based on criteria specified in the *Diagnostic and Statistical Manual of Mental Disorders, Fourth Edition* (DSM-IV) (American Psychiatric Association, 1994). The prevalence of

TABLE 7-1 Prevalence of Mental Illness and Drug and Alcohol Dependence and Abuse in U.S. Prisoners

Condition	Jails (%)	State Prisons (%)	Federal Prisons (%)
Mental Illness	64	56	45
Drug and/or Alcohol Dependence or Abuse (combined total)	68		
Drug Dependence or Abuse	53	53	45
Alcohol Dependence or Abuse	47		

NOTES: James and Glaze (2006) use data from the Survey of Inmates in State and Federal Correctional Facilities, 2004, and the Survey of Inmates in Local Jails, 2002, to examine mental disorders among jail and prison inmates. Karberg and James (2005) use data from the Survey of Inmates in Local Jails, 2002, to study drug and alcohol dependence and abuse among jail inmates. Mumola and Karberg (2006) use data from the Survey of Inmates in State and Federal Correctional Facilities, 2004, to examine drug use, abuse, and dependence among state and federal prisoners.
SOURCES: James and Glaze (2006); Karberg and James (2005); Mumola and Karberg (2006).

mental health problems is most striking in jails (64 percent); the prevalence is slightly lower in state and federal prisons but still is 56 percent and 45 percent, respectively. The prevalence of mental health problems is higher among whites than among blacks and Hispanics: 71 percent of whites in jails, compared with 63 percent of blacks and 51 percent of Hispanics, and 62 percent of whites in state prisons, compared with 55 percent of blacks and 46 percent of Hispanics. These figures may misrepresent the state of mental illness among the incarcerated as a result of self-reporting bias or to the extent that the accuracy of traditional measures of mental health varies by race and ethnicity (James and Glaze, 2006).

By some estimates, 10-25 percent of prisoners in the United States suffer from *serious* mental health problems, such as major affective disorders or schizophrenia (Ditton, 1999; Fazel and Danesh, 2002; Haney, 2006; Steadman et al., 2009); corresponding estimates for jail inmates are nearly 15 percent for men and 31 percent for women (Steadman et al., 2009). By comparison, an earlier study estimates that 5 percent of the general population has a serious mental illness, although the rates are not directly comparable across different time periods and studies, given variations in survey questions and measures (Kessler et al., 1996).

The presence of large concentrations of mentally ill persons within prisons and jails has been noted for almost a hundred years (Fazel and Danesh, 2002; Morgan et al., 2010; Torrey, 1995), but attention to this issue has increased since the closing of mental hospitals in the 1970s. Between 1970 and 2002, the number of public psychiatric hospital beds fell from 207 to 20 per 100,000 population (Yoon, 2011). Deinstitutionalization was intended to shift patients to more humane care in the community, but insufficient funding instead left many people without access to treatment altogether (Baillargeon et al., 2010b; Lamb and Weinberger, 2005; Lamb et al., 2004). As a result, mentally ill individuals likely became at greater risk of incarceration.

Although nationwide studies are not available, small-scale studies show the high rate of criminal justice involvement among those with mental illness who are receiving mental health services. In San Diego, for example, 12 percent of mental health service recipients were incarcerated during a 1-year period; in Los Angeles, 24 percent of Medicaid clients receiving mental health services were arrested over a 10-year period (Cuellar et al., 2007; Hawthorne et al., 2012). Mental illness frequently becomes de facto criminalized when those affected by it use illegal drugs, sometimes as a form of self-medication (Harris and Edlund, 2005), or engage in behaviors that draw attention and police response. Even with appropriate training, police have diverted such people into the criminal justice system rather than the mental health system because of time or resource constraints (e.g., through "mercy bookings," when it appears that no mental health resources are available for a person in need) (Lamb and Weinberger, 2005; Lamb et al., 2004; Morabito, 2007; Yoon, 2011).

Substance Abuse

Given the contribution of the war on drugs to the dramatic rise in incarceration (see Chapters 2 and 3), high rates of drug addiction among prisoners can be expected. Estimates of inmates with a history of substance abuse are somewhat uncertain, in part because of reliance on multiple, sometimes unvalidated, diagnostic instruments (Belenko and Peugh, 2005; Mears et al., 2002). However, national estimates (James and Glaze, 2006; Karberg and James, 2005; Mumola and Karberg, 2006) can serve as a useful overview and enable comparisons between prisons and jails (see Table 7-1).

Grant and colleagues (2004) report a 9 percent prevalence of substance use disorders within the U.S. population. In contrast, the Bureau of Justice Statistics reports that 68 percent of jail inmates have symptoms consistent with DSM-IV definitions of dependence or abuse. About 47 percent of jail inmates have alcohol dependence or abuse, compared with 54 percent of jail inmates with drug dependence or abuse, indicating a substantial population dealing with both substances simultaneously (Karberg and James, 2005). Among jail inmates, 78 percent of whites compared with 64 percent of blacks and 59 percent of Hispanics meet the criteria for substance dependence or abuse (Karberg and James, 2005). Rates are lower in state prisons—59 percent for whites, 50 percent for blacks, and 51 percent for Hispanics (Mumola and Karberg, 2006). In 2004, 17 percent of prisoners and 18 percent of federal inmates reported that "they committed their current offense to obtain money for drugs" (Bureau of Justice Statistics, n.d.-a).

Neuroscience research has demonstrated that addiction is a disease of the brain. Drug addiction is a chronic but treatable condition (see Box 7-1). Relapse is frequent, but with rates comparable to those for failure to adhere to treatment for other medical conditions, such as hypertension and diabetes (McLellan et al., 2000). The perception of addiction as a moral failing rather than a medical issue may have contributed to the low availability of treatment in the community. As a result, drug dependence remains left largely in the hands of the criminal justice system instead of the health care system—i.e., criminalized rather than medicalized. Simply incarcerating someone does not constitute effective treatment; without medical treatment, individuals are prone to relapse to drug use and too often to criminal behavior that results in reincarceration. The available evidence on drug treatment provided in correctional facilities is discussed later in this chapter.

BOX 7-1
Principles of Drug Abuse Treatment for
Criminal Justice Populations

1. Drug addiction is a brain disease that affects behavior.
2. Recovery from drug addiction requires effective treatment, followed by management of the problem over time.
3. Treatment must last long enough to produce stable behavioral changes.
4. Assessment is the first step in treatment.
5. Tailoring services to fit the needs of the individual is an important part of effective drug abuse treatment for criminal justice populations.
6. Drug use during treatment should be carefully monitored.
7. Treatment should target factors that are associated with criminal behavior.
8. Criminal justice supervision should incorporate treatment planning for drug abusing [individuals], and treatment providers should be aware of correctional supervision requirements.
9. Continuity of care is essential for drug abusers re-entering the community.
10. A balance of rewards and sanctions encourages pro-social behavior and treatment participation.
11. [Individuals] with co-occurring drug abuse and mental health problems often require an integrated treatment approach.
12. Medications are an important part of treatment for many drug abusing [individuals].
13. Treatment planning for drug abusing [individuals] living in or re-entering the community should include strategies to prevent and treat serious, chronic medical conditions, such as HIV/AIDS, hepatitis B and C, and tuberculosis.

SOURCE: Excerpted from National Institute on Drug Abuse (2012).

Many inmates have both a mental illness and a history of substance abuse. In jails, more than 70 percent of those with a serious mental illness have a co-occurring substance abuse disorder; the corresponding percentage in the general population is about 25 percent (Kessler et al., 1996; Ditton, 1999; James and Glaze, 2006; Steadman et al., 2009). Again, the rates are not directly comparable across different studies and time periods, but the health care community finds the potential differences striking (National Research Council and Institute of Medicine, 2013). Co-occurring disorders can complicate detection and effective treatment, especially when staff or diagnostic instruments are insufficiently sensitive, or where overcrowding or understaffing reduces the time spent on medical screening.

Infectious Diseases

Contagious diseases such as tuberculosis (TB) have traditionally been a major health problem in correctional facilities. One study found that in 1997, an estimated 40 percent of all those in the United States with TB passed through a correctional facility, while another study found that jail and prison inmates, respectively, had up to 17 times and 4 times the TB prevalence of the general population (Hammett et al., 2002). More recently, however, TB has been largely controlled in the United States, in contrast with some other world regions. In 2010, the lowest ever rate (3.4 cases per 100,000 population) and number of cases (10,528) were reported, and only 4.3 percent of the cases diagnosed were in a correctional facility (Centers for Disease Control and Prevention, 2012). Outbreaks are still possible in prisons and jails, however, because the presence of large numbers of people in enclosed, poorly ventilated spaces is highly conducive to the spread of TB (Centers for Disease Control and Prevention, 2004). Worldwide, transmission behind bars has been estimated to contribute to 6.3-8.5 percent of the TB cases in the community (Baussano et al., 2010).

Rates of sexually transmitted diseases (STDs) among people who pass through correctional facilities, particularly jails,[2] are higher than those in the general population (Centers for Disease Control and Prevention, 2011c; Hammett, 2006; Khan et al., 2011); according to the Centers for Disease Control and Prevention (CDC) (2011c), "prevalence rates for Chlamydia and gonorrhea in these settings are consistently among the highest observed in any venue." Prevalence is especially high among female inmates, in whom syphilis seropositivity may be as high as 28 percent, compared with 10 percent among male inmates (Parece et al., 1999). However, reported rates may understate the true prevalence in facilities that do not perform universal screening or among sex workers, who often are released from jail before testing is conducted (National Commission on Correctional Health Care, 2002).

HIV prevalence also is higher in correctional populations than in the population at large, although local and regional estimates vary substantially across facilities and states depending on testing policies and practices (Desai et al., 2002; Maruschak, 2012; Centers for Disease Control and Prevention, 2011b). States or facilities that test primarily when requested by the inmate will likely underdiagnose HIV compared with states with opt-out testing (i.e., testing is automatic unless the inmate refuses) or with mandatory testing. That said, the prevalence of diagnosed HIV in correctional facilities declined from 194 cases per 10,000 inmates in 2001 to 146 cases per

---

[2]Screening for STDs is often conducted within jails for both those serving jail sentences and those who will be entering prison.

10,000 in 2010, but remains two to seven times higher than in the general population, with an overall prevalence of 1.5 percent (range 0.3 percent to 5.5 percent) among state and federal prisoners (Centers for Disease Control and Prevention, 2009; Maruschak, 2012).

CDC recommends HIV testing for all inmates (Centers for Disease Control and Prevention, 2009). National surveys of prisons in 2004 and jails in 2002 revealed that 77 percent of federal prisoners, 69 percent of state prisoners, and 18.5 percent of jail inmates reported being tested for HIV since their incarceration (Maruschak, 2004, 2006). A large portion of incarcerated individuals are at risk for HIV because of addiction, injection drug use, sexual practices, and high-risk social networks. An estimated 17 percent of all Americans living with HIV pass through a correctional facility (jail or prison) annually. This includes 22-28 percent of all black men with HIV and 22-33 percent of all Hispanic men with HIV (Spaulding et al., 2009). Correctional facilities have played an important role in diagnosing HIV in people who have not previously been tested (Beckwith, 2010). They also are being studied as an important venue not only for diagnosing the 25 percent of people living with HIV that do not know they are infected but also, through treatment and linkage to care after release, for playing a critical role in the prevention of further HIV transmission (Granich et al., 2011).

People living with HIV frequently have other health problems, including coexisting infectious diseases. Because injection drug use is a common route of transmission for both HIV and hepatitis C virus (HCV) infections, HIV/HCV coinfection is especially common; in one study, 65 percent of prisoners with HIV also had HCV (Solomon et al., 2004). HCV by itself (monoinfection) is a "silent" infection, often without symptoms; it can remain unsuspected and undiagnosed until a late stage. Point estimates of HCV prevalence among correctional populations vary widely. An estimated 16-41 percent of prisoners carry HCV antibodies, and 12-31 percent have advanced to chronic infection, a rate 8-20 times higher than in the general population (Boutwell et al., 2005; Centers for Disease Control and Prevention, 2011a; Larney et al., 2013; Spaulding et al., 2006).

Although HCV now outpaces HIV in new cases and deaths in the community (Ly et al., 2012), it has not yet gained the same awareness among the public, including correctional administrators, which may be one reason HCV testing remains far less frequent than testing HIV (Varan et al., 2012). In addition, CDC has yet to promulgate recommendations for universal testing of prisoners for HCV as it has for HIV (Macalino et al., 2005). The high price tag for a course of HCV treatment (well over $50,000 and rising) may also discourage prisons and jails from broad-based testing, because diagnosis could require treatment on the part of the correctional facility.

Chronic Conditions and Special Populations

Chronic diseases, such as hypertension, asthma, and diabetes, as well as health conditions in special populations, have only recently become a substantial focus for researchers in correctional health. Chronic conditions now constitute a growing percentage of correctional health care needs as the result of a confluence of trends, especially the increase in chronic disease among younger Americans and the aging of the correctional population (see below). One study estimates that 39-43 percent of all inmates have at least one chronic condition (Wilper et al., 2009).

With few exceptions, the prevalence of almost all chronic conditions is higher among both prison and jail inmates than in the general population (Binswanger et al., 2009). In a national study, inmates had 1.2-fold more hypertension than the general population. Even in the youngest age group (18-33), 10 percent of jail inmates and 11 percent of prison inmates had hypertension, compared with 7 percent of nonincarcerated individuals in the same age group, and patterns were similar for other common chronic conditions (e.g., asthma) (Binswanger et al., 2009). Other local studies have found that inmates are similar to the general population on measures of hypertension, diabetes, and heart disease risk (Harzke et al., 2010; Khavjou et al., 2007). Since not all inmates receive medical screening for chronic conditions, however, these conditions may have been underreported among prisoners.[3]

Certain populations present unique health care challenges within correctional facilities. Incarcerated juveniles generally are held separately from adults; however, about 10 percent are held in adult prisons (see Chapter 6). In either setting, they are highly vulnerable and, like adult prisoners, have a higher disease burden than their nonincarcerated peers. More than two-thirds of incarcerated adolescents report a health care need. Dental decay, injury, and prior abuse are common, and 20 percent are parents or expecting (American Academy of Pediatrics Committee on Adolescence, 2011). Studies have found a high prevalence of STDs among incarcerated adolescents, as well as engagement in high-risk behaviors associated with HIV, STDs, and hepatitis and limited access to health care (see the review by Joesoef et al., 2006). A study of adherence to standards of the National Commission on Correctional Health Care found that fewer than half of juvenile detention facilities complied with recommended screening for health care needs upon admission (Gallagher and Dobrin, 2007).

Prisoners with disabilities also tend to be overlooked. Disabilities that are relatively minor in society at large can constitute serious impediments to well-being in prison. Living in correctional facilities entails activities of

---

[3]Note such conditions in the general population may also be underreported.

daily living (ADLs) that pose particular challenges to people with physical or developmental disabilities. For instance, regular ADLs include bathing and dressing, but ADLs in prison also can involve getting on and off an upper bunk, dropping to the floor for alarms, and hearing and promptly following orders against extensive background noise (Williams et al., 2006).

Finally, incarcerated veterans generally are not less healthy than the correctional population as a whole, with the exception of high rates of posttraumatic stress disorder (PTSD) (Tsai et al., 2013a, 2013b; Greenberg and Rosenheck, 2009, 2012). At the same time, they have the advantage of access to resources in the Department of Veterans Affairs (VA) upon reentry. Some correctional systems coordinate with the VA to ensure that veterans succeed in linking to VA care following release from incarceration.

The aging incarcerated population and women within correctional facilities are discussed further below.[4]

The Aging Incarcerated Population

From 1990 to 2012, the U.S. population aged 55 or older increased by about 50 percent. In that same period, the U.S. incarcerated population aged 55 or older in the state and federal prison systems increased by some 550 percent as the prison population doubled (Williams et al., 2012). The overall percentage of older adults within prison systems remains small compared with the vast majority of those 40 and under; however, those 55 and older generally are in poorer health than those younger than 55 (Williams and Abraldes, 2010; Williams et al., 2012).

As in the general population, older compared with younger inmates tend to have higher rates of typical chronic health conditions (e.g., congestive heart failure, diabetes, chronic obstructive pulmonary disease) and serious life-limiting illnesses. A Texas study, for example, found that 41 percent of prisoners aged 45-54 had at least one chronic condition, compared with 65 percent of those 55 or older (Harzke et al., 2010).[5] Older inmates also may have high rates of additional geriatric syndromes, such as cognitive impairment or dementia, and disabilities or impaired ability to perform ADLs. Like inmates with disabilities, older inmates may not be able to drop to the floor as instructed in response to an alarm or, worse, be unable to get back up again after the alarm is over, or have difficulty climbing on or

---

[4]Much of the information in the next two sections comes from the aforementioned workshop on health and incarceration (National Research Council and Institute of Medicine, 2013).

[5]The prevalence of chronic diseases may be underestimated in this study because prisoners under age 50 were not screened for many conditions after intake. In addition, most studies are based on self-reported symptoms or diagnoses, and prisoners also may not trust correctional staff (Harzke et al., 2010), be concerned about stigma associated with some health problems, or be ignorant of their own health conditions.

off their assigned bunk. Given the aging trend during the period of rising incarceration rates and the greater prevalence of health conditions among older inmates, prisons increasingly are becoming a critical delivery site for nursing home-level care and care for serious chronic illnesses (National Research Council and Institute of Medicine, 2013). As discussed later, many prisons lack the resources for such care.

The rapidly increasing population of older adults in correctional facilities underscores the importance of screening and, more important, re-screening, for cognitive impairment, dementia, and disability. Currently, a disability assessment generally is performed only at intake, even if an individual is incarcerated for decades. Older prisoners will best serve their time if placed in correctional housing appropriate to their cognitive and physical abilities. In the New York prison system, for example, as the proportion of inmates over 50 rose to 11 percent in 2006, a dementia unit was created when needs of the afflicted inmates were not served in general facilities. Many fear the need for nursing home-type care could be a growing trend if incarceration rates are not reduced (Becker, 2012; Hill, 2007).

The Health of Female Inmates

Although female inmates make up only about 10 percent of the correctional population, they have higher rates of disease than male inmates and additional reproductive health issues. Rates of mental illness are substantially higher among female than male inmates, particularly because they have high rates of childhood sexual abuse and PTSD (Binswanger et al., 2010; Lewis, 2006). A systematic review found particularly large variation in estimates of the prevalence of alcohol dependence/abuse by gender, in part because of multiple diagnostic instruments and methodologies. Nonetheless, 18-30 percent of male prison inmates exhibited alcohol dependence/abuse, only slightly in excess of figures for the U.S. general public, while at 10-29 percent prevalence, female prisoners were two to four times as likely as nonincarcerated women to have alcohol dependence/abuse (Fazel et al., 2006).

An estimated 5 to 6 percent of women entering prisons and jails are pregnant (Clarke and Adashi, 2011). The data on birth outcomes vary, but in general, babies weigh more the longer a woman is incarcerated. Reasons for these better birth outcomes likely include better access to prenatal care; decreased substance use; and for some, stable housing and regular meals. These outcomes for the incarcerated underscore the need for services in communities for highly vulnerable populations.

Studies also have shown that most women who enter incarceration pregnant conceived within 3 months of leaving a prior incarceration (Clarke et al., 2010). This finding suggests the value of correctional facilities providing family planning services. In fact, about 70 percent of women in the criminal justice system who are at risk of an unplanned pregnancy say they want to start using a contraceptive method (Clarke et al., 2006).

The prevalence of STDs (tested for on entry to prison or jail) is about 10 to 20 times higher in the incarcerated than in the general population, and at least twice as high as in the incarcerated male population (Hammett, 2009). In addition, 25-40 percent of female inmates have abnormal pap smears, compared with 7 percent of women in the general population (Nijhawan et al., 2010). Screening and treating women for such infections is important, as the health consequences of these diseases are much greater for women than for men.

HEALTH CARE IN CORRECTIONAL FACILITIES

Correctional facilities are health care providers of last resort for many people who lack access to care in the community; however, there is much uncertainty about the quantity and quality of care across these institutions. In this section, we acknowledge the legal basis for health care within correctional facilities and associated costs for both inmates and facilities. We discuss the difficulty of assessing the quality of care across correctional facilities because of the lack of uniform standards, the disconnect between correctional health care and that provided within the community, and the variations in correctional health providers and availability of treatments. We close with a reflection on the role of correctional health care in offsetting health disparities.

Legal Basis

The 1976 Supreme Court decision in *Estelle v. Gamble* found that deliberate indifference to serious medical needs of the incarcerated constitutes a violation of the Eighth Amendment prohibition of cruel and unusual punishment. *Estelle v. Gamble* led to expanded health care services for inmates, especially through a series of subsequent lawsuits or threatened litigation (Greifinger, 2010; Metzner, 2012). Indeed, the main oversight of health care in correctional settings, aside from voluntary accreditation, has been through the court system. The duty of correctional facilities to provide health care was recently reinforced in *Brown v. Plata* (2011),[6] which resulted in California's being ordered to reduce overcrowding in prisons because of the associated failure to provide adequate health care to all inmates.

---

[6]*Brown v. Plata*, 131 S. Ct. 1910 (2011).

Some have argued that the constitutionally mandated standards of care for inmates are quite low (Human Rights Watch, 2003), especially given the need to demonstrate "deliberate indifference" in lawsuits alleging inadequate care and the limitations imposed by the Prison Litigation Reform Act of 1996 (Wool, 2010). That act was intended to reduce "frivolous" lawsuits. However, critics argue that it has effectively cut off access to legal remedies for many prisoners and their advocates—for instance, through the requirement that prisoners pay filing fees from their prison accounts and especially by means of the "exhaustion rule," which requires prisoners to exhaust all avenues of administrative appeal before filing a case (Gibbons and Katzenbach, 2006; Wool, 2010).

Costs

To see a health care provider, inmates generally must submit a sick call slip and often must pay a fee. Copayments have been implemented in the federal system, about 70 percent of state prisons, and an unknown number of jails. While copayments usually are small sums (e.g., $2.00-5.00), even this low cost has been a substantial deterrent for inmates making $0.07-$0.13 per hour, who often put off health care requests as long as possible (Awofeso, 2005; Fisher and Hatton, 2010; Gibbons and Katzenbach, 2006). Some systems, notably accredited facilities, do provide waivers for copayments, at least for some types of care, such as that for communicable diseases and true emergency and follow-up care; copayments also can be waived for incarcerated people who are medically indigent. A 2003 CDC report on a multistate outbreak of antibiotic-resistant staph infections in correctional facilities cites copayments, along with staff shortages, as hindering access to timely care, which contributed to the spread of the infection (Centers for Disease Control and Prevention, 2003).

Comprehensive data are lacking on costs to correctional facilities for providing health care. The Bureau of Justice Statistics reports that in 2001, state prisons spent 12 percent of their operating expenditures, or $3.3 billion, on health care for prisoners. There was wide variation by state, ranging from $5,601 (Maine) to $860 (Louisiana) per inmate per year, with an average of $2,625 per inmate per year, or $7.19 per day (Stephan, 2004).

Generally, all medical costs are borne by the correctional institution, given the prohibition on using Medicaid or Medicare funds to treat prisoners. One small exception, which correctional facilities increasingly are taking advantage of, is the use of Medicaid funds to provide care in the event of overnight hospitalization outside of the correctional institution. The pending implementation of the Patient Protection and Affordable Care Act (ACA) and accountable care organizations may offer the opportunity to fund at least some care for pretrial detainees in jails (National Research Council and Institute of Medicine, 2013).

Standards

There are a number of international guidelines for prisoner care, especially those framed by the United Nations High Commissioner for Human Rights (United Nations, 2005) and the World Health Organization (2007), but the United States has either not ratified or not regularly monitored and enforced such international agreements. Standards for correctional health care also have been established by the American Public Health Association, the American Correctional Association, and the National Commission on Correctional Health Care. About 500 of more than 3,000 facilities have been accredited, but no systematic studies are available to provide any evidence of conditions following adoption of these standards (Stern et al., 2010). Uniform quality-of-care standards for correctional systems and facilities, which would permit comparisons to identify better- and worse-performing facilities or improvements in care delivery over time, currently are lacking. The quality measures employed and the underlying data systems on which measures rely continue to vary substantially (Asch et al., 2011; Damberg et al., 2011). In part, this variation results from the difficulties of translating quality measures used in free society to correctional facilities. In addition, there are no measures for the quality of health care during the period of transition into or out of correctional facilities, perhaps the most perilous time from a health perspective.

Screening

Some correctional facilities have served as important public health collaborators in screening for and diagnosing various infectious diseases. During the 1990s, for instance, a third of all HIV cases in Rhode Island were diagnosed at the state's correctional facilities (Beckwith et al., 2010; Desai et al., 2002). Hamden County jail in Massachusetts, which partners with community health centers, facilitates continuous care delivery by assigning new inmates, based on their zip code, to care from staff of community health centers while inside the facility and developing individualized discharge plans linking inmates to their local health centers upon release (Conklin et al., 2002). A number of other facilities have sought partnerships with community-based medical and public health practitioners to ensure that care begun during incarceration is continued following release (Lincoln et al., 2006; Wang et al., 2008; Zaller et al., 2008). Continuity of care following release is discussed in greater detail later in this chapter.

Overall, however, a disconnect exists between correctional health care and state or local public health departments in diagnosis and in planning and delivery of care for inmates and those released into the community. Testing policies and procedures remain inconsistent across states and facilities. In jails, where many people remain for under 48 hours, testing follow-through (receipt of test results and establishment of a treatment regime) is especially challenging.

Correctional Health Care Providers

The structures, quantity, and quality of correctional care vary widely both among the states and within state and local systems. The picture of who provides care in correctional facilities overall is incomplete. The largest systems typically have a full range of in-house medical services, whereas municipal and local jails often rely on arrangements with local providers. Many correctional doctors, nurses, and other health care workers are still government employees, but about 10 percent of all prisoners are held in privately owned prisons. As of 2004, 32 states contracted with private industry (e.g., Correctional Healthcare Companies, Inc.) for some or all of their medical services, accounting for approximately $3 billion of the estimated $7.5 billion allocated for correctional health care (Bedard and Frech, 2009; Mellow and Greifinger, 2007). In 2005, 40 percent of all inmate medical care was provided by for-profit companies (von Zielbauer, 2005); 77 of 88 federal institutions surveyed for a Bureau of Prisons report had comprehensive contracts for medical services with such companies (Office of Inspector General, 2008). Others have contracted with academic medical centers, a partnership some scholars have argued could facilitate correctional systems' integration into the medical community at large, instead of their remaining relegated to its fringes (Kendig, 2004). No comprehensive studies have as yet established whether the type of provider (public, private, or academic) is correlated with the quality of care provided or any clinical outcomes.

A number of state audits and anecdotal evidence suggest that private health care services to correctional facilities are particularly marked by substandard care (Bedard and Frech, 2009; Robbins, 1999). For instance, a state audit in Maryland, where health care services were contracted out among six different companies, found that 8 of 37 medical contractor employees were not present as scheduled during a site visit, including 6 scheduled to perform the required intake medical exams used to screen new arrivals for critical health problems and suicide risk (Office of Legislative Audits, 2007). Timekeeping records also showed that 48 percent of employees were working 12 hours or more per day, contravening a state cap of 8 hours designed to ensure quality of care. And the Maryland audit found a failure to respond to sick call requests in a timely manner in 39-45 percent of cases, more than 2,700 appointment cancellations in a 6-month period, and regular medication dispensing errors.

The substandard practices documented in the Maryland audit are offered for illustrative purposes, not as especially egregious examples. Insufficient levels of health care staffing and poor access to health care providers are common in correctional facilities, and may be more so where health care services have been contracted out (Bedard and Frech, 2009; Lindquist and Lindquist, 1999; Robbins, 1999). The health outcomes associated with staffing shortages were highlighted in testimony during *Brown v. Plata*, which specifically linked overcrowding to the failure to abide by constitutionally required provider-to-patient ratios. California had vacancies among 25 percent of its budgeted physicians, 39 percent of its nurse practitioners, and 54 percent of its psychiatrists, and the federal court declared even the number of positions in the budget insufficient to meet inmate needs. *Brown v. Plata* further revealed that the conditions of care created by overcrowding had resulted in a staff culture of "cynicism and fear," which made it even more difficult to attract competent clinicians and presumably affected the care provided by existing staff. The California staffing shortfalls became especially notorious in association with holding conditions for inmates awaiting treatment, particularly the mentally ill, who were held in phone booth-sized cages without access to toilets for extended periods of time.[7]

In the absence of a systemic overview of care provided in correctional facilities, it is impossible to know how representative such examples are, but anecdotal reports from other states also indicate extensive waiting periods. However, the committee recognizes that many correctional health care providers across the country are highly trained and deeply committed to their patients' well-being.

Drug Treatment

As noted earlier, a body of evidence shows that drug addiction is a chronic brain disease that can be treated effectively (Chandler et al., 2009; Volkow and Li, 2005). The principles of drug abuse treatment of the National Institute on Drug Abuse presented earlier in Box 7-1 suggest that drug treatment, in parallel with sanctions for individuals involved with the criminal justice system, can be effective in leading toward recovery from drug addiction as well as reducing criminal behavior (see also Matejkowski et al., 2011; Nordstrom and Williams, 2012). Nationwide, the current levels of treatment for substance abuse/dependence are insufficient to meet the needs of those involved in the criminal justice system. By one estimate, 70-85 percent of state prisoners were in need of drug treatment, while only

---

[7] *Brown v. Plata*, 131 S. Ct. 1910 (2011).

13 percent received care (in a 1996 study by the Center on Addiction and Substance Abuse reported in Mears et al. [2002]). Another survey found that on average, fewer than 10 percent of inmates had access to drug treatment services at any given time (Chandler et al., 2009).

Drug treatment administered by the criminal justice system has taken several approaches: assignment to interventions within the community, referral to drug courts where treatment is merged with judicial oversight, treatment while incarcerated within prisons and jails, and/or participation in reentry programs when prisoners transition from prison back to the community. Interventions for the incarcerated include drug and alcohol education, group counseling, therapeutic communities, relapse prevention, case management, cognitive behavioral therapy, medication-assisted therapy, and others (Taxman et al., 2013). Drug treatment is most effective through proper routine screening, diagnosis of the type of substance use disorder and matching patients to appropriate evidence-based practice that continues beyond incarceration into the community (Friedmann et al., 2007). The latter is perhaps most critical given the chronic relapsing nature of addiction as well as the high number of stressors and triggers that individuals face upon reentry.

Research on drug treatment among incarcerated populations is limited but improving; there have been several recent meta-analyses of incarceration-based drug treatment. One examines four types of therapeutic communities, group counseling, boot camps, and narcotic maintenance programs (Mitchell et al., 2012). The authors find the strongest support for therapeutic communities in reducing both recidivism and relapse to substance use. They find support for group counseling, but because of the often eclectic nature of such counseling, disentangling its effects on substance use from other program attributes remains challenging. The authors find no effects at all for correctional boot camps oriented toward drug-involved individuals. They find less support for medication-assisted therapies for opiate addiction on reducing recidivism in their review, but several other studies find they are associated with reduced drug use and criminal behavior (Egli et al., 2009; Hedrich et al., 2011; Perry et al., 2013).

A recent randomized trial of heroin-dependent prisoners receiving methadone treatment prior to release and postrelease (Gordon et al., 2008) found that individuals "who received methadone plus counseling were significantly less likely to use heroin or engage in criminal activity than those who received only counseling" (Chandler et al., 2009, p. 184). Another randomized trial also confirmed the importance of counseling in addition to methadone treatment (McKenzie et al., 2012). That study compared outcomes between individuals who initiated methadone maintenance treatment just weeks prior to release with those who received only counseling and were referred to treatment at the time of release. Individuals who initiated methadone treatment prior to release were significantly more likely to enter treatment in the community postrelease and did so within fewer days. The study also found that these individuals reported less heroin use, other opiate use, and injection drug use at 6-month follow-up. Additional studies have demonstrated the importance of continuity of care, often finding that when treatment is provided in prison and after release, treatment effects are magnified (Butzin et al., 2006; Larney et al., 2012; Martin et al., 1999; Mitchell et al., 2012).

Despite growing evidence of the usefulness of drug treatment programs (Chandler et al., 2009), survey results show that few correctional facilities have adopted evidence-based treatments, relying more frequently on less effective drug education services (Chandler et al., 2009; McCarty and Chandler, 2009). A survey by the Substance Abuse and Mental Health Services Administration found that 57 percent of prisons and jails provided self-help programs such as Narcotics Anonymous, but only 16 percent provided detoxification (Substance Abuse and Mental Health Services Administration, 2000). Moreover, detoxification and treatment of withdrawal most often entailed use of analgesics such as Tylenol (Oser et al., 2009), which do not treat underlying addiction and leave prisoners vulnerable to relapse and overdose upon release. Although methadone maintenance has been found effective in reducing heroin use (Centers for Disease Control and Prevention, 2002), HIV risk behaviors and transmission, and overdose deaths (Institute of Medicine, 1995), U.S. prison authorities have largely rejected its use (Nunn et al., 2009; Rich et al., 2005).

To some extent, correctional facilities simply mirror structural and organizational problems of the broader health care system in treating substance abuse/dependence (Taxman et al., 2009) and the general lack of understanding of drug addiction and evidence-based treatments, but these problems are exacerbated in the correctional setting. Correctional health care staffs generally do not include physicians familiar with addiction medicine who can educate correctional authorities about addiction as a medical condition; as a result, addiction frequently is omitted from the list of medical conditions for which treatment must be provided (Chandler et al., 2009). The lack of proper medical management of an addiction frequently undermines successful treatment of other, coexisting health conditions, such as HIV or diabetes, that require ongoing adherence to treatment (Chandler et al., 2009; Humphreys, 2012).

Health Disparities

Given the substantial racial/ethnic disparities in both incarceration (see Chapter 2) and health (Institute of Medicine, 2001, 2012) in the United States, it is important to address the relationship between correctional health care and health disparities. The preceding discussion of the potential public health role of correctional facilities as places to diagnose and treat the medically underserved suggests that capitalizing on these opportunities for care and especially for linkage to care after release could help offset health disparities in the community. Rosen and colleagues (2012), for example, found that black inmates were more likely than white inmates to see a provider for some condition, such as a heart problem, although what care actually was provided as a result of those visits is unknown.

Mortality rates in prison appear to support the argument that incarceration is associated with a reduction in health disparities. The state prison mortality rate in 2009 was 366/100,000 for whites, compared with 225/100,000 for blacks and 195/100,000 for Hispanics (Noonan and Carson, 2011). These figures reflect a black mortality rate that is 57 percent lower than that in the general black population and a white rate that is 10 percent higher than that in the general white population (Mumola, 2007; Spaulding et al., 2011). (Jails, where most inmates remain for only a few days, have much lower mortality rates [Noonan, 2007; Spaulding et al., 2011].) Patterson examined mortality data for 29 states from 1985 to 1998 and found that rates among both black and white prisoners resembled those among nonincarcerated whites (Patterson, 2010). Similar trends were identified in Georgia's 15-year survival rates between 1991 and 2006 and a comparison of standardized mortality rates in North Carolina using 1995-2005 data (Mumola, 2007; Noonan, 2007; Rosen et al., 2011; Spaulding et al., 2011). The striking difference between mortality for African Americans in and out of prison should draw attention to the context of their lives outside of prison and consideration of how that context has changed over time, particularly during this period of increased incarceration.

With some methodological variation, these studies all agree that blacks are less likely to die in than outside prison, while whites do not appear to share that advantage. Possible explanations include theories on the temporarily eliminated risk of vehicle- and firearm-related mortality that plays a prominent role in some communities; the provision of health care during incarceration; and a "healthy worker" effect,[8] whereby those in poor health are observed to be largely kept out of the criminal justice system. The latter theory is discounted on its face because the health profiles of prison and jail inmates in general are worse than those of the general population. However, the theory may play a role in the reduced disparities among inmates compared with the general population because incarceration casts a broad net into the black population, capturing a large number of relatively healthy

---

[8]The healthy worker effect, initially observed in studies of occupational diseases, explains that workers usually exhibit lower overall death rates than the general population because the severely ill and chronically disabled are ordinarily excluded from employment (Last, 1995).

black men. Thus the relatively small racial disparities in overall inmate mortality rates (Patterson, 2010; Rosen et al., 2008; Spaulding et al., 2011) may simply reflect the fact that nonincarcerated versus incarcerated young black males are at excess risk of dying, particularly from vehicular and gunshot injuries, rather than any relevant benefit of incarceration for blacks compared with whites. As discussed in subsequent chapters, however, in the long run, incarceration, as a disruptive life event experienced disproportionately by young black and Hispanic men, may have adverse effects on employment, homelessness, marriage, and other social determinants of health that end up concentrated among nonwhite families (Binswanger et al., 2012; Iguchi et al., 2005; London and Myers, 2006; Massoglia, 2008a, 2008b; Pager et al., 2009a; Schnittker and John, 2007).

IMPACT OF INCARCERATION ON HEALTH

As discussed above, a significant number of people enter prisons and jails with serious health conditions, and these institutions are required to provide them with an adequate level of medical care. Access to health care in prisons and jails is especially important for black men, who outside of prison, on average, have lower access to care than white men (Rosen et al., 2012). Prisoners are often, but far from always, willing to participate in whatever preventive health care services are available (Nijhawan et al., 2010). For example, a South Dakota study found that 43 percent of uninsured incarcerated women qualifying for CDC's WISEWOMAN Program completed all the intervention sessions, compared with 4 percent of their nonincarcerated peers (Khavjou et al., 2007). A 2008 federal audit found that federal prisons provided preventive care health services to more than 90 percent of inmates (Office of the Inspector General, 2008).

This section examines what is known about inmates' health changes over the course of incarceration, looking particularly at how the prison conditions and violence experienced by inmates may affect their physical and mental health. Unfortunately, the available evidence is limited, and we can only conclude that, overall, health probably improves during incarceration in some ways but deteriorates in others.

Conditions of Incarceration and Health

For people living especially chaotic lives, incarceration can offer respite and stabilization. In addition to access to health care, it provides stable meals; a structured day; and reduced access to alcohol, drugs, and cigarettes. As discussed in more detail in Chapter 6, however, many daily conditions of incarceration have direct negative impacts on mental health. They also affect physical health.

Incarceration is related to the incidence of infectious diseases (i.e., new cases of infection) in complex ways. On the negative side, the near-capacity occupancy of many facilities and the overcrowding of others continue to raise concerns about transmission of airborne infections, especially diseases such as TB and influenza. On the positive side, compared with some other world regions, there is little incidence of infectious diseases, particularly those requiring blood-to-blood transmission, within U.S. correctional facilities. However, evidence is growing regarding postrelease transmission rates. For one thing, the primary paths of transmission for HIV and HCV—sex and drug use—are less frequent in than out of prison[9] (Blankenship et al., 2005). Thus the vast majority of HIV and HCV incidence among the incarcerated population in the United States occurs before incarceration or shortly after release from prison or jail (Beckwith et al., 2010). HIV incidence is slightly higher among inmates than in the general population (0.08 per 100 person-years versus 0.02 per 100 person-years), but it is much higher among people who are released and reincarcerated (2.92 per 100 person-years), indicating that the highest risk is in the periods between release and reincarceration rather than during the prison or jail stay itself (Gough et al., 2010). Inmates with HIV who remain incarcerated have lower viral loads and higher CD4 counts (i.e., their HIV is better controlled) than those who have been released and reincarcerated, meaning that those cycling repeatedly through the correctional system are not only less healthy but also more infectious (Baillargeon et al., 2010a).

The effects of incarceration on general health and chronic diseases are more difficult to evaluate. Aggregate information on health behaviors and associated changes in health during incarceration is lacking, and although health behaviors of the incarcerated (physical activity, nutrition, and smoking) are now receiving increased attention from researchers, their findings are mixed or limited. For example, studies from the United Kingdom and Australia provide contradictory evidence on the amount of physical activity among men and women in correctional facilities compared with the general population (Herbert et al., 2012; Plugge et al., 2009). With respect to nutrition, the nutritional value of prison meals is far from ideal because energy-dense (high-fat, high-calorie) foods are common, although prison meals may be better than those normally consumed by people living especially chaotic lives. One of the few studies to measure inmates more than once found that 71 percent of women gained weight over a 2-week period after admission to jail, on average 1.1 pounds per week (Clarke and Waring, 2012).

---

[9]Note, however, that sex and drug use often are conducted in a riskier manner in prison than on the outside, given limited access to condoms and injection and sterilization equipment, limited privacy, and a coercive environment (Blankenship et al., 2005).

The prison environment may exacerbate health conditions such as asthma because of poor ventilation, overcrowding, and stress (which may trigger asthma attacks) (Wang and Green, 2010). Smoking is a serious problem, with a prevalence of 60-80 percent and secondhand smoke concentrations from 1.5 to 12 times greater than in the average smoker's home. There is an ongoing trend toward smoke-free correctional facilities, but although 60 percent of prison systems have total smoking bans and 27 percent more ban smoking inside, smoking remains common among prisoners (Kauffman et al., 2011). A survey of female inmates in Rhode Island also found a strong inverse correlation between the number of incarcerations and willingness to remain abstinent from smoking after release (Nijhawan et al., 2010). Thus despite some improvements with smoking bans (Ritter et al., 2012), both smoking and exposure to secondhand smoke during incarceration likely are contributors to ongoing deterioration of health, including asthma, among prisoners.

More evidence is available regarding the effects of incarceration on mental health. Two conditions are particularly associated with a serious degeneration of mental health: overcrowding and confinement in isolation units (see the discussion in Chapter 6). Strains on staffing and facilities, mentioned above in the context of *Brown v. Plata*, have had serious repercussions for wait times and holding conditions for the mentally ill. In addition to their often untreated illness, mentally ill prisoners are more likely than other prisoners to incur disciplinary infractions and suffer punishment as a result (James and Glaze, 2006; O'Keefe and Schnell, 2007), and they also are more likely to be victimized, including sexual victimization, in the course of their confinement (Beck et al., 2013; Blitz et al., 2008; Wolff et al., 2007).

In extreme cases, some prisoners react to the psychic stresses of imprisonment by taking their own lives. Various studies have documented somewhat higher rates of suicide among prisoners than in the general population (Bland et al., 1990; Hayes, 1989; Mumola and Noonan, 2007; Mumola, 2005).[10] Significant reductions in the rate of suicides in U.S. prisons have been achieved over the past several decades. Thus, suicide rates in prison dropped from 34 per 100,000 in 1980 to 16 per 100,000 in 1990, and largely stabilized after that (Mumola, 2005). Most experts believe that the reduction occurred largely because of proactive steps taken by prison officials and staff. For example, the main agency that accredits correctional

---

[10]According to data from the National Center for Health Statistics and the Bureau of Justice Statistics, the overall rate of suicide in the United States in 2002 was 11 per 100,000, as compared with 14 per 100,000 for prisoners (McKeown et al., 2006; Mumola, 2005). A match of the rates according to the demographic makeup of the prisoner population would likely make this differential even smaller.

facilities now requires, as a precondition for accreditation, that prisons screen incoming inmates for suicide risk and provide treatment for those found to be at risk and that they have implemented a program of suicide prevention (American Correctional Association, 2003, Standard 4-4373). Nonetheless, suicide remains the leading cause of death in local jails and in the top five causes of deaths in state prisons (among cancer, heart disease, liver disease, and respiratory disease) (Noonan, 2012).

Rates of prison suicide appear to be a product both of the number of traumas and risk factors to which prisoners were exposed before incarceration and the harshness of the prison conditions they experience during their confinement (Liebling, 1995). Thus, although researchers have identified individual factors and background characteristics that help predict suicide in different groups of incarcerated male prisoners, they also have identified institutional factors—the severity of environmental stressors—that play a significant role in the levels of anxiety, depression, and suicidality from which prisoners suffer (Cooper and Berwick, 2001). Many experts believe that, despite being one of the leading causes of prison fatalities, suicide is "potentially the most preventable cause of death in prisons" (Salive et al., 1989, p. 368) and that psychotherapeutic and other kinds of prison interventions can have a significant effect in further reducing suicide rates (e.g., Patterson and Hughes, 2008).

Violence and Health

A review of the health effects of incarceration must take account of violence and injury, both self- or other-inflicted and accidental. Violence and injury are considered public health issues in free society but generally are viewed as disciplinary or management problems in correctional facilities (Sung, 2010). With the decline of HIV and TB rates, injuries are now the most common health problem in correctional facilities (Sung, 2012). Fifteen percent of state prisoners surveyed by the Bureau of Justice Statistics reported violence-related injuries, and 22 percent reported accidental injuries (Sung, 2010). A New York City jail study found that 66 percent of all inmate injuries were intentional, and 39 percent of those injuries were serious enough to require care beyond the means of the facility's medical staff (Ludwig et al., 2012). Among jail inmates nationally, 13 percent reported being injured either through violence or accidentally (Sung, 2012). In a study of one jurisdiction, 32 percent of male prison inmates reported a physical assault in a 6-month period (Wolff and Jing, 2009). In a study among U.S. prisoners, 14 percent of white men and 18 percent of black men sustained fight-related injuries, although some may have forgone medical treatment for their injuries in keeping with prison culture (Rosen et al., 2012).

Certain types of injury are becoming the focus of concern. Traumatic brain injury (TBI) may have distinctive repercussions for not only long-term health but also recidivism, as it is associated with violence and criminal justice involvement (Farrer and Hedges, 2011). Although few data are available on TBIs suffered during incarceration, a meta-analysis found consistently and substantially higher lifetime prevalence among prisoners than in the general population (Farrer and Hedges, 2011), indicating the need for greater attention to targeted treatment and/or behavioral interventions for inmates with a TBI history.

Self-injury also is common. According to one study, about 50 percent of female prison inmates engaged in self-injury (e.g., cutting or ingesting foreign objects, as distinct from suicidal behaviors), although only about half of respondent states kept data on this behavior. The study also found that self-injury was most common for those held in segregation units (Appelbaum et al., 2011).

More data are available on sexual assault as a result of the 2003 Prison Rape Elimination Act, which required the collection and analysis of data on sexual assault in correctional facilities (Fellner, 2010). This important legislation is a good example of the federal government's taking an active role in responding to a problem within the nation's prisons. Sexual assault not only places victims at risk of physical injury during the assault but also increases the risk of STDs, including HIV, and mental health repercussions, including depression and suicide. Interviews with inmates reveal that many still do not report sexual assault, however, either because they fear repercussions from other inmates or correctional authorities or because they are unable to discuss the experience (Jenness et al., 2010). In a survey of parolees by the Bureau of Justice Statistics, nearly 10 percent of former state prisoners reported at least one episode of sexual victimization during their most recent incarceration (Bureau of Justice Statistics, 2012b). In a survey of current inmates, more than 4 percent of prison inmates and 3 percent of jail inmates reported sexual assault (Beck et al., 2013).

The increase in data collection as a result of the Prison Rape Elimination Act also has allowed a better understanding of both victims and perpetrators. A substantial proportion of incidents involving staff were reported as consensual (without coercion or force) and between male inmates and female staff (Beck et al., 2010; Bureau of Justice Statistics, 2012b). However, female inmates were far more likely than males to report being pressured into sexual activity by staff (82 percent of female victims versus 55 percent of male victims) (Beck et al., 2010). Based on self-report, women also were more subject to sexual victimization by other inmates; 14 percent reported such assaults, compared with 4 percent of men (Bureau of Justice Statistics, 2012b). Women who have previously been abused are at especially heightened risk of sexual assault during incarceration (Beck and

Harrison, 2008; Moloney et al., 2009). Inmates who reported their sexual orientation as other than heterosexual (12 percent of such prisoners and 8.5 percent of such jail inmates [Beck et al., 2013]) or who had experienced sexual victimization prior to incarceration also were at higher risk (Beck, 2010; Beck and Harrison, 2008; Beck et al., 2013; Wolff and Jing, 2009). Bisexual or gay men were 10 times as likely to be victimized as straight men (Bureau of Justice Statistics, 2012b).

While the Prison Rape Elimination Act required all states to collect and report all allegations of such incidents and to note whether they had been "substantiated" through investigation, serious questions continue to be raised about the completeness and reliability of the data acquired. For example, the extreme state-by-state variability in numbers of "substantiated" claims of sexual abuse perpetrated by staff members against inmates reported in 2006 (e.g., none of 152 allegations substantiated in Florida as compared with 6 of 7 substantiated in West Virginia) led one researcher to conclude "that not only are state practices of dealing with the allegations of sexual abuse strikingly different, but that some of them are also suspiciously perfunctory in determining whether evidence was (in)sufficient to show that the alleged incident occurred" (Kutateladze, 2009, p. 201).

HEALTH FOLLOWING RELEASE

In this section, we discuss the importance of continuity of care during the transition from medical care in prisons or jails to that in the community. Unfortunately, such continuity often is absent.

Some changes in health status may not fully manifest until long after release from incarceration. Evidence on the longer-term outcomes for health conditions among former prisoners is limited, but some studies have found associations between previous incarceration and heightened risk of asthma, hypertension, and stress-related diseases (Massoglia, 2008a; Wang and Green, 2010; Wang et al., 2009; Mallik-Kane and Visher, 2008). For most, the period immediately following release from prison is especially risky. While, as discussed earlier, mortality rates within prisons and jails are comparable to those among the general population for white males and lower than among nonincarcerated peers for black males, ex-prisoners are nearly 13 times more likely than the general population to die in the 2 weeks following release (Binswanger et al., 2007; Patterson, 2010; Rosen et al., 2011; Spaulding et al., 2011).

Studies show that prisoners are at great risk of suicide shortly after being released from prison (e.g., Pratt et al., 2006). In addition, those recently released are 129 times more likely than the general population to die of an overdose (Binswanger et al., 2007). Release from incarceration often is accompanied by stress and anxiety as people struggle to reestablish housing, employment, and social relations. Often people return to the same situations and social networks in which they were involved before being incarcerated and end up returning to the same patterns of drug use and other criminal behavior. The elevated risk of overdose in the days following release reflects the insufficient nature of drug treatment during (and after) incarceration. During periods of absolute or relative abstinence from regular opiate use, such as incarceration, individuals lose their tolerance to opiates, which puts them at high risk for overdose and death. Drug treatment during incarceration often is undermined by a return to the original environment. Research in behavioral science has shown that environmental triggers can dominate individual motivation (Volkow et al., 2011). As discussed earlier, interventions that follow in-prison drug treatment programs with postrelease treatment have been shown to be more effective.

Access to Health Care After Release

Almost 80 percent of inmates are without private or public insurance upon reentry, making it difficult for them to access health care services (Mallik-Kane and Visher, 2008). Because unemployment is high among those formerly incarcerated, Medicaid is a particularly important source of coverage; however, a large number of these individuals have been ineligible for Medicaid. Moreover, those who are enrolled in Medicaid often lose their coverage during incarceration (Wakeman et al., 2009). Despite federal guidance suggesting that states only suspend Medicaid during incarceration, many states terminate it altogether and take no steps to reenroll incarcerated individuals when they leave prison or jail. As a result, many lack health insurance and thus access to most health care during the critical reentry period. Implementation of the ACA in 2014 will extend Medicaid eligibility to a substantial number of those previously without insurance (Phillips, 2012). It remains to be seen how many and how well states will coordinate between Medicaid and correctional systems to facilitate the enrollment of incarcerated individuals. Enrolling these newly eligible people in Medicaid upon release should improve access to health care, reduce reliance on emergency departments, and sustain the benefit of care received in prison.

The need to improve the outcomes of prisoner reentry through assistance with employment, housing, and other transitional needs that ultimately affect health is receiving growing attention, as evidenced by the work of the Council of State Governments' Reentry Policy Council, the National Governors Association, the Transition from Prison to Community Program of the National Institute of Corrections, and many others (Travis, 2007). Correctional authorities also are increasingly addressing the problem of linkage to community-based care through discharge planning, a term that refers broadly to the process of helping prisoners prepare to make the transition from incarceration back into the community. Until recently, however, only about 10 percent of those released from state prisons in need of discharge planning actually received it (Mellow and Greifinger, 2007). There are examples of relatively successful programs, such as the previously noted Hampden County jail program (Conklin et al., 2002), transition clinics (Wang et al., 2010), and specialty HIV programs (Rich et al., 2001; Booker et al., 2013). Even in these closely coordinated programs, however, through which community providers are incorporated into prerelease correctional care, a number of inmates frequently fail to receive follow-up care upon release. In general, those diagnosed with mental illness are more likely than others to receive discharge planning (Baillargeon et al., 2010b), but they also are more likely to be homeless and to rely extensively on emergency department health care after release. Moreover, even though inmates with mental illnesses generally are given a short supply of medications upon release, their medication maintenance has been found to decline with time (Mallik-Kane and Visher, 2008).

To date there have been only piecemeal studies of health care and health status upon return to the community for those diagnosed with HIV, although two major multisite studies, funded by the Health Resources and Services Administration and the National Institutes of Health, are currently under way (Draine et al., 2011; Montague et al., 2012). A study in Texas (2004-2007) found that even when a free prescription for HIV medications was provided, only 5 percent filled it in time to avoid an interruption in their HIV treatment, and only 30 percent had filled it after 2 months (Baillargeon et al., 2009). Only 28 percent were enrolled in outpatient care in the community within 3 months of release (Baillargeon et al., 2010a). Qualitative studies elsewhere have identified factors ranging from transportation to provider attitudes that account for the failure to link to care even when financial assistance is provided (Fontana and Beckerman, 2007; Marlow et al., 2010; Nunn et al., 2010). Because people with HIV often have other health problems as well, the need to see multiple providers also can make treatment more difficult to sustain.

Community Health

Several studies are now examining networks of STD/HIV transmission associated with incarceration. These networks have been linked to the removal of young men from the community or to their return; either way, they reflect the disruption of stable relationships and a sex-ratio imbalance, both of which are risk factors for STD/HIV transmission (Johnson and Raphael, 2009; Khan et al., 2008, 2011; Rogers et al., 2012; Thomas et al., 2008). Given the disproportionate incarceration rates of young black and Hispanic men discussed in earlier chapters, incarceration has been speculated to contribute the lion's share of racial disparities in HIV/AIDS rates (Johnson and Raphael, 2009), and its role in community health may hold true for other health disparities as well. This association between incarceration and racial disparities in rates of HIV/AIDS is not simply a reflection of drug use, as this study controlled for drug use. Furthermore, community rates of drug use are comparable between blacks and whites and consistently higher among incarcerated whites than among incarcerated blacks, which would decrease the impact of racial disparities on drug-related HIV transmission.

The importance of partnering with correctional facilities in addressing community health was revealed in Chicago. There, following the discontinuation of universal jail-based screening, the number of male STD cases reported citywide plummeted—not because actual STDs were declining but because so many men were no longer being tested. The effects were visible in the accompanying rise in documented STD cases among women in Chicago, again the result of incarcerated men no longer being diagnosed and treated (Broad et al., 2009).

In addition, a recent paper examines across states how growing populations of former prisoners affect rates of communicable diseases, such as chlamydia, HIV, syphilis, and TB (Uggen et al., 2012b). The authors report that the prevalence of a given disease in communities with a high rate of individuals returning from prison decreases or increases, respectively, depending on whether the disease is routinely screened for and treated within prisons. This finding points to the importance of screening and treatment for vulnerable populations, and not necessarily to the value of incarceration.

KNOWLEDGE GAPS

As is evident from the discussion in this chapter, much remains unknown about the health and health care of the incarcerated. It is known, however, that this population bears a heavy burden of disease, and that there are many opportunities to improve the health not only of the incarcerated but also of the communities to which they return. We offer the following areas as research priorities to fill knowledge gaps regarding the health and health care of the incarcerated.

Public Health Opportunities

There is need for systematic study of ways to capitalize on public health opportunities associated with incarceration, particularly for infectious diseases such as HIV, HCV, and STDs, and also for mental illness and substance abuse. Understanding which components of the criminal justice system are or can be beneficial to individual and public health and which are detrimental is a priority. Research should help in identifying and developing strategies and interventions that can optimize the former and minimize the latter. Furthermore, it is important to understand what is necessary to implement such interventions and what short- and long-term health, public health, and criminal justice outcomes can be expected.

Research is needed to understand the extent to which underlying health issues, especially substance abuse and mental illness, contribute to incarceration and recidivism. Research in this area also needs to examine how treating those underlying conditions can prevent incarceration and reduce recidivism.

The ACA presents an unprecedented opportunity to extend health insurance coverage to many who previously lacked it and to link them to medical care, mental health care, and addiction treatment services. Understanding how best to capitalize on this opportunity and how to measure the outcomes is a top research priority.

Several special populations that present unique challenges to providing optimal or even adequate health care in correctional settings need to be better understood. These populations include women prisoners, especially those who are pregnant; prisoners who are elderly and disabled; those with cognitive impairment, including TBI; those who are severely mentally ill; youth; and others.

Data Standardization and Quality Improvement

Research is needed to identify a set of universal measures of the quality of health care and outcomes in correctional institutions. A system also is needed that fosters improvements over time in care within correctional institutions, as well as in the linkages between them and community health care. Ultimately, it would be ideal to have not only universal measures of the quality of care and outcomes, but also a fully integrated medical system with the same standards of care inside correctional facilities and out, as well as seamless care transitions. The quality and quantity of medical and mental health care provided in correctional institutions vary widely, and in the absence of standardized quality measures, the quality of the treatment provided cannot be known.

CONCLUSION

The incarcerated population bears a disproportionate burden of many diseases, not only posing challenges for the provision of care but also creating opportunities for screening, diagnosis, treatment, and linkage to treatment after release. The evidence suggests that improving the health of the vulnerable populations who become incarcerated and their communities will require integrating multiple strategies, including (1) diversion options, (2) comprehensive screening and care, and (3) continuity of care after release.

When asked about reducing correctional medical costs, a correctional administrator replied, "No problem, just stop sending me sick prisoners."[11] Correctional institutions have essentially no control over who enters and leaves. To reduce the burden of disease in correctional facilities, diversion strategies in the court system could potentially connect individuals to more appropriate treatment, particularly those with histories of mental illness and substance abuse given their high prevalence in incarcerated populations.

In light of the high prevalence of infectious diseases such as HIV, HCV, and STDs and of mental illness and substance use disorders, as well as general medical problems, among disadvantaged populations that are incarcerated, programs for comprehensive screening, diagnosis, and treatment of these individuals would likely improve their health while capitalizing on public health opportunities. Some prisons and a few jails have become important public health partners by screening most inmates for various health conditions, but many facilities screen only a few inmates for a limited number of health needs, so that many illnesses go undiagnosed and untreated.

A strong focus on reentry services, including linkages to health insurance and medical care, also is needed. Given the statistics on mortality and morbidity, relapse to substance abuse, and high emergency room use after release, many have argued that linkage to care after release is critically important to preserve individual and community health and reduce costly and often avoidable hospitalizations. Linkage to care postrelease can sustain treatments begun on the inside. In practice, however, such linkage rarely occurs in a systematic and comprehensive fashion. As a consequence, many of the diagnoses that are made and treatments that are begun during incarceration do not translate into improved health after release. Expensive and inefficient emergency room care and preventable hospitalizations result, and the investments made in health during incarceration are lost.

The ACA promises to be a turning point in the nation's health care, and—given the expansion of Medicaid eligibility; the mandate to enroll disadvantaged populations; and the inclusion of prevention, early intervention, and treatment for mental health problems and substance use disorders as essential health benefits—will provide unprecedented access to care for many people being released from correctional facilities. Yet while the ACA could remove some of the financial barriers to care, other structural and

---

[11]Personal conversation with Scott Allen, MD, medical director, Rhode Island Department of Corrections.

individual barriers, such as insufficient discharge planning, community care providers, and ancillary services, likely exist.

Finally, monitoring the broader, population-level outcomes of reduced incarceration and improved screening, health care, and postrelease linkages to health insurance and care will be important to determine their societal benefits.

8

Consequences for Employment
and Earnings

This chapter reviews the labor market literature to examine the extent
to which the experience of serving time in prison affects subsequent
labor market outcomes. In the best of worlds, those who were incarcerated would serve their time and receive treatment if necessary, and upon
release would be able to return to work or find meaningful employment.
For many ex-prisoners, however, labor market prospects after prison are
bleak. Several studies of ex-prisoner populations report that roughly half
remain jobless up to a year after their release. For example, a longitudinal
study of 740 males exiting prisons in Illinois, Ohio, and Texas, conducted
by the Urban Institute (Visher et al., 2010), found that only 45 percent were
formally employed 8 months after release (65 percent had been employed
at some point since release). Similarly, a study of 46,000 Ohio ex-prisoners
released in 1999 and 2000 found that 42.5 percent remained unemployed
1 year after release (Sabol, 2007, based on linked unemployment insurance
data). Other small-scale studies have found even lower rates of employment following release (Petersilia, 2003; Festen and Fischer, 2002; Nelson
et al., 1999).

For the most part, available employment research does not examine
the effects of rising rates of incarceration. Therefore, we cannot directly
address how the employment outcomes of ex-prisoners may have changed
as the experience of incarceration became more widespread. In addition, the
effect of incarceration, as measured in most studies, may reflect the effect
of a conviction with or without incarceration (see below for exceptions).
Nonetheless, we believe the findings discussed here suggest an increasing
labor market impact of incarceration, at least in terms of the numbers

affected, and notably concentrated among certain populations whose over-representation among the incarcerated is discussed elsewhere in this report.

Because the ex-prisoner population is skewed toward prime-age men, much of the literature salient to the discussion in this chapter focuses on men; only a few studies focus on women, as noted below. The chapter begins with a discussion of the possible mechanisms through which incarceration reduces wages and employment among former prisoners. A review of the various approaches used to estimate the impact of incarceration on subsequent employment and earnings follows. The available evidence evaluating program and policy interventions aimed at improving the employment outcomes of those previously incarcerated is then considered.

MECHANISMS

In a recent research review, Pager (2007) identifies three mechanisms that could explain the poor employment outcomes for ex-prisoners: (1) selection, (2) transformation, and (3) labeling. All three mechanisms are likely to contribute to some extent, with some perhaps being more dominant than others for certain types of inmates or institutional experiences.

Selection

Virtually all research on employment and earnings finds that people who have been incarcerated do very poorly in the labor market; there is less consensus as to whether these poor outcomes are an effect of incarceration. As discussed elsewhere in this report, those who are incarcerated have certain characteristics associated with both the risk of incarceration and poor labor market outcomes: they average less than 12 years of schooling; have low levels of functional literacy; score low on cognitive tests; often have histories of drug addiction, mental illness, violence, and/or impulsive behavior; and have little work experience prior to incarceration, with at least one-quarter to one-third of inmates being unemployed at the time of their incarceration (Travis, 2005; Bureau of Justice Statistics, 1994). Unemployment and low wages among the formerly incarcerated may therefore result not from incarceration but from preexisting low employability and productivity.

As noted in earlier chapters and discussed further in Chapter 10, many of the incarcerated come from marginalized communities. Because of shifts in the American labor market (Wilson, 1987, 1997; Kalleberg, 2011), these communities often have fewer quality jobs and more unstable, low-paying, low-quality jobs—the kind of jobs for which those released from prison are most likely to compete when they are able to compete at all. And it is to those neighborhoods—where others are marginally employed and where the social networks needed to link to quality employment are most disrupted or nonexistent—that most men and women released from prison return. It may be, then, that the employment challenges of the formerly incarcerated are driven largely by characteristics of those who end up in prison and the communities from which they come, rather than by any direct consequence of incarceration itself.

Transformation

This second explanation suggests that the experience of incarceration changes inmates in ways that are detrimental to their job readiness. Here there is likely to be significant heterogeneity in effects, with variation across both inmates and institutions. While some inmates advance their education, develop job skills, and/or stabilize their lifestyle during their time in prison, many others are worse off when they leave prison than when they arrived as a result of a range of disruptive and debilitating features of prison life. Moreover, behaviors that are adaptive for survival in prison—a taciturn demeanor, a suspicious approach to human relationships, and resistance to authority, for example (Irwin and Austin, 1997, p. 121)—often are counterproductive for stable employment (see the discussion in Chapters 6 and 7).

In addition, extended periods of absence from the labor market can erode skills and create large gaps in work histories, in turn raising questions about individuals' preparation for work. Extended periods away also can disrupt social and familial relationships (Hagan, 1993), which often are critical to securing employment. (The consequences of incarceration for families are discussed further in Chapter 9.)

Labeling

The legal and social stigma of a criminal record,[1] especially now that criminal record information is widely available to employers, may mean that mere contact with the criminal justice system can have lasting employment consequences. The labeling due to criminal conviction can result in both legal and social exclusion. Formal exclusion is imposed through the web of federal and state laws that restrict those with a criminal record from a range of labor market activities (Olivares et al., 1996; Petersilia, 2003).

The number of barred occupations and limits on employment for those with a criminal record has increased substantially during this period. The nature of the restrictions can vary from bans for anyone with a criminal record to bans for certain crimes; the restrictions can be time-limited or

---

[1]Employers often lack information on incarceration from official record sources, so many hiring decisions likely are made on the basis of convictions rather than time served.

lifetime bans. Some restrictions offer employers hiring discretion, and some provide the job seeker avenues for demonstrating rehabilitation. These hiring restrictions have been adopted by legislatures and state agencies overtime in response to diverse events. As such, these policies are spread across chapters of state laws and records and have become quite complex to navigate for those seeking employment, those seeking to hire, as well as those trying to aid persons with criminal records. There are also a number of federal and local restrictions. Neither the number of legal restrictions nor the jobs subject to restrictions have been quantified nationally.[2] However, some states have initiated inventories of their policies and restrictions. Florida, for example, identified state-created restrictions on 40 percent of the jobs in large employment sectors (Mills, 2008).

Beyond legal restrictions, employers express a reluctance to hire individuals with a criminal record, which often is viewed as a sign of untrustworthiness or unreliability (Holzer, 1996). Over time, employers have become increasingly likely to ask job applicants about their criminal history and substantially more likely to conduct official criminal background checks to verify applicants' reports on their prior criminal convictions (Bureau of Justice Statistics, 2003; SEARCH, 2005). To the extent that job applicants are eliminated from consideration on the basis of their criminal record, the labeling consequences of criminal justice contact will result in reduced opportunities for employment. These dynamics could likewise cause ex-inmates to concentrate their job search outside the formal sector of the labor market.

APPROACHES TO STUDYING EMPLOYMENT EFFECTS

This section reviews the various approaches that can be used to study the effects of incarceration on employment. We caution that, when assessing the labor market consequences of incarceration, much of the existing literature takes as its relevant comparison group those who are similar to incarcerated individuals in all ways apart from the criminal conviction that led to their incarceration. The "effect" in this case captures the consequences of both the conviction and the period of incarceration.

---

[2]The American Bar Association has begun assembling a database of collateral consequences of conviction for each U.S. jurisdiction. This work is supported through the National Institute of Justice under a provision in the Court Security Improvement Act of 2007. To date, this database contains more than 30,000 state laws that restrict access to employment, occupational and professional licenses, and other basic rights. The database is expected to include information from all states by 2014. For more information, see http://www.abacollateralconsequences. org/ [May 2013].

Surveys of Employer Attitudes

Surveys of employers have examined attitudes toward hiring individuals with a criminal record. In contrast with other sensitive topics, such as race or gender, employers do not appear reluctant to express negative views about those who have had trouble with the law. According to Holzer (1996), for example, roughly 40 percent of employers in a sample of four large urban labor markets reported that they would not knowingly hire someone with a criminal record (see also Holzer et al., 2004a, 2004b, 2006, 2007; Husley, 1990, pp. 40-41; Pager, 2007, Chapter 7). Another 25-35 percent of the employers responded "it depends" (Holzer et al., 2004a; Pager and Quillian, 2005), which suggests that at least for some employers, the type of crime or the circumstances of the conviction provide relevant information beyond the simple fact of conviction. Overall, though, the plurality of employers appear highly reluctant to hire those with a prior criminal record.

Some survey research suggests that employer attitudes vary by type of occupation, with greater restrictions being placed on sales and clerical jobs than on those entailing more manual skill (Husley, 1990, p. 43; Holzer, 1996, pp. 58-62; Pager, 2007, Chapter 7). Employers filling positions that require contact with customers and handling of cash are less receptive than those with jobs not requiring these tasks (Stoll et al., 2004). Large firms are more willing than small firms to hire someone with a criminal record (although the latter firms are less likely to conduct criminal background checks); manufacturing firms are more likely to hire such an individual than those in finance, insurance, or real estate; and employers located in the central city are more willing to do so than those in the suburbs (Stoll et al., 2004, p. 219). Characteristics of the offense and program participation also appear to matter. In particular, violent and property crimes evoke more negative reactions than drug crimes, and employers appear to be responsive to evidence of rehabilitation, such as participation in a drug treatment program or transitional work (Holzer, 2007; Pager, 2007).

Survey research allows for the exploration of a wide range of considerations among employers. At the same time, the validity of survey research is dependent on the accuracy of respondents' reports. Although employers in general appear willing to express their honest views about employing individuals with a criminal record, some ambiguity remains in determining how employer attitudes correspond to subsequent actions (Pager and Quillian, 2005). Employer attitudes are only one factor shaping hiring decisions, and abstract survey responses do not take into account other relevant considerations, such as those related to the available labor pool, the number of vacancies, and the process of conducting a criminal background check.

Nevertheless, it appears that given the choice, employers would consistently prefer to avoid hiring individuals with a criminal record.

It is worth noting that the legal system can be hard on employers, holding them liable for acts of their employees under "negligent hiring laws," which could shape hiring decisions. Complicating matters, existing laws can impose contradictory expectations, with negligent hiring laws and fair employment laws often working at cross purposes (Watstein, 2009; Pager, 2007). Little is known about how the legal context shapes employer behavior with respect to applicants with a criminal record, and case law points to rather ambiguous patterns (e.g., Mukamal, 2003). Some states have recently adopted laws, in conjunction with other reforms, designed to limit the liability of employers that hire people with a criminal record (Rodriguez et al., 2011). More research is needed to understand what specific concerns underlie employers' reluctance to hire such individuals.

Ethnographic and Other Qualitative Studies

Researchers who have studied firsthand the experiences of individuals released from prison have consistently documented the range of hardships facing those seeking employment (Sullivan, 1989; Duneier, 1999; Anderson, 1999; Goffman, 2009; Gonnerman, 2004). In a study of black men in Chicago, Young (2003, p. 95) concludes, "Nothing created as great a stigma for them than the possession of a criminal record. Each knew very well that a record was a severe detriment to finding work." Sullivan (1989, p. 69) documents some of the concrete experiences in which employment difficulties appeared to follow directly from criminal justice involvement. "Gaspar Cruz lost one job that he had held for a year after his employer found out that he had been in jail. . . . Miguel Tirado lost four different jobs in the course of a six-month period during which he had to make weekly court appearances. He did not want to tell his employers that he had to go to court and could not otherwise explain his absences." Sullivan also finds that individuals who had assistance through employment services or personal networks were more likely to obtain a job than those without such help.

These cases illustrate the stigma and subsequent disruption associated with incarceration, as well as the importance of the reentry context. Eli Anderson's (1999, p. 244) research illustrates the psychological toll exacted by such experiences. He describes John Turner, a young man whose initially minor contact with the criminal justice system triggered a sequence of adverse events. "After John had finished completing the successive weekends in jail, there was no job waiting for him. He then looked for a new job, without success, for many weeks. The places where he inquired told him they needed no help or that they would call him—which they never did. As his best efforts repeatedly proved unsuccessful, he became increasingly demoralized" (see also Harding, 2003). These accounts suggest a possible negative feedback cycle through which repeated encounters with rejection may lead to cynicism and withdrawal from formal labor market activity (see also Black, 2009).

Ethnographic studies offer a detailed view of the complex pathways that lead from prison to home. However, this complexity makes it difficult to draw simple conclusions about the net impact of any single factor. As Goffman's (2009) recent study shows—criminal justice entanglements can sometimes become an excuse invoked by young men to relieve themselves of the responsibility of getting a job, regardless of whether they could have done so absent the criminal record. Yet even without a clear causal story, the pervasive finding that respondents *perceive* their record to be a significant impediment to finding work is important in its own right. To the extent that individuals become discouraged in their search for work or avoid formal employment opportunities preemptively, real distortions in labor market outcomes based on these supply-side responses may occur.

Experimental Approaches to Studying Criminal Stigma

With experimental methods, researchers can control for nonrandom selection into a treatment group (e.g., incarceration) to isolate causal pathways. Several studies have used experiments to examine the labeling effects of incarceration on employment decisions. Much of the rigorous work accomplished to date was inspired by a classic study by Schwartz and Skolnick (1962) in which researchers prepared four fictitious resumes to present to prospective employers for an unskilled hotel job. Three of the four résumés reflected varying levels of criminal justice contact related to an assault charge, ranging from conviction to arrest to acquittal; the fourth résumé reflected no criminal record. Each of the applicants with a criminal record was less likely to be considered for the job relative to the noncriminal control, even when the individual had subsequently been cleared of any wrongdoing. Although the severity of the criminal record mattered, these results suggest that mere contact with the criminal justice system can have serious negative effects on employment.

Several later studies have formalized and extended Schwartz and Skolnick's design, varying the types of crimes committed by the hypothetical applicants or the national context (Finn and Fontaine, 1985; Boshier and Johnson, 1974; Buikhuisen and Dijksterhuis, 1971). Most recently, Pager (2003) and Pager and colleagues (2009b) conducted a series of experimental in-person audit studies of entry-level jobs in Milwaukee and New York City, respectively. In these studies, résumés reflecting equivalent schooling and work histories were assigned to pairs of trained testers, with one tester in the pair receiving a criminal record condition; the member of each pair receiving this condition alternated each week. The results from both cities indicate that employers strongly disfavored job seekers with a criminal record (with reductions in callbacks of 30-60 percent), the penalty of a criminal record being especially large for blacks.[3]

Beyond the effect of a criminal record in these studies, the direct effect of race also loomed large. In both Milwaukee and New York, blacks with a clean record experienced callback rates similar to those of whites with a felony conviction. Some have argued that contemporary racial discrimination can in part be explained by employers' concerns about crime, with race being used as a proxy for criminality (Pager, 2007; Alexander, 2012). Holzer and colleagues (2006) suggest that employers who are reluctant to hire those with a criminal record and who conduct criminal background checks are more likely to hire blacks than those who do not conduct background checks (who may instead engage in statistical discrimination) (see also Bushway, 2004). To the extent that the growth of incarceration and racial disproportionality therein may contribute to perceptions of widespread criminality among young black men, the estimated impact of incarceration on employment may be understated. In this case, the rise of incarceration may have consequences above and beyond its individual-level effects. Pervasive contact with the criminal justice system at today's scale has consequences for racial stratification that extend well beyond individuals behind bars.

Experimental studies offer a rigorous measure of causality, eliminating many of the problems of selection endemic to observational research. At the same time, experiments have their limitations. For one thing, the applicant profile used in experiments cannot capture the diversity of characteristics represented among the ex-prisoner population; estimates then may be generalizable only to those of the chosen profile (e.g., conviction type, age, education level). Further, experiments rely on samples of help-wanted ads and direct application procedures. To the extent that ex-prisoners find work through networks or intermediaries, audit studies may overestimate the barriers they encounter in the open labor market. Likewise, job applicants with a criminal record may apply to systematically different kinds of jobs from those that are audited, further limiting the external validity of the results. Despite these limitations, field experiments provide compelling evidence that, under specific conditions, the stigma of a criminal record is substantial for those seeking employment.

---

[3]In Milwaukee, whites with no criminal record received callbacks 30 percent of the time, compared with 17 percent for whites with a criminal record, 14 percent for blacks with no criminal record, and 5 percent for blacks with a criminal record. In New York City, whites with no criminal record received callbacks or job offers 31 percent of the time, compared with 22 percent for whites with a criminal record, 25 percent for blacks with no criminal record, and 10 percent for blacks with a criminal record.

Analysis of Survey Data

It may be possible to address limits on the external validity of audit studies by analyzing surveys drawn from the population of workers with an incarceration record. Using survey results to analyze the labor market effects of incarceration is challenging because few data collections follow people in and out of institutional settings. Panel data from the 1979 and 1997 cohorts of the National Longitudinal Survey of Youth (NLSY) are exceptional because interviews are conducted with respondents if they become incarcerated. Likewise, the Fragile Families Survey of Child Well-Being, a panel survey of mainly low-income parents in urban areas, began interviewing incarcerated male respondents a few years after the first-round survey was fielded. Information on the incarceration status of survey respondents also has been collected indirectly, with retrospective reports for the NLSY cohorts, Fragile Families, and the National Youth Survey and with an item for survey nonresponse in the Panel Study of Income Dynamics, which records incarceration as a reason for noninterview.

Besides the possibility of population inference, survey data provide detailed measurement of labor market outcomes. Respondents often are asked about their current employment status, earnings, occupation, hours worked, job tenure, and multiple job holding. Measures of earnings are not confined to those on which taxes and unemployment insurance contributions are assessed.

Against these advantages, survey data have two main limitations. First, surveys may measure criminal justice system involvement imprecisely or with error. Questions about prior incarceration in the NLSY79 and the Fragile Families Survey, for example, do not obtain information about the timing of incarceration, preventing estimation of the pre/postincarceration difference in earning. Survey respondents also may be unwilling to report prior incarceration, and some may count short terms of jail incarceration while others count only imprisonment. Problems of measurement can be overcome when incarceration is directly observed, with survey interviews conducted in prison being recorded. This direct observation of incarceration has been used in a number of studies of wages and family income (e.g., Western, 2002; Raphael, 2007; Geller et al., 2011).

The second important limitation of survey data is that sample sizes for incarcerated respondents are relatively small. In the NLSY79, around 7 percent of approximately 5,000 male respondents reported incarceration or were interviewed in prison at some point before age 40. With such small samples, analyses of population subsets, say, by race or age, will have low statistical power.

Data limitations aside, all observational studies—survey, qualitative, and administrative—pose the problem of nonrandom selection into incarceration. Survey studies have dealt with this threat to causal inference in three main ways. First, to adjust for selection on observables, survey analysis has controlled for variables that are unusual in standard labor market studies but useful for the estimation of incarceration effects. Measures of drinking, smoking, drug use, aggressive or impulsive personality, juvenile incarceration and criminal involvement, and domestic violence all have been used as controls in regression analyses of employment and income. Second, panel data studies can control for all time-invariant factors correlated with incarceration and earnings with individual-level fixed effects. Finally, Lalonde's (1986) classic study of the National Supported Work Demonstration shows that treatment effects estimated with observational data can be aligned with experimental results when analysis is restricted to subsets of the population likely to receive the treatment. Researchers have thus analyzed subsets of crime-involved survey respondents instead of entire samples (Western, 2006, Chapter 5; Grogger, 1995).

Each of these strategies defines different comparison groups for the estimation of incarceration's consequences. Regression adjustment compares formerly incarcerated workers with observably similar workers who have not been incarcerated. Fixed effects analysis removes cross-sectional variation and compares the formerly incarcerated with themselves prior to incarceration. Sample restrictions compare the formerly incarcerated with those who are not incarcerated but observably at risk of incarceration, including those who may later be incarcerated.

Table 8-1 summarizes several studies of survey data. The survey studies consistently indicate reductions in employment, wages, and annual incomes associated with incarceration. The findings suggest that employment declines 10 to 20 percent after incarceration. A similar incarceration consequence is estimated for hourly wages. In one analysis of the 1979 cohort of the NLSY, annual incomes are estimated to fall by more than 30 percent (Western, 2006). In the general population, wages grow strongly with age at least until the mid-40s. Formerly incarcerated respondents in the NLSY exhibit very little earnings growth, a pattern clearly evident in the administrative data as well.

Use of Administrative Data

While survey studies are relatively rare, a number of researchers have analyzed administrative data linking court or correctional records to earnings data obtained from state unemployment insurance (UI) systems. Analyzing administrative records enables the collection of very large samples, often with thousands of formerly incarcerated workers. Administrative data also can provide detailed information about the court process and sentencing. Thus studies have been able to distinguish prison from jail incarceration

TABLE 8-1 Analyses of the Labor Market Effects of Incarceration Using Survey Data

Study	Data Source	Outcome Studied	Negative Effect?
Freeman (1992)	NLSY79	Annual employment	Yes
	BYS	Current employment	Yes
	ICY	Current employment	Yes
Western (2006)	NLSY79	Hourly wages	Yes
		Annual employment	Yes
		Annual earnings	Yes
Raphael (2007)	NLSY79	Annual employment	Yes
		Hourly wages	Mixed
Apel and Sweeten (2010)	NLSY97	Annual employment	Yes
		Hourly wages	No

NOTE: BYS = 1989 Boston Youth Survey; ICY = 1979-1980 Inner City Youth Survey; NLSY = National Longitudinal Survey of Youth.

(Grogger, 1995), and the random assignment of judges to cases has been a source of exogenous variation used to identify incarceration effects through an instrumental variables approach (Kling, 2006; Loeffler, 2012).

Despite their advantages, administrative data suffer from three main limitations. First, court and correctional records used for analysis often include relatively little covariate information. Detailed controls for such factors as schooling, work experience, juvenile criminal involvement, or cognitive ability that are available in survey data are rarely included in administrative records.

Second, most administrative studies are based on linkage of court and UI records. Record linkage generally is based on names, social security numbers, and dates of birth. These identifiers can be unreliable in court records for a population for whom varying identifying information is presented. Some of the difficulty posed by the quality of identifiers for record linkage is reflected in the match rate between criminal records and UI earnings histories. Match rates of around 60 to 70 percent are common, so earnings for 30 to 40 percent of the administrative samples remain unobserved.[4] Little is known about the biases that might be introduced by match failure, although it appears unlikely to be randomly distributed.

---

[4]As discussed further below, these poor match rates are likely due to some combination of inferior data quality and the prevalence of sample members who have not worked in UI-covered employment.

The third difficulty posed by administrative studies concerns the measurement of earnings with UI records. If the formerly incarcerated are working in non-UI-covered (e.g., informal or casual) or interstate jobs, they will not be included in UI records. Indeed, a longitudinal study of ex-prisoners in three states found that 8 months after release, respondents were more likely to have received income from informal work (47 percent) than from formal employment (41 percent) (Visher et al., 2011). Likewise, analyzing a sample of male youth with a prior arrest, Kornfeld and Bloom (1999) show that UI earnings are 70 to 100 percent lower than self-reported earnings. Holzer (2009, p. 252) similarly observes "that the very low quarterly employment rates [in UI data] are dramatically lower than those found in any of the NLSY studies or in any other survey of those incarcerated." Holzer (2009) goes on to note that the direction of bias will depend on the incidence of underreporting before and after incarceration. If younger (preincarceration) workers are more involved in casual employment and postincarceration workers are more involved in the formal labor market while on parole or subject to child support obligations, the post-pre difference will be biased upwards (i.e., will lead to the inaccurate conclusion that incarceration is associated with higher rates of employment). Indeed, in a study by Piehl (2009, p. 8), individuals in a prerelease program in Maryland referred to the onerous requirement that they participate in formal employment despite more lucrative opportunities to be found in informal (non-UI-covered) work. To the extent that the formal requirements of parole induce movement from informal to formal employment, pre/postincarceration estimates of employment based on administrative records may overstate the relative employment successes of those recently released from prison. In summary, the limitations of administrative data may contribute to both noise and a positive bias in the estimation of incarceration's effects on labor market outcomes.

Despite these challenges, several studies yield evidence of the negative effects of incarceration on quarterly employment and earnings (see Table 8-2). Grogger (1995) and Waldfogel (1994) both report reductions in employment of around 5 percent. These two studies also report similar earnings losses of 10 to 30 percent. Grogger's (1995) analysis is able to distinguish the effects of arrest, probation, jail incarceration, and imprisonment. Six quarters after admission to incarceration, Grogger (1995) reports large negative effects of jail and prison on earnings and employment. The imprisonment effect may reflect time out of the labor market due to incarceration, although jail terms typically are shorter than a year, so low

TABLE 8-2 Analyses of the Labor Market Effects of Incarceration Using Administrative Data

Study	Data Source	Outcome Studied	Negative Effect?
Waldfogel (1994)	Probation reports	Monthly income	Yes
		Monthly employment	Yes
Grogger (1995)	UI and court (California)	Quarterly UI employment	Yes
		UI quarterly earnings	Yes
Kling (2006)	UI and court records (California and Florida)	Quarterly UI employment	No
		UI quarterly earnings	No
		UI poverty	No
Sabol (2007)	UI and DOC (Ohio)	Quarterly UI employment	Mixed
Pettit and Lyons (2007)	UI and DOC (Washington)	Quarterly UI employment	Mixed
Lalonde and Cho (2008)*	UI and DOC (Illinois)	Quarterly UI employment	No
Loeffler (2012)	UI and jail (Cook County, Illinois)	Quarterly UI employment	No

NOTE: DOC = department of corrections; UI = unemployment insurance.
*Analysis is confined to women enrolled in welfare and social service programs.

employment and earnings after a year are interpreted as postrelease effects.[5] Negative long-term effects of imprisonment also were found in a sample of prisoners in Washington State (Pettit and Lyons, 2007) and in Ohio (Sabol, 2007). Characteristic of recent studies using administrative data, Pettit and Lyons (2007) and Sabol (2007) also find small increases in UI employment immediately after release compared with preincarceration levels, perhaps reflecting the necessity of formal-sector employment as a condition of parole (see, e.g., Piehl, 2009, p. 8).

Several recent studies of administrative data provide much weaker evidence for the negative effects of incarceration on labor market outcomes. In

---

[5]Note that Grogger was unable to observe actual release dates, and thus some estimates may be biased downward (away from zero) because of continued incarceration. Estimates for jail populations are less affected by this concern as it is uncommon for inmates to remain in jail longer than 1 year.

particular, studies by Kling (2006), Loeffler (2012), and Lalonde and Cho (2008) all suggest that incarceration has no significant negative effect on these outcomes. In contrast to much of the research comparing those who have and have not been incarcerated, Kling (2006) studies the effects of the length of incarceration among those serving time in prison. Analyzing UI data for federal prisoners in California and state prisoners in Florida, he finds small short-term gains in UI employment and earnings for those serving longer sentences. Kling (2006, pp. 873-874) speculates that additional programming, particularly work releases, may be associated with improved employment for those serving longer sentences. He also provides a set of analyses in which the causal effect of incarceration is identified by comparing otherwise similar individuals who received shorter or longer prison sentences as a result of the relative leniency of the judges to which they were randomly assigned (an instrumental variables approach). The instrumental variables point estimates also indicate a positive (although insignificant) effect of incarceration on employment.

Analyzing data from Cook County, Illinois, Loeffler (2012) also uses the random assignment of judges to identify the effect of incarceration. Similar to Kling's (2006) results, Loeffler's instrumental variables estimates have standard errors about 10 times larger than least-squares standard errors, and none of the Cook County incarceration effects is significant. Instrumental variables estimates are sometimes taken as a gold standard, although these assessments never consider the cost of bias reduction in additional variance. Loeffler's employment data come from administrative UI records, representing a 67 percent match rate for his sample. As with other analyses based on UI data, positive effects may reflect the short-term impact of parole supervision for the subset of ex-inmates who are moved into formal employment. Little is known about the work activities of the 33 percent of the sample not identified by UI records, or about the distribution of non-UI-covered work before and after the relevant periods of supervision.

Finally, Lalonde and Cho (2008) analyze linked incarceration and UI records for a sample of welfare-enrolled women in Illinois state prison in the 1990s. Examining employment dynamics surrounding incarceration, they find that quarterly UI employment is above preprison levels for three quarters after incarceration. They find that the positive effects of prison on employment are largest for women with children. This increase in employment may be due to greater financial need experienced by those with dependants. The positive employment consequence may also be confounded with 1996 welfare reform that imposed more stringent work requirements on poor single women with children applying for welfare.

Discussion

The balance of quantitative results points to the negative consequences of incarceration for employment. These consequences have been found in survey data (Freeman, 1992; Western, 2006; Raphael, 2007) and administrative data (Waldfogel, 1994; Grogger, 1995; Pettit and Lyons, 2007; Sabol, 2007) with a reasonably stringent variety of specifications fitting individual fixed effects. A few recent studies of administrative data find no negative effect, as well as short-term positive effects that may reflect increased formal-sector employment while under community supervision and shifting institutional conditions associated with welfare reform.

Studies of the labor market experiences of people released from incarceration have adopted a wide variety of methods, examined both the supply and demand sides of the labor market, and analyzed different kinds of qualitative and quantitative data in a wide range of times and places. With such heterogeneity in research designs, it is not surprising that the many different findings of these studies fail to point in a single direction. Still, several general conclusions can be drawn, and specific areas in which more research is needed can be identified.

Studies employing a variety of methods point to similar conclusions. Audit studies of employers and analyses of survey data on formerly incarcerated respondents consistently show the negative effect of incarceration on employment. Survey analyses also show the negative effect on earnings and, less consistently, on hourly wages. The estimated effects in these studies often are substantively large, with reductions in employment outcomes of 10 to 30 percent. Audit studies and survey analyses also are able to impose strong controls for selection—experimentally in the case of audit studies and through a combination of fixed effects, regression adjustment, and sample restrictions in the case of survey analyses. This evidence for the negative effect of incarceration is buttressed by qualitative research, employer surveys, and some but not all studies of administrative data.

Yet a few recent administrative studies reject the hypothesis of a negative incarceration effect and show small increases in employment immediately after release. An urgent question here concerns the utility of administrative data for describing the employment experiences of the formerly incarcerated. The nonrandom observation of employment and earnings in administrative data produced by incomplete record linkage and incomplete UI coverage of postrelease work likely introduces bias, although the direction and magnitude of that bias are poorly understood.

Aggregate Studies

Looking beyond the consequences for individuals, researchers have asked whether the impact of incarceration on labor market outcomes is sufficiently large to result in distortions in aggregate patterns of employment. As the numbers of incarcerated individuals have grown exponentially, it has become important to consider such macro-level consequences. Two lines of research have studied the aggregate significance of incarceration for the labor market: the first views incarceration as a source of "invisible inequality" unmeasured by standard methods such as household surveys; the second assesses the effects of incarceration on aggregate outcomes such as the unemployment rate for different segments of the labor market.

The hypothesis of invisible inequality claims that large institutionalized populations significantly distort official measures of employment based on household surveys (Western and Beckett, 1999; Western and Pettit, 2005). The simplest analyses have compared employment-to-population ratios based on household surveys with adjusted employment ratios that include prison and jail inmates in the population count. Note that these analyses make no claim about the causal effect of incarceration. They simply aim to measure population counts more accurately than the usual household surveys, yielding more accurate estimates of labor utilization and economic well-being in the population. When inmates are included in the denominator of these employment ratios, conventional statistics, particularly for low-educated black men, are altered substantially. According to Western and Pettit (2010, p. 12), "Conventional estimates of the employment rate show that by 2008, around 40 percent of African American male dropouts were employed. . . . Once prison and jail inmates are included in the population count (and among the jobless), employment among young African American men with little schooling fell to around 25 percent by 2008. Indeed, by 2008 these men were more likely to be locked up than employed." Official statistics based on household surveys thus overlook the degree to which contemporary employment patterns are affected by high rates of incarceration.

The second line of research on aggregate effects examines whether the micro-level effects of incarceration accumulate to produce large effects on aggregate measures such as the unemployment rate. Holzer and colleagues (2005) thus examine the aggregate relationship between incarceration and employment among young black men, but in this case focus on the longer-term impact of those reentering society after incarceration. Using data from the outgoing rotation groups of the Current Population Survey between 1979 and 2000 and controlling for a range of state-level social and demographic characteristics with state and year dummies, the authors find that a

1 percent rise in incarceration of blacks (lagged by 3 years to match typical reentry flows) is associated with a roughly 1 percent decline in employment and labor force participation among young black men. Controlling for similar patterns among whites—using a difference-in-difference approach in which effects for whites are attributed to omitted variables—yields comparable results (see also Freeman and Rodgers, 1999).

Sabol and Lynch (2003) use county-level data to estimate the aggregate effects of changes in incarceration on family structure and employment. Their instrumental variables approach relies on an indicator for states that did or did not adopt mandatory or determinate sentencing laws during the 1980s. The sentencing variables are correlated with imprisonment, but not related to changes in family structure or employment. Using data from 280 counties in 96 metropolitan areas, the authors find that the annual number of male prisoners released back into the county from which they were sentenced is negatively related to employment levels among black men; the effects for whites are not significant. Change models show similar effects, but with state fixed effects, these results are not significant.

Useem and Piehl (2008) rely on aggregate data to investigate both the short-term effects of incarceration on employment via population removal and the longer-term consequences for reentry. Based on analyses that include state-level incarceration rates (lagged at multiple intervals) with state and year fixed or random effects, their results yield smaller estimates than those of previous researchers, suggesting that the aggregate impact of incarceration may be less than previously indicated. One key difference among estimates is that the Useem-Piehl analyses focus on employment outcomes for men of all ages, whereas the effects of incarceration may be concentrated among young men.

Overall, these aggregate analyses generate mixed findings about the overall relationship between incarceration and employment: while the general aggregate association between incarceration and employment may be quite weak, this relationship appears more substantial among prime-age men, and particularly black men with no college education. Perhaps not surprisingly, these results suggest that labor market distortions are likely to be greatest among those demographic groups most affected by the high levels of incarceration (e.g., young black men). Of course, aggregated data present only a coarse view of this relationship, and state-level data in particular may obscure important within-state heterogeneity. Paired with the individual-level analyses discussed above—pointing to employment and wage penalties experienced by ex-prisoners, in some cases more so for blacks—these results help tell a fuller story about the negative impact of incarceration on labor market outcomes.

PROGRAMS AND POLICIES FOR IMPROVING
EMPLOYMENT OUTCOMES

The challenge of improving the employment outcomes of ex-prisoners is in many ways similar to that of improving the employment outcomes of all low-skilled men. Spotty work histories, low education, and poor social capital make the transition to stable employment difficult. For a thorough review of the challenges and possibilities of increasing employment among poor men, see Mead (2011). In this section, we briefly review the state of the evidence on reentry programs that focus on employment and then discuss recent efforts to limit employer access to criminal record information as a strategy for increasing the employment opportunities of those released from incarceration.

Employment Reentry Programs

Western (2008, pp. 10-13) categorizes four types of programs aimed at increasing employment and reducing recidivism "among people with criminal records: (1) transitional employment programs; (2) residential and training programs for disadvantaged youth; (3) prison work and education programs; and (4) income supplements for the unemployed." Evaluations of such programs are limited, but a growing body of findings indicates that intensive and directive interventions, provided immediately after release, are more likely to be successful than less concerted services.

Transitional employment programs provide temporary subsidized work to those released from prison. Participants often work in small groups with a high level of supervision to support the development of behaviors useful for permanent employment. They also have access to job placement services. Several of these programs have been tested empirically. A study of the National Supported Work (NSW) demonstration, carried out during the 1970s, found positive employment effects as well as reduced recidivism for older participants but not for those younger than age 26. According to Western (2008, p. 10), the "early randomized experiment . . . placed parolees and probationers in construction industry jobs. Three years after entry to the program, about 42 percent of NSW clients over the age of twenty-six had been rearrested, compared with 54 percent in the control group (Uggen, 2000). NSW participants over age twenty-six were also less likely to report illegal earnings. There were no significant differences between program and control groups among those aged twenty-six and younger."

A 3-year evaluation of the Center for Employment Opportunities (CEO) in New York City, using random assignment, found that the effects of increased employment early in the follow-up period declined over time. At the first-year follow-up, there was little difference in employment and earnings between the program and control groups. However, the evaluation found that CEO significantly reduced recidivism, especially for participants that enrolled within 3 months of being released from prison. The researchers also conducted a cost-benefit analysis and determined that because of reduced criminal justice system expenditures, the financial benefits exceeded the costs (Redcross et al., 2012). Since the evaluation, CEO has improved its program to address low job retention after participants leave the program. According to Mead (2011, p. 62), "CEO created a retention unit to follow up with clients on the job and address problems there. It also has instituted Rapid Rewards, a bonus of up to $200 a year . . . for achieving certain milestones in job retention. The program claims to have improved its job retention rate at 180 days after placement from 40 to 60 percent."

Another program in New York, the ComALERT Program, provides substance abuse treatment with subsidized employment and housing. An evaluation of this program found that "participation was associated with significant improvements in employment and a 18 percent reduction in arrest rates compared to a matched control group with similar demographics and criminal history" (Jacobs and Western, 2007; Western, 2008, p. 10).

The Transitional Jobs Reentry Demonstration (TJRD), an evaluation using rigorous random assignment, tested transitional employment programs for former prisoners in four cites (Chicago, Detroit, Milwaukee, and St. Paul) (Jacobs, 2012). It was designed to examine whether transitional employment programs were more effective than less costly options—those that provided services for job search, referral, and placement but no subsidized employment. The study found that at first-year follow-up, during a period of recession and increased unemployment rates in the four cities, early employment gains for the program group faded as transitional jobs ended, and in contrast with CEO, there was no difference in recidivism between the program and control groups, although the researchers note that most subsequent "prison admissions were for violations of parole rules, not new crimes" (Redcross et al., 2010, p. iii). The results of this study support findings of earlier evaluations that transitional employment programs have yet to be effective at helping former prisoners obtain and hold permanent jobs. However, participation in the transitional jobs is generally high, suggesting that former prisoners welcome the income and the opportunity to work.

Residential and training programs for disadvantaged youth target a specific population and offer services, often combined, such as housing, drug treatment, education, and job training. According to Western (2008, p. 13), the "Opportunity to Succeed (OPTS) program (1994-97) provided mandatory substance-abuse treatment in intensive residential placements, as well as job readiness training. A year after random assignment, the treatment group had accumulated an extra month of full-time employment and were 9 percent more likely to have held a full-time job. Recidivism was also modestly lower in the treatment group, although the program effect was not significant" (Rossman et al., 1999).

Job Corps, established by the Economic Opportunity Act of 1964 and operated now under the Workforce Investment Act of 1998, is a national program targeting economically disadvantaged youth aged 16 to 24. A comprehensive experimental evaluation, using random assignment from 1994 to 1996 and data collection covering a 48-month period after assignment, found that Job Corps improves outcomes for participants—with large effects in obtainment of general equivalency diplomas (GEDs) and vocational certificates and increased earnings for disadvantaged youth—but at a high financial cost (Schochet et al., 2008). The researchers conclude that for older participants, the benefits appear to offset the costs and note that across the full sample, "benefits exceed costs for the participants themselves [thus] effectively redistribut[ing] resources toward low-income youth" (Schochet et al., 2008, p. 1883). The evaluation found employment and earnings gains across a number of subgroups of participants, including those who had been arrested for less serious crimes[6] prior to participation. The study examined the program's impact on crime and found that the program group was significantly less likely than the control group to be arrested, particularly for less serious crimes, during the first 2 years of follow-up. The program group also was less likely to be convicted and spend time in jail.

More conventional vocational training is provided in a nonresidential setting under the Job Training Partnership Act (now called the Workforce Investment Act). An earlier evaluation of this program found no effect on earnings and rearrest rates among the male participants with prior arrest records (Bloom et al., 1997), which may be because the program is not intensively directive, having a focus on general job skills aimed largely at adults.

A recent study examined training programs that target industry-specific needs for a given area to prepare disadvantaged populations to fill local positions and connect them with employers (Maguire et al., 2010). A random assignment research design was used to study three such "sectoral employment" programs in Boston, Milwaukee, and New York City. Seventeen percent of the adult sample (N = 1014) had been formerly incarcerated. The 2-year evaluation found that the nonprofit-led sector-focused training programs did increase the earnings of the program group compared with the control group across a range of program participants. Notably, at two

---

[6]Disorderly conduct and trespassing were considered less serious crimes. Serious crimes included aggravated assault, burglary, murder, and robbery (Schochet et al., 2008).

of the three program sites, formerly incarcerated individuals showed significant earnings gains.

Another intensive residential program for disadvantaged youth—the National Guard Youth ChalleNGe Program—was evaluated with a random assignment design (Millenky et al., 2011). This program combines a 20-week quasimilitary residential phase with a 1-year postresidential-supported mentoring phase. Researchers surveyed the sample of 1,200 young people 3 years after the start of the study (or about 1.5 years after the end of the 17-month ChalleNGe Program) and found that the program group was more likely than the control group to have obtained education credentials (GED, high school diploma, or college credits) and to be employed, earning about 20 percent more than the control group. The evaluation found no statistically significant difference between the groups in whether they had been arrested (about 50 percent of both groups) or convicted (about 25 percent) by the 3-year point. The study did find significant effects on arrests or convictions after 1 or 2 years, but the effects were not significant after 3 years (Bloom et al., 2009; Millenky et al., 2010). The program is open only to youth aged 16 to 18 who are drug free and not "heavily" involved with the justice system,[7] so the above findings may not apply to youth who have substance abuse problems or have committed serious crimes and/or been in contact with the adult criminal justice system.

Prison work and education programs, offered by nearly all state and federal prison systems, are provided to prisoners either throughout their sentence or just prior to release. These programs serve multiple purposes, such as addressing deficient education and skills, reducing idleness, and providing social benefits. As discussed in Chapter 6, it is possible with available statistics to estimate how many prisons offer such programs and how many prisoners participate, but much is unknown about correctional education and employment, such as the quality and the level of engagement and completion. Unfortunately, most studies compare those who participated in such programs with those who did not, thus biasing the findings toward those who self-select to participate, and little information is collected about the characteristics of participants in comparison with those that do not participate. Nonetheless, a number of recent meta-analyses and reviews conclude that programs such as basic education, GED, postsecondary education, and vocational training can be cost-effective, have lowered the risk of recidivism, and hold promise for increasing future employment, while correctional industries and work programs are less or not effective (Cecil et al., 2000; Davis et al., 2013; Fabelo, 2002; Gerber and Fritsch,

---

[7]Those "heavily" involved with the justice system included those currently on parole or on probation for anything other than juvenile status offenses, serving time or awaiting sentencing, under indictment or charged, or convicted of a felony or a capital offense.

1995; MacKenzie, 2006, 2012; Steurer et al., 2001; Western, 2008; Wilson et al., 1999, 2000).

Western (2008, p. 13) points to three large-scale studies whose findings indicate the beneficial effects of prison education:

> The PREP study (1983-85) found that participation in vocational training and work programs was associated with reduced rates of reincarceration in federal prison as long as twelve years after release (Saylor and Gaes, 1997). The Three-State Recidivism Study (1997-98), named for study groups in Maryland, Minnesota, and Ohio, examined a variety of educational programs including basic education, GED preparation, and secondary and postsecondary schooling. Although the study does not distinguish the effects of different types of educational programs, those who participated in classes in prison were only 48 percent likely to be rearrested after a year, compared with a 57 percent rearrest rate for the comparison group (Steurer et al., 2001). Program participants had higher earnings in the first year after release, but this earnings advantage disappeared after three years. Similar to the Three-State Recidivism Study, the Florida GED study (1994-99) found no enduring gains to earnings or employment for those who obtained a GED in prison. Still, some immediate improvements in earnings were found, particularly for nonwhite GED holders (Tyler and Kling, 2007).

It is difficult to draw strong conclusions about the impact of prison work and education programs on later criminal behavior and employment because participants often are involved in other institutional services. Thus, the possibility that the impact is due to a combination of factors and not the program alone cannot be ruled out. Does the link between education and training and recidivism depend only on cognitive and/or skill change or some combination of such change and increased opportunities for additional schooling or employment in the community? Strong arguments have been made about the importance of gender- and race/ethnicity-sensitive programming. However, evidence is insufficient to know whether such "responsive" programming would increase academic progress, be more effective in reducing recidivism, or assist in employment success. Work programs face additional challenges if the institutional goals of producing products and maintaining facilities conflict with rehabilitation goals for work programs. Considering the large number of vocational and academic education, prison industry, and work programs, the research in this area is sparse and severely limited by flaws in the research methodology. More rigorous research using randomized trials would greatly increase knowledge of how to provide effective, evidence-based correctional education and work programs.

Finally, **income supplements** involve paying unemployment benefits to released prisoners to spur economic opportunities. Western (2008, p. 13) reviews early research on income supplements:

> Beginning in 1971, the Baltimore LIFE (Living Insurance for Ex-Prisoners) experiment (1972-74) randomly allocated released state prisoners to a thirteen-week treatment consisting of weekly $252 payments and job placement in some cases, while a control group received no treatment. After twelve months, 49.5 percent of the treatment group had been rearrested compared with 56.9 percent of the controls (Mallar and Thornton, 1978). The LIFE program was replicated on a larger scale in Texas and Georgia in the TARP (Transitional Aid for Released Prisoners) experiment (1975-77). The TARP participants had higher rates of unemployment than the control group, however, and were no less likely to recidivate (Rossi et al., 1980).

Limits on Access to Criminal Records

Beyond programs that directly intervene in the job readiness or placement of ex-prisoners, one final approach to improving their employment outcomes is to reduce the labeling consequences of their criminal record. "Ban the Box" campaigns have received popular support in recent years, promoting policies that limit employers' exposure to criminal background information until later in the hiring process. As of August 2013, Ban the Box legislation had been passed in more than 50 cities and counties.[8] In most cases, the legislation applies primarily to city employers, but it extends in some locations to vendors or private contractors doing business with the city. Unfortunately, no systematic evaluation of the impact of Ban the Box legislation has yet been conducted. Whether or how—through increased supply or demand—these policies affect the overall employment rates of ex-prisoners is currently unknown.

Efforts also have been made to regulate the dissemination of criminal record information. For example, the Criminal Offender Record Information (CORI) reform in Massachusetts prohibits the dissemination of misdemeanor records after 5 years from release from supervision or custody or after 10 years for felony convictions (except for murder, manslaughter,

---

[8] As of August 2013, Ban the Box legislation had been passed in Alameda County, Atlanta, Atlantic City, Austin, Baltimore, Berkeley, Boston, Bridgeport, Buffalo, Cambridge, Canton, Carrboro, Carson, Chicago, Cincinnati, Cleveland, Compton, Cumberland County, Detroit, Durham City, Durham County, East Palo Alto, Hartford, Jacksonville, Kalamazoo, Kansas City, Memphis, Minneapolis, Multnomah County, Muskegon County, New Haven, New York, Newark, Newport News, Norfolk, Norwich, Oakland, Philadelphia, Pittsburgh, Portsmouth, Providence, Richmond, San Francisco, Santa Clara, Seattle, Spring Lake, St. Paul, Tampa, Travis County, Washington, DC, Wilmington, and Worcester (National Employment Law Project, 2013).

or sex offenses). This legislation goes well beyond the provisions in most states. While most states make some provision for the sealing or expungement of records (Love, 2006), particularly in the case of nonviolent or first-time offenses, credit reporting agencies and criminal background services typically are subject to little oversight in distributing this information. At present, there exists no federal legislation comparable to the Fair Credit Reporting Act, which prohibits credit agencies from disseminating information dating back more than 7 years. Again, little evidence is available with which to evaluate how the regulation of criminal record information at the state or federal levels may affect the employment rates of ex-prisoners. In considering policies of this kind, it is useful to keep in mind that the predictive value of a criminal record declines over time. Seven to 10 years following an arrest, the likelihood of arrest for young men with a record looks indistinguishable from that of those with no criminal history (Kurlycheck et al., 2006; Blumstein and Nakamura, 2009; see also Chapter 3). Thus there may be good reason to pursue policies that regulate the introduction of stigmatizing information beyond this window.

KNOWLEDGE GAPS

We offer the following observations regarding gaps in knowledge on the issues examined in this chapter and suggestions for addressing those gaps.

Directions for Future Research

Current research findings do not make it possible to distinguish among the effects of criminal behavior, criminal conviction, and the experience of incarceration as they relate to subsequent labor market experiences. A clearer understanding of the mechanisms by which criminal justice involvement leads to poor employment outcomes is critical for addressing the central policy concern of whether and to what extent reductions in or alternatives to incarceration can improve employment outcomes.

Research more explicitly comparing estimates derived from administrative data on employment and earnings with those derived from survey data would be useful. A better understanding is needed of the extent to which discrepancies across these literatures are the result of poor data matches, poor data coverage (e.g., of informal or casual employment), supervision effects, errors in self-reports, or something else.

The collection of longitudinal data tracking individuals before and after their contact with the criminal justice system is needed. Partnering with existing longitudinal studies (e.g., the Panel Study of Income Dynamics [PSID], AdHealth) would be a useful avenue to explore. Tracking participation in the informal labor market would enable a better under-standing of the continuum of economic activity that characterizes the survival strategies of ex-prisoners.

Labor Market Context

Attention to the broader labor market context is needed in examining the consequences of incarceration. Limited research has focused on the question of how tight or slack labor markets may affect the reentry experiences of individuals leaving prison. Going forward, it will be important to understand how macroeconomic conditions interact with criminal justice policy to produce observed labor market outcomes.

Little is known about how formal barriers and the experience of prison affect the job search strategies of former prisoners. Do the experiences of overcrowding, prison violence, the quality of health care, or prison staff interactions, for example, influence, whether positively or negatively, the trajectories of inmates following release? To what extent do the supply-side adaptations of ex-prisoners (e.g., search intensity, search strategy) produce distortions in their labor market outcomes? Both qualitative and quantitative research would be useful in understanding how perceived and real barriers to employment affect ex-prisoners' persistence and placement in the labor market.

Programs to Improve Employment and Other Outcomes

Large-scale, long-term, and experimental evaluations of in-prison education and therapeutic programming, job training, and job placement programs are critical for directing policy activity in this area. Policy development to date has been to some extent stymied by contradictory findings among relatively small-scale studies. Investment is needed in broader evaluations that can inform efforts to improve experiences during and after imprisonment. The interdependence between employment and other reentry outcomes also needs to be considered. The experimental evaluation of CEO's transitional employment program, for example, found that early placement in transitional work significantly reduced recidivism but had no measurable effect on longer-term employment. This puzzling finding warrants further research into the role of early intervention in the postrelease process, how short- and long-term employment may be linked, and how they in turn are linked to recidivism. Evaluations of programs that address the needs of ex-prisoners across multiple dimensions (e.g., housing, substance abuse, employment) may likewise better inform understanding of pathways to desistance than those focused on employment alone. Institutional aspects of work and reentry programs need to be examined. What allowed CEO to generate impacts where NSW largely failed? How are such programs built and improved over time? Answering these questions will require field research, of which there has as yet been far too little.

CONCLUSION

Research to date on the employment and earnings consequences of incarceration has taken many forms, from employer surveys to ethnographic observation, survey research, analysis of administrative data, and studies of aggregate effects. Results across this broad field vary, but the bulk of the evidence supports the conclusion that incarceration is associated with poor employment outcomes. Employers express a reluctance to hire those with a criminal record, and field experiments confirm this reluctance in measures of real-world behavior. Individuals see having a criminal record as a significant barrier to employment, although little is known about how these perceptions may affect one's strategy or persistence in job search.

Evidence from survey research consistently finds a significant negative relationship between incarceration and employment, wages, and annual income. Studies using administrative data come to somewhat more mixed conclusions, with some recent work reporting a boost in employment immediately following incarceration. In most cases, however, that boost is short-lived, giving way to longer-term null or negative effects. The aggregate effects of incarceration, or of having a criminal record are difficult to detect for general populations, but appear significant for young black men. These results suggest both the direct consequences for the employment prospects of those returning from prison and the consequences for the broader population of young black men, who are viewed with suspicion in the labor market by virtue of membership in a high incarceration group.

As noted throughout this report, the incarcerated population in the United States disproportionately comprises individuals with low levels of schooling and histories of mental illness and substance abuse—generally poor human capital and "work readiness." These individuals also often have quite limited access to social networks that could yield jobs with high growth prospects. The experience of incarceration thus both reflects and exacerbates persistent labor market inequalities.

Considering the mechanisms by which incarceration affects employment is critical to our evaluation of potential policy alternatives. For example, if the negative consequences of incarceration for employment are due primarily to its "transformative" impact on the physical, psychological, or social well-being of inmates—through attrition of human capital, weakening of prosocial ties, or development of coping mechanisms incompatible with life on the outside—then substituting community supervision for prison would reduce those consequences. If, on the other hand, the consequences of incarceration for employment are due primarily to the stigma of having serious criminal justice contact, policies reducing incarceration by assigning individuals to other formal sanctions (e.g., probation, fines, treatment) would do little to reduce this labeling effect. Many of these alternative sanctions also come with a permanent criminal record. To the extent that the employment consequences associated with incarceration are driven in part by the effect of a criminal record (with or without incarceration), policies aimed at mitigating these consequences must go beyond reducing the numbers of people behind bars.

The evaluation literature examining programs designed to improve postrelease employment outcomes yields a mixed record (see also reviews by Mead, 2011, Chapter 4; Bushway and Reuter, 2002; Bloom, 2006; and Visher et al., 2005). These programs vary greatly in their content and in their clients. Many appear to generate only short-term effects or effects that generalize only to subsets of the population. Less intensive interventions, such as the income supplements of TARP and the training under the Job Training Partnership Act, and interventions directed at male youth have been unsuccessful. More intensive interventions that are directive as to desired behavior tend to be more successful, particularly if they target adults who are known to be motivated to desist from crime. The results of CEO and ComALERT also suggest that timely interventions focused on the period immediately after prison release are likely to have a greater chance of success.

Most program evaluations conducted to date have focused on the reentry process. Less is known about the impact of policies designed to reduce the flow of individuals into prison, which may represent a more powerful mechanism through which to mitigate the negative consequences of incarceration for employment. To the extent that incarceration results in a decay of human capital, a disruption of family ties, or psychological/interpersonal adaptations not conducive to stable employment, programs or policies focused on front-end diversion may have greater scope for success. At the same time, as noted above, it is important to remember that the problems of criminal activity and a criminal record present their own difficulties for employment, even absent incarceration.

9

Consequences for Families and Children

The dramatic increase in incarceration rates since 1972 has stimulated widespread interest in how this trend is affecting families and children. As incarceration rates increased, more families and children had direct experience with imprisonment of a parent (see Figure 9-1). In a calculation of the number of minor children with fathers in prison or jail in the two decades from 1980 to 2000, Western and Wildeman (2009) found that the number of children with an incarcerated father increased from about 350,000 to 2.1 million, about 3 percent of all U.S. children in 2000. According to the most recent estimates from the Bureau of Justice Statistics, 53 percent of those in prison in 2007 had minor children. In that year, an estimated 1.7 million children under age 18 had a parent in state or federal prison (Glaze and Maruschak, 2008). The racial and ethnic disparities of the prison population are reflected in the disparate rates of parental incarceration. In 2007, black and Hispanic children in the United States were 7.5 and 2.7 times more likely, respectively, than white children to have a parent in prison (Glaze and Maruschak, 2008; see also Box 9-1). While the consequences for families and children can be expected to vary by race and ethnicity, much of the research reviewed for this study does not distinguish outcomes by these characteristics. For the few studies that do, the differences and similarities are noted in the text.

This chapter reviews the empirical evidence on the consequences of incarceration for family behavior and child well-being. We focus on incarceration of men because it is more common than that of women and is the subject of the bulk of the available research. The literature on men's incarceration is large and includes ethnographic studies as well as quantitative

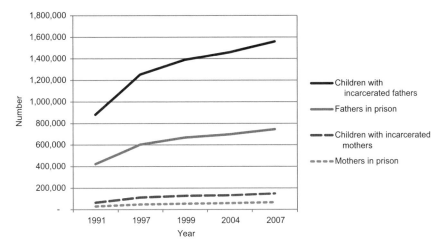

FIGURE 9-1 Estimated number of parents in state and federal prisons and their minor children, by inmate's gender.
SOURCE: Data from Glaze and Maruschak (2008).

analyses of survey data and administrative records. The literature on women's incarceration is limited but growing. Most of the literature examining the consequences of maternal incarceration for families and children is primarily qualitative or limited to specific field sites. While the risk of maternal imprisonment for children is quite small, it has grown much more rapidly in recent years than the risk of paternal imprisonment (Kruttschnitt, 2010; Wildeman, 2009). The number of children with a mother in prison increased 131 percent from 1991 to 2007 (see Figure 9-1), while the number with a father in prison increased 77 percent (Glaze and Maruschak, 2008). As discussed in Chapter 6, incarcerated mothers are more likely than incarcerated fathers to have lived with their children prior to incarceration. In a 2004 survey of inmates, 55 percent of female inmates in state prisons who were parents, compared with 36 percent of male inmates, reported living with their children in the month before arrest. Incarcerated parents in federal prisons were more likely to report living with their children before arrest (73 percent of female inmates, compared with 46 percent of male inmates). In addition, incarcerated mothers are more likely than incarcerated fathers to have come from single-parent households (42 percent versus 17 percent in state prisons, and 52 percent versus 19 percent in federal prisons) (Glaze and Maruschak, 2008).

The available literature on the consequences of incarceration for families and children focuses on incarceration per se and does not examine the

---

BOX 9-1
Racial and Ethnic Differences in the Cumulative
Risk of Parental Imprisonment

Wildeman (2009) calculated the probability that a child would have experienced a parent being sent to prison by the child's teenage years. This cumulative risk of parental imprisonment was calculated for two different birth cohorts of children. For white children born in 1978, Wildeman (2009) found that 2.2 to 2.4 percent had experienced a mother or father being sent to prison by age 14. For a birth cohort born 12 years later, in 1990, the cumulative risk of parental imprisonment for white children had increased to 3.6 to 4.2 percent. Among black children, parental imprisonment in the 1978 cohort was 13.8 to 15.2 percent, compared with 25.1 to 28.4 percent in the 1990 cohort. Similar estimates were developed by Pettit and colleagues (2009), who found that in 2009, 15 percent of white children whose parents had not completed high school had experienced a parent being sent to prison by age 17. Among Hispanic children with similarly low-educated parents, 17 percent had experienced parental imprisonment by age 17. The comparable percentage for African American children is 62 percent (Pettit et al., 2009).

---

specific effects of the increasing rates of incarceration. Therefore, we cannot discuss any changes in the consequences for families and children of the incarcerated during this period. We consider what is currently known about the potential consequences for individuals, positive and negative, as a result of having a partner or parent incarcerated and believe that the numbers affected have risen. A few studies, however, discussed later, look at the effect of increasing incarceration on the marriage market and childbearing.

Most studies find that incarceration is associated with weaker family bonds and lower levels of child well-being. Men with a history of incarceration are less likely to marry or cohabit and more likely to form unstable partnerships than those who have never been incarcerated, and children of incarcerated fathers tend to exhibit more problems in childhood and adolescence. The picture is not entirely negative, however. There is evidence from at least one state, for example, that increased rates of incarceration are associated with lower rates of nonmarital childbearing. Moreover, some studies find that the negative association between incarceration and family outcomes is limited to families in which the father was living with the family prior to imprisonment. Finally, there is evidence that in cases in which a father is violent, incarceration may actually improve his family's well-being. The few studies that have examined the consequences for children of incarcerated mothers tend to focus on separation from children and housing stability. These studies often find persistent disadvantage in terms of poor education and financial circumstances, substance abuse, mental illness, domestic abuse, or a combination of these. At this time, findings on the effects of maternal incarceration on child well-being are mixed.

In this chapter, we begin by reviewing available research on the consequences of men's incarceration for families. We then examine the small but growing literature on mothers' incarceration. Next, we discuss the methodological limitations of existing studies in this area. The chapter ends with a review of knowledge gaps and concluding remarks.

INCARCERATION OF PARTNERS AND FATHERS

For this review, we looked at both quantitative research and ethnographic studies. Our review of quantitative studies was limited to studies published within the past decade[1] that meet four criteria: (1) they are based on probability samples; (2) response rates are good, and sample attrition is low; (3) they include good measures of incarceration and family/child outcomes; and (4) the temporal ordering of incarceration and the outcome of interest is correct. We gave special attention to studies that attempt to deal with omitted variable bias. (For other reviews of the incarceration literature, see Hagan and Dinovitzer, 1999; Murray et al., 2009; Schnittker et al., 2011; Wakefield and Uggen, 2010; Wildeman and Western, 2010; and Wildeman and Muller 2012). Our review criteria would exclude most studies linking outcomes to the developmental stage of the child(ren) because these studies typically are based on small, purposive samples. As a result, our review represents a partial look at the literature on the consequences of incarceration for families and children.

Ethnographic studies generally do not allow for statements about causality; however, they describe the experiences of women with incarcerated partners and their children and reveal potential mechanisms for explaining the link between incarceration and family well-being. A key goal of our assessment is to determine whether the use of more complex statistical methods produces findings that are consistent with those from ethnographic studies and quantitative analyses using simpler statistical methods. To the extent that the findings from the various studies tell a similar story, we have greater confidence in the results.

In this section, we review the consequences of incarceration of men in four domains—(1) male-female relationships, (2) economic well-being, (3) parenting, and (4) child well-being.

---

[1]Recent quantitative work does a better job than older studies of accounting or controlling for possible confounding and unmeasured variables.

Male-Female Relationships

An extensive body of qualitative research examines relationship dynamics between incarcerated men and their female partners. These studies find that although these men view marriage as a desirable goal (Braman, 2004), incarceration (in addition to the father's criminal activity) poses difficulties for maintaining a relationship, and for those who are not yet married, it makes marriage less feasible than for those not incarcerated.

Relationship problems of the incarcerated are attributable to several factors. First, women grow weary of the time, energy, and money required to maintain a relationship with an incarcerated partner. Studies find that while family members often view their role as one of moral and emotional support, making regular visits and phone calls and sending letters and packages to prisoners can be difficult and costly (Grinstead et al., 2001), particularly when visits require long-distance travel and hours of waiting (Christian, 2005; Comfort, 2003; Braman, 2004). Second, women may undergo emotional strain from not knowing what their partner is experiencing while incarcerated (Ferraro et al., 1983) or from feeling socially excluded (some report feeling as if they themselves were incarcerated). Upon visiting their partners, for example, women often are subject to searches, removal of personal belongings, and the enforcement of strict rules (Fishman, 1990; Comfort, 2003; Braman, 2004). Similarly, following release, partners may become subject to some terms of the parolee's supervision, such as searches of their residence or car (Comfort, 2008). Third, either partner may perceive an imbalance in the relationship. Often, this is because men are unable to contribute as much financially while incarcerated. However, Braman (2004) finds that the perceived imbalance is not always material. Incarceration may diminish trust between partners and augment the perception that individuals need to look out for themselves first, that others are selfish, and that relationships are exploitive. Moreover, Goffman (2009) finds that former prisoners and men on parole may feel the need to avoid or carefully navigate their relationships with partners who may use the criminal justice system as a way to control their behavior (e.g., a woman may threaten to call her partner's parole officer if he continues arriving home late, becomes involved with another woman, or does not contribute enough money to the household). In communities with high levels of incarcerated males, the overall gender imbalance also may shape behavior, making men more inclined to seek other partners (Braman, 2004).

Despite these findings, it is important to note that incarceration is not always harmful to relationships. Edin and colleagues (2004) find that while incarceration may strain the bonds between parents who are in a relationship prior to incarceration, it more often proves beneficial to couples whose relationship has been significantly hindered by lifestyle choices (almost always substance abuse) prior to incarceration. For some of these men, incarceration serves as a turning point, a time to rehabilitate and rebuild ties with their child's mother—at least a cooperative friendship if not a romantic relationship. There is also evidence that marriage prevents dissolution of relationships. Indeed, Braman (2004) reports that wives of incarcerated men often say they would have left their husband had they not been married to him.

Consistent with the ethnographic literature, quantitative studies find that incarceration increases the economic costs of maintaining a relationship and imposes considerable psychological strain on the wives and partners of men in prison, especially those who were living with the man prior to his incarceration. At the same time, these studies highlight the fact that for some couples, prison is a time when men can change their lives and reestablish family relationships. A large number of quantitative studies have examined the association between incarceration and such behaviors as marriage, cohabitation, divorce, and repartnering (Apel et al., 2010; Charles and Luoh, 2010; Lewis, 2010; Lopoo and Western, 2005; Massoglia et al., 2011; Turney and Wildeman, 2012; Waller and Swisher, 2006; Western and McLanahan, 2001; Western et al., 2004). One study examines nonmarital childbearing (Mechoulan, 2011). Some of these studies focus on young adults or men in general, while others focus on parents only. All adjust for observed characteristics, and many employ rigorous methods.

Lewis (2010) and Waller and Swisher (2006) find evidence that fathers' incarceration reduces subsequent marriage and cohabitation. More rigorous studies, however, suggest that these effects are not causally related. Using a lagged dependent variable (LDV) model, Lopoo and Western (2005) find no association between men's incarceration and later marriage. Similarly, using data from a cohort of Dutch men convicted of a crime, Apel and colleagues (2010) find no effect of incarceration on marriage after the first year postrelease. Both studies do, however, find a strong positive effect on divorce/separation. Married men who were incarcerated were three times more likely to divorce than married men who were convicted but not incarcerated. These researchers also report that the effect of incarceration on divorce was stronger among men without children and those convicted of serious offenses. This study is especially noteworthy because, by focusing exclusively on men with a criminal conviction, it can distinguish the effects of incapacitation from those of conviction.

Two studies use state-level variables to examine how variation in marriage market conditions due to increasing incarceration rates affect women's marriage and fertility. Using state-level, race-specific incarceration rates as an indicator of marriage market conditions, Charles and Luoh (2010) find a negative effect of incarceration on the prevalence of marriage among women. They also find a modest and positive effect of incarceration on women's education and labor force participation. Using a similar approach but more detailed information on mothers' behavior, Mechoulan (2011) finds a weak negative effect of male incarceration on black women's probability of marriage and a strong negative effect on young black women's nonmarital childbearing. This study also finds a positive link between men's incarceration and women's education and employment. The Mechoulan study is of particular interest because it highlights the possible benefits of high rates of male incarceration: namely, more education for women and the prevention of unintended pregnancies among young black women. The author is careful to note that his analysis does not identify the mechanisms underlying these changes in women's behavior, which could be due to the increased incapacitation of more promiscuous men or changes in women's sexual behavior. The author also notes that his findings are driven primarily by changes in incarceration rates in one state—Texas—making it difficult to generalize to other parts of the United States.

In addition to the studies described above, which focus on men rather than fathers, at least one study attempts to estimate the effect of fathers' incarceration on the stability of parents' unions. Using data from the Fragile Families Study, Turney and Wildeman (2012) find that father's incarceration increases the likelihood that the mother will end her relationship with him and form a partnership with a new man. The researchers aim to identify the effect of incarceration by employing a rich set of control variables (including couple's relationship quality); they also limit their sample to couples in which the father has a history of incarceration and compare couples who experienced a recent incarceration with those who did not. The latter results can be interpreted as the effect of a repeat incarceration for men with a history of imprisonment.

The studies described above have several limitations. First, those that use state-level incarceration rates to estimate the effect of incarceration on marriage and divorce must assume that marital status does not affect incarceration (whereas many people would argue it does) or that a third variable—such as social norms—is not causing both high rates of incarceration and high rates of union instability. A second limitation of most studies is that they ignore unions formed by cohabiting couples. Because marriage is rare among men at high risk of incarceration, at least in the United States, the failure to include cohabiting unions makes it difficult to draw strong conclusions about the effect of incarceration on union stability. A third limitation is that most studies do not compare the effect of incarceration with that of other types of forced separation. The one study that makes this comparison (Massoglia et al., 2011) finds that the destabilizing effects of incarceration are similar to those of military deployment, which suggests that the negative consequences of incarceration are due not to stigma but to the stress associated with incapacitation or possibly changes in fathers' behavior. Both war and incarceration are likely to expose men to violence and undermine their relationship skills.

Economic Well-Being

According to the Bureau of Justice Statistics, more than half of fathers in state prison report being the primary breadwinner in their family (Glaze and Maruschak, 2008). Thus the partners and children of these men are likely to experience a loss of economic resources while the provider is in prison. This effect also is likely to persist after the father returns home, given what is known about the link between incarceration and unemployment (see Chapter 8). Ethnographic studies generally concur that the incarceration of a partner or father can lead to increased economic hardship for members of his family. Financial circumstances are one of the most frequently cited sources of stress or strain among partners of incarcerated individuals (Carlson and Cavera, 1992; Ferraro et al., 1983). Many affected families already were living in unfavorable economic circumstances prior to the incarceration, and many were dependent on public assistance or other financial support. Even so, Arditti and colleagues (2003) find that these families become even more impoverished following the partner's or father's incarceration.

The increased economic stress among families affected by incarceration is due to several factors. One is the extra expenses (collect calls, travel costs, sending money and packages) reported by women trying to maintain a relationship with the incarcerated individual (Grinstead et al., 2001; Christian, 2005; Arditti et al., 2003). Other new expenditures include attorney or other legal fees or job loss stemming from increased work-family conflict (Arditti et al., 2003).

Consistent with the ethnographic literature, quantitative studies indicate that the families of men with an incarceration history experience a good deal of economic insecurity and hardship, resulting in greater use of public assistance among mothers and children. Three studies examine the link between fathers' incarceration and mothers' material hardship (including housing insecurity) (Geller et al., 2009; Geller and Walker, 2012; Schwartz-Soicher et al., 2011); two other studies examine the relationship between fathers' incarceration and mothers' welfare use (Sugie, 2012; Walker, 2011); and one study examines the association between fathers' incarceration and children's homelessness (Wildeman, forthcoming). All of these studies are based on data from the Fragile Families Study.

Geller and Walker (2012) find that the partners of incarcerated fathers are at increased risk of experiencing homelessness and other types of housing insecurity. These authors use a lagged measure of housing insecurity and a rich set of early-life and contemporaneous covariates. They also distinguish between recent and early incarceration and find that part of the effect of incarceration on housing insecurity is due to a reduction in financial resources (father's earnings or partner's financial contributions). In a third study examining housing insecurity, Wildeman (forthcoming) uses propensity score models and finds that recent paternal incarceration is associated with an increased risk of child homelessness, especially among black children. Foster and Hagan (2007) also find an association with increased homelessness among adolescent girls.

One study in this group examines the influence of fathers' incarceration on other types of material hardship besides housing. Employing several strategies for determining causality, including fixed effects models, a lagged dependent variable, and a placebo test used to examine whether future incarceration is related to current behaviors, Schwartz-Soicher and colleagues (2011) find strong evidence that paternal incarceration leads to increased material hardship for mothers and children, measured as mothers' reports of the difficulty faced by their family in meeting basic needs. Finally, two studies examine whether fathers' incarceration increases mothers' participation in public assistance programs. Using propensity score matching, Walker (2011) finds some evidence that incarceration may increase the probability of mothers' receipt of both food stamps and Temporary Assistance for Needy Families (TANF). In contrast, using fixed effects models and a more recent wave of data, Sugie (2012) finds that recent paternal incarceration is associated with mothers' receipt of food stamps and Medicaid/State Children's Health Insurance Program (SCHIP) assistance, but not TANF. Neither of these studies attempts to estimate the cost of these benefits to taxpayers. On balance, the evidence that father's incarceration increases the family's material hardship and housing insecurity is strong, especially when the father was living in the household prior to incarceration.

Parenting

Ethnographic work examining the effects of incarceration on parenting focuses primarily on fathers, including their contact with the child and their financial contributions to the family. In discussing these findings, it is important to note that men do not father in a vacuum. Key concepts that influence the experiences of an incarcerated father and his children are his relationship with the child's mother and his own behavior and lifestyle before his arrest.

The father's relationship with his child's mother appears to play an important role in the father-child relationship during incarceration and after his release from prison. Fathers who lived with their child prior to incarceration are more likely than nonresident fathers to stay in contact with the child (Martin, 2001). In addition, while some mothers and families provide encouragement for continuing contact between the child and his or her father, others promote social exclusion (Nurse, 2004). For example, some family members refuse to bring the child when making visits (Martin, 2001), and some fathers feel that mothers use the incarceration to justify limiting or prohibiting contact or painting a negative view of the father so the child does not want to interact with him (Edin et al., 2004).

The father's lifestyle prior to his incarceration and the quality of the father-child relationship also are important influences on the parenting effects of incarceration. As Edin and colleagues (2004) note, if the father's severe substance abuse or criminal activity prior to incarceration was enough to prevent him from making financial contributions to the family or developing a close relationship with his child(ren) prior to his arrest, then his incarceration may serve as a time to rebuild bonds, even allowing parents and children to communicate more frequently (Giordano, 2010). Some fathers believe their incarceration will serve as an example to their children, discouraging them from making similar mistakes (Martin, 2001). On the other hand, among fathers who previously experienced frequent contact with their children, incarceration almost always proves to be detrimental—breaking bonds in terms of physical closeness and financial contributions and eroding relationships that may already have been fragile. Most often, this is because the mother ends her relationship with the father or becomes involved with another man (Edin et al., 2004). Martin (2001) also finds that fathers themselves sometimes refuse to accept visits from their child(ren) to protect themselves and their child(ren) emotionally.

Four quantitative studies examine the association between fathers' incarceration and three outcomes: coparenting, engagement in activities with the child, and contact with the child (Geller and Garfinkel, 2012; Turney and Wildeman, 2012; Waller and Swisher, 2006; Woldoff and Washington, 2008). Generally, researchers find a negative association between fathers' prior or recent incarceration and each of these behaviors.

Waller and Swisher (2006) find a negative association between recent and past incarceration and father-child contact and engagement that is mediated by the father-mother relationship. Similarly, using more rigorous methods and controlling for characteristics likely to be associated with both criminal justice contact and family stability, Geller and Garfinkel (2012) find reductions in father-child contact for resident and nonresident fathers who become incarcerated and weaker coparenting relationships with the child's mother following release. Turney and Wildeman (2012) use a variety of estimation strategies, including lagged dependent variables, fixed effects, propensity score matching, and conditioning on ever-incarcerated fathers. They find that among fathers who were living with their children, the negative effects of incarceration are robust across all measures of involvement (engagement, shared responsibility in parenting, and cooperation in parenting) and all strategies. They find further that lower levels of father involvement are due to changes in the quality of the parental relationship, changes in fathers' economic conditions, and changes in fathers' health. Effects are similar across racial/ethnic groups. These researchers also examine the effects of fathers' incarceration on mothers' parenting and find that they are much weaker. Among fathers who were not living with their children prior to incarceration, however, the effects are smaller and disappear in fixed effects and other models. The latter finding is likely due to the fact that a large proportion of nonresident fathers have no contact with their children (Amato et al., 2009). Taken together, these studies indicate that incarceration reduces paternal involvement in families in which the father was living with the child prior to incarceration. A major limitation is that the analyses for incarcerated fathers are based on one source of data—the Fragile Families Study.

Child Well-Being

Negative outcomes for children are commonly reported in open-ended interviews with fathers and their families. Mothers and some fathers believe their children perform more poorly or have more difficulties in school following their father's incarceration (Braman, 2004; Martin, 2001; Arditti et al., 2003). And many parents report negative behavioral changes in their children, including becoming more private or withdrawn (Braman, 2004), not listening to adults (Martin, 2001), becoming irritable, or showing signs of behavioral regression (Arditti et al., 2003). Some studies also provide evidence of changes in children's emotional or mental health, with children experiencing such feelings as shame or embarrassment about their father's incarceration; emotional strain, including a belief that the father did not want to live at home; a loss of trust in the father (Martin, 2001); grief or depression (Arditti et al., 2003); or even guilt (Giordano, 2010).

Despite these negative experiences, periods of incarceration are not always viewed as the most challenging circumstance these children face (Giordano, 2010). A father's severe substance addiction or violent behavior at home may lead some children to feel happier when their father is incarcerated. Imprisonment may give the father an opportunity to receive help for his problems and even communicate more with the child (Edin et al., 2004). In such cases, a father's release from prison may be emotionally complex, being both a happy and stressful life event for the child.

In summary, qualitative studies for the most part indicate that fathers' incarceration is stressful for children, increasing both depression and anxiety as well as antisocial behavior. There is also evidence that children of fathers who are violent or have serious substance abuse problems are happier when their father is removed from the household.

The majority of quantitative studies focus on children's problem behaviors, which include both internalizing problems (depression and anxiety) and externalizing problems (aggression and delinquency). Early and persistent aggression and conduct problems are known to be associated with a host of negative outcomes in adulthood, including criminal behavior (Farrington, 1991; Babinski et al., 2003). A few studies investigate the influence of fathers' incarceration on physical health, cognitive ability, and grades and educational attainment.

The strongest and most consistent findings regarding effects of fathers' incarceration on child well-being are for behavior problems and delinquency (also see the meta-analysis of Murray et al., 2012a). Most studies examining behavior problems focus on young children. However, results of these studies generally are consistent with those of studies looking at older children. In both age groups, researchers find that fathers' incarceration increases externalizing behaviors, especially aggression.

Adjusting for other characteristics, Craigie (2011) finds a positive association between fathers' incarceration and children's externalizing behavior problems among blacks (see also Perry and Bright, 2012) and Hispanics, but not whites. Comparing a sample of children whose fathers were incarcerated after their birth with children whose fathers had been incarcerated before birth, Johnson (2009) finds a positive association between incarceration and externalizing behavior, but only for the former children. Walker (2011) uses propensity score matching and finds a similar association with aggressive behavior at age 5 (but not at age 3, when aggressive behavior is more common). Using similar methods, Haskins (2012) finds a positive association between fathers' incarceration and externalizing behavior and attention problems at age 5. Using a series of placebo tests, fixed effects models, and propensity score matching, Wildeman (2010) finds that paternal incarceration increases physical aggression among boys but not girls (see also Geller et al., 2009), particularly among children whose fathers were incarcerated for a nonviolent offense or were not abusive to the child's mother prior to incarceration. Using a similar set of tests, Geller and colleagues (2012) find that the effect of incarceration on young children's aggressive behaviors is nearly twice as large for boys as for girls, but significant for both genders; they find significant (though weaker) effects for fathers who were not living with their child prior to incarceration. Aggressive behavior is much more common among boys than among girls in this age group, which may account for the gender difference in children's response to father's incarceration. Finally, Wakefield and Wildeman (2011) find that across all age groups (young children to young adults), fathers' incarceration increases aggression, especially among boys.

These researchers find no evidence that increased behavior problems and aggression resulting from paternal incarceration differ by race. However, they do note that in cases in which there is a history of domestic abuse, paternal incarceration may actually reduce aggressive behavior in children. These findings are consistent with research of Jaffe and colleagues (2003) showing that children's response to their father's exit from the household depends on the nature of the mother-father relationship, and suggest that the association between incarceration and aggression is complex.

Another type of problem behavior examined by researchers is delinquency, specifically among older children. Using nationally representative longitudinal data, Roettger and Swisher (2011) find fathers' incarceration to be positively associated with the propensity of adolescent and young adult males for delinquency and risk of arrest. They find no interactions with race or ethnicity and note that father's incarceration both before and after birth is associated with these outcomes, although the relationships are stronger when the incarceration occurred during the child's life. Using data from the Pittsburgh Youth Study, Murray and colleagues (2012b) find that parental incarceration is not associated with boys' marijuana use but is positively associated with theft; in this study, the associations are stronger among white than among black youth. Parenting and peer processes following parental incarceration explained about half of the association. Neither of these studies examines the effect of fathers' incarceration on delinquency among adolescent girls. Using a nationally representative sample of Dutch men convicted in 1977, van de Rakt and colleagues (2012) find a moderate positive association between paternal imprisonment and child convictions (odds 1.2 times greater than for children whose fathers never went to prison). The effect was especially pronounced when the father was imprisoned before the child's twelfth birthday. Again, this study is noteworthy because it is able to estimate the effect of incarceration net of conviction.

The evidence for children's internalizing behavior (depression and anxiety) is more mixed. Craigie (2011) and Geller and colleagues (2012) find no evidence of an effect on internalizing behavior among young children. Similarly, Murray and colleagues (2012b) find no significant influence on depression among adolescents. In contrast, Wakefield and Wildeman (2011) find that paternal incarceration increases internalizing behavior among adolescents and young adults. Part of this disparity in results may be due to the fact that internalizing of problems (depression) often does not appear until adolescence.

Two studies examine the effects of incarceration on children's physical health. Using state and year fixed effects, Wildeman (2012) finds that paternal incarceration increases the risk of early infant mortality, but only among infants whose fathers were not abusive. Similarly, Roettger and Boardman (2012) find that fathers' incarceration is positively associated with higher body mass index (BMI) in young adult women, an effect that operates primarily through depression. Foster and Hagan (2007) find evidence that fathers' absence due to incarceration increases daughters' risk of physical and sexual abuse and neglect.

Finally, a few studies examine the effects of fathers' incarceration on children's cognitive ability and academic performance, with somewhat mixed results. Using propensity score matching, Walker (2011) finds a negative effect of incarceration on cognitive ability at age 5, whereas Haskins (2012) and Geller and colleagues (2012), using similar and more rigorous methods, find no effect at age 5. Murray and colleagues (2012b) find no relationship between parental incarceration and academic performance after adjusting for youth behavior prior to incarceration. Hagan and Foster (2012) find a negative association between fathers' incarceration (at the individual and school levels) and children's grade point average (GPA), educational attainment, and college completion. Finally, Foster and Hagan (2009), using matching techniques, find a negative effect of incarceration on years of education, even after adjusting for GPA and other characteristics, with variation by race/ethnicity. On balance, the findings for education suggest that insofar as fathers' incarceration has a causal effect on educational attainment, it operates primarily through behavior problems and socioemotional adjustment rather than through cognitive ability.

INCARCERATION OF MOTHERS

More than 200,000 women are in jails or prisons in the United States, representing nearly one-third of incarcerated females worldwide (Walmsley, 2012). The past three to four decades have seen rapid growth in women's incarceration rates—a rise of 646 percent since 1980 compared with a 419 percent rise for men (Mauer, 2013; Frost et al., 2006). Prior to 2000, most of this growth occurred among African American women. In 2000, black women were imprisoned at six times the rate of white women (Guerino et al., 2011; Mauer, 2013). Between 2000 and 2009, however, the rate declined for black women by 31 percent while continuing to increase for white and Hispanic women (by 47 and 23 percent, respectively). Mauer (2013) suggests that much of this recent shift was due to a reduction in drug-related incarcerations among black women and an increase in methamphetamine prosecutions among white women.

As the rate of women's incarceration has grown, so has the risk of maternal imprisonment (Kruttschnitt, 2010). One in 30 children born in 1990 had a mother incarcerated by age 14, compared with 1 in 60 born in 1978 (Wildeman, 2009). Scholars have been examining the experiences of incarcerated women and their children for decades, with a majority of studies using small convenience samples and qualitative methods (for reviews, see Bloom and Brown, 2011; Henriques and Manatu-Rupert, 2001; and Myers et al., 1999). These studies highlight the prevalence of economic and educational disadvantage, substance use, mental illness, and domestic abuse among mothers with an incarceration history, with some mothers portraying jail or prison as a "safe haven" from battering and problems related to substance addiction (Richie, 1996; Greene et al., 2000; Henriques and Jones-Brown, 2000).

Nearly two-thirds of mothers in state prisons were living with their child(ren) prior to their incarceration, many in single-parent households (Glaze and Maruschak, 2008; Mumola, 2000). Thus, a predominant theme in the literature on incarcerated mothers is mother-child separation. Using single-prison samples, Poehlmann (2005b, 2005c) describes the initial separation as one of intense distress for both mothers and children (see also Fishman, 1983). During the incarceration period, mother-child contact may be limited as a result of travel costs or mother-caregiver relationship issues (Bloom and Steinhart, 1993; Hairston, 1991). Less mother-child contact may be associated with mothers' increased depressive symptoms (Poehlmann, 2005b). Other studies find that maternal incarceration is associated with a host of negative child outcomes, including poor academic performance, classroom behavior problems, suspension, and delinquency (see the review of Myers et al., 1999). Poehlmann (2005a) examines the role of caregiver arrangements and modified home environments during mothers' incarceration and finds that among children of incarcerated mothers, cognitive outcomes may be influenced by caregiver socioeconomic characteristics and the quality of the home environment. This topic merits more attention in future research.

A few recent studies use longitudinal data and more rigorous methods to examine the effect of maternal incarceration on child academic performance, housing arrangements, and behavioral outcomes. Using data from two large samples of children in Chicago public schools and propensity score and fixed effects modeling techniques, Cho (2009a, 2009b) finds no association between maternal incarceration and children's standardized test scores, but a negative effect on grade retention in the years immediately following mother's prison entry. Another study (Cho, 2011), using administrative records and event history analysis, finds that adolescents are at higher risk of dropping out of school in the year their mother enters jail or prison.

Two studies use data from the Fragile Families Study to examine the effect of maternal incarceration on housing instability. Geller and colleagues (2009) find that incarceration is associated with an increase in the likelihood of residential mobility. Wildeman (forthcoming) finds no effect on child homelessness. This latter finding may be due to the fact that children of incarcerated mothers are more likely than children of incarcerated fathers to enter foster care (Dallaire, 2007; Mumola, 2000).

Finally, Wildeman and Turney (forthcoming) use data from the Fragile Families Study to examine the effect of maternal incarceration on child behavior problems. Using propensity score models for both parent and teacher reports, they find no association between mothers' incarceration and children's behavior problems at age 9. Dallaire (2007), however, finds that adult children of incarcerated mothers are more likely than adult children of incarcerated fathers to be incarcerated.

Taken together, then, the small amount of evidence on the effect of maternal incarceration on overall child well-being is mixed. This subject, too, deserves more attention in future research.

METHODOLOGICAL LIMITATIONS

To put the above discussion in proper context, it is important to note the major limitations of the studies reviewed. First, all of the ethnographies and many of the quantitative studies are based on convenience samples obtained in specific cities or communities. While these studies provide rich descriptions of the family lives of men and women with an incarceration history, and while they generate a multitude of intriguing hypotheses, their findings may not be generalizable to families in other cities or other parts of the country.

Second, although a number of more recent quantitative studies use probability samples of the national population, these studies are based on only three data sets: the Fragile Families Study, the National Longitudinal Study of Adolescent Health, and the Panel Study of Income Dynamics. At this time, these are the only large, nationally representative data sets that include information on incarceration. The field would benefit and more would be known about outcomes for families if other large national surveys did more to capture data from families with incarcerated or previously incarcerated parents.

A third limitation involves the measurement of other criminal justice contact or criminal behavior. With a few exceptions, studies do not take account of factors that precede incarceration (offending, arrests, and convictions), so the consequences of imprisonment are not sharply distinguished from those of other factors.

A fourth, and perhaps most important, limitation of the literature is that all of the studies are based on observational rather than experimental data. Men who go to prison are different from other men in ways that are likely to affect their family relationships as well as their chances of incarceration. As noted elsewhere in this report (see Chapters 2 and 7), men and women with an incarceration history are less educated and more likely to have mental health problems and alcohol and drug addictions than the general population. In turn, their families are likely to be unstable and to experience economic hardships and their children to be at risk of doing less well in school regardless of whether the father or mother spends time in jail;

BOX 9-2
Techniques for Dealing with Omitted Variable Bias

Researchers use a variety of statistical techniques to deal with the problem of omitted variable bias. The oldest and most widely used is to control for all of the characteristics that might affect both incarceration and family well-being. Unfortunately, this technique is limited because the data sets available for examining the effects of incarceration do not measure all the relevant characteristics.

A second technique is to measure the outcome variable of interest before and after fathers' incarceration to see whether spending time in prison is associated with a change in the outcome. This approach—the lagged dependent variable (LDV) model—requires longitudinal data and allows the researcher to estimate the effect of incarceration net of the factors that affect the preincarceration outcome. In one of the studies we examined (Geller et al., 2012), for example, the researchers controlled for children's behavior problems at age 3 and looked at whether those whose fathers went to jail or prison when the children were between ages 3 and 5 were more likely to exhibit behavior problems at age 5 than those whose fathers did not go to jail or prison. Longitudinal data also allow the researcher to conduct a placebo test to see whether fathers' future incarceration predicts current family problems. In the example given above, the researchers looked at whether children whose fathers were incarcerated when the children were between ages 3 and 5 showed higher levels of behavior problems at age 3. A positive outcome would indicate that something other than incarceration was causing the behavior problems.

Other researchers use longitudinal data to estimate a fixed effects model, which examines the association between a change in incarceration and a change in behavior. While this model does a better job than the LDV model of controlling for omitted variable bias, it does not eliminate the possibility that a change in an omitted variable might have led to the incarceration as well as the change in behavior. Continuing with the previous example, a father might have become

---

that is, the correlation between incarceration and family hardship may be due to conditions other than incarceration. The failure to take account of characteristics that affect incarceration as well as social and economic hardships leads to what researchers call "omitted variable bias." This problem is endemic in the literature on incarceration effects.

The best way to deal with omitted variable bias is to run an experiment in which people are randomly assigned to incarceration status. Because people cannot be randomly assigned to prison,[2] researchers have used a

---

[2]Note, however, that some studies have tested an overnight stay in jail as treatment (Sherman and Berk, 1984). In their study of police interventions for family violence, Sherman and Berk (1984), for example, found that a night in jail was not strongly associated with reduced offending. In addition, researchers have considered differing practices as natural experiments. In a recent study, Loeffler (2013) used randomization to judges, which led to variation in time

unemployed during the 2-year period after the child reached age 3 and before age 5 and responded by engaging in criminal activity that ultimately led to incarceration. In this case, the father's unemployment and criminal behavior may also have a role in the child's increasing behavior problems, or may be the primary causes rather than incarceration.

A fifth technique is to use a state policy, or natural experiment, to estimate the effect of incarceration on family well-being. For example, several researchers have used state differences in race-specific incarceration rates to determine whether these policies and practices affect family formation behaviors, such as marriage, divorce, and nonmarital childbearing. By using a state-level measure of incarceration, the researcher avoids the problem of omitted variable bias at the individual level. But the problem still exists at the aggregate level unless the researcher can find a policy or practice that affects an individual's chances of incarceration but is unrelated to the outcome of interest except via this pathway.

Finally, some researchers use a propensity score matching approach, which entails calculating a probability of incarceration for each man (or father) in the study, and then comparing the family outcomes of men with the same probability (or propensity) but different incarceration experiences to see whether they differ. Although this approach does not deal with omitted variable bias—propensity scores are based on observed variables only—it has certain advantages over standard regression analyses and may yield more accurate estimates of the association between incarceration and outcomes of interest. One of the more convincing studies is one that starts with a sample of convicted men, constructs a matched sample of men with the same propensity for incarceration, and then looks at whether those who were incarcerated had different outcomes than those who did not go to jail or prison (Apel et al., 2010). This study found that men who were incarcerated were more likely to divorce than their counterparts who were not incarcerated.

variety of statistical techniques to deal with the problem of omitted variable bias (see Box 9-2).

KNOWLEDGE GAPS

As discussed above, the studies reviewed in this chapter have several limitations. A more robust research program is needed to answer the questions considered here with greater confidence. We offer the following observations on how to address some of the knowledge gaps in this area.

---

served, to assess the effects of incarceration on crime and unemployment. While this approach has limitations, it would provide additional information to be considered along with findings based on the other approaches to dealing with omitted variable bias.

Understanding Variations

More work is needed to understand how the effects of fathers' incarceration on families and children vary depending on living arrangements prior to incarceration, the quality of relationships, and the ages and developmental stages of affected children. Information on the level of involvement and quality of the parental relationship prior to conviction could be incorporated into an experiment, as well as longitudinal data collection. Note, however, that measuring fathers' residence would be a challenge because men who are likely to spend time in prison and jail also are likely to be involved in multiple households before and after release.

Still missing is important descriptive information that bears on the causal questions at hand. The field would benefit from tackling the problem of omitted variables by observing them. How dangerous, violent, drug involved, and/or mentally unstable are the individuals who go to prison? What do their personal histories (as children) of family instability and family violence look like? How does incarceration contribute to family complexity—multiple partners, attachments, and households?

The collection of longitudinal data tracking individuals before and after their contact with the criminal justice system is needed. Partnering with existing longitudinal studies would be a useful avenue to explore to this end. Indicators of the quality of family life need to be tracked to better understand the influences on spousal and/or parental behaviors.

Aggregate Effects

Little attention has to date been paid to estimating the aggregate effects of high rates of incarceration on family stability, poverty and economic well-being, and child well-being. Given that incarceration is concentrated among men with low education, one might expect that recent trends in incarceration have affected aggregate poverty rates as well as trends in family structure and intergenerational mobility. To address aggregate effects, better estimates are needed of the proportion of families and children exposed to incarceration and the differential effects of incarceration depending on living arrangements and the quality of preincarceration relationships. Estimates also are needed of the proportion of families likely to benefit from a family member's incarceration.

CONCLUSION

This chapter has reviewed the literature on the consequences of parental incarceration for the children and families of those incarcerated, a question of importance at any level of incarceration but particularly in the current era of high U.S. incarceration rates. Our literature review has included both recent ethnographic studies and quantitative analyses and studies using convenience samples as well as population-based samples. Such a review represents a partial look at the literature on the consequences of incarceration for families and children; a more thorough review would be beyond the scope of this study. Nonetheless, our review suffices to provide a sense of the consequences. Although the evidence from individual studies is limited and findings across some studies are mixed, our review leads to the conclusion that parental incarceration, on balance, is associated with poorer outcomes for families and children. Whether these associations reflect causality is much less certain.

We find consistent evidence, in both the ethnographic and quantitative studies, of a link between men's incarceration and instability in male-female unions. We find a strong and consistent link between fathers' incarceration and family economic hardship, including housing insecurity, difficulty meeting basic needs, and use of public assistance. Incarceration tends to reduce fathers' involvement in the lives of their children after release, in large part because it undermines the coparenting relationship with the child's mother. Finally, both ethnographic and quantitative studies indicate that fathers' incarceration increases children's behavior problems, notably aggression and delinquency. The consequences are especially pronounced among boys and among children who were living with and positively involved with their father at the time of his incarceration. Recent surveys indicate that roughly 4 of 10 incarcerated fathers report living with their children prior to incarceration. Of interest, although father's incarceration is associated with poorer grades and lower educational attainment, it is not associated with lower cognitive ability. Rather, school failure appears to arise from social-emotional problems rather than a lack of intellectual capacity.

In reviewing the literature on the consequences of parental incarceration for the families and children of those incarcerated, we have been mindful of the broad charge to this committee. Ideally, the research evidence would help in determining whether the dramatic increase in incarceration rates over the past four decades, viewed as a distinct phenomenon, has affected, for better or worse, the families and children of those incarcerated. There are, however, no studies explicitly examining the effect of the prison buildup on the families and children of incarcerated parents. As a statistical matter, the number of children with a parent in prison continued to grow with increasing incarceration, reaching an estimated 1.7 million in 2007. Thus we might hypothesize that greater numbers of individuals and families have experienced the predominantly negative consequences of a partner's or parent's incarceration as the extent of incarceration has expanded, but that hypothesis has not been tested. There remain unanswered questions about the aggregate effects of the incarceration buildup. Nonetheless, the close correlation between having a partner or parent who has been incarcerated and poor outcomes among families and children is unmistakable.

10

Consequences for Communities

Previous chapters have examined the impact of the historic rise in U.S. incarceration rates on crime, the health and mental health of those incarcerated, their prospects for employment, and their families and children. In those discussions, the unit of analysis is the individual before and after incarceration and, secondarily, his or her familial networks. Here, our focus is on the community, especially the urban neighborhoods from which most prisoners come.

At the most prosaic level, we use the term *community* here to denote the geographically defined neighborhood where the individuals sent to prison lived before their arrest and to which, in most cases, they will return after they are released from prison. Scholars have long been interested in the aggregate correlates and consequences of incarceration, but research has tended until quite recently to examine larger social units such as nations, states, and counties. Relatively few studies have examined the units of analyses that are the focus of this chapter—urban communities or neighborhoods. We are most interested in how neighborhoods have borne the brunt of the historic increase in rates of incarceration.

Two questions frame the chapter. We begin by assessing the spatial distribution of incarceration: To what extent is incarceration concentrated by place, and what are the characteristics of the communities most affected by high rates of incarceration? For example, how uneven is the geographic spread of incarceration within American cities, and how does it differ across neighborhoods that vary by economic conditions or the racial and ethnic distribution of residents? These are largely descriptive questions, but ones that are essential for scientific understanding of the problem at hand.

The second question on which we focus here is: What are the consequences for communities of varying levels of incarceration? For example, how have neighborhoods with high rates of incarceration fared relative to those with lower rates? The incidence of crime is one key outcome, but our analysis also considers a broad conception of community life that includes economic well-being (e.g., the concentration of poverty) and the complex set of relationships that create or undermine a sense of connection, belonging, and purpose. Recent research has focused in particular on the dynamics of informal social control and the perceived legitimacy of the criminal justice system. We are also interested in whether the nearly 5-fold increase in per capita rates of incarceration, viewed from the perspective of affected communities, has had positive or negative effects on local neighborhoods.

The second question on the consequences of incarceration is largely causal in nature and puts strict demands on the evidence, which we assess in the third section of the chapter. Our review reveals that, while there is strong evidence that incarceration is disproportionately concentrated in a relatively small number of communities, typically urban neighborhoods, tests of the independent *effects* of incarceration on these communities are relatively sparse. Moreover, the studies that do exist have a number of problems that preclude drawing clear or consistent inferences about what is cause and what is effect. A major problem is that incarceration at the neighborhood level is entangled with a large number of preexisting social disadvantages, especially the concentration of high levels of poverty and violence. We believe this to be an important finding in itself. Indeed, even if incarceration has no estimable unique effect on community-level indicators, the intense concentration of incarceration added to existing social inequalities constitutes a severe hardship faced by a small subset of neighborhoods.

In short, we conclude in this chapter that (1) incarceration is concentrated in communities already severely disadvantaged and least capable of absorbing additional adversities, but (2) there exist no reliable statistical estimates of the unique effect of the spatial concentration of incarceration on the continuing or worsening social and economic problems of these neighborhoods. Based on the existing evidence, we thus are unable to estimate with confidence the magnitude of incarceration's effects on communities. We reach this cautious conclusion fully aware of the unprecedented levels of criminal justice involvement, particularly incarceration, in the communities of interest. Accordingly, in the fourth section of the chapter, we recommend steps that can be taken to fill knowledge gaps in this area and provide a more rigorous assessment of competing claims. We also conclude that causal questions are not the only ones of interest and that further research is needed to examine variation over time and geographic scale in the spatial concentration of disadvantage and incarceration.

SPATIAL CONCENTRATION OF HIGH
RATES OF INCARCERATION

Our review of the evidence underscores the fact that incarceration is concentrated in specific places, and the dramatic increases in incarceration have been concentrated disproportionately in those neighborhoods. In other words, rates of incarceration are highly uneven, with some communities experiencing stable and disproportionately high rates and others seeing very few if any residents imprisoned. The communities and neighborhoods with the highest rates of incarceration tend to be characterized by high rates of poverty, unemployment, and racial segregation. In particular, the geography of incarceration is contingent on race and concentrated poverty, with poor African American communities bearing the brunt of high rates of imprisonment. These same places also have high levels of violence and frequent contact with criminal justice institutions (e.g., the police, probation and parole, and the court system). The spatial inequality of incarceration is a general phenomenon across the United States and is seen in multiple cities. To illustrate, we consider four cities: Chicago, Seattle, New York City, and Houston.

Chicago provides an example of the spatial inequality in incarceration (Sampson and Loeffler, 2010). West Garfield Park and East Garfield Park on the city's West Side, both almost all black and very poor, stand out as the epicenter of incarceration, with West Garfield having a rate of admission to prison more than 40 times higher than that of the highest-ranked white community (Sampson, 2012, p. 113). This is a difference of kind, not simply degree.

A second example is Seattle, which is demographically very different from Chicago. The highest levels of incarceration in Seattle are in the Central District and the Rainer Valley. Only a few census tracts in the city or even within these neighborhoods are majority black, but the plurality of the population in those places is African American, and the residents have the city's highest levels of economic disadvantage. Here, too, incarceration is concentrated in the most disadvantaged places (Drakulich et al., 2012).

To provide a visual perspective that captures the neighborhood concentration of incarceration and its social context by race and income, Figures 10-1 and 10-2 show an aerial view of two other cities, again very different from one another and located in different parts of the country; in this case, moreover, the cities also have very different levels of incarceration.[1] Figure 10-1 shows the distribution of incarceration in the country's most populous city, New York City, which had an overall prison admission rate of

---

[1]These maps were produced for the committee by Eric Cadora of the Justice Mapping Center (http://www°.justicemapping.org/about-us/).

1.8 per 1,000 residents in 2009 (the most recent year for which data with fine-tuned geographic coordinates were available). Figure 10-2 focuses on the country's fourth most populous city—Houston, Texas. Even though Houston has an admission rate more than triple that of New York City, at 6.3 per 1,000 in 2008, a substantial neighborhood concentration of imprisonment still is seen in both cities.

In New York City (Figure 10-1), incarceration is concentrated in such neighborhoods as Central and East Harlem, the South Bronx, and pockets of Brooklyn near Bedford Stuyvesant and East New York, almost all of which are black or Hispanic and are characterized by concentrated poverty (see legend graphs). By contrast, many neighborhoods of the city are virtually incarceration free, as, for example, are most of Queens and Staten Island. Overall, just 15 of the city's 65 community districts account for more than half of those sent to prison over the course of the year. These communities have twice the poverty rate of the rest of the city and are more than 90 percent minority, compared with less than 60 percent among the remaining areas.

Figure 10-2 shows that, while having much higher levels of incarceration than New York City, Houston has rates of removal to prison that are also highly uneven. Incarceration rates are highest in a sector extending south of downtown (e.g., Third Ward, South Union) and to the northeast (e.g., Kashmere Gardens). As in New York City, these neighborhoods are disproportionately black or Hispanic and poor (see legend graphs). Overall, these neighborhoods represent less than 20 percent of the city's population yet generate more than half of the admissions to state prison. Also as in

FIGURE 10-1 Distribution of incarceration in New York City (2009). People admitted to prison per 1,000 adults by census tract of residence with community district borders.
NOTE: About half (52 percent) of the people sent to prison from New York City in 2009 came from 15 of the city's 65 community districts. These 15 community districts have the highest prison admission rates among the city's community districts and are labeled on the map according to rank from 1 to 15. They are collectively labeled "Highest (15)" and compared with the city's remaining 50 community districts, labeled "Remaining (50)," in the figure above.
SOURCE: Prepared for the committee by the Justice Mapping Center, Rutgers University School of Criminal Justice: Maps designed and produced by Eric Cadora and Charles Swartz.

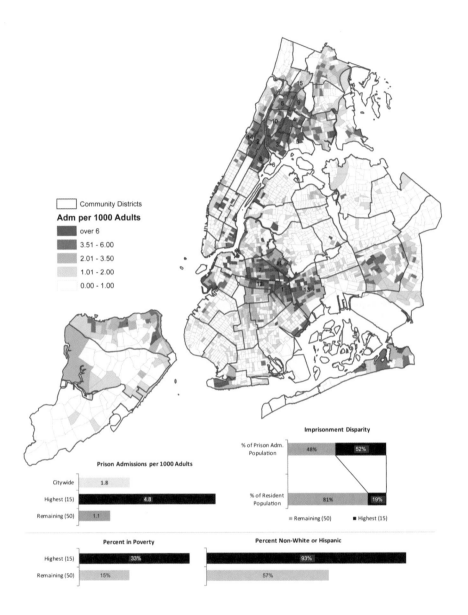

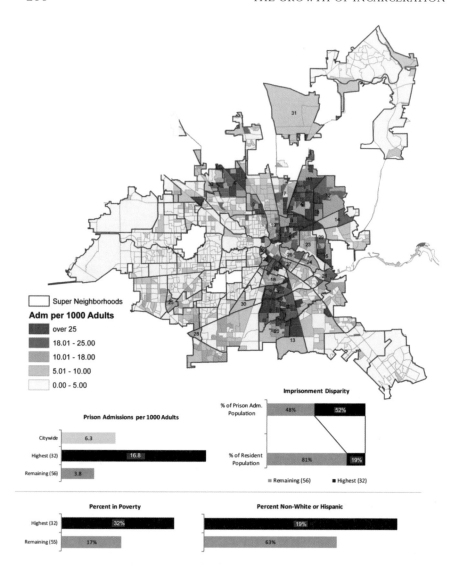

New York City, wide swaths of Houston—especially the western, southeastern, and far northeastern parts of the city—see little incarceration.

Thus, whether in Chicago in the midwest, New York City in the northeast, Houston in the central southern portion of the country, or Seattle in the northwest, as in other cities across the United States, geographic inequality in incarceration is the norm, with black and poor communities being disproportionately affected. The level and cost of this kind of spatial concentration can be surprisingly high. In their analysis of the residential blocks in Brooklyn, New York City, with the highest incarceration rates, Cadora and Swartz (1999) find that approximately 10 percent of men aged 16 to 44 were admitted to jail or prison each year. In a subsequent study, they calculate the costs of incarcerating the men from those blocks. For blocks with the highest rates of incarceration, the taxpayers of New York were spending up to $3 million a year per block to house those incarcerated from that block (Cadora et al., 2003).

Did these communities experience the same (or greater, or lesser) increase in per capita rates of incarceration as the country as a whole? Although not at the neighborhood level, a study by Lynch and Sabol (2001) sheds light on this question. They determined that in 1984, early in the prison buildup, about half of the 220,000 individuals released from state prisons returned to "core counties," which the authors define as those with a central city. In 1996, by contrast, two-thirds of the reentry cohort, which had grown to 500,000 individuals, returned to these counties. In absolute numbers, this shift from 110,000 to 330,000 individuals returning to the nation's urban centers represents a tripling of the reentry burden shouldered by these counties in just 12 years.

Evidence also indicates that the link between concentrated disadvantage and incarceration impacts some demographic groups more than others.

FIGURE 10-2 Distribution of incarceration in Houston, Texas (2008). People admitted to prison per 1,000 adults by census block-group of residence with super neighborhood borders.
NOTE: About half (52 percent) of the people sent to prison from Houston in 2008 came from 32 of the city's 88 super neighborhoods. These 32 super neighborhoods have the highest prison admission rates among the city's super neighborhoods and are labeled on the map according to rank from 1 to 32. They are collectively labeled "Highest (32)" and compared with the city's remaining 56 super neighborhoods, labeled "Remaining (50)," in the figure above.
SOURCE: Prepared for the committee by the Justice Mapping Center, Rutgers University School of Criminal Justice: Maps designed and produced by Eric Cadora and Charles Swartz.

Heimer and colleagues (2012) find that black women's imprisonment increases when the African American population is concentrated in metropolitan areas and poverty rates rise, but that white women's rates are unaffected by changes in poverty. Unfortunately, data are insufficient at the neighborhood level from the 1970s to the present to allow finer-grained conclusions about differential rates of increase by disadvantage. Overall, however, Figures 10-1 and 10-2, along with data from other cities around the country, demonstrate that incarceration is highly uneven spatially and is disproportionately concentrated in black, poor, urban neighborhoods.

COMPETING VIEWS ON THE COMMUNITY-LEVEL EFFECTS OF INCARCERATION

Two competing hypotheses frame the conceptual case for the differential effects of incarceration, by community, on crime and other aspects of well-being. One hypothesis, which might be termed the classic view (reviewed in depth in Chapter 5), is that incarceration has a deterrent and/or incapacitative effect (National Research Council, 1978a; Levitt, 2004). Common sense suggests that crime will be reduced as increased incarceration takes criminally active individuals off the streets or deters others in the community from committing crimes. According to this view, one need only point to the low levels of crime in the modern era, and then to the high rates of incarceration, and conclude that the two phenomena are causally linked. Yet, as discussed in Chapter 5, this simple causal claim is not easily sustained at the national level for a number of methodological reasons, and it is equally problematic at the neighborhood level. Moreover, again as noted in Chapter 5, deterrence appears to be linked more closely to the certainty of being apprehended than to the severity of punishment. Incarceration does incapacitate, but the marginal effects are smaller than they at first appear because the free population has less criminal propensity than the incarcerated population. At very high rates of incarceration, therefore, the marginal incapacitative effect may be quite small. At the community level, the overall effects of incarceration are equally difficult to estimate for methodological reasons.

The second, very different hypothesis is that incarceration—at least at high levels—has a criminogenic, or positive, effect on crime independent of other social-ecological factors. According to this view, to the extent that high incarceration rates disrupt a community's stability, they weaken the forces of informal social control in ways that result in more crime. This hypothesis may initially appear to be counterintuitive, as one wonders how the removal and incarceration of many more people convicted of crimes could lead to an increase in crime. Yet this hypothesis is rooted in a scientific understanding of the role of informal social control in deterring criminal behavior.

The most forceful argument for this hypothesis is made by Clear (2007) and his colleagues (Rose and Clear, 1998; Clear et al., 2003). These authors argue for an interpretation of incarceration as a dynamic of "coercive mobility"—the involuntary churning of people going from the community to prison and back—generating residential instability that is a staple of social disorganization theory (Bursik, 1988; Sampson and Groves, 1989). The effects of imprisonment at one point in time thus are posited to destabilize neighborhood dynamics at a later point, which in turn increases crime. Destabilization is hypothesized to occur mainly through residential and family instability, weakened political and economic systems, and diminished social networks. Clear (2007, p. 5) argues as follows: "Concentrated incarceration in those impoverished communities has broken families, weakened the social control capacity of parents, eroded economic strength, soured attitudes toward society, and distorted politics; even after reaching a certain level, it has increased rather than decreased crime."

Another mechanism, hypothesized by Sampson (1995), works through increased unemployment and imbalanced sex ratios arising from the disproportionate removal of males in the community. Thus, for example, where there are fewer males, especially employed males, per female rates of family disruption are higher. These changes in high incarceration communities are thought to disrupt social control and other features of the neighborhood that inhibit or regulate crime. Of course, it is also possible that incarceration may have no effect on crime, or only a small one (see Chapter 5). It is important as well to note that the above two hypotheses are not mutually exclusive. Incarceration at moderate levels could decrease crime while disrupting the social organization of communities and increasing crime at high levels.

ASSESSING THE EVIDENCE

Relatively few studies have directly assessed the coercive mobility hypothesis or the more traditional crime reduction hypothesis at the neighborhood level, and among existing studies the evidence is conflicting. Similar to a recent review by Harding and Morenoff (forthcoming), our efforts yielded fewer than a dozen studies directly addressing the questions raised in this chapter.

In a study of Tallahassee, Florida, Clear and colleagues (2003) report that after a neighborhood reaches a certain concentration of prison admissions, the effect of more admissions is to increase crime (see also Clear, 2007). Hence the relationship between prison input and crime in this study is curvilinear, with high levels of imprisonment having criminogenic effects.

However, the same study finds that releases from prison are positively associated with higher crime rates the following year, which the authors note could be explained in several different ways.[2] Another study of Tallahassee finds similar nonlinear results (Dhondt, 2012).

Renauer and colleagues (2006) attempted to replicate the Tallahassee studies in Portland, Oregon. They argue that testing nonlinear effects is problematic with the models used in prior research.[3] Using three different estimation techniques, they find a significant negative relationship between incarceration and violent crime at moderate levels but a positive relationship at high levels. They identify the tipping point of high incarceration as a rate of 3.2 admissions per 1,000, but only 4 of 95 neighborhoods they examined met or exceeded this level. These results do not hold for property crime, and the results for violence are sensitive to outliers. In a study of New York City, Fagan and colleagues (Fagan and West, 2013; Fagan et al., 2003) find no overall effect of incarceration on homicide at the neighborhood level. By contrast, Lynch and Sabol (2004b) report that removing and incarcerating people in Baltimore reduced crime at the neighborhood level. Overall, then, while some research finds that incarceration, depending on its magnitude, has both positive and negative associations with crime, the results linking incarceration to crime at the neighborhood level are mixed across studies and appear to be highly sensitive to model specifications.

The coercive mobility hypothesis advanced by Rose and Clear (1998) focuses on the effects of incarceration not only on crime but also on the social organization of neighborhoods. They argue that high rates of incarceration, controlling for crime rates, undermine key social characteristics of neighborhoods, such as social networks, community cohesion, informal controls, and respect for the law—in other words, legitimate systems of order and the political and social structure within a community. Lynch and Sabol (2004b) tested this hypothesis in Baltimore by estimating the effect of prison admissions on informal social control, community solidarity, neighboring (i.e., individuals interacting with others and meaningfully engaging in behaviors with those living around them), and voluntary associations (see

---

[2]"Routine-activities theory," for example, suggests that "releasing ex-offenders into the community increases the number of offenders in the community and that an increase in crime is, therefore, not surprising." Another interpretation, consistent with a "social disorganization framework," is that released ex-offenders "are people whose arrival in the community constitutes a challenge to the community's capacity for self-regulation" (Clear et al., 2003, pp. 55-56).

[3]Clear and colleagues (2003) estimate a negative binomial model for count data. Relying on Hannon and Knapp (2003), Renauer and colleagues (2006) argue that negative binomial models and log transformations may "bend" the data toward artifactual support for nonlinear relationships. They therefore recommend robustness checks using a variety of estimation techniques to determine the sensitivity of results to model specification.

also Lynch and Sabol, 2004a). Their findings are mixed. Using an instrumental variables approach, the authors find that incarceration in the form of removal had a positive effect on informal social control but a negative effect on community cohesion. Adjusting for control variables, they find no effect of incarceration on neighboring and membership in voluntary associations. Drakulich and colleagues (2012) report that as the number of released inmates increases in census tracts, crime-inhibiting collective efficacy is reduced, although the authors indicate that this effect is largely indirect and is due to the turmoil created in a given neighborhood's labor and housing markets.[4] We were surprised by the absence of research on the relationship between incarceration rates and direct indicators of a neighborhood's residential stability, such as population movement, household mobility, and length of residence in the community.

Two studies examine human capital and the link between incarceration and a neighborhood's economic status. Fagan and West (2013) find that jail and prison admissions were associated with lower median income, although the association was larger for jail than for prison. Piquero and colleagues (2006) report that the association of high rates of incarceration with lower income and human capital was strongest for blacks.

A closely related question is whether incarceration influences attitudes toward the law, and if so, to what extent. Clear and Rose (1999) find that Tallahassee residents familiar with someone who had been imprisoned were more skeptical of the power of government or community to enforce social norms than those who had not been exposed to incarceration. A later study (Rose et al., 2001) finds that Tallahassee residents with a family member in prison were more isolated from other people and less likely to interact with neighbors and friends. Finally, research has established that concentrated disadvantage is strongly associated with cynical and mistrustful attitudes toward police, the law, and the motives of neighbors—what Sampson and Bartusch (1998) call "legal cynicism." And research also has shown that communities with high rates of legal cynicism are persistently violent (Kirk and Papachristos, 2011). Consistent with the hypothesis of Clear and Rose (1999), then, high rates of incarceration may add to distrust of the criminal justice system; however, few studies have directly addressed this issue.

---

[4]If one assumes an effect of incarceration on communities due to such coercive reentry, then the question arises of whether the underlying mechanism is compositional or contextual. A compositional effect could occur if releasing individuals from prison (churning) puts active criminals back into the community, driving up the crime rate even with no change to the neighborhood's social organization. A contextual effect could occur if the return (or removal) of individuals disrupts neighborhood social organization, leading in turn to higher crime rates. Future studies are needed to distinguish these (nonexclusive) mechanisms if the process by which incarceration affects communities is to be fully understood.

Methodological Challenges to Causal Inference

When attempting to estimate the effects of incarceration on crime or other dimensions of community life, such as informal social control, researchers encounter a host of methodological challenges. The challenges addressed in this section are equally relevant whether the object of study is crime or community life more broadly.

One simple but large obstacle is that much of the research on the relationship between community or neighborhood characteristics and incarceration is cross-sectional. Although longitudinal assessments are no panacea, disentangling cause and effect at a single point in time is difficult. The important questions on these topics—such as whether incarceration reduces or increases community crime or informal social control—are about social processes over time, which require longitudinal data to be thoroughly tested. Such neighborhood data have yet to be assembled across all the decades of the prison boom. Instead, cause-and-effect questions have been addressed using a small number of cross-sectional data sets, usually for limited periods of time. At the outset, then, the database from which to assess the evidence is neither large nor robust, a point to which we return in the chapter's concluding section.

A second problem, whether one is using cross-sectional data or making longitudinal predictions with explicit temporal ordering, arises from the high correlation and logical dependencies between crime rates and incarceration at the community level. These factors make it difficult to (1) disentangle what is causal and what is spurious, and (2) control for prior crime in estimating the independent influence of incarceration. For example, crime is expected to influence incarceration and vice versa, and both are embedded in similar social contexts. Incarceration also is conditional on conviction, which in turn is conditional on arrest, which in turn is strongly related overall to differences in crime commission. The interdependent nature of criminal justice processing is complicated by the fact that incarceration rates are highest in communities with a long history of social deprivation. Communities with high rates of incarceration and violent crime, in other words, tend to be characterized by the persistent concentration of poverty and racial segregation (Sampson, 2012, Figures 1 and 2). To the extent that incarceration is closely associated with crime rates and other long-hypothesized causes of crime at the community level, large analytic challenges arise. The remainder of this section probes the nature of these challenges in more detail.

A body of research in criminology suggests that crime and violence have deleterious effects on community well-being through mechanisms, such as selective outmigration, the segregation of minorities in disadvantaged environments, fear, disorder, legal cynicism, diminished collective efficacy and altruism, and general community decline (Bursik, 1986; Liska and Bellair, 1995; Morenoff and Sampson, 1997; Skogan, 1986, 1990). There is also compelling evidence that exposure to violence among children leads to decreases in learning and increased risk of future violence, producing self-reinforcing "cycles of violence" (National Research Council and Institute of Medicine, 2001; Sharkey, 2010) and incarceration that are concentrated in selected communities. The result is that what appear to be incarceration effects at the community level may instead be caused by prior crime or violence.

Consider just the relationship between incarceration and crime rates. Evidence from Chicago indicates that the two are highly correlated across neighborhood, defined and measured in different ways, and time period (Sampson and Loeffler, 2010). In a set of follow-up analyses conducted for this report, we examined the *concurrent* association between incarceration and crime rates in Chicago community areas averaging approximately 38,000 residents. These are the two variables of central interest to the coercive mobility, criminogenic, and deterrence or crime control hypotheses. The linear relationship is near unity (0.96) in the period 2000-2005: there are no low crime, high incarceration communities and no low incarceration, high crime communities that would support estimating a causal relationship. The concurrent relationship between concentrated disadvantage in 1990 and incarceration in 1990-1995 is also extremely high—0.89.

We then examined the *predictive* relationship between incarceration and crime and at a lower level of aggregation, the census tract. Multicollinearity, or overlap among variables, is typically less of an issue at lower levels of aggregation.[5] Yet the 1995-2000 crime rate in Chicago census tracts is strongly, positively associated with imprisonment between 2000 and 2005 (R = .85, p <.01). Among more than 800 census tracts, only 1 was an outlier neighborhood that plausibly could be said to have high crime and low (or lower than expected) incarceration. Only 9 tracts combined no incarceration with varied rates of crime, and then only up to the middle of the crime distribution.

Furthermore, crime tends to be highly correlated over time, and controlling for prior crime is one of the major strategies employed by researchers to adjust for omitted variable bias when attempting to estimate the independent effect of incarceration (see Chapter 9 for a discussion of omitted variable bias). As Clear (2007, p. 164) notes: "Controlling for the

---

[5]The geographic unit of analysis varies across the studies we examined, but the most common unit in neighborhood-level research is the census tract, an administratively defined area meant to reflect significant ecological boundaries and averaging about 4,000 residents. One reason census tract data are commonly used is that they allow linkage to a rich array of sociodemographic variables collected by the U.S. Census Bureau.

previous year's crime rate removes a great deal of variance in crime rate and places a substantial statistical burden on the capacity of other variables in the model to explain the much reduced variance that is left." Clear's observation underscores the problem that arises with regression equations examining crime residuals from prior crime, regardless of whether incarceration is the independent variable. The existing literature predominantly finds persistently high correlations of crime rates over time, again meaning that only a handful of neighborhoods are supporting empirical estimates of independent effects of either incarceration or crime. Renauer and colleagues (2006, p. 366), for example, find that the correlation of violent crime from one year to the next was 0.99 across Portland neighborhoods. The effects of incarceration in this study thus are estimated on a tiny residual.

Arrest rates also are strongly correlated with imprisonment rates at the community level (0.75 at the tract level in Chicago) and not just with crime itself, making it difficult to disentangle the causal impact of incarceration from that of arrest. And of course, incarceration is definitionally dependent on conviction. These facts are important because a large literature in criminology suggests that arrest and conviction are in themselves disruptive and stigmatizing, just as incarceration is hypothesized to be (Becker, 1963; Goffman, 1963; Sutherland, 1947).[6] Attributing the criminogenic effects of these multiple prior stages of criminal justice processing (another kind of punishment) solely to incarceration is problematic without explicit modeling of their independent effects. Specifically, if criminal justice processing prior to incarceration is causally important, the appropriate counterfactual in a test meant to assess the specific role of high rates of incarceration in a community's social fabric would be an equally high-crime community with high-arrest rates but low imprisonment. Because neighborhoods with high levels of imprisonment tend to have high rates of crime and criminal justice processing, this comparison is difficult to find.

This close interdependence extends beyond the criminal justice system. Indeed, there is a strong concentration in the same communities not just of crime, arrests, and incarceration but also of multiple social disadvantages—often over long periods of time. It has long been known that the neighborhoods from which convicted felons are removed and sent to prison are troubled, marginal places. At the other end of the process, released inmates typically return to the disadvantaged places and social networks they left behind (Kirk, 2009). Even when not returning to the same neighborhood,

---

[6]Recent evidence suggests that arrest in adolescence is strongly associated with later school failure (Kirk and Sampson, 2013), and low educational attainment is known to be strongly related to both criminal involvement and incarceration. Crutchfield and colleagues (2012) find that early juvenile arrest is positively associated with later juvenile arrest, holding self-reported crime constant. Evidence also indicates that early arrest may predict young adult criminality and later conviction, holding self-reported crime involvement constant.

they return to places much like those from which they were removed (Bobo, 2009). These communities are characterized by high levels of social disadvantage, including poverty; unemployment; dropping out of school; family disruption; and, not surprisingly, high rates of crime, violence, and criminal justice processing in the form of arrests and convictions (Sampson, 2012).

The correlation of neighborhood disadvantage with race and incarceration presents an additional problem of interpretation when one is attempting to assess the effects of incarceration. Massoglia and colleagues (2013) use a nationally representative data set and find that only whites live in significantly more disadvantaged neighborhoods after than before prison. For blacks and Hispanics, incarceration has no overall effect on neighborhood attainment once preprison context is controlled for. The authors attribute this racial variation in the effect of incarceration to the high degree of racial neighborhood inequality: black ex-prisoners on average come from severely disadvantaged areas, while white ex-prisoners generally come from much better neighborhoods and so have more to lose from a prison spell. The authors conclude that their results "demonstrate the importance of controlling for pre-prison neighborhood characteristics when investigating the effects of incarceration on residential outcomes" (p. 142).

The situation of historically correlated adversities in most neighborhoods of the United States makes it difficult to estimate the unique causal impact of incarceration. The use of instrumental variables is one statistical approach with which researchers have attempted to address the fundamental causal identification problem. The idea is to seek exogenously or randomly induced variation in incarceration, such as one would obtain in an experiment. But we found that the empirical results of the handful of such studies are highly conflicting. Moreover, regardless of what direction of relationship obtains, the assumptions necessary to support identification restrictions often are arbitrary, and none of the studies of which we are aware uses experimentally induced variation. For example, one study that finds a deterrent effect of incarceration at the community level hinges on the assumption that drug arrests (the excluded instrument) are related to incarceration but not later crime (Lynch and Sabol, 2004b). This assumption is violated if, say, increases in drug arrests lead to competition among dealers that in turn results in a cascade of violence, or if the visibility of arrests leads residents to reduce crime through a deterrence mechanism. In both of these scenarios, the instrument has an effect on crime not operating through incarceration. Other studies have tried to use dependent variables thought to be decoupled from simultaneity or endogeneity, such as adult incarceration rates predicting juvenile delinquency as the outcome (unpublished paper described in Clear [2007, p. 171]). But the existing evidence on the intergenerational transmission of violence (Farrington et al., 2001) renders this strategy problematic as well.

Our review thus suggests a number of serious challenges to existing estimates of the neighborhood-level effects of incarceration. An independent assessment reaches much the same conclusion concerning the fragility of causal estimates in prior research (Harding and Morenoff, forthcoming). The authors conclude that the empirical evidence in published studies on neighborhoods and incarceration is equivocal: "Existing studies are few in number, based on relatively small numbers of neighborhoods, and heavily reliant on static cross-neighborhood comparisons that are very susceptible to omitted variable bias and reverse causality. Moreover, the findings are inconsistent across studies and even within studies when using different estimation techniques." To this we would add that although fixed effects longitudinal analyses have been used to control stable characteristics of the community and thereby omitted variable bias, crime, incarceration, arrest, poverty, most of the other confounders discussed in this section are time varying. It is possible that time-varying counterfactual models of neighborhood effects would be useful in addressing this problem (see, e.g., Wodtke et al., 2011).

Is High Incarceration Different?

As noted earlier, the coercive mobility hypothesis predicts that incarceration at low to moderate levels will reduce crime or imprisonment but at high levels will increase crime. Our examination of the evidence on this hypothesis revealed that nonlinear effects have not been systematically investigated in a sufficient number of studies or in ways that yield clear answers. Clear (2007, pp. 163-165) reviews six studies testing the nonlinear pattern and concludes that there is partial support for the coercive mobility hypothesis. At the same time, Clear notes that a number of problems hinder such estimates, including influential observations that are typically those with the highest incarceration rates. A related issue is that there is no consensus definition, whether theoretical or empirical, of what constitutes "high incarceration." In the study by Renauer and colleagues (2006), for example, a high incarceration neighborhood is defined empirically as one with more than 3 prison admissions per 1,000 residents, meaning that more than 0.5 percent of the population was admitted to prison. More worrisome, the authors report that only a handful of neighborhoods (four) met this criterion, yet these neighborhoods accounted for the positive effect of incarceration on crime (the effect was negative for moderate incarceration). In addition, when a nonlinear cubic model is estimated with terms for incarceration, incarceration squared, and incarceration cubed, these constituent terms tend to be highly correlated (even when transformed), and thus estimates often are highly unstable or, again, highly influenced by a few observations.

These studies point to an important conclusion: if there is a nonlinear pattern such that incarceration *reduces* crime at one point and *increases* it at another, then it is important to know precisely what the net effect is and where the tipping point lies. Based on our review, the challenges to estimating the countervailing influences of incarceration have not yet been resolved. In short, if incarceration has both positive and negative effects and at different time scales and tipping points, single estimates at one point in time or at an arbitrary point in the distribution yield misleading or partial answers (Sampson, 2011).

Additional Perspectives

Although the confounding among community crime rates, incarceration rates, and multiple dimensions of inequality makes it difficult to draw causal inferences, this high degree of correlation is itself substantively meaningful. Indeed, the fact that communities that are already highly disadvantaged bear the brunt of both crime and current incarceration policies sets up a potentially reinforcing social process. Sampson and Loeffler (2010), for example, argue that concentrated disadvantage and crime work together to drive up the incarceration rate, which in turn deepens the spatial concentration of disadvantage and (eventually) crime and then further incarceration—even if incarceration reduces some crime in the short run through incapacitation. In such a reinforcing system with possible countervailing effects at the aggregate temporal scale, estimating the overall net effect of incarceration is difficult if not impossible, even though it may be causally implicated in the dynamics of community life.

A growing ethnographic literature is focused on understanding the effect of incarceration on community life. Although not estimating cause and effect, these studies draw on interviews, fieldwork, and observation to provide a description of the consequences of incarceration.

Two studies offer insight into the social processes and mechanisms through which incarceration may influence the social infrastructure of urban communities. Rios (2011) considers the impact of the rise in incarceration on the structure of urban communities and institutions in Oakland, California. He argues that youth are subjected to social control efforts as a consequence of punitive practices among families, schools, convenience stores, police, parole officers, and prisons. According to this view, community institutions have been restructured from their original design in the wake of the growth in incarceration to focus on punishing marginalized boys living under conditions of extreme supervision and criminalization. In a study of a poor Philadelphia community, Goffman (2009) examines how imprisonment and the threat of imprisonment have undermined individual relationships to family, employment, and community life. Men "on the run" and their families or associates develop strategies for avoiding confinement and coping with the constant surveillance of their community.

Gowan's (2002) ethnographic research in San Francisco and St. Louis reveals that incarceration often led to periods of homelessness after release because of disrupted social networks, which substantially increased the likelihood of reincarceration resulting from desperation and proximity to other former inmates. Studying a group of men and women returning to Seattle neighborhoods after incarceration, Harris (2011) finds that an important determinant of successful reentry was individual-level change, but those she interviewed were aware of the importance of the cultural and structural barriers to their success, including employment and housing challenges, as well as the proximity to others in the neighborhood who were still "in the life."

In his analysis of family dynamics based on a series of case studies in Washington, DC, Braman (2002) compares relationships between men and women in high and low incarceration neighborhoods. In communities with many of their men behind bars, there were only 62 men for every 100 women, compared with a ratio of 94 men to 100 women in low incarceration neighborhoods. Braman (2002, p. 123) describes the consequences of this gender imbalance: "Men and women in neighborhoods where incarceration rates are high described this as both encouraging men to enter into relationships with multiple women, and encouraging women to enter into relationships with men who are already attached." It is not clear, however, whether gender imbalance can be attributed to incarceration as opposed to differentials in violence rates, mortality, or other social dynamics occurring in inner-city African American communities.

The studies cited above add richness to the findings presented in this report on the impact of high incarceration rates on families and children (Chapter 9) and U.S. society (Chapter 11). They also underscore the importance of undertaking a rigorous, extensive research program to examine incarceration's effects at the community level.

KNOWLEDGE GAPS

As detailed above, research on the effects of incarceration on communities has confronted a number of analytic challenges to drawing causal inferences. Moreover, the data available for this purpose leave much to be desired. State corrections departments maintain data for their own administrative purposes (e.g., locating parolees, collecting fines or restitution), so they often do not maintain information researchers need to test either the aggregate deterrence or coercive mobility hypothesis. Researchers have been able to obtain data that have allowed partial tests, but good-quality and temporally relevant geocoded data documenting both the communities from which the incarcerated are removed and those to which they return are needed to substantially advance understanding of these processes.

Beyond the collection and dissemination of georeferenced data, we believe the existing evidence justifies a rigorous program of research on communities, crime, and crime control—including incarceration. Based on our review, we see at least four potentially useful directions for future research: (1) comparative qualitative studies of the communities from which the incarcerated come and to which they return; (2) research taking advantage of natural experiments that induce exogenous change in prison admissions or releases; (3) longitudinal or life-course examination of individuals as they are arrested, convicted, and admitted to and released from prison; and (4) study of neighborhood-level relationships among crime, cumulative neighborhood disadvantage, and criminal justice processing over time, including over the full period of the historic rise in incarceration. We stress the importance of studying incarceration not in isolation but in the context of the other criminal justice experiences and social adversities typically faced by prisoners.

Comparative Qualitative Studies

As indicated above, some scholars have studied high incarceration neighborhoods through ethnography. Because it is difficult to generalize from single sites, there is a need for more qualitative studies, in diverse jurisdictions, of what happens in communities in which large numbers of people are imprisoned and large numbers of formerly incarcerated people live. Collaborative and comparative ethnographies are especially important, and researchers need to probe more widely multiple aspects of criminal justice processing and social deprivation. In particular, it is important to examine prior exposure to violence and state sanctions such as arrest and court conviction alongside incarceration, especially if Feeley's (1979) well-known argument that "the process is the punishment" is correct.

Natural Experiments

Some states have recently undergone rapid change in their criminal justice procedures as a result of court orders or other events that are arguably uncorrelated with underlying social conditions. California, for example, recently began a large-scale release of inmates under court order, providing an opportunity to study how the unexpected return of ex-prisoners to selected communities is causally linked to social conditions and crime rates. In the Boston area, mistaken and fraudulent work in a crime lab led to the voiding of hundreds of criminal convictions. Studying the impact of these exogenous changes might improve on prior attempts to use arbitrarily defined instrumental variables and thus prove useful in teasing out the various hypotheses on coercive mobility and the return of prisoners to communities. We caution, however, that an unbiased causal estimate is not the whole story. Often, where strong identification can be obtained, it is scientifically uninteresting because the estimate is for a highly atypical sample or a specific policy question that lacks broad import. The criminological research community needs to balance concern for unbiased causal estimates against external and substantive validity.

Life-Course Perspectives

Considerable observational research has focused on individuals released from prison, much of it looking at recidivism (National Research Council, 2007). Studying parolees, for example, Hipp and colleagues (2010) find that the social context of the neighborhoods and nearby neighborhoods to which they returned and the availability of social services in those neighborhoods were important predictors of their success or failure after release. Researchers could advance understanding of the processes discussed here by beginning to focus more on the communities where individuals returning from prison reside under naturally occurring or equilibrium conditions and by taking into account knowledge gained from life-course criminology. For example, the concept of "turning points" has been proposed to explain the effects of incarceration on later criminal and other social behaviors (Sampson and Laub, 1993). Neighborhoods can have turning points as well, allowing researchers to examine the aggregate deterrence and coercive mobility hypotheses in new ways, potentially building an understanding of how communities react when larger numbers of formerly incarcerated people live in them. Crucially, however, future research of this sort is dependent on the availability of a new generation of high-quality data matched to specific geographic coordinates in the criminal history.[7]

Neighborhood-Level Relationships

Feedback loops and cumulative processes not easily ascertained in experiment-like conditions are important to study. One area deserving further research is the likely reciprocal interaction whereby community vulnerability, violence, and incarceration are involved in negative feedback loops. As we have noted, disadvantaged communities are more likely than more advantaged communities to have high rates of incarceration, and

---

[7]We recognize that there are potentially serious confidentiality and institutional review board (IRB) concerns with respect to geographically identifiable data on arrestees and prisoners. Further work is needed in this area as well.

there is suggestive evidence that this connection increases their likelihood of becoming even more disadvantaged in the future (Clear, 2007; Sampson, 2012). Moreover, if disadvantaged communities disproportionately produce prisoners, they will disproportionately draw them back upon release, which in turn will generate additional hardships in terms of surveillance imposed on the community (Goffman, 2009), the financial strains of housing and employment support and addiction treatment, and potential recidivism. These feedback loops need further testing but conceptually are consistent with the persistent challenges faced by high incarceration communities. Simulation and agent-based models developed to understand neighborhood change (Bruch and Mare, 2006) may be useful in further understanding the complex dynamics of incarceration and crime.

CONCLUSION

Incarceration, broadly speaking, represents an interrelated sequence of events, experiences, and institutions. It is important to consider how the components and correlates of incarceration may have differential importance for any given community characteristic. As many researchers have observed, admissions and releases may have significantly different outcomes because they are very different social processes. As noted in Chapter 5, moreover, incarceration is not itself a policy but a policy product. Greater clarity is therefore needed as to what "incarceration" means: juvenile justice practices, admissions, releases, community supervision, and the incarceration rate (i.e., how many former residents are currently incarcerated) are related but different, and further research is needed on the precise mechanisms that relate them. The important point for this chapter is that incarceration represents the final step in a series of experiences with the criminal justice system such that incarceration by itself may not have much of an effect on communities when one also considers arrest, conviction, or other forms of state social control (Feeley, 1979).

High incarceration communities are deeply disadvantaged in other ways. We have underscored that prior exposure to violence and persistent disadvantage represent major challenges to estimating independent effects of incarceration at the community level beyond prior criminal justice processing. We want to emphasize that this problem is different from that described in Chapter 5 concerning the impact of incarceration on crime in the United States as a whole. In studies of communities, the effect of incarceration on crime cannot at present be estimated with precision. Specifically, unless researchers can locate high incarceration but socially advantaged communities with low arrest rates and low crime rates or low incarceration communities with high arrest and high crime rates and concentrated disadvantage, they will find it difficult or impossible to estimate the unique effect of incarceration. Even if located, any such communities would be highly atypical by definition, and the findings on those communities would thus lack general import.

It is also unclear whether incarceration has the same community impact for whites and blacks. As discussed in earlier chapters, increased incarceration is known to have occurred disproportionately among African Americans (Pettit, 2012; Western, 2006) and in poor African American neighborhoods (Sampson and Loeffler, 2010). What is as yet unknown is whether increased incarceration has systematic differential effects on black compared with white communities, and whether there are reinforcing or reciprocal feedback loops such that incarceration erodes community stability and therefore reinforces preexisting disadvantages in the black community.

Although the available evidence is inconclusive, existing theoretical accounts are strong enough to warrant new empirical approaches and data collections that can shed further light on the relationship between incarceration and communities. It is important to emphasize here that adjudicating the relationship between competing hypotheses is difficult because of how neighborhoods are socially organized in U.S. society. This is a substantive reality rather than a mere statistical nuisance. Indeed, durable patterns of inequality lead to the concentration in the same places, often over long periods of time, of multiple social ills such as exposure to violence, poverty, arrest, and incarceration—especially in segregated African American communities. Thus, while legacies of social deprivation on a number of dimensions mean that the unique effect of incarceration is confounded and imprecisely estimated, perhaps the larger point is that the harshest criminal sanctions are being meted out disproportionately in the most vulnerable neighborhoods. The long-run consequences of historically correlated adversities, although difficult to quantify, remain a priority for research. So, too, is descriptive work on the variability across communities and time in the degree to which incarceration is geographically entangled with other social adversities. The dual concentration of disadvantage and incarceration is of considerable significance in its own right.

11

Wider Consequences for U.S. Society

The effects of high rates of incarceration extend far beyond the millions of people who have served time in jail or prisons and the families and communities they have left behind. The committee found that the increase in incarceration rates has also had broader effects on U.S. society—on civic and political participation, on fundamental notions of citizenship, on the allocation of public resources, and on the functioning of the polity and government. These effects are only beginning to receive sustained scholarly and analytical attention.

More specifically, we found that the extraordinary growth of the U.S. penal system has begun to alter how major governing and public institutions operate. It also has begun to compromise the quality of important demographic, political, and socioeconomic databases, producing misleading findings about trends in economic growth, political participation, unemployment, poverty, internal migration, and public health. Furthermore, many people, including prisoners, parolees, probationers, convicted sex offenders, and others with a criminal record, are now routinely denied a range of rights as well as access to many public benefits because of previous or current involvement with the criminal justice system. The result is a growing number of people who are "partial citizens" or "internal exiles" in the United States (Manza and Uggen, 2006, p. 9; Simon, 2007, p. 164). As the number of people in the United States with a criminal record has grown, the criminal justice system is increasingly serving as a major gateway to a much larger system of stigmatization and long-term marginalization. This trend has some similarities with earlier patterns of legal discrimination and racial segregation (Alexander, 2010, p. 12). For U.S. citizens, a criminal record, especially a felony conviction, often confers a legal, political, and social status that falls far short of full citizenship.

Another major societal consequence is that the penal system has been consuming larger portions of many government budgets. As a result, less money is available to spend on education, health care, economic development, state and local police, and other key government interventions and services to aid historically disadvantaged groups and improve the health and well-being of the population as a whole.

As this chapter demonstrates, some of the effects of high incarceration rates on U.S. society are straightforward. Others are more difficult to assess because they are subtle and because standard social, demographic, and economic databases are inadequate. Furthermore, it is difficult to separate the effects of the rise in incarceration rates from those of coinciding social, economic, and political changes. The upward turn in the incarceration rate that began in 1973 came amid a period of tumultuous changes in the United States, as discussed in Chapter 4. Those changes included large-scale social and political unrest, the migration of minority and immigrant populations into cities, white flight to suburbs, expanding civil rights, transformations in family structure, changes in welfare and other key social programs, deindustrialization, the decline of organized labor, rising income inequality, and many others. In reviewing the empirical evidence, we attempted to distinguish carefully the effects of high rates of incarceration from those of other contemporaneous changes.

In this chapter, we begin by examining the new gradations of citizenship resulting from the growing numbers of people not confined in jails or prisons but nonetheless entangled with the penal system. We then look at the political consequences of how prisoners are enumerated in the U.S. census and of the disenfranchisement, in all but two U.S. states, of prisoners and those with a criminal record. Next we turn to the effect of the exclusion of inmates from standard social surveys on estimates derived from the survey results. This is followed by a discussion of the fiscal burden imposed by high rates of incarceration.

NEW GRADATIONS OF CITIZENSHIP

Focused on the sharp increase in the number of people serving time in jail or prison, analysts have only just begun to pay attention to the remarkable rise in the number of people who are not confined to jail or prison but are nonetheless enmeshed in the penal system. As noted in Chapter 2, on any given day, in addition to the more than 2 million people confined in jail or prison, another 5 million are on probation or parole or under some form of community supervision—altogether about 1 of every 31 U.S. adults (Glaze et al., 2010). By age 23, at least a third of Americans have been arrested, compared with an estimated 22 percent in the mid-1960s (Brame et al., 2012, pp. 21-27). At least 16 million people have a criminal record that includes a felony conviction. In some major cities, 80 percent of young African American men now have a criminal record (Street, 2002). This involvement with the penal system curtails the citizenship of those affected in a number of ways.

Probationers and Parolees

Many of the 5 million people currently serving parole and probation are subject to a matrix of controls intended to both encourage and condition their reentry to society and deter the commission of further crimes. Although some of these practices are not new, the number of people exposed to them has grown considerably as rates of crime, conviction, and incarceration have grown. Furthermore, technological, legal, and other developments have made it easier and less costly to maintain elaborate surveillance systems that extend beyond the prison. Probation and parole officers are permitted to regulate many aspects of the lives of the people they are supervising—everything from where probationers and parolees live and with whom they associate to whether they are permitted to keep beer in their refrigerator or carry a cell phone. Law enforcement officers also are permitted to conduct warrantless searches of probationers and parolees that are not subject to the standard Fourth Amendment protections, and many probationers and parolees are subject to frequent unannounced drug tests (Petersilia, 2003, pp. 81-83; Travis, 2005).

In her ethnographic study of "life on the run" in a disadvantaged neighborhood in Philadelphia, Goffman (2009) details the extensive systems of policing and supervision that have accompanied the rise of incarceration rates. She demonstrates how these developments have fostered a climate of fear and suspicion that penetrates all aspects of daily life in these neighborhoods, including intimate and family relations, labor force participation, and access to medical care. Goffman describes how men on probation or parole and those with outstanding warrants, even for trivial offenses, avoid the police and the courts at all costs—even when they are the victims of violent attacks and other serious crimes—out of a justified fear they will be sent to prison or jail (Goffman, 2009, p. 353).

Extensions of Punishment

As noted in Chapter 8, punishment for many does not end after they have served their prison sentence or successfully completed their probation or parole. Many ex-felons (and even some former misdemeanants) are subjected to what is commonly known as "civil death," or the loss of certain civil rights due to a criminal conviction. This loss of rights and privileges pushes them further to the political, social, and economic margins. Travis (2005) terms these legal extensions of incarceration "invisible punishment." In November 2011, the American Bar Association released a database identifying 38,000 punitive provisions that apply to people convicted of crimes (American Bar Association Criminal Justice Section, 2011).

States deny those with a criminal record licenses to work in many professions, including plumbing; food catering; and even haircutting, a popular trade in many prisons (Hull, 2006, p. 33; Legal Action Center, n.d.). Numerous states suspend or revoke the driver's licenses of people convicted of drug offenses, even when those offenses did not involve a driving-related incident. Many states provide no means for obtaining restricted driver's licenses that would allow those convicted of drug offenses to get to work, school, or treatment. Individuals with felony convictions sometimes must forfeit all or some of their pension, disability, or veteran's benefits. Many are ineligible for public housing, student loans, food stamps, and other forms of public assistance (Simon, 2007, pp. 194-198; Alexander, 2010, Chapter 4). Dozens of states and the federal government ban former felons from jury service for life. As a result, nearly one-third of African American men in the United States are estimated to be permanently ineligible to serve as jurors (Kalt, 2003, pp. 67, 170-171). These developments, together with the persistence of extensive racial discrimination in jury selection, compound the problem of the gross underrepresentation of African Americans on juries.[1]

Some jurisdictions forbid employers to discriminate against job applicants based solely on their criminal record unless their offense is directly relevant to performing the job (see, e.g., National Employment Law Project [2012]). But applicants with a criminal record are still disproportionately denied jobs (see Chapter 8), and rejected job seekers have great difficulty obtaining redress in the courts (Hull, 2006, pp. 32-34). The problem of employment discrimination against people with a criminal record has grown as the numbers arrested and convicted have escalated and as background checks have become less costly and easier for employers to conduct.[2] Pager's (2007) seminal audit study of employment, race, and criminal history, discussed in Chapter 8, reveals that the stigma of a criminal conviction

---

[1]See Equal Justice Initiative (2010) for more on how racial discrimination remains an important factor in the operation of juries despite landmark Supreme Court decisions that supposedly curtailed the use of race in jury selection.

[2]More than 90 percent of employers surveyed conducted criminal background checks in 2009 (Society for Human Resource Management, 2010), up from 66 percent in 1996 (Society for Human Resource Management, 2004, p. 19). Many employers rely on unregulated private firms to conduct these checks, which often contain information that is inaccurate, incomplete, or misleading (Bushway et al., 2007).

presents an enormous barrier to employment for black applicants and a considerable barrier for white applicants (Pager, 2007).

In 2012, the Equal Employment Opportunity Commission approved a new policy making it more difficult for employers to use background checks to systematically rule out hiring anyone with a criminal record. The Commission acknowledged that employers may legally consider criminal records in their hiring decisions, but determined that across-the-board exclusion of all applicants with a conviction could violate employment discrimination law because of the potentially disparate effects on racial and ethnic minorities. "National data supports a finding that criminal record exclusions have a disparate impact based on race and national origin," according to the agency (as quoted in Greenhouse, 2012).

Political Disenfranchisement

As a result of the rise in the incarceration rate, a growing proportion of U.S. citizens—especially from poorer and minority communities—is now excluded from key aspects of civic and political life. The widespread practice in the United States of denying the right to vote to people with a criminal conviction raises questions about how the growth of the prison population is transforming conceptions of citizenship and affecting democratic institutions. As Chief Justice Earl Warren declared in the landmark 1964 *Reynolds v. Sims* decision: "The right to vote freely for the candidate of one's choice is of the essence of a democratic society, and any restrictions on that right strike at the heart of representative government."[3]

Recent presidential elections drew public attention to the plight of the millions of Americans barred from voting by a maze of state laws that deny the right to vote to people who have completed their sentence, as well as probationers, parolees, and prisoners.[4] Other established democracies generally place far fewer restrictions on the right to vote for people with a criminal conviction, including those in prison. The United States not only disenfranchises most of its prisoners but also routinely disenfranchises people who have completed their sentence—an exceptional practice in most other Western democracies.[5] Numerous states also disenfranchise

---

[3]*Reynolds v. Sims*, 377 U.S. 533 (1964), 555. This decision declared unconstitutional legislative districts across states that were not of comparable population sizes.

[4]According to a 2002 public opinion poll, only about one-third of Americans endorse allowing people currently in prison to vote. However, a majority of Americans favor restoring voting rights to ex-felons—with the magnitude of the majority varying depending on the nature of the offense (Manza et al., 2004).

[5]At least 18 European countries place no restrictions on the right to vote for those imprisoned, while about half a dozen, including England, do not allow prisoners to vote. Some European countries restrict prisoners' right to vote based on the crime committed or their length

nonincarcerated individuals who are serving probation or parole (Manza and Uggen, 2006, pp. 38-39).

The political impact of laws disenfranchising felons in the United States is so large because the number of people with a criminal conviction is so large and those laws also have racial origins and racial consequences. After the Civil War, public officials carefully tailored their felon disenfranchisement laws so as to circumvent the Fifteenth Amendment and thus restrict the vote of newly freed blacks (Uggen et al., 2006; Brown-Dean, 2004; Hull, 2006; Manza and Uggen, 2006, Chapter 2; Pettus, 2005, Chapters 3-5). The U.S. Supreme Court has generally upheld such laws, except in instances of clear and convincing evidence that they were enacted with a racially discriminatory intent.[6]

As of 2010, nearly 6 million people were disenfranchised because of a felony conviction—a 5-fold increase since 1976. This figure represents about 2.5 percent of the total U.S. voting-age population, or 1 in 40 adults. One of every 13 African Americans of voting age, or approximately 7.7 percent, is disenfranchised. This rate is about three times greater than the disenfranchisement rate for non-African Americans (Uggen et al., 2012a, p. 1).

The distribution of disenfranchised felons varies greatly by state, race, and ethnicity because of variations in state disenfranchisement statutes and state incarceration rates. In the three states with the highest rates of African American disenfranchisement—Florida, Kentucky, and Virginia—more than one in five African Americans is disenfranchised (Uggen et al., 2012a, p. 2). In Arizona and Florida, an estimated 9 to 10 percent of voting-age Latino citizens are disenfranchised because of their criminal record (Demeo and Ochoa, 2003). New research suggests that administrative practices—such as providing former felons with incomplete or inaccurate information about their voting rights—sometimes turn temporary voting bans into de facto lifelong disenfranchisement (Allen, 2011). Experts disagree about the magnitude of the impact of the disenfranchisement of those with a criminal record on the outcome of close elections.[7]

---

of sentence. For example, Germany's ban extends only to prisoners whose crime targeted the integrity of the state or of the democratic polity. Most European countries do not restrict the right to vote of convicted individuals who are not incarcerated (White, 2013, pp. 8-9, 47-57).

[6]For a summary of the key felon disenfranchisement legal decisions, see Manza and Uggen (2006, pp. 28-34).

[7]Manza and Uggen (2006, p. 192) estimate that if Florida had not banned an estimated 800,000 former felons from voting in the 2000 election, Al Gore would likely have carried the state and won the White House. Burch (2012, p. 5) disputes this claim, arguing that Manza and Uggen's results "are based on estimates of turnout and vote choice of the non-felon population, with no evidence based on the behavior of actual offenders." Manza and Uggen (2006, pp. 192-196) also contend that the Democratic Party would likely have controlled the U.S. Senate for much of the 1990s, as well as several additional governorships, had former felons been permitted to vote. Hjalmarsson and Lopez (2010) agree with Manza and Uggen's analysis

Since the mid-1990s, about two dozen states have amended their statutes and policies to expand the eligibility to vote for citizens with felony convictions. By 2010, an estimated 800,000 people had regained the right to vote thanks to the repeal of or amendments to lifetime disenfranchisement laws, the extension of voting rights to parolees and probationers, and the relaxation of restrictions on the process of restoring voting and other rights (Porter, 2010). However, some of the measures designed to ease restrictions on voting rights have since been reversed (Sample, 2011, p. 37; Porter, 2010, p. 12).

The impact of penal policies on political participation extends beyond official barriers to voting such as felon disenfranchisement statutes. Evidence shows that those who have contact with the criminal justice system are more likely than others to withdraw from political and civic life. Having a criminal conviction may be a more significant factor than formal legal barriers to voting in depressing voter turnout among those affected (Burch, 2007). After controlling for socioeconomic status, criminality, and other key variables, contact with the criminal justice system—from being stopped by the police to serving time in prison—appears to have a cumulatively negative effect not only on voter registration and turnout but also on involvement in civic groups and trust in the government (Weaver and Lerman, 2010, p. 827; see also Cohen, 2010; Bobo and Thompson, 2006). New research suggests that, all things being equal, the family and fellow community members of felons and ex-felons also are more likely to be politically disengaged and to perceive the criminal justice system as unfair and illegitimate (Sugie, 2013; Muller and Schrage, 2014; Lee et al., 2013; Burch, forthcoming; Lerman and Weaver, 2014). Because police stops, arrests, and convictions are concentrated within certain racial and ethnic groups and in certain geographic areas, growing contact with the criminal justice system and the related rise in incarceration and restrictions on citizenship appear to be creating a phenomenon that Burch calls "concentrated disenfranchisement" (Burch, 2007, Chapters 5 and 6).

THE U.S. CENSUS AND POLITICAL REPRESENTATION

The way prisoners are enumerated in the decennial census not only affects the accuracy and quality of demographic data (see the discussion of "invisible inequality" below) but also raises important political questions. In every state except Maine and Vermont, imprisoned felons are barred from voting. Yet disenfranchised prisoners are included in the census's population tallies for the jurisdictions where prisons are located. These

---

that Gore would have won the 2000 election had former felons in Florida been permitted to vote but dispute some of their conclusions about control of the U.S. Senate.

tallies are used for congressional reapportionment and for redistricting of state house and senate seats, city councils, and other government bodies. Prisoners counted as part of those local populations have bolstered the electoral representation of those jurisdictions.

Enumerating prisoners in this manner dilutes the votes of urban and rural areas that do not have a prison within their jurisdiction. For example, nearly 40 percent of the inmates in Pennsylvania's state prisons come from Philadelphia, which has no state prisons in its city limits (Elliott-Engel, 2009). For census and redistricting purposes, these Philadelphia citizens—nearly all of whom are black or Latino—are considered residents of the counties where they are imprisoned. These tend to be predominantly white, rural districts.[8]

The evidence of political inequities in redistricting due to the way the U.S. Census Bureau counts prisoners is "compelling" according to a report of the National Research Council (2006, p. 9). If prisoners in Texas were enumerated in their home county rather than where they are incarcerated, Houston would likely have one additional state representative in the latest round of redistricting (*Houston Chronicle*, 2011). Likewise, an analysis by the Prison Policy Initiative (Wagner, 2002) finds that several Republican seats in the New York State Senate would be in jeopardy if prisoners in upstate correctional institutions were counted in their home neighborhood in New York City.

Under growing political pressure to revise how it enumerates prisoners, the U.S. Census Bureau announced in early 2010 that it would begin collecting and providing to states data on the size of the population living in group quarters such as prisons. This decision has made it easier for states, should they so choose, to redraw districts based on counts that enumerate prisoners in their home neighborhood, not where they happen to be serving their prison sentence. Since 2010, several states, including New York, Maryland, California, and Delaware, have enacted laws that call for counting prisoners at their last address for purposes of redistricting rather than as "residents" of the jurisdiction in which they are incarcerated (Clark, 2012).

INVISIBLE INEQUALITY

The contribution of higher rates of incarceration to the growth in political, social, and economic inequality in the United States can be difficult to discern because of the way standard social surveys account for

---

[8]Nearly 200 counties nationwide now have at least 5 percent of their "residents" in prison, and about 20 counties have more than 20 percent of their "residents" incarcerated in prison (Lotke and Wagner, 2004). In one city council district in Anamosa, Iowa, 96 percent of the inhabitants were incarcerated (Wagner, 2011).

individuals incarcerated in prison and jail. Government-collected survey data are widely used to measure such key social indicators as trends in unemployment, wage inequality, high school completion, voting participation, and mortality and morbidity. With the growth in the size of the prison population, whether and how one counts jail and prison inmates has large implications for the resulting estimates. Most general population data collections exclude current inmates by design. As a consequence, measures commonly used to assess the well-being of the U.S. population will be biased, and the time trend in these measures will generally be overly positive, especially for historically disadvantaged groups, concealing the extent of deprivation in American society.

The U.S. Census

Politicians and policy makers at all levels of government—from Washington to state capitals to city halls—routinely use the census and other federal surveys to identify problems and target resources. Since the 1930s, these federal surveys have been central to determining how federal government funds are allocated to state and local jurisdictions.[9]

Undercounting of historically disadvantaged groups has been a perennial problem for the decennial census. Since the mid-twentieth century, the size of the census undercount has diminished, thanks in part to improved statistical techniques; greater investments in data collection; and growing political pressure, especially from urban areas and advocacy groups, to enumerate marginalized groups fully and accurately. Nonetheless, the undercount of African Americans remains considerable, estimated to be as high as 3 percent in the 2000 census.[10] Because this problem is well understood, users can apply the weights provided by the Census Bureau

[9]Pettit (2012, Table 2.1) calculates that 16 percent of the federal budget—or more than 3 percent of gross domestic product (GDP)—is currently allocated to state and local governments through grants-in-aid based on formulas derived from the census and other federal surveys. Lotke and Wagner (2004, p. 602) estimate the total amount of money reallocated because of the way inmates are counted as a "consistent, low-level distortion in funding formulations" on the order of $100 per person. With the caveat that it is difficult to generalize, they also note that the money is more likely displaced from small counties without prisons than from counties with large populations.

[10]An estimated 5 percent of African American men were excluded from the 2000 U.S. census (Robinson et al., 2002, cited in Pettit, 2012, p. 30). Much of the undercount of African Americans and other minorities likely is due to their "higher rates of residential mobility and instability, homelessness, and residence in highly concentrated urban areas"—the same factors that are highly correlated with people who have spent time in jail or prison (Pettit, 2012, pp. 30-31). The Census Bureau itself reports an undercount of 2.1 percent of the black population in 2010, essentially unchanged from the 1.8 percent it estimated for 2000 (U.S. Census Bureau, 2012).

to compensate for the undercount. More troubling is that the census also appears to be doing a worsening job of enumerating how many people are inmates. From 1980 to 2000, census estimates of the size of the jail and prison population reasonably matched Bureau of Justice Statistics (BJS) figures, but since then, the census and BJS data have been diverging dramatically (Pettit, 2012, p. 31).

For certain purposes, the decennial census has been severely compromised by the growth in numbers of people incarcerated. Distortions resulting from the way the census enumerates prisoners have led to misleading conclusions on such matters as economic growth, migration, household income, and racial composition. For the 2010 census, the Census Bureau chose to continue the practice of enumerating prisoners as residents of the towns and counties where they are incarcerated. But most inmates have no personal or civic ties to these communities and almost always return to their home neighborhood upon release. In the 2000 census, 56 counties nationwide—or 1 in 50—with declining populations were reported to be growing because of the inclusion of their incarcerated populations in census counts (Heyer and Wagner, 2004). As former U.S. Census Bureau Director Kenneth Prewitt (quoted in Wagner, 2012) explains, "Current census residency rules ignore the reality of prison life. . . . Counting people in prison as residents of their home communities offers a more accurate picture of the size, demographics and needs of our nation's communities."

Other Databases

Other major social surveys, such as the Current Population Survey (CPS), do an even worse job than the decennial census of incorporating marginalized populations, especially young black men, in their data collection. The CPS and many other leading federal surveys are based on periodic statistical sampling of people living in households. This practice omits the growing population of people confined to jails and prisons. Furthermore, these household-based surveys tend to undercount young black men who are not in prison or jail because many of these men maintain a loose connection (at best) to a household. Pettit (2012, p. 32) estimates that 16 percent or more of black men are rendered invisible in standard household surveys because of these two factors. Users of these databases could adjust for the jail and prison population, but often do not.

The leading surveys used to assess health outcomes, notably the National Health Interview Survey, the National Health and Nutrition Examination Survey, and the National Survey of Family Growth, are modeled on the CPS and therefore also undercount marginalized populations not attached to households. They also do not statistically sample inmates, even though it is well established that imprisonment exacerbates many public health problems—notably the rates of transmission of communicable diseases, such as hepatitis C, HIV/AIDS, and tuberculosis—and even though prisoners and former prisoners are much more likely to test positive for these diseases than the general population (Pettit, 2012, pp. 94-96; see also Chapter 7). Although it is theoretically possible for researchers to combine information from inmate surveys and surveys of the nonincarcerated population, federal surveys specifically designed to gauge the health status of inmates "are not always comparable to those conducted with the non-institutionalized population" (Pettit, 2012, p. 96).

When researchers incorporate the impact of the growth of the incarcerated population into their analyses of trends in leading measures of inequality, the picture of widening inequalities is at odds with conventional narratives that stress a narrowing of the black-white gap in such critical areas as wages, employment, education, and political participation. Research accounting for the incarcerated population challenges claims about the achievements of the economic expansion of the 1990s, widely regarded as the largest peacetime economic expansion in U.S. history. With the incarcerated population factored in, the unemployment rate for males would have been at least 2 percentage points higher by the mid-1990s (Western and Beckett, 1999, p. 1052). Furthermore, the jobless rate for young black males in 2000 would have been 32 percent, not the official 24 percent (Western, 2006, p. 90). Although researchers disagree about the assumptions underlying these estimates and the actual magnitude of the distortion in the unemployment rate, these "thought experiments" are at least "worthwhile reminders that when we use labor force statistics to assess how we are doing, we are omitting a large segment of the population" (Useem and Piehl, 2008, p. 152).

As another example, including inmates in analyses of high school dropout rates increases the dropout rate for young black men by about 40 percent over conventional estimates. This finding suggests that the black-white gap in high school graduation rates has not narrowed since the early 1990s (Pettit, 2012, pp. 50-64). Analyses of wage trends that incorporate inmates also suggest that the relative wages of young black men have not improved over the past two decades and that claims about the recent shrinking of the black-white wage gap are overstated (Pettit, 2012, pp. 64-67).

Voter Turnout

For more than half a century, the country's plummeting voter turnout rate has been a cause of national concern and been vigorously debated. But most analyses of voter turnout fail to consider the large and growing number of noncitizens, prisoners, people on parole or probation, and ex-felons who have been disenfranchised by electoral laws. By not doing so, they tend to misestimate the extent and sources of the overall decline in voter turnout in the United States (Manza and Uggen, 2006, pp. 176-177).[11]

Conventional accounts of growing political participation among African Americans based on national surveys, such as the CPS and the National Election Study, also appear to be off the mark. The much heralded narrowing of the black-white gap in voter turnout in recent years likely is due not to rising voter turnout among blacks but to the exclusionary effects of high rates of incarceration and to declines in turnout among whites. Claims that voter turnout among young black men reached record levels in the 2008 election and exceeded that of young white men for the first time do not hold up once the incarcerated population is factored in (Rosenfeld et al., 2011; Pettit, 2012, Chapter 5).

The U.S. Census Bureau (2013, p. 3) recently reported that African Americans voted at a higher rate than whites in the 2012 presidential election. This was the first time blacks outvoted whites since the Census Bureau started publishing voting rates by eligible citizenship population in 1996. However, the Census Bureau analysis did not consider the institutionalized population, which is composed primarily of people residing in correctional institutions and nursing homes. If the hundreds of thousands of African Americans who are incarcerated and therefore ineligible to vote were factored in, the turnout figures for blacks in the 2012 presidential election would have been substantially reduced, perhaps below the turnout rate for whites.

PUBLIC COSTS AND FISCAL PRESSURES

The corrections system and the public safety system more broadly (that is, police, prosecutors, and the courts) command a larger share of government budgets than was the case 30 years ago. Budgetary allocations for corrections have outpaced budget increases for nearly all other key government services (often by wide margins), including education, transportation, and public assistance (Pew Center on the States, 2009, p. 11). Today, state spending on corrections is the third highest category of general fund expenditures in most states, ranked behind Medicaid and education.[12] Corrections budgets have skyrocketed at a time when spending for other key social services and government programs has slowed or contracted. As a result, the criminal justice system increasingly is the main provider of health care,

---

[11]Manza and Uggen (2006) build on earlier work by McDonald and Popkin (2001).

[12]The actual fiscal burden of the corrections system is probably much higher. A Vera Institute of Justice survey of 40 states added 13.9 percent to those states' 2010 corrections spending totals for other corrections-related expenditures recorded elsewhere, including current and accruing contributions to employee health care and pensions, some capital costs, and some hospital and health care for prisoners (Henrichson and Delaney, 2012, p. 2).

substance abuse treatment, mental health services, job training, education, and other critical social and economic supports for the most disadvantaged groups in U.S. society.

Between 1972 and 2010, public expenditures for building and operating the country's prisons and jails increased sharply, keeping pace with the increase in the number of people held in those facilities. From fiscal year 1985 to 2012, corrections spending increased from 1.9 percent to 3.3 percent of state budgets, or from $6.7 to $53.2 billion (U.S. Census Bureau, n.d.-a; Census of Government Finances historical tables; National Association of State Budget Officers, 2013). State corrections spending accounted for 7 percent or more of combined states' general fund expenditures from fiscal year 2008 through fiscal year 2012 (National Association of State Budget Officers, 2013, p. 1). Over 20 years beginning with fiscal year 1980, only Medicaid grew more rapidly as a proportion of state budgets.

At the local level, government spending for jails totaled $26.8 billion in fiscal year 2010. Corrections spending rose from 1.2 percent of all local spending in 1985 to 1.6 percent in 2010 (U.S. Census Bureau, n.d.-a; Census of Government Finances historical tables). At the federal level, spending for the Bureau of Prisons—both operations and capital—totaled $6.5 billion in fiscal year 2011. As a percentage of the federal budget, spending by the Bureau of Prisons has risen from 0.05 to 0.2 percent of total outlays since 1985. Still, spending on incarceration remains a tiny fraction of the federal budget (James, 2013a, 2013b).[13]

Adjusted for inflation, states' combined corrections spending from 1980 to 2009 increased by just over 400 percent, while the number of prisoners increased by 475 percent. Local spending for jails and federal spending for prisons followed similar patterns. Figure 11-1 shows inflation-adjusted trends in spending for incarceration since 1980 for all three levels of government.

The increase in government spending for corrections since 1980 has been driven almost entirely by increased numbers of prisoners.[14] Adjusted for inflation, annual costs per prisoner at all three levels of government

---

[13]The federal government and some states, mainly in the south and west, have funded private entities to administer some prisons and other detention facilities. In 2011, 7.2 percent of state prisoners were in privately run institutions, an increase from 6.4 percent in 2000 but a smaller percentage than in 2010. In 2011, 14.5 percent of federal prisoners were housed in private institutions, more than double the percentage in 2000 (Glaze and Parks, 2012, Appendix Table 1).

[14]As discussed in Chapter 1, the increased numbers of people incarcerated at any one time are a function of both the numbers sentenced and the average length of time they are incarcerated. A 2012 study shows that the cohort of state prisoners released in 2009 were in custody almost 3 years, 9 months—an average prison stay that was 12 months, or 36 percent, longer than the average stay of those released in 1990 (Pew Center on the States, 2012).

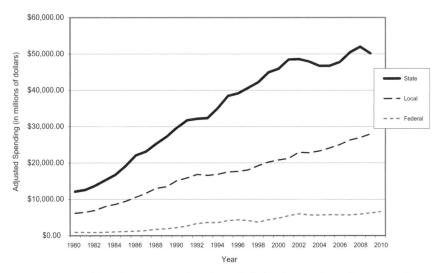

FIGURE 11-1 Trends in state, local, and federal spending for corrections, 1980-2010.
NOTE: Amounts shown are adjusted to 2011 dollars.
SOURCE: Data from U.S. Census Bureau (n.d.-a).

are about the same as they were 30 years ago and have fluctuated during this period only slightly. In 2010 dollars, federal spending per prisoner was around $30,000 per year at the beginning of the 1980s and was $31,000 in 2010. State spending per prisoner was about $37,000 per year (in 2010 dollars) in both 1980 and 2008, the last year for which these figures have been calculated.[15] Similarly, local spending for jails was $33,000 per year per inmate in 2010 dollars in 1980 and almost the same in 2008.

Spending per prisoner varies greatly among the states, partly reflecting differences in facilities and services for prisoners, including rehabilitation programming and health care. In 2010, a survey of annual costs in 40 states showed a range of $14,603 per prisoner in Kentucky to $60,076 per prisoner in New York (Henrichson and Delaney, 2012, Figure 4, p. 10).[16]

---

[15]This figure applies total state corrections spending to the numbers incarcerated. If this percentage is used to exclude the amounts spent on probation or parole, average state spending per prisoner is around $33,000, or comparable to the average for local governments.

[16]These estimates include corrections-related expenditures recorded outside the corrections budgets of those states, including current and accruing contributions to employee health care and pensions, some capital costs, and some hospital and health care for prisoners (Henrichson and Delaney, 2012).

Corrections spending can be considered part of a larger set of expenditures related to public safety that also includes police, courts, and prosecution. Combining these functions, the country was spending around $90 billion annually on state and federal public safety, including corrections, by the end of the prison boom, about 6.8 percent of all state and local spending in 2010 (U.S. Census of Governments). This represents a significant shift in public resources, particularly at the state level. While varying by state, policing is largely a local government responsibility; 87 percent of combined state and local police spending in 2010 was by local governments. In contrast, 63 percent of combined state and local corrections spending that year was by state governments. Spending for judicial and legal functions was split almost evenly between the two levels but with wide variation from state to state.

The growth of state corrections spending has slowed with the stabilization of the incarceration rate; cutbacks in staffing, correctional programs, and other services in some jails and prisons; and the levying of more fees on those convicted and their families for everything from a doctor's visit in prison to parole supervision on the outside. But with the aging of the prison population (as discussed in Chapter 7) and mounting medical costs, correctional budgets will continue to be under substantial pressure for years to come.

CONCLUSION

Our review of the evidence demonstrates that, in this era of expanded penal control, incarceration has become a key element of the U.S. approach to dealing with marginality and social dysfunction. High levels of incarceration documented throughout this report have exacerbated social, economic, and political inequalities. Punishment has been extended beyond prison by laws and practices that restrict the rights of former felons and render them second-class citizens. The disenfranchisement of felons and ex-felons and the way in which prisoners are enumerated in the U.S. census have combined to weaken the political power of low-income and minority communities. Enumerating prisoners in the jurisdictions where they are serving their sentences—and not in the communities to which they will return—dilutes the votes of those urban and rural areas that do not contain prisons.

Standard survey tools used to measure key social, economic, and other indicators obscure the relationship between high rates of incarceration and inequality. Failure to include in these surveys the large population of people involved with the criminal justice system calls into question assessments of the well-being of the U.S. population, and especially of historically disadvantaged groups.

High rates of incarceration have had important and far-reaching collateral consequences. A growing proportion of people in the United States—especially from poorer and minority communities—has been increasingly marginalized in civic and political life. These developments are creating a distinct political and legal universe for whole categories of people. These "partial citizens" or "internal exiles" are now routinely denied a range of rights and access to many public benefits. These consequences pose a significant risk to achievement of the nation's aspirations for democratic self-government and social and racial justice.

With the rise in the incarceration rate over the past four decades, a uniquely American form of social policy has emerged that has clear implications for the quality of American democracy. The criminal justice system has become central to how the nation deals with social dysfunction. Corrections spending has grown as a share of government budgets. This system of laws and punishments is meting out stigma and producing social stratification on a large scale and has become a key contributor to the political, social, and economic marginalization of African Americans and members of other groups that have historically been disadvantaged in the United States.

The new penal regime of tougher criminal sanctions, high rates of incarceration, and severely reduced opportunities for the millions of people with a criminal record has not yet drawn widespread public concern. That is partly because these developments have been legitimized so that they appear to be natural, inevitable, necessary, and just, despite the social and political inequalities that result. The net result is the risk that the American criminal justice system will advance social control at the expense of social justice.

The increase in incarceration rates has taken place against the backdrop of deindustrialization and the collapse of inner-city livelihoods, as discussed in Chapter 4. Those sent to prison tend to come from the poorest, most violent, and segregated communities, and imprisonment tends to leave them even more likely to remain poor, unemployed, and socially isolated (Western, 2006), as elaborated in Chapter 10. Incarceration and other kinds of contact with the criminal justice system thus both reflect and exacerbate inequality in the United States.

Race and ethnicity play a crucial role in these developments. On one level, the disproportionate number of blacks, Hispanics, and other historically disadvantaged groups among the incarcerated, though striking, is not altogether surprising. The social deprivation and spatial isolation of the poor and the less educated, many of whom are members of minority groups living in urban areas, tend to foster criminal acts that result in a prison sentence or other penal sanctions. Members of these groups also are at heightened risk of drawing severe sanctions because of intense state surveillance in their communities (see, e.g., Duneier, 1999; Anderson, 1999; Bourgois,

1995; Wilson, 1968, Chapter 2; Herbert, 1997). The limited legal, social, and other resources available to them once they have become involved in the criminal justice system compound the problem.

On another level, the fact that racial and ethnic minorities constitute a large portion of the nation's prison population must still be questioned on grounds of social justice. Even if the American criminal justice system were entirely free of racial or ethnic discrimination and bias—a highly elusive goal—the fact that blacks, Hispanics, and members of other historically disadvantaged groups dominate the country's prison and jail populations is deeply troubling. Incarceration ought not to be assessed only in terms of the personal culpability of those behind bars or otherwise caught up in the penal system; collective issues touching on race and citizenship must also be addressed.

Standard justifications of the present U.S. penal regime overlook the many ways in which the broader society was involved in creating and maintaining the damaged, neglected, and feared communities that today produce the country's highest rates of serious violent crime. Urban districts of concentrated disadvantage—such as North Philadelphia, the West Side of Chicago, the East Side of Detroit, or South Central Los Angeles—have persisted as the result of complex forces and interests ranging far beyond their borders. The antisocial behavior of some people from these communities reflects personal shortcomings, but it also reflects the shortcomings of society as a whole. The overarching question for criminal justice policy is whether long and harsh prison sentences are the most appropriate and effective way of responding to the antisocial behavior of the residents of these hard-pressed communities.

12

The Prison in Society:
Values and Principles

The transformation of U.S. punishment policy during the rise in incarceration reflected not just deep changes in society, but also a change in thinking. The country experienced a tumultuous period of economic and political change, rapidly rising crime rates, and changing race relations. The politics of criminal justice policy became much more punitive. Policy makers enacted laws that were meant to send many more people to prison and keep them there longer. These changes reflect a shift in emphasis among competing values. Public and professional discourses moved from a focus on rehabilitation as the predominant purpose of punishment to just deserts, or retribution, as the primary goal. Stated in colloquial terms, "tough on crime," "do the crime, do the time," and "adult time for adult crime" became the public narrative.

The preceding chapters of this report assessed the scientific evidence on the causes and consequences of high rates of incarceration in the United States. In the next chapter, the committee considers the policy implications of that evidence. However, questions regarding the appropriate use of prison in a democratic society cannot be resolved solely by reference to evidence, nor can a society decide whether prison rates are too high only by weighing narrowly quantifiable costs against benefits. Accordingly, the committee explored the scholarly literatures on the purposes of punishment, the role of prisons in democratic societies, and the normative principles[1] that have traditionally limited the penal power of the state. This chapter

---

[1]Political theorists and legal analysts have often observed that public policy necessarily embodies ethical judgments about means or ends. These judgments are informed by normative principles: basic ideals or values—often embedded in history, institutions, and public

documents important shifts in prevailing ways of thinking that reinforced the growth in the use of prison. An assessment of this literature was an essential step for the committee in addressing its charge to discuss the policy implications of the scientific evidence on high rates of incarceration.

HISTORICAL DEVELOPMENT

Early in the twentieth century, the goal of rehabilitation of offenders was central to mainstream thinking about the purposes of punishment. Incarceration was widely seen as an opportunity to address the needs and remedy the defects of the criminal offender (Rothman, 1971, 1980; Garland, 1991, 2001). The rehabilitative ideal was regularly compromised in practice and too rarely truly attained. There was nonetheless a positive transformative purpose that was supposed to be central to the institutional design of the prison, the nature of correctional programming, the use of probation and parole, and the day-to-day practices of sentencing judges (Allen, 1981).

In the shifting political climate of the 1970s, however, skepticism about the appropriateness and the effectiveness of rehabilitation grew. From the 1970s on, two sometimes incompatible goals were increasingly invoked: to link the severity of punishments closely to the seriousness of crimes and to prevent crime, principally through deterrence and incapacitation. Andrew von Hirsch (1976), reporting for the Committee for the Study of Incarceration, detailed a theory of punishment based on retribution and deterrence in his book *Doing Justice*, and he added the phrase "just deserts" to the nation's criminal justice vocabulary. Numerous other philosophers, criminal lawyers, and correctional officials urged that retribution be recognized as the primary purpose of punishment (e.g., Morris, 1966; Morris, 1974; Fogel, 1979). As von Hirsch (1976, 2007) observed, punishment is a blaming institution that censures offenders for criminal conduct. Retribution, for Von Hirsch, was to be moderated by a principle of fairness and by a fundamental commitment to apportioning punishments to offenders' relative blameworthiness. Others urged a shift away from rehabilitation as a goal and toward crime prevention. In *Thinking about Crime*, James Q. Wilson (1975) channeled public anxiety and anger about street crime, repudiated rehabilitation as an achievable objective, and argued that deterrence and incapacitation should be viewed as the preeminent goals of punishment.

These works signaled a shift in values. The emphasis on rehabilitation was replaced by an emphasis on punishment as a symbol of moral accountability and as a means to control crime.

---

understanding—that offer a yardstick by which good governance is measured (see, e.g., Gillroy and Wade 1992).

The notion that punishments should aim to prevent crime dates from the work of Cesare Beccaria (1764) and Jeremy Bentham (1830, 1970), who pioneered the modern theory of deterrence in the late eighteenth and early nineteenth centuries (see Chapter 5). Early in the twentieth century, positivist thinkers, typified by Enrico Ferri (1921) in Europe and by Jerome Michael and Herbert Wechsler (1937) in the United States, laid preventive foundations for what came to be called indeterminate sentencing. In this sentencing framework, offenders should be imprisoned if they threatened public safety and should be released when they ceased to do so (Pifferi, 2012). Otherwise, they should be kept in prison and thereby incapacitated until they ceased to present an unacceptable safety threat.

The retributive and crime control mission of punishment gained renewed emphasis beginning in the 1970s. Research on incapacitation and deterrence burgeoned (Greenwood and Abrahamse, 1982; National Research Council, 1978a). Among policy makers and practitioners, deterrence, incapacitation, and offender accountability became the predominant objectives of punishment. Proponents of legislative proposals to make sentencing laws more punitive invoked theories of deterrence and incapacitation. Crime control was a key goal for measures such as mandatory minimums, three-strikes, truth-in-sentencing, and sentences of life without parole.

As the goals of crime control and offender accountability ascended, however, long-standing principles that limited harsh punishment receded from political debate and crime policy. The magnitude of the increase in incarceration rates after 1972 and the speed with which it occurred demonstrate the transformation of the purposes of punishment.

In both classical and contemporary retributive theories, punishments may or must be imposed because they are deserved, but to be just they must be closely apportioned to the seriousness of the crime. In both classical and contemporary consequentialist theories,[2] punishments may or must be imposed if doing so will achieve valid preventive goals, but to be just they must be no more severe than is needed for them to be effective.

Many recent sentencing laws sought to be punitive, and were, but failed to assure that punishments were apportioned to the seriousness of offenders' crimes. Many recent sentencing laws sought to prevent crime through deterrence and incapacitation, but failed to ensure that punishments were no more severe than was necessary to achieve their aims. Today, with little evidence of a sizable reduction in crime that is attributable to a more than 4-fold increase in incarceration over nearly 40 years, and with the possibility of real social harm from excessive use of incarceration, old principles of restrained punishment need to be reemphasized.

---

[2]Utilitarian, positivist, and other theories that justify actions by reference to their effects, or consequences, are called "consequentialist" theories.

Principles for the restrained use of punishment—similar to the values of crime control and offender accountability—have deep roots in normative theories of jurisprudence and social policy. Some emerge from historical and contemporary efforts to justify the imposition of pain on convicted offenders. Others emerge from broader concerns about the nature of citizenship in a free society. These principles of restraint can curb the rush to punish by appealing to ideas of fairness and by underlining the steadfast mutual obligations that arise from citizens' common membership in the social compact.

The following sections trace the scholarly literature and the intellectual lineage of the principles that should inform the use of incarceration and the role of prison in U.S. society. Each section distills a core principle that acts as a constraint on the power of the state to punish individuals who have violated the law. These principles provided guidance to the committee as we weighed the evidence of the causes and consequences of high rates of incarceration in the United States. Taken together, these normative principles describe a broad conception of justice to which the nation's public institutions should aspire:

- *Desert and proportionality*: Punishments are said to be deserved, and therefore just, only to the extent that their severity is apportioned to the seriousness of the crimes for which they are imposed. Because of myriad differences in the circumstances of offenses and offenders, punishments may sometimes justly be less severe than is maximally deserved but should never be more severe.
- *Parsimony:* Punishments for crime, and especially lengths of prison sentences, should never be more severe than is necessary to achieve the retributive or preventive purposes for which they are imposed.
- *Citizenship:* The conditions and consequences of punishments for crime, especially terms of imprisonment, should not be so severe or so enduring as to violate an individual's fundamental status as a member of society.
- *Social justice:* Prisons should be instruments of justice. Their collective effect should be to promote, and not to undermine, society's aspirations for a fair distribution of rights, resources, and opportunities.

Each of these principles recognizes that the forcible deprivation of liberty through incarceration is an awesome state power that is vulnerable to misuse, threatening the republican values that underpin the legitimacy of the prison and of the state. These principles of restraint are complements, not alternatives, to recent emphases on offender accountability and crime control. Offender accountability and crime control are unquestionably important values but, unbalanced by principles of restraint, they have

precipitated unconstrained growth in incarceration. The principles of restraint help set limits on the scale of incarceration and point toward new
approaches.

DESERT AND PROPORTIONALITY

The principle of proportionality should guide the distribution of punishment across the full range of crimes. Proportionality requires that crimes
be sentenced in relation to their seriousness and the extent of the offender's
moral culpability. Ideas about proportionality are as old as humankind.
Plato and Aristotle wrote about them. In modern times, they are developed most fully in philosophical writing on retribution and desert. That
literature dates from the eighteenth and early nineteenth century writings
of Immanuel Kant (1965 [1798]). Kant believed that respect for the moral
autonomy of human beings requires that offenders be held accountable
for their wrongdoing in strict proportion to its seriousness. He proposed a
"principle of equality" under which harms brought into the world by offenders would be returned to them as punishment in "like kind." That is
not now and never has been practicable in absolute terms. No one can make
a compelling case for why any particular crime deserves to be punished to
a uniquely appropriate degree. However, that has not significantly inhibited
the development of retributive theories of punishment.

Modern writing makes the case not for absolutely deserved but for
relatively deserved punishments (e.g., von Hirsch 1976, 1992; Duff 1986,
2001; Robinson 2008). What is seen as important is that comparably
serious crimes are punished in comparable ways, and that more serious
ones are punished more severely than less serious ones (and, of course,
vice versa). Proportionality thus provides guidance in setting relative levels
of punishment across the full range of offenses, not the absolute level of
severity of punishment for any particular offense. Once crimes have been
ranked according to their seriousness, the principle of proportionality offers a benchmark by which severity can be calibrated. There is wide public
agreement about the relative seriousness of various crimes (Roberts and
Stalans, 1997; Darley 2010; Robinson, 2013).

At this time, the committee believes, most people—including legislators,
judges, and practitioners—share and support common intuitions about
deserved punishments and proportionality. However, this has not always
been true in the United States, as we show in Chapter 3. During the half
century when indeterminate sentencing systems were ubiquitous, many
people believed that punishments should be individualized to take account
of offenders' rehabilitative prospects and to reflect public safety needs for
their incapacitation. The existence of widely held intuitions about retributive punishment were acknowledged but disparaged as old-fashioned and

unseemly. Retributive ideas had little influence (e.g., Michael and Wechsler, 1937). Proportionality in the contemporary sense was simply not seen as important.

That view changed in the 1970s when rehabilitation lost credibility and support as a primary aim of punishment. Indeterminate sentencing fell from favor. Partly by default and partly because they fit with contemporaneous concerns for individual rights, procedural fairness, and transparency and accountability in government, retributive ideas became much more influential. Absence of proportionality underlay major critiques of unwarranted disparities in indeterminate sentencing. Proportionality was seized upon as a plausible and principled basis for setting standards for sentencing by the developers of determinate sentencing laws and newly invented guidelines systems.

Sentencing guidelines were widely adopted by state and local U.S. jurisdictions during the 1970s and 1980s. Ideas about proportionality provided a framework for creating comprehensive systems for setting sentences for criminal offenses. Guidelines typically took the form of two-dimensional grids that specified sentences according to the severity of the offense and the offender's criminal history. (See Chapter 3 for a discussion of these developments and the social science evidence concerning their largely positive effects.) Well-designed, well-managed systems successfully reduced disparities, made sentencing predictable, made the system more transparent, and held judges accountable. They also provided important tools for rational and economic policy making. Early guidelines systems in Minnesota, Washington, and Oregon not only made sentencing more consistent, predictable, and transparent, but also enhanced financial planning and correctional management (Tonry, 1996).

The gains in justice, rationality, and cost-effectiveness that proportionality ideas fostered ultimately proved short-lived. The core ideas about justice and equal treatment that motivated support for proportionality were eroded by the adoption of mandatory minimum sentences, three-strikes laws, and other measures that readily imposed incarceration. Such laws often disconnected the severity of punishments from the seriousness of crimes. Low-level drug crimes often were punished as severely as serious acts of violence. Under three strikes laws, some misdemeanors and minor property felonies were punished as severely as homicides, rapes, and robberies. In other Western countries that enacted mandatory minimum sentence laws, judges were almost always authorized to disregard the minimums in the "interest of justice." By contrast, U.S. laws almost never give judges that discretion (Tonry, 2009b).

PARSIMONY

"Parsimony," like proportionality, is an old idea but one that is salient in the current debate. Jeremy Bentham (1830, 1970) believed that the measure of a good law or policy is whether it maximizes human happiness. He regarded all infliction of pain, including on offenders, as an "evil" but as justifiable if its imposition prevented greater pain for others. If that test could not be satisfied, a principle of parsimony (sometimes he used the term frugality) forbade imposition of the punishment. Immanuel Kant was, of course, not a utilitarian and did not believe moral matters could be evaluated by weighing costs and benefits (1965 [1798]). However, an idea akin to parsimony is central to classical retributive theories and to contemporary ideas about proportionality in punishment. By all such accounts, and by definition, any punishment that is more or "disproportionately" severe than is deserved is unjust. The word parsimony is not used by retributivists but the underlying concept is the same: Any punishment that is more severe than is required to achieve valid and applicable purposes is to that extent morally unjustifiable. It is excessive. During the indeterminate sentencing period, the term "least restrictive alternative" was used to express the concept, for example, in the *Model Sentencing Act* of the Advisory Committee of Judges of the National Council on Crime and Delinquency (1972).

The idea of parsimony as a restraint on punishment expresses the normative belief that infliction of pain or hardship on another human being is something that should be done, when it must be done, as little as possible. The late University of Chicago law professor Norval Morris likened it to a "Hippocratic criminal justice" oath according to which criminal punishments should do no harm beyond that which is minimally required in order to achieve valid social purposes (Tonry, 1994, 2004). The legitimate social purposes served by punishment have come to be defined as retribution, deterrence, incapacitation, and rehabilitation. Retribution reflects "society's official view of what a criminal deserves," and Morris (1982, p. 161) adds, "it is not finely tuned." Deterrence, incapacitation, and rehabilitation are more utilitarian, intended to promote public safety.

Morris (1974) offered a highly influential account of punishment that takes parsimony seriously. Called "limiting retributivism," Morris's theory posits that for every crime, wide agreement can be reached that some punishments would be unjustly severe and others would be unduly lenient. He described unjustly severe and unduly lenient punishments as "undeserved" and possible punishments that lay between them as "not undeserved." The phrasing is awkward but it is based on the view that it is unlikely that widespread agreements can be reached about punishments that are uniquely "deserved" for particular crimes but highly likely that wide agreements can be reached that particular punishments are unjustly severe or unduly lenient.

The range of allowable "not undeserved punishments" is however only the starting point. Within that range, Morris said, any punishment could in theory be appropriate, but the presumptions in a free society, consistent with Bentham's notion of parsimony, should favor liberty. Thus the presumption in every case should be that punishments should be imposed at the bottom end of the allowable range. Overcoming the presumption would require that good evidence be available to show that a more severe punishment would achieve demonstrable preventive effects. The American Law Institute (2011) explicitly adopted Morris's limiting retributivism as the theoretical basis of the *Model Penal Code—Sentencing*. It is reflected in the laws of states that have adopted systems of presumptive sentencing guidelines (Frase, 2013).

Parsimonious use of criminal punishments may have benefits larger than sparing offenders unnecessary suffering and saving public monies. Greater restraint in the use of punishment could, for example, advance public safety. When punishments are unduly severe and affect large numbers of people in particular communities, crime may flourish as justice institutions lose legitimacy, time in prison becomes a predictable feature of young men's lives, and the deterrent effect of prison is dulled (Muller and Schrage, 2014; Nagin, 1998).

Social justice may also be more enhanced by parsimonious use of punishment. The concentration of incarceration mainly among poor and minority men in severely disadvantaged communities means that the negative effects of incarceration, including diminution of the life chances of the children of those incarcerated, are also socially concentrated. Throughout this report, we presented evidence showing that those incarcerated face risks to economic opportunities and well-being, and that family members and neighborhoods may also be affected. Parsimonious use of punishment may not only minimize unnecessary use of penal sanctions including imprisonment, but also limit the negative and socially concentrated effects of incarceration, thereby expanding the distribution of rights, resources, and opportunities more broadly throughout U.S. society.

CITIZENSHIP

The principle of citizenship is a basic tenet of jurisprudence and constitutional government. Citizenship denotes a core set of fundamental rights accruing to all persons by virtue of their membership in a political community. T.H. Marshall (1950) describes how citizenship establishes basic civil rights to self-expression and recourse to the courts; political rights to the franchise; and in the modern era through social policy, a basic right to human welfare. Together, the rights of citizenship establish a minimum standard of human dignity and protections against state action that compromises, abridges, or undermines the capacity of citizens to exercise those rights.

Incarceration tests the limits of citizenship. Penal confinement necessarily restricts freedom of action in ways that are experienced by no other citizens. Still, the idea that there are basic standards and rights to which all citizens remain entitled is reflected in two precepts of public policy that are widely although not universally applied: that the restrictions associated with incarceration are temporary, and that the nature of penal confinement must respect human dignity. Underlying measures for the temporary and dignified character of punishment is the concept of what Meyer (2010) describes as human connectedness among the members of a political community that serves to limit the penal power of the state.

The temporary character of incarceration is reflected in the fact that the overwhelming majority of prisoners ultimately will return to free society, and underscores why time spent in prison should not serve to compromise their successful re-entry when they do. The many mechanisms for discretionary release that accelerate the prisoner's return to the community and hasten the full restoration of rights—from parole, through the expiration of collateral consequences, to executive pardons—also underscore the time-limited, temporary nature of the prison experience and the importance given to restoring full citizenship rights as soon as possible.[3]

The need to maintain human dignity for incarcerated individuals is well established by international standards (e.g., United Nations Office on Drugs and Crime, 2006). Many legal and correctional organizations in the United States also openly value human dignity and acknowledge the importance of protecting it during penal confinement. The American Correctional Association takes "humanity" as its first principle of correctional supervision, stating, "The dignity of individuals, the rights of all people and the potential for human growth and development must be respected" (American Correctional Association, 2002). In its Standards on Treatment of Prisoners, the American Bar Association (2010, Standard 23-7.1) endorses a similar principle: "Correctional authorities should treat prisoners in a manner that respects their human dignity, and should not subject them to harassment, bullying, or disparaging language or treatment, or to invidious discrimination based on race, gender, sexual orientation, gender identity,

---

[3]For a history of parole release in the United States and its connection to the reforming impulse of the Progressive movement, see Rothman (1980). Office of the Pardon Attorney (1996) catalogs state and federal collateral consequences and mechanisms for the restoration of rights. Meyer (2010) reviews the normative theory of mercy and its connection to Kantian theories of retribution.

religion, language, national origin, citizenship, age, or physical or mental disability."

Some of the most authoritative statements on this issue can be found in the United States Supreme Court's Eighth Amendment jurisprudence, which has evolved to embody a standard of basic decency in prohibiting cruel and unusual punishment. Thus in the landmark capital case *Furman v. Georgia*, Justice William O. Brennan famously wrote that "punishment must not by its severity be degrading to human dignity." More recently, Justice Kennedy echoed these sentiments when, speaking directly about the way that harsh conditions of confinement could adversely and unconstitutionally affect the treatment of prisoners, he wrote that: "Prisoners retain the essence of human dignity inherent in all persons. Respect for that dignity animates the Eighth Amendment prohibition against cruel and unusual punishment" [*Brown v. Plata*, 131 S.Ct. 1910 (2011), p. 1928].

The legal scholar Robert Cover's observation that "[t]he experience of the prisoner is, from the outset, an experience of being violently dominated, and it is colored from the beginning by the fear of being violently treated" [cited in *Brown v. Plata*, p. 1608] serves as a reminder of the power of imprisonment and a caution against losing sight of the old adage that persons are sent to prison *as* punishment not for (more) punishment. In this context, the principle of citizenship requires that the punishment of prison should not be so severe that it causes damage to prisoners, places them at serious risk of significant harm, or compromises their chances to lead a fulfilling and successful life after they are released.

Yet during the past decades of high rates of incarceration, as we have noted, the growth of incarceration strained fidelity to the principle of citizenship. Under pressure to accommodate and manage truly unprecedented and rapidly increasing numbers of prisoners and a multitude of other challenging problems, the limiting principle that acknowledges and protects the essence of human dignity inherent in all prisoners was at times compromised. Moreover, although the goal of rehabilitation may have been rarely attained, it nonetheless served as a kind of restraining edge against the worst excesses of imprisonment. If, at least in theory, prisoners were supposed to be released from prison better off than they entered, then there were some implicit limits to what prison administrators and officials could knowingly tolerate or practice. When the nation relinquished its commitment to rehabilitation, this implicit limit was relaxed.

To be sure, there were some measurable positive changes that occurred in the nature of imprisonment, even during these otherwise challenging times. As we have noted earlier in this report, lethal violence has significantly declined overall in U.S. prisons, and that many prisons and entire prison systems continued to be well managed and adequately staffed and supported. As we have also noted, however, although systematic and comprehensive research on the quality of life and other more subtle indices of the experience of incarceration is limited, evidence of problematic practices, conditions, and forms of treatment persists.

The principle of citizenship—and respect for human dignity—would require review of certain conditions of confinement. Our review suggests, for example, that lengthy periods of isolation or administrative segregation can place prisoners at risk of significant psychological harm (see Chapter 6). Other evidence suggests that, partly as a result of serious overcrowding, prisoners have experienced reduced access to educational, vocational, and rehabilitative programs; and little or no adequate preparation for the return to free society. Prisoners who return to free society emotionally damaged, socially marginalized, or unprepared to obtain gainful employment may never be able to become fully functioning and participating members of the community, violating the most basic tenets of the principles of citizenship.

SOCIAL JUSTICE

The legal and political theory of punishment is largely silent on the social context in which criminal behavior arises. Criminal punishment is treated as a state-sanctioned blaming of offenders for moral failure, with limits imposed on the state to preserve core rights of citizenship. Justice is served by the equal treatment of suspects, defendants, and the incarcerated. This view of criminal punishment typically neglects the social or economic circumstances of crime, or the social inequality that often grows as cases move from arrest, to conviction, and then incarceration. The equation of justice with equal treatment in the courts is striking since the authorities deal overwhelmingly with the poor. We have seen from our review of incarceration statistics that, in the period of high incarceration rates, imprisonment has become commonplace for recent birth cohorts of men, particularly minorities, with very little schooling. Pervasive incarceration among poor men raises the question: What is the significance of poverty and social inequality for the U.S. system of punishment as an instrument of justice?

Classical conceptions of justice took little notice of the social inequalities that frequently divided the citizenry. Liberal justice of the eighteenth century insisted on a basic equality among men, in the language of the Declaration of Independence. Still, the liberal justice of equal rights failed to deliver citizenship to enslaved populations in the United States, and widely failed to deliver the franchise to women. Other deep social and economic inequalities persisted through the liberal revolutions of the eighteenth and nineteenth centuries.

By the early twentieth century, normative theorists—deeply concerned by the problems of poverty and social inequality—advocated for social policy to help redress unequal life chances produced by the rapidly indus-trializing economies of Western Europe and the United States. In 1912, R.H. Tawney's treatise on *Equality* reflected on the inadequate education and slum housing of the English working class, leading him to call for not merely "an open road, but . . . an equal start" (Tawney 1912, p. 143). Nearly 40 years later, T.H. Marshall (1987 [1950]) described how public education, health care, and income assistance were establishing a dignified standard of living as a basic social right. Political philosophers explicitly made the connection between poverty and injustice. John Rawls (1971) in his monumental *Theory of Justice* argued that a just society would provide for the fair distribution of "primary goods," which included not only wealth and income, but powers and opportunities and the social bases of self-respect. Amartya Sen (1992) went further, arguing that justice de-manded not only a fair distribution of the means to freedom, but freedom itself in the form of human capabilities. The central thread running through all this writing surpassed the idea of equal treatment to include the allevia-tion of poverty and inequality, not as a matter of charity, but as a matter of justice.[4] In this account, the state played a central role in promoting the opportunities of the most disadvantaged.

The normative theory of social justice developed in parallel with the modern social policy instruments for poverty reduction and equal oppor-tunity. Throughout the twentieth century, public health and education systems, cash assistance programs, and social insurance were all charged with improving the well-being and life chances of the disadvantaged and the unfortunate (Esping-Andersen 1990; Katz 1996).

Key elements of the modern criminal justice system also shared in this policy history. David Rothman (1980) has shown how, in the United States, indeterminate sentencing, the juvenile court, and and parole release and supervision all had their roots in the same progressive movement of the early twentieth century that also championed public sanitation and sec-ondary school education. David Garland (2001) called this perspective on correctional policy, "penal welfarism," underlining its aspirations to affirm citizenship and provide opportunity to society's most marginal members. This perspective was eclipsed as incarceration rates increased. Sentencing guidelines replaced indeterminate sentencing, discretionary parole release was widely abandoned and incarceration was used more readily.

Although correctional policy clearly changed as incarceration rates increased, the over-representation of the poor in the criminal justice sys-tem did not. The challenge to penal policy of advancing social justice thus

---

[4]The language of social justice came to be widely adopted by legal philosophers and political theorists (e.g., Ackerman 1980; Nussbaum 1998; Miller 1999; Barry 2005).

remains no less urgent than when penal welfarism first emerged as a policy philosophy in the early twentieth century.

In this context, the principle of social justice requires that a penal system avoid adding to social inequality or reduced opportunity. This goal of limiting penal harm recognizes that the power of incarceration is vast and may be socially damaging to those who are incarcerated, their families, and their communities. Minimizing penal harm is imperative because of the severe social and economic disadvantage of those at greatest risk of incarceration.

Reducing the negative effects of incarceration, however, is a minimal goal. More ambitiously, by helping to provide order and predictability in daily life and by reducing violence and other crime in the poorest communities, the criminal justice system can be expected to contribute positively to social justice. In this case, social justice is served by improvements in public safety. More than a general reduction in crime, however, social justice is particularly advanced where crime is reduced among poor and marginal populations. Improving public safety most for the poorest, for whom crime rates are highest, provides for a fairer distribution of rights, resources, and opportunities. Because rates of violence tend to be highest in the poorest communities, the goal of public safety is closely aligned with the value of social justice. Public safety consistent with social justice goes beyond the traditional focus on the detection, apprehension, and prosecution of crimes to also encompass prevention, and the mitigation of the social and economic conditions in which crime tends to flourish. In contrast, if the criminal justice system preserves or exacerbates racial, economic, and other inequalities, social justice is compromised.

Incarceration not only is associated with race, poverty and their correlates, incarceration has also become highly prevalent in the nation's poorest communities. Incarceration and social inequality are closely entwined. Our review of the evidence on the effects of incarceration suggests that the most troubled communities have not clearly become safer as a result of the growth of incarceration, and they may have suffered significant negative effects. In this respect, high incarceration rates have likely failed to deliver social justice. Through its intimate connection to social inequality, the criminal justice system also risks losing its legitimacy, particularly in the communities where its effects are felt most deeply.

CONCLUSION

In the domain of justice, empirical evidence by itself cannot determine public policy. Tacit conceptions of fairness and human welfare can remain hidden in the sober accounting of costs and benefits. Even more challenging, the social science evidence is often incomplete and uncertain. Moreover, an explicit and transparent account of normative principles has been notably missing from the significant policy shifts that propelled the rise in incarceration rates over the last four decades. As a committee, we worried that respect was lost for incarceration as an awesome state power in a liberal society. In this chapter, we have elaborated a set of key normative principles with deep roots in jurisprudence and theories of governance. These principles help supplement the large body of empirical evidence we have reviewed, indicating future directions for policy and research.

CONCLUSION: In the domain of justice, empirical evidence by itself cannot point the way to policy, yet an explicit and transparent expression of normative principles has been notably missing as U.S. incarceration rates dramatically rose over the last four decades. Normative principles have deep roots in jurisprudence and theories of governance and are needed to supplement empirical evidence to guide future policy and research.

13

Findings, Conclusions, and Implications

Originating in a period of rising crime rates and social foment and driven by punitive sentencing policy, the steep increase in incarceration in the United States was carried out with little regard for an objective evaluation of benefits or possible harms. This committee was charged with assessing the causes of the steep increase and the consequences that followed.

In this chapter, we first summarize the findings and state our conclusions from the review of the evidence presented in the preceding chapters. We next consider the implications of these findings for public policy. In so doing, we draw on the long-standing normative principles of jurisprudence and public policy that historically guided deliberations on the use of incarceration as a response to crime. Our findings and conclusions, supplemented by these normative principles, lead us to the main recommendation that federal and state policy makers should take steps to significantly reduce the rate of incarceration in the United States. We then make specific suggestions for reform in the areas of sentencing policy, prison policy, and social policy. The next section offers recommendations for further research. The final section presents concluding thoughts.

FINDINGS AND CONCLUSIONS

History

The U.S. rate of incarceration in 2007 was more than four and one-half times the rate in 1972 (Chapter 2 details these trends). By 2012, the prison

334

and jail population had grown to 2.23 million people, and the United States had by far the highest reported rate of incarceration in the world. Today, adult incarceration rates of the Western European democracies average around 100 per 100,000, and in the common law countries of Australia and Canada, the rates are only slightly higher. The U.S. rate in 2012 was seven times higher, at 707 per 100,000. At this level of penal confinement, the United States (accounting for about 5 percent of the world's population) holds close to 25 percent of the global incarcerated population.

CONCLUSION: The growth in incarceration rates in the United States over the past 40 years is historically unprecedented and internationally unique.

The growth of incarceration rates, beginning in 1972, followed a tumultuous period of social and political change (see Chapter 4). From 1962 to 1972, the annual number of homicides had climbed from 8,530 to 18,670. Homicide was just one indicator of declining public safety, as the overall violent crime rate doubled in that same decade (Maguire, n.d., Table 3.106.2011). If rising crime were the only new social trend of the 1960s, the link between crime and incarceration might be clear-cut. But political activism and race relations also came to a boil. Civil rights action and conservative reaction produced a contentious and sometimes violent politics that blurred the line between protest and disorder. The civil rights acts themselves upended the racial order of the south and outlawed discrimination in labor and housing markets across the country. In short, the period of rising crime accompanied a period of intense political conflict and a transformation of U.S. race relations.

Cities also were transformed. Riotous unrest culminated in the Kerner Commission (1968) report that surveyed dozens of incidents of disorder in 23 cities. The Commission, struggling to untangle a complex mix of crime, racial inequality, and politics, famously concluded that the nation was moving to "two societies, one black, one white—separate and unequal." Rising crime and disorder were accompanied by declining manufacturing sector employment in inner cities, classically described in William Julius Wilson's (1987) *The Truly Disadvantaged*. In Wilson's analysis, the outmigration of whites and working class blacks left behind pockets of concentrated disadvantage. These poor, racially segregated neighborhoods were characterized not just by high rates of crime but also by an array of other problems, including high rates of unemployment and widespread single parenthood. It was in these neighborhoods, decades later, where the effects of incarceration were felt most strongly.

Historic changes in politics, race relations, and urban life provided the context in which policy makers wrestled with the crime problem. Rising crime rates gained a prominent place in national policy debates. Crime and race sometimes were conflated in political conversation. Public policy of the 1960s was moving in a liberal direction, through an expansion of social programs and stronger rights for criminal defendants and prisoners, but these measures did not appear to stem the rise in crime. The debates about crime unfolded in a setting where crime policy was mostly made at the state and local levels. Local elected officials—including state legislators who enacted sentencing policies and, in many places, judges and prosecutors who decided individual cases—were highly attuned to their constituents' concerns about crime. Under these conditions, punishment policy moved in a more punitive direction.

Across all branches and levels of government, the policies governing criminal processing and sentencing were reformed to expand the use of incarceration. Prison time was increasingly required for lesser offenses. Time served was significantly increased for violent crimes and for repeat offenses. Drug crimes, particularly street dealing in urban areas, became policed and punished more severely (see Chapter 3). These changes in punishment policy—the enactment of mandatory sentence laws, long sentences for violence and repeat offenses, and intensified criminalization of drug-related activity—were the main and proximate drivers of the growth in incarceration.

CONCLUSION: The unprecedented rise in incarceration rates can be attributed to an increasingly punitive political climate surrounding criminal justice policy formed in a period of rising crime and rapid social change. This provided the context for a series of policy choices —across all branches and levels of government—that significantly increased sentence lengths, required prison time for minor offenses, and intensified punishment for drug crimes.

Consequences

When evaluating criminal justice policies, researchers and policy makers may turn first to the effects on crime rates. Most studies conclude that rising incarceration rates reduced crime, but the evidence does not clearly show by how much. A number of studies also find that the crime-reducing effects of incarceration become smaller as the incarceration rate grows, although this may be reflecting the aging of prison populations. As with many rigorous assessments of large historical events, a high level of scientific certainty about the effects of increased incarceration rates is elusive. The relationships between incarceration, crime, sentencing policy, social inequality, and the dozens of other variables that describe the growth of incarceration are complex, variable across time and place, and mutually determining.

Because of the great scientific challenge of separating cause and effect from the surrounding array of social forces, the impact of increased incarceration on crime cannot be calculated precisely. There is only weak evidence that increased prison populations from the 1970s to the 2000s led to large aggregate reductions in crime rates (see Chapter 5).

CONCLUSION: The increase in incarceration may have caused a decrease in crime, but the magnitude is highly uncertain and the results of most studies suggest it was unlikely to have been large.

Although increasing prison admissions and increases in time served in prison both fueled incarceration rates, research has best illuminated the effects of time served. Long sentences are characteristic of the period of high incarceration rates, but research indicates it is the certainty of apprehension, not an increase in the duration of long sentences, that actively deters would-be offenders. The marked decline in offending with age also means that the incapacitation effect of long sentences is likely to be small (see Chapter 5).

CONCLUSION: The incremental deterrent effect of increases in lengthy prison sentences is modest at best. Because recidivism rates decline markedly with age, lengthy prison sentences, unless they specifically target very high-rate or extremely dangerous offenders, are an inefficient approach to preventing crime by incapacitation.

What are the effects of increased incarceration on prisoners and their families? The committee began to consider these effects by reviewing research on prison conditions and the health of the prison population. Increased rates of incarceration may have altered prison conditions in ways that are, on balance, harmful to some prisoners and undermine their chances of living a normal life when released. Although the rate of lethal violence in prison declined, increased rates of incarceration were accompanied by overcrowding, decreased opportunity for rehabilitative programs, and a growing burden on medical and mental health services. Psychological research shows that many aspects of prison life—material deprivations, restricted movement, the absence of personal privacy, and high levels of uncertainty and fear, for example,—are significant sources of stress that damage the emotional well-being of some of those incarcerated (see Chapter 6).

Medical and epidemiological research indicates that these stressors are focused on a population that carries a high burden of disease and experiences a high rate of mental illness. Incarceration is associated with overlapping afflictions of substance use, mental illness, and risk for infectious diseases (HIV, viral hepatitis, sexually transmitted diseases, and others).

People who have been inadequately treated while in prison and after release face higher risks of suicide, relapse to drug addiction, and drug-overdose death than the general public (see Chapter 7).

Outside of the prison, incarceration is strongly correlated with negative social and economic outcomes. The people who have been incarcerated have very low earnings, high rates of unemployment, and experience little earnings growth over the life course. Because of school failure, criminal involvement, mental health problems and related challenges, those who go to prison have very poor economic opportunities even before incarceration. These pre-existing traits make it difficult to precisely estimate the economic effects of incarceration. Still, the experience of incarceration may undermine the productivity and employment opportunities of those incarcerated. Controlled experiments further show that job seekers with criminal records face extreme reluctance from prospective employers, and criminal records can have lasting employment consequences (see Chapter 8).

Family instability in the lives of former prisoners and behavioral problems among their children is also well-established. Studies have documented the large increase in the number of children with incarcerated parents and have described the range of poor outcomes that may be associated with having a parent in prison. The evidence shows a strong relationship between a father's incarceration and family hardship, including housing insecurity and behavioral problems in children, though it is difficult to draw causal inferences about that relationship. Studies that focus exclusively on incarcerated men have found that partners and children of male prisoners are particularly likely to experience adverse outcomes if the men were positively involved with their families prior to incarceration (see Chapter 9).

Beyond the research on individuals and families, the committee also explored the consequences of high incarceration rates for communities (see Chapter 10). The escalating rates of incarceration have been concentrated in poor and largely urban African American and Hispanic communities. As a result of the shift in penal policy toward greater use of prison, large number of residents of these communities, mostly poor men with little schooling, have experienced the cycle of arrest, detention, imprisonment, release, and supervision in the community, often followed by a return to prison for violating parole conditions or for a new crime. Given the challenge of drawing strong causal inferences, it is difficult to determine precisely the impact of this high concentration of the growth in incarceration on the levels of crime in these communities. Yet the evidence is clear that the large increase in incarceration has been concentrated in high-crime, disadvantaged minority communities and has transformed the character of life in poor urban neighborhoods.

The committee also reviewed evidence on the consequences of the growth of the prison population for civic and social life more broadly (see Chapter 11). High rates of incarceration are associated with lower levels of civic and political engagement among former prisoners and their families and friends. The quality of important demographic, political, and socioeconomic databases were compromised. High incarceration rates served as a gateway to a much larger system of stigmatization and legal, political, and social marginalization. The high cost of the penal system for state budgets also transformed incarceration into a major function of state government.

In summary, over the decades reviewed in this report, policy makers aggressively promoted measures that greatly increased incarceration rates. They adopted imprisonment as a key tool for crime control. Very long sentences became commonplace for repeat offenses and serious violence, and drug offenses were prosecuted more aggressively. Prison time was often mandated for offenses that previously were punished through community sanctions. Throughout this significant shift in penal policy, the possibility of negative social consequences was either not considered or disregarded. Nor did policy makers adequately consider the possibility that the crime reduction effects of the prison expansion might be modest. Yet the evidence reviewed by this committee indicates that the large increase in incarceration rates probably did not substantially reduce crime. At the same time, the available evidence suggests the prison expansion may have resulted in negative effects on prisoners, their families and the larger society. The committee recognizes that a great deal of scientific uncertainty characterizes scholarly efforts to assess these two effects. In carrying out its charge to assess the available evidence, and cognizant of this uncertainty, the committee concludes that, despite a profound change in penal policy in the U.S., large benefits failed to clearly materialize, and social harm may have resulted.

CONCLUSION: The change in penal policy over the past four decades may have had a wide range of unwanted social costs, and the magnitude of crime reduction benefits is highly uncertain.[1]

Race is a theme that runs through many of the chapters of this report. Racial disparities in incarceration have been observed since the relevant data were first available in the nineteenth century. Incarceration rates escalated rapidly for African Americans to levels six and seven times higher than those of whites, and reached extraordinary levels among young African American men with little schooling. Estimates indicate that by 2010, one-third of all African American male high school dropouts under age 40

---

[1]See Appendix A for a supplementary statement by Ricardo Hinojosa on this and other similar committee findings.

were in prison or jail, compared to an incarceration rate of 0.7 percent in the population as a whole (see Chapter 2). Much of the significance of the social and economic consequences of incarceration is rooted in the high absolute level of incarceration for minority groups and in the large racial and ethnic disparities in incarceration rates. Research on the spatial distribution of incarceration indicates that prisoners are overwhelmingly drawn from poor minority neighborhoods that also suffer from an array of other socioeconomic disadvantages. In the era of high incarceration rates, prison admission and return became commonplace in minority neighborhoods with high levels of crime, poverty, family instability, poor health, and residential segregation (see Chapter 10). Large racial disparities in incarceration focused any negative effects of incarceration disproportionately on African Americans, the poor in particular, and transformed their collective relationship to the state.

> CONCLUSION: People who live in poor and minority communities have always had substantially higher rates of incarceration than other groups. As a consequence, the effects of harsh penal policies in the past 40 years have fallen most heavily on blacks and Hispanics, especially the poorest.

Implications

The findings and conclusions presented here do not easily lend themselves to a simple calculation of costs and benefits. The policies that produced very high rates of incarceration grew out of a historical period of rapid change and social conflict. By greatly expanding the use of penal confinement, the policies charted a new direction for the American criminal justice system. No other Western democracy went so far down this path. Through the 1990s and 2000s, crime rates fell significantly, but the evidence indicates it is unlikely that the rise in incarceration rates played a powerful role in this trend. Against weak evidence for large benefits, there is also the chance of significant social costs for individuals who are incarcerated, their families, and communities. The strong correlation of incarceration with unemployment, poverty, family disruption, poor health and drug addiction is very clear. Causality is harder to disentangle, but experiments and statistical adjustment point to the real possibility of negative social effects. These correlations and negative effects are concentrated almost entirely in poor, especially poor minority, communities. For policy and public life, the size of the effects of incarceration may be less important than the overwhelming evidence of the correlation between very high levels of incarceration, race, poverty, and the myriad of accompanying social problems.

The committee struggled with the meaning of these conclusions. Across the many perspectives and specializations represented by our members, we agreed that basic questions of justice cannot be answered by science alone, particularly in this context where the problem is complex, many different kinds of evidence—quantitative and qualitative—are relevant, and scientific certainty was often elusive. The decision to deprive another human being of his or her liberty is, at root, anchored in beliefs about the just relationship between the individual and society and the role of criminal sanctions in preserving the social compact. Thus, good justice policy is necessarily based on a combination of empirical research and explicit normative commitments.

CONCLUSION: In the domain of justice, empirical evidence by itself cannot point the way to policy, yet an explicit and transparent expression of normative principles has been notably missing as U.S. incarceration rates dramatically rose over the past four decades. Normative principles have deep roots in jurisprudence and theories of governance and are needed to supplement empirical evidence to guide future policy and research.

To frame the policy implications of the evidence presented in this report, we return to the normative principles first presented in Chapter 1 and elaborated in Chapter 12. The committee noted that, over the past 40 years, principles that would restrain the use of prison as a response to crime were given less weight in public discourse than the crime control mission for punishment. The principle of proportionality—that the sanction imposed for violation of the criminal law should be proportionate to the seriousness of the crime—is challenged by harsh sentences for minor offenses. The principle of parsimony—that the criminal sanction imposed for an offense should be sufficient but not greater than the punishment necessary to achieve sentencing goals—is inconsistent with overly long sentences. The principle of citizenship—the notion that the consequences of a prison sentence should not be so severe as to substantially weaken one's status as a member of society—is tested by conditions of confinement that can be considered inhumane. Finally, the principle of social justice, as applied to prisons—that prisons should promote, not diminish, a fair distribution of resources, rights, and opportunities—is strained when incarceration becomes pervasive in poor and minority communities.

In weighing the scientific evidence on the causes and consequences of the high rates of incarceration in the United States, and then considering the implications of that evidence for public policy, the committee found it instructive to refer to the principles that govern the use of imprisonment for crime control and define the proper role of prison in a democratic society. The committee recognizes that a range of values might influence society's response to crime. The imposition of the criminal sanction is considered a validation of the social compact. The prevention and control of crime is also recognized as a long-established purpose of the criminal justice system. As is documented in Chapter 12, striking the appropriate balance between these competing values lies at the heart of the policy discourse in a democracy. Yet, Chapter 12 also shows that recent policy discussions have retreated from the principles that constrain the power of the state to punish, respect the human dignity of persons incarcerated, and are troubled by the intimate connection between prisons, racial inequality and poverty. As the committee considered the implications of its findings and conclusions, we affirmed the importance of reviving these principles and striking a new balance in the nation's penal policies.

ROLE OF POLICY

The growth of the prison population can be traced to policies expanding the use of imprisonment for felony convictions, imposing longer sentences on those committed to prison, and intensifying punishment for the sale and use of drugs. Proponents of those policies argued that more prison and longer sentences would reduce crime. The committee concluded that research indicates that the large increase in incarceration rates has not clearly yielded sizable reductions in crime. Furthermore, while the research does not clearly indicate the magnitude of the impact of incarceration on crime, there is strong evidence that increasing long sentences has promoted neither deterrence nor incapacitation.

The cost of expanding the penal system has been substantial. The financial costs are borne by taxpayers, who provide funding for local jails, state and federal prisons, and the operations of the larger criminal justice apparatus associated with institutions of incarceration. The opportunity cost is also considerable. Spending on prisons diverts resources from more effective public safety strategies, services for crime victims, or programs designed to help achieve effective reintegration of people who have been released from prisons. The burden of incarceration also falls on the millions of incarcerated individuals and, the evidence suggests, their families and neighborhoods. More broadly, as a consequence of the unprecedented rise in incarceration rates, the larger society bears the costs of an expanded share of the population that struggles with the stigma and negative effects of the prison experience.

To recognize the high cost of incarceration does not deny that, in specific cases, prison sentences are an appropriate societal response to the crimes committed. Nor does this assessment of the costs of prison overlook the fact that, in certain cases, incarceration will prevent crime. Similarly, incarceration has certainly improved life for some of those sent to prison.

Yet the weight of the scientific evidence on the consequences of high rates of incarceration, when viewed in light of the principles of proportionality, parsimony, citizenship, and social justice outlined above, suggests that too many people are in prison in the United States and that, overall, their sentences are too long.

The nation cannot yet accurately estimate the long-term consequences of imprisoning so many of its citizens. However, the current evidence is troubling and leads to our overarching policy recommendation.

RECOMMENDATION: Given the small crime prevention effects of long prison sentences and the possibly high financial, social, and human costs of incarceration, federal and state policy makers should revise current criminal justice policies to significantly reduce the rate of incarceration in the United States. In particular, they should reexamine policies regarding mandatory minimum sentences and long sentences. Policy makers should also take steps to improve the experience of incarcerated men and women and reduce unnecessary harm to their families and their communities.

Based on our analysis of the evidence, we urge policy makers at the state and national levels to reconsider policies in three distinct domains: (1) sentencing policy, (2) prison policy, and (3) social policy. Doing so will require political will. Just as the expansion of the penal system was driven by changes in policy, it must be reversed through policy choices. Most fundamentally, reversing course will require state and federal policy makers to significantly reform sentencing policy. More specifically, as discussed below, they should consider reforms to the current regime of long sentences, mandatory minimum sentences, and the overall enforcement strategies regarding drug laws. In addition, reversing course will require changes in the use of discretion available under current laws to police, prosecutors, parole decision makers, community corrections officials, and other actors in the criminal justice system. The development of new penal policies will depend, in turn, on a new public consensus that current policies have been, on balance, more harmful than effective and are inconsistent with U.S. history and notions of justice. Making this case to the public will require determined political leadership.

Before turning to our suggestions in the three policy domains, we note that, although our overarching recommendation involves issues of sentencing and prison policy, a broader menu of alternatives is necessarily implicated when reforming sentencing policies to reduce incarceration rates. To support the recommended change in policy direction, jurisdictions would likely have to review a range of allied programs, such as community-based alternatives to incarceration, probation and parole, prisoner reentry, diversion from prosecution, and crime prevention initiatives. Correctional programs, such as cognitive-behavioral therapies aimed at changing criminal behavior, also are likely to be an important part of the needed change in direction (MacKenzie, 2006). Assessing the effectiveness of these programs is beyond this committee's charge, but we note the importance of viewing the above recommendation in the context of this larger policy framework. We return to this issue in our discussion of research needs below.

Sentencing Policy

The evidence we reviewed does not provide a roadmap for comprehensive sentencing reform. Just as research does not indicate precisely whether a sentence for a specific crime is too short or too long, it does not specify an optimal sentence reduction. Other values may also shape sentencing policy. For example, many sentencing reforms of recent years were intended to reduce racial disparities, and policy makers must be careful not to reverse any resulting gains in sentence proportionality. More important, and consistent with our emphasis on the importance of values and the need for political leadership, we recognize that the details of strategies for reducing incarceration levels will depend on a complex interplay between the public and policy makers. However, the evidence does identify some types of policies that drove the prison buildup; imposed sizable social, financial, and human costs; failed to produce commensurate public safety benefits; and were inconsistent with the normative principles articulated above. Three dimensions of sentencing policy are particularly appropriate for reexamination: long sentences, mandatory minimum sentences, and enforcement of drug laws.

Long Sentences

The case for reducing long sentences is compelling. As this report has documented (see Chapters 2 and 3), the steady growth in incarceration rates has been significantly fuelled by longer prison sentences. A variety of statutory enactments have driven these results, including laws imposing truth-in-sentencing, life without parole, and three strikes enhancements. In addition to these changes in sentencing policy, states also have reduced or eliminated the use of discretionary parole release, increased the level of returns to prison for parole violations, reduced the use of "good time" provisions to accelerate release eligibility and cut back on the use of halfway houses, educational release programs and compassionate release options. These policy shifts significantly increased the average time served for a felony conviction.

Yet, as reviewed in this report, research shows that long sentences have little marginal effect on crime reduction through either deterrence or incapacitation. The deterrent value of long sentences is minimal, as the decision to commit a crime is more likely influenced by the certainty and swiftness of punishment than by the severity of the criminal sanction. Research on criminal careers shows that recidivism rates decline markedly with age. Prisoners serving long sentences necessarily age as they serve their time and their risk of re-offending declines over time. Accordingly, unless sentencing judges can specifically target very high-rate or extremely dangerous offenders, imposing long prison sentences is an inefficient way to prevent crime. Finally, the evidence is clear that long prison sentences incur substantial costs to state and federal budgets and will likely add significant future costs as the prison population ages.

Efforts to reduce incarceration rates by reducing long sentences could usefully follow the initiatives undertaken by the federal government and by many states. The U.S. Congress has curtailed the length of the sentence for crack cocaine offenses, and the U.S. Sentencing Commission has retroactively applied sentencing guideline changes for current prisoners (U.S. Sentencing Commission, 2013a). Between 2006 and 2011, 29 states shortened sentences with the aim of reducing prison populations. Some, including Michigan and Mississippi, modified truth-in-sentencing laws to accelerate parole eligibility. California, Indiana, and South Carolina scaled back their three strikes enhancements. Other states reduced sentence lengths by authorizing credits for "good time" that directly affected prison release and parole eligibility. Since 2001, these reforms have been implemented in at least 16 states (Arkansas, California, Colorado, Delaware, Georgia, Kansas, Louisiana, Mississippi, Nevada, North Carolina, Ohio, Pennsylvania, South Carolina, Vermont, Wisconsin, and Wyoming). Although the precise impact of these reforms on average sentence length has yet to be determined, it is reasonable to assume that they have contributed to the overall decline in incarceration rates among the states (Vera Institute of Justice, 2010).

If the policy reforms designed to reduce long prison sentences were prospective and applied only to new convictions, then prison populations would decline only slowly. More immediate effects could be obtained by re-examining and reforming the policies governing release from prison. For example, the state and federal governments could reconsider policies that abolished or restricted discretionary parole release, or curtailed the use of work release, educational release and half-way houses. They could follow the example of states that are considering the establishment or expansion of geriatric or medical parole, also called "compassionate release." According to the National Conference of State Legislators, between 2000 and 2012, 29 states reformed their rules governing the medical release of inmates;

the changes frequently included compassionate release for the elderly and terminally ill (National Conference of State Legislators, 2012).

Finally, policy makers could implement reforms that would reduce the flow of individuals back to prison because their parole (or probation) has been revoked for technical violations of the conditions of their release. States that have pursued this reform strategy have substantially reduced the flow of people returning to prison. From 2001 through 2010, at least 9 states (Alabama, California, Colorado, Florida, Kentucky, Louisiana, South Carolina, South Dakota, and Washington) enacted these and related legislative measures (Vera Institute of Justice, 2010). Between 2007 and 2013, 13 states (Arkansas, Georgia, Hawaii, Kansas, Kentucky, Louisiana, Nevada, North Carolina, Pennsylvania, South Carolina, South Dakota, Texas, and West Virginia) authorized graduated responses for parole violations, providing front-line officers with a continuum of community-based sanctions to keep more parolees in the community while still maintaining accountability for violations (Pew Charitable Trusts, 2007).

These and other reforms offer a broad menu of policy options that together could significantly reduce the average length of stay in U.S. prisons. They are best combined with a more fundamental re-examination of overall sentence length under state and federal laws. As was noted in Chapter 2, the use of longer prison terms has been a critical driver of high rates of incarceration. A thorough inquiry into the value of longer sentences, including life sentences without the option of parole, resulting in the establishment of new sentencing parameters, could produce substantial reduction in the nation's prison population in the long run. Cutting back the maximum sentence length for specified offenses would not yield savings in prison time until many years from now, but such a policy reform would be consistent with the normative values outlined in this report and would pose little risk to public safety.

Mandatory Minimum Sentences

Between 1975 and 1995, all 50 states and the U.S. Congress reduced the discretion available to sentencing judges by passing laws requiring imprisonment for a wide variety of offenses. Prior to these enactments, judges could impose noncustodial sanctions such as probation, restitution, or community service. As a result of these new mandatory minimum penalties, custodial sentences have increasingly been imposed for minor offenses. Mandatory minimum sentences were also enacted for drug offenses, murder, aggravated rape, felonies involving firearms and felonies committed by individuals with prior felony convictions. Over the decades covered by this report, mandatory minimums were the most frequently enacted sentencing law change in the U.S. (see Chapter 3).

The stated reason for these sentencing enactments was crime prevention. Policy makers asserted that requiring prison sentences for designated
offenses would deter others from committing crimes. Yet the weight of
evidence reviewed in this report is strong that such enactments have few, if
any, deterrent effects. As is discussed in Chapter 5, three reports of panels
convened by the National Research Council have reviewed the research
literature on the deterrent effect of such laws and have concluded that the
evidence is insufficient to justify the conclusion that these harsher punishments yield measurable public safety benefits. At the same time, there
is substantial evidence in the research literature that the imposition of
mandatory minimum sentences creates incentives for practitioners—police,
prosecutors and judges—to circumvent these penalties.

A broad strategy for reducing the nation's prison population would
also entail review of mandatory minimum sentences in general. A number
of states have undertaken such a review. Between 2001 and 2010, 12 states
(Delaware, Georgia, Hawaii, Indiana, Louisiana, Michigan, Minnesota,
Nevada, New Jersey, New York, Rhode Island, and South Carolina) relaxed
their mandatory minimum sentence laws (Vera Institute of Justice, 2010).
Statutory reform is not required to reach this result; changes in prosecutorial policy could also change the dynamics of sentencing. In recent instructions to U.S. attorneys, Attorney General Eric Holder has limited the use
of mandatory minimums by federal prosecutors for some classes of drug
cases (Holder, 2013a, 2013b).

The principles of proportionality and parsimony also call for a reexamination of penal policies mandating imprisonment for minor offenses.
Allowing judges to exercise greater discretion in the imposition of a criminal sentence recognizes that any term of imprisonment is a severe sanction that must be imposed deliberately with clear reference to the facts of
specific cases. The research also indicates that these reforms would reduce
the practice of circumventing mandatory penalties. Finally, the evidence
strongly suggests that reforms envisioned here would reduce the nation's
prison population without posing significant risks to public safety.

Enforcement of Drug Laws

The law enforcement strategy known as the war on drugs has been
a significant driver of the increase in U.S. incarceration rates. Over the
decades of the prison buildup, the incarceration rate for drug offenses
increased tenfold—twice the rate for other crimes. Prison admissions for
drug offenses grew rapidly, increasing from about 10,000 state prison commitments for drugs in 1980, to about 120,000 admissions by 1990, and
peaking at 157,000 admissions in 2008 (see Chapter 5). Yet, as reported in
a 2001 report of the National Research Council, these dramatic increases

in imprisonment for drug crimes did not clearly reduce drug use and were accompanied by a significant decline in drug prices from the 1980s to the 1990s. The evidence of high costs—particularly the high costs of incarceration—and of the apparently low effectiveness of the current drug enforcement strategy should compel a fresh look at alternatives. Furthermore, the disparate impact of the war on drugs on communities of color and the high rates of incarceration for drug offenses among African Americans and Hispanics make a reduction in drug-related incarceration an urgent priority.

Reducing incarceration rates requires reassessment of the nation's war on drugs and the implementation of more effective responses. This reassessment should recognize that abuse of illegal drugs is both a health policy and a justice policy issue. Alternatives that rely more on health care measures might well reduce the social and economic costs of imprisonment and improve public health. A fresh look at drug policy should also confront the realities of current enforcement policies. Over the period of U.S. history covered in this report, the arrest rate for drugs increased substantially— from about 200 per 100,000 adults in 1980 to over 400 per 100,000 in 2009 (see Chapter 5). A more effective response that relied less on arrests would also reduce the reliance on prisons. One promising approach is the law enforcement intervention piloted in High Point, North Carolina. Reflecting principles of focused deterrence, this approach, since replicated widely across the U.S., has shown that a coordinated multiagency response to overt drug markets can effectively address their adverse effects with limited reliance on arrests and therefore reduced reliance on incarceration (Kennedy, 2011).

In addition to high levels of arrests, sentencing for drug offenses has also become more punitive. As mentioned above, reforms to limit mandatory minimum sentences and long sentences for drug offenses would reduce incarceration rates. Recent reductions in incarceration resulting from the reform of U.S. sentencing guidelines for crack cocaine offenses and of New York's Rockefeller Drug Laws illustrate the potential benefits of reducing the use of incarceration for drug crimes.

Other strategies might be even more effective in addressing the underlying issue of drug use within the contours of the criminal justice system. A number of states and the federal government have taken steps to this end. For example, the development of drug treatment courts and prosecutorial diversion programs offer innovative possibilities that could reduce both drug use and incarceration rates. Recent innovative probation reforms, such as project HOPE (Hawaii Opportunity Probation with Enforcement), which mixes swift and certain sanctions with a regime of drug testing, represent promising efforts to treat problems of drug abuse without relying extensively on incarceration.

A full assessment of the evidence of effectiveness of these and other programmatic innovations is beyond the scope of this report. But what is clear is that reducing the nation's reliance on incarceration will require a thorough and sustained fresh look at the current approach to drug use and drug crimes.

Other Sentencing Policy Considerations

Although the above measures do not exhaust the options for sentencing reform, we view reduced use of long sentences, review of mandatory minimum sentences, and a revised approach to drug law enforcement as three key main ways in which incarceration could be significantly reduced. Recent reform efforts also have addressed other phases of correctional supervision, notably community corrections. As was mentioned above, a shift in sentencing policy away from reliance on incarceration would necessarily require closer examination of the effectiveness of alternatives to incarceration, including the effectiveness of parole and probation supervision. Similarly, any well-conceived plan for reducing prison populations should consider the effectiveness of short-term and longer-term assistance to parolees. A 2008 National Research Council report on parole policies includes the recommendation that both in-prison and postrelease parole programs be redirected to providing a variety of supports to parolees and others released from prison at the time of release and suggests that no one should leave prison without an immediately available support program and a plan for life postrelease (National Research Council, 2008, p. 82).

Prison Policy

Even if incarceration rates are significantly reduced, prisons will remain indispensable to the nation's system of punishment. In parallel with our general recommendation to reduce the level of incarceration, we urge reduction of the potentially harmful effects of incarceration through reaffirmation of the principle of citizenship and recognition of the public character of penal institutions.

Reaffirmation of the Principle of Citizenship

The principle of citizenship requires that a person's status as a member of a community not be fundamentally diminished by incarceration. In our view, respect for citizenship demands that punishment by incarceration not be so severe, or have such lasting negative consequences, that the person punished is forever excluded from full participation in mainstream society. Stated affirmatively, the principle of citizenship requires that prisons operate to respect the autonomy and dignity of those incarcerated, consistent with the goal of administering safe and orderly institutions.

The principle of citizenship suggests a rigorous review of the conditions of confinement and of the legal disabilities and restrictions imposed on those who have been incarcerated. In particular, policies and practices that result in long periods of administrative segregation from the general population, deprivation of meaningful human contact, overcrowding, and unnecessarily high levels of custody all require rigorous review. Prison authorities and legislatures should consider reestablishing the commitment to programming and rehabilitation that was deemphasized during the period of rising incarceration. Conditions of confinement should be reviewed with the objective of increasing prisoners' chances of reentering society with social relationships intact and better prepared to make a positive, productive transition. Review of these conditions and the policies that regulate them is compelling because, with rare exceptions, all those incarcerated in the nation's prisons and jails will be released to return to their communities (Travis, 2005). The principle of citizenship also demands a broad review of the penalties and restrictions faced by the formerly incarcerated in their access to the social benefits, rights, and opportunities that might otherwise promote their successful reintegration following release from prison. In short, the state's decision to deprive a person of liberty temporarily should not lead to permanently diminished citizenship.

The Prison as a Mainstay of Justice

Despite the nation's great reliance on prisons, the public has few opportunities for a comprehensive and critical examination of the state of penal institutions and how they operate. Compared with other areas of social policy that require similar expenditures of billions of dollars, prisons in many states are subject to relatively little oversight. Through laws, such as the Prison Litigation Reform Act, the role of courts in reviewing conditions of confinement has been restricted (see Chapter 6). Many new prisons were sited in remote areas where they are not readily visible or accessible. The locations and forbidding design of many prisons stand as metaphors for this reality: prisons are far from the public mind and appear closed to public view.

The committee urges policy makers to elevate the public profile and transparency of prisons in recognition of their important role in U.S. society. The broad topics of concern might include the quality of life in prisons, public accountability for expenditures, designation of expected in-prison and postrelease outcomes for prisoners, standards for health and mental health care, limits on the use of administrative segregation, and access by researchers (see Chapter 6). Prison conditions and practices can be improved over time through continuing outside scrutiny. Policy makers might also consider establishing or reinforcing independent monitoring and oversight of prisons, including independent commissions of the sort that operate in other Western nations.[2] U.S. policy makers would benefit from discussions with their counterparts in some other nations where oversight of corrections policies and practices is more rigorous and systematic than is the case in most U.S. prison systems.

Social Policy

If incarceration rates are reduced, many people who would have been incarcerated will continue residing in their communities, often under community supervision. These are largely poor men and women with very low levels of schooling and poor employment histories, many of whom also have histories of substance abuse and mental illness. Their criminal responsibility is real, but embedded in a context of social and economic disadvantage. The close connections between crime, incarceration, and poverty have implications for reforms aimed at reducing high incarceration rates as well as those aimed at reducing criminal behaviors in the first place.

With fewer people in prison, there may be a greater need for social services in the community. It will be necessary to carefully assess available services to determine if there are sufficient quality services in accessible locations to meet the needs of otherwise imprisoned members of the community. Drug treatment, health care, employment, and housing will face especially strong demand. Sustainably reducing incarceration will depend in part on whether communities can meet the needs of those who would otherwise be locked up. If large numbers of intensely disadvantaged prime-age men and women are resituated in poor communities without appropriate social supports, the effects could be broadly harmful and could discredit decisions to reduce the use of incarceration.

Here, the historical example of the deinstitutionalization of the mentally ill offers a cautionary example. Deinstitutionalization, gradually unfolding through the 1950s and 1960s, was originally conceived to be buttressed by an array of community-based mental health services. Instead, state mental hospitals were shuttered, and policy makers were reluctant to

---

[2]In some U.S. states, independent oversight is provided by an ombudsman or inspector general. In the United Kingdom, Her Majesty's Inspectorate of Prisons conducts announced and unannounced inspections assessing prisons against established standards for inmate safety, health care, respectful conduct among staff and inmates, programming, reentry, and administrative segregation (Her Majesty's Inspectorate of Prisons, 2012). Similar independent oversight through the Council of Europe is provided by the European Committee for the Prevention of Torture and Inhuman or Degrading Treatment or Punishment. An annotated bibliography of writings on independent prison oversight is provided by Deitch (2010).

support community-based programs. Homelessness and other hardships among the mentally ill resulted from the deficit of treatment and other services. Significant reductions in prison population without community planning risks similar problems. Responsibly reducing incarceration will require a parallel expansion of social services.

Policy research on released prisoners emphasizes the importance of employment, housing, and health services (e.g., Travis, 2005; Seiter and Kadela, 2003; Mead, 2011). Employment programs provide a variety of services, from job readiness training to subsidized work (see Chapter 8). Although evaluation research provides uneven evidence that labor market programs can boost employment and reduce recidivism, such programs often are intrinsically valuable when they provide income support and structure the time of program clients. There have been few evaluations of subsidized housing programs.[3] However, housing insecurity is common among those at risk of incarceration (see Chapter 9), and like employment programs, housing support often meets serious needs of program clients. Evaluation research also indicates that recidivism can be significantly reduced when social opportunity programs, such as those providing employment, are combined with programs that address criminogenic behaviors (see MacKenzie, 2006, 2012).

The need for health services for released prisoners, including drug and mental health treatment, is similarly serious. The Patient Protection and Affordable Care Act (ACA) presents an unprecedented opportunity to extend health insurance coverage to this population. Improving the health of this and other disadvantaged populations will require continuity of health care from custody to community. Comprehensive screening, diagnosis, and treatment—particularly for infectious diseases such as HIV, hepatitis C virus, and sexually transmitted diseases and for mental illness and substance use disorders—would address broader public health and improve health for those at risk of incarceration. Improving health insurance coverage and medical care is especially important given the evidence on the effectiveness of substance abuse treatment (see Chapter 7). Recent meta-analyses have indicated that drug treatment is associated with reductions in both drug use and recidivism after release (Egli et al., 2009; Mitchell et al., 2012).

In many places, programs already address some of the needs of those diverted or released from incarceration. Prisoner reentry programs have been introduced in all 50 states and a number of local jurisdictions. In various locations, education and transitional employment programs, community health and substance abuse treatment, and community investment

---

[3]One notable evaluation is that of the ComALERT reentry program in Brooklyn, which includes a large residential population. It was found that the program delivered reductions in arrests and improvements in employment (Jacobs and Western, 2007).

and neighborhood capacity building have been implemented as part of a comprehensive approach to reducing reliance on incarceration (Pew Center on the States, 2010; Council of State Governments Justice Center, 2013). These developments have been spurred by federal initiatives under the Second Chance Act and the Justice Reinvestment Act. The exploration of social policy supports, in tandem with reduced incarceration, would reflect recognition that the growth in incarceration was in part a response to real social problems in poor communities for which comprehensive approaches are needed. Using policy tools such as the ACA combined with investments in employment, housing, and health care can also provide support to vulnerable populations at the earliest possible time before involvement with the criminal justice system begins.

RECOMMENDED RESEARCH

As noted throughout this report, the committee encountered a variety of gaps in data and empirical research. Most generally, our review of the research revealed great variation in how incarceration is experienced. To a significant degree, this variation reflects broad differences in routines, management, and organizational culture across correctional facilities. These differences in prison conditions are reflected in data on levels of custody. A rough national measure of confinement conditions is also derived from statistics on overcrowding. But beyond these rudimentary indicators, detailed knowledge about the spectrum of conditions of prison life is sparse. Given the extent to which carceral policies in the United States have diverged from those of other affluent democracies in the past four decades, cross-national comparative studies could be expected to shed light on several of the research questions posed below. Across jurisdictions in the United States, great variation also is seen in penal codes and their application in the courts. Variation in incarceration rates has grown across states as the national incarceration rate has increased.

Looking forward, we see several key priorities for research. We begin with one overarching recommendation:

> **RECOMMENDATION: Given the prominent role played by prisons in U.S. society, the far-reaching impact of incarceration, and the need to develop policies that reduce reliance on imprisonment as a response to crime, public and private research institutions and statistical agencies should support a robust research and statistics program commensurate with the importance of these issues.**

More specifically, we recommend support for research aimed at developing a better understanding of (1) the experience of being incarcerated and its effects, (2) alternative sentencing policies, and (3) the impact of incarceration on communities. (A more detailed discussion is presented in Appendix C.)

Understanding the Experience of Incarceration and Its Effects

Understanding the effects of conditions of confinement on those incarcerated and their chances for successful reentry after prison is important, yet there has been too little systematic research on these questions. Some studies have examined the effects of sentence length on employment and recidivism, and a large literature evaluates prison programs, but researchers know little about interstate variation in sentence lengths and prison conditions (National Research Council, 2012a). Knowledge also is inadequate about the effects on postprison life of overcrowding, victimization in prison, administrative segregation, long-term isolation, mental health treatment, staffing levels, custody levels, and staff training. Most research on social and economic effects treats prison as a black box, with little detailed study of what takes place inside and its potential effects. Because correctional facilities vary so greatly, mapping the differences across facilities would fill a first-order gap in knowledge with immediate policy significance.

A research agenda in this area could assist in the development of standards for conditions of confinement. A national statistical series would allow for cross-jurisdiction comparisons of the dimensions of the prison experience, including such variables as time served and sentence length by crime type, the quality and outcomes of different types of programming, the nature and extent of visitation, the number of prisoners held in different housing configurations, and responses to rule infractions. On the critical issue of health care and treatment of mental illness, a national database would allow for a better understanding of the health consequences of incarceration and the effectiveness of various health and mental health interventions. Another priority for future research is the collection of longitudinal data tracking individuals before and after their contact with the criminal justice system, including prison. Current research often cannot distinguish among the effects of criminal behavior, criminal conviction, and the experience of incarceration as they relate to such outcomes as recidivism, employment, and family life. The ability to make these distinctions is important both to the research community and to policy makers.

Understanding Alternative Sentencing Policies

As the debate over sentencing policy continues to explore alternatives to incarceration, understanding the effectiveness of these alternatives is a key policy priority. Understanding the available options and assessing their costs and benefits will require a broad research agenda. At its core, this agenda should include further research on the effects of incarceration on crime rates so that alternative interventions can be compared with the prison sentence. Priority should be given to investigating the magnitude of deterrence as a function of sentence length and to establishing whether other components of the certainty of punishment beyond the certainty of apprehension (such as the probability of imprisonment given conviction) are effective deterrents. Such studies should include estimates of the long-lagged effects on crime, through deterrence or other mechanisms, of specific sentencing policies. Another priority is the development of a comprehensive database that would allow for cross-state comparisons of postconviction sentencing practices over time, as has also been recommended by the National Research Council (2012a).

The research agenda should include an extensive portfolio of evaluations of various sentencing policies that do not involve incarceration so that policy makers can assess available options. This portfolio should include, but not be limited to, evaluations of programs explicitly designed to serve as alternatives to incarceration. These evaluations should be rigorous, be open to replication, and inform the development of standards of best practice to help policy makers invest in these programs instead of prisons. The evaluations should include assessment of the deterrent effects of these sentencing alternatives, as well as estimates of their cost-effectiveness. Similarly, rigorous evaluations should be conducted of in-prison programs designed to facilitate successful reentry and community-based programs committed to reintegration of formerly incarcerated men and women. This research agenda should also yield a better understanding of the impact of various impediments to reintegration, such as legal exclusions from certain employment sectors and restrictions on voting and public housing.

Understanding the Impact of Incarceration on Communities

Throughout this report, we have reviewed strong evidence of the extreme concentration of incarceration in poor communities and in the poorest segments of the population. Much of the research on the effects of incarceration has focused on individual-level outcomes for formerly incarcerated individuals and sometimes their families. Yet because of the extreme social concentration of incarceration, the most important effects may be systemic, for groups and communities. If African American male high school dropouts have a high expectation of going to prison at some point in their lives, that expectation may change the behavior of all the men in the group, not just those actually going to prison. If a third of the young men in a poor community are incarcerated, skewing gender balance and disrupting family relations, incarceration may have community-level effects that shape the social context of community residents, even if their families are not involved in the criminal justice system. Too little is known about these effects.

A rigorous program of research on communities, crime, and crime control (including incarceration) should include comparative qualitative studies of the communities from which the incarcerated come and to which they return; research that takes advantage of "natural experiments" that induce exogenous change in prison admissions or releases; longitudinal or life-course examination of individuals as they are arrested, convicted, and admitted to and released from prison; and the study of neighborhood-level relationships among crime, cumulative neighborhood disadvantage, and criminal justice processing.

Future research also should focus on estimating the aggregate effects of high rates of incarceration on family stability, poverty, economic well-being, and child well-being. As with micro-level research, causal inference is challenging because family stability, poverty, and economic well-being may themselves contribute to local incarceration rates. Also similar to micro-level research, changes in policy or criminal justice practice may induce exogenous variation in incarceration that might enable causal inferences. At the family level, studies should examine how the effect of a parent's incarceration varies depending on living arrangements prior to incarceration and the quality of relationships with partners and children.

CONCLUDING THOUGHTS

Our examination of the causes and consequences of high rates of incarceration in the United States, informed by a set of normative principles, leads us to conclude that the nation's incarceration levels are unnecessarily high. We urge a systematic review of the nation's current sentencing policies with one main goal: a significant reduction in U.S. rates of incarceration. We also urge that the nation take positive steps to treat all prisoners humanely and fairly and to provide prisons with appropriate resources. Finally, to complement a reduction in incarceration and ensure that it does not further disadvantage poor communities, we urge a review of social policies to address the needs for health care, housing, and employment of those who would otherwise be in custody under conditions of high incarceration rates.

The potential impact of the proposed reforms is great. If the share of discretionary funds now allocated to prisons and jails were reduced, savings would accrue to governments and could be used to support other public priorities. Rethinking the proper application of prison sentences could result in a better balance of responsibilities among prosecutors, courts, and legislators consistent with long-established principles of sentencing. A focus on effective alternatives to incarceration and improved coordination between prison programs and community organizations would strengthen the capacity of the public and private sectors to support reintegration for those convicted of serious crimes. Lowering incarceration rates also would reduce the number of people damaged by imprisonment, limit harmful family separations, keep more workers in the labor market, and mitigate the stigma now associated with time in prison. Improving the quality of life in the nation's prisons would likely contribute to better physical and mental health, enhance human capital, and improve family relationships.

More fundamentally, reducing the nation's reliance on imprisonment as a response to crime, together with a parallel reduction in the collateral consequences of incarceration, would recognize appropriate limits on the power of the state, promote social inclusion and racial justice, and enhance the quality of citizenship for those who have been incarcerated. Based on our assessment of the research, we believe a reduction in the nation's incarceration rates—if implemented with all the necessary policy supports— would achieve these benefits with little if any impact on public safety.

In this report, we have attempted to illuminate what Associate Supreme Court Justice Anthony Kennedy has called the "hidden world of punishment." In a keynote speech to the American Bar Association in 2003, Justice Kennedy warned that if we look closely at America's prisons, "we should be startled by what we see." After reviewing the history of the American prison buildup, the costs of incarceration, and the human toll of imprisonment, Justice Kennedy concluded, "Our resources are misspent, our punishments too severe, our sentences too long." He ended his speech by reminding his audience that "the more than 2 million inmates in the United States are human beings whose minds and spirits we must try to reach." With these words, Justice Kennedy anticipated the conclusions of this committee.

References

Abramsky, S. (2007). *American Furies: Crime, Punishment, and Vengeance in the Age of Mass Imprisonment*. Boston, MA: Beacon Press.

Ackerman, B. (1980). *Social Justice in the Liberal State*. New Haven, CT: Yale University Press.

Aebi, M.F., and Delgrande, N. (2013). *Council of Europe Annual Penal Statistics. Space 1. Survey 2011*. Available: http://www3.unil.ch/wpmu/space/files/2013/05/SPACE-1_2011_English.pdf#page=41and°zoom=auto,0,135 [August 2013].

Aharoni, E., and Friedland, A.J. (2012, November). Punishment without reason: Isolating retribution in lay punishment of criminal offenders. *Psychology, Public Policy, and Law, 18*(4), 599-625.

Alexander, M. (2010). *The New Jim Crow: Mass Incarceration in the Age of Colorblindness*. New York: The New Press.

Alexander, M. (2012 reprint). *The New Jim Crow: Mass Incarceration in the Age of Colorblindness*. New York: The New Press.

Allen, F.A. (1959). Criminal justice, legal values and the rehabilitative ideal. *Journal of Criminal Law, Criminology, and Police Science, 50*(3), 226-232.

Allen, F.A. (1975). The judicial quest for penal justice: The Warren Court and the criminal cases. *University of Illinois Law Forum, 4*, 518-542.

Allen, F.A. (1981). *The Decline of the Rehabilitative Ideal: Penal Policy and Social Purpose*. New Haven, CT: Yale University Press.

Allen, J. (2011). Documentary disenfranchisement. *Tulane Law Review, 86*, 389-464.

Allen-Hagen, B. (1991). *Public Juvenile Facilities: Children in Custody 1989*. Washington, DC: Office of Juvenile Justice and Delinquency Prevention, U.S. Department of Justice.

Alschuler, A. (1978). Sentencing reform and prosecutorial power. *University of Pennsylvania Law Review, 126*, 550-577.

Amato, P. R., Meyers, C.E., and Emery, R.E. (2009). Changes in nonresident father-child contact from 1976 to 2002. *Family Relations, 58*(1), 41-53.

American Academy of Pediatrics Committee on Adolescence. (2011). Health care for youth in the juvenile justice system. *Pediatrics, 128*(6), 1219-1235.

American Bar Association. (2010, February). *Standards for Treatment of Prisoners. Section VII, Standard 23-7.1 Respect for Prisoners.* Available: http://www.americanbar.org/publications/criminal_justice_section_archive/crimjust_standards_treatmentprisoners.html#23-7.1 [July 23, 2013].

American Bar Association Criminal Justice Section. (2011, November 20). *Adult Collateral Consequences Project News.* Available: http://isrweb.isr.temple.edu/projects/accproject/blog.cfm?RecordID=1 [June 26, 2012].

American Civil Liberties Union. (1995). *Status Report: State Prisons and the Courts. National Prison Project of the ACLU Foundation.* Washington, DC: American Civil Liberties Union.

American Correctional Association. (2002). *Past, Present and Future.* Available: https://www.aca.org/pastpresentfuture/principles.asp [July 23, 2013].

American Correctional Association. (2003). *Standards for Adult Correctional Institutions.* 4th ed. Alexandria, VA: American Correctional Association.

American Friends Service Committee. (1971). *Struggle for Justice: A Report on Crime and Punishment in America.* New York: Hill and Wang.

American Law Institute. (1962). *Model Penal Code.* Proposed Official Draft. Philadelphia, PA: American Law Institute.

American Law Institute. (2011). *Model Penal Code—Sentencing.* Tentative Draft No. 2. Philadelphia, PA: American Law Institute.

American Psychiatric Association. (1994). *Diagnostic and Statistical Manual of Mental Disorders, Fourth Edition (DSM-IV).* Washington, DC: American Psychiatric Association.

American Psychiatric Association. (2000). *Diagnostic and Statistical Manual of Mental Disorders, 4th Edition, Text Revision (DSM-IV-TR).* Washington, DC: American Psychiatric Association.

American Psychiatric Association. (2012). *Position Statement on the Segregation of Prisoners with Serious Mental Illness.* Available: http://www.dhcs.ca.gov/services/MH/Documents/2013_04_AC_06c_APA_ps2012_PrizSeg.pdf [February 1, 2014].

Anderson, E. (1990). *Streetwise: Race, Class, and Change in an Urban Community.* Chicago, IL: University of Chicago Press.

Anderson, E. (1999). *Code of the Street: Decency, Violence, and the Moral Life of the Inner City.* New York: W.W. Norton.

Andrews, D., and Bonta, J. (2006). *The Psychology of Criminal Conduct.* 4th ed. Cincinnati, OH: Anderson Publishing.

Apel, R., and Nagin, D.S. (2011). General deterrence: A review of recence evidence. In J.Q. Wilson and J. Petersilia (Eds.), *Crime and Public Policy* (pp. 411-436). Oxford, England: Oxford University Press.

Apel, R., and Sweeten, G. (2010). The impact of incarceration on employment during the transition to adulthood. *Social Problems, 57*(3), 448-479.

Apel, R., Blokland, A.J., Nieuwbeerta, P., and van Schellen, M. (2010). The impact of imprisonment on marriage and divorce: A risk set matching approach. *Journal of Quantitative Criminology, 26*(2), 269-300.

Appelbaum, K.L., Savageau, J.A., Trestman, R.L., Metzner, J.L., and Baillargeon, J. (2011). A national survey of self-injurious behavior in American prisons. *Psychiatric Services, 62*(3), 285-290.

Arditti, J.A., Lambert-Shute, J., and Joest, K. (2003). Saturday morning at the jail: Implications of incarceration for families and children. *Family Relations, 52*(3), 195-204.

Arthur D. Little, Inc., and Goldfarb and Singer, Esqs. (1981). *An Evaluation of Parole Guidelines in Four Jurisdictions.* Washington, DC, and Cambridge, MA: Arthur D. Little, Inc.

Asch, S.M., Damberg, C.L., Hiatt, L., Teleki, S.S., Shaw, R., Hill, T.E., Benjamin-Johnson, R., Eisenman, D.P., Kulkarni, S.P., Wang, E., Williams, B., Yesus, A., and Grudzen, C.R. (2011). Selecting performance indicators for prison health care. *Journal of Correctional Health Care, 17*(2), 138-149.

Ashworth, A., von Hirsch, A., and Roberts, J. (Eds.). (2009). *Principled Sentencing: Readings on Theory and Policy.* 3rd ed. Oxford, England: Hart Publishing.

Austin, A. (2010). *Criminal Justice Trends—Key Legislative Changes in Sentencing Policy, 2000-2010.* New York: Vera Institute of Justice.

Austin, J., Jones, C., Kramer, J., and Renninger, P. (1994). *National Assessment of Structured Sentencing.* Washington, DC: U.S. Department of Justice, Bureau of Justice Assistance.

Austin, J., Johnson, K.D., and Gregorion, M. (2000). *Juveniles in Adult Prison and Jails: A National Assessment.* NCJ 182503. Washington, DC: U.S. Department of Justice, Bureau of Justice Assistance.

Austin, J., Cadora, E., Clear, T.R., Dansky, K., Greene, J., Gupta, V., Mauer, M., Porter, N., Tucker, S., and Young, M.C. (2013). *Ending Mass Incarceration: Charting a New Justice Reinvestment.* Washington, DC: The Sentencing Project.

Avi-Itzhak, B., and Shinnar, R. (1973). Quantitative models in crime control. *Journal of Criminal Justice, 1*(3), 185-217.

Awofeso, N. (2005). Making prison health care more efficient. *British Medical Journal, 331*(7511), 248-249.

Babinski, L.M., Hartsough, C.S., and Lambert, N.M. (2003). Childhood conduct problems, hyperactivity-impulsivity, and inattention as predictors of adult criminal activity. *Journal of Child Psychology and Psychiatry, 40*(3), 347-355.

Baillargeon, J., Giordano, T.P., Rich, J.D., Wu, Z.H., Wells, K., Pollock, B.H., and Paar, D.P. (2009). Accessing antiretroviral therapy following release from prison. *Journal of the American Medical Association, 301*(8), 848-857.

Baillargeon, J., Giordano, T.P., Harzke, A.J., Baillargeon, G., Rich, J.D., and Paar, D.P. (2010a). Enrollment in outpatient care among newly released prison inmates with HIV infection. *Public Health Report, 125*(Suppl. 1), 64-71.

Baillargeon, J., Hoge, S.K., and Penn, J.V. (2010b). Addressing the challenge of community reentry among released inmates with serious mental illness. *American Journal of Community Psychology, 46*(3-4), 361-375.

Baldus, D.C., Woodworth, G.G., and Pulaski, C.A., Jr. (1990). *Equal Justice and the Death Penalty: A Legal and Empirical Analysis.* Boston, MA: Northeastern University Press.

Bambra, C., Gibson, M., Sowden, A., Wright, K., Whitehead, M., and Petticrew, M. (2010). Tackling the wider social determinants of health and health inequalities: Evidence from systematic reviews. *Journal of Epidemiology and Community Health, 64*(4), 284-291.

Barker, V. (2009). *The Politics of Imprisonment: How the Democratic Process Shapes the Way America Punishes Offenders.* New York: Oxford University Press.

Barnett, C. (2000). *The Measurement of White-Collar Crime Using Uniform Crime Report (UCR) Data.* (NCJ 202866). Washington, DC: U.S. Department of Justice, Federal Bureau of Investigation, Criminal Information Services Division.

Barry, B. (2005). *Why Social Justice Matters.* New York: Wiley.

Baumer, E.P. (2010). Reassessing and redirecting research on race and sentencing. Draft manuscript prepared for Symposium on the Past and Future of Empirical Sentencing for Research, School of Criminal Justice, University at Albany.

Baussano, I., Williams, B.G., Nunn, P., Beggiato, M., Fedeli, U., and Scano, F. (2010). Tuberculosis incidence in prisons: A systematic review. *PLOS Medicine, 7*(12), e1000381.

Beccaria, C. (1986). *On Crimes and Punishment.* (H. Paolucci, Trans.). New York: Macmillan. (Orig. work published 1764).

Beccaria, C. (2007). *On Crimes and Punishments.* (A. Thomas and J. Parzen, Trans.). Toronto: University of Toronto Press. (Orig. work published 1764).

Beck, A.T. (1999). *Prisoners of Hate: The Cognitive Basis of Anger, Hostility and Violence.* New York: Harper Collins.

Beck, A. (2010). *Sexual Victimization in Prisons and Jails Reported by Inmates, 2008-2009.* Washington, DC: U.S. Department of Justice, Bureau of Justice Statistics.

Beck, A. (2012). *PREA Data Collection Activities, 2012.* Washington, DC: U.S. Department of Justice, Bureau of Justice Statistics.

Beck, A.J., and Blumstein, A. (2012, October 31). *Trends in Incarceration Rates: 1980-2010.* Paper prepared for the National Research Council Committee on the Causes and Consequences of High Rates of Incarceration, Washington, DC.

Beck, A., and Harrison, P. (2008). *Sexual Victimization in Local Jails Reported by Inmates, 2007.* Washington, DC: U.S. Department of Justice, Bureau of Justice Statistics.

Beck, A. and Mumola, C.J. (1999). *Prisoners in 1998.* Washington, DC: U.S. Department of Justice, Bureau of Justice Statistics.

Beck, A.J., and Shipley, B.E. (1989). *Recidivism of Prisoners Released in 1983.* Washington, DC: U.S. Department of Justice, Bureau of Justice Statistics.

Beck, A., Harrison, P., Berzofsky, M., Caspar, R., and Krebs, C. (2010). *Sexual Victimization in Prisons and Jails Reported by Inmates, 2008-2009.* Washington, DC: U.S. Department of Justice, Bureau of Justice Statistics.

Beck, A.J., Berzofsky, M., Caspar, R. and Krebs, C. (2013). *Sexual Victimization in Prisons and Jails Reported by Inmates, 2011-12.* NCJ 241399. Washington, DC: U.S. Department of Justice, Bureau of Justice Statistics.

Becker, A.L. (2012, February 27). State seeking nursing home to take sick, disabled prisoners. *The CT Mirror.*

Becker, H. (1963). *Outsiders: Studies in the Sociology of Deviance.* New York: Free Press.

Beckett, K. (1997). *Making Crime Pay: Law and Order in Contemporary American Politics.* New York: Oxford University Press.

Beckett, K., and Herbert, S. (2011). *Banished.* New York: Oxford University Press.

Beckett, K., and Sasson, T. (2004). *The Politics of Injustice.* 2nd ed. Beverly Hills, CA: SAGE.

Beckett, K., Nyrop, K., Pfingst, L., and Bowell, M. (2005). Drug use, drug possession arrests, and the question of race. *Social Problems, 52*(3), 419-441.

Beckett, K., Nyrop, K., and Pfingst, L. (2006). Race, drugs, and policing: Understanding disparities in drug delivery arrests. *Criminology, 44*(1), 105-137.

Beckwith, C.G. (2010). Routine jail-based HIV testing—Rhode Island, 2000-2007. *Morbidity and Mortality Weekly Report, 59*(24), 740-745.

Beckwith, C.G., Zaller, N.D., Fu, J.J., Montague, B.T., and Rich, J.D. (2010). Opportunities to diagnose, treat, and prevent HIV in the criminal justice system. *Journal of Acquired Immune Deficiency Syndromes, 55*(Suppl. 1), S49-S55.

Bedard, K., and Frech, H.E., III. (2009). Prison health care: Is contracting out healthy? *Health Economics, 18*(11), 1248-1260.

Beha, J.A., II. (1977). "And Nobody Can Get You Out": The Impact of a Mandatory Prison Sentence for the illegal carrying of a firearm on the use of firearms and on the administration of criminal justice in Boston. *Boston University Law Review, 57,* 96-146 (Part 1), 289-233 (Part 2).

Belcher, J. (1988). Are jails replacing the mental health system for the homeless mentally ill? *Community Mental Health Journal, 24*(3), 185-195.

Belenko, S., and Peugh, J. (2005). Estimating drug treatment needs among state prison inmates. *Drug and Alcohol Dependence, 77*(3), 269-281.

Bench, L., and Allen, T. (2003). Investigating the stigma of prison classification: An experimental design. *The Prison Journal, 83*(4), 367-382.

Bennett, W.J., Dilulio, J.J., and Waters, J.P. (1996). *Body Count: Moral Poverty . . . and How to Win America's War against Crime and Drugs.* New York: Simon and Schuster.

Bentham, J. (1970). The utilitarian theory of punishment. In J. Bentham, J.H. Burns, and H.L.A. Hart (Eds.), *An Introduction to Principles of Morals and Legislation.* London: Athlone Press. (Orig. work published 1789).

Bentham, J. (1988). *The Principles of Morals and Legislation.* Amherst, NY: Prometheus Books. (Orig. work published 1789).

Bentham, J. (2008). *The Rationale of Punishment.* Amherst, NY: Kessinger. (Orig. work published 1830).

Bernburg, J., Krohn, M., and Rivera, C. (2006). Official labeling, criminal embeddedness, and subsequent delinquency: A longitudinal test of labeling theory. *Journal of Research in Crime and Delinquency, 43*(1), 67-88.

Besci, Z. (1999). Economics and crime in the states. *Federal Reserve Bank of Atlanta Economic Review First Quarter,* 38-49.

Binswanger, I.A., Stern, M.F., Deyo, R.A., Heagerty, P.J., Cheadle, A., Elmore, J.G., and Koepsell, T.D. (2007). Release from prison—a high risk of death for former inmates. *New England Journal of Medicine, 356*(2), 157-165.

Binswanger, I.A., Krueger, P.M., and Steiner, J.F. (2009). Prevalence of chronic medical conditions among jail and prison inmates in the U.S.A. compared with the general population. *Journal of Epidemiology and Community Health, 63*(11), 912-919.

Binswanger, I.A., Merrill, J.O., Krueger, P.M., White, M.C., Booth, R.E., and Elmore, J.G. (2010). Gender differences in chronic medical, psychiatric, and substance-dependence disorders among jail inmates. *American Journal Public Health, 100*(3), 476-482.

Binswanger, I.A., Redmond, N., Steiner, J.F., and Hicks, L.S. (2012). Health disparities and the criminal justice system: An agenda for further research and action. *Journal of Urban Health, 89*(1), 98-107.

Biondi, M. (2006). *To Stand and Fight: The Struggle for Civil Rights in Postwar New York City.* Cambridge, MA: Harvard University Press.

Bishop, D.M., and Frazier, C. (2000). Consequences of transfer. In J. Fagan and F. Zimmerman (Eds.), *The Changing Borders of Juvenile Justice* (pp. 227-276). Chicago, IL: University of Chicago Press.

Black, T. (2009). *When a Heart Turns Rock Solid: The Lives of Three Puerto Rican Brothers On and Off the Streets.* New York: Pantheon Books.

Blackmon, D. (2009). *Slavery by Another Name: The Re-Enslavement of Black Americans from the Civil War to World War II.* New York: Anchor Books.

Blair, I.V., Judd, C.M., Sadler, M.S., and Jenkins, C. (2002). The role of Afrocentric features in person perception: Judging by features and categories. *Journal of Personality and Social Psychology, 83*(1), 5-25.

Blair, I.V., Judd, C.M., and Fallman, J.L. (2004). The automaticity of race and afrocentric facial features in social judgments. *Journal of Personality and Social Psychology, 87*(6), 763-778.

Blair, I.V., Chapleau, K.M., and Judd, C.M. (2005). The use of Afrocentric features as cues for judgment in the presence of diagnostic information. *European Journal of Social Psychology, 35*(1), 59-68.

Bland, R., Newman, S., Dyck, R. and Orn, H. (1990). Prevalence of psychiatric disorders and suicide attempts in a prison population. *Canadian Journal of Psychiatry, 35*(5), 407-413.

Blankenship, K.M., Smoyer, A.B., Bray, S.J., and Mattocks, K. (2005). Black-white disparities in HIV/AIDS: The role of drug policy and the corrections system. *Journal of Health Care for the Poor and Underserved, 16*(4, Suppl. B), 140-156.

Bleich, J. (1989). The politics of prison crowding. *California Law Review, 77,* 1125-1180.

Blitz, C., Wolff, N., and Shi, J. (2008). Physical victimization in prison: The role of mental illness. *International Journal of Law and Psychiatry, 31*(5), 385-393.

Blomberg, T.G. and Lucken, K. (2000). *American Penology: A History of Control.* New York: Aldine de Gruyter.

Bloom, D. (2006). *Employment Focused Programs for Ex-Prisoners: What Have We Learned, What Are We Learning, and Where Should We Go From Here?* New York: National Poverty Center.

Bloom, B., and Brown, M. (2011). Incarcerated women: Motherhood on the margins. In J.M. Lawston and A.E. Lucus (Eds.), *Razor Wire Women: Prisoners, Activists, and Artists* (pp. 51-66). Albany, NY: SUNY Press.

Bloom, B., and D. Steinhart. (1993). *Why Punish the Children? A Reappraisal of the Children of Incarcerated Mothers in America.* San Francisco, CA: National Council on Crime and Delinquency.

Bloom, H.S., Orr, L.L., Cave, G., Bell, S.H., Doolittle, F., and Lin, W. (1997). The benefits and costs of JTPA programs: Key findings from the National JTPA study. *The Journal of Human Resources, 32*(3), 549-576.

Bloom, D., Gardenhire-Crooks, A., and Mandsager, C. (2009). *Reengaging High School Dropouts: Early Results of the National Guard Youth ChalleNGe Program Evaluation.* New York: MDRC.

Blue, E. (2012). *Doing Time in the Depression: Everyday Life in Texas and California Prisons.* New York: New York University Press.

Blumstein, A. (1982). On racial disproportionately of the United States' prison populations. *Journal of Criminal Law and Criminology, 73*(3), 1259-1281.

Blumstein, A. (1993). Racial disproportionality of US prison populations revisited. *University of Colorado Law Review, 64*(3), 743-760.

Blumstein, A., and Beck, A.J. (1999). Population growth in US prisons, 1980-1996. In M. Tonry and J. Petersilia (Eds.), *Crime and Justice: A Review of Research* (Vol. 26, pp. 17-61). Chicago, IL: University of Chicago Press.

Blumstein, A., and Beck, A.J. (2005). Reentry as a transient state between liberty and recommitment. In J. Travis and C. Visher (Eds.), *Prisoner Reentry and Crime in America* (pp. 50-79). Cambridge, UK: Cambridge University Press.

Blumstein, A., and Beck, A.J. (2012, July 9). Trends in U.S. Incarceration Rates (1980-2010). Presentation to the National Research Council Committee on Causes and Consequences of High Rates of Incarceration. Washington, DC.

Blumstein, A., and Cohen, J. (1980). *Sentencing of Convicted Offenders: An Analysis of the Public's View.* Pittsburgh, PA: Carnegie-Mellon University, Urban Systems Institute.

Blumstein, A., and Nakamura, K. (2009). Redemption in the presence of widespread background checks. *Criminology, 47*(2), 327-359.

Blumstein, A., and Wallman, J. (2006). The crime drop and beyond. *Annual Review of Law and Social Science, 2*, 125-146.

Bobo, L.D. (2001). Racial attitudes and relations at the close of the twentieth century. In N.J. Smelser, W.J. Wilson, and F. Mitchell (Eds.), *America Becoming: Racial Trends and Their Consequences* (Vol. 1, pp. 262-299). Washington, DC: National Academy Press.

Bobo, L.D. (2009). Crime, urban poverty, and social science. *Du Bois Review: Social Science Research on Race, 6*, 273-278.

Bobo, L.D., and Johnson, D. (2004). A taste for punishment: Black and white Americans' views on the death penalty and the War on Drugs. *Du Bois Review, 1*(1), 151-180.

Bobo, L.D., and Thompson, V. (2006). Unfair by design: The war on drugs, race, and the legitimacy of the criminal justice system. *Social Research, 73*(2), 445-472.

Bobo, L.D., and Thompson, V. (2010). Racialized mass incarceration: Poverty, prejudice, and punishment. In H.R. Markus and P. Moya (Eds.), *Doing Race: 21 Essays for the 21st Century* (pp. 322-355). New York: W.W. Norton.

Bonczar, T.P. (2003). *Prevalence of Imprisonment in the U.S. Population, 1974-2001.* Washington, DC: U.S. Department of Justice, Bureau of Justice Statistics.

Bonczar, T.P., and Beck, A.J. (1997). *Lifetime Likelihood of Going to State or Federal Prison.* Washington, DC: U.S. Department of Justice, Office of Justice Programs, Bureau of Justice Statistics.

Bonczar, T.P., and Glaze, L.E. (2011). *Adults on Parole, Federal and State-By-State, 1975-2010.* Washington, DC: U.S. Department of Justice, Office of Justice Programs, Bureau of Justice Statistics.

Bonta, J., and Gendreau, P. (1990). Reexamining the cruel and unusual punishment of prison life. *Law and Human Behavior, 14*(4), 347-372.

Booker, C.A., Flygare, C.T., Solomon, L., Ball, S.W., Pustell, M.R., Bazerman, L.B., Simon-Levine, D., Teixeira, P.A., Cruzado-Quinones, J., Kling, R.N., Frew, P.M., and Spaulding, A.C. (2013). Linkage to HIV care for jail detainees: Findings from detention to the first 30 days after release. *AIDS and Behavior, 17*(Suppl. 2), S128-S136.

Boshier, R., and Johnson, D. (1974). Does conviction affect employment opportunities? *British Journal of Criminology, 14,* 264-268.

Bound, J., and Freeman, R. (1992). What went wrong? The erosion of relative earnings and employment among young black men in the 1980s. *Quarterly Journal of Economics, 107*(1), 201-232.

Bourgois, P. (1995). *In Search of Respect: Selling Crack in El Barrio.* New York: Cambridge University Press.

Bourgois, P. (2002). *In Search of Respect: Selling Crack in El Barrio.* 2nd ed. New York: Cambridge University Press.

Boutwell, A.E., Allen, S.A., and Rich, J.D. (2005). Opportunities to address the hepatitis C epidemic in the correctional setting. *Clinical Infectious Diseases, 40*(Suppl. 5), S367-S372.

Braithwaite, J. (2001). *Restorative Justice and Responsive Regulation.* Oxford, England: Oxford University Press.

Braithwaite, J., and Pettit, P. (1990). *Not Just Deserts: A Republican Theory of Criminal Justice.* New York: Oxford University Press.

Braman, D.S. (2002). *Families and Incarceration.* Dissertation. New Haven, CT: Yale University.

Braman, D.S. (2004). *Doing Time on the Outside: Incarceration and Family Life in Urban America.* Ann Arbor: University of Michigan Press.

Brame, R., Turner, M.G., Paternoster, R., and Bushway, S.D. (2012). Cumulative prevalence of arrest from ages 8 to 23 in a national sample. *Pediatrics, 129*(1), 21-27.

Braveman, P., Egerter, S., and Williams, D.R. (2011). The social determinants of health: Coming of age. *Annual Review of Public Health, 32,* 381-398.

Briggs, C., Sundt, J., and Castellano, T. (2003). The effect of supermaximum security prisons on aggregate levels of institutional violence. *Criminology, 41*(4), 1341-1376.

Broad, J., Cox, T., Rodriguez, S., Mansour, M., Mennella, C., Murphy-Swallow, D., Raba, J.M., and Wong, W. (2009). The impact of discontinuation of male STD screening services at a large urban county jail: Chicago, 2002-2004. *Sexually Transmitted Diseases, 36*(Suppl. 2), S49-S52.

Brock, T., Doolittle, F., Fellerath, V., and Wiseman, M. (1997, October). *Creating New Hope: Implementation of a Program to Reduce Poverty and Reform Welfare.* New York: Manpower Demonstration Research Corporation.

Brodsky, S., and Scogin, F. (1988). Inmates in protective custody: First data on emotional effects. *Forensic Reports, 1,* 267-280.

Brown-Dean, K.L. (2004). *One Lens, Multiple Views: Felon Disenfranchisement Laws and American Political Inequality*. Dissertation. Columbus: Ohio State University.

Bruch, E.E., and Mare, R.D. (2006). Neighborhood choice and neighborhood change. *American Journal of Sociology, 112*, 667-709.

Buchanan, K. (2007). Impunity: Sexual abuse in women's prisons. *Harvard Civil Rights-Civil Liberties Law Review, 42*, 45-87.

Buikhuisen, W., and Dijksterhuis, F.P.H. (1971). Delinquency and stigmatisation. *British Journal of Criminology, 11*, 185-187.

Bumiller, K. (2008). *In an Abusive State: How Neoliberalism Appropriated the Feminist Movement Against Sexual Violence*. Durham, NC: Duke University Press.

Burch, T.R. (2007). *Punishment and Participation: How Criminal Convictions Threaten American Democracy*. Dissertation. Cambridge, MA: Harvard University.

Burch, T.R. (2012). Did disenfranchisement laws help elect President Bush? New evidence on the turnout rates and candidate preferences of Florida's ex-felons. *Political Behavior, 34*(1), 1-26.

Burch, T. (forthcoming). Mass imprisonment and political participation: Evidence from North Carolina. *The ANNALS of the American Academy of Political and Social Science*.

Bureau of Justice Statistics. (n.d.-a). *Drug and Crime Facts*. Washington, DC: U.S. Department of Justice, Bureau of Justice Statistics.

Bureau of Justice Statistics. (n.d.-b). *Federal Justice Statistics Program*. Federal Bureau of Prisons SENTRY Database, Fiscal Year End 2010. Available: http://bjs.ojp.usdoj.gov/fjsrc/ [February 1, 2014].

Bureau of Justice Statistics. (1985). *Data Quality of Criminal History Records*. NCJ-98079. Washington, DC: U.S. Department of Justice, Bureau of Justice Statistics.

Bureau of Justice Statistics. (1994). *Comparing Federal and State Prison Inmates, 1991*. Washington, DC: U.S. Department of Justice, Bureau of Justice Statistics.

Bureau of Justice Statistics. (2003). *Compendium of State Privacy and Security Legislation: 2002 Overview*. NCJ 200030. Washington DC: U.S. Department of Justice, Bureau of Justice Statistics.

Bureau of Justice Statistics. (2012a). *Immigration Offenders in the Federal Justice System, 2010*. NCJ 238581. Washington, DC: U.S. Department of Justice, Bureau of Justice Statistics.

Bureau of Justice Statistics. (2012b). *PREA Data Collection Activities, 2012*. Washington, DC: U.S. Department of Justice, Bureau of Justice Statistics.

Bursik, R.J. (1986). Delinquency rates as sources of ecological change. In J.M. Byrne and R.J. Sampson (Eds.), *The Social Ecology of Crime* (pp. 63-76). New York: Springer-Verlag, Inc.

Bursik, R.J. (1988). Social disorganization and theories of crime and delinquency: Problems and prospects. *Criminology, 35*, 677-703.

Bushway, S.D. (2004). Labor market effects of permitting employer access to criminal history records. *Journal of Contemporary Criminal Justice, 20*(3), 276-291.

Bushway, S.D., and Reuter, P. (2002). Labor markets and crime risk factors. In D. Farrington, D.L. MacKenzie, L. Sherman, and B.C. Welsh (Eds.), *Evidence-Based Crime Prevention* (pp. 198-240). London: Routledge.

Bushway, S.D., Nieuwbeerta, P., and Blokland, A. (2007). Private providers of criminal history records: Do you get what you pay for?" In S. Bushway, M.A. Stoll, and D.F. Weiman (Eds.), *Barriers to Reentry? The Labor Market for Released Offenders in Post-Industrial America* (pp. 174-200). New York: Russell Sage Foundation.

Bushway, S.D., Nieuwbeerta, P. and Blokland, A. (2011). The predictive value of criminal background checks: Do age and criminal history affect time to redemption? *Criminology, 49*(1), 27-60.

Butterfield, F. (1995). *All God's Children: The Bosket Family and the American Tradition of Violence*. New York: Vintage Books.

Butzin, C.A., O'Connell, D.J., Martin, S.S., and Inciardi, J.A. (2006). Effect of drug treatment during work release on new arrests and incarceration. *Journal of Criminal Justice, 34*(5), 557-565.

Cacioppo, S., and Cacioppo, J. (2012). Decoding the invisible forces of social connection. *Frontiers in Integrative Neuroscience, 6*, 51.

Cadora, E., and Swartz, C. (1999, August 22). *The Center for Alternative Sentencing and Employment Services (CASES), Community Justice Project*. Washington, DC: National Institute of Justice, Crime Mapping Research Center.

Cadora, E., Swartz, C., and Gordon, M. (2003). Criminal justice and health and human services: An exploration of overlapping needs, resources, and interests in Brooklyn neighborhoods. In J. Travis and M. Waul (Eds.), *Prisoners Once Removed: The Impact of Incarceration and Reentry on Children, Families, and Communities* (pp. 285-311). Washington, DC: Urban Institute Press.

California Department of Corrections and Rehabilitation Expert Panel on Adult Offender Reentry and Recidivism Reduction Programs. (2007). *Report to the State Legislature. A Roadmap for Effective Offender Programming in California*. Sacramento: California Department of Corrections and Rehabilitation.

Campbell, M.C. (2007). Criminal disenfranchisement reform in California: A deviant case study. *Punishment and Society, 9*(2), 177-199.

Canela-Cacho, J., Blumstein, A., and Cohen, J. (1997). Relationship between the offending frequency (λ) of imprisoned and free offenders. *Criminology, 35*, 133-176.

Carlson, K. (1982). *Mandatory Sentencing: The Experience of Two States*. Washington, DC: National Institute of Justice, U.S. Department of Justice.

Carlson, B.E., and Cavera, N. (1992). *Inmates and Their Wives: Incarceration and Family Life*. Westport, CT: Greenwood Press.

Carroll, L. (1998). *Lawful Order: A Case Study of Correctional Crisis and Reform*. New York: Garland Publishing.

Carrow, D.M., Feins, J., Lee, B.N.W., and Olinger, L. (1985). *Guidelines without Force: An Evaluation of the Multi-Jurisdictional Sentencing Guidelines Field Test*. Cambridge, MA: Abt Associates.

Carson, E.A., and Golinelli, D. (2013, July). *Prisoners in 2012—Advance Counts*. NCJ 242467. Washington, DC: U.S. Department of Justice, Bureau of Justice Statistics.

Carson, E.A., and Sabol, W.J. (2012). *Prisoners in 2011*. NCJ 239808. Washington, DC: U.S. Department of Justice, Bureau of Justice Statistics.

Carter, D.T. (1995). *The Politics of Rage: George Wallace, the Origins of the New Conservatism, and the Transformation of American Politics*. New York: Simon & Schuster.

Caulkins, J.P., and Chandler, S. (2006). Long-run trends in incarceration of drug offenders in the U.S. *Crime & Delinquency, 52*(4), 619-641.

Caulkins, J.P., and Reuter, P. (2010). How drug enforcement affects drug prices. In M. Tonry (Ed.), *Crime and Justice: A Review of Research* (Vol. 39, pp. 213-272). Chicago, IL: University of Chicago Press.

Cavadino, M., and Dignan, J. (2006). *Penal Systems: A Comparative Approach*. 4th ed. London: SAGE.

Cecil, D.K., Drapkin, D.A., MacKenzie, D.L., and Hickman, L.J. (2000). The effectiveness of adult basic education and life-skills programs in reducing recidivism: A review and assessment of the research. *Journal of Correctional Education, 51*, 207-226.

Center for Constitutional Rights. (2009). *Racial Disparity in NYPD Stops-and-Frisks: The Center for Constitutional Rights Preliminary Report on UF-250 Data from 2005 through June 2008.* Available: http://ccrjustice.org/files/Report-CCR-NYPD-Stop-and-Frisk.pdf [February 1, 2014].

Centers for Disease Control and Prevention. (2002). *Methadone Maintenance Treatment.* Available: http://www.cdc.gov/idu/facts/methadonefin.pdf [November 2013].

Centers for Disease Control and Prevention. (2003). Methicillin-resistant Staphylococcus aureus infections in correctional facilities—Georgia, California, and Texas, 2001-2003. *Morbidity and Mortality Weekly Report, 52*(41), 992-996.

Centers for Disease Control and Prevention. (2004). Tuberculosis transmission in multiple correctional facilities—Kansas, 2002-2003. *Morbidity and Mortality Weekly Report, 53*(32), 734-738.

Centers for Disease Control and Prevention. (2009). *HIV Testing Implementation Guidance for Correctional Settings: HIV Testing.* Available: http://www.cdc.gov/hiv/topics/testing/resources/guidelines/correctional-settings/pdf/Correctional_Settings_Guidelines.pdf [November 2013].

Centers for Disease Control and Prevention. (2011a). *Correctional Facilities and Viral Hepatitis.* Available: http://www.cdc.gov/hepatitis/Settings/corrections.htm [March 2013].

Centers for Disease Control and Prevention. (2011b). HIV screening of male inmates during prison intake medical evaluation—Washington, 2006-2010. *Morbidity and Mortality Weekly Report, 60*(24), 811-813.

Centers for Disease Control and Prevention. (2011c). *STDs in Persons Entering Corrections Facilities.* Available: http://www.cdc.gov/std/stats10/corrections.htm [March 2013].

Centers for Disease Control and Prevention. (2012). *Reported Tuberculosis in the United States, 2011.* Available: http://www.cdc.gov/tb/statistics/reports/2011/default.htm [March 2013].

Centers for Disease Control and Prevention. (2013). *Social Determinants of Health.* Available: http://origin.glb.cdc.gov/socialdeterminants/FAQ.html [July 2013].

Chandler, R.K., Fletcher, B.W., and Volkow, N.D. (2009). Treating drug abuse and addiction in the criminal justice system: Improving public health and safety. *Journal of the American Medical Association, 301*(2), 183-190.

Charles, K.K., and Luoh, M.C. (2010). Male incarceration, the marriage market, and female outcomes. *Review of Economics and Statistics, 92*(3), 614-627.

Chávez-Garcia, M. (2012). *States of Delinquency: Race and Science in the Making of California's Juvenile Justice System.* Berkeley and Los Angeles: University of California Press.

Chen, K., and Shapiro, J. (2007). Do harsher prison conditions reduce recidivism? A discontinuity-based approach. *American Law and Economics Review, 9*, 1-29.

Child Trends. (n.d.). *Juvenile Detention.* Available: http://www.childtrends.org/?indicators=juvenile-detention [July 2013].

Chiricos, T.G., and Crawford, C. (1995). Race and imprisonment: A contextual assessment of the evidence. In D. Hawkins (Ed.), *Ethnicity, Race, and Crime* (pp. 281-309). Albany: State University of New York Press.

Cho, R.M. (2009a). Impact of maternal imprisonment on children's probability of grade retention. *Journal of Urban Economics, 65*(1), 11-23.

Cho, R.M. (2009b). The impact of maternal imprisonment on children's educational achievement: Results from children in Chicago public schools. *Journal of Human Resources, 44*(3), 772-797.

Cho, R.M. (2011). Understanding the mechanism behind maternal imprisonment and adolescent school dropout. *Family Relations, 60*(3), 272-289.

Christian, J. (2005). Riding the bus: Barriers to prison visitation and family management strategies. *Journal of Contemporary Criminal Justice, 21*(1), 31-48.

Churchill, W. (1910). William Churchill's House of Commons speech, given as Home Secretary, July 20, 1910.

Clark, M. (2012, October 12). *Could a Recount of Prisoners Affect Elections.* Available: http://www.pewstates.org/projects/stateline/headlines/could-a-recount-of-prisoners-affect-elections-85899422906 [February 1, 2014].

Clark, J., Austin, J., and Henry, A.D. (1997). *"Three Strikes and You're Out": A Review of State Legislation.* Available: https://www.ncjrs.gov/pdffiles/165369.pdf [February 1, 2014].

Clarke, J.G., and Adashi, E.Y. (2011). Perinatal care for incarcerated patients: A 25-year old woman pregnant in jail. *Journal of the American Medical Association, 305*(9), 923-929.

Clarke, J.G., and Waring, M.E. (2012). Overweight, obesity, and weight change among incarcerated women. *Journal of Correctional Health Care, 18*(4), 285-292.

Clarke, J.G., Rosengard, C., Rose, J., Hebert, M.R., Phipps, M.G., and Stein, M.D. (2006). Pregnancy attitudes and contraceptive plans among women entering jail. *Women and Health, 43*(2), 111-130.

Clarke, J.G., Phipps, M., Tong, I., Rose, J., and Gold, M. (2010). Timing of conception for pregnant women returning to jail. *Journal of Correctional Health Care, 16*(2), 133-138.

Clear, T.R. (2007). *Imprisoning Communities: How Mass Incarceration Makes Disadvantaged Neighborhoods Worse.* Oxford, England: Oxford University Press.

Clear, T.R., and Rose, D. (1999). *When Neighbors Go to Jail: Impact on Attitudes about Formal and Informal Social Control.* Washington, DC: National Institute of Justice Research in Brief.

Clear, T.R., Rose, D.R., Waring, E., and Scully, K. (2003). Coercive mobility and crime: A preliminary examination of concentrated incarceration and social disorganization. *Justice Quarterly, 20*, 33-64.

Clemmer, D. (1958). *The Prison Community.* New York: Holt, Rinehart, and Winston.

Coggeshall, J. (1991). Those who surrender are female: Prisoner gender identities as cultural mirror. In P. Frese and J. Coggeshall (Eds.), *Transcending Boundaries: Multi-disciplinary Approaches to the Study of Gender* (pp. 81-95). New York: Bergin and Garvey.

Cohen, J. (1978). The incapacitative effect of imprisonment: A critical review of the literature. In A. Blumstein, J. Cohen, and D. Nagin (Eds.), *Deterrence and Incapacitation; Estimating the Effects of Criminal Sanctions on Crime Rates* (pp. 187-243). Washington, DC: National Academy Press.

Cohen, J. (1983). Incapacitation as a strategy for crime control: Possibilities and pitfalls. In N. Morris and M. Tonry (Eds.), *Crime and Justice: A Review of Research* (Vol. 5, pp. 1-84). Chicago, IL: University of Chicago Press.

Cohen, J. (1986). Research on criminal careers: Individual frequency rates and offense seriousness. In National Research Council, A. Blumstein, J. Cohen, J. Roth, and C.A. Visher (Eds.), *Criminal Careers and Career Criminals* (Vol. 1, pp. 292-418). Washington, DC: National Academy Press.

Cohen, C.J. (1999). *The Boundaries of Blackness: AIDS and the Breakdown of Black Politics.* Chicago, IL: University of Chicago Press.

Cohen, F. (2004). The limits of the judicial reform of prisons: What works, what does not. *Criminal Law Bulletin, 40*, 421-465.

Cohen, C.J. (2010). *Democracy Remixed: Black Youth and the Future of American Politics.* New York: Oxford University Press.

Cohen, D.K., and Lindblom, C.E. (1979). *Usable Knowledge: Social Science and Social Problem Solving.* New Haven, CT: Yale University Press.

Cohen, J., and Tonry, M. (1983). Sentencing reforms and their impacts. In National Research Council, A. Blumstein, J. Cohen, S.E. Martin, and M. Tonry (Eds.), *Research on Sentencing: The Search for Reform* (Vol. 2, pp. 305-459). Washington, DC: National Academy Press.

Cole, R., and Call, J. (1992). When courts find jail and prison overcrowding unconstitutional. *Federal Probation, 56*, 29-39.

Coley, R.J., and Barton, P.E. (2006). *Locked Up and Locked Out: An Educational Perspective on the U.S. Prison Population.* Princeton, NJ: Educational Testing Service.

Colorado Department of Corrections. (2012.) *Administrative Segregation and Classification System Analysis and Review Process.* Available: http://www.aclu.org/files/assets/co_adseg_rept_jan2012.pdf [November 21, 2013].

Comfort, M.L. (2003). In the tube at San Quentin: The "secondary prisonization" of women visiting inmates. *Journal of Contemporary Ethnography, 32*(1), 77-107.

Comfort, M.L. (2008). *Doing Time Together: Love and Family in the Shadow of Prison.* Chicago, IL: University of Chicago Press.

Commission on Social Determinants of Health. (2008). *Closing the Gap in a Generation: Health Equity through Action on the Social Determinants of Health.* Geneva, Switzerland: World Health Organization.

Comptroller General of the United States. (1973). *Development of a Nationwide Criminal Data Exchange System: Need to Determine Cost and Improve Reporting.* Washington, DC: U.S. General Accounting Office.

Conklin, T., Lincoln, T., and Wilson, R. (2002). *A Public Health Manual for Correctional Health Care.* Ludlow, MA: Hampden County Sheriff's Department and Massachusetts Public Health Association.

Cook, P.J. (1980). Research in criminal deterrence: Laying the groundwork for the second decade. In N. Morris and M. Tonry (Eds.), *Crime and Justice: A Review of Research* (Vol. 2, pp. 211–268). Chicago, IL: University of Chicago Press.

Cooke, M., and Goldstein, J. (1989). Social isolation and violent behavior. *Forensic Reports, 2*(4), 287-294.

Cooper, C., and Berwick, S. (2001). Factors affecting psychological well-being of three groups of suicide prone prisoners. *Current Psychology, 20*(2), 169-182.

Cormier, B., and Williams, P. (1966). Excessive deprivation of liberty. *Canadian Psychiatric Association Journal, 11*, 470-484.

Cornelius, G.F. (2012). Jails: Pretrial detention, and short-term confinement. In J. Petersilia and K.R. Reitz (Eds.), *The Oxford Handbook of Sentencing and Corrections* (pp. 389-415). New York: Oxford University Press.

Council of State Governments Justice Center. (2013). *Reentry Matters: Strategies and Successes of Second Chance Act Grantees Across the United States.* New York: Council of State Governments Justice Center. Available: http://csgjusticecenter.org/wp-content/uploads/2013/1/ReentryMatters.pdf [February 2014].

Countryman, M.J. (2007). *Up South: Civil Rights and Black Power in Philadelphia.* Philadelphia, PA: University of Pennsylvania Press.

Cox, V., Paulus, P., and McCain, G. (1984). Prison crowding research: The relevance for prison housing standards and a general approach regarding crowding phenomena. *American Psychologist, 39*, 1148-1160.

Craigie, T.L. (2011). The effect of paternal incarceration on early child behavioral problems: A racial comparison. *Journal of Ethnicity in Criminal Justice, 9*(3), 179-199.

Crawford, C. (2000). Gender, race, and habitual offender sentencing in Florida. *Criminology, 38*(1), 263-280.

Crawford, C., Chiricos, T., and Kleck, G. (1998). Race, racial threat, and sentencing of habitual offenders. *Criminology, 36*(3), 481-511.

Crayton, A., and Neusteter, S.R. (2008, March 31). *The Current State of Correctional Education.* Paper presented at the Reentry Roundtable on Education, John Jay College of Criminal Justice, New York.

Crutchfield, R.D., Weis, J.G., Engen, R.L., and Gainey, R.R. (1995). *Racial and Ethnic Disparities in the Prosecution of Felony Cases in King County.* Olympia, WA: Washington State Minority and Justice Commission.

Crutchfield, R.D., Fernandes, A., and Martinez, J. (2010). Racial and ethnic disparity and criminal justice: How much is too much? *Journal of Criminal Law and Criminology, 100*(3), 903-932.

Crutchfield, R.D., Skinner, M.L., Haggerty, K.P., McGlynn, A., and Catalano, R.F. (2012). Racial disparity in police contacts. *Race and Justice, 2*(3), 179-202.

Cuellar, A.E., Snowden, L.M., and Ewing, T. (2007). Criminal records of persons served in the public mental health system. *Psychiatric Services, 58*(1), 114-120.

Cullen, F. (1995). Assessing the penal harm movement. *Journal of Research in Crime and Delinquency, 32*(3), 338-358.

Cullen, F.T., and Gendreau, P. (2000). Assessing correctional rehabilitation: Policy, practice, and prospects. In J. Horney (Ed.), *Criminal Justice 2000: Policies, Processes, and Decisions of the Criminal Justice System* (Vol. 3, pp. 109-176). Washington, DC: U.S. Department of Justice, National Institute of Justice.

Cullen, F.T., Fisher, B.S., and Applegate, B.K. (2000). Public opinion about punishment and corrections. In M. Tonry (Ed.), *Crime and Justice: A Review of Research* (Vol. 27, pp. 1-79). Chicago, IL: University of Chicago Press.

Cullen, F., Jonson, C., and Nagin, D. (2011). Prisons do not reduce recidivism: The high cost of ignoring science. *The Prison Journal, 91*(Suppl.), S48-S65.

D'Atri, D. (1975). Psychophysiological responses to crowding. *Environment and Behavior, 7,* 237-252.

Dallaire, D.H. (2007). Children with incarcerated mothers: Developmental outcomes, special challenges and recommendations. *Journal of Applied Developmental Psychology, 28*(1), 15-24.

Damberg, C.L., Shaw, R., Teleki, S.S., Hiatt, L., and Asch, S.M. (2011). A review of quality measures used by state and federal prisons. *Journal of Correctional Health Care, 17*(2), 122-137.

Darley, J.M. (2010). Citizens' assignments of punishments for moral transgressions: A case study in the psychology of punishment. *Ohio State Journal of Criminal Law, 8,*101-117.

Darley, J.M., and Pittman, T.S. (2003). The psychology of compensatory and retributive justice. *Personality and Social Psychology Review, 7,* 324-336.

Dasgupta, N., Benaji, M., and Abelson, R. (1999). Group entitavity and group perception: Associations between physical features and psychological judgment. *Journal of Personality and Social Psychology, 77*(5), 991-1003.

Davis, K.C. (1969). *Discretionary Justice: A Preliminary Inquiry.* Baton Rouge: Louisiana State University Press.

Davis, L.M., Bozick, R., Steele, J.L., Saunders, J., and Miles, J.N.V. (2013). *Evaluating the Effectiveness of Correctional Education: A Meta-Analysis of Programs That Provide Education to Incarcerated Adults.* Santa Monica, CA: RAND Corporation.

Dawson, M.D. (2011). *Not in Our Lifetimes: The Future of Black Politics.* Chicago, IL: University of Chicago Press.

Dawson, R.O. (1969). *Sentencing.* Boston, MA: Little, Brown and Company.

de Beaumont, G., and de Tocqueville, A. (1970). *On the Penitentiary System in the United States and Its Application in France.* (F. Lieber, Trans.). New York: Augustus M. Kelly. (Orig. work published 1833).

de Giorgi, A. (2006). *Re-Thinking the Political Economy of Punishment: Perspectives on Post-Fordism and Penal Politics.* Aldershot, England: Ashgate Publishing.

Deitch, M. (2010). Annotated bibliography on independent prison oversight. *Pace Law Review, 30*(5), 1687-1690.

Deitch, M., Barstow, A., Lukens, L., and Reyna, R. (2009). *From Time Out to Hard Time: Young Children in the Adult Criminal Justice System.* Austin: The University of Texas at Austin, LBJ School of Public Affairs.

Demeo, M.J., and Ochoa, S.A. (2003, December). *Diminished Voting Power in the Latino Community: The Impact of Felony Disenfranchisement Laws in Ten Targeted States.* Los Angeles, CA: Mexican American Legal Defense and Educational Fund.

Demuth, S., and Steffensmeier, D. (2004). Ethnicity effects on sentencing outcomes in large urban courts: Comparisons among white, black, and Hispanic defendants. *Social Science Quarterly, 85*(4), 991-1011.

Dershowitz, A. (1976). *Fair and Certain Punishment.* Columbus, OH: McGraw-Hill.

Desai, A.A., Latta, E.T., Spaulding, A., Rich, J.D., and Flanigan, T.P. (2002). The importance of routine HIV testing in the incarcerated population: The Rhode Island experience. *AIDS Education and Prevention, 14*(5, Suppl. B), 45-52.

Dhondt, G. (2012). The bluntness of incarceration: Crime and punishment in Tallahassee neighborhoods, 1995 to 2002. *Crime, Law and Social Change, 57*, 1-18.

DiCataldo, F., Greer, A., and Profit, W. (1995). Screening prison inmates for mental disorder: An examination of the relationship between mental disorder and prison adjustment. *Bulletin of the American Academy of Psychiatry and Law, 23*(4), 573-585.

DiIulio, J.J., Jr. (1987). *Governing Prisons: A Comparative Study of Correctional Management.* New York: Cornell University Press.

DiIulio, J.J., Jr., and Piehl, A.M. (1991). Does prison pay? *Brookings Review*, 28-35.

Dills, A.K., Miron, J.A., and Summers, G. (2008). *What Do Economists Know about Crime?* Working Paper No. 13759. Cambridge, MA: National Bureau of Economic Research.

Dingeman, M.K., and Rumbaut, R.G. (2010). The immigration-crime nexus and post-deportation experiences. *University of La Verne Law Review, 31*(2), 363-402.

Ditton, P.P. (1999). *Mental Health and Treatment of Inmates and Probationers.* Washington, DC: U.S. Department of Justice, Bureau of Justice Statistics.

Ditton, P.M., and Wilson, D.J. (1999). *Truth in Sentencing in State Prisons.* Washington, DC: U.S. Department of Justice, Bureau of Justice Statistics.

Dixon, T., and Maddox, K. (2005). Skin tone, crime news, and social reality judgments: Priming the stereotype of the dark and dangerous black criminal. *Journal of Applied Social Psychology, 35*(8), 1555-1570.

Dobson, K.S., and Khatri, N. (2000). Cognitive therapy: Looking backward, looking forward. *Journal of Clinical Psychology, 56*(7), 907-923.

Donohue, J.J. (2007). *Assessing the Relative Benefits of Incarceration: The Overall Change over the Previous Decades and the Benefits on the Margin.* New Haven, CT: Yale University.

Doob, A., and Webster, C. (2003). Sentence severity and crime: Accepting the null hypothosis. In M. Tonry (Ed.), *Crime and Justice: A Review of Research* (Vol. 30, pp. 143-195). Chicago, IL: University of Chicago Press.

Dostoevsky, F. (1861). *The House of the Dead.*

Drago, F., Galbiati, R., and Vertova, P. (2011). Prison conditions and recidivism. *American Law and Economics Review, 13*(1), 103-130.

Draine, J., Ahuja, D., Altice, F.L., Arriola, K.J., Avery, A.K., Beckwith, C.G., Booker, C.A., Ferguson, A., Figueroa, H., Lincoln, T., Ouellet, L.J., Porterfield, J., Spaulding, A.C., and Tinsley, M.J. (2011). Strategies to enhance linkages between care for HIV/AIDS in jail and community settings. *AIDS Care, 23*(3), 366-377.

Drakulich, K.M., Crutchfield, R.D., Matsueda, R.L., and Rose, K. (2012). Instability, informal control, and criminogenic situations: Community effects of returning prisoners. *Crime, Law, and Social Change, 57*, 493-519.

Duff, R.A. (1986). *Trials and Punishments*. Cambridge: Cambridge University Press.

Duff, R.A. (2001). *Punishment, Communication, and Community*. New York: Oxford University Press.

Duncan, M., and Corner, J. (2012). *Severe and Multiple Disadvantage: A Review of Key Texts*. London: Lankelly Chase Foundation.

Duneier, M. (1999). *Sidewalk*. New York: Farrar, Strauss, and Giroux.

Durkheim, E. (1984). *The Division of Labour in Society*. London: Palgrace Macmillan.

Durlauf, S.N., and Nagin, D.S. (2011a). Imprisonment and crime: Can both be reduced? *Criminology and Public Police, 10*(1), 13-54.

Durlauf, S.N., and Nagin, D.S. (2011b). The deterrent effect of imprisonment. In P.J. Cook, L. Jens, and J. McCrary (Eds.), *Controlling Crime: Strategies and Tradeoffs* (pp. 43-94). Chicago, IL: University of Chicago Press.

Durlauf, S., Navarro, S., and Rivers, D. (2008). On the interpretation of aggregate crime regressions. In A. Goldberger and R. Rosenfeld (Eds.), *Crime Trends*. Washington, DC: The National Academies Press.

Durlauf, S., Navarro, S., and Rivers, D. (2010). Understanding aggregate crime regressions. *Journal of Econometrics, 158*(2), 306-317.

Eberhardt, J.L., Goff, P.A., Purdie, V.J., and Davies, P.G. (2004). Seeing black: Race, crime, and visual processing. *Journal of Personality and Social Psychology, 87*(6), 876-893.

Eberhardt, J.L., Davies, P.G., Purdie-Vaughns, V.J., and Johnson, S.L. (2006). Looking death-worthy: Perceived stereotypicality of black defendants predicts capital-sentencing outcomes. *Psychological Science, 17*(5), 383-386.

Edin, K., Nelson, T.J., and Paranal, R. (2004). Fatherhood and incarceration as potential turning points in the criminal careers of unskilled men. In M. Pattillo, D. Weiman, and B. Western (Eds.), *Imprisoning America: The Social Effects of Mass Incarceration* (pp. 46-75). New York: Russell Sage Foundation.

Edsall, M.D., and Edsall, T.B. (1992). *Chain Reaction: The Impact of Race, Rights, and Taxes on American Politics*. New York: W.W. Norton.

Egli, N., Pina, M., Skovbo Christensen, P., Aebi, M., and Killias, M. (2009). Effects of drug substitution programs on offending among drug addicts. *Campbell Systematic Reviews, 5*(3). Available: http://campbellcollaboration.org/lib/project/79/ [November 2013].

Elk, M., and Sloan, B. (2011, August 1). *The Hidden History of ALEC and Prison Labor*. Available: http://www.thenation.com/print/article/162478/hidden-history-alec-and-prison-labor [February 1, 2014].

Elliott-Engel, A. (2009, June 26). *Report: Census Prisoner Count Dilutes Urban Political Clout*. Available: http://www.law.com/jsp/pa/PubArticlePA.jsp?id=1202431781399&Report_Census_Prisoner_Count_Dilutes_Urban_Political_Clout&slreturn=20130726142839 [February 1, 2014].

Engel, R.S., and Calnon, J.M. (2004). Examining the influence of drivers' characteristics during traffic stops with police: Results from a national survey. *Justice Quarterly, 21*(1), 49-90.

Engel, R.S., and Swartz, K. (2013). Race, crime, and policing. In S. Bucerius and M. Tonry (Eds.), *The Oxford Handbook of Ethnicity, Crime, and Immigration*, Chapter 6. New York: Oxford University Press.

Entman, R. (1992). Blacks in the news: Television, modern racism, and cultural change. *Journalism Quarterly, 69*(2), 341-361.

Equal Justice Initiative. (2010, August). *Illegal Racial Discrimination in Jury Selection*. Montgomery, AL: Equal Justice Initiative.

Esping-Andersen, G. (1990). *Three Worlds of Welfare Capitalism*. Princeton: Princeton University Press.

Fabelo, T. (2002). The impact of prison education on community reintegration of inmates: The Texas case. *The Journal of Correctional Education*, *53*(3), 106-110.

Fagan, J., and West, V. (2013). Incarceration and the economic fortunes of urban neighborhoods. In R. Rosenfeld, M. Edberg, X. Fang, and C. Florence (Eds.), *Economics and Youth Violence: Current Perspectives* (pp. 207-254). New York: New York University Press.

Fagan, J., West, V., and Hollan, J. (2003). Reciprocal effects of crime and incarceration in New York City neighborhoods. *Fordham Urban Law Journal*, *30*, 1551.

Fairlie, R.W., and Sundstrom, W.A. (1999, January). The emergence, persistence, and recent widening of the racial employment gap. *Industrial and Labor Relations Review*, *52*(2), 252-270.

Farrer, T.J., and Hedges, D.W. (2011). Prevalence of traumatic brain injury in incarcerated groups compared to the general population: A meta-analysis. *Progress in Neuro-Psychopharmacology and Biological Psychiatry*, *35*(2), 390-394.

Farrington, D.P. (1986). Age and crime. In M. Tonry and N. Morris (Eds.), *Crime and Justice: A Review of Research* (Vol. 7, pp. 189-250). Chicago, IL: University of Chicago Press.

Farrington, D.P. (1991). Childhood aggression and adult violence: Early precursors and later-life outcomes. In D.J. Pepler and K.H. Rubin (Eds.), *The Development and Treatment of Childhood Aggression* (pp. 5-29). Hillsdale, NJ: Lawrence Erlbaum.

Farrington, D.P. (2003). Developmental and life-course criminology: Key theoretical and empirical issues. *Criminology*, *41*, 221-255.

Farrington, D.P., Jolliffe, D., Loeber, R., Stouthamer-Loeber, M., and Kalb, L.M. (2001). The concentration of offenders in families, and family criminality in the prediction of boys' delinquency. *Journal of Adolescence*, *24*(5), 579-596.

Fazel, S., and Baillargeon, J. (2011). The health of prisoners. *Lancet*, *377*(9769), 956-965.

Fazel, S., and Danesh, J. (2002). Serious mental disorder in 23000 prisoners: A systematic review of 62 surveys. *Lancet*, *359*(9306), 545-550.

Fazel, S., Bains, P., and Doll, H. (2006). Substance abuse and dependence in prisoners: A systematic review. *Addiction*, *101*(2), 181-191.

Federal Bureau of Investigation. (1990). *Age-Specific Arrests Rates and Race-Specific Arrests Rates for Selected Offenses, 1965-1988*. NCJ 122713. Washington, DC: U.S. Department of Justice, Uniform Crime Reporting Program, Federal Bureau of Investigation.

Federal Bureau of Investigation. (1993). *Age-Specific Arrests Rates and Race-Specific Arrests Rates for Selected Offenses, 1965-1992*. Washington, DC: U.S. Department of Justice, Uniform Crime Reporting Program, Federal Bureau of Investigation.

Feeley, M.M. (1979). *The Process Is the Punishment: Handling Cases in a Lower Criminal Court*. New York: Russell Sage Foundation.

Feeley, M.M. (1983). *Court Reform on Trial: Why Simple Solutions Fail*. New York: Basic.

Feeley, M.M., and Rubin, E.L. (1998). *Judicial Policy Making and the Modern State: How the Courts Reformed America's Prison*. Cambridge, UK: Cambridge University Press.

Fellner, J. (2010). Ensuring progress: Accountability standards recommended by the National Prison Rape Elimination Commission. *Pace Law Review*, *30*(5), 1625-1645.

Ferraro, K.J., Johnson, J.M., Jorgensen, S.R., and Bolton, F.G., Jr. (1983). Problems of prisoners' families: The hidden costs of imprisonment. *Journal of Family Issues*, *4*(4), 575-591.

Ferri, E. (1921). *Relazione sul Progetto Preliminare di Codice Penale Italiano*. Milan: L'Universelle.

Festen, M., and Fischer, S. (2002). *Navigating Reentry: The Experiences and Perceptions of Ex-Offenders Seeking Employment*. Chicago, IL: Urban League.

Festinger, L. (1954). A theory of social comparison processes. *Human Relations*, *7*, 117.

Feucht, T., and Keyser, A. (1999, October). Reducing drug use in prisons: Pennsylvania's approach. *National Institute of Justice Journal*, 11-15.

Finn, P. (1984). Prison crowding: The response of probation and parole. *Crime & Delinquency*, 30, 141-153.

Finn, R.H., and Fontaine, P.A. (1985). The association between selected characteristics and perceived employability of offenders. *Criminal Justice and Behavior*, 12(3), 353-365.

Fisher, A.A., and Hatton, D.C. (2010). A study of women prisoners' use of co-payments for health care: Issues of access. *Women's Health Issues*, 20(3), 185-192.

Fishman, L.T. (1990). *Women at the Wall: A Study on Prisoners' Wives Doing Time on the Outside*. Albany: State University of New York Press.

Fishman, S.F. (1983). The impact of incarceration on children of offenders. *Journal of Children in Contemporary Society*, 15(1), 89-99.

Flamm, M.W. (2005). *Law and Order: Street Crime, Civil Unrest, and the Crisis of Liberalism in the 1960s*. New York: Columbia University Press.

Fletcher, B., Shinor, L., and Moon, D. (1993). *Women Prisoners: A Forgotten Population*. Westport, CT: Praeger.

Fleming, M. (1974). *The Price of Perfect Justice: The Adverse Effects of Current Legal Doctrine on the American Courtroom*. New York: Basic Books.

Fogel, D. (1979). *We Are the Living Proof: The Justice Model for Corrections*. Cincinnati, OH: Anderson.

Fontana, L., and Beckerman, A. (2007). Recently released with HIV/AIDS: Primary care treatment needs and experiences. *Journal of Health Care for the Poor and Underserved*, 18(3), 699-714.

Forman, J. (2012). Racial critiques of mass incarceration: Beyond the new Jim Crow. *New York University Law Review*, 87(1).

Fortner, M.J. (2013). The carceral state and the crucible of black politics: An urban history of the Rockefeller drug laws. *Studies in American Political Development*, 27(1), 14-35.

Foster, H., and Hagan, J. (2007). Incarceration and intergenerational social exclusion. *Social Problems*, 54(4), 399-433.

Foster, H., and Hagan, J. (2009). The mass incarceration of parents in America: Issues of race/ethnicity, collateral damage to children, and prison reentry. *The ANNALS of the American Academy of Political and Social Science*, 623(1), 179-194.

Frankel, M. (1973). *Criminal Sentences—Law Without Order*. New York: Hill and Wang.

Frase, R.S. (1997). Sentencing principles in theory and practice. In M. Tonry (Ed.), *Crime and Justice: A Review of Research* (Vol. 22, pp. 364-433). Chicago, IL: University of Chicago Press.

Frase, R.S. (2005). Sentencing guidelines in Minnesota, 1978-2003. In M. Tonry (Ed.), *Crime and Justice: A Review of Research* (Vol. 32, pp. 131-132). Chicago, IL: University of Chicago Press.

Frase, R.S. (2009). Limiting excessive prison sentencing. *University of Pennsylvania Journal of Constitutional Law*, 11(1), 43-46.

Frase, R.S. (2013). *Just Sentencing: Principles and Procedures for a Workable System*. New York: Oxford University Press.

Freeman, R.B. (1992). Crime and the employment of disadvantaged youths. In G. Peterson and W. Vroman (Eds.), *Urban Labor Markets and Job Opportunities*. Washington, DC: Urban Institute Press.

Freeman, R.B., and Rodgers, W.M., III. (1999). *Area Economic Conditions and the Labor Market Outcomes of Young Men in the 1990s Expansion*. Working Paper No. 7073. Cambridge, MA: National Bureau of Economic Research.

Friedmann, P.D., Taxman, F.S., and Henderson, C.E. (2007). Evidence-based treatment practices for drug-involved adults in the criminal justice system. *Journal of Substance Abuse Treatment*, 32(3), 267-277.

Fries, A., Anthony, R.W., Cseko, A., Jr., Gaither, C.S., and Schulman, E. (2008). *The Price and Purity of Illicit Drugs, 1981-2007*. Working Paper P-4369. Alexandria, VA: Institute for Defense Analyses.

Frost, N., Greene, J., and Pranis, K. (2006). *The Punitiveness Report Hard Hit: The Growth in Imprisonment of Women, 1977-2004*. New York: Women's Prison Association.

Gaes, G.G. (1985). The effects of overcrowding in prison. In N. Morris and M. Tonry (Eds.), *Crime and Justice: An Annual Review of Research* (Vol. 6, pp. 95-146). Chicago, IL: University of Chicago Press.

Gaes, G.G., and Camp, S. (2009). Unintended consequences: Experimental evidence for the criminogenic effect of prison security level placement on post-release recidivism. *Journal of Experimental Criminology*, 5, 139-162.

Gaes, G.G., Flanagan, T.J., Motiuk, L., and Stewart, L. (1999). Adult correctional treatment. In M. Tonry and J. Petersilia (Eds.), *Crime and Justice: A Review of Research* (Vol. 26, pp. 361-426). Chicago, IL: University of Chicago Press.

Gallagher, C.A., and Dobrin, A. (2007). Can juvenile justice detention facilities meet the call of the American Academy of Pediatrics and National Commission on Correctional Health Care? A national analysis of current practices. *Pediatrics*, 119(4), e991-e1001.

Garland, D. (1991). Sociological perspectives on punishment. In M. Tonry (Ed.), *Crime and Justice: A Review of Research* (Vol. 14, pp. 115-165). Chicago, IL: University of Chicago Press.

Garland, D. (2001). *The Culture of Control: Crime and Social Order in Contemporary Society*. Chicago, IL: University of Chicago Press.

Garland, D. (2010). *Peculiar Institution: America's Death Penalty in an Age of Abolition*. Cambridge, MA: Harvard University Press.

Garland, D. (2013). Punishment and social solidarity. In J. Simon and R. Sparks, *The SAGE Handbook of Punishment and Society* (Ch. 1). London: SAGE.

Geller, A., and Garfinkel, I.S. (2012). *Paternal Incarceration and Father Involvement in Fragile Families*. Presented at the Annual Meeting of the Population Association of America, San Francisco, CA.

Geller, A., and Walker, A. (2012). *Partner Incarceration and Women's Housing Insecurity*. Fragile Families Working Paper WP12-02-FF. Princeton, NJ: Center for Research on Child Wellbeing.

Geller, A., Garfinkel, I., Cooper, C.E., and Mincy, R.B. (2009). Parental incarceration and child well-being: Implications for urban families. *Social Science Quarterly*, 90(5), 1186-1202.

Geller, A., Garfinkel, I., and Western, B. (2011). Paternal incarceration and support for children in fragile families. *Demography*, 48(1), 25-47.

Geller, A., Cooper, C.E., Garfinkel, I., Schwartz-Soicher, O., and Mincy, R.B. (2012). Beyond absenteeism: Father incarceration and child development. *Demography*, 49(1), 49-76.

Gendreau, P., Freedman, N., Wilde, G., and Scott, G. (1972). Changes in EEG alpha frequency and evoked response latency during solitary confinement. *Journal of Abnormal Psychology*, 79(1), 54-59.

Gerber, J., and Fritsch, E.J. (1995). Adult academic and vocational correctional education programs: A review of recent research. *Journal of Offender Rehabilitation*, 22, 119-142.

Gest, T. (2001). *Crime and Politics: Big Government's Erratic Campaign for Law and Order*. Oxford: Oxford University Press.

Gibbons, J., and Katzenbach, N. (2006). Confronting confinement: A report of The Commission on Safety and Abuse in America's Prisons. *Washington University Journal of Law and Policy*, 22, 385-560.

Gibbs, J. (1982). The first cut is the deepest: Psychological breakdown and survival in the detention setting. In R. Johnson and H. Toch (Eds.), *The Pains of Imprisonment* (pp. 97-113). Thousand Oaks, CA: SAGE.

Gibson, L., Holt, J., Fondacaro, K., Tang, T., Powell, T. and Turbitt, E. (1999). An examination of antecedent traumas and psychiatric co-morbidity among male inmates with PTSD. *Journal of Traumatic Stress, 12*(3), 473-484.

Gillespie, W. (2003). *Prisonization: Individual and Institutional Factors Affecting Inmate Conduct.* New York: LFB Scholarly Publishing.

Gillespie, W. (2005). A multilevel model of drug abuse inside prison. *The Prison Journal, 85*(2), 223-246.

Gilmore, R.W. (2007). *Golden Gulag: Surplus, Crisis, and Opposition in Globalizing.* Berkeley and Los Angeles, CA: University of California Press.

Gillroy, J. M., and Wade, M.L. (1992). *The Moral Dimensions of Public Policy Choice: Beyond the Market Paradigm.* Pittsburgh: University of Pittsburgh Press.

Giordano, P.C. (2010). *Legacies of Crime: A Follow-up of the Children of Highly Delinquent Girls and Boys.* New York: Cambridge University Press.

Glaze, L.E. (2011). *Correctional Populations in the U.S., 2010.* NCJ 236319. Washington, DC: U.S. Department of Justice, Bureau of Justice Statistics.

Glaze, L.E., and Bonczar, T.P. (2011). *Probation and Parole in the United States, 2010.* NCJ 236019. Washington, DC: U.S. Department of Justice, Bureau of Justice Statistics.

Glaze, L.E., and Herberman, E.J. (2013). *Correctional Populations in the United States, 2012.* Washington, DC: U.S. Department of Justice, Bureau of Justice Statistics.

Glaze, L.E., and Maruschak, L.M. (2008). *Parents in Prison and Their Minor Children.* NCJ 222984. Washington, DC: U.S. Department of Justice, Bureau of Justice Statistics.

Glaze, L.E., and Parks, E. (2012). *Correctional Populations in the U.S., 2011.* NCJ 239972. Washington, DC: U.S. Department of Justice, Bureau of Justice Statistics.

Glaze, L.E., Bonczar, T.P., and Zhang, F. (2010). *Probation and Parole in the United States, 2009.* Washington, DC: U.S. Department of Justice, Bureau of Justice Statistics.

Goff, A., Rose, E., Rose, S., and Purves, D. (2007). Does PTSD occur in sentenced prison populations? A systematic literature review. *Criminal Behavior and Mental Health, 17,* 152-162.

Goffman, E. (1963). *Sigma: Notes on the Management of Spoiled Identity.* New York: Simon and Schuster.

Goffman, A. (2009). On the run: Wanted men in a Philadelphia ghetto. *American Sociological Review, 74*(3), 339-357.

Goldin, C., and Katz, L. (2008). *The Race between Education and Technology.* Cambridge, MA: Belknap Press for Harvard University Press.

Gonnerman, J. (2004). *Life on the Outside: The Prison Odyssey of Elaine Bartlett.* New York: Picador.

Goodstein, L. (1979). Inmate adjustment to prison and the transition to community life. *Journal of Research in Crime and Delinquency, 16*(2), 246-272.

Gopnik, A. (2012, January 30). *The Caging of America: Why Do We Lock So Many People Up?* Available: http://www.newyorker.com/arts/critics/atlarge/2012/01/30/120130crat_atlarge_gopnik [February 1, 2014].

Gordon, D. (1989). The topography of criminal justice: A factor analysis of the "get-tough" policy trend. *Criminal Justice Policy Review, 3*(2), 184-207.

Gordon, S.C., and Huber, G.A. (2007). The effect of electoral competitiveness on incumbent behavior. *Quarterly Journal of Political Science, 2,* 107-138.

Gordon, M.S., Kinlock, T.W., Schwartz, R.P., and O'Grady, K.E. (2008). A randomized clinical trial of methadone maintenance for prisoners: Findings at 6 months post-release. *Addiction, 103*(8), 1333-1342.

Gottfredson, S. (1984). Institutional responses to prison crowding. *New York University Review of Law and Social Change, 12*(1), 259-273.

Gottfredson, S.D., and Taylor, R.B. (1987). Attitudes of correctional policymakers and the public. In S.D. Gottfredson and S. McConville (Eds.), *America's Correctional Crisis: Prison Populations and Public Policy* (pp. 55-75). New York: Greenwood Press.

Gottfredson, D.M., Wilkins, L.T., and Hoffman, P.B. (1978). *Guidelines for Parole and Sentencing.* Lanham, MD: Lexington.

Gottschalk, M. (2006). *The Prison and the Gallows: The Politics of Mass Incarceration in America.* New York: Cambridge University Press.

Gottschalk, M. (forthcoming). *Caught: The Prison State and the Lockdown of American Politics.* Princeton: Princeton University Press.

Gough, E., Kempf, M.C., Graham, L., Manzanero, M., Hook, E.W., Bartolucci, A., and Chamot, E. (2010). HIV and hepatitis B and C incidence rates in U.S. correctional populations and high risk groups: A systematic review and meta-analysis. *BMC Public Health, 10,* 777.

Government Accountability Office. (2012, September). *Bureau of Prisons: Growing Inmate Crowding Negatively Affects Inmates, Staff, and Infrastructure.* GAO-12-743. Washington, DC: Government Accountability Office.

Government Accountability Office. (2013, May). *Improvements Needed in Bureau of Prisons' Monitoring and Evaluation of Impact of Segregated Housing.* GAO-13-429. Washington, DC: Government Accountability Office.

Gowan, T. (2002). The nexus: Homelessness and incarceration in two American cities. *Ethnography, 3*(4), 500-534.

Gramlich, J. (2013, March 13). *Leahy-Paul Bill Would Relax Federal Sentencing Laws.* Roll Call. Available: http://www.rollcall.com/news/leahy_paul_bill_would_relax_federal_sentencing_laws-223332-1.html [December 2013].

Granich, R., Gupta, S., Suthar, A.B., Smyth, C., Hoos, D., Vitoria, M., Simao, M., Hankins, C., Schwartlander, B., Ridzon, R., Bazin, B., Williams, B., Lo, Y.R., McClure, C., Montaner, J., and Hirnschall, G. (2011). Antiretroviral therapy in prevention of HIV and TB: Update on current research efforts. *Current HIV Research, 9*(6), 446-469.

Grant, B.F., Stinson, F.S., Dawson, D.A., Chou, S.P., Dufour, M.C., Compton, W., Pickering, R.P., and Kaplan, K. (2004). Prevalence and co-occurrence of substance use disorders and independent mood and anxiety disorders. Results from the national epidemiologic survey on alcohol and related conditions. *Archives of General Psychiatry, 61*(8), 807-816.

Grassian, S. (1983). Psychopathological effects of solitary confinement. *American Journal of Psychiatry, 140*(11), 1450-1454.

Grassian, S., and Friedman, N. (1986). Effects of sensory deprivation in psychiatric seclusion and solitary confinement. *International Journal of Law and Psychiatry, 8*(1), 49-65.

Grassian, S., and Kupers, T. (2011). The Colorado study vs. the reality of supermax confinement. *Correctional Mental Health Report, 13,* 1-4.

Grebler, L., Moore, J., and Guzman, R. (1970). *The Mexican-American People: The Nation's Second Largest Minority.* New York: The Free Press.

Greenberg, G.A., and Rosenheck, R.A. (2009). Mental health and other risk factors for jail incarceration among male veterans. *Psychiatric Quarterly, 80*(1), 41-53.

Greenberg, G.A., and Rosenheck, R.A. (2012). Incarceration among male veterans: Relative risk of imprisonment and differences between veteran and nonveteran inmates. *International Journal of Offender Therapy and Comparative Criminology, 56*(4), 646-667.

Greenberg, D.F., and West, V. (2001). State prison populations and their growth, 1971-1991. *Criminology, 39*(3).

Greenberg, E., Dunleavy, E., and Kutner, M. (2007). *Literacy Behind Bars: Results from the 2003 National Assessment of Adult Literacy Prison Survey.* NCES 2007-473. Washington, DC: U.S. Department of Education, National Center for Education Statistics.

Greene, S., Haney, C., and Hurtado, A. (2000). Cycles of pain: Risk factors in the lives of incarcerated mothers and their children. *The Prison Journal, 80*(1), 3-23.

Greenhouse, S. (2012, April 26). Equal opportunity panel updates hiring policy. *The New York Times.*

Greenwald, A.G., and Krieger, L.H. (2006). Implicit bias: Scientific foundations. *California Law Review,* 945.

Greenwood, P., and Hawken, A. (2002). *An Assessment of the Effect of California's Three-Strikes Law.* Toronto, Ontario: Greenwood Associates.

Greifinger, R.B. (2010). Thirty years since Estelle v Gamble: Looking forward, not wayward. In R.B. Greifinger (Ed.), *Public Health Behind Bars: From Prisons to Communities* (pp. 1-10). New York: Springer.

Grinstead, O., Faigeles, B., Bancroft, C., and Zack, B. (2001). The financial cost of maintaining relationships with incarcerated African American men: A survey of women prison visitors. *Journal of African American Studies, 6*(1), 59-69.

Grogger, J. (1995). The effect of arrest on the employment and earnings of young men. *Quarterly Journal of Economics, 110*(1), 51-72.

Gross, K. (2006). *Colored Amazons: Crime, Violence, and Black Women in the City of Brotherly Love, 1880-1910.* Durham, NC: Duke University Press.

Gross, S.R., and Mauro, R. (1989). *Death and Discrimination: Racial Disparities in Capital Sentencing.* Boston, MA: Northeastern University Press.

Guerino, P., Harrison, P.M., and Sabol, W.J. (2011). *Prisoners in 2010.* NCJ 236096. Washington, DC: U.S. Department of Justice, Bureau of Justice Statistics.

Gullone, E., Jones, T., and Cummins, R. (2000). Coping styles and prison experience as predictors of psychological well-being in male prisoners. *Psychiatry, Psychology and Law, 7*(2), 170-181.

Gusfield, J.R. (1963). *Symbolic Crusade. Status Politics and the American Temperance Movement.* Urbana: University of Illinois Press.

Hagan, J. (1993). The social embeddedness of crime and unemployment. *Criminology, 31,* 465-491.

Hagan, J. (1995). The imprisoned society: Time turns a classic on its head. *Sociological Forum, 10*(3), 520-524.

Hagan, J. (2010). *Who Are the Criminals? The Policies of Crime Policy from the Age of Roosevelt to the Age of Reagan.* Princeton, NJ: Princeton University Press.

Hagan, J., and Bumiller, K. (1983). Making sense of sentencing: A review and critique of sentencing research. In National Research Council, A. Blumstein, J. Cohen, S.E. Martin, and M.H. Tonry (Eds.), *Research on Sentencing: The Search for Reform* (Vol. II, pp. 1-54). Washington, DC: National Academy Press.

Hagan, J., and Dinovitzer, R. (1999). Collateral consequences of imprisonment for children, communities, and prisoners. *Crime and Justice, 26,* 121-162.

Hagan, J., and Foster, H. (2012). Intergenerational school effects of mass imprisonment in America. *Sociology of Education, 85*(3), 259-286.

Hairston, C.F. (1991). Family ties during imprisonment: Important to whom and for what? *Journal of Society and Social Welfare, 18*(1), 87-104.

Haldeman, H.R. (1994). *The Haldeman Diaries—Inside the Nixon White House.* New York: G.P. Putnam's Sons.

Hallinan, J.T. (2001). *Going up the River: Travels in a Prison Nation.* New York: Random House.

Hammett, T.M. (2006). HIV/AIDS and other infectious diseases among correctional inmates: Transmission, burden, and an appropriate response. *American Journal of Public Health, 96*(6), 974-978.

Hammett, T.M. (2009). Sexually transmitted diseases and incarceration. *Current Opinion in Infectious Diseases, 22*(1), 77-81.

Hammett, T.M., Harmon, M.P., and Rhodes, W. (2002). The burden of infectious disease among inmates of and releasees from U.S. correctional facilities, 1997. *American Journal of Public Health, 92*(11), 1789-1794.

Haney, C. (2003). Mental health issues in long-term solitary and "Supermax" confinement. *Crime & Delinquency, 49*(1), 124-156.

Haney, C. (2005). The contextual revolution in psychology and the question of prison effects. In A. Liebling and S. Maruna (Eds.), *The Effects of Imprisonment* (pp. 66-93). Devon, UK: Willan Publishing.

Haney, C. (2006). *Reforming Punishment: Psychological Limits to the Pains of Imprisonment.* Washington, DC: American Psychological Association Books.

Haney, C. (2010). Demonizing the "Enemy": The role of "Science" in declaring the "War on Prisoners." *Connecticut Public Interest Law Journal, 9*(2), 185-242.

Haney, C. (2011). The perversions of prison: On the origins of hypermasculinity and sexual violence in confinement. *American Criminal Law Review, 48*, 121-141.

Haney, C., and Lynch, M. (1997). Regulating prisons of the future: A psychological analysis of supermax and solitary confinement. *New York University Review of Law and Social Change, 23*, 477-570.

Hannon, L., and Knapp, P. (2003). Reassessing nonlinearity in the urban disadvantage/violent crime relationship: An example of methodological bias from log transformation. *Criminology, 41*, 1427-1448.

Hanson, A., (2010). Correctional suicide: Has progress ended? *Journal of the American Academy of Psychiatry and the Law, 38*(1), 6-10.

Harding, D.J. (2003). Jean Valjean's dilemma: The management of ex-convict identity in the search for employment. *Deviant Behavior, 24*, 571-595.

Harding, D.J., and Morenoff, J.D. (Forthcoming). Incarceration, prisoner reentry, and communities. *Annual Review of Sociology.*

Harrington, M.P., and Spohn, C. (2007). Defining sentence type: Further evidence against use of the total incarceration variable. *Journal of Research in Crime and Delinquency, 44*(1), 36-63.

Harris, A. (2011). Constructing clean dreams: Accounts, future selves, and social and structural support as desistance work. *Symbolic Interaction, 34*(1), 63-85.

Harris, K.M., and Edlund, M.J. (2005). Self-medication of mental health problems: New evidence from a national survey. *Health Services Research, 40*(1), 117-134.

Harzke, A.J., Baillargeon, J.G., Pruitt, S.L., Pulvino, J.S., Paar, D.P., and Kelley, M.F. (2010). Prevalence of chronic medical conditions among inmates in the Texas prison system. *Journal of Urban Health, 87*(3), 486-503.

Haskins, A.R. (2012). *Unintended Consequences of Mass Imprisonment: Effects of Paternal Incarceration on Child School Readiness.* Fragile Families Working Paper WP11-18-FF. Princeton, NJ: Center for Research on Child Wellbeing.

Hawken, A. (2010). Behavioral triage: A new model for identifying and treating substance-abusing offenders. *Journal of Drug Policy Analysis, 3*(1), 1-5.

Hawken, A., and Kleiman, M. (2009). *Managing Drug Involved Probationers with Swift and Certain Sanctions: Evaluating Hawaii's HOPE.* Washington, DC: U.S. Department of Justice, National Institute of Justice.

Hawkley, L., and Cacioppo, J. (2003). Loneliness and pathways to disease. *Brain, Behavior, and Immunity, 17*(Suppl. 1), S98-S105.

Hawthorne, W.B., Folsom, D.P., Sommerfeld, D.H., Lanouette, N.M., Lewis, M., Aarons, G.A., Conklin, R.M., Solorzano, E., Lindamer, L.A., and Jeste, D.V. (2012). Incarceration among adults who are in the public mental health system: Rates, risk factors, and short-term outcomes. *Psychiatric Services, 63*(1), 26-32.

Hay, D. (1975). Property, authority, and the criminal law. In D. Hay, P. Linebaugh, and E.P. Thompson (Eds.), *Albion's Fatal Tree: Crime and Society in Eighteenth Century England* (pp. 17-63). New York: Pantheon.

Hayes, L. (1989). National study of jail suicides: Seven years later. *Psychiatric Quarterly, 60*(1), 7-29.

Heckman, C., Cropsey, K., and Olds-Davis, T. (2007). Posttraumatic stress disorder treatment in correctional settings: A brief review of the empirical literature and suggestions for future research. *Psychotherapy: Theory, Research Practice, Training, 44*(1), 46-53.

Hedrich, D., Alves, P., Farrell, M., Stover, H., Moller, L., and Mayet, S. (2011). The effectiveness of opoid maintenance treatment in prison settings: A systematic review. *Addiction, 107*(3), 501-517.

Hegel, G.W.F. (1991). Wrong. In A.W. Wood (Ed.), *Elements of the Philosophy of Right.* (H.B. Nisbet, Trans.). Cambridge, UK: Cambridge University Press. (Orig. work published 1821).

Heimer, K., Lang, J.B., Johnson, K.R., Rengifo, A.F., and Stemen, D. (2012). Race and women's imprisonment: Poverty, African American presence, and social welfare. *Journal of Quantitative Criminology, 28*(2), 219-244.

Helland, E., and Tabarrok, A. (2007). Does three strikes deter? A nonparametric estimation. *Journal of Human Resources, 42*, 309-330.

Hemmens, C., and Marquart, J. (1999). Straight time: Inmate's perceptions of violence and victimization in the prison environment. *Journal of Offender Rehabilitation, 28*(3/4), 1-21.

Henrichson, C., and Delaney, R. (2012). *The Price of Prisons, What Incarceration Costs Taxpayers.* New York: Vera Institute of Justice, Center on Sentencing and Corrections.

Henriques, Z.W., and Jones-Brown, D.D. (2000). Prisons as "safe havens" for African-American women. In M. Markowitz and D.D. Jones-Brown (Eds.), *The System in Black and White: Exploring the Connections Between Race, Crime, and Justice* (pp. 267-273). Westport, CT: Praeger.

Henriques, Z.W., and Manatu-Rupert, N. (2001). Living on the outside: African American women before, during, and after imprisonment. *The Prison Journal, 81*(1), 6-19.

Her Majesty's Inspectorate of Prisons. (2012). *Expectations.* Available: http://www.justice.gov.uk/downloads/about/hmipris/adult-expectations-2012.pdf [February 1, 2014].

Herbert, S. (1997). *Policing Space: Territoriality and the Los Angeles Police Department.* Minneapolis: University of Minnesota Press.

Herbert, K., Plugge, E., Foster, C., and Doll, H. (2012). Prevalence of risk factors for non-communicable diseases in prison populations worldwide: A systematic review. *Lancet, 379*(9830), 1975-1982.

Herival, T., and Wright, P. (2007). *Prison Profiteers: Who Makes Money from Mass Incarceration.* New York: The New Press.

Herman, J. (1992). A new diagnosis. In J. Herman (Ed.), *Trauma and Recovery* (pp. 115-129). New York: Basic Books.

Heumann, M., and Loftin, C. (1979). Mandatory sentencing and the abolition of plea bargaining: The Michigan Felony Firearms Statute. *Law and Society Review, 13*, 393-430.

Heyer, R., and Wagner, P. (2004). *Too Big to Ignore: How Counting People in Prisons Distorted 2000 Census.* Cincinnati, OH: Prison Policy Initiative. Available: www.prisonersofthecensus.org/toobig/toobig.html [May 2011].

Hicks, C.D. (2010). *Talk with You Like a Woman: African American Women, Justice, and Reform in New York, 1890-1935.* Chapel Hill, NC: University of North Carolina Press.

Hildalgo, J.C. (2010, October 29). *Hispanics and Proposition 19*. Washington, DC: Cato.

Hill, C. (2004). Gangs. *Corrections Compendium, 29*, 8-23.

Hill, C. (2009). Gangs/security threat groups. *Corrections Compendium, 34*, 23-37.

Hill, M. (2007, May 29). New York prison creates dementia unit. *The Washington Post.*

Hindelang, M.J., Gottfredson, M.R., Dunn, C.S., and Parisi, N. (1977). *Sourcebook of Criminal Justice Statistics, 1976*. Albany, NY: Criminal Justice Research Center.

Hinton, E. (2012). *From Social Welfare to Social Control: Federal War in American Cities, 1968-1988*. New York: Columbia University.

Hipp, J.R., Petersilia, J., and Turner, S. (2010). Parolee recidivism in California: The effect of neighborhood context and social service agency characteristics. *Criminology, 48*, 947-979.

Hjalmarsson, R. (2009). Crime and expected punishment: Changes in perceptions at the age of criminal majority. *American Law and Economics Review, 11*(1), 209-248.

Hjalmarsson, R., and Lopez, M. (2010). The voting behavior of young disenfranchised felons: Would they vote if they could? *American Law and Economics Review, 12*(2), 265-279.

Hochschild, J.L., and Weaver, V. (2007). The skin color paradox and the American racial order. *Social Forces, 86*(2), 643-670.

Hocking, F. (1970). Extreme environmental stress and its significance for psychopathology. *American Journal of Psychotherapy, 24*(1), 4-26.

Hoffman, A. (1977). *Unwanted Mexican Americans in the Great Depression—Repatriation Pressures, 1929-1939*. Tucson, AZ: University of Arizona Press.

Holder, E., Jr. (2013a, August 12). *Department Policy on Charging Mandatory Minimum Sentences and Recidivist Enhancements in Certain Drug Cases*. Memorandum. Available: http://www.jdsupra.com/legalnews/us-attorney-general-eric-holders-memora-07918/ [November 2013].

Holder, E., Jr. (2013b, August 12). *Attorney General Eric Holder Delivers Remarks at the Annual Meeting of the American Bar Association's House of Delegates, San Francisco, CA*. Available: http://www.justice.gov/iso/opa/ag/speeches/2013/ag-speech-130812.html [November 2013].

Holzer, H.J. (1996). *What Employers Want: Job Prospects for Less-Educated Workers*. New York: Russell Sage Foundation.

Holzer, H.J. (2007). *Collateral Costs: The Effects of Incarceration on the Employment and Earnings of Young Workers*. Discussion Paper 3118. Bonn, Germany: Institute for the Study of Labor.

Holzer, H.J. (2009). Workforce development programs as an antipoverty strategy: What do we know? What should we do? In M. Cancian and S. Danziger (Eds.), *Changing Poverty, Changing Policies* (pp. 301-323). New York: Russell Sage Foundation.

Holzer, H.J., Raphael, S., and Stoll, M. (2004a). How willing are employers to hire ex-offenders? *Focus, 23*(2), 40-43.

Holzer, H.J., Raphael, S., and Stoll, M. (2004b). Will employers hire former offenders? Employer preferences, background checks and their determinants. In M. Pattillo, D. Weiman, and B. Western (Eds.), *Imprisoning America: The Racial Effects of Mass Incarceration* (pp. 205-246). New York: Russell Sage Foundation.

Holzer, H.J., Offner, P., and Sorensen, E. (2005). Declining employment among young black less-educated men: The role of incarceration and child support. *Journal of Policy Analysis and Management, 24*(2), 329-350.

Holzer, H.J., Raphael, S., and Stoll, M. (2006). Perceived criminality, criminal background checks and the racial hiring practices of employers. *Journal of Law and Economics, 49*.

Holzer, H.J., Raphael, S., and Stoll, M.A. (2007). The effect of an applicant's criminal history on employer hiring decisions and screening practices: Evidence from Los Angeles. In S. Bushway, M. Stoll, and D. Weiman (Eds.), *Barriers to Reentry? The Labor Market for Released Prisoners in Post-Industrial America* (pp. 117-150). New York: Russell Sage Foundation.

Hope, M., and Young, J. (1984). From back wards to back alleys: Deinstitutionalization and the homeless. *Urban and Social Change Review, 17,* 7-11.

HoSang, D. (2010). *Racial Propositions: Ballot Initiatives and the Making of Postwar California.* Berkeley: University of California Press:

Houston Chronicle. (2011, April 27). Counting Houston inmates would change map. Available: http://blog.chron.com/texaspolitics/2011/04/counting-houston-inmates-would-change-map/?utm_source=feedburnerandutm_medium=feedandutm_campaign=Feed%2525253A+houstonchronicle%2525252Ftexaspolitics+%25252528Texas+Politics%25252529 [December 2012].

Huber, G.A., and Gordon, S.C. (2004). Accountability and coercion: Is justice blind when it runs for office? *American Journal of Political Science, 48*(2), 247-263.

Hudson, B. (1984). The rising use of imprisonment: The impact of "decarceration" policies. *Critical Social Policy, 4*(11), 46-59.

Huey, M., and McNulty, T. (2005). Institutional conditions and prison suicide: Conditional effects of deprivation and overcrowding. *The Prison Journal, 85*(4), 490-514.

Hull, E.A. (2006). *The Disenfranchisement of Ex-Felons.* Philadelphia, PA: Temple University Press.

Human Rights Watch. (2003). *Ill-Equipped: U.S. Prisons and Offenders with Mental Illness.* New York: Human Rights Watch.

Humphreys, K. (2012). Federal policy on criminal offenders who have substance use disorders: How can we maximize public health and public safety? *Substance Abuse, 33*(1), 5-8.

Hunt, G., Riegel, S., Morales, T., and Waldorf, D. (1993). Changes in prison culture: Prison gangs and the case of the "Pepsi Generation." *Social Problems, 40*(3), 398-409.

Husley, L.F. (1990). *Attitudes of Employers with Respect to Hiring Released Prisoners.* Mankato, MN: Mankato State University.

Iguchi, M.Y., Bell, J., Ramchand, R.N., and Fain, T. (2005). How criminal system racial disparities may translate into health disparities. *Journal of Health Care for the Poor and Underserved, 16*(4, Suppl. B), 48-56.

Institute of Medicine. (1995). *Federal Regulation of Methadone Treatment.* R.A. Rettig and A. Yarmolinsky (Eds.). Committee on Federal Regulation of Methadone Treatment Division of Biobehavioral Sciences and Mental Disorders. Washington, DC: National Academy Press.

Institute of Medicine. (2001). *Crossing the Quality Chasm: A New Health System for the 21st Century.* Washington, DC: National Academy Press.

Institute of Medicine. (2012). *How Far Have We Come in Reducing Health Disparities? Progress Since 2000: Workshop Summary.* Washington, DC: The National Academies Press.

International Centre for Prison Studies. (2012). *World Prison Brief.* Available: http://www.prisonstudies.org/info/worldbrief/ [May 2013].

International Centre for Prison Studies. (2013). *World Prison Brief.* Available: http://www.prisonstudies.org/world-prison-brief [January 2014].

Irwin, J. (1970). *The Felon.* Englewood Cliffs, NJ: Prentice-Hall.

Irwin, J. (2005). *The Warehouse Prison: Disposal of the New Dangerous Class.* Los Angeles, CA: Roxbury Publishing.

Irwin, J., and Austin, J. (1997). *It's About Time: America's Imprisonment Binge.* 2nd ed. Belmont, CA: Wadsworth.

Jacobs, E. (2012). *Returning to Work after Prison: Final Results from the Transitional Jobs Reentry Demonstration.* New York: MDRC.

Jacobs, D., and Carmichael, J.T. (2001). The politics of punishment across time and space: A pooled time-series analysis of imprisonment rates. *Social Forces, 80*(1), 61-91.

Jacobs, D., and Helms, R. (2001). Toward a political sociology of punishment: Politics and changes in the incarcerated population. *Social Science Research, 30*(2), 171-194.

Jacobs, E., and Western, B. (2007). *Report on the Evaluation of the ComALERT Prisoner Reentry Program.* Brooklyn, NY: Office of the Kings County District Attorney.

Jacobson, M. (2005). *Downsizing Prisons: How to Reduce Crime and End Mass Incarceration.* New York: New York University Press.

Jacoby, J.E. (1980). *The American Prosecutor: A Search for Identity.* Lexington, MA: D.C. Heath.

Jaffe, S.R., Moffitt, T.E., Caspi, A., and Taylor, A. (2003). Life with (or without) father: The benefits of living with two biological parents depend on the father's antisocial behavior. *Child Development, 74*(1), 109-126.

James, D.J., and Glaze, L.E. (2006). *Mental Health Problems of Prison and Jail Inmates.* Washington, DC: U.S Department of Justice, Bureau of Justice Statistics.

James, N. (2013a). *The Bureau of Prisons (BOP): Operations and Budget.* R42486. Washington, DC: Congressional Research Service.

James, N. (2013b). *The Federal Prison Population Buildup: Overview, Policy Changes, Issues, and Options.* R42937. Washington, DC: Congressional Research Service.

Janssen, V. (2009). When the "jungle" met the forest: Public work, civil defense, and prison camps in postwar California. *Journal of American History, 96*(3), 702-726.

Jargowsky, P.A. (1997). *Poverty and Place: Ghettos, Barrios, and the American City.* New York: Russell Sage Foundation.

Jenness, V., Maxson, C., Sumner, J., and Matsuda, K. (2010). Accomplishing the difficult but not impossible: Collecting self-report data on inmate-on-inmate sexual assault in prison. *Criminal Justice Law Review, 21*(1), 3-30.

Joesoef, M.R., Kahn, R.H., and Weinstock, H.S. (2006). Sexually transmitted diseases in incarcerated adolescents. *Current Opinion in Infectious Diseases, 19*(1), 44-48.

Johnson, D. (2008). Racial prejudice, perceived injustice, and the black-white gap in punitive attitudes. *Journal of Criminal Justice, 36*(2), 198-206.

Johnson, R.C. (2009). Ever-increasing levels of parental incarceration and the consequences for children. In S. Raphael and M.A. Stoll (Eds.), *Do Prisons Make Us Safer? The Benefits and Costs of the Prison Boom* (pp. 177-206). New York: Russell Sage Foundation.

Johnson, R., and Raphael, S. (2009). The effects of male incarceration dynamics on Acquired Immune Deficiency Syndrome infection rates among African American women and men. *Journal of Law and Economics, 52*(2), 251-293.

Johnson, R., and Raphael, S. (2012). How much crime reduction does the marginal prisoner buy? *Journal of Law and Economics, 55*(2), 275-310.

Johnson, W., Benett, K., and Flanagan, T. (1997). Getting tough on prisoners: Results from the National Corrections Executive Survey, 1995. *Crime & Delinquency, 43*(1), 24-41.

Johnston, L.D., O'Malley, P.M., Bachman, J.G., and Schulenberg, J.E. (2012). *Monitoring the Future: National Survey Results on Drug Use, 1975-2007.* Volume 2: College Students and Adults Ages 19-50. Bethesda, MD: National Institute of Drug Abuse.

Joint Committee on New York Drug Law Evaluation. (1978). *The Nation's Toughest Drug Law: Evaluating the New York Experience.* Washington, DC: U.S. Government Printing Office.

Jolls, C., and Sunstein, C.R. (2006). The law of implicit bias. *California Law Review, 94,* 969-996.

Jones, P.D. (2010). *The Selma of the North: Civil Rights Insurgency in Milwaukee*. Cambridge, MA: Harvard University Press.

Jonson, C.L. (2010). *The Impact of Imprisonment of Reoffending: A Meta-Analysis*. Available: http://cech.uc.edu/content/dam/cech/programs/criminaljustice/docs/phd_dissertations/Jonson-Cheryl-Lero.pdf [February 1, 2014].

Jose-Kampfner, C. (1990). Coming to terms with existential death: An analysis of women's adaptation to life in prison. *Social Justice, 17*(2), 110-124.

Kabler, P. (2013, March 21). Prison overcrowding bill passes Senate. *The Charleston Gazette*. Available http://www.wvgazette.com/News/201303210067 [February 2014].

Kalleberg, A.L. (2011). *Good Jobs, Bad Jobs: The Rise of Polarized and Precarious Employment Systems in the United States, 1970s-2000s*. New York: Russell Sage Foundation, American Sociological Association Rose Series in Sociology.

Kalt, B.C. (2003). The exclusion of felons from jury service. *American University Law Review, 53*(1), 67.

Kamisar, Y. (2005). How Earl Warren's twenty-two years in law enforcement affected his work as chief justice. *Ohio State Journal of Criminal Law, 3*(11), 11-32.

Kant, I. (1965). The penal law and the law of pardon. In J. Ladd (transl.), *The Metaphysical Elements of Justice*. Indianapolis, IN: Liberal Arts Press/Bobbs-Merrill. (Orig. work published 1798).

Karberg, J., and James, D. (2005). *Substance Dependence, Abuse, and Treatment of Jail Inmates, 2002*. Washington, DC: U.S Department of Justice, Bureau of Justice Statistics.

Katz, M. (1996). *In the Shadow of the Poorhouse: A Social History of Welfare in America*. New York: Basic Books.

Kauffman, R.M., Ferketich, A.K., Murray, D.M., Bellair, P.E., and Wewers, M.E. (2011). Tobacco use by male prisoners under an indoor smoking ban. *Nicotine & Tobacco Research, 13*(6), 449-456.

Kendig, N.E. (2004). Correctional health care systems and collaboration with academic medicine. *Journal of the American Medical Association, 292*(4), 501-503.

Kennedy, D.M. (2011). *Don't Shoot: One Man, A Street Fellowship, and the End of Violence in Inner-City America*. New York: Bloomsbury USA.

Kennedy, R. (1997). *Race, Crime, and the Law*. New York: Pantheon Books.

Kessler, D., and Levitt, S. (1999). Using sentence enhancements to distinguish between deterrence and incapacitation. *Journal of Law and Economics, 42*, 348-363.

Kessler, R.C., Sonnega, A., Bromet, E., Hughes, M., and Nelson, C.B. (1995). Posttraumatic stress disorder in the National Comorbidity Survey. *Archives of General Psychiatry, 52*(12), 1048-1060.

Kessler, R.C., Nelson, C.B., McGonagle, K.A., Edlund, M.J., Frank, R.G., and Leaf, P.J. (1996). The epidemiology of co-occurring addictive and mental disorders: Implications for prevention and service utilization. *American Journal of Orthopsychiatry, 66*(1), 17-31.

Khan, M.R., Miller, W.C., Schoenbach, V.J., Weir, S.S., Kaufman, J.S., Wohl, D.A., and Adimora, A.A. (2008). Timing and duration of incarceration and high-risk sexual partnerships among African Americans in North Carolina. *Annals of Epidemiology, 18*(5), 403-410.

Khan, M.R., Epperson, M.W., Mateu-Gelabert, P., Bolyard, M., Sandoval, M., and Friedman, S.R. (2011). Incarceration, sex with an STI- or HIV-infected partner, and infection with an STI or HIV in Bushwick, Brooklyn, NY: A social network perspective. *American Journal of Public Health, 101*(6), 1110-1117.

Khavjou, O.A., Clarke, J., Hofeldt, R.M., Lihs, P., Loo, R.K., Prabhu, M., Schmidt, N., Stockmyer, C.K., and Will, J.C. (2007). A captive audience: Bringing the WISEWOMAN program to South Dakota prisoners. *Women's Health Issues, 17*(4), 193-201.

King, M. (1992). Male rape in institutional settings. In G. Mezey and M. King (Eds.), *Male Victims of Sexual Assault* (pp. 67-74). Oxford, England: Oxford University Press.

King, R.S., Mauer, M., and Huling, T. (2003). *Big Prisons, Small Towns: Prison Economics in Rural America*. Washington, DC: The Sentencing Project. Available: http://prison.ppjr.org/files/tracy%20huling%20prisons%20economy%20study.pdf [February 1, 2014].

Kirk, D.S. (2009). A natural experiment on residential change and recidivism: Lessons from Hurricane Katrina. *American Sociological Review*, 74(3), 484-505.

Kirk, D.S., and Papachristos, A.V. (2011). Cultural mechanisms and the persistence of neighborhood violence. *American Journal of Sociology*, 116(4), 1190-1233.

Kirk, D.S., and Sampson, R.J. (2013). Juvenile arrest and collateral educational damage in the transition to adulthood. *Sociology of Education*, 86, 336-362.

Kirschenman, J., and Neckerman, K.M. (1991). We'd love to hire them but . . . the meaning of race for employers. In C. Jencks and R. Peterson (Eds.), *The Urban Underclass* (pp. 203-234). Washington, DC: Brookings Institution.

Kjellstrand, J.M., and Eddy, J.M. (2011). Parental incarceration during childhood, family context, and youth problem behavior across adolescence. *Journal of Offender Rehabilitation*, 50(1), 18-36.

Kleiman, M.A.R. (1997). The problem of replacement and the logic of drug law enforcement. *Drug Policy Analysis Bulletin*, 3, 8-10.

Kleiman, M.A.R. (2009). *When Brute Force Fails: How to Have Less Crime and Less Punishment*. Princeton, NJ: Princeton University Press.

Kleiman, M.A.R., Caulkins, J.P., and Hawken, A. (2011). *Drugs and Drug Policy: What Everyone Needs to Know*. New York: Oxford University Press.

Klein, S., Tolbert, M., Bugarin, R., Cataldi, E.F., and Tasuchek, G. (2004). *Correctional Education: Assess the Status of Prison Programs and Information Needs*. Washington, DC: U.S. Department of Education, Office of Safe and Drug-Free Schools.

Kline, S. (1989). *Children in Custody, 1975-85: Census of Public and Private Juvenile Detention, Correctional, and Shelter Facilities, 1975, 1977, 1979, 1983, and 1985*. NCJ 114065. Washington, DC: U.S. Department of Justice, Bureau of Justice Statistics.

Kling, J.R. (2006). Incarceration length, employment and earnings. *American Economic Review*, 96(3), 863-876.

Knox, G.W. (2005). *The problem of gangs and security threat groups (STG's) in American prisons today: Recent research findings from the 2004 prison gang survey*. Available: http://www.ngcrc.com/corr2006.html [November 2013].

Kohler-Hausmann, J. (2010). The "Attila the Hun Law": New York's Rockefeller drug laws and the making of a punitive state. *Journal of Social History*, 44(1), 71-95.

Korn, R. (1988a). The effects of confinement in the high security unit at Lexington. *Social Justice*, 15(1), 8-19.

Korn, R. (1988b). Follow-up report on the effects of confinement in the high security unit at Lexington. *Social Justice*, 15(1), 20-29.

Kornfeld, R., and Bloom, H.S. (1999). Measuring program impacts on earnings and employment: Do unemployment insurance wage reports from employers agree with surveys of individuals? *Journal of Labor Economics*, 17(1), 168-197.

Kramer, J., and Ullmer, J. (2008). *Sentencing Guidelines: Lessons from Pennsylvania*. Boulder, CO: Lynne Reinner.

Kress, J.M. (1980). *Prescription for Justice: The Theory and Practice of Sentencing Guidelines*. Cambridge, MA: Ballinger.

Kruse, K.M., and Sugrue, T.J. (Eds.). (2006). *The New Suburban History*. Chicago, IL: University of Chicago Press.

Kruttschnitt, C. (2010). The paradox of women's imprisonment. *Daedalus*, 139(3), 32-42.

Krysan, M. (2012). From color caste to color blind, Part III: Contemporary era racial attitudes, 1976-2004. In H.L. Gates, Jr., C. Steele, L.D. Bobo, M. Dawson, G. Jaynes, L. Crooms-Robinson, and L. Darling-Hammond (Eds.), *The Oxford Handbook of African American Citizenship, 1865-Present* (pp. 235-278). New York: Oxford University Press.

Kupers, T. (1999). *Prison Madness: The Mental Health Crisis Behind Bars and What We Must Do About It.* San Francisco, CA: Jossey-Bass.

Kupers, T., Dronet, T., Winter, M., Austin, J., Kelly, L., Cartier, W., Morris, T.J., Hanlon, S.F., Sparkman, E.L., Kumar, P., Vincent, L.C., Norris, J., Nagel, K., and McBride, J. (2009). Beyond supermax administrative segregation: Mississippi's experience rethinking prison classification and creating alternative mental health programs. *Criminal Justice and Behavior, 36*(10), 1037-1050.

Kurlychek, M.C., Brame, R., and Bushway, S. (2006). Scarlet letters and recidivism: Does an old criminal record predict future offending? *Criminology and Public Policy, 5*(3), 483-504.

Kurlychek, M., Brame, R., and Bushway, S.D. (2007). Enduring risk? Old criminal records and predictions of future criminal involvement. *Crime & Delinquency, 53*(1), 64-83.

Kutateladze, B. (2009). *Is America Really So Punitive? Exploring a Continuum of U.S. State Criminal Justice Policies.* El Paso, TX: LFB Scholarly Publishing.

Lacey, N. (2008). *The Prisoners' Dilemma: Political Economy and Punishment in Contemporary Democracies.* Cambridge, UK: Cambridge University Press.

Lacey, N. (2010) American imprisonment in comparative perspective. *Daedalus, 139*(3): 102-114.

Lalonde, R.J. (1986). Evaluating the econometric evaluations of training programs with experimental data. *The American Economic Review, 76*(4), 604-620.

Lalonde, R.J., and Cho, R.M. (2008). The impact of incarceration in state prison on the employment prospects of women. *Journal of Quantitative Criminology, 24,* 243-265.

Lamb, H.R., and Weinberger, L.E. (2005). The shift of psychiatric inpatient care from hospitals to jails and prisons. *Journal of the American Academy of Psychiatry and the Law, 33*(4), 529-534.

Lamb, H.R., Weinberger, L.E., and Gross, B.H. (2004). Mentally ill persons in the criminal justice system: Some perspectives. *Psychiatric Quarterly, 75*(2), 107-126.

Land, K.C., McCall, P.L., and Cohen, L.E. (1990). Structural covariates of homicide rates: Are there any invariances across time and social space? *American Journal of Sociology, 95,* 922-963.

Lane, R. (1989). On the social meaning of homicide trends in America. In T.R. Gurr (Ed.), *Violence in America.* Newbury Park, CA: SAGE.

Langan, P.A. (1985). Racism on trial: New evidence to explain the racial composition of prisons in the United States. *Journal of Criminal Law and Criminology, 76*(3), 666-683.

Langan, P.A. (1991a). America's soaring prison population. *Science, 251*(5001), 1568-1573.

Langan, P.A. (1991b). *Race of Prisoners Admitted to State and Federal Institutions, 1926-86.* NCJ-125618. Washington, DC: U.S. Department of Justice, Bureau of Justice Statistics.

Langan, P.A., and Levin, D.J. (2002). *Recidivism of Prisoners Released in 1994.* NCJ 193427. Washington, DC: U.S. Department of Justice, Bureau of Justice Statistics.

Lappi-Seppälä, T. (2008). Trust, welfare, and political culture: Explaining differences in national penal policies. In M. Tonry (Ed.), *Crime and Justice: A Review of Research* (Vol. 37, pp. 313-387). Chicago, IL: University of Chicago Press.

Larney, S., Toson, B., Burns, L., and Dolan, K. (2012). Effect of prison-based opioid substitution treatment and post-release retention in treatment on risk of re-incarceration. *Addiction, 107*(2), 372-380.

Larney, S., Kopinski, H., Beckwith, C., Zaller, N., Des Jarlais, D., Hagan, H., Rich, J.D., van den Bergh, B.J., and Degenhardt, L. (2013). The incidence and prevalence of hepatitis C in prisons and other closed settings: Results of a systematic review and meta-analysis. *Hepatology, 58*(4), 1215-1224.

Last J. (1995). *A Dictionary of Epidemiology.* 3rd ed. Oxford, UK: Oxford University Press.

Laub, J.H., and Sampson, R.J. (2003). *Shared Beginnings, Divergent Lives: Delinquent Boys to Age 70.* Cambridge, MA: Harvard University Press.

Lawrence, C., and Andrews, K. (2004). The influence of perceived prison crowding on male inmates' perception of aggressive events. *Aggressive Behavior, 30*(4), 273-283.

Lawrence, S., Mears, D.P., Dubin, G., and Travis, J. (2002). *The Practice and Promise of Prison Programming.* Washington, DC: Urban Institute Press.

Lee, C. (2007). Hispanics and the death penalty: Discriminatory charging practices in San Joaquin County, California. *Journal of Criminal Justice, 35*(1), 17-27.

Lee, D.S., and McCrary, J. (2009). *The Deterrent Effect of Prison: Dynamic Theory and Evidence.* Princeton, NJ: University of Princeton, Industrial Relations Section.

Lee, H., Porter, L.C., and Comfort, M. (2013). The collateral consequences of family member incarceration: Impacts on civic participation and perceptions of legitimacy and fairness. *The ANNALS of the American Academy of Political and Social Science, 651*(1), 44-73.

Leese, M., Stuart, T. and Snow, L. (2006). An ecological study of factors associated with rates of self-inflicted death in prisons in England and Wales. *International Journal of Law and Psychiatry, 29*(5), 355-360.

Legal Action Center. (n.d.). *After Prison: Roadblocks to Reentry: A Report on State Legal Barriers Facing People with Criminal Records.* Available: http://www.lac.org/roadblocks-to-reentry/main.php?view=overview [January 24, 2013].

Lerman, A.E. (2009a). *Bowling Alone (With My Own Ball and Chain): Effects of Incarceration and the Dark Side of Social Capital.* Princeton, NJ: Princeton University.

Lerman, A.E. (2009b). The people prisons make: Effects of incarceration on criminal psychology. In S. Raphael and M. Stoll (Eds.), *Do Prisons Make Us Safer? The Benefits and Costs of the Prison Boom* (pp. 151-176). New York: Russell Sage Foundation.

Lerman, A.E., and Weaver, V. (2014). Staying out of sight: Concentrated policing and local political action. *The ANNALS of the American Academy of Political and Social Science, 651*(1), 202-219.

Levitt, S.D. (1996). The effect of prison population size on crime rates: Evidence from prison overcrowding legislation. *Quarterly Journal of Economics, 111*(2), 319-352.

Levitt, S.D. (1998). Juvenile crime and punishment. *Journal of Political Economy, 106,* 1156-1185.

Levitt, S.D. (2004). Understanding why crime fell in the 1990s: Four factors that explain the decline and six that do not. *Journal of Economic Perspectives, 18*(1), 163-190.

Levitt, S.D. (2006). The case of the critics who missed the point: A reply to Webster et al. *Criminology & Public Policy, 5*(3), 449-460.

Levitt, S.D., and Venkatesh, S.A. (2000). An economic analysis of a drug selling gang's finances. *Quarterly Journal of Economics, 115*(3), 755-789.

Lewis, C. (2006). Treating incarcerated women: Gender matters. *The Psychiatric Clinics of North America, 29*(3), 773-789.

Lewis, C.E., Jr. (2010). Incarceration and family formation. In W.E. Johnson, Jr. (Ed.), *Social Work with African American Males: Health, Mental Health, and Social Policy* (pp. 293-310). New York: Oxford University Press.

Lichtenstein, A. (1996). *Twice the Work of Free Labor: The Political Economy of Convict Labor in the New South.* New York: Verso.

Lieb, R., and Boerner, D. (2001). Sentencing reform in the other Washington. In M. Tonry (Ed.), *Crime and Justice: A Review of Research* (Vol. 28, pp. 71-136). Chicago, IL: University of Chicago Press.

Liebling, A. (1995). Vulnerability and prison suicide. *British Journal of Criminology, 35*(2), 173-187.

Liebling, A. (2011). Moral performance, inhumane and degrading treatment and prison pain. *Punishment and Society, 13*(3), 530-550.

Liedka, R.V., Piehl, A.M., and Useem, B. (2006). The crime control effect of incarceration: Does scale matter? *Criminology and Public Policy, 5*(2), 245-275.

Lin, A. (2002). *Reform in the Making: The Implementation of Social Policy in Prison.* Princeton, NJ: Princeton University Press.

Lincoln, T., Kennedy, S., Tuthill, R., Roberts, C., Conklin, T.J., and Hammett, T.M. (2006). Facilitators and barriers to continuing healthcare after jail: A community-integrated program. *Journal of Ambulatory Care Management, 29*(1), 2-16.

Lindquist, C.H., and Lindquist, C.A. (1999). Health behind bars: Utilization and evaluation of medical care among jail inmates. *Journal of Community Health, 24*(4), 285-303.

Lipsey, M.W., Landenberger, N.A., and Wilson, S.J. (2007). Effects of cognitive-behavioral programs for criminal offenders. *Campbell Systematic Reviews, 6.*

Liska, A.E., and Bellair, P.E. (1995). Violent-crime rates and racial composition: Convergence over time. *American Journal of Sociology, 101*(3), 578-610.

Loeffler, C.E. (2012). *Does Imprisonment Alter the Life-Course? Evidence on Crime and Employment from a Natural Experiment.* Cambridge, MA: Harvard University.

Loeffler, C.E. (2013). Does imprisonment alter the life course? Evidence on crime and employment from a natural experiment. *Criminology, 51*(1), 137-166.

Loftin, C., and McDowall, D. (1981). "One with a gun gets you two": Mandatory sentencing and firearms violence in Detroit. *The ANNALS of the American Academy of Political and Social Science, 455*(1), 150-167.

Loftin, C., and McDowall, D. (1984). The deterrent effects of the Florida felony firearm law. *Journal of Criminal Law and Criminology, 75*(1), 250-259.

Loftin, C., Heumann, M., and McDowall, D. (1983). Mandatory sentencing and firearms violence: Evaluating an alternative to gun control. *Law and Society Review, 17*(2), 287-318.

London, A., and Myers, N. (2006). Race, incarceration, and health: A life-course approach. *Research on Aging, 28*(3), 409-422.

Lopoo, L.M., and Western, B. (2005). Incarceration and the formation and stability of marital unions. *Journal of Marriage and Family, 67*(3), 721-734.

Losel, F., and Schmucker, M. (2005). The effectiveness of treatment for sexual offenders: A comprehensive meta-analysis. *Journal of Experimental Criminology, 1*(1), 117-146.

Lotke, E., and Wagner, P. (2004). Prisoners of the Census: Electoral and financial consequences of counting prisoners where they go, not where they come from. *Pace Law Review, 24,* 587-608.

Love, M. (2006). *Relief from the Collateral Consequences of Conviction: A State-by-State Resource Guide.* Buffalo, NY: William S. Hein & Co., Inc.

Love, M.C., Roberts, J., and Klingele, C.M. (2013). *Collateral Consequences of a Criminal Conviction: Law, Policy and Practice.* Washington, DC: National Association of Criminal Defense Lawyers and Thompson Reuters (West).

Lovell, D., and Toch, H. (2011). Some observations about the Colorado Segregation Study. *Correctional Mental Health Report, 13,* 3-6, 14.

Lovell, D., Johnson, L., and Cain, K. (2007). Recidivism of supermax prisoners in Washington State. *Crime & Delinquency, 53*(4), 633-656.

Ludwig, A., Cohen, L., Parsons, A., and Venters, H. (2012). Injury surveillance in New York City jails. *American Journal of Public Health, 102*(6), 1108-1111.

Ludwig, J. and Raphael, S. (2003). Prison sentence enhancements: The case of project exile. In J. Ludwig and P.J. Cook (Eds.), *Evaluating Gun Policy: Effects on Crime and Violence*. Washington, DC: Brookings Institution Press.

Lukes, S., and A. Scull. (1983). Introduction. In S. Lukes and A. Scull (Eds.), *Durkheim and the Law*. Oxford, England: Martin Roberston.

Ly, K.N., Xing, J., Klevens, R.M., Jiles, R.B., Ward, J.W., and Holmberg, S.D. (2012). The increasing burden of mortality from viral hepatitis in the United States between 1999 and 2007. *Annals of Internal Medicine, 156*(4), 271-278.

Lynch, M. (2010). *Sunbelt Justice: Arizona and the Transformation of American Punishment*. Stanford, CA: Stanford University Press.

Lynch, J.P., and Addington, L.A. (2006). *Understanding Crime Statistics: Revisiting the Divergence of the NCVS and UCR*. New York: Cambridge University Press.

Lynch, J.P., and Sabol, W.J. (2001). *Prisoner Reentry in Perspective: Crime Policy Report*. Vol. 3. Washington, DC: The Urban Institute. Available: http://www.urban.org/pdfs/410213_reentry.pdf [February 1, 2014].

Lynch, J.P., and Sabol, W.J. (2004a). Assessing the effects on mass incarceration on informal social control in communities. *Criminology and Public Policy, 3*(2), 267-294.

Lynch, J.P., and Sabol, W.J. (2004b). Effects of incarceration on informal social control in communities. In D. Weiman, B. Western, and M. Pattillo (Eds.), *Imprisoning America: The Social Effects of Mass Incarceration* (pp. 135-164). New York: Russell Sage Foundation.

Macalino, G.E., Dhawan, D., and Rich, J.D. (2005). A missed opportunity: Hepatitis C screening of prisoners. *American Journal of Public Health, 95*(10), 1739-1740.

MacCoun, R., and Martin, K.D. (2009). Drugs. In M. Tonry (Ed.), *Handbook on Crime and Public Policy* (pp. 501-523). New York: Oxford University Press.

MacDonald, J., and Sampson, R.J. (2012). The world in a city: Immigration and America's changing cities. *The ANNALS of the American Academy of Political and Social Science, 641*, 6-15.

MacDonald, M., and Stöver, H. (2005). Editorial. *International Journal of Prisoner Health, 1*(1)1-6.

MacKenzie, D.L. (2000). Evidence-based corrections: Identifying what works. *Crime & Delinquency, 46*(4), 457-471.

MacKenzie, D.L. (2006). *What Works in Corrections? Reducing the Criminal Activities of Offenders and Delinquents*. Cambridge, UK: Cambridge Press.

MacKenzie, D.L. (2008). *Structure and Components of Successful Education Programs*. Paper presented at the Reentry Roundtable on Education, John Jay College of Criminal Justice, New York.

MacKenzie, D.L. (2012). The effectiveness of corrections-based work and academic and vocational education programs. In J. Petersilia and K.R. Reitz (Eds.), *The Oxford Handbook of Sentencing and Corrections* (pp. 492-520). New York: Oxford University Press.

MacKenzie, D.L., and Goodstein, L. (1995). Long-term incarceration impacts and characteristics of long-term offenders. In T. Flanagan (Ed.), *Long-Term Imprisonment: Policy, Science, and Correctional Practice* (pp. 64-74). Thousand Oaks, CA: SAGE.

Maddox, K.B., and Gray, S.A. (2002). Cognitive representations of black Americans: Re-exploring the role of skin tone. *Personality and Social Psychology Bulletin, 28*(2), 250-259.

Maguire, K. (Ed.). (n.d.). *Sourcebook of Criminal Justice Statistics Online*. Albany, NY: University at Albany, Hindelang Criminal Justice Research Center. Available: http://www.albany.edu/sourcebook [June 2013].

Maguire, S., Freely, J., Clymer, C., Conway, M., and Schwartz, D. (2010). *Tuning In to Local Labor Markets: Findings from the Sectoral Employment Impact Study*. Public/Private Ventures.

Mallar, C.D., and Thornton, C.V.D. (1978). Transitional aid for released prisoners: Evidence from the LIFE experiment. *Journal of Human Resources, 13*(2), 208-236.

Mallik-Kane, K., and Visher, C. (2008). *Health and Prisoner Reentry: How Physical, Mental, and Substance Abuse Conditions Shape the Process of Reintegration.* Washington, DC: Urban Institute Press.

Mallik-Kane, K., Parthasarathy, B., and Adams, W. (2012, September). *Examining Growth in the Federal Prison Population, 1998-2010.* Washington, DC: Urban Institute Press.

Manza, J., and Uggen, C. (2006). *Locked Out: Felon Disenfranchisement and American Democracy.* New York: Oxford University Press.

Manza, J., Brooks, C., and Uggen, C. (2004). Public attitudes toward felon disenfranchisement in the United States. *Public Opinion Quarterly, 68*(2), 275-286.

Marlow, E., White, M.C., and Chesla, C.A. (2010). Barriers and facilitators: Parolees' perceptions of community health care. *Journal of Correctional Health Care, 16*(1), 17-26.

Marmot, M. (2005). Social determinants of health inequalities. *Lancet, 365*(9464), 1099-1104.

Marshall, T.H. (1950). *Citizenship and Social Class: And Other Essays.* Cambridge, UK: Cambridge University Press.

Martin, S.E. (1984). Interests and politics in sentencing reform: The development of sentencing guidelines in Pennsylvania and Minnesota. *Villanova Law Review, 29,* 21-113.

Martin, J.S. (2001). *Inside Looking Out: Jailed Fathers' Perceptions about Separation from Their Children.* New York: LFB Scholarly Publishing.

Martin, S.S., Butzin, C.A., Saum, C.A., and Inciardi, J.A. (1999). Three-year outcomes of therapeutic community treatment for drug-involved offenders in Delaware: From prison to work release to aftercare. *Prison Journal, 79*(3), 294-320.

Martinson, R. (1974). What works?—Questions and answers about prison reform. *Public Interest, 35*(2), 22-54.

Maruschak, L.M. (2004). *HIV in Prisons and Jails, 2002.* Washington, DC: U.S. Department of Justice, Bureau of Justice Statistics.

Maruschak, L.M. (2006). *HIV in Prisons, 2004.* Washington, DC: U.S. Department of Justice, Bureau of Justice Statistics.

Maruschak, L.M. (2012). *HIV in Prisons, 2001-2010.* Washington, DC: U.S. Department of Justice, Bureau of Justice Statistics.

Marvell, T.B. (1995). Sentencing guidelines and prison population growth. *Journal of Criminal Law and Criminology, 85*(3), 696-706.

Marvell, T.B., and Moody, C.E. (1994). Prison population growth and crime reduction. *Journal of Quantitative Criminology, 10*(2), 109-140.

Marvell, T.B., and Moody, C.E. (1996). Determinate sentencing and abolishing parole: The long-term impacts on prisons and crime. *Criminology, 34*(1), 107-128.

Massoglia, M. (2008a). Incarceration as exposure: The prison, infectious disease, and other stress-related illnesses. *Journal of Health and Social Behavior, 49*(1), 56-71.

Massoglia, M. (2008b). Incarceration, health, and racial disparities in health. *Law and Society Review, 42*(2), 275-305.

Massoglia, M., Remster, B., and King, R.D. (2011). Stigma or separation? Understanding the incarceration-divorce relationship. *Social Forces, 90*(1), 133-155.

Massoglia, M., Firebaugh, G., and Warner, C. (2013). Racial variation in the effect of incarceration on neighborhood attainment. *American Sociological Review, 78,* 142-165.

Matejkowski, J., Festinger, D.S., Benishek, L.A., and Dugosh, K.L. (2011). Matching consequences to behavior: Implications of failing to distinguish between noncompliance and nonresponsivity. *International Journal of Law and Psychiatry, 34*(4), 269-274.

Mauer, M. (2013). *The Changing Racial Dynamics of Women's Incarceration.* Washington, DC: The Sentencing Project.

Mazon, M. (1984). *The Zoot-Suit Riots: The Psychology of Symbolic Annihilation*. Austin: University of Texas Press.

McCain, G., Cox, V., and Paulus, P. (1976). The relationship between illness complaints and degree of crowding in a prison environment. *Environment and Behavior, 8*(2), 283-290.

McCarty, D., and Chandler, R.K. (2009). Understanding the importance of organizational and system variables on addiction treatment services within criminal justice settings. *Drug and Alcohol Dependence, 103*(Suppl. 1), S91-S93.

McClellan, D., Farabee, D., and Crouch, B. (1997). Early victimization, drug use, and criminality: A comparison of male and female prisoners. *Criminal Justice and Behavior, 24*(4), 455-476.

McCorkle, R. (1992). Personal precautions to violence in prison. *Criminal Justice and Behavior, 19*(2), 160-173.

McCoy, C., and McManimon, P. (2004). *New Jersey's "No Early Release Act": Its Impact on Prosecution, Sentencing, Corrections, and Victim Satisfaction*. Final Report. Washington, DC: U.S. Department of Justice.

McDonald, K. (2003). Marginal youth, personal identity, and the contemporary gang: Reconstructing the social world? In L. Dontos, D. Brotherton, and L. Barrios (Eds.), *Gangs and Society: Alternative Perspectives* (pp. 62-74). New York: Columbia University Press.

McDonald, M.P., and Popkin, S. (2001). The myth of the vanishing voter. *American Political Science Review, 95*, 963-974.

McDowall, D., Loftin, C., and Wiersema, B. (1992). A comparative study of the preventive effects of mandatory sentencing laws for gun crimes. *Journal of Criminal Law and Criminology, 83*(2), 378-394.

McGirr, L. (2002). *Suburban Warriors: The Origins of the New American Right*. Princeton, NJ: Princeton University Press.

McKenzie, M., Zaller, N., Dickman, S.L., Green, T., Parihk, A., Friedmann, P.D., and Rich, J.D. (2012). A randomized trial of methadone initiation prior to release from incarceration. *Substance Abuse, 233*(1), 19-29.

McKeown, R., Cuffe, S., and Schulz, R. (2006). Suicide rates by age group, 1970-2002: An examination of recent trends. *American Journal of Public Health, 96*(10), 1744-1751.

McLellan, A.T., Lewis, D.C., O'Brien, C.P., and Kleber, H.D. (2000). Drug dependence, a chronic medical illness: Implications for treatment, insurance, and outcomes evaluation. *Journal of the American Medical Association, 284*(13), 1689-1695.

McLennan, R.M. (2008). *The Crisis of Imprisonment: Protest, Politics, and the Making of the American Penal State, 1776-1941*. New York: Cambridge University Press.

Mead, L. (2011). *Expanding Work Programs for Poor Men*. Washington, DC: AEI Press.

Meares, T. (1997). Charting race and class differences in attitudes toward drug legalization and law enforcement: Lessons for federal criminal law. *Buffalo Criminal Law Review, 1*(1), 137-174.

Mears, D., and Bales, W. (2009). Supermax incarceration and recidivism. *Criminology, 47*(4), 1131-1166.

Mears, D., Winterfield, L., Hunsaker, J., Moore, G., and White, R. (2002). *Drug Treatment in the Criminal Justice System: The Current State of Knowledge*. Washington, DC: Urban Institute Press.

Mechoulan, S. (2011). The external effects of black male incarceration on black females. *Journal of Labor Economics, 29*(1), 1-35.

Meissner, D., Kerwin, D.M., Chishti, M., and Bergeron, C. (2013). *Immigration Enforcement in the United States: The Rise of a Formidable Machinery*. Washington, DC: Migration Policy Institute.

Mellow, J., and Greifinger, R.B. (2007). Successful reentry: The perspective of private correctional health care providers. *Journal of Urban Health, 84*(1), 85-98.

Mendelberg, T. (2001). *The Race Card: Campaign Strategy, Implicit Messages, and the Norm of Equality.* Princeton, NJ: Princeton University Press.

Merritt, N., Fain, T., and Turner, S. (2006). Oregon's get tough sentencing reform: A lesson in justice system adaptation. *Criminology and Public Policy, 5*(1), 5-36.

Messemer, J.E. (2011). The historical practice of correctional education in the United States: A review of the literature. *International Journal of Humanities and Social Sciences, 1*(17), 91-100.

Messinger, S.L., and Johnson, P.E. (1978). California's determinate sentencing statute: History and issues. In National Institute of Law Enforcement and Criminal Justice, Law Enforcement Assistance Administration *Proceedings of the Special Conference on Determinate Sentencing* (pp. 13-58), June 2-3, 1977, Boalt Hall of Law, University of California, Berkeley.

Messinger, S.L., Berecochea, J.E., Rauma, D., and Berk, R.A. (1985). Foundations of parole in California. *Law and Society Review, 19*(16), 69-106.

Metzner, J.L. (2012). Commentary: Treatment for prisoners: A U.S. perspective. *Psychiatric Services, 63*(3), 276.

Meyer, L.R. (2010). *The Justice of Mercy.* Ann Arbor, MI: The University of Michigan Press.

Michael, J., and Wechsler, H. (1937). A rationale of the law of homicide. *Columbia Law Review, 37*, 701-761 (Part I), 1261-1335 (Part II).

Miles, T.J., and Ludwig, J. (2007). The silence of the Lambdas: Deterring incapacitation research. *Journal of Quantitative Criminology, 23*, 287-301.

Millenky, M., Bloom, D., and Dillon, C. (2010). *Making the Transition: Interim Results of the National Guard Youth ChalleNGe Evaluation.* New York: MDRC.

Millenky, M., Bloom, D., Muller-Ravett, S., and Broadus, J. (2011). *Staying the Course: Three-Year Results of the National Guard Youth ChalleNGe Evaluation.* New York: MDRC.

Miller, D. (1999). *Principles of Social Justice.* Cambridge, MA: Harvard University Press.

Miller, J.L., Rossi, P.H., and Simpson, J.E. (1986). Perceptions of justice: Race and gender differences in judgments of appropriate prison sentences. *Law & Society Review, 20*(3), 313-334.

Miller, M.L., and Wright, R.F. (2008). The black box. *Iowa Law Review, 94*, 125-196.

Mills, L. (2008). *Inventorying and Reforming State-Created Employment Restrictions Based on Criminal Records: A Policy Brief and Guide.* Baltimore, MD: The Annie E. Casey Foundation.

Minton, T.D. (2011). *Jail Inmates at Midyear 2010—Statistical Tables.* NCJ 233431. Washington, DC: U.S Department of Justice, Bureau of Justice Statistics.

Minton, T.D. (2013). *Jail Inmates at Midyear 2012—Statistical Tables.* NCJ 241264. Washington, DC: U.S. Department of Justice, Bureau of Justice Statistics.

Mitchell, O. (2005). A meta-analysis of race and sentencing research: Explaining the inconsistencies. *Journal of Quantitative Criminology, 21*(4), 439-466.

Mitchell, O., and Caudy, M.S. (2013, January 22). Examining racial disparities in drug arrests. *Justice Quarterly.*

Mitchell, O., Wilson, D.B., and MacKenzie, D.L. (2012). The effectiveness of incarceration-based drug treatment on criminal behavior: A systematic review. *Campbell Systematic Reviews, 8*(18). Available: http://campbellcollaboration.org/lib/project/20/ [November 2013].

Moloney, K.P., van den Bergh, B.J., and Moller, L.F. (2009). Women in prison: The central issues of gender characteristics and trauma history. *Public Health, 123*(6), 426-430.

Montague, B.T., Rosen, D.L., Solomon, L., Nunn, A., Green, T., Costa, M., Baillargeon, J., Wohl, D.A., Paar, D.P., and Rich, J.D. (2012). Tracking linkage to HIV care for former prisoners: A public health priority. *Virulence, 3*(3), 319-324.

Morabito, M.S. (2007). Horizons of context: Understanding the police decision to arrest people with mental illness. *Psychiatric Services, 58*(12), 1582-1587.

Morash, M., and Schram, P. (2002). *The Prison Experience: Special Issues of Women in Prison.* Long Grove, IL: Waveland Press.

Morenoff, J., and Sampson, R.J. (1997). Violent crime and the spatial dynamics of neighborhood transition: Chicago, 1970-1990. *Social Forces, 76*(1), 31-64.

Morgan, S., and Winship, C. (2007). *Counterfactuals and Causal Inference: Methods and Principles for Social Research.* Cambridge, UK: Cambridge University Press.

Morgan, R., Fisher, W., Duan, N., Mandracchia, J., and Murray, D. (2010). Prevalence of criminal thinking among state prison inmates with serious mental illness. *Law and Human Behavior, 34*(4), 324-336.

Morris, H. (1966). Persons and punishment. *The Monist, 52*, 475-501.

Morris, N. (1974). *The Future of Imprisonment.* Chicago, IL: University of Chicago Press.

Morris, N. (1982). *Madness and the Criminal Law.* Chicago, IL: University of Chicago Press.

Morris, N. (1995). The contemporary prison, 1965-present. In N. Morris and D. Rothman (Eds.), *The Oxford History of the Prison: The Practice of Punishment in Western Society* (pp. 202-231). New York: Oxford University Press.

Morris, N. (2000). Prisons in the USA: Supermax—the bad and the mad. In L. Fairweather and S. McConville (Eds.), *Prison Architecture: Policy, Design, and Experience* (pp. 98-108). London: Architectural Press.

Morris, N., and Howard, C. (1964). *Studies in Criminal Law.* Oxford: Clarendon Press.

Morris, N., and Tonry, M.H. (1990). *Between Prison and Probation: Intermediate Punishments in a Rational Sentencing System.* New York: Oxford University Press.

Moynihan, D.P. (1993). Iatrogenic government—social policy and drug research. *The American Scholar, 62*(3), 351-362.

Muhammad, K.G. (2010). *The Condemnation of Blackness: Race, Crime, and the Making of Modern Urban America.* Cambridge, MA: Harvard University Press.

Mukamal, D. (2003). *Negligent Hiring Case Law in New York.* Research memo prepared for the Legal Action Center, Washington, DC.

Muller, C. (2012). Northward migration and the rise of racial disparity in American incarceration, 1880-1950. *American Journal of Sociology, 118*(2), 281-326.

Muller, C., and Schrage, D. (2014). Mass imprisonment and trust in the law. *The ANNALS of the American Academy of Political and Social Science, 651*(1), 139-158.

Mullings, J., Hartley, D., and Marquart, J. (2004). Exploring the relationship between alcohol use, childhood maltreatment, and treatment needs among female prisoners. *Substance Use and Misuse, 39*(2), 277-305.

Mulvey, E.P., and Schubert, C. (2011). Youth in prison and beyond. In B.C. Feld and D.M. Bishop (Eds.), *Oxford Handbook on Juvenile Crime and Juvenile Justice* (pp. 843-867). New York: Oxford University Press.

Mumola, C.J. (2000). *Incarcerated Parents and their Children.* NCJ 182335. Washington, DC: U.S. Department of Justice, Bureau of Justice Statistics.

Mumola, C. (2005, August). *Suicide and Homicide in State Prisons and Local Jails.* NCJ 210036. Washington, DC: U.S. Department of Justice, Bureau of Justice Statistics.

Mumola, C. (2007). *Medical Causes of Death in State Prisons, 2001-2004.* NCJ 216340. Washington, DC: U.S. Department of Justice, Bureau of Justice Statistics.

Mumola, C.J., and Beck, A.J. (1997). *Prisoners in 1996.* Washington, DC: U.S. Department of Justice, Bureau of Justice Statistics.

Mumola, C., and Karberg, J. (2006). *Drug Use and Dependence, State and Federal Prisoners, 2004.* NCJ 213530. Washington, DC: U.S. Department of Justice, Bureau of Justice Statistics.

Mumola, C., and Noonan, M. (2007). *Statistical Tables: Deaths in Custody* (last updated June 16, 2009). Washington, DC: U.S. Department of Justice, Bureau of Justice Statistics.

Murakawa, N. (2008). The origins of the carceral crisis: Racial order as "law and order" in postwar American politics. In J. Lowndes, J. Novkov, and D.T. Warren (Eds.), *Race and American Political Development* (pp. 235-255). New York: Routledge.

Murakawa, N. (Forthcoming). *The First Civil Right: Racial Proceduralism and the Construction of Carceral America*. New York: Oxford University Press.

Murch, D. (2010). *Living for the City: Migration, Education, and the Rise of the Black Panther Party in Oakland, California*. Chapel Hill: University of North Carolina Press.

Murray, J., Farrington, D.P., Sekol, I., and Olsen, R.F. (2009). Effects of parental imprisonment on child antisocial behaviour and mental health: A systematic review. *Campbell Systematic Reviews, 4*, 1-105.

Murray, J., Farrington, D.P., and Sekol, I. (2012a). Children's antisocial behavior, mental health, drug use, and educational performance after parental incarceration: A systematic review and meta-analysis. *Psychological Bulletin, 138*(2), 175-210.

Murray, J., Loeber, R., and Pardini, D. (2012b). Parental involvement in the criminal justice system and the development of youth theft, marijuana use, depression, and poor academic performance. *Criminology, 50*(1), 255-302.

Musto, D.F. (1999). *The American Disease: Origins of Narcotics Control*. New York: Oxford University Press.

Musto, D., and Korsmeyer, P. (2002). *The Quest for Drug Control: Politics and Federal Policy in a Period of Increasing Substance Abuse, 1963-1981*. New Haven, CT: Yale University Press.

Myers, B.J., Smarsh, T.M., Amlund-Hagan, K., and Kennon, S. (1999). Children of incarcerated mothers. *Journal of Child and Family Studies, 8*(1), 11-25.

Myrdal, G. (1944). *An American Dilemma: The Negro Problem and Modern Democracy*. New York: Harper and Brothers.

Nagin, D. (1998). Criminal deterrence research at the outset of the twenty-first century. In M. Tonry (Ed.), *Crime and Justice: A Review of Research* (Vol. 23, pp. 1-42). Chicago, IL: University of Chicago Press.

Nagin, D.S. (2005). *Group-based Modeling of Development*. Cambridge, MA: Harvard University Press.

Nagin, D.S. (2013a). Deterrence: A review of the evidence by a criminologist for economists. *Annual Review of Economics, 5*, 83-105.

Nagin, D.S. (2013b). Deterrence in the twenty-first century: A review of the evidence. In M. Tonry (Ed.), *Crime and Justice: A Review of Research* (Vol. 42, pp. 199-263). Chicago, IL: University of Chicago Press.

Nagin, D.S., Cullen, F.T., and Jonson, C.L. (2009). Imprisonment and reoffending. In M. Tonry (Ed.), *Crime and Justice: A Review of Research* (Vol. 38, pp. 115-200). Chicago, IL: University of Chicago Press.

National Advisory Commission on Civil Disorders. (1968, February 29). *The Report of the National Advisory Commission on Civil Disorders*. New York: Bantam Books.

National Advisory Commission on Criminal Justice Standards and Goals. (1973). *Report on the Criminal Justice System*. Washington, DC: U.S. Government Printing Office.

National Association of State Budget Officers. (2013). *State Spending for Corrections: Long-term Trends and Recent Criminal Justice Policy Reforms*. Washington, DC: National Association of State Budget Officers.

National Center for State Courts. (2006). *The NCSC Sentencing Attitudes Survey: A Report on the Findings*. Williamsburg, VA: National Center for State Courts. Available: http://www.ncsc.org/sitecore/content/microsites/csi/home/Topics/~/media/Microsites/Files/CSI/The%20NCSC%20Sentencing%20Attitudes%20Survey.ashx [February 1, 2014].

National Commission on Correctional Health Care. (2002). *The Health Status of Soon-to-be-Released Inmates: A Report to Congress*. Chicago, IL: National Commission on Correctional Health Care.

National Commission on Reform of Federal Criminal Laws. (1971). *Final Report: A Proposed New Federal Criminal Code*. Washington, DC: U.S. Government Printing Office.

National Conference of State Legislators. (2012). *Medical Release of Inmates: Recent State Enactments*. Available: http://www.ncsl.org/issues-research/justice/state-sentencing-and-corrections-legislation.aspx [July 11, 2013].

National Council on Crime and Delinquency. (1972). *Model Sentencing Act*. 2nd ed. Hackensack, NJ: National Council on Crime and Delinquency.

National Employment Law Project. (2012). *States Adopt Fair Hiring Standards: Reducing Barriers to Employment of People with Criminal Records*. New York: National Employment Law Project.

National Employment Law Project. (2013). *Ban the Box: Major U.S. Cities and Counties Adopt Fair Hiring Policies to Remove Unfair Barriers to Employment of People with Criminal Records*. New York: National Employment Law Project.

National Institute for Literacy. (2002). *State Correctional Education Programs: State Policy Update*. Washington, DC: National Institute for Literacy.

National Institute on Drug Abuse. (2012). *Principles of Drug Abuse Treatment for Criminal Justice Populations: A Research-Based Guide*. Bethesda, MD: National Institute on Drug Abuse, National Institutes of Health. Available: http://www.drugabuse.gov/publications/principles-drug-abuse-treatment-criminal-justice-populations [July 2013].

National Research Council. (1978a). *Deterrence and Incapacitation: Estimating the Effects of Criminal Sanctions on Crime Rates*. A. Blumstein, J. Cohen, and D. Nagin (Eds.). Washington, DC: National Academy Press.

National Research Council. (1978b). *Knowledge and Policy: The Uncertain Connection*. L.E. Lynn (Ed.). Washington, DC: National Academy Press.

National Research Council. (1979). *The Rehabilitation of Criminal Offenders: Problems and Prospects*. L. Sechrest, S.O. White, and E. Brown (Eds.). Panel on Research on Rehabilitative Techniques, Committee on Research on Law Enforcement and Criminal Justice. Assembly of Behavioral and Social Sciences. Washington, DC: National Academy Press.

National Research Council. (1983). *Research on Sentencing: The Search for Reform*. Panel on Sentencing Research. A. Blumstein, J. Cohen, S.E. Martin, and M.H. Tonry (Eds.). Committee on Research on Law Enforcement and the Administration of Justice, Commission on Behavioral and Social Sciences and Education. Washington, DC: National Academy Press.

National Research Council. (1986). *Criminal Careers and "Career Criminals."* Panel on Research on Criminal Careers. A. Blumstein, J. Cohen, J.A. Roth, and C.A. Visher (Eds.). Committee on Research on Law Enforcement and the Administration of Justice, Commission on Behavioral and Social Sciences and Education. Washington, DC: National Academy Press.

National Research Council. (1993). *Understanding and Preventing Violence, Volume 1*. Panel on the Understanding and Control of Violent Behavior. A.J. Reiss and J.A. Roth (Eds.). Committee on Law and Justice, Commission on Behavioral and Social Sciences and Education. Washington, DC: National Academy Press.

National Research Council. (2001). *Informing America's Policy on Illegal Drugs: What We Don't Know Keeps Hurting Us*. Committee on Data and Research for Policy on Illegal Drugs. C.F. Manski, J.V. Pepper, and C.V. Petrie (Eds.). Committee on Law and Justice and Committee on National Statistics. Commission on Behavioral and Social Sciences and Education. Washington, DC: National Academy Press.

National Research Council. (2006). *Once, Only Once, and in the Right Place: Residence Rules in the Decennial Census.* Panel on Residence Rules in the Decennial Census. D.L. Cork and P.R. Voss (Eds.). Committee on National Statistics, Division of Behavioral and Social Sciences and Education. Washington, DC: The National Academies Press.

National Research Council. (2007). *Parole, Desistance from Crime, and Community Integration.* Committee on Community Supervision and Desistance from Crime. Committee on Law and Justice, Division of Behavioral and Social Sciences and Education. Washington, DC: The National Academies Press.

National Research Council. (2008). *Understanding Crime Trends Workshop Report.* Committee on Understanding Crime Trends. A.S. Goldberger and R. Rosenfeld (Eds.). Committee on Law and Justice, Division of Behavioral and Social Sciences and Education. Washington, DC: The National Academies Press.

National Research Council. (2009). *Ensuring the Quality, Credibility, and Relevance of U.S. Justice Statistics.* Panel to Review the Programs of the Bureau of Justice Statistics. R. Groves and D.L. Cork (Eds.). Committee on National Statistics and Committee on Law and Justice, Division of Behavioral and Social Sciences and Education. Washington, DC: The National Academies Press.

National Research Council. (2011). *Budgeting for Immigration Enforcement: A Path to Better Performance.* Committee on Estimating Costs of Immigration Enforcement in the Department of Justice. S. Redburn, P. Reuter, and M. Majmundar (Eds.). Committee on Law and Justice, Division of Behavioral and Social Sciences and Education. Washington, DC: The National Academies Press.

National Research Council. (2012a). *Deterrence and the Death Penalty.* Committee on Deterrence and the Death Penalty. D.S. Nagin and J.V. Pepper (Eds.). Committee on Law and Justice, Division of Behavioral and Social Sciences and Education. Washington, DC: The National Academies Press.

National Research Council. (2012b). *Using Science as Evidence in Public Policy.* Committee on the Use of Social Science Knowledge in Public Policy. K. Prewitt, T.A. Schwandt, and M.L. Straf (Eds.). Center for Education, Division of Behavioral and Social Sciences and Education. Washington, DC: The National Academies Press.

National Research Council. (2013). *Reforming Juvenile Justice: A Developmental Approach.* Committee on Assessing Juvenile Justice Reform. R.J. Bonnie, R.L. Johnson, B.M. Chemers, and J.A. Schuck (Eds.). Committee on Law and Justice, Division of Behavioral and Social Sciences and Education. Washington, DC: The National Academies Press.

National Research Council and Institute of Medicine. (2001). *Juvenile Crime, Juvenile Justice.* Panel on Juvenile Crime: Prevention, Treatment, and Control. J. McCord, C.S. Widom, and N.A. Crowell (Eds.). Committee on Law and Justice and Board on Children, Youth, and Families. Washington, DC: National Academy Press.

National Research Council and Institute of Medicine. (2013). *Health and Incarceration: A Workshop Summary.* A. Smith, Rapporteur. Committee on Law and Justice, Division of Behavioral and Social Sciences and Education and Board on the Health of Select Populations, Institute of Medicine. Washington, DC: The National Academies Press.

Navarro, A. (2000). *La Raza Unida Party: A Chicano Challenge to the U.S. Two-Party Dictatorship.* Philadelphia, PA. Temple University Press.

Neal, D., and Armin, R. (2013, May). *The Prison Boom and the Lack of Black Progress After Smith and Welch.* Chicago, IL: University of Chicago.

Nellis, A. (2013). *Life Goes On: The Historic Rise in Life Sentences in America.* Washington, DC: The Sentencing Project.

Nellis, A., and King, R.S. (2009). *No Exit: The Expanding Use of Life Sentences in America.* Washington, DC: The Sentencing Project.

Nelson, M., Deess, P., and Allen, C. (1999). *The First Month Out: Post-Incarceration Experiences in New York City*. New York: Vera Institute of Justice.

New York State Division of Criminal Justice Services. (2012). *2009 Drug Law Changes—June 2012 Update*. Albany, NY: New York State Division of Criminal Justice Services.

Newman, D. (1966). *Conviction*. Boston, MA: Little, Brown and Company.

Nicholson-Crotty, S. (2004). The impact of sentencing guidelines on state-level sanctions: An analysis over time. *Crime & Delinquency, 50*(3), 395-411.

Nieuwbeerta, P., Nagin, D.S., and Blokland, A.A. (2009). The relationship between first imprisonment and criminal career development: A matched samples comparison. *Journal of Quantitative Criminology, 25*, 227-257.

Nijhawan, A.E., Salloway, R., Nunn, A.S., Poshkus, M., and Clarke, J.G. (2010). Preventive healthcare for underserved women: Results of a prison survey. *Journal of Women's Health, 19*(1), 17-22.

Noonan, M. (2007). *Mortality in Local Jails, 2000-2007*. NCJ 222988. Washington, DC: U.S. Department of Justice, Bureau of Justice Statistics.

Noonan, M. (2012). *Mortality in Local Jails and State Prisons, 2000-2010—Statistical Tables*. NCJ 239911. Washington, DC: U.S. Department of Justice, Bureau of Justice Statistics.

Noonan, M., and Carson, E. (2011). *Prison and Jail Deaths in Custody, 2000-2009—Statistical Tables*. NCJ 236219. Washington, DC: U.S. Department of Justice, Bureau of Justice Statistics.

Nordstrom, B.R., and Williams, A.R. (2012). Drug treatments in criminal justice settings. *Psychiatric Clinics of North America, 35*(2), 375-391.

Nunn, A., Zaller, N., Dickman, S., Trimbur, C., Nijhawan, A., and Rich, J.D. (2009). Methadone and buprenorphine prescribing and referral practices in U.S. prison systems: Results from a nationwide survey. *Drug and Alcohol Dependence, 105*(1-2), 83-88.

Nunn, A., Cornwall, A., Fu, J., Bazerman, L., Loewenthal, H., and Beckwith, C. (2010). Linking HIV-positive jail inmates to treatment, care, and social services after release: Results from a qualitative assessment of the COMPASS Program. *Journal of Urban Health, 87*(6), 954-968.

Nurse, A.M. (2004). Returning to strangers: Newly paroled young fathers and their children. In M. Patillo, D. Weiman, and B. Western (Eds.), *Imprisoning America: The Social Effects of Mass Incarceration* (pp. 21-45). New York: Russell Sage Foundation.

Nussbaum, M.C. (1998). *Sex and Social Justice*. New York: Oxford University Press.

O'Connor, A. (2008). The privatized city: The Manhattan Institute, the urban crisis, and the conservative counterrevolution in New York. *Journal of Urban History, 34*(2), 333-353.

Office of Inspector General. (2004, March). *The Federal Bureau of Prisons Inmate Release Preparation and Transitional Reentry Programs*. Audit Report 04-16. Washington, DC: U.S. Department of Justice.

Office of Inspector General. (2008). *The Federal Bureau of Prison's Efforts to Manage Inmate Health Care*. Audit Report 08-08. Washington, DC: U.S. Department of Justice. Available: http://www.justice.gov/oig/reports/BOP/a0808/final.pdf [July 2013].

Office of Juvenile Justice and Delinquency Prevention. (1983). *Children in Custody: Advance Report on the 1982 Census of Public Juvenile Facilities*. Washington, DC: Office of Juvenile Justice and Delinquency Prevention, U.S. Department of Justice.

Office of Legislative Audits. (2007). *Performance Audit Report: Inmate Healthcare*. Baltimore, MD: Maryland General Assembly, Office of Legislative Audits.

Office of the Pardon Attorney. (1996). *Civil Disabilities of Convicted Felons: A State-by-State Survey*. Washington, DC: U.S. Department of Justice.

Offner, P., and Holzer, H. (2002). *Left Behind in the Labor Market: Recent Employment Trends Among Young Black Men*. Washington, DC: The Brookings Institution.

Ohlin, L. (1956). *Sociology and the Field of Corrections*. New York: Russell Sage Foundation.

O'Keefe, M., and Schnell, M. (2007). Offenders with mental illness in the correctional system, *Journal of Offender Rehabilitation, 45*(1-2), 81-104.

O'Keefe, M.L., Klebe, K.J., Metzner, J., Dvoskin, J., Fellner, J., and Stucker, A. (2013). A longitudinal study of administrative segregation. *Journal of the American Academy of Psychiatry and the Law, 41*(1), 49-60.

Olivares, K.M., Burton, V.S., Jr., and Cullen, F. (1996). The collateral consequences of a felony conviction: A national study of state legal codes 10 years later. *Federal Probation, 60*(3), 10-17.

Oser, C.B., Knudsen, H.K., Staton-Tindall, M., Taxman, F., and Leukefeld, C. (2009). Organizational-level correlates of the provision of detoxification services and medication-based treatments for substance abuse in correctional institutions. *Drug and Alcohol Dependence, 103*(Suppl. 1), S73-S81.

Oshinsky, D.M. (1997). *Worse than Slavery: Parchman Farm and the Ordeal of Jim Crow Justice*. New York: Free Press.

Ostfeld, A. (1987). *Stress, Crowding, and Blood Pressure in Prison*. Hillsdale, NJ: Erlbaum.

Owen, B. (1998). *"In the Mix": Struggle and Survival in Women's Prison*. Albany: State University of New York Press.

Owens, E.G. (2009). More time, less crime? Estimating the incapacitative effects of sentence enhancements. *Journal of Labor Economics, 53*, 551-579.

Pager, D. (2003). The mark of a criminal record. *American Journal of Sociology, 108*, 937-975.

Pager, D. (2007). *Marked, Race, Crime, and Finding Work in an Era of Mass Incarceration*. Chicago, IL: University of Chicago Press.

Pager, D., and Quillian, L. (2005). Walking the talk: What employers say versus what they do. *American Sociological Review, 70*(3), 355-380.

Pager, D., Western, B., and Bonikowski, B. (2009a). Discrimination in a low-wage labor market: A field experiment. *American Sociological Review, 74*(5), 777-799.

Pager, D., Western, B., and Sugie, N. (2009b). Sequencing disadvantage: Barriers to employment facing young black and white men with criminal records. *The ANNALS of the American Academy of Social and Political Science, 623*(1), 195-213.

Papadopoulos, F., and Tsakloglou, P. (2006). *Social Exclusion in the EU: A Capability-based Approach*. London: European Institute.

Parece, M.S., Herrera, G.A., Voigt, R.F., Middlekauff, S.L., and Irwin, K.L. (1999). STD testing policies and practices in U.S. city and county jails. *Sexually Transmitted Diseases, 26*(8), 431-437.

Parisi, N., Gottfredson, M.R., Hindelang, M.J., and Flanagan, T.J. (1979). *Sourcebook of Criminal Justice Statistics, 1978*. Albany, NY: Criminal Justice Research Center.

Parker, R.N., and Horwitz, A.V. (1986). Unemployment, crime, and imprisonment: A panel approach. *Criminology, 24*(4), 751-773.

Parnas, R.I., and Salerno, M.B. (1978). The influence behind, substance and impact of the new determinate sentencing law in California. *University of California at Davis Law Review, 11*, 29-41.

Paterline, B., and Petersen, D. (1999). Structural and social psychological determinants of prisonization. *Journal of Criminal Justice, 27*(5), 427-441.

Patterson, E.J. (2010). Incarcerating death: Mortality in U.S. state correctional facilities, 1985-1998. *Demography, 47*(3), 587-607.

Patterson, E.J., and Preston S.H. (2008). Estimating mean length of stay in prison: Methods and applications. *Journal of Quantitative Criminology, 24*(1), 33-49.

Patterson, R., and Hughes, E. (2008). Review of completed suicides in the California Department of Corrections and Rehabilitation, 1999-2004. *Psychiatric Services, 59*(6), 676-682.

Paulus, P., Cox, V., and McCain, G. (1988). *Prison Crowding: A Psychological Perspective*. New York: Springer-Verlag.

Peffley, M., and Hurwitz, J. (2010). *Justice in America: The Separate Realities of Blacks and Whites*. New York: Cambridge University Press.

Perkinson, R. (2010). *Texas Tough: The Rise of America's Prison Empire*. New York: Metropolitan Books.

Perry, A.R., and Bright, M. (2012). African American fathers and incarceration: Paternal involvement and child outcomes. *Social Work in Public Health*, 27(1-2), 187-203.

Perry, A.E., Neilson, M., Martyn-St James, M., Glanville, J.M., McCool, R., Duffy, S., Godfrey, C., and Hewitt, C. (2013). Pharmacologic interventions for drug-using offenders. *Cochrane Database of Systematic Reviews, 12*.

Petersilia, J. (2003). *When Prisoners Come Home: Parole and Prisoner Reentry*. New York: Oxford University Press.

Petersilia, J., Greenwood, P.W., and Marvin, L. (1978). *Criminal Careers of Habitual Felons*. Santa Monica, CA: RAND Corporation.

Petrosino, A., Turpin-Petrosino, C., and Guckenburg, S. (2010). *Formal System Processing of Juveniles: Effects on Delinquency*. Oslo, Norway: The Campbell Collaboration.

Pettit, B. (2012). *Invisible Men: Mass Incarceration and the Myth of Black Progress*. New York: Russell Sage Foundation.

Pettit, B., and Western, B. (2004). Mass imprisonment and the life course: Race and class inequality in U.S. incarceration. *American Sociological Review, 69*(2), 151-169.

Pettit, B., and Lyons, C. (2007). Status and the stigma of incarceration: The labor market effects of incarceration by race, class, and criminal involvement. In D. Weiman, S. Bushway, and M. Stoll (Eds.), *Barriers to Re-entry: The Impact of Incarceration on Labor Market Outcomes* (pp. 203-226). New York: Russell Sage Foundation.

Pettit, B., Sykes, B., and Western, B. (2009). *Technical Report on Revised Population Estimates and NLSY-79 Analysis Tables for the Pew Public Safety and Mobility Project*. Cambridge, MA: Harvard University.

Pettus, K.I. (2005). *Felony Disenfranchisement in America: Historical Origins, Institutional Racism, and Modern Consequences*. New York: LFB Scholarly Publishing.

Pew Center on the States. (2009). *One in 31: Behind Bars in America 2008*. Washington, DC: Pew Charitable Trusts.

Pew Center on the States. (2010). *Prison Count 2010*. Philadelphia, PA: Pew Charitable Trusts. Available: http://www.pewstates.org/research/reports/prison-count-2010-85899372907 [February 2014].

Pew Center on the States. (2012). *Time Served: The High Cost, Low Return of Longer Prison Terms*. Washington, DC: Pew Charitable Trusts.

Pew Charitable Trusts. (2007, November). *When Offenders Break the Rules: Smart Responses to Parole and Probation Violations*. Available: http://www.pewtrusts.org/uploadedFiles/wwwpewtrustsorg/Reports/sentencing_and_corrections/Condition-Violators-Briefing.pdf [July 12, 2013].

Phelps, M.S. (2011). Rehabilitation in the punitive era: The gap between rhetoric and reality in U.S. prison programs. *Law and Society Review, 45*(1), 33-68.

Phillips, K. (1969). *The Emerging Republican Majority*. New York: Arlington House.

Phillips, J. (2001). Cultural construction of manhood in prison. *Psychology of Men and Masculinity, 2*(1), 13-23.

Phillips, S.D. (2012). *The Affordable Care Act: Implications for Public Safety and Corrections Populations*. Washington, DC: The Sentencing Project.

Phillips, S.D., and Harm, N.J. (1997). Women prisoners: A contextual framework. *Women and Therapy, 20*(4), 1-9.

Piehl, A.M. (2009). *Preparing Prisoners for Employment: The Power of Small Rewards.* Center for Civic Innovation at the Manhattan Institute. Available: http://www.manhattaninstitute.org/pdf/cr_57.pdf [November 2013].

Piehl, A.M., and DiIulio, J.J., Jr. (1995, Winter). Does prison pay? Revisited: Returning to the crime scene. *Brookings Review*, 21-25.

Pifferi, M. (2012). Individualization of punishment and the rule of law. *American Journal of Legal History*, 52, 325-376.

Piquero, A.R., and Blumstein, A. (2007). Does incapacitation reduce crime? *Journal of Quantitative Criminology*, 23(4), 267-286.

Piquero, A.R., West, V., Fagan, J., and Holland, J. (2006). Neighborhood, race, and the economic consequences of incarceration in New York City, 1985-1996. In R.D. Peterson, L. Krivo, and J. Hagan (Eds.), *The Many Colors of Crime: Inequalities of Race, Ethnicity and Crime in America* (pp. 256-276). New York: New York University Press.

Pizzi, W.T., Blair, I.V., and Judd, C.M. (2005). Discrimination in sentencing on the basis of Afrocentric features. *Michigan Journal of Race and Law*, 10(2), 327-353.

Plugge, E.H., Foster, C.E., Yudkin, P.L., and Douglas, N. (2009). Cardiovascular disease risk factors and women prisoners in the UK: The impact of imprisonment. *Health Promotion International*, 24(4), 334-343.

Poehlmann, J. (2005a). Children's family environment and intellectual outcomes during maternal incarceration. *Journal of Marriage and Family*, 67(5), 1275-1285.

Poehlmann, J. (2005b). Incarcerated mothers' contact with children, perceived family relationships, and depressive symptoms. *Journal of Family Psychology*, 19(3), 350-357.

Poehlmann, J. (2005c). Representations of attachment relationships in children of incarcerated mothers. *Child Development*, 76(3), 679-696.

Pollock, J. (1997). The social world of the prisoner. In J. Pollock (Ed.), *Prisons: Today and Tomorrow* (pp. 218-269). Gaithersburg, MD: Aspen Publishers.

Porporino, F. (1990). Difference in response to long-term imprisonment: Implications for the management of long-term offenders. *The Prison Journal*, 70(1), 35-45.

Porter, N.D. (2010, October). *Expanding the Vote: State Felony Disenfranchisement Reform, 1997-2010.* Washington, DC: The Sentencing Project.

Porter, N.D. (2013). *The State of Sentencing 2012—Developments in Policy and Practice.* Washington, DC: The Sentencing Project.

Powell, T., Holt, J., and Fondacaro, K. (1997). The prevalence of mental illness among inmates in a rural state. *Law and Human Behaviour*, 21(4), 427-438.

Powers, M., and Faden, R. (2006). *Social Justice: The Moral Foundation of Public Health.* New York: Oxford University Press.

Pratt, D., Appleby, L., Webb, R., and Shaw, J. (2006). Suicide in recently released prisoners: A population-based cohort study. *Lancet, 368*(9530), 119-123.

Prendergast, M.L., Campos, M., Farabee, D., Evans, W.K., and Martinez, J. (2004). Reducing substance use in prison: The California Department of Corrections drug reduction strategy project. *The Prison Journal*, 84(2), 265-280.

President's Commission on Law Enforcement and the Administration of Justice. (1967). *The Challenge of Crime in a Free Society.* Washington, DC: U.S. Government Printing Office.

President's Committee on Civil Rights. (1947). *To Secure These Rights: The Report of the President's Committee on Civil Rights.* Washington, DC: U.S. Government Printing Office.

Quinnipiac University. (2012). *Cutting Stop and Frisk Won't Increase Crime, More New Yorkers Tell Quinnipiac University Poll; Voters Oppose Soda Limits, Back Liquor Crackdown.* Available: http://www.quinnipiac.edu/institutes-centers/polling-institute/new-york-city/release-detail?ReleaseID=1788 [August 16, 2012].

Rachlinksi, J.J., Johnson, S.L., Wistrich, A.J., and Guthrie, C. (2009). Does unconscious racial bias affect trial judges? *Notre Dame Law Review*, 84(3), 1195-1246.

Raphael, S. (2006). The deterrent effects of California's Proposition 8: Weighing the evidence. *Criminology and Public Policy, 5*(3), 471-478.

Raphael, S. (2007). Boosting the earnings and employment of low-skilled workers in the United States: Making work pay and reducing barriers to employment and social mobility. In T.J. Bartik and S.M. Houseman (Eds.), *A Future of Good Jobs? America's Challenge in the Global Economy* (pp. 245-305). Kalamazoo, MI: W.E. Upjohn Institute.

Raphael, S., and Stoll, M. (2009). Why are so many Americans in prison? In S. Raphael and M. Stoll (Eds.), *Do Prisons Make Us Safer? The Benefits and Costs of the Prison Boom* (pp. 27-72). New York: Russell Sage Foundation.

Raphael, S., and Stoll, M.A. (2013). *Why Are So Many Americans in Prison?* New York: Russell Sage Foundation.

Rawls, J. (1971). *A Theory of Justice.* Boston, MA: Harvard University Press.

Redcross, C., D. Bloom, G.L. Azurdia, J.M. Zweig, and N. Pindus. (2009). *Transitional Jobs for Ex-prisoners: Implementation, Two Year Impacts and Costs of the Center for Employment Opportunities (CEO) Prisoner Reentry Program.* New York: MDRC.

Redcross, C., Bloom, D., Jacobs, E., et al. (2010). *Work After Prison: One-Year Findings from the Transitional Jobs Reentry Demonstration.* New York: MDRC.

Redcross, C., Millenky, M., Rudd, T., and Levshin, V. (2012). *More Than a Job: Final Results from the Evaluation of the Center for Employment Opportunities (CEO) Transitional Jobs Program.* OPRE Report 2011-18. Washington, DC: Office of Planning, Research and Evaluation, Administration for Children and Families, U.S. Department of Health and Human Services.

Redding, R.E. (2008). *Juvenile Transfer Laws: An Effective Deterrent to Delinquency?* Available: http://works.bepress.com/richard_redding/6 [July 2013].

Reekie, I.H. (1930). Report on the Select Committee on Capital Punishment. *The Howard Journal of Criminal Justice, 3*(1), 67-73.

Reeves, J.L., and Campbell, R. (1994). *Cracked Coverage: Television News, the Anti-Cocaine Crusade, and the Reagan Legacy.* Durham, NC: Duke University Press.

Reitz, K. (1997). Sentencing guideline systems and sentence appeals: A comparison of federal and state experiences. *Northwestern University Law Review, 91,* 1441-1506.

Reitz, K. (2006). Don't blame determinacy: US incarceration growth has been driven by other forces. *Texas Law Review, 84,* 1787-1802.

Reitz, K. (2012). The 'traditional' indeterminate sentencing model. In J. Petersilia and K. Reitz (Eds.), *The Oxford Handbook of Sentencing and Corrections* (pp. 270-298). New York: Oxford University Press.

Remington, F. (1969). Introduction. In R. Dawson (Ed.), *Sentencing: The Decision as to Type, Length, and Conditions of Sentence.* Boston, MA: Little, Brown and Company.

Renauer, B.C, Cunningham, W.S., Feyerherm, B., O'Connor, T., and Bellatty, P. (2006). Tipping the scales of justice: the effect of overincarceration on neighborhood violence. *Criminal Justice Policy Review, 17*(3), 362-379.

Reuter, P. (1992). Hawks ascendant: The punitive trend of American drug policy *Daedalus, 121*(3), 15-52.

Reuter, P. (2013). Why has U.S. drug policy changed so little over 30 years? In M. Tonry (Ed.), *Crime and Justice in America, 1975-2025* (Vol. 42, pp. 75-140). Chicago, IL: University of Chicago Press.

Reuter, P., MacCoun, R.J., and Murphy, P. (1990). *Money from Crime: The Economics of Drug Dealing in Washington, DC.* Santa Monica, CA: RAND Drug Policy Research Center.

Rhodes, L., and Lovell, D. (2011). Is "adaptation" the right question? Addressing the larger context of administrative segregation: Commentary on One Year Longitudinal Study of the Psychological Effects of Administrative Segregation. *Corrections & Mental Health.* Washington, DC: National Institute of Corrections. Available: http://community.nicic. gov/blogs/mentalhealth/archive/2011/06/21/is-adaptation-the-right-question-addressing-the-larger-context-of-administrative-segregation.aspx [February 1, 2014].

Rich, J.D., Holmes, L., Salas, C., Macalino, G., Davis, D., Ryczek, J., and Flanigan, T. (2001). Successful linkage of medical care and community services for HIV-positive offenders being released from prison. *Journal of Urban Health, 78*(2), 279-289.

Rich, J.D., Boutwell, A.E., Shield, D.C., Key, R.G., McKenzie, M., Clarke, J.G., and Friedmann, P.D. (2005). Attitudes and practices regarding the use of methadone in U.S. state and federal prisons. *Journal of Urban Health, 82*(3), 411-419.

Rich, J.D., Wakeman, S.E., and Dickman, S.L. (2011). Medicine and the epidemic of incarceration in the United States. *New England Journal of Medicine, 364*(22), 2081-2083.

Rich, W.D., Sutton, L.P., Clear, T.D., and Saks, M.J. (1982). *Sentencing by Mathematics: An Evaluation of the Early Attempts to Develop Sentencing Guidelines.* Williamsburg, VA: National Center for State Courts.

Richie, B. (1996). *Compelled to Crime: The Gender Entrapment of Battered Black Women.* New York: Routledge.

Richie, B.E. (2012). *Arrested Justice: Black Women, Violence, and America's Prison Nation.* New York: New York University Press.

Rideau, W., and Sinclair, B. (1998). Prison: The sexual jungle. In A. Scacco (Ed.), *Male Rape: A Casebook of Sexual Aggressions* (pp. 3-29). New York: AMS Press.

Rieder, J. (1985). *Canarsie: The Jews and Italians of Brooklyn Against Liberalism.* Cambridge, MA: Harvard University Press.

Rios, V. (2011). *Punished: Policing the Lives of Black and Latino Boys.* New York: New York University Press.

Ritchie, B. (2004). Feminist ethnographies of women in prison. *Feminist Studies, 30*(2), 438-450.

Ritter, C., Huynh, C.K., Etter, J.F., and Elger, B.S. (2012). Exposure to tobacco smoke before and after a partial smoking ban in prison: Indoor air quality measures. *Tobacco Control, 21*(5), 488-491.

Robbins, I.P. (1999). Managed health care in prisons as cruel and unusual punishment. *Journal of Criminal Law and Criminology, 90*(1), 195-237.

Roberts, J.V. (1997). American attitudes about punishment: Myth and reality. In M. Tonry and K. Hatlestad (Eds.), *Sentencing Reform in Overcrowded Times: A Comparative Perspective.* New York: Oxford University Press.

Roberts, J.V., and Stalans, L.J. (1997). *Public Opinion, Crime, and Criminal Justice.* Boulder, CO: Westview.

Roberts, J.V., and Stalans, L.J. (1998). Crime, criminal justice, and public opinion. In M. Tonry (Ed.), *The Handbook of Crime and Punishment* (pp. 31-57). New York: Oxford University Press.

Roberts, J.V., and Stalans, L.J. (2000). *Crime, Criminal Justice, and Public Opinion.* Boulder, CO: Westview Press.

Roberts, J.V., Stalans, L.S., Indermaur, D., and Hough, M. (2003). *Penal Populism and Public Opinion: Lessons from Five Countries.* New York: Oxford University Press.

Robinson, P.H. (1999). *Would You Convict?: Seventeen Cases That Challenged the Law.* New York: New York University Press.

Robinson, P.H. (2008). *Distributive Principles of Criminal Law: Who Should Be Punished How Much.* New York: Oxford University Press.

Robinson, P.H. (2013). *Intuitions of Justice and the Utility of Desert*. New York: Oxford University Press.

Robinson, P.H., and Darley, J.M. (2004). Does criminal law deter? A behavioural science investigation. *Oxford Journal of Legal Studies, 24*(2), 173-205.

Robinson, J.G., West, K., and Adlakha, A. (2002). Coverage of the population in Census 2000: Results from demographic analysis. *Population Research and Policy Review, 21*(1-2), 19-38.

Rodriguez, M.N., Farid, E., and Porter, N. (2011). *State Reforms Promoting Employment of People with Criminal Records: 2010-11 Legislative Round-Up*. New York and Washington, DC: National Employment Law Project, National H.I.R.E. Network, and Sentencing Project.

Roettger, M.E., and Boardman, J.D. (2012). Parental incarceration and gender-based risks for increased body mass index: Evidence from the National Longitudinal Study of Adolescent Health in the United States. *American Journal of Epidemiology, 175*(7), 636-644.

Roettger, M.E., and Swisher, R.R. (2011). Associations of fathers' history of incarceration with sons' delinquency and arrest among black, white, and Hispanic males in the United States. *Criminology, 49*(4), 1109-1147.

Rogers, S.M., Khan, M.R., Tan, S., Turner, C.F., Miller, W.C., and Erbelding, E. (2012). Incarceration, high-risk sexual partnerships and sexually transmitted infections in an urban population. *Sexually Transmitted Infections, 88*(1), 63-68.

Romilly, S.S. (1820). Sir Samuel Romilly's speeches. In J. Michael and H. Wechsler (Eds.), *Criminal Law and Its Administration*. Chicago, IL: Foundation Press.

Room, R., Fischer, B., Hall, W., Lenton, S., and Reuter, P. (2013). *Cannabis Policy: Moving Beyond Stalemate*. New York: Oxford University Press.

Rose, D.R., and Clear, T.R. (1998). Incarceration, social capital and crime: Examining the unintended consequences of incarceration. *Criminology, 36*, 441-479.

Rose, D.R., Clear, T.R., and Ryder, J. (2001). Addressing the unintended consequences of incarceration through community-oriented services at the neighborhood level. *Corrections Management Quarterly, 3*, 62-71.

Rosen, D.L., Schoenbach, V.J., and Wohl, D.A. (2008). All-cause and cause-specific mortality among men released from state prison, 1980-2005. *American Journal of Public Health, 98*(12), 2278-2284.

Rosen, D.L., Wohl, D.A., and Schoenbach, V.J. (2011). All-cause and cause-specific mortality among black and white North Carolina state prisoners, 1995-2005. *Annals of Epidemiology, 21*(10), 719-726.

Rosen, D.L., Hammond, W.P., Wohl, D.A., and Golin, C.E. (2012). Disease prevalence and use of health care among a national sample of black and white male state prisoners. *Journal of Health Care for the Poor and Underserved, 23*(1), 254-272.

Rosenfeld, R. (2007). Explaining the divergence between UCR and NCVS aggravated assault trends. In J.P. Lynch and L.A. Addington (Eds.), *Understanding Crime Statistics: Revisiting the Divergence of the NCVS and the UCR* (pp. 251-268). New York: Cambridge University Press.

Rosenfeld, J., Pettit, B., Laird, J., and Sykes, B. (2011, September 1-4). *Incarceration and Racial Inequality in Voter Turnout*. Paper presented at the annual meeting of the American Political Science Association, Seattle, WA.

Ross, L., and Nisbett, R. (1991). *The Person and the Situation: Perspectives of Social Psychology*. New York: McGraw-Hill.

Rossi, P.H., Berk, R.A., and Lenihan, K.J. (1980). *Money, Work, and Crime: Experimental Evidence*. New York: Academic Press.

Rossman, D., Froyd, P., Pierce, G., McDevitt, J., and Bowers, W. (1979). *The Impact of the Mandatory Gun Law in Massachusetts.* Washington, DC: U.S. Government Printing Office.

Rossman, S., Sridharan, S., Gouvis, C., Buck, J., and Morley, E. (1999). *Impact of the Opportunity to Succeed Aftercare Program for Substance-Abusing Felons: A Comprehensive Final Report.* Washington, DC: Urban Institute Press.

Rothman, D.J. (1971). *The Discovery of Asylum: Social Order and Disorder in the New Republic.* Boston, MA: Little, Brown and Company.

Rothman, D.J. (1980). *Conscience and Convenience: The Asylum and Its Alternatives in Progressive America.* Boston, MA: Little, Brown and Company.

Rothman, D.J. (2002a). *Conscience and Convenience: The Asylum and Its Alternatives in Progressive America.* Hawthorne, NY: Aldine de Gruyter.

Rothman, D.J. (2002b). *The Discovery of the Asylum: Social Order and Disorder in the New Republic.* Hawthorne, NY: Aldine de Gruyter.

Rubenstein, D. (1982). The older person in prison. *Archives of Gerontology and Geriatrics, 3,* 287-296.

Rumbaut, R.G. (2009). Undocumented immigration and rates of crime and imprisonment: Popular myths and empirical realities. In A. Khashu (Ed.), *The Role of Local Police: Striking a Balance Between Immigration Enforcement and Civil Liberties* (pp. 119-139). Washington, DC: Police Foundation.

Rumbaut, R.G., and Ewing, W. (2007, Spring). *The Myth of Immigrant Criminality.* Washington, DC: Immigration Policy Center.

Rusche, G. (1978). Labor market and penal sanction. *Crime and Justice, 10,* 2-8. (Originally published in 1933.).

Ruth, H., and Reitz, K.R. (2003). *The Challenge of Crime: Rethinking Our Response.* Cambridge, MA: Harvard University Press.

Sabol, W. (2007). Local labor-market conditions and post-prison employment experiences of offenders released from Ohio state prisons. In S. Bushway, M.A. Stoll, and D.F. Weiman (Eds.), *Barriers to Reentry? The Labor Market for Released Prisoners in Post-Industrial America* (Ch. 9, pp. 257-303). New York: Russell Sage Foundation.

Sabol, W.J., and Lynch, J.P. (2003). Assessing the longer-run effects of incarceration: Impact on families and employment. In D. Hawkins, S. Myers, Jr., and R. Stone (Eds.), *Crime Control and Social Justice: The Delicate Balance* (pp. 3-26). Westport, CT: Greenwood Press.

Sabol, W.J., Rosich, K., Kane, K.M., Kirk, D., and Dubin, G. (2002). *The Influences of Truth-in-Sentencing Reforms on Changes in States' Sentencing Practices and Prison Populations.* Washington, DC: Urban Institute Press.

Sabol, W.J., West, H.C., and Cooper, M. (2009). *Prisoners in 2008.* NCJ 228417. Washington, DC: U.S. Department of Justice, Bureau of Justice Statistics.

Salive, M., Smith, G., and Brewer, T. (1989). Suicide mortality in the Maryland state prison system, 1979 through 1987. *Journal of the American Medical Association, 262*(3), 365-369.

Sample, B. (2011, August). Voting rights must be "earned" back, says Iowa governor. *Prison Legal News.*

Sampson, R.J. (1987). Urban black violence: The effect of male joblessness and family disruption. *American Journal of Sociology, 93*(2), 348-383.

Sampson, R.J. (1995). Unemployment and imbalanced sex ratios: Race-specific consequences for family structure and crime. In M.B. Tucker and C. Mitchell-Kernan (Eds.), *The Decline in Marriage among African Americans: Causes, Consequences, and Policy Implications* (pp. 229-254). New York: Russell Sage Foundation.

Sampson, R.J. (2011). The incarceration ledger: Toward a new era in assessing societal consequences. *Criminology and Public Policy, 10*(3), 819-828.

Sampson, R.J. (2012). *Great American City: Chicago and the Enduring Neighborhood Effect*. Chicago, IL: University of Chicago Press.

Sampson, R.J., and Bartusch, D.J. (1998). Legal cynicism and (subcultural?) tolerance of deviance: The neighborhood context of racial differences. *Law and Society Review, 32*(4), 777-804.

Sampson, R.J., and Groves, W.B. (1989). Community structure and crime: Testing social-disorganization theory. *American Journal of Sociology, 94*(4), 774-802.

Sampson, R.J., and Laub, J. (1993). *Crime in the Making: Pathways and Turning Points through Life*. Cambridge, MA: Harvard University Press.

Sampson, R.J., and Lauritsen, J.L. (1997, January 1). Racial and ethnic disparities in crime and criminal justice in the United States. *Crime and Justice: A Review of Research, 21*, 311-374.

Sampson, R.J., and Loeffler, C. (2010). Punishment's place: The local concentration of mass incarceration. *Daedalus, 139*(3), 20-31.

Sampson, R.J., and Wilson, W.J. (1995). Toward a theory of race, crime, and urban inequality. In J. Hagan and R.D. Peterson (Eds.), *Crime and Inequality* (pp. 37-54). Stanford, CA: Stanford University Press.

Sapsford, R. (1978). Life sentence prisoners: Psychological changes during sentence. *British Journal of Criminology, 18*(2), 128-145.

Savelsberg, J.J. (1994). Knowledge, domination, and criminal punishment. *American Journal of Sociology, 99*(4), 911-943.

Saylor, W.G., and Gaes, G.G. (1997). Training inmates through industrial work participation and vocational and apprenticeship instruction. *Corrections Management Quarterly, 1*(2), 32-43.

Schachter, S. (1959). *The Psychology of Affiliation*. Stanford, CA: Stanford University Press.

Scharff-Smith, P. (2006). The effects of solitary confinement on prison inmates: A brief history and review of the literature. In M. Tonry (Ed.), *Crime and Justice: A Review of Research* (Vol. 34, pp. 441-528). Chicago, IL: University of Chicago Press.

Scharf-Smith, P. (2011). The effects of solitary confinement: Commentary on One Year Longitudinal Study of the Psychological Effects of Administrative Segregation. *Corrections & Mental Health*. Washington, DC: National Institute of Corrections.. Available: http://community.nicic.gov/blogs/mentalhealth/archive/2011/06/21/the-effects-of-solitary-confinement-commentary-on-one-year-longitudinal-study-of-the-psychological-effects-of-administrative-segregation.aspx [February 1, 2014].

Schlanger, M. (2003). Inmate litigation. *Harvard Law Review, 116*(6), 1557-1706.

Schlanger, M., and Shay, G. (2008). Preserving the rule of law in America's jails and prisons: The case for amending the Prison Litigation Reform Act. *University of Pennsylvania Journal of Constitutional Law, 11*, 139-154.

Schlosser, E. (1998, December). The prison-industrial complex. *The Atlantic*. Available: http://www.theatlantic.com/magazine/archive/1998/12/the-prison-industrial-complex/304669/ [March 9, 2013].

Schlossman, S., and Spillane, J. (1994). *Bright Hopes, Dim Realities: Vocational Innovation in American Correctional Education*. Berkeley: University of California, Berkeley, National Center for Research in Vocational Education.

Schnittker, J., and John, A. (2007). Enduring stigma: The long-term effects of incarceration on health. *Journal of Health and Social Behavior, 48*(2), 115-130.

Schnittker, J., Massoglia, M., and Uggen, C. (2011). Incarceration and the health of the African American community. *Racial Inequality and Health, 8*(1), 133-141.

Schochet, P.Z., Burghardt, J., and McConnell, S. (2008). Does Job Corps work? Impact findings from the National Job Corps Study. *American Economic Review, 98*(5), 1864-1886.

406 THE GROWTH OF INCARCERATION

Schoenwald, J.M. (2002). *A Time for Choosing: The Rise of Modern American Conservatism.* New York: Oxford University Press.

Schwartz, R., and Skolnick, J. (1962). Two studies of legal stigma. *Social Problems, 10*(2), 133-142.

Schwartz-Soicher, O., Geller, A., and Garfinkel, I. (2011). The effect of paternal incarceration on material hardship. *Social Service Review, 85*(3), 447-473.

Scott, G., and Gendreau, P. (1969). Psychiatric implications of sensory deprivation in a maximum security prison. *Canadian Psychiatric Association Journal, 14*(4), 337-341.

Scull, A. (1977). *Decarceration: Community Treatment and the Deviant—A Radical View.* Englewood Cliffs, NJ: Prentice-Hall.

SEARCH. (2005). *Report of the National Task Force on the Commercial Sale of Criminal Justice Record Information.* Sacramento, CA: SEARCH, The National Consortium for Justice Information and Statistics.

Secret, P.E., and Johnson, J.B. (1989). Racial differences in attitudes toward crime control. *Journal of Criminal Justice, 17*(5), 361-375.

Seiter, R., and Kadela, K. (2003). Prisoner reentry: What works, what does not, and what is promising. *Crime & Delinquency, 49*(3), 360-388.

Sellin, T. (1938). *Culture, Conflict, and Crime.* New York: Social Science Research Council.

Sen, A.K. (1985). *Commodities and Capabilities.* Oxford: Oxford University Press.

Shalev, S. (2009). *Supermax: Controlling Risk through Solitary Confinement.* Portland, OR: Willan Publishing.

Shalev, S., and Lloyd, M. (2011). Though this be method, yet there is madness in't: Commentary on One Year Longitudinal Study of the Psychological Effects of Administrative Segregation. *Corrections & Mental Health,* 1-7. Washington, DC: National Institute of Corrections. Available: http://community.nicic.gov/blogs/mentalhealth/archive/2011/06/21/though-this-be-method-yet-there-is-madness-in-t-commentary-on-one-year-longitudinal-study-of-the-psychological-effects-of-administrative-segregation.aspx [February 1, 2014].

Shane-DuBow, S., Brown, A.P., and Olsen, E. (1985). *Sentencing Reform in the United States: History, Content, and Effect.* Washington, DC: U.S. Government Printing Office.

Sharkey, P. (2010). The acute effect of local homicides on children's cognitive performance. *Proceedings of the National Academy of Sciences, 107,* 11733-11738.

Sherman, L.W. (1998). *Evidence-based policing.* Washington, DC: The Police Foundation.

Sherman, L.W., and Berk, R.A. (1984). The specific deterrent effects of arrest for domestic assault. *American Sociological Review, 49*(2), 261-272.

Sherman, L.W., Gottfredson, D., MacKenzie, D., Eck, J., Reuter, P., and Bushway, S. (1997). *Preventing Crime: What Works, What Doesn't, What's Promising.* Washington, DC: A Report to the U.S. Congress prepared by National Institute of Justice.

Shermer, E.T. (Ed.). (2013). *Barry Goldwater and the Transformation of the American Political Landscape.* Tucson: University of Arizona Press.

Sickmund, M., Sladky, T.J., Kang, W., and Puzzanchera, C. (2011). *Easy Access to the Census of Juveniles in Residential Placement.* Available: http://www.ojjdp.gov/ojstatbb/ezacjrp/ [July 2013].

Simon, J. (2007). *Governing through Crime: How the War on Crime Transformed American Democracy and Created a Culture of Fear.* New York: Oxford University Press.

Simon, J., and Sparks, R. (2013). Introduction: Punishment and society: The emergence of an academic field. In J. Simon and R. Sparks (Eds.), *The SAGE Handbook of Punishment and Society* (pp. 1-21). London, UK: SAGE.

Simpson, S.S. (2011). Making sense of white collar crime: Theory and research. *The Ohio State Journal of Criminal Law, 8,* 481-502.

Skarbek, D. (2011). Governance and prison gangs. *American Political Science Review, 105*(4), 702-716.

Skarbek, D. (2012). Prison gangs, norms, and organizations. *Journal of Economic Behavior and Organization, 82*(1), 96-109.

Skogan, W. (1986). Fear of crime and neighborhood change. In J. Albert, J. Reiss, and M. Tonry (Eds.), *Communities and Crime* (pp. 203-229). Chicago, IL: University of Chicago Press.

Skogan, W. (1990). *Disorder and Decline: Crime and the Spiral of Decay in American Cities.* Berkeley: University of California Press.

Smith, J.P., and Welch, F.R. (1989). Black economic progress after Myrdal. *Journal of Economic Literature, 27*(2), 519-564.

Smith, K.B. (2004). The politics of punishment: Evaluating political explanations of incarceration rates. *Journal of Politics, 66*(3), 925-938.

Smith, M.E., and Dickey, W.J. (1999). *Reforming Sentencing and Corrections for Just Punishment and Public Safety.* Washington, DC: U.S. Department of Justice, National Institute of Justice.

Smith, P., Goggin, C., and Gendreau, P. (2004). *The Effects of Prison Sentences and Intermediate Sanctions on Recidivism: General Effects and Individual Differences.* Unpublished Manuscript. New Brunswick, Canada: University of New Brunswick, Department of Psychology.

Smykla, J., and Williams, J. (1996). Co-corrections in the United States of America, 1970-1990: Two decades of disadvantages for women prisoners. *Women and Criminal Justice, 8*(1), 61-76.

Snell, T.L. (2011). *Capital Punishment 2010—Statistical Tables.* NCJ 236510. Washington, DC: U.S. Department of Justice, Bureau of Justice Statistics.

Snyder, H.N. (2011). *Arrest in the United States, 1980-2009.* NCJ 234319. Washington, DC: U.S. Department of Justice, Office of Justice Programs, Bureau of Justice Statistics.

Society for Human Resource Management. (2004, January). *SHRM Workplace Violence Study.* Available: http://www.shrm.org/Research/SurveyFindings/Documents/Workplace%20Violence%20Survey.pdf [February 1, 2014].

Society for Human Resource Management. (2010, January 22). *Background Checking: Conducting Criminal Background Checks.* Available: http://www.shrm.org/Research/SurveyFindings/Articles/Pages/BackgroundCheckCriminalChecks.aspx [February 1, 2014].

Solinger, R., Johnson, P., Raimon, M., Reynolds, T., and Tapia, R. (2010). *Interrupted Life: Experiences of Incarcerated Women in the United States.* Berkeley: University of California Press.

Solomon, L., Flynn, C., Muck, K., and Vertefeuille, J. (2004). Prevalence of HIV, syphilis, hepatitis B, and hepatitis C among entrants to Maryland correctional facilities. *Journal of Urban Health, 81*(1), 25-37.

Soothill, K., and Francis, B. (2009). When do ex-offenders become like non-offenders? *Howard Journal of Criminal Justice, 48*(4), 373-387.

Sorensen, J., and Wallace, D.H. (1999). Prosecutorial discretion in seeking death: An analysis of racial disparity in the pretrial stages of case processing in a Midwestern county. *Justice Quarterly, 16*(3), 559-578.

Spaulding, A.C., Weinbaum, C.M., Lau, D.T., Sterling, R., Seeff, L.B., Margolis, H.S., and Hoofnagle, J.H. (2006). A framework for management of hepatitis C in prisons. *Annals of Internal Medicine, 144*(10), 762-769.

Spaulding, A.C., Seals, R.M., Page, M.J., Brzozowski, A.K., Rhodes, W., and Hammett, T.M. (2009). HIV/AIDS among inmates of and releasees from U.S. correctional facilities, 2006: Declining share of epidemic but persistent public health opportunity. *PLoS One, 4*(11), e7558.

Spaulding, A.C., Seals, R.M., McCallum, V.A., Perez, S.D., Brzozowski, A.K., and Steenland, N.K. (2011). Prisoner survival inside and outside of the institution: Implications for health-care planning. *American Journal of Epidemiology, 173*(5), 479-487.

Spelman, W. (2000). What recent studies do (and don't) tell us about imprisonment and crime. In M. Tonry (Ed.), *Crime and Justice: A Review of Research* (Vol. 27, pp. 419–494). Chicago, IL: University of Chicago Press.

Spelman, W. (1994). *Criminal Incapacitation.* New York: Plenum Press.

Spelman, W. (2009). Crime, cash, and limited options: Explaining the prison boom. *Criminology and Public Policy, 8*(1), 29-77.

Spitzer, S. (1991). [Review of] A Cultural History of the French Revolution. *Contemporary Sociology, 20*(1), 102-103.

Spohn, C. (2009). Race, sex, and pretrial detention in federal court: Indirect effects and cumulative disadvantage. *University of Kansas Law Review, 57*, 879-902.

Spohn, C. (2013). Racial disparities in prosecution, sentencing, and punishment. In S. Bucerius and M. Tonry (Eds.), *The Oxford Handbook of Ethnicity, Crime, and Immigration* (pp. 166-193). New York: Oxford University Press.

Spohn, C., and Holleran, D. (2002). The effect of imprisonment on recidivism rates of felony offenders: A focus on drug offenders. *Criminology, 40*(2), 329-347.

Steadman, H.J., Osher, F.C., Robbins, P.C., Case, B., and Samuels, S. (2009). Prevalence of serious mental illness among jail inmates. *Psychiatric Services, 60*(6), 761-765.

Stein, M., Walker, J., Hazen, A., and Forde, D. (1997). Full and partial posttraumatic stress disorder: Findings from a community survey. *American Journal of Psychiatry, 154*(8), 1114-1119.

Steiner, B. (2009). Assessing static and dynamic influences on inmate violence levels. *Crime & Delinquency, 55*(1), 134-161.

Steiner, B., and Wooldredge, J. (2009). Rethinking the link between institutional crowding and inmate misconduct. *The Prison Journal, 89*(2), 205-233.

Stemen, D., Rengifo, A., and Wilson, J. (2006). *Of Fragmentation and Ferment: The Impact of State Sentencing Policies on Incarceration Rates, 1975-2002.* Washington, DC: National Institute of Justice.

Stephan, J.J. (2004). *State Prison Expenditures, 2001, Special Report.* NCJ 202949. Washington DC: U.S. Department of Justice, Bureau of Justice Statistics.

Stephan, J.J., and Karberg, J. (2003). *Census of State and Federal Correctional Facilities, 2000.* Washington, DC: U.S. Department of Justice, Bureau of Justice Statistics.

Stern, M.F., Greifinger, R.B., and Mellow, J. (2010). Patient safety: Moving the bar in prison health care standards. *American Journal of Public Health, 100*(11), 2103-2110.

Steurer, S., Smith, L., and Tracy, A. (2001). *Three State Recidivism Study.* Lanham, MD: U.S. Department of Education, Office of Correctional Education Association.

Stewart-Winter, T. (Forthcoming). Queer law and order: Sex, criminality, and policing in the age of mass incarceration. *Journal of Urban History.*

Stith, K., and Cabranes, J. (1998). *Fear of Judging: Sentencing Guidelines in the Federal Courts.* Chicago, IL: University of Chicago Press.

Stoll, M.A., Raphael, S., and Holzer, H.J. (2004). Black job applicants and the hiring officer's race. *Industrial and Labor Relations Review, 57*(2), 267-287.

Stolzenberg, L., and D'Alessio, S.J. (1997). "Three strikes and you're out": The impact of California's new mandatory sentencing law on serious crime rates. *Crime & Delinquency, 43*(4), 457-469.

Street, P. (2002). *The Vicious Circle: Race, Prison, Jobs, and Community in Chicago, Illinois, and the Nation.* Chicago, IL: Chicago Urban League, Department of Research and Planning.

Struckman-Johnson, C., and Struckman-Johnson, D. (2006). A comparison of sexual coercion experiences reported by men and women in prison. *Journal of Interpersonal Violence, 21*(12), 1591-1615.

Stuntz, W.J. (2011). *The Collapse of American Criminal Justice.* Cambridge, MA: Harvard University Press.

Subcommittee on Penitentiaries and Corrections. (1978). *The Problem of Prison Overcrowding and its Impact on the Criminal Justice System, United States Senate Committee on the Judiciary, Ninety-Fifth Congress, First Session, December 13, 1977.* Washington, DC: U.S. Government Printing Office.

Substance Abuse and Mental Health Services Administration. (2000). *Substance Abuse Treatment in Adult and Juvenile Correctional Facilities: Findings from the Uniform Facility Data Set 1997 Survey of Correctional Facilities.* Washington, DC: Department of Health and Human Services, Substance Abuse and Mental Health Services Administration.

Sugie, N.F. (2012). Punishment and welfare: Paternal incarceration and families' receipt of public assistance. *Social Forces, 90*(4), 1403-1427.

Sugie, N.F. (2013). *Chilling Effects: Diminished Political Participation among Partners of Ex-Felons.* Available: http://crcw.princeton.edu/workingpapers/WP11-19-FF.pdf [February 1, 2014].

Sugrue, T.J. (1996). *Origins of the Urban Crisis: Race and Inequality in Postwar Detroit.* Princeton, NJ: Princeton University Press.

Sullivan, M.L. (1989). *"Getting Paid": Youth Crime and Work in the Inner City.* Ithaca, NY: Cornell University Press.

Sung, H.E. (2010). Prevalence and risk factors of violence-related and accident-related injuries among state prisoners. *Journal of Correctional Health Care, 16*(3), 178-187.

Sung, H.E. (2012). Nonfatal violence-related and accident-related injuries among jail inmates in the United States. *The Prison Journal, 90*(3), 353-468.

Sutherland, E. (1947). *Principles of Criminology.* Philadelphia, PA: Lipincott.

Sweeten, G., Piquero, A.R., and Steinberg, L. (2013). Age and the explanation of crime, revisited. *Journal of Youth and Adolescence, 42*(6), 921-938.

Sykes, B. (2013, March 12). *Documentation and Methods for Incarceration Rates in the United States, 1972-2010.* Paper prepared for the National Academy of Sciences Committee on the Causes and Consequences of High Rates of Incarceration, Washington, DC.

Sykes, G.M. (1958). *The Society of Captives: A Study of a Maximum Security Prison.* Princeton, NJ: Princeton University Press.

Sylvester, S.F., Reed, J.H., and Nelson, D.O. (1977). *Prison Homicide.* Jamaica, NY: Spectrum Publications.

Tartino, C., and Levy, M. (2007). Density, inmate assaults, and direct supervision jails. *Criminal Justice Policy Review, 18*(4), 395-417.

Task Force on Community Preventive Services. (2007). Recommendation against policies facilitating the transfer of juveniles from juvenile to adult justice systems for the purpose of reducing violence. *American Journal of Preventive Medicine, 32*(4), 5-6.

Taxman, F.S., Henderson, C.E., and Belenko, S. (2009). Organizational context, systems change, and adopting treatment delivery systems in the criminal justice system. *Drug and Alcohol Dependence, 103*(Suppl. 1), S1-S6.

Taxman, F., Pattavina, A., Caudy, M., Byrne, J., and Durso, J. (2013). The empirical basis for the RNR model with an updated RNR conceptual framework. In F.S. Taxman and A. Pattavina (Eds.), *Simulation Strategies to Reduce Recidivism: Risk Need Responsivity (RNR) Modeling in the Criminal Justice System* (Chapter 4). New York: Springer.

Taylor, A. (1961). Social isolation and imprisonment. *Psychiatry, 24*, 373-376.

Tewskbury, R., Ericson, D.J., and Taylor, J.M. (2000). Opportunities lost: The consequences of eliminating Pell grant eligibility for correctional education students. *Journal of Offender Rehabilitation, 31*(1/2), 43-56.

Theoharis, J., and Woodard, K. (2003). *Freedom North: Black Freedom Struggles Outside the South, 1940-1980.* New York: Palgrave Macmillan.

Thernstrom, S., and Thernstrom, A. (1997). *America in Black and White: One Nation, Indivisible.* New York: Simon and Schuster.

Thomas, J.C., Levandowski, B.A., Isler, M.R., Torrone, E., and Wilson, G. (2008). Incarceration and sexually transmitted infections: A neighborhood perspective. *Journal of Urban Health, 85*(1), 90-99.

Thompson, H.A. (2001). *Whose Detroit? Politics, Labor, and Race in a Modern American City.* Ithaca, NY: Cornell University Press.

Thompson, H.A. (2010). Why mass incarceration matters: Rethinking crisis, decline, and transformation in postwar American history. *Journal of American History, 97*(3), 703-734.

Thompson, H.A. (2012). The prison industrial complex: A growth industry in a shrinking economy. *New Labor Forum, 21*(3), 39-47.

Thornberry, T., and Call, J. (1983). Constitutional challenges to prison overcrowding: The scientific evidence of harmful effect. *Hastings Law Journal, 35*(2), 313-351.

Thornicroft, G. (1991). Social deprivation and rates of treated mental disorder: Developing statistical models to predict psychiatric service utilization. *British Journal of Psychiatry, 158*, 475-484.

Toch, H. (1975). *Men in Crisis: Human Breakdowns in Prison.* New York: Aldine.

Toch, H. (1977). *Living in Prison: The Ecology of Survival.* New York: Free Press.

Toch, H. (2001). The future of supermax confinement. *The Prison Journal, 81*(3), 376-388.

Toch, H., and Adams, K. (2002). *Acting Out: Maladaptive Behavior in Confinement.* Washington, DC: American Psychological Association.

Tonry, M. (1994). Proportionality, parsimony, and interchangeability of punishments. In A. Duff and D. Garland (Eds.), *A Reader on Punishment* (pp. 133-160). New York: Oxford University Press.

Tonry, M. (1996). *Sentencing Matters.* New York: Oxford University Press.

Tonry, M. (2001). Punishment policies and patterns in Western countries. In M. Tonry and R.S. Frase (Eds.), *Sentencing and Sanctions in Western Countries* (pp. 3-28). New York: Oxford University Press.

Tonry, M. (2004). *Thinking About Crime: Sense and Sensibility in American Penal Culture.* New York: Oxford University Press.

Tonry, M. (Ed.). (2007a). *Crime, Punishment, and Politics in Comparative Perspective.* Chicago, IL: University of Chicago Press.

Tonry, M. (2007b). Determinants of penal policies. In M. Tonry (Ed.), *Crime, Punishment, and Politics in Comparative Perspective* (pp. 1-48). Chicago, IL: University of Chicago Press.

Tonry, M. (2009a). Explanations of American punishment policies: A national history. *Punishment and Society, 11*(3), 377-394.

Tonry, M. (2009b). The mostly unintended effects of mandatory penalties: Two centuries of consistent findings. In M. Tonry (Ed.), *Crime and Justice: A Review of Research* (Vol. 38, pp. 65-114). Chicago, IL: University of Chicago Press.

Tonry, M. (2011a). *Punishing Race: An American Dilemma Continues.* New York: Oxford University Press.

Tonry, M. (2011b). *Why Punish? How Much?* New York: Oxford University Press.

Tonry, M. (2012, April 26). *Sentencing.* Presentation to the Robina Institute Annual Conference. Crime and Justice in America, 1975-2025, University of Minnesota Law School, Minneapolis.

Tonry, M., and Melewski, M. (2008). The malign effects of drug and crime control policies on black Americans. *Crime and Justice*, 37(1), 1-44.

Torrey, E.F. (1995). Jails and prisons—America's new mental hospitals. *American Journal of Public Health*, 85(12), 1611-1613.

Travis, J. (2000). *But They All Come Back: Rethinking Prisoner Reentry*. Washington, DC: U.S. Department of Justice, National Institute of Justice.

Travis, J. (2005). *But They All Come Back: Facing the Challenges of Prisoner Reentry*. Washington, DC: Urban Institute Press.

Travis, J. (2007). Reflections on the reentry movement. *Federal Sentencing Reporter*, 20(2), 84-87. Available: http://www.jjay.cuny.edu/extra/president_articles/ReflectionsOntheReentryMovement.pdf [July 2013].

Tsai, J., Rosenheck, R.A., Kasprow, W.J., and McGuire, J.F. (2013a). Risk of incarceration and clinical characteristics of incarcerated veterans by race/ethnicity. *Social Psychiatry and Psychiatric Epidemiology*, 48(11), 1777-1786.

Tsai, J., Rosenheck, R.A., Kasprow, J.W., and McGuire, J.F. (2013b). Risk of incarceration and other characteristics of Iraq and Afghanistan era veterans in state and federal prisons. *Psychiatric Services*, 64(1), 36-43.

Turner, R. (1983). Direct, indirect, and moderating effects of social support on psychological distress and associated conditions. In H. Kaplan (Ed.), *Psychosocial Stress: Trends in Theory and Research* (pp. 105-155). New York: Academic Press.

Turner, S., Fain, T., Greenwood, P.W., Chen, E.Y., and Chiesa, J.R. (2001). *National Evaluation of the Violent Offender Incarceration/Truth-in-Sentencing Incentive Grant Program*. Santa Monica, CA: RAND Corporation.

Turney, K., and Wildeman, C. (2012). *Redefining Relationships: Countervailing Consequences of Paternal Incarceration for Parenting*. Fragile Families Working Paper WP12-06-FF. Princeton, NJ: Center for Research on Child Wellbeing.

Tyler, J.H., and Kling, J.R. (2007). Prison-based education and reentry into the mainstream labor market. In S. Bushway, M.A. Stoll, and D.F. Weiman (Eds.), *Barriers to Reentry? The Labor Market for Released Prisoners in Post-Industrial America* (pp. 227-256). New York: Russell Sage Foundation.

Uggen, C. (2000). Work as a turning point in the life course of criminals: A duration model of age, employment, and recidivism. *American Sociological Review*, 65(4), 529-546.

Uggen, C., Manza, J., and Thompson, M. (2006). Citizenship, democracy, and the civic reintegration of criminal offenders. *The ANNALS of the American Academy of Political and Social Sciences*, 605, 281-310.

Uggen, C., Shannon, S., and Manza, J. (2012a, July). *State-Level Estimates of Felon Disenfranchisement in the United States, 2010*. Washington, DC: The Sentencing Project.

Uggen, C., Schnittker, J., Massoglia, M., and Shannon, S. (2012b). *The Contingent Effect of Incarceration on State Health Outcomes*. Paper presented at the American Society of Criminology Meeting, Chicago, IL, November 16.

Ulmer, J.T., Kurlychek, M.C., and Kramer, J.H. (2007). Prosecutorial discretion and the imposition of mandatory minimum sentences. *Justice Quarterly*, 44(4), 427-458.

United Nations. (1990, December 14). *Basic Principles for the Treatment of Prisoners*. Available: http://www.un.org/documents/ga/res/45/a45r111.htm [July 2013].

United Nations. (2005). *Human Rights and Prisons: Manual on Human Rights Training for Prison Officals*. New York and Geneva, Switzerland: Office of the United Nations High Commissioner for Human Rights. Available: http://www.ohchr.org/Documents/Publications/training11en.pdf [July 2013].

United Nations Office on Drugs and Crime. (2006). *Compendium of United Nations Standards and Norms in Crime Prevention and Criminal Justice*. New York: United Nations.

U.S. Census Bureau. (n.d.-a). *Federal, State, and Local Governments.* Available: http://www.
census.gov/govs/ and http://www2.census.gov/pub/outgoing/govs/special60/ [February
1, 2014].

U.S. Census Bureau. (n.d.-b). *U.S. and World Population Clock.* Available: http://www.census.
gov/popclock/ [January 17, 2014].

U.S. Census Bureau. (2012, May 22). *Census Bureau Releases Estimates of Undercount and
Overcount in the 2010 Census.* Available: http://www.census.gov/newsroom/releases/
archives/2010_census/cb12-95.html [February 1, 2014].

U.S. Census Bureau. (2013). *The Diversifying Electorate—Voting Rates by Race and Hispanic
Origin in 2012 (and Other Recent Elections).* Washington, DC: U.S. Department of
Commerce, Economics and Statistics Administration. Available: http://www.census.gov/
prod/2013pubs/p20-568.pdf [February 1, 2014].

U.S. Department of Commerce. (2010). *Statistical Abstract of the United States: 2010.* Washington, DC: Bernan Press.

U.S. Department of Justice. (1992). *The Case for More Incarceration.* Available: https://www.
ncjrs.gov/pdffiles1/Digitization/139583NCJRS.pdf [February 1, 2014].

U.S. National Commission on the Causes and Prevention of Violence. (1969). *To Establish
Justice, To Insure Domestic Tranquility: Final Report.* Transmitted to President Richard
M. Nixon, December 10. Washington, DC: U.S. Government Printing Office.

U.S. Sentencing Commission. (1991). *Special Report to Congress: Mandatory Minimum
Penalties in the Federal Criminal Justice System.* Washington, DC: U.S. Sentencing
Commission.

U.S. Sentencing Commission. (2007, May). *Report to the Congress: Congress and Fed-
eral Sentencing Policy.* Available: http://www.ussc.gov/Legislative_and_Public_Affairs/
Congressional_Testimony_and_Reports/Drug_Topics/200705_RtC_Cocaine_Sentencing_
Policy.pdf [February 1, 2014].

U.S. Sentencing Commission. (2013a). *Preliminary Crack Retroactivity Data Report; Fair Sen-
tencing Act.* Available: http://www.ussc.gov/Research_and_Statistics/Federal_Sentencing_
Statistics/FSA_Amendment/2013-04_USSC_Prelim_Crack_Retro_Data_Report_FSA.pdf
[July 11, 2013].

U.S. Sentencing Commission. (2013b). *Sourcebook of Federal Sentencing Statistics—2012.*
Washington, DC: U.S. Sentencing Commission.

Unnever, J.D. (2013). Race, crime, and public opinion. In S. Bucerius and M. Tonry (Eds.),
The Oxford Handbook of Ethnicity, Crime, and Immigration (pp. 70-106). New York:
Oxford University Press.

Unnever, J.D., Cullen, F.T., and Lero Jonson, C.N. (2008). Race, racism, and support for capital punishment. In M. Tonry (Ed.), *Crime and Justice: A Review of Research* (Vol. 37,
pp. 45-96). Chicago, IL: University of Chicago Press.

Useem, B., and Piehl, A. (2006). Prison buildup and disorder. *Punishment and Society, 8*(1),
87-115.

Useem, B., and Piehl, A.M. (2008). *Prison State: The Challenge of Mass Incarceration.* New
York: Cambridge University Press.

Valdez, A. (2005). Mexican American youth and adult prison gangs in a changing heroin
market. *Journal of Drug Issues, 35*(4), 843-868.

van de Rakt, M., Murray, J., and Nieuwbeerta, P. (2012). The long-term effects of paternal
imprisonment on criminal trajectories of children. *Journal of Research in Crime and
Delinquency, 49*(1), 81-108.

van den Haag, E. (1975). *Punishing Criminals.* New York: Basic Books.

van der Kolk, B. (1987). The role of the group in the origin and resolution of the trauma
response. In B. van der Kolk (Ed.), *Psychological Trauma* (pp. 153-172). Washington,
DC: American Psychiatric Publishing.

Varan, A., Mercer, D., Stein, M., and Spaulding, A. (2012). *State Prison System Surveillance of Hepatitis C Exposure: Limited Data Show Declining Share of U.S. Epidemic.* Paper presented at the Fifth Academic and Health Policy Conference on Correctional Health, Atlanta, GA.

Vaugh, M.S. (1993). Listening to the experts: A national study of correctional administrators' responses to prison overcrowding. *Criminal Justice Review, 18*(1), 12-25.

Vega, W.A., Rodriguez, M.A., and Gruskin, E. (2009). Health disparities in the Latino population. *Epidemiological Review, 31*(1), 99-112.

Vera Institute of Justice. (2010). *Criminal Justice Trends: Key Legislative Changes in Sentencing Policy, 2001-2010.* Available: http://www.vera.org/sites/default/files/resources/downloads/Sentencing-policy-trends-v1alt-v4.pdf [July 2013].

Vieraitis, L., Kovandzic, T., and Marvell, T. (2007). The criminogenic effect of imprisonment: Evidence from state panel data, 1974-2002. *Criminology and Public Policy, 6*(3), 589-622.

Visher, C.A. (1986). The Rand inmate survey: A reanalysis. In National Research Council, A. Blumstein, J. Cohen, J.A. Roth, and C.A. Visher (Eds.), *Criminal Careers and Career Criminals* (Vol. 2, pp. 161-211). Washington, DC: National Academy Press.

Visher, C.A., Winterfield, L., and Coggeshall, M.B. (2005). Ex-offender employment programs and recidivism: A meta-analysis. *Journal of Experimental Criminology, 1*(3), 295-315.

Visher, C.A., Debus-Sherrill, S.A., and Yahner, J. (2011). Employment after prison: A longitudinal study of former prisoners. *Justice Quarterly, 28*(5), 698-718.

Vitiello, M. (1991). Reconsidering rehabilitation. *Tulane Law Review, 65,* 1011-1154.

Vollaard, B. (2012). Preventing crime through selective incapacitation. *The Economic Journal, 123*(567), 262-284.

Volkow, N., Baler, R.D., and Goldstein, R.Z. (2011). Addiction: Pulling at the neural threads of social behaviors. *Neuron, 69*(4), 599-602.

Volkow, N.D., and Li, T-K. (2005). Drugs and alcohol: Treating and preventing abuse, addiction and their medical consequences. *Pharmacology & Therapeutics, 108*(1), 3-17.

Vollaard, B. (2012). Preventing crime through selective incapacitation. *The Economic Journal, 123*(567), 262-284.

von Hirsch, A. (1976). *Doing Justice: The Choice of Punishments.* New York: Hill and Wang.

von Hirsch, A. (1992). Proportionality in the philosophy of punishment. In M. Tonry (Ed.), *Crime and Justice: A Review of Research* (Vol. 16, pp. 55-98). Chicago, IL: University of Chicago Press.

von Hirsch, A. (2007). The "desert" model for sentencing: Its influence, prospects, and alternatives. *Social Research, 74*(2), 413-434.

von Hirsch, A., and Hanrahan, K.J. (1979). *The Question of Parole: Retention, Reform, or Abolition?* Cambridge, MA: Ballinger Publishing.

von Zielbauer, P. (2005, February 27). As health care in jails goes private, 10 days can be a death sentence. *New York Times,* A1, A32.

Wagner, P. (2002, April 22). *Importing Constituents: Prisoners and Political Clout in New York.* Available: http://www.prisonpolicy.org/importing/importing.html [January 21, 2013].

Wagner, P. (2011, July 18). *Wisconsin Sees Dramatic Prison-Based Gerrymandering in New State, County, City Districts.* Available: http://www.prisonersofthecensus.org/news/2011/07/18/wi-districts/ [May 12, 2012].

Wagner, P. (2012, July 15). *Beginning of the End for "Prison-Based Gerrymandering."* Available: http://articles.washingtonpost.com/2012-07-13/opinions/35486912_1_prison-population-census-counts-census-bureau [December 2012].

Wakefield, S., and Uggen, C. (2010). Incarceration and stratification. *Annual Review of Sociology, 36*(1), 387-406.

Wakefield, S., and Wildeman C. (2011). Mass imprisonment and racial disparities in childhood behavioral problems. *Criminology and Public Policy, 10*(3), 793-817.

Wakeman, S.E., McKinney, M.E., and Rich, J.D. (2009). Filling the gap: The importance of Medicaid continuity for former inmates. *Journal of General Internal Medicine, 24*(7), 860-862.

Waldfogel, J. (1994). The effect of criminal conviction on income and the trust "reposed in the workmen." *The Journal of Human Resources, 29*(1), 62-81.

Walker, S.P. (2011). *The Effects of the Incarceration of Fathers on the Health and Wellbeing of Mothers and Children.* Dissertation. College Park: University of Maryland.

Walker, S., Spohn, C., and DeLone, M. (2006). *The Color of Justice: Race, Ethnicity, and Crime in America.* 4th ed. Belmont, CA: Wadsworth.

Waller, M., and Swisher, R.R. (2006). Fathers' risk factors in fragile families: Implications for 'health' relationships and father involvement. *Social Problems, 53*(3), 392-420.

Walmsley, R. (2012). *World Female Imprisonment List.* 2nd ed. London, England: International Centre for Prison Studies.

Walters, G. (2003). Changes in criminal thinking and identity in novice and experienced inmates. *Criminal Justice and Behavior, 30*(4), 399-421.

Walters, R., Callagan, J., and Newman, A. (1963). Effect of solitary confinement on prisoners. *American Journal of Psychiatry, 119*, 771-773.

Wang, E.A., and Green, J. (2010). Incarceration as a key variable in racial disparities of asthma prevalence. *BMC Public Health, 10*, 290.

Wang, E.A., White, M.C., Jamison, R., Goldenson, J., Estes, M., and Tulsky, J.P. (2008). Discharge planning and continuity of health care: Findings from the San Francisco County jail. *American Journal of Public Health, 98*(12), 2182-2184.

Wang, E.A., Pletcher, M., Lin, F., Vittinghoff, E., Kertesz, S.G., Kiefe, C.I., and Bibbins-Domingo, K. (2009). Incarceration, incident hypertension, and access to health care: Findings from the Coronary Artery Risk Development in Young Adults (CARDIA) study. *Archives of Internal Medicine, 169*(7), 687-693.

Wang, E.A., Hong, C.S., Samuels, L., Shavit, S., Sanders, R., and Kushel, M. (2010). Transitions clinic: Creating a community-based model of health care for recently released California prisoners. *Public Health Reports, 125*(2), 171-177.

Ward, D., and Kassenbaum, G. (2009). *Women's Prisons: Sex and Social Structure.* New Brunswick, NJ: Aldine Transaction.

Watstein, R.D. (2009). Out of jail and out of luck: The effect of negligent hiring liability and the criminal record revolution on an ex-offender's employment prospects. *Florida Law Review, 69*, 581-609.

Weaver, V.M. (2007). Frontlash: Race and the development of punitive crime policy. *Studies in American Political Development, 21*(2), 230-265.

Weaver, V., and Lerman, A.E. (2010). Political consequences of the carceral state. *American Political Science Review, 104*(4), 827.

Webster, C.M., Doob, A., and Zimring, F. (2006). Proposition 8 and crime rates in California: The case of the disappearing deterrent. *Criminology and Public Policy, 5*(3), 417-448.

Weiman, D.F., and Weiss, C. (2009). The origins of mass incarceration in New York State: The Rockefeller Drug Laws and the local war on drugs. In S. Raphael and M.A. Stoll (Eds.), *Do Prisons Make Us Safer? The Benefits and Costs of the Prison Boom.* New York: Russell Sage Foundation.

Weisburd, D., Einat, T., and Kowalski, M. (2008). The miracle of the cells: An experimental study of interventions to increase payment of court-ordered financial obligations. *Criminology and Public Policy, 7*(1), 9-36.

Wells, J.B., Minor, K.I., Angel, E., Carter, L., and Cox, M. (2002). *A Study of Gangs and Security Threat Groups in America's Adult Prisons and Jails.* Indianapolis, IN: National Major Gang Task Force.

Western, B. (2002). The impact of incarceration on wage mobility and inequality. *American Sociological Review, 67*(4), 477-498.

Western, B. (2006). *Punishment and Inequality in America.* New York: Russell Sage Foundation.

Western, B. (2008). *From Prison to Work: A Proposal for a National Prisoner Reentry Program.* Washington, DC: The Brookings Institution. Available: http://www.brookings.edu/papers/2008/12_prison_to_work_western.aspx [July 2013].

Western, B., and Beckett, K. (1999). How unregulated is the U.S. labor market? The penal system as a labor market institution. *American Journal of Sociology, 104*(4), 1030-1060.

Western, B., and McLanahan S. (2001). Fathers behind bars: The impact of incarceration on family formation. *Contemporary Perspectives in Family Research, 2*(1), 309-324.

Western, B., and Muller, C. (2013). Mass incarceration, macrosociology and the poor. *The ANNALS of the American Academy of Social and Political Science, 647(1),* 166-189.

Western, B., and Pettit, B. (2005). Black-white wage inequality, employment rates, and incarceration. *American Journal of Sociology, 111,* 553-578.

Western, B., and Pettit, B. (2010). Incarceration & social inequality. *Daedalus, 139*(3), 8-19.

Western, B., and Wildeman, C. (2009). The black family and mass incarceration. *The ANNALS of the American Academy of Social and Political Science, 621,* 221-242.

Western, B., Lopoo, L., and McLanahan, S. (2004). Incarceration and the bonds among parents in fragile families. In M. Patillo, D. Weiman, and B. Western (Eds.), *Imprisoning America: The Social Effects of Mass Incarceration* (pp. 21-45). New York: Russell Sage Foundation.

Western, B., Kleykamp, M., and Rosenfeld, J. (2006). Economic inequality and the rise in U.S. imprisonment. *Social Forces, 84*(4), 2291-2301.

White, I. (2013, July 4). *Prisoners' Voting Rights.* London, UK: House of Commons Library. Available: http://www.parliament.uk/briefing-papers/SN01764.pdf [February 1, 2014].

Whitfield, D. (2008). *Economic Impact of Prisons in Rural Areas: A Literature Review.* Kerry, Ireland: European Services Strategy Unit. Available: http://summerlandbc.files.wordpress.com/2011/03/prison-impact-review-rural-towns.pdf [February 1, 2014].

Whitmer, G. (1980). From hospitals to jails: The fate of California's deinstitutionalized mentally ill. *American Journal of Orthopsychiatry, 50*(1), 65-75.

Wildeman, C. (2009). Parental imprisonment, the prison boom, and the concentration of childhood disadvantage. *Demography, 46*(2), 265-280.

Wildeman, C. (2010). Paternal incarceration and children's physically aggressive behaviors: Evidence from the Fragile Families and Child Wellbeing Study. *Social Forces, 89*(1), 285-309.

Wildeman, C. (2012). Imprisonment and infant mortality. *Social Problems, 59*(2), 228-257.

Wildeman, C. (Forthcoming). Parental incarceration, child homelessness, and the invisible consequences of mass imprisonment. *The ANNALS of the American Academy of Social and Political Science.*

Wildeman, C., and Muller, C. (2012). Mass imprisonment and inequality in health and family life. *Annual Review of Law and Social Science, 8,* 11-30.

Wildeman, C., and Turney, K. (Forthcoming). Positive, negative, or null? The effects of maternal incarceration on children's behavioral problems. *Demography.*

Wildeman, C., and Western, B. (2010). Incarceration in fragile families. *Future of Children, 20*(2), 181-201.

Williams, B., and Abraldes, R. (2010). Growing older: Challenges of prison and reentry for the aging population. In R.B. Greifinger (Ed.), *Public Health Behind Bars: From Prisons to Communities* (pp. 56-72). New York: Springer.

Williams, B.A., Lindquist, K., Sudore, R.L., Strupp, H.M., Willmott, D.J., and Walter, L.C. (2006). Being old and doing time: Functional impairment and adverse experiences of geriatric female prisoners. *Journal of the American Geriatrics Society, 54*(4), 702-707.

Williams, B.A., Stern, M., Mellow, F., Safer, M., and Greifinger, R.B. (2012). Aging in correctional custody: Setting a policy agenda for older prisoner health care. *American Journal of Public Health, 102*(8), 1475-1481.

Wilper, A.P., Woolhandler, S., Boyd, J.W., Lasser, K.E., McCormick, D., Bor, D.H., and Himmelstein, D.U. (2009). The health and health care of U.S. prisoners: Results of a nationwide survey. *American Journal of Public Health, 99*(4), 666-672.

Wilson, D.B., Gallagher, C.A., Coggeshall, M.B., and MacKenzie, D.L. (1999). A quantitative review and description of corrections based education, vocation and work programs. *Corrections Management Quarterly, 3,* 8-18.

Wilson, D.B., Gallagher, C.A., and MacKenzie, D.L. (2000). A meta-analysis of corrections-based education, vocation, and work programs for adult offenders. *Journal of Research in Crime and Delinquency, 37*(4), 347-368.

Wilson, J.P., and Raphael, B. (Eds.). (1993). *International Handbook of Traumatic Stress Syndromes.* New York: Plenum Press.

Wilson, J.Q. (1968). *Varieties of Police Behavior: The Management of Law and Order in Eight Communities.* Cambridge, MA: Harvard University Press.

Wilson, J.Q. (1975). *Thinking about Crime.* New York: Basic Books.

Wilson, W.J. (1987). *The Truly Disadvantaged: The Inner City, the Underclass, and Public Policy.* Chicago, IL: University of Chicago Press.

Wilson, W.J. (1997). *When Work Disappears: The World of the Urban Poor.* New York: Alfred A. Knopf.

Wodtke, G.T., Harding, D.J., and Elwert, F. (2011). Neighborhood effects in temporal perspective: The impact of long-term exposure to concentrated disadvantage on high school graduation. *American Sociological Review, 76*(5), 713-736.

Woldoff, R.A., and Washington, H.M. (2008). Arrested contact: The criminal justice system, race, and father engagement. *The Prison Journal, 88*(2), 179-206.

Wolff, N., and Jing, S. (2009). Contextualization of physical and sexual assault in male prisons: Incidents and their aftermath. *Journal of Correctional Health Care, 15*(1), 58-77.

Wolff, N., Blitz, C., and Shi, J. (2007). Rates of sexual victimization in prison for inmates with and without mental disorders. *Psychiatric Services, 58*(8), 1087-1094.

Wool, J. (2010). Litigating for better medical care. In R.B. Greifinger (Ed.), *Public Health Behind Bars: From Prisons to Communities* (pp. 25-41). New York: Springer.

Wooldredge, J. (1999). Inmate experiences and psychological well-being. *Criminal Justice and Behavior, 26*(2), 235-250.

World Health Organization. (2007). *Health in Prisons: A WHO Guide to the Essentials in Prison Health.* Available: http://www.euro.who.int/__data/assets/pdf_file/0009/99018/E90174.pdf [July 2013].

Wright, K.N. (2005). Designing a national performance measurement system. *The Prison Journal, 85*(3), 368-393.

Wright, R. (2002). Counting the cost of sentencing in North Carolina, 1980-2000. In M. Tonry (Ed.), *Crime and Justice: A Review of Research* (Vol. 29, pp. 39-112). Chicago, IL: University of Chicago Press.

Yoon, J. (2011). Effect of increased private share of inpatient psychiatric resources on jail population growth: Evidence from the United States. *Social Science and Medicine, 72*(4), 447-455.

Young, A. (2003). *The Minds of Marginalized Black Men: Making Sense of Mobility, Opportunity, and Future Life Chances*. Princeton, NJ: Princeton University Press.

Zaller, N.D., Holmes, L., Dyl, A.C., Mitty, J.A., Beckwith, C.G., Flanigan, T.P., and Rich, J.D. (2008). Linkage to treatment and supportive services among HIV-positive ex-offenders in Project Bridge. *Journal of Health Care for the Poor and Underserved, 19*(2), 522-531.

Zalman, M. (1987). Sentencing in a free society: The failure of the President's Crime Commission to influence sentencing policy. *Justice Quarterly, 4*(4), 545-569.

Zamble, E. (1992). Behavior and adaptation in longterm prison inmates: Descriptive longitudinal results. *Criminal Justice and Behavior, 19*(4), 409-425.

Zatz, M. (1987). The changing forms of racial/ethnic biases in sentencing. *Journal of Research in Crime and Delinquency, 25*, 69-92.

Zeisel, H., and Diamond, S.S. (1977). Search for sentencing equity: Sentence review in Massachusetts and Connecticut. *American Bar Foundation Research Journal, 2*(4), 881, 883-940.

Zimring, F.E., Hawkins, G., and Kamin, S. (2001). *Punishment and Democracy: Three Strikes and You're Out in California*. New York: Oxford University Press.

Zinger, I., Wichmann, C., and Andrews, D.A. (2001). The psychological effects of 60 days in administrative segregation. *Canadian Journal of Criminology, 43*(1), 47-88.

Zlotnick, C. (1997). Posttraumatic stress disorder (PTSD), PTSD comorbidity, and childhood abuse among incarcerated women. *Journal of Nervous and Mental Disease, 185*(12), 761-763.

Appendix A

Supplementary Statement by Ricardo H. Hinojosa

I respect the views of the members of the study committee who have worked hard over the last 2 years to forge a consensus based on their review of the body of published scholarly research regarding the causes and consequences of the rise of incarceration in the United States. Although I have not personally engaged in academic research, my expertise and views on these matters are based on 30 years as a federal district judge sentencing thousands of individuals, reviewing their presentence reports, and presiding over their sentencing hearings as well as having served for more than 10 years on the United States Sentencing Commission. My views are not meant to represent views of the federal judiciary nor the United States Sentencing Commission.

Based on my experience I have concerns about certain research findings, statements and conclusions in the report. My experience leads me to question statements and conclusions regarding the effect of incarceration rates on crime prevention (e.g., Chapter 13, p. 339, lines 29-31, which also appear in other parts of the report) and the underlying causes of high incarceration rates. My experience leads me to place less emphasis on racial and political factors as causes of the increase of incarceration rates (e.g., Chapter 4, p. 108, lines 29-32; p. 113, lines 33-36; p. 115, lines 21-34; p. 116, lines 1-9; p. 120, lines 18-25, which also appear in other parts of the report) and more emphasis on high crime rates and socioeconomic factors such as school dropout rates as factors contributing to policies that increased incarceration. However, I do not write separately on the matters in this report about which I may have concerns because I concur with the recommendations in this report, which are important, ripe for consideration and need to be addressed by the public and the policy makers.

Appendix B

Data Sources

This appendix summarizes and critiques major sources of descriptive statistics used in this report and by many scholars of incarceration.

HISTORICAL AND COMPARATIVE INCARCERATION RATES

The adult incarcerated population is generally counted as the number of people held in jails and prisons. Prison population counts have been reported by the Bureau of Justice Statistics (BJS) in a continuous time series dating back to 1925. Counts of the jail population are available in a continuous time series from 1980, although earlier years are available periodically through special BJS collections and in the U.S. census. The scale of a penal system is usually measured by an incarceration rate that expresses the number incarcerated per 100,000 of the resident population. The annual rates are usually formed with census population counts and intercensus estimates.

The rate of state and federal imprisonment 1925-2012 (Figure 2-1 in Chapter 2) was taken from Maguire (n.d., Table 6.28.2012). Data for jail incarceration 1980-2011 were taken from Maguire (n.d., Table 6.1.2011). Figures for 2012 are from Glaze and Herberman (2013). Data on jail incarceration 1972-1979 were taken from Hindelang et al. (1977, p. 632) and Parisi et al. (1979). Missing years were interpolated. International incarceration rates in Aebi and Delgrande (2013) for European countries and Walmsley (2012) for Australia, Canada, and New Zealand provided data and methodologies for comparative considerations. Figure 2-2 on international comparisons was created with most recent rates available from International Centre for Prison Studies (2013).

Growth in federal and state prison populations and local jail populations 1972-2010 are for men and women under age 65. These data were compiled by Bryan Sykes, University of Washington, Seattle, and are described below.

Data on counts of the total correctional population and its constituent prison, jail, parole, and probation populations (Figure 2-4 in Chapter 2) were taken from Maguire (n.d., Table 6.1.2011). Data for the 1972-1979 period were taken from the *Sourcebook of Criminal Justice Statistics* (1982).

Data on state imprisonment rates 2000-2010 are for sentenced prisoners under the jurisdiction of state correctional authorities (Figure 2-4) and were taken from Maguire (n.d., Table 6.28.2011). Data for 1972 are from the *Sourcebook of Criminal Justice Statistics* (1982, p. 471).

DATA AND METHODS FOR DISAGGREGATED INCARCERATION RATES

Data for incarceration by sex, race, ethnicity, age, and education were constructed by Bryan Sykes and Becky Pettit at the University of Washington, Seattle. Estimates of persons incarcerated by sex, race, age, and education are for the period 1972-2010. Unlike many BJS series, microdata from prison and jail surveys of inmates were used to obtain estimates of the prison and jail populations for non-Hispanic blacks, non-Hispanic whites, and Hispanics. To obtain these estimates, Sykes and Pettit used aggregated data on penal populations from BJS. Aggregated data for the entire time series are available by facility type, not for specific sex, race/ethnicity, age, and education groups. Data on inmate totals come from the *Sourcebook of Criminal Justice Statistics Online.*[1] Data for federal and state inmates 1982-1984 and 1986-1989 were provided by BJS. Jail counts are for the last business day in June; state and federal prison counts are for December 31 of the year.

Following methods outlined in Pettit and Western (2004), Western (2006), and Pettit (2012), microdata from BJS correctional surveys were used to estimate proportions of inmates within sex, racial/ethnic, age, and education groups. The Survey of Inmates of Local Jails (1972, 1978, 1983, 1989, 1996, 2002), the Survey of Inmates of State Correctional Facilities (1974, 1979, 1986, 1991, 1997, 2004), and the Survey of Inmates of Federal Correctional Facilities (1991, 1997, 2004) were used to interpolate

---

[1]See http://www.albany.edu/sourcebook/pdf/t612010.pdf [August 2013].

between survey years (within facility type).[2] Estimates for state inmates prior to 1974 were assumed to follow the distributions of the 1974 Survey of Inmates of State Correctional Facilities, while estimates for federal inmates prior to 1991 were assumed to follow the distributions of the 1991 Survey of Inmates of Federal Correctional Facilities. Estimates for inmates after the last survey year (2002 Survey of Inmates of Local Jails, 2004 Survey of Inmates of State Correctional Facilities, and 2004 Survey of Inmates of Federal Correctional Facilities) were calculated based on the demographic distributions of respondents in the last survey. These proportions were applied to aggregated population counts of inmates by facility type to obtain the demographic distributions of prison and jail inmates.

The U.S. civilian population was obtained from the weighted March Current Population Survey (CPS) for 1972-2010.[3] Because the CPS is a household-based, noninstitutional sample, we constructed a series of civilian incarceration rates in which the weighted population totals from the March CPS were adjusted to include inmate totals from BJS, as outlined in Pettit (2012) and Pettit et al. (2009). This analysis reports civilian incarceration rates of men and women by race and educational attainment for different age intervals. Race is coded as non-Hispanic white, non-Hispanic black, Hispanic, and non-Hispanic other. Educational attainment was measured as less than high school, high school, and some college education. Age was disaggregated into 5-year age groups except for those aged 18-19. However, the grouped table of the analysis collapses these age categories into 18-19, 20-39, and 40-64 to minimize small cell counts and extreme variability for demographic groups in which incarceration is less prevalent.

---

[2]For more information on BJS surveys of correctional institutions, see http://www.bjs. gov/index.cfm?ty=dcdetail&iid=274; http://www.bjs.gov/index.cfm?ty=dcdetail&iid=275; and http://www.bjs.gov/index.cfm?ty=dcdetail&iid=273 [August 2013].

[3]These data are publicly available from the Minnesota Population Center (https://cps.ipums. org/cps/ [August 2013].

Appendix C

Incarceration in the United States: A Research Agenda

This report on the causes and consequences of high rates of incarceration identifies a variety of areas in which research is notably missing or critically inconclusive. The report outlines a research agenda in three parts—(1) on the experience of being incarcerated and its effects, (2) on alternative sentence policies, and (3) on the impact of incarceration on communities. This appendix elaborates on this research agenda, describing several of the key research priorities in greater detail.

Much of the research on the consequences of incarceration is directed at what statisticians call the identification of causal effects—isolating independent changes in incarceration and studying how outcomes vary as a result. Although researchers have focused on the challenge of identification, our review suggests that many of the main research priorities for the field are of a more fundamental kind, of data and measurement and of conceptualization.

We describe four main research priorities that follow from our detailed review of the causes and consequences of incarceration: (1) research on the effects of incarceration should specify more precisely the treatment whose effect is being estimated; (2) research should examine the heterogeneity of incarceration effects across individuals and operating at different levels; (3) causal questions are only a subset of significant research questions, and researchers should also study the whole structure of conditions of disadvantage that are correlated with incarceration; and (4) significant data limitations currently restrict the full development of the research program on incarceration, and new data are needed on conditions of confinement, on sentencing, and on the course people follow as they move through the criminal justice system.

SPECIFYING THE TREATMENT

A number of chapters of this report note in different ways that research on "the effects of incarceration" is sometimes poorly specified from policy and scientific perspectives. Research on causal effects typically contrasts a group receiving a "treatment" with a comparison or "control" group. Average differences for some outcome of interest between the treatment and control groups provide an estimate of the causal effect of the treatment, provided the two groups are identical in expectation in all relevant respects except for their assignment to the treatment or control group (Morgan and Winship, 2007, review methods and concepts). Scientific debates often surround whether treatment and control groups are identical in all relevant respects and what those respects might be.

In research on the effects of incarceration, the content of the treatment ("incarceration") and the content of the control ("not incarceration") often are not precisely specified and may not be informative for policy (Nagin et al., 2009). The effects we associate with incarceration and review in this report—from specific deterrence, through behavioral reform, to diminished job skills and psychological trauma—are linked not only to the deprivation of liberty but also to the conditions of penal confinement. The effects of incarceration may vary greatly depending on conditions of overcrowding, the quality of health and treatment services, order and safety in specific facilities, exposure to administrative segregation, and so on. This report, particularly in Chapter 6, shows that the conditions of penal confinement vary enormously across jurisdictions, as well as across facilities within jurisdictions. Still, there is very little research in any domain—on recidivism, health, employment, families—that measures the actual content of the "treatment" of incarceration and then relates it to the large number of post-incarceration outcomes of scientific and policy interest.

Just as the conditions of confinement typically remain unspecified, the conditions faced by the comparison group remain undescribed in most research. Comparison groups may, for example, serve less time, be under community supervision, participate in diversion, or just be free and unsupervised in the community. Each of these control conditions implies a different kind of contrast with the treatment condition of incarceration.

In studying the effects of incarceration, future research should attempt to specify the treatment and control conditions more systematically. Researchers could usefully study the effects of specific conditions of incarceration in contrast to some specific community alternative. The contrast in outcomes from conditions of confinement and a clearly defined community alternative would serve as a test for theories describing how incarceration influences later outcomes. A contrast between well-defined conditions of confinement and a well-defined community alternative also would have the advantage of enabling clear interpretation of causal estimates. Such estimates can provide precise guidance to policy makers.

If incarcerated study subjects are drawn from a range of facilities, then the research design should ideally describe the variety of institutional conditions from which the treatment group is drawn. If study subjects are drawn from a variety of security levels, for example, the treatment could be interpreted as an average over those conditions. The same point applies to the control conditions. The design should ideally specify the range of conditions obtaining for the control group. Often in program evaluation, control group subjects may seek programs or treatment outside the experiment. This kind of extra-experimental program participation should be reflected in the interpretation of treatment effects. Well-designed evaluations will assign subjects to alternative, lower-dose program conditions. In these cases, the contrast that defines the treatment effect is clearly specified.

For example, the evaluation of the Center for Employment Opportunity's (CEO) transitional jobs programs for New York parolees assigned control group subjects to a jobs resource room. In the control condition, parolees searched online jobs databases with program staff, whereas members of the treatment group worked in subsidized employment (Redcross et al., 2009). In the CEO evaluation, control group subjects were clearly occupied in alternative program activities, although even in this case the control group may have been contaminated by extracurricular program participation outside of the experiment. If participation in these extra-experimental programs has effects, this will alter the baseline against which the tested program is assessed. Improvements in baseline measurement of treatments and controls may be achieved with surveys of all experimental subjects before assignment to program conditions (see, e.g., Brock et al., 1997).

Research on deterrence and incapacitation also indicates the importance of specifying the treatment precisely. The strongest evidence on the effects of incarceration on crime concern the small deterrent effect of long sentences. As indicated in Chapter 5, research on the "total effect" of incarceration on crime addresses a question that is poorly specified from a scientific and policy viewpoint. Changes in the incarceration rate can be obtained with a wide variety of policies affecting, say, the initial decision to incarcerate, the length of sentences, and parole release. Most important, different people are being incarcerated under each policy alternative. Thus each policy change, even if yielding an identical change in the rate of incarceration, has different implications for deterrence and incapacitation. Moreover, policy makers do not control the incarceration rate itself but instead control policies defining the use of incarceration in contrast to noncustodial alternatives. Future research should thus study the effects of specific sentencing policies. Policies defining sentence length and the certainty of incarceration given an arrest emerged as strong research priorities in our review of the work on deterrence and incapacitation.

Analysis of a habitual offender enhancement in the Netherlands by Vollaard (2012) offers a good example of analysis of a specific policy measure, with a clearly defined comparison group. The habitual offender enhancement was introduced at different times in different localities, and offending rates were compared before and after its adoption. Three things stand out in the Vollaard study: (1) the analysis estimates the effect of a discrete change in sentencing policy; (2) the analysis examines how the policy effect evolves over time (it declines); and (3) the analysis offers a detailed account of the policy's implementation, describing how the courts applied it and the kinds of offenses being prosecuted (mostly those committed by indigent heroin addicts). By focusing on a specific policy intervention and describing its implementation, Vollaard (2012) offers a sharp definition of the treatment effect as it actually came to operate at the research site.

THE HETEROGENEITY OF INCARCERATION EFFECTS

The "effect of incarceration" is a coarsely defined quantity because the conditions of incarceration vary greatly, and the policies that yield marginal increments in incarceration also show significant variation. Our review of the research indicated further that evidence for the effects of incarceration may be weak because the effects are likely to vary significantly across individuals, social contexts, and units of analysis.

Studying the heterogeneity of the effects of incarceration may be one way of addressing the disparity in results reported in the research literature and the larger debate over incarceration's positive and negative effects. Incarceration may successfully deter crime, but perhaps only in a subset of the population. Similarly, incarceration may diminish human capital and reduce employment opportunities, but only for certain kinds of people.

Evidence for the heterogeneity of incarceration effects is abundant. For example, experimental audit studies of employers suggest that the stigma of a criminal record is greater for an African American job seeker with a criminal record than for a white job seeker with a criminal record (Pager, 2007; Pager and Quillian, 2005). Another line of research suggests that high-status respondents are more likely than low-status respondents to be deterred by public punishments (Nagin, 1998, 2013). In both cases, the effects of criminal stigma vary in different ways across population. In ethnographic research, Edin and colleagues (2006) find that incarceration is generally destabilizing for poor families with children, although for some, incarceration of a violent spouse can help restore order to the household.

In some cases, the authors find, incarceration offers a period of reflection in which people can decide to desist permanently from crime.

In these examples, the effect of incarceration appears to vary with different individual-level characteristics and dispositions. Other research suggests that incarceration may also vary across social contexts. For example, the negative effects of incarceration on child well-being may depend on whether fathers are resident in the household. Where incarceration is associated with dissolution of the household, its negative economic effects for children are greater (Geller et al., 2012). In general, the negative effects of incarceration may be greater where those going to prison are embedded in the prosocial roles of worker and resident father.

These examples do not suggest any systematic account of the heterogeneity of the effects of incarceration, but they do suggest that incarceration may vary greatly in its effects. Currently, there is little understanding of whether this variation is systematic, perhaps unfolding in similar ways in different domains.

In contrast with the usual ideas about the heterogeneity of causal effects, incarceration may have different effects for different social units. The effects of incarceration on individuals, for example, may be quite different from the effects on families or neighborhoods. The idea that incarceration has aggregate-level effects, beyond the individuals incarcerated, turns on external effects whereby those who have not been incarcerated are somehow affected by the incarceration of others. It is easy to think about these external effects in the case of families. The incarceration of a husband for domestic violence may make a family safer through the husband's incapacitation. At the community level, Clear (2007) argues that the population turnover associated with incarceration may be criminogenic for the wider neighborhood, as the informal social ties that would otherwise sustain public safety are undermined. In labor markets or marriage markets with high incarceration rates, employers and prospective spouses may assume that potential employees or spouses have previously been incarcerated even when they have not, with the effect of reducing overall rates of employment or marriage. As discussed in Chapter 10, compelling empirical tests are difficult to design, but these kinds of equilibrium effects are seldom studied and go beyond a simple summation of the individual-level effects of incarceration.

Some outcomes gain their social significance through their prevalence in a group or community. For example, the legitimacy of criminal justice authorities and the level of public health are viewed as aggregate-level phenomena because they describe environments or social contexts that may themselves have individual-level effects.

In the context of a steep socioeconomic disparity in incarceration, the effects of high rates of incarceration on institutional legitimacy appear to be a strong research priority. The legitimacy of criminal justice authority is not just the sum of individual beliefs about prison and police. Institutional legitimacy suggests a set of beliefs and values that are shared within a community. The causal force of legitimacy depends on the prevalence of shared beliefs about the propriety of criminal justice authorities. To the extent that community residents feel that criminal justice authorities are legitimate, they may feel more compelled to comply with directions, actively assist in investigations, and desist from crime. Legitimacy produces these behavioral responses not only because of individual beliefs but also because individuals act out social expectations accompanying the role of being a community member. Although there is a large literature on criminal justice legitimacy, particularly police legitimacy, the level of community-wide support for criminal justice authorities often is inferred from individual-level opinions and attitudes (Unnever, 2013). In a context of high incarceration rates that are spatially concentrated, the effects of incarceration on institutional legitimacy may be more complex than the simple summation of individual beliefs.

Like legitimacy, public health has collective significance, providing a social context for individual effects. Given clear evidence of the high rates of infectious disease in the incarcerated population and the individual health effects of incarceration, understanding the effects of incarceration on public health in the aggregate is a key research priority. An example of this type of research is provided by Johnson and Raphael (2009), who examine the impact of incarceration on racial disparities in AIDS infection. Their analysis predicts the age- and race-specific rate of AIDS in each state as a function of the incarceration rate. The key conceptual contribution of this research design involves predicting the prevalence of AIDS among women from the incarceration rate of men. The authors find that nearly all the black-white disparity in AIDS among women is related to the racial disparity in incarceration among men. Although only a first contribution to a larger research program on the public health effects of high rates of incarceration, this analysis underlines the importance of studying aggregate-level effects whereby those beyond the penal system are nevertheless affected by it.

BEYOND CAUSALITY

Much of the discussion of future priorities for research on high rates of incarceration has focused on questions about causal effects. Research showing the close correlation among incarceration, crime, race, poverty, addiction, mental illness, family instability, neighborhood poverty, and residential segregation is noted throughout this report. The correlation of incarceration with an array of other measures of social and economic marginality has been observed at the individual level, across families, at the level of neighborhoods and states, and over time.

These correlations are so dense, with all factors apparently being endogenous, that it is difficult or impossible to draw causal linkages among them. What may be more significant here is simply the fact of high intercorrelation. The various correlates of disadvantage cluster in a complex or syndrome that should be studied in its own right. The research priority may shift from assigning causal priority to describing how this complex has arisen and changed over time. In that process, incarceration plays a key role. Something in the nature of the relationship among the state and society, race relations, and social inequality has been transformed by the substantial growth in prison and jail populations. Whatever its effects, life in poor, high-crime communities now is also characterized by very high levels of criminal justice supervision in addition to well-documented social problems of unemployment, housing insecurity, nonmarital births, family complexity, high school dropouts, and so on.

Under conditions of high incarceration rates, the structure of correlation among incarceration, street crime, and social and economic disadvantage emerges as an important social fact. Sampson (2012) makes similar arguments about the persistence of segregation and poverty in Chicago neighborhoods. European students of "social exclusion" and "multiple disadvantage" also emphasize the highly correlated character of the many dimensions of social inequality (see Duncan and Corner, 2012; Papadopoulos and Tsakloglou, 2006).

At least three kinds of research questions emerge from this perspective. First, at a purely descriptive level, what kinds of social conditions are most closely correlated with incarceration, and how does the structure of these correlations vary across time and space? Answering this question would help in identifying and describing the cluster of social conditions in which prison time is now commonplace.

Second, how can variation in the pattern of correlations be described in a way that would be useful for analysis? Research in other fields has viewed this as a problem of scale construction, in which a variety of factors are combined to measure an underlying construct. However, this approach does not quite capture the idea that it is not a score on a scale but the strength of association of incarceration with other variables that may be consequential for social science and for policy. Motivation for examining the pattern of correlation—rather than trying to isolate the effects of individual factors—might derive from both a high level of interaction operating with incarceration and its correlates and a high level of feedback or endogeneity operating among the factors. In this context, efforts to assess individual causal effects will result in misspecification. Studying the cluster of conditions and variations in the cluster across time and space emerges as an important research priority.

Third, what social dynamics are associated with those times and places in which incarceration is closely correlated with a variety of other markers of social and economic disadvantage? Research on urban ecology and inequality and on social exclusion in poor European communities argues that each factor, in a setting of clustered disadvantages, may reduce opportunity and social mobility only a little, but a whole cluster of disadvantages may have a much larger impact. Thus, the reproduction of social inequality and persistent poverty results not only from historic levels of poverty but also from the myriad social conditions with which poverty is correlated. Such contexts of strongly correlated social and economic disadvantage are characterized by "hysteresis" in which prevailing social conditions become self-sustaining.

NEW DATA COLLECTION

The research agenda described here indicates the importance of significant new data collection. First, new research will need data on the conditions of confinement. Second, new research will need longitudinal data that include observations before and after incarceration. Third, new research will require better measurement of sentencing policy at the city, state, and national levels.

Conditions of Confinement

In his classic ethnography, Sykes (1958) precisely detailed nearly every aspect of the conditions of confinement in a maximum security prison in New Jersey, documenting everything from how the physical space of the prison was laid out, to the rigid schedule inmates kept, to how men dealt with the myriad deprivations of prison life, to the infractions that would get them put in the hole. In so doing, Sykes provided a compelling portrait of how even within the same prison, the conditions of confinement could vary dramatically, with often important implications for prisoners not only during their confinement but also after their release.

Unfortunately, existing data do not provide even the most basic information regarding the conditions of confinement faced by prisoners. Existing data do not, for instance, make it possible to differentiate prison incarcerations from jail incarcerations. In a similar vein, the data provide little to no insight into the level of overcrowding in facilities, the programming available (ranging from educational, to vocational, to anger management, to drug treatment), or any other characteristics of the institutions. To illustrate this point, consider two of the best longitudinal data sets available for exploring the consequences of incarceration and two studies using some of the best data collected within prisons.

To start with the within-prison data, Haney (2003) and Lerman (2009b) both use data on prisons in California to show how sensory deprivation and security level shape mental health and criminal propensities. These are both compelling studies, to be sure, but the fact that they are so exemplary in this field suggests just how limited the available data are.

Turning to existing longitudinal data, both the National Longitudinal Survey of Youth 1979 (NLSY79) and the Fragile Families and Child Wellbeing Study (FFCW) have been used for some of the most highly cited studies on the consequences of incarceration (e.g., Lopoo and Western, 2005; Western, 2002; Wildeman, 2010). Yet neither of these sources includes a single question on the conditions of confinement, making it impossible to tell what component of the incarceration experience is driving any effects or, on an even more basic level, whether these effects are driven by prison or jail incarceration. For example, it is nearly impossible to analyze variation in incarceration outcomes by type of criminal conviction (beyond broad violent versus nonviolent distinctions available in only a few data sets), security level of the confinement institution, or reentry services utilized after release. Such variability is of tremendous theoretical and practical importance, but rigorous analysis of these contextual factors currently remains beyond the reach of social scientists.

Because information is lacking on the conditions of confinement, therefore, it remains impossible to know how the conditions of confinement could be varied to minimize the consequences of incarceration (and reduce recidivism rates), with or without sizable decreases in incarceration.

Longitudinal Data

The preceding sections have cited a series of methods that have been underused in the study of the consequences of incarceration. But what are the data demands for these methods? The data demands for many of these methods—especially those that require some source of exogenous variation in incarceration—are quite steep. With existing longitudinal data, one needs to design a clever experiment or rely on a natural experiment.

But what are the data demands for some of the methods that rely on longitudinal data? To consider one of the simpler—and more often utilized—methods, running a fixed effects model requires that the data include measures both before and after the incarceration experience. With an event such as incarceration, where the effects of current and prior incarceration likely differ and are both of interest, this requires a minimum of three data points—although many more data points would be better because the effects of ever having been incarcerated might change over time. To again consider the same two excellent longitudinal data sets, what measures of incarceration are available in the NLSY79 and the FFCW? Twenty-four waves of the NLSY79 are currently available, all of which include information on current incarceration. Because of the large number of waves of data, analysts using these data can also construct a measure of prior incarceration, although this measure likely captures only prior prison incarcerations, not jail incarcerations.

The FFCW data, which are in many ways the broadly representative data set that includes the second-best measures of incarceration, illustrates just how badly needed are repeated measures of incarceration. As of this writing, the FFCW had five waves of data (at the child's birth and around ages 1, 3, 5, and 9), with an additional wave of data (around age 15) currently in the field. So what incarceration measures do these data include? At birth and age 1, the measures of paternal incarceration are very limited, with only fathers currently incarcerated being counted with confidence as having been incarcerated since the child's birth. Between ages 1 and 3, the measures of paternal incarceration improve markedly, with some information not only on whether the father is currently incarcerated but also on whether he was incarcerated since the last interview, which makes it possible to easily run a fixed effects model (or other fairly rigorous models). The measures of paternal incarceration available at age 5 are the strongest and enable use of a range of modeling strategies. Yet by age 9, the vast majority of fathers currently incarcerated were not followed into the prison, leading to much lost information on them. So the second-best data set traditionally used to consider this topic has five waves of data, one of which contains excellent incarceration data (age 5), three of which contain incarceration data that are good but not great (ages 1, 3, and 9), and one of which contains essentially no incarceration data. That this is the data set with the second-best incarceration data suggests how badly more data are needed.

Although the NLSY79 likely provides a much better measure of prison incarceration than jail incarceration, it provides no information on incarcerations occurring between waves and can be used only to consider a small range of outcomes for adult men (labor market outcomes, marriage and divorce, and health). Still, the NLSY79 provides an ideal model for how to measure incarceration consistently over a long survey. To grasp the consequences of incarceration for individuals and society more fully, future data must contain more complete, repeated measures not only of incarceration but also of crime, arrest, conviction, probation, and parole.

Sentencing Policy

Finally, more information on specific sentencing policies and practices at the national, state, and jurisdictional levels are needed to understand the role of policy in shaping incarceration rates, recidivism risks, and inequality in both. No reliable national database tracking the sanction regime of each of the 50 states and the federal government is available (National Research Council, 2012). By sanction regime is meant the sanctions that are legally available for the punishment of various crimes, as well as measurements of the actual administration of the legally available options (e.g., sentence length, time served). Without such data, it is impossible to make systematic cross-state comparisons of sentencing practices and their potential outcomes (e.g., effects on crime rates). The sanction regime also extends beyond the penal code prescribing the duration of sentences.

Case studies indicate the many dimensions of criminal sanction. For example, some jurisdictions have adopted policies and enforcement measures that restrict the movement of formerly incarcerated men and women, limiting their access to public spaces (e.g., Beckett and Herbert, 2011) and creating novel risks for rearrest. This example also illustrates how sentencing policy shapes not only the kind of punishment received but also who receives it. If sanctions are attached to presence in certain urban areas, or similarly if sentence enhancements are associated with urban density (close to a school zone, for example), then minority populations who are predominantly urban residents may be at great risk of sanction. If sentence enhancements are added to third-time felonies, then longer sentences will be served by older people with relatively long criminal histories.

Chapter 3 addresses the potential slippage between penal policies and their implementation in the courts. While analysis of the implementation of specific sentencing policies is a key supplement to understanding policy effects, opportunities for analysis across jurisdictions and over time would nevertheless be important for extending understanding of the crime and other social effects of the precise levers driving variation in incarceration rates.

Appendix D

Biographical Sketches of Committee Members

JEREMY TRAVIS (*Chair*) is president of John Jay College of Criminal Justice. Prior to his appointment in 2004, Mr. Travis served 4 years as a senior fellow affiliated with the Justice Policy Center at the Urban Institute in Washington, DC, where he launched a national research program focused on prisoner reentry into society. From 1994 to 2000, he directed the National Institute of Justice, the research arm of the U.S. Department of Justice. He was deputy commissioner for legal matters for the New York City Police Department (NYPD) from 1990 to 1994, chief counsel to the U.S. House Judiciary Subcommittee on Criminal Justice in 1990, special advisor to New York City Mayor Edward I. Koch from 1986 to 1989, and special counsel to the police commissioner of the NYPD from 1984 to 1986. Before joining city government, he served as law clerk to then-U.S. Court of Appeals Judge Ruth Bader Ginsburg, currently a member of the U.S. Supreme Court. He was executive director of the New York City Criminal Justice Agency from 1977 to 1979 and served 6 years at the Vera Institute of Justice. Mr. Travis has taught courses on criminal justice, public policy, history, and law at Yale College, New York University Wagner Graduate School of Public Service, New York Law School, The George Washington University, and John Jay College of Criminal Justice. He is the author of *But They All Come Back: Facing the Challenges of Prisoner Reentry* (Urban Institute Press, 2005), co-editor (with Christy Visher) of *Prisoner Reentry and Crime in America* (Cambridge University Press, 2005), and co-editor (with Michelle Waul) of *Prisoners Once Removed: The Impact of Incarceration and Reentry on Children, Families, and Communities* (Urban Institute Press, 2003). He is chair of the Committee on Law and Justice of the National Research Council and a member of the Board of Trustees of the Urban Institute. He earned a J.D., cum laude, from the New York University School of Law; an M.P.A. from the New York University Wagner Graduate School of Public Service; and a B.A., cum laude, in American studies from Yale College.

BRUCE WESTERN (*Vice Chair*) is professor of sociology, the Daniel and Florence Guggenheim professor of criminal justice policy and management and the director of the Malcolm Wiener Center for Social Policy at Harvard University. Before going to Harvard, Dr. Western was a member of the Sociology Department at Princeton University from 1993 to 2007. He has edited or authored several books including *Between Class and Market: Postwar Unionization in the Capitalist Democracies* (1997), *Imprisoning America: The Social Effects of Mass Incarceration* (edited with Mary Patillo and David Weiman, 2004), and *The Great Recession* (edited with David Grusky and Christopher Wimer 2011). The 2006 book, *Punishment and Inequality in America*, examines the causes, scope, and consequences of the growth in incarceration rates in the United States from the 1970s to the 2000s. The book won the Albert J. Reiss Award for distinguished scholarly publication of the Crime, Law, and Deviance Section of the American Sociological Association, and the Michael Hindelang Award from the American Society for Criminology. Western was a Jean Monnet fellow at the European University Institute, a visiting fellow at the Russell Sage Foundation, a Guggenheim fellow, and an elected member of the American Academy of Arts and Sciences. He received his B.A. (Hons.) in government from the University of Queensland, Australia, and his Ph.D. in sociology from the University of California, Los Angeles.

JEFFREY A. BEARD was appointed as secretary of the California Department of Corrections and Rehabilitation by Governor Edmond G. Brown, Jr., on December 27, 2012. He is responsible for the management of the Corrections Department, which houses 132,785 adult inmates and 870 juveniles, supervises 57,755 parolees, and has more than 50,000 employees and a budget of $9 billion. He will also serve as chairman of both the Board of State and Community Corrections and the Prison Industry Board. He began his criminal justice career in 1972 with the Pennsylvania Department of Corrections (PaDoC) as a corrections counselor. He served in various positions within the PaDoC, including superintendent in two institutions, one of which he activated in 1987 and another that he took over after two serious riots in November 1989. He then served as deputy commissioner and executive deputy secretary until he was appointed secretary of the PaDoC by Governor Tom Ridge in January 2001. He was reappointed by Governor Ed Rendell in February 2003 and February 2007. He remained with the PaDoC until August 2010, when he retired as secretary of corrections. During his retirement, he served as a consultant and/or instructor to the National Institute of Corrections, corrections agencies, and various companies on correctional matters, security, performance measures, mental health issues, evidence-based programs, and assessment. In early 2011, he became a professor of practice with the Justice Center for Research at Pennsylvania State University. In this capacity, he served as an advisor and consultant. He holds a B.S. in psychology and an M.Ed and Ph.D. in counseling, all from Pennsylvania State University.

ROBERT D. CRUTCHFIELD is a professor of sociology at the University of Washington. His current research focuses on neighborhoods and crime, social inequality as a cause of crime, and racial inequality in the criminal justice system. He has written extensively on labor markets and crime and on racial and ethnic disparities in prosecution, sentencing, and imprisonment. He is a fellow of the American Society of Criminology and a past vice president of that organization, and he has served as chair of the American Sociological Association's Crime, Law, and Deviance Section. From 2005 to 2011, he served on the National Research Council's Committee on Law and Justice. Prior to his academic career, he was a juvenile probation officer and an adult parole officer in Pennsylvania. He also served on the Washington State Juvenile Sentencing Commission. He holds a B.A. from Thiel College, Greenville, Pennsylvania, and an M.A. and Ph.D. from Vanderbilt University.

TONY FABELO is division director of research at the Council of State Governments (CSG) Justice Center. He is in charge of designing, developing, and implementing a research agenda for the Justice Center. He also provides technical assistance to state and local governments to help them increase public safety and make more efficient uses of state and local taxpayer dollars. Before joining CSG, he was a senior research associate with the JFA Institute. He worked with the Texas Criminal Justice Policy Council between 1984 and 2003, and was appointed by Governor Ann Richards to head this state research and evaluation agency in 1991. He continued to serve as director under Governor George W. Bush and Governor Rick Perry. During his tenure on the council, he advised five governors from both sides of the aisle. In his different capacities in Texas, he has assisted every legislature since 1985 in developing criminal justice policies, including crafting the major Justice Reinvestment initiative adopted by the Texas legislature in 2007. The U.S. Attorney General appointed him to the Office of Justice Programs Science Advisory Panel in 2010. He received his B.A. in political science from Loyola University and his M.A. and Ph.D. from the University of Texas at Austin.

MARIE GOTTSCHALK is a professor in the Department of Political Science at the University of Pennsylvania. She specializes in American politics, with a focus on criminal justice, health policy, the U.S. political economy, organized labor, the welfare state, and the comparative politics of public policy. She is the author of, among other works, *The Prison and the Gallows: The Politics of Mass Incarceration in America* (Cambridge, 2006), which won the 2007 Ellis W. Hawley Prize from the Organization of American Historians, and *The Shadow Welfare State: Labor, Business, and the Politics of Health Care in the United States* (Cornell, 2000). She is a former editor and journalist and was a university lecturer for 2 years in the People's Republic of China. In 2001-2002, she was a visiting scholar at the Russell Sage Foundation in New York; and in 2009, she was named a distinguished lecturer in Japan by the Fulbright Program. She formerly served on the American Academy of Arts and Sciences national task force on the challenge of mass incarceration. Her latest book, *Caught: The Prison State and the Lockdown of American Politics*, will be published by Princeton University Press in fall 2014. She holds a B.A. in history from Cornell University, an M.P.A. from Princeton University's Woodrow Wilson School of Public and International Affairs, and an M.A. and Ph.D. in political science from Yale University.

CRAIG W. HANEY is distinguished professor of psychology and director of the Program in Legal Studies at the University of California, Santa Cruz. His research concerns the application of social psychological principles and data to various legal, constitutional, and civil rights issues. He has specialized in the assessment of institutional environments, especially the psychological effects of incarceration, as well as the study of criminogenic social histories of persons accused or convicted of serious violent crimes. He has toured and inspected correctional institutions across the country and conducted research on the psychological effects of different forms of imprisonment. His research, writing, and testimony have been cited in numerous opinions that address the constitutionality of various conditions of prison confinement. He writes widely about criminal justice issues, the psychology of imprisonment, and both the determinants and consequences of American prison policy. His book *Death by Design: Capital Punishment as a Social Psychological System* (Oxford, 2005) received the Herbert Jacobs Prize from the Law & Society Association as that year's most outstanding book on law and society, and *Reforming Punishment: Psychological Limits to the Pains of Imprisonment* (APA Books, 2006), was nominated for a National Book Award. He holds a B.A. from the University of Pennsylvania and a J.D. and Ph.D. (in psychology) from Stanford University.

CHIEF JUDGE RICARDO H. HINOJOSA has served on the U.S. District Court for the Southern District of Texas since 1983, and became Chief Judge of that District on November 13, 2009. From June 2003-present, Chief Judge Hinojosa has served on the United States Sentencing Commission, including serving as chair from August 2004-December 2008, acting chair from January 2009-October 2009, and vice chair from June 2013 to the present. He graduated Phi Beta Kappa with honors from the University of Texas at Austin in 1972 and received his law degree from Harvard Law School in 1975. He was selected to serve as a briefing attorney with the Texas Supreme Court from 1975-1976. He entered private practice with the firm of Ewers & Toothaker in McAllen, Texas, and became partner in 1979. Prior to becoming a federal judge, he served as member (1979-1983) and chairman (1981-1983) of the Pan American University Board of Regents. He serves as a member of the Fifth Circuit Judicial Council (2009-present) and as a member of the Budget Committee of the Judicial Conference of the United States (2003-present). He is a member of the American Law Institute (2011-present). He has also served as a member of the U.S. Supreme Court Fellows Commission (2004-2008) and as a member of the Committee on Defender Services of the Judicial Conference of the United States (1996-2002). He served as an adjunct professor at the University of Texas School of Law, teaching a federal sentencing seminar (2001-2003). In May 2011, Chief Judge Hinojosa was selected as the recipient of the 29th Annual Edward J. Devitt Distinguished Service to Justice Award.

GLENN C. LOURY is Merton P. Stoltz professor of the social sciences and professor of economics at Brown University. Previously, he taught economics at Harvard, Northwestern, and the University of Michigan. He has made scholarly contributions to the fields of welfare economics, game theory, industrial organization, natural resource economics, and the economics of income distribution. He has been a scholar in residence at Oxford University, Tel Aviv University, the University of Stockholm, the Delhi School of Economics, the Institute for the Human Sciences in Vienna, and the Institute for Advanced Study at Princeton. He has received a Guggenheim Fellowship to support his work. He is a fellow of the American Academy of Arts and Sciences, a fellow of the Econometric Society, and a member of the American Philosophical Association and was elected vice president of the American Economic Association for 1997. His book *One by One, From the Inside Out: Essays and Reviews on Race and Responsibility in America* won the 1996 American Book Award and the 1996 Christianity Today Book Award. He was chosen by his Boston University colleagues to present the prestigious University Lecture for the 1996-1997 academic year. He was recently elected as a member of the

Council on Foreign Relations and as a fellow of the American Academy of Arts and Sciences. He has published more than 200 essays and reviews on racial inequality and social policy. His recent work includes "Color-Blind Affirmative Action," accepted for forthcoming publication in the *Journal of Law, Economics and Organization* (with Roland Fryer and Tolga Yuret); "Valuing Identity: Trans-Generational Justice: Compensatory vs. Interpretative Approaches," in *Reparations*, edited by Jon Miller (Oxford University Press, 2006); and "Racial Stigma: Toward a New Paradigm for Discrimination Theory," in *Understanding Poverty*, edited by A. Banerjee, R. Benabou, and D. Mookherjee (Oxford University Press, 2005). His books include *The Anatomy of Racial Inequality* (Harvard University Press, 2002) and *Ethnicity, Social Mobility and Public Policy: Comparing the U.S. and the U.K.* (Cambridge University Press, 2005). He received his B.A. in mathematics from Northwestern University and his Ph.D. in economics from the Massachusetts Institute of Technology.

SARA S. MCLANAHAN is William S. Tod professor of sociology and public affairs at Princeton University and director of the Bendheim-Thoman Center for Research on Child Wellbeing. She is principal investigator of the Fragile Families Study and editor-in-chief of *The Future of Children*, a journal dedicated to providing research on policies designed to improve child health and well-being. She is a past president of the Population Association of America and has served on the boards of the American Sociological Association and the Population Association of America. She is a member of the National Academy of Sciences and currently serves on the boards of the William T. Grant Foundation, the Russell Sage Foundation, and the Robert Wood Johnson Health and Society Scholars Program. She is the author of many articles and books, including *Fathers Under Fire: The Revolution in Child Support Enforcement* (1998), *Growing Up with a Single Parent* (1994), and *Single Mothers and Their Children: A New American Dilemma* (1986). She earned her Ph.D. in sociology from the University of Texas at Austin.

LAWRENCE M. MEAD is a professor of politics and public policy at New York University, where he teaches public policy and American government, and a visiting scholar at the American Enterprise Institute. He has been a visiting professor at Harvard, Princeton, and the University of Wisconsin and a visiting fellow at Princeton and the Hoover Institution at Stanford. He is an expert on the problems of poverty and welfare in the United States. Among academics, he was the principal exponent of work requirements in welfare. He is a leading scholar of the politics and implementation of welfare reform and work programs for men, and his many books and articles on these subjects have helped shape social policy in the United States and abroad. He testifies regularly to Congress on poverty, welfare, and social policy. He received his B.A. in political science at Amherst College and his M.A. and Ph.D. in political science at Harvard University.

KHALIL GIBRAN MUHAMMAD is director of the Schomburg Center for Research in Black Culture, The New York Public Library. He is a former professor of African American history at Indiana University. He spent 2 years as an Andrew W. Mellon postdoctoral fellow at the Vera Institute of Justice, a nonprofit criminal justice reform agency in New York City, before joining the faculty of Indiana University. He is the author of *The Condemnation of Blackness: Race, Crime, and the Making of Modern Urban America*, which won the American Studies Association John Hope Franklin Publication Prize, awarded annually to the best published book in American studies. As an academic, he is at the forefront of scholarship on the enduring link between race and crime that has shaped and limited opportunities for African Americans. He is now working on his second book, *Disappearing Acts: The End of White Criminality in the Age of Jim Crow*, which traces the historical roots of the changing demographics of crime and punishment so evident today. He has been an associate editor of *The Journal of American History*. He received a B.A. in economics from the University of Pennsylvania and a Ph.D. in American history from Rutgers University, specializing in twentieth century U.S. and African American history.

DANIEL S. NAGIN is Teresa and H. John Heinz III university professor of public policy and statistics in the Heinz College, Carnegie Mellon University. He is an elected fellow of the American Society of Criminology and of the American Society for the Advancement of Science and is the 2006 recipient of the American Society of Criminology's Edwin H. Sutherland Award. His research focuses on the evolution of criminal and antisocial behaviors over the life course, the deterrent effect of criminal and non-criminal penalties on illegal behaviors, and the development of statistical methods for analyzing longitudinal data. His work has appeared in such diverse outlets as *American Economic Review, American Sociological Review, Journal of the American Statistical Association, American Journal of Sociology, Archives of General Psychiatry, Criminology, Child Development, Psychological Methodology, Law & Society Review, Crime and Justice Annual Review, Operations Research*, and *Stanford Law Review*. He is also the author of *Group-based Modeling of Development* (Harvard University Press, 2005). He received his Ph.D. from the H. John Heinz III School of Public Policy and Management, Carnegie Mellon University.

DEVAH PAGER is a professor of sociology and public policy at Harvard University. Previously, she was an associate professor of sociology and co-director of the Joint Degree Program in Social Policy at Princeton University and faculty associate of the Office of Population Research and the Woodrow Wilson School. Her research focuses on institutions affecting racial stratification, including education, labor markets, and the criminal justice system. Her recent research has involved a series of field experiments studying discrimination against minorities and those with criminal records in the low-wage labor market. Her book *Marked: Race, Crime, and Finding Work in an Era of Mass Incarceration* (University of Chicago, 2007) investigates the racial and economic consequences of large-scale imprisonment for contemporary U.S. labor markets. She holds master's degrees from Stanford University and the University of Cape Town and a Ph.D. from the University of Wisconsin–Madison.

ANNE MORRISON PIEHL is an associate professor of economics and director of the Program in Criminal Justice at Rutgers University and a research associate at the National Bureau of Economic Research. She conducts research on the economics of crime and criminal justice. Her current work analyzes the causes and consequences of the prison population boom; determinants of criminal sentencing outcomes; and the connections between immigration and crime, both historically and currently. She recently testified before the U.S. Sentencing Commission and the U.S. House of Representatives Subcommittee on Immigration and served on the New Jersey Commission on Government Efficiency and Reform Corrections/Sentencing Task Force. Before joining Rutgers in 2005, she was on the faculty of the John F. Kennedy School of Government, Harvard University. She received her A.B. from Harvard University and her Ph.D. from Princeton University.

JOSIAH D. RICH is a professor of medicine and epidemiology at Brown University and attending physician at the Miriam Hospital, with expertise in infectious diseases and addiction. He has authored more than 150 peer-reviewed publications, predominantly on the overlap among infectious diseases, addictions, and incarceration. He is principal investigator for several projects focused on incarcerated populations. He is the director and co-founder of the Center for Prisoner Health and Human Rights at the Miriam Hospital Immunology Center. He is also a co-founder of the nationwide Centers for AIDS Research (CFAR) Collaboration in HIV in Corrections (CFAR/CHIC) initiative. He has advocated for public health policy changes to improve the health of people with addiction, including improving legal access to sterile syringes and increasing drug treatment for the incarcerated and formerly incarcerated populations. He received his B.A. from Columbia

University, his M.D. from the University of Massachusetts, and his M.P.H. from the Harvard School of Public Health.

ROBERT J. SAMPSON is Henry Ford II professor of the social sciences at Harvard University and past president of the American Society of Criminology. Before joining the Harvard faculty in 2003, he taught at the University of Chicago and was a research fellow at the American Bar Foundation. He is a fellow of the American Academy of Arts and Sciences, the American Philosophical Society, and the American Society of Criminology and an elected member of the National Academy of Sciences. In June 2011, he and his colleague John Laub received the Stockholm Prize in Criminology. His main research interests focus on crime, the life course, neighborhood effects, and the social structure of the contemporary city. His most recent book—*Great American City: Chicago and the Enduring Neighborhood Effect*—was published in paperback by the University of Chicago Press in June 2013. He received an M.A. and Ph.D. from the State University of New York at Albany.

HEATHER ANN THOMPSON is an associate professor of history in the Department of African American Studies and the Department of History at Temple University. She is writing the first comprehensive history of the Attica Prison Rebellion of 1971 and its legacy for Pantheon Books. She has also written numerous scholarly articles on the current crisis of mass incarceration, including: "Why Mass Incarceration Matters: Rethinking Crisis, Decline and Transformation in Postwar American History" (*Journal of American History*, December 2010), "Downsizing the Carceral State: The Policy Implications of Prisoner Guard Unions" (*Criminology and Public Policy*, August, 2011), "Rethinking Working Class Struggle through the Lens of the Carceral State: Toward a Labor History of Inmates and Guards" (*Labor: Working Class Studies of the Americas*, Fall, 2011), and "Criminalizing Kids: The Overlooked Reason for Failing Schools" (*Dissent*, October, 2011). She earned a B.A. and M.A. in history from the University of Michigan and a Ph.D. in history from Princeton University.

MICHAEL TONRY is a professor of law at the University of Minnesota, specializing in criminal law. He teaches courses in criminal law, jurisprudence, and comparative law. In 1990, he was named Marvin J. Sonosky chair of law and public policy. From 1999 to 2004, he was also professor of law and public policy and director of the Institute of Criminology at Cambridge University. Since 2001, he has been a visiting professor at the University of Lausanne, Switzerland. He has also been a senior fellow of The Netherlands Institute for the Study of Crime and Law Enforcement, Leiden, since 2003. From 2000 to 2010, he was editor of *Criminology in*

Europe. He edits *Crime and Justice: A Review of Research*, the Oxford University Press series *Studies in Crime and Public Policy*, the Oxford University Press series *Oxford Handbooks on Criminology and Criminal Justice*, and the Oxford University Press series *Studies in Penal Theory and Philosophy* (with Antony Duff). He received his A.B. from the University of North Carolina at Chapel Hill; his LL.B. from Yale; and his Ph.D. (h.c.) from the Free University, Amsterdam.

AVELARDO VALDEZ is a professor in the School of Social Work at the University of Southern California. A primary focus of his research is on the relationship between substance abuse and violence and health issues among high-risk groups. His research projects have been among "hidden populations," such as youth and prison gang members, injecting and noninjecting heroin users, and sex workers on the U.S./Mexico border. He is a recipient of federal grants from the National Institutes of Health and National Institute on Drug Abuse. He has published more than 75 journal articles and book chapters and academic publications, including two books. His most recent book is entitled *Mexican American Girls and Gang Violence: Beyond Risk* (2007). He obtained his Ph.D. in sociology at the University of California, Los Angeles.